2023
California 60 Hour Qualifying Education

Table of Contents

Quick Start Guide

WELCOME to the most advanced tax learning system in the United States: Prendo365 powered by Latino Tax Professionals! Our tax education is a powerful, user-friendly e-learning system. An optional textbook is available. The following instructions will provide the steps to create and/or log in to your Prendo365 account.

First-Time User Purchased Online or Through Sales Rep

Step 1: After purchase, open the email you received from adressmailer@workato.com with subject line "Welcome to Prendo365 – DO NOT REPLY" – it contains a password and username to access your created account. Check your spam/junk folder if you do not see it.

Step 2: At login, you MUST complete and save the required fields marked with a red asterisk to continue.

Step 3: Scroll down to "Courses" on the left side of your dashboard and click on your course icon to begin!

First-Time User Through Instructor or Office Manager

Step 1: Enter prendo365.com into your preferred browser then hit enter. (We recommend Google Chrome or Firefox for best user experience.)

Step 2: Click on the "Register" button on the top right.

Step 3: Your username is your email*. (Remember which email and password you used). Complete all required fields.

Step 4: If you have an instructor, click on the drop-down menu, "*do you have an instructor*" and select your instructor. Otherwise, click on the "I Accept the terms of the privacy policy" and click "Next."

Step 5: Enter your PTIN and State information for Continuing Education Credits, if applicable. If you do not have a PTIN, type "N/A." Complete all required fields. You will receive an email from edsupport@latinotaxpro.com. If you do not receive the email within 15 minutes, check your spam folder.

Step 6: Open the email you received from edsupport@latinotaxpro.com — it contains your temporary password. Click the link to confirm your registration and use the temporary password provided to sign in.

Step 7: Enter the temporary password and then create a new password that you will remember. Click "Save Changes."

Step 8: Scroll down to "Courses" on the list to the left side of your dashboard and click on your course icon to begin!

*If you receive a message that your email is already in the system, an account has been created by a staff member, instructor, or by purchasing online. Click on "Forgot your password?" to reset your password or chat at prendo365.com.

Returning User

Step 1: Enter Prendo365.com in your preferred browser. Hit enter.

Step 2: Click the "Sign In" button.

Step 3: Enter your username and password. Forgot your password? Click "Forgot your password?"

Step 4: Click "Sign In."

Step 5: Haven't started your course yet? Find your course on the dashboard. On the left side under "Courses" open your course by clicking on the thumbnail. Then click on "Start Learning Now."

Step 6: Started your course already? Find your course once again on the dashboard under "Courses" and click on the thumbnail to open. Then choose "Resume Where You Left Off" to go to the last section completed.

Still have questions? Chat at prendo365.com, email questions to edsupport@latinotaxpro.com or call 866.936.2587.

You have been placed into a group with other tax pros taking the same course! This community is for you to SHARE knowledge and CONNECT with others.

HOW TO ACCESS YOUR ACCOUNT

1. Once you're in your Prendo365 account, click on the 3 lines on the top left corner to open the menu.
2. With the menu open, click on "Visit the Community" to continue.
3. YOU NEED TO CLICK "Continue with your existing Prendo365 account" to enter your information.
4. You're in! Agree to the Code of Conduct, upload a profile picture, and start posting in the Community!

Have a question? Call or text us for questions at (866) 936-2587!

Course Description

This course completes the requirement for the California Tax Education Council (CTEC) registration. This course provides the student with a basic understanding of federal and state tax law. Our courses are designed to be convenient, easy to use, affordable, and bilingual. Increasing your knowledge of tax law and practice will help you grow your business and increase profits!

This course meets the 60-hour Qualifying Education requirement (45 hours of Federal Tax Law, which includes the required 2 hours of Ethics and 15 hours of California Tax Law) imposed by the state of California to become a California Registered Tax Preparer (CRTP).

In this beginner qualifying education course, you will learn:

> ➤ How to prepare a federal individual tax return.
> ➤ How to prepare Schedule A, Schedule C, Schedule E, and Schedule F.
> ➤ The requirements for each filing status, dependents, standard and itemized deductions.
> ➤ Which form to use and how it flows to Form 1040.
> ➤ Credits the taxpayer qualifies for and how to properly complete each form.
> ➤ How and when to submit an amendment and an extension to file your tax return.

Our proprietary Professional Training System, Prendo365.com, combines traditional textbook courses with online interactive chapter eBooks, chapter videos, chapter review questions and exam and chapter Practice Tax Returns (PTR) exercises.

In our textbooks and chapter eBooks, you will have content for specific line or area of Form 1040, and several review questions to test your knowledge on the material you have learned. After finishing reading the material or watching the chapter videos, the student will complete a required chapter exam and a Practice Tax Return (PTR) exercise which will only focus on the material you learned for individual chapters and must complete a PTR short test. Remember, each chapter in the course is the foundation for the next.

Practice Tax Returns are in PDF format and include links to the necessary forms to complete a tax return by hand. The Practice Tax Return will have their own set of review questions. Returns containing Schedule A are prepared with state income tax withholding on line 5 and the additional state-specific taxes such as CASDI. PTRs are based on the material covered in the chapter.

Review questions and PTRs may be taken as many times as necessary to achieve the required score. If you have obtained a score of 70% or better, but choose to obtain a higher score, Prendo365 records the most recent score, even if it is less than your prior score.

This course has been approved by the California Tax Education Council (CTEC) (2080-QE-001), which fulfills the 60-hour qualifying education requirement imposed by the state of California for individuals who are not a certified public accountant (CPA), enrolled agent (EA), or an attorney. A listing of additional requirements to register as a tax preparer may be obtained by contacting CTEC at www.CTEC.org or 1-877-850-2832.

Included in this course:

> ➤ **Textbook Study Guide** (Purchased separately).
> ➤ **eBook** (The online course includes an eBook for every chapter).
> ➤ **Online Questions** "To Test Your Knowledge" (not required to pass the course).
> ➤ **Online Practice Tax Returns** (PTR). There is a quiz at the end of each chapter.
> ➤ **Online Finals**. You will have three final exams to complete the course.

This course has been copyrighted and published by Latino Tax Professionals Association, LLC.

Chapter Introduction

Each chapter begins with an introductory paragraph that will give the student an overview of what is covered in the chapter.

Chapter Objectives

Each chapter is designed to build upon the others. The chapter objectives state the framework for the material presented in the chapter.

Chapter Resources

The chapter resources serve as a guide for students when more research may be needed on a particular topic. Our editorial team has created this list of resources to make it easier to begin researching.

Textbook and eBook Chapter Part Review Questions "To Test Your Knowledge"

The content of each chapter is divided into several parts. You will find review questions at the end of each chapter part. LTP encourages the student not to skip these but read and learn from the answers and feedback. These review questions are not graded and are not part of the final grade you need to pass this course.

Chapter Questions "To Test Your Knowledge"

There is a short quiz at the end of each chapter. The online review questions are designed to help the student recall subject matter from the chapter. These review questions are not graded and are not part of the final grade you need to pass this course.

Final Exams

Students must pass three separate final exams with a 70% grade or better. The Ethics chapter final exam is included at the end of the chapter and consists of 10 questions. The federal tax law final consists of 215 questions, and the California tax law consists of 75 final questions. Students are encouraged to complete the individual chapter review in preparation for the final.

Practice Tax Returns

LTP has created practice tax returns (PTR) to assist the student in understanding tax preparation. Each PTR is based on a scenario encompassing the course content that has been included up to that point. For example, if a lesson covers income, the tax calculations will not reflect any credits that have not yet been discussed in the course, even if the taxpayer in the scenario would have qualified for them. Ideally, the student would prepare the PTR by hand and then answer the PTR review questions on the website. LTP does not discourage software preparation.

When preparing a Schedule A, there are 2 choices for Taxes You Paid; State Tax Withheld or Sales Tax. PTR instructions will use a fixed Sales Tax when preparing the tax return. Be aware that individual states, and county and city could vary in rate and tax withheld.

Note: The IRS and the states update their tax forms and tax law at the end of the current year therefore you will be learning tax law and using tax year 2022 forms and schedule to complete the course.

Textbook Updates

The digital version of the textbook is updated throughout the year to always contain the most recent information. The physical copy of the textbook will also be updated periodically. Notifications are inside Prendo365 indicated by the bell in the upper right of the screen.

LTP Mission

LTP promotes entrepreneurship, education, diversity, and knowledge among tax preparation businesses across the nation — a number that is growing every year. Not only do we provide education, we provide support for tax professionals who pursue opening their own tax preparation businesses or for current business owners who strive to expand their businesses.

> ➤ Our **GOAL** is to help you grow your practice and increase your profits.
> ➤ Our **VISION** is to give you the best education, leadership, and business-skill training available.
> ➤ Our **MISSION** is to give tax professionals a unified, powerful voice on a national level.

LTP believes the best way to begin tax preparation is by understanding Form 1040 efficiently. The chapters in this textbook are designed to give the student basic instructions. When the chapter is completed, the student will go online and complete multiple-choice review questions with feedback for review.

LTP Commitment

This publication is designed to provide accurate and authoritative information on the matter covered. It is presented with the understanding that Latino Tax Professionals is not engaged in rendering legal or accounting services or other professional advice and assumes no liability in connection with its use. Pursuant to Circular 230, this text has been prepared with due diligence; however, the possibility of mechanical or human error does exist. The text is not intended to address every situation that may arise. Consult additional sources of information, as needed, to determine the solution of tax questions.

Tax laws are constantly changing and are subject to differing interpretations. In addition, the facts and circumstances of a particular situation may not be the same as those presented here. Therefore, the student should do additional research to understand fully the information contained in this publication.

Federal law prohibits unauthorized reproduction of the material in this manual. All reproduction must be approved in writing by Latino Tax Professionals. This is not a free publication. Illegal distribution of this publication is prohibited by international and United States copyright laws and treaties. Any illegal distribution by the purchaser can subject the purchaser to penalties of up to $100,000 per copy distributed. No claim is made to original government works; however, within this product or publication, the following are subject to LTP's copyright:

1. Gathering, compilation, and arrangement of such government materials
2. The magnetic translation and digital conversion of data if applicable
3. The historical statutory and other notes and references
4. The commentary and other materials

Our Editorial and Production Team

Authors: Kristeena S. Lopez, MA Ed, EA
Carlos C. Lopez, MDE, EA

Editor: Fernando Cabrera, MA

Contributing Staff: Niki Young, BS, EA
Fernando Cabrera, MA
Andres Santos, EA
Timur Taluy, BS
Roberto Pons, EA
Ricardo Rivas, EA
Pascual Garcia, EA

Graphic Designers: Susan Espinoza, BS
David Lopez

ISBN: 9798398389746

Made in California, USA

Published Date: June 14, 2023

Chapter 1 Due Diligence and Preparer Penalties

Prerequisite

This course is designed for people with zero to basic tax knowledge and Form 8867. A beginning tax preparer will learn terminology that is industry specific. If you are afraid to learn, then this course may not be for you. This course will help the student with a new career if one is willing to take the time and energy to learn all you possibly can. This course will have a final exam that consists of 10 questions and must be passed with a 70% or better. You may retake the exam until you pass. Our online learning system randomizes the test questions and shuffles the answers.

Objectives

At the end of this lesson, the student will:

> ➢ Identify the due diligence requirements of the tax preparer when completing a tax return with refundable credits.
> ➢ Clarify what documentation the IRS requires to be maintained when preparing specific credits used on tax returns.
> ➢ Understand what documents the tax preparer should maintain for their records.
> ➢ Recognize what credits are on Form 8867.
> ➢ Know who is the paid preparer.

Resources

Form 886 Form 8867 Circular 230	Instructions Form 8867 Publication 596

Table of Contents

Part 1 Due Diligence

"Ethics" is defined as the discipline of dealing with what is good and bad and with moral duty and obligation. It is a set theory or system of principles or moral values. It is also the rules and standards governing the conduct of a person or the members of a profession (e.g., tax practice ethics).

The rules and standards governing the conduct of tax professionals are contained in Circular 230. These rules and standards are the ethics of tax practice. "Ethical behavior" is defined as "of ethics or relating to ethics." In addition, it is being in accordance with or conforming to the accepted principles of right and wrong that govern the conduct of a profession (i.e., professional standards of conduct).

Most people would define ethics as "doing the right thing," which leads one to believe that individuals will, as a matter of common sense and conscience, instinctively react in an ethical manner in all situations. As evidenced by financial scandals involving Bernie Madoff and Lehman Brothers, this is not always true. "Doing the right thing" was not the basis for the decisions made by leaders of those organizations. As a result, many have become generally disillusioned and untrusting of the business community.

The U.S. Treasury Department requires all attorneys, certified public accountants, enrolled agents, enrolled actuaries, and registered tax return preparers to annually complete continuing education, including two hours of ethics or professional conduct.

Introduction

This course will cover basic due diligence and tax preparer penalties. Due diligence are actions that an individual will perform to satisfy a legal requirement. The Internal Revenue Service has a guideline for their requirements known as Circular 230. This chapter will give a brief description of the rules and regulations that govern the tax preparer outlined in Circular 230.

The dictionary definition of due diligence is "the care that a reasonable person exercises to avoid harm to other persons or to their property." Due diligence should always be a part of our daily decision process. In business due diligence refers to practicing prudence by carefully assessing associated costs and risks prior to completing the transaction.

Form 8867 was first introduced in 2006. The form was originally created for the paid preparer to report earned income credit and the paid preparer penalty was $100. In 2011 the penalty was raised to $500. The penalty amount is for each failure to comply with the diligence requirements. For tax year 2021, the penalty amount was $540 for each failure. For 2022 the penalty is $545 for each failure to comply with all due diligence requirements. The 2022 Form 8867 reports all refundable credits and head of household filing status. A tax preparer could be fined a total of $2,180 per Form 8867 for not completing their due diligence.

When the taxpayer files a return with the following credits and filing status the tax preparer needs to complete an accurate Form 8867, which then is attached to the taxpayer's return. The following are found on Form 8867 that require the preparer to ask question to determine if the taxpayer qualify for credits and filing status:

1. Earned Income Credit (EIC).
2. Child Tax Credit (CTC).
3. Additional Child Tax Credit (ACTC).
4. Other Dependent Credit (ODC).
5. American Opportunity Tax Credit (AOTC).
6. Head of Household Status

Purpose of Form 8867

What is due diligence? The Internal Revenue Service (IRS) requires a tax preparer who prepares a return for a client that claims certain credits or head-of-household status thoroughly interview and question the taxpayer. This includes collecting documentation to show that the taxpayer is qualified for the tax advantage.

The paid preparer is required to perform due diligence when preparing tax returns with or without refundable credit. Treasury regulations Section 6695(g) requires the paid tax preparer to meet certain requirements when interviewing the client. Questions must be asked that will give the preparer enough information to complete Form 8867. IRS provides guidelines on how to interview.

The following guidelines have been set forth by the IRS.

1. Meet the knowledge requirement by interviewing the taxpayer, asking adequate questions, contemporaneous documenting the questions and the taxpayer's responses on the return or in your notes, reviewing adequate information to determine if the taxpayer is eligible to claim the credits(s) and/or head of household (HOH) filing status, and to figure the amount(s) of the credit(s) claimed.
2. Complete Form 8867 truthfully and accurately and complete actions described on Form 8867 for any applicable credit(s) claimed and HOH filing status, if claimed.
3. Submit Form 8867 in the manner required.
4. Keep all five of the following records for 3 years from the latest of the dates specified later.
   a. A copy of Form 8867.
   b. The applicable worksheet(s) or if tax preparer created their own for any credits claimed.
   c. Copies of any documents provided by the taxpayer on which the preparer relied to determine the taxpayer's eligibility for the credit(s) and/or HOH filing status and to figure amount(s) of the credits.

    d. A record of how, when, and from whom the information used was obtained to prepare Form 8867 and the applicable worksheet(s).

    e. A record of any additional information tax preparer relied upon, including questions asked and the taxpayer's responses, to determine taxpayer's eligibility for the credit(s) and/or HOH filing status and to figure the amount(s) of the credits(s).

Contemporaneous Documenting

Contemporaneous documents are files or notes that were created at the time of the interview with the taxpayer. Documentation is an important part of due diligence. The tax professional needs to be diligent in keeping records of how the tax return was prepared. Documents proving the taxpayer's income, expenses, credits claimed on the tax return and how the tax return was prepared should be kept. Documentation could save the preparer a due diligence penalty. Good intention of saving the taxpayers documentations and not doing keeping records of how the return was prepared, is only a good intention, and will not save the tax preparer from a due diligence penalty. There are three words that could save a preparer from penalties: DOCUMENT, DOCUMENT, & DOCUMENT.

Documentation should be completed during the interview of the client no matter how the interview takes place, such as in person, via phone, or virtually. When determining HOH filing status, make sure that the individual has paid more than half of the cost of keeping up a home with a qualifying dependent. (Discussed in more detail in the Filing Status Chapter).

Reasonable inquiries include asking pertinent questions, which should result in the needed information to complete Form 8867. Certain questions should determine age of taxpayer and/or dependents to help determine filing status and which credit(s) the taxpayer may qualify for.

The following questions are samples to determine taxpayer's filing status:

➢ Were you single on December 31st?
➢ Were you married on December 31st?
➢ Did you live apart the entire year from your spouse?
➢ Do you have qualifying children?
➢ Did the qualifying children live with you the entire year?
➢ How many months did the qualifying children live with you?
➢ Does anyone else live in your house?
➢ Do you live with another taxpayer? If so, what is that individual's relationship to you? Parent, in-laws, cousin, grandchild, etc.?

Creating Form 8867 Truthfully and Accurately

When completing Form 8867, each year is considered. Questions that were asked in the past only relate to the past, and not to the current tax year. It may seem like the same questions are being asked over and over with the same results, but this is essential. People's lives change, and the tax professional must ask the taxpayer about any changes. Asking the same questions to understand the taxpayer's situation is critical to preparing an accurate and truthful return. Even records furnished by the taxpayer must support the credits, income, and expenses claimed on the tax return.

Submitting Form 8867 Truthfully and Accurately

Tax preparer needs to complete Form 8867 by answering the questions that pertain to the taxpayer. Completing Form 8867 is not a cookie-cutter procedure. Every taxpayer is unique and so are the questions asked to determine due diligence for the taxpayer and the tax preparer.

Refundable Credits Due Diligence

Tax preparers must take additional steps to safeguard their compliance with the refundable credits' due diligence. Ignoring tax law could result in penalties and other consequences for the paid tax preparer and their clients. A paid tax preparer who prepares returns with *Earned Income Tax Credit* (EITC), *Child Tax Credit* (CTC), *Other Dependent Credit* (ODC), or the *American opportunity tax credit* (AOTC) must meet due diligence requirements. These requirements focus on accurately determining the client's eligibility and the amount of each credit. The four requirements are:

1. Complete and submit Form 8867 (Treasury Reg. §1.6695-2(b)(1)).
2. Compute the credits (Treasury Reg. §1.6695-2(b)(2)).
3. Knowledge of who and what is required for credits (Treasury Reg. §1.6695-2(b)(3)).
4. Keep records for three years (Treasury Reg. §1.6695-2(b)(4)).

Most due diligence penalties are a result of failure to comply with the knowledge requirement. To meet the knowledge requirement, one should:

➢ Ask questions regarding the information provided by the client to determine if the client truly can claim the credits or filing status.
➢ Assess if the information given is complete. Collect additional information if facts seem to be missing.
➢ Determine if the information is consistent; recognize contradictory statements, and statements you know are true.
➢ Conduct a thorough, in-depth interview with each client, every year. Don't rely on the statement "everything is the same as last year".
➢ Ask enough questions to realize the prepared tax return is correct and complete.
➢ Document, at the time of the interview, any questions asked and the clients' answers.

Documents must be kept for three years from the latest of:

➢ The due date of the return (not including extensions).
➢ The date the tax return was electronically filed.
➢ For a paper return, the date the return was presented to the client for signature.

Señor 1040 Says: The paid tax preparer cannot solely rely on software for their refundable credit due diligence. Professional software may not comply with Treasury Regulation 1.6695(b)(3). It is the paid tax preparer's due diligence responsibility to make sure that they have complied with Treasury Regulation 1.6695.

Most Common EIC Errors

1. Claiming EIC for a child who does not meet the qualifying child requirements.
2. Filing as single or head of household when married.
3. Incorrectly reporting income or expenses.

Consequences of Filing EIC Returns Incorrectly

Tax professionals should know that clients come to them to prepare an accurate tax return. The client trusts a tax professional to know and understand the guidelines to prepare correct tax returns. If a tax preparer incorrectly files EIC returns, it will affect their client, themselves, and, if an employee, their employer.

The following are some basic consequences that can occur when a paid tax preparer files an incorrect EIC tax return for his/her client.

> ➤ The client must pay back the amount in error as well as interest on the amount.
> ➤ The client may have to file Form 8862 for up to 10 years.
> ➤ The client may be banned from claiming EIC for the next 2 years if the error is because of reckless or intentional disregard of the rules.
> ➤ The client may be banned from claiming EIC for the next 10 years if the error is because of fraud.

If the IRS examines a refundable tax credit return for a preparer, and the IRS finds that the preparer did not meet the four due diligence requirements (IRC §6694), they may be given a penalty:

> ➤ A $560 penalty for returns completed in 2023 for each failure to comply with due diligence requirements.
> ➤ The penalty is $1,000 or 50% of the income derived by tax preparer with the respect to the return or claim for refund

Remember the four due diligence requirements are:

1. Complete and submit Form 8867 (Treasury Reg. §1.6695-2(b)(1))
2. Compute the credits (Treasury Reg. §1.6695-2(b)(2))
3. Knowledge of who and what is required for credits (Treasury Reg. §1.6695-2(b)(3))
4. Keep records for three years (Treasury Reg. §1.6695-2(b)(4))

Example: Anet prepared a tax return for Lewis. Lewis qualified for refundable credits. Anet was audited and had no documentation and was assessed a penalty for not completing her due diligence on Form 8867. Her penalty for failure to meet the due diligence requirements containing EIC, CTC/ACTC/ODC, or AOTC filed in 2021 is $545 per credit per return. The amount Anet will be assessed for Lewis' return is $545.00 x 4 = $2,180.00.

If the tax preparer receives a return-related penalty, they can also face:

1. Loss of their tax preparer designation.
2. Suspension or expulsion from IRS e-file program.
3. Other disciplinary action by the IRS Office of Professional Responsibility (OPR).
4. Injunctions barring the preparer from preparing tax returns or imposing conditions on the tax returns they have prepared.

The IRS can also penalize the employer if an employee fails to comply with the EIC due diligence requirements.

Questions to ask to determine if the taxpayer qualifies for Earned Income Credit

Although Form 8867 is a paid preparer due diligence form, it provides answers to help tax professionals to determine appropriate questions to ask the taxpayer.

1. Did the child live with you for over half the year?
2. Have you supported the child the entire year?
3. Have you ever been disallowed to claim earned income credit?
4. Have you ever had to file Form 8862?

The tax professional should not rely on the above questions only.

To stay current on EIC changes and due diligence, go to www.irs.gov/eitc.

Most Common Child Tax Credit (CTC), Additional Child Tax Credit (ACTC), and/or Other Dependent Credit (ODC) Errors

1. Claiming the CTC/ACTC/ODC for a qualifying child or qualifying person who does not meet the age requirement.
2. Claiming the CTC/ACTC/ODC for a qualifying child or qualifying person who does not meet the dependency requirements.
3. Claiming the CTC/ACTC/ODC for a qualifying child or qualifying person who does not meet the residency requirement.
4. Not understanding that some credits are reduced based on income amounts.

Questions to ask to determine if the taxpayer qualifies for CTC/ACTC/ODC

1. Did the qualifying child live with the taxpayer for more than half the year?
2. Is the qualifying child a citizen, national, or resident of the United States?
3. Has the custodial parent released the qualifying dependent to the taxpayer?
4. Has the taxpayer supported the child? (Just paying child support is not supporting the child).

The tax professional should not rely on the above questions only.

Consequences of Filing CTC/ACTC/ODC Returns Incorrectly

The following are some basic consequences that can occur when a paid tax preparer files an incorrect CTC/ACTC/ODC tax return for his/her client.

➢ The client must pay back the difference in income, as well as interest and penalties.
➢ The tax preparer may get bad publicity from an angry client(s).
➢ The tax preparer may have to pay a due diligence interest and penalties because of reckless or intentional disregard of the rules or other penalties that apply.
➢ The tax preparer could be disciplined by Office of Professional Responsibility (OPR).

Most Common American opportunity tax credit (AOTC) Errors

1. Claiming AOTC for a student who did not attend an eligible educational institution.
2. Claiming AOTC for a student who did not pay qualifying college expenses.
3. Claiming AOTC for a student for too many years.
4. Preparer did not ask for Form 1098-T.

Questions to ask to determine if the taxpayer qualifies for AOTC

1. Did the qualifying child attend a higher education institution?
2. Was the qualifying child at least a half-time student?
3. Did the qualifying child receive Form 1098-T? (Did box 5 have an amount larger than box 1?)
4. How many years has the taxpayer claimed this credit?
5. Is the student under age 24?
6. Was the student convicted of a felony drug possession or distribution before the end of the tax year?

Consequences of Filing AOTC Returns Incorrectly

➢ The client must pay back the amount in error as well as interest and penalties.
➢ The tax preparer may get some bad publicity from the angry client(s).
➢ The tax preparer could pay due diligence interest and penalties because of reckless or intentional disregard of the rules.
➢ The tax preparer could be disciplined by Office of Professional Responsibility (OPR).

Determining Head of Household (HOH) Filing Status

The information here is specifically what the tax preparer and taxpayer need to know about answering and completing Form 8867.

Head of household filing status was included on Form 8867 for 2021 tax returns. To be considered HOH, taxpayer must have a qualifying dependent and claim dependency exemption for the qualifying child who lived with the taxpayer more than half the year (exceptions may apply). Some documentation that the tax preparer should obtain when interviewing the taxpayer are official birth documents, marriage certificates, adoption agency letter or placement letter, or pertinent court documents to verify residence and relationship to the child.

The taxpayer must file Head of Household (HOH) if he or she meets any of the following criteria on December 31st of the tax year being filed:

➢ The taxpayer must be considered unmarried on the last day of the year.
➢ A qualifying child or relative lived in the home for more than half the year (there are exceptions for temporary absences). Children of divorced or separated parents, or of parents who lived apart, can be claimed based on the residency test in most cases.
➢ The taxpayer paid for more than half the cost of keeping up the home for the tax year.

Other items that could be useful to claim residency for the qualifying child are school, medical, daycare, or social services records. If the taxpayer brings in school records, then the letter should be written on school letterhead with a photo of the child on the letter. If the daycare provider is a relative, such as grandparents, siblings, or other relatives, then the tax preparer should require another letter of proof that is not from a relative.

Other items needed to determine HOH could be:

1. Qualifying person test.
2. Cost of keeping up a home test.
3. Divorce decree or separation agreement if applicable.
4. Documents that prove you and your spouse did not live together for the last 6 months of the year.

a. Utility bills
b. Lease agreement
c. A letter from clergy or social services.

As a tax preparer the more information you gather, the better off you are in determining filing status.

> *Señor 1040 Says:* To qualify for HOH **all** eligibility requirements must be met.

Questions to ask to determine if the taxpayer qualifies for Head of Household

Below are sample questions to ask to determine a taxpayer's best filing status:

1. Are you single?
2. Are you married?
3. Do you have children?
4. Did the children live with you the entire year?
5. How many months did the children live with you?
6. What documentation do you have to prove the child(ren) lived with you?
7. Does anyone else live in your house?
8. Do you live with another taxpayer?

It is necessary that the tax professional determines the correct filing status by asking pertinent questions such as above.

Self-employed Taxpayer's Due Diligence

Refundable credits due diligence regarding Schedule C requires the paid preparer to take additional steps to ensure that the taxpayer filing a Schedule C with refundable credits complies with tax law. Per Internal Revenue Code (IRC) section 6695(g), paid tax preparers are required to make additional inquiries of taxpayers who appear to be making inconsistent, incorrect, or incomplete claims for the credit.

Paid tax return preparers can generally rely on the taxpayer's representations until it involves EIC due diligence requirements. The paid tax preparer must take additional steps to determine the net self-employment income used to calculate refundable credits eligibility is correct and complete. The additional inquiries made to comply with due diligence and the client's response must be documented. The statute requires the return preparer to be reasonable, well-informed, and knowledgeable in tax law.

It is very important that the information is documented, and the paid tax preparer can prove that they have asked these or similar questions that will arrive at the same goal. The paid tax preparer should ask sufficient questions to taxpayers claiming self-employment income. Some questions that need to be asked include:

The paid tax preparer should ask sufficient questions to taxpayers claiming self-employment income. Some questions that need to be asked include:

1. Does the client have and conduct a business?
2. Does the client have records to support the documentation of the income and expenses claimed on the return?
3. Can the client reconstruct the documentation, if necessary?
4. Has the client included all income and related expenses reported on the Schedule C?

Reporting Schedule C Income Common Errors

The most common income reporting errors are from Schedule C. Self-employed taxpayers filing a Schedule C must report the correct gross income and all related deductions on their return. The knowledge requirement must be satisfied for correct and complete information. Clients who claim income without expense on a Schedule C should be able to answer probing questions, especially if the client claims they have no records to support the numbers given. Once again, be prepared to ask probing questions with supporting documentation supplied to determine the correct facts.

Example: Esperanza has a cleaning business, and she tells her paid preparer:

➤ She did not receive Form 1099.
➤ She was self-employed.
➤ She earned $12,000.
➤ She had no related expenses to the cleaning business.

Questions to ask should include:

➤ Do you have records of the amount of money you received from house cleaning?
➤ How much did you charge to clean a house?
➤ How many houses did you clean?
➤ Who provided the cleaning supplies?
➤ If you provided the cleaning supplies, how much did you spend weekly?
➤ Did you provide your own transportation to clean the houses?

Ultimately, the goal is for the paid tax preparer to feel confident that the prepared return is correct and complete, and the paid preparer knows that they have complied with their EIC due diligence requirements.

Best Practice Guidelines

By following these best practices when providing advice and preparing tax return submissions to the IRS, tax advisors are better able to provide their clients with the highest possible representation quality concerning federal tax matters.

Tax professional best practices include the following:

➤ Communicate clearly with clients regarding the terms of the engagement. This means determining what the client is seeking and what he or she expects from the practitioner. In turn, make sure the client understands the scope and type of services that will be rendered.
➤ Establish the facts. Determine which facts are relevant to the matter at hand and evaluate the reasonableness of any assumptions or representations.
➤ Relate the applicable law to the relevant facts and arrive at a conclusion based on this support.

➢ Advise the client based on the meaning of any findings. Inform him or her of any tax repercussions as a result of any actions or lack thereof (e.g., accuracy-related penalties, interest, etc.).

➢ Act fairly and with integrity in practice before the IRS.

A practitioner, when advising a client to take a position on a tax return, document, affidavit, or other paperwork submitted to the IRS or when preparing or signing a tax return as a preparer, may generally rely in good faith, without verification, upon information furnished by the client.

The practitioner may not, however, ignore the implications of information furnished to or actually known by the practitioner and must make reasonable inquiries if the information as furnished appears to be incorrect, incomplete, or inconsistent with an important fact or other factual assumption.

Tax advisors responsible for overseeing a firm's practice of providing advice on federal tax issues and preparing or assisting in the preparation of submissions to the IRS should take reasonable steps to ensure that the firm's procedures for all members, associates, and employees are consistent with these best practices.

Document Guidelines and Procedures

A practitioner may not willfully, recklessly, or through gross incompetence sign a tax return or claim for refund that the tax practitioner knows or reasonably should know contains any of the following:

➢ An unreasonable basis.

➢ An unreasonable position as described in §6694(a)(2) of the IRC Code.

➢ A willful attempt by the practitioner to understate the tax liability or to intentionally disregard the rules and regulations as described in §6694(b)(2).

A paid tax preparer who guarantees a specific amount of refund is an example of the kind of action for this penalty. Others would include if the preparer intentionally disregards information given by the taxpayer to reduce the taxpayer's liability; in this case, the preparer is guilty of a willful attempt to understate tax liability. This does not mean that the preparer may not rely in good faith on the information furnished by the taxpayer. However, the tax preparer must make reasonable inquiries if the information furnished by the taxpayer appears to be incorrect or incomplete.

If the tax professional receives a request for documents, records, or information concerning one of their clients from the IRS or the OPR, he or she must comply with the request unless the tax professional reasonably believes that the information is privileged. If the requested information is not in the tax professional or the tax professional client's possession, the tax professional must promptly inform the requesting IRS or OPR personnel of that fact.

A practitioner may not advise a client to take a position on a document, affidavit, or any other paper(s) submitted to the Internal Revenue Service unless the position is not frivolous. A position is frivolous if it purposefully contains or omits information that demonstrates an intentional disregard of a rule or regulation. If challenged, it is the taxpayer's responsibility to prove to the IRS that a position is not frivolous, and it is then up to the IRS to make the final decision thereof.

A practitioner may not advise a client to submit any document, affidavit, or other paper to the IRS under the following circumstances:

> ➤ If the purpose of the submission is to delay or impede the administration of the federal tax laws.
> ➤ The information is frivolous.
> ➤ The content omits information or demonstrates an intentional disregard of a rule or regulation unless the practitioner also advises the taxpayer to submit a document that shows evidence of a good faith challenge to the rule or regulations.

A practitioner must inform the client of any penalties that are reasonably likely to apply to the client with a position that was taken on the tax return. The tax preparer also needs to inform the client on how to avoid penalties.

The tax practitioner may generally rely in good faith upon any information provided by the taxpayer without having to verify the information the client has given. However, the tax practitioner cannot ignore any potential implications of the documentation that was given to him or any actual knowledge he may have of any errors thereof. A reasonable inquiry about the information furnished is necessary if the taxpayer's provided information seems to be inconsistent or incomplete.

Standards of Competence for Tax Professionals

A practitioner must possess the appropriate level of knowledge, skill, thoroughness, and preparation necessary for competent engagement in practice before the Internal Revenue Service. A practitioner may become competent for the matter for which the practitioner has been engaged through various methods, such as consulting with experts in the relevant area or studying the relevant law.

If the tax professional is not competent in a subject matter, they may consult another individual who the tax professional knows or believes has established competence in the field of study. When the tax professional does consult with another individual, they must consider the requirements of Internal Revenue Code §7216.

Compliance Procedures

Any practitioner who has or shares principal authority and responsibility for overseeing a firm's practice of providing advice concerning federal tax issues must take reasonable steps to ensure that the firm has adequate procedures to raise awareness and to promote compliance with Circular 230 by the firm's members, associates, and employees, and that all such employees are complying with the regulations governing practice before the IRS. These compliance procedures are stated in full in Circular 230 subparts A, B, and C, which can be found on the IRS website.

Any individual or individuals who share principal authority will be subject to discipline for failing in the following ways through willfulness, recklessness, or gross incompetence:

> ➤ The individual does not take reasonable steps to ensure the procedures of the firm are adequate.
> ➤ The individual does not take reasonable steps to ensure the firm's procedures are properly followed.
> ➤ The individual fails to take prompt action to correct any noncompliance despite knowing (or being in a situation where it was the individual's duty to know) that one or more individuals who are associated with or employed by the individual are engaged in a pattern or practice that does not comply with the firm's position.

Taxpayers should receive and be advised to keep copies of the following:

> ➢ Form 8879 (PIN program).
> ➢ Any Form W-2, Form 1099, etc., and any other backup material for their return.
> ➢ A copy of the return that was electronically filed, in a form they can understand.
> ➢ A copy of Form 9325, *General Information for Taxpayers Who File Electronically*, which tells taxpayers the procedure to follow if they do not receive their refund.
> ➢ For those who request a bank product, a copy of the signed bank application and the disclosure statement.

Taxpayer Information Retention

The tax professional must provide a complete copy of the return to the taxpayer. Tax professionals may provide the copy in any media, including electronic, that is acceptable to both the taxpayer and the tax professional. The copy does not have to contain the Social Security number of the client. A complete copy of a taxpayer's return includes Form 8453 and other documents that the tax professional cannot electronically transmit, when applicable, as well as the electronic portion of the return.

The electronic portion of the return can be contained on a replica of an official form or on an unofficial form. However, on an unofficial form, the tax professional must reference data entries to the line numbers or descriptions on an official form. If the taxpayer provided a completed paper return for electronic filing and the information on the electronic portion of the return is identical to the information provided by the taxpayer, the tax professional does not have to provide a printout of the electronic portion of the return to the taxpayer.

The tax professional should advise the taxpayer to retain a complete copy of his/her return and any supporting material. The tax professional should advise their clients that, if needed, they must file an amended return as a paper return and mail it to the submission processing center that handles the taxpayer's paper return.

Part 1 Review Questions

To obtain the maximum benefit from this chapter, LTP recommends that you complete each of the following questions, and then compare them to the answers with feedback that immediately follows. Under governing self-study standards, vendors must present review questions intermittently throughout each self-study course.

These questions and explanations are not part of the final examination and will not be graded by LTP.

DDPP1.1
Which of the following procedures is not a best practice for the tax professional?

a. Communicate clearly with the client regarding the terms and condition of the LTPA website.
b. Act fairly and with integrity.
c. Advise clients on whether they may avoid accuracy-related penalties if the client relies on that person's advice.
d. Establish facts to arrive at a conclusion supported by those facts.

DDPP1.2

Vicente prepared Esperanza's tax return but did not ask her any questions to determine if she qualified for Earned Income Tax Credit (EITC). Which of the following statements is not a paid tax preparer EITC due diligence requirement?

    a. Complete and maintain copies of all worksheets and additional questions asked.
    b. Does not have to complete the appropriate refundable credit worksheets.
    c. Know the law and use that knowledge of the law to ensure the client is being asked the right questions to get all relevant information.
    d. Complete and submit Form 8867 with each EITC return.

DDPP1.3

Deborah is a new client to Gloria. Deborah owns a cleaning business and has a part-time W-2 job. Total gross wages reported on her W-2 were $8,500. Her cleaning business earned $7,000 with no expenses. Deborah has 3 children under the age of 17. Which of the following questions does Gloria not have to ask Deborah?

    a. Does Deborah have a business license?
    b. Does Deborah have a business checking account?
    c. What proof does Deborah have of her income?
    d. Does Deborah want Gloria to do her bookkeeping?

DDPP1.4

IRC Section _____ contains the income tax regulations pertaining to due diligence requirements for tax professional.

    a. 6695
    b. 4321
    c. 2295
    d. 8867

DDPP1.5

Which of the following is a due diligence requirement?

    a. Incomplete Form 8863
    b. Keep a copy of all information provided
    c. Have the client sign a declaration of truth statement
    d. Advising the client, the burden of proof is on them, is enough to protect the tax preparer

DDPP1.6

Due Diligence is requiring tax preparers to take additional steps to ensure Schedule C filers are truly in business. Which of the following steps is NOT a due diligence compliance check?

    a. Business license
    b. Bank statements of the business
    c. Proof of income such as 1099s
    d. Tax preparer visits the client's business office

DDPP1.7
Preparer penalties for due diligence non-compliance include:

a. $560 penalty for each failure to comply
b. $1,000 penalty for unreasonable position
c. $5,000 penalty for recklessness or intent
d. All the answers are penalties

DDPP1.8
The paid tax preparer must exercise _____ when preparing tax returns and determine _____ of representations made by themselves to their clients or to the IRS.

a. due diligence/correctness
b. regularly/accurately
c. good faith/evaluation
d. due diligence/faithfulness

DDPP1.9
Which of the following practitioner who has the responsibility of oversight for tax return preparation could be subject to disciplinary action if the procedures are not followed correctly?

a. A practitioner who knows of an employee's engagement in practices not in compliance with Circular 230, and the practitioner take prompt action to correct the noncompliance.
b. An employee engages in a noncompliant practice due to the practitioner's failure to take reasonable steps to ensure compliance with Circular 230.
c. A practitioner who fails to ensure adequate procedures; however, the firm's members, associates, and employees all comply with Circular 230.
d. A practitioner who does not know of an employee's noncompliance with Circular 230.

DDPP1.10
Which of the following practitioner who has the responsibility of oversight for tax return preparation could be subject to disciplinary action if the procedures are not followed correctly?

a. A practitioner who knows of an employee's engagement in practices not in compliance with Circular 230, and the practitioner take prompt action to correct the noncompliance.
b. An employee engages in a noncompliant practice due to the practitioner's failure to take reasonable steps to ensure compliance with Circular 230.
c. A practitioner who fails to ensure adequate procedures; however, the firm's members, associates, and employees all comply with Circular 230.
d. A practitioner who does not know of an employee's noncompliance with Circular 230.

Part 1 Review Questions Answers

DDPP1.1
Which of the following procedures is not a best practice for the tax professional?

a. **Communicate clearly with the client regarding the terms and conditions of the LTPA website.**
b. Act and with integrity.
c. Advise clients on whether they may avoid accuracy-related penalties if the client relies on that person's advice.
d. Establish facts to arrive at a conclusion supported by those facts.

Feedback: Review section *Best Practice Guidelines.*

DDPP1.2
Vicente prepared Esperanza's tax return but did not ask her any questions to determine if she qualified for Earned Income Tax Credit (EITC). Which of the following statements is not a paid tax preparer EITC due diligence requirement?

    a. Complete and maintain copies of all worksheets and additional questions asked.
    b. Does not have to complete the appropriate refundable credit worksheets.
    c. Know the law and use that knowledge of the law to ensure the client is being asked the right questions to get all relevant information.
    d. Complete and submit Form 8867 with each EITC return.

Feedback: Review section *Purpose of Form 8867.*

DDPP1.3
Deborah is a new client to Gloria. Deborah owns a cleaning business and has a part-time W-2 job. Total gross wages reported on her W-2 were $8,500. Her cleaning business earned $7,000 with no expenses. Deborah has 3 children under the age of 17. Which of the following questions does Gloria not have to ask Deborah?

    a. Does Deborah have a business license?
    b. Does Deborah have a business checking account?
    c. What proof does Deborah have of her income?
    d. Does Deborah want Gloria to do her bookkeeping?

Feedback: Review section *Self-employed Taxpayer's Due Diligence.*

DDPP1.4
IRC Section _____ contains the income tax regulations pertaining to due diligence requirements for tax professional.

    a. 6695
    b. 4321
    c. 2295
    d. 8867

Feedback: Review section *Self-employed Taxpayer's Due Diligence.*

DDPP1.5
Which of the following is a due diligence requirement?

    a. Incomplete Form 8863
    b. Keep a copy of all information provided
    c. Have the client sign a declaration of truth statement
    d. Advising the client, the burden of proof is on them, is enough to protect the tax preparer

Feedback: Review section *Document Guidelines and Procedures*

DDPP1.6
EITC Due Diligence is requiring tax preparers to take additional steps to ensure Schedule C filers are truly in business. Which of the following steps is NOT an EITC compliance check?

    a. Business license
    b. Bank statements of the business
    c. Proof of income such as 1099s
    d. Tax preparer visits the client's business office

Feedback: Review section *Self-employed Taxpayer's Due Diligence.*

DDPP1.7
Preparer penalties for due diligence non-compliance include:

    a. $560 penalty for each failure to comply
    b. $1,000 penalty for unreasonable position
    c. $5,000 penalty for recklessness or intent
    d. All of the answers are penalties

Feedback: Review section *Consequences of Filing EIC Returns Incorrectly*

DDPP1.8
The paid tax preparer must exercise _____ when preparing tax returns and determine _____ of representations made by themselves to their clients or to the IRS.

    a. due diligence/correctness
    b. regularly/accurately
    c. good faith/evaluation
    d. due diligence/faithfulness

Feedback: Review section *Best Practices Guidelines*

DDPP1.9
Which of the following practitioner who has the responsibility of oversight for tax return preparation could be subject to disciplinary action if the procedures are not followed correctly?

    a. A practitioner who knows of an employee's engagement in practices not in compliance with Circular 230, and the practitioner take prompt action to correct the noncompliance.
    b. An employee engages in a noncompliant practice due to the practitioner's failure to take reasonable steps to ensure compliance with Circular 230.
    c. A practitioner who fails to ensure adequate procedures; however, the firm's members, associates, and employees all comply with Circular 230.
    d. A practitioner who does not know of an employee's noncompliance with Circular 230.

Feedback: Review section *Best Practices Guidelines*

DDPP1.10
Which of the following practitioner who has the responsibility of oversight for tax return preparation could be subject to disciplinary action if the procedures are not followed correctly?

   a. A practitioner who knows of an employee's engagement in practices not in compliance with Circular 230, and the practitioner take prompt action to correct the noncompliance.
   b. An employee engages in a noncompliant practice due to the practitioner's failure to take reasonable steps to ensure compliance with Circular 230.
   c. A practitioner who fails to ensure adequate procedures; however, the firm's members, associates, and employees all comply with Circular 230.
   d. A practitioner who does not know of an employee's noncompliance with Circular 230.

Feedback: Review section *Best Practices Guidelines*

Part 2 Office of Professional Responsibility (OPR)

OPRs Mission

The Office of Professional Responsibility (OPR) follows a mission to ensure that all tax practitioners, tax preparers, and third parties in the tax system adhere to professional standards and follow the law. OPR is the governing body responsible for interpreting and applying Circular 230 to all who prepare tax returns, whether they are signing or non-signing tax practitioners. OPR has exclusive responsibility for practitioner conduct and discipline.

OPR has oversight of practitioner conduct as well as exclusive responsibility with respect to practitioner discipline, including disciplinary proceedings and sanctions. The OPR may, after notice and an opportunity for a conference, perform the following disciplinary proceedings:

   ➢ Disqualify an appraiser from further submissions in connection with tax matters.
   ➢ Propose a monetary penalty on any practitioner who engages in conduct subject to sanction. The monetary penalty may be proposed against the individual or a firm or both and can be done in addition to another form of discipline.
   ➢ Negotiate an appropriate level of discipline with a practitioner or initiate an administrative proceeding to Censure, Suspend, or Disbar the practitioner.
      o Censure: A public reprimand in which an offender is included on a quarterly list issued by the IRS that states the offender's city and state, name, professional designation, and the effective date(s) of the censure. If censured, offenders can still prepare taxes, but they are more closely monitored, and their newly-sullied names and reputations can negatively impact their businesses. This is the lightest form of punishment.
      o Suspend: If a taxpayer is suspended, it means they cannot prepare any returns for one to fifty-nine months; how long a taxpayer is suspended is determined by the OPR on a case-by-case basis.
      o Disbar: If a taxpayer is disbarred, he or she cannot prepare any returns whatsoever for at least five years.

These penalties and punishments are connected to the activities that the tax preparer has been associated with on behalf of the employer, for it is the employer's legal responsibility to know what their employees are doing as the employer may be liable for the actions of their employee.

Example: Omar Tax Service (OTS), as an entity subject to the Circular 230 guidelines, needs to have a person in charge of ensuring all OTS and IRS procedures are followed and handled correctly. If employee Travis is caught preparing returns in some way that is non-compliant with these guidelines, there are two potential scenarios:

1. If Omar Tax Service did not have someone to ensure the procedures of both the IRS and OTS were being followed correctly, then OTS is liable for their employee's actions.
2. If OTS did have somebody in place to ensure all procedures were followed properly, and did so in full compliance with Circular 230, then Travis is considered a rogue employee, and OTS may not be liable for his actions because OTS correctly followed all the required procedures.

OPR's Authority

OPR oversees the conduct of tax practice. The oversight extends to all individuals who make a presentation to the IRS relating to a taxpayer's rights, privileges, or liabilities under the laws or regulations administered by the IRS. This authority generally extends to any individual who interacts with federal tax administration in person, orally, in writing, or by the preparation and submission of documents.

OPR oversees a practitioner's conduct and discipline, including disciplinary proceedings and sanctions. After serving a practitioner a notice and granting them an opportunity for a conference, OPR could negotiate an appropriate level of discipline with the practitioner; or could in fact initiate an administrative proceeding to censure (a public reprimand), suspend (one to fifty-nine months), or disbar (five years) the practitioner.

Rules Overseeing the Authority to Practice

The Circular 230 is the written guideline that governs those who represent taxpayers before the IRS. The rules and regulations found in Circular 230 are overseen by the Office of Professional Responsibility (OPR). In this section you will find a detailed list of each section of the Circular 230 and the rules and guidelines contained within each part. It is imperative that the paid tax preparer learns these guidelines and understands his or her individual responsibility to prepare tax returns accurately based on tax law and the information provided by the taxpayer.

Information Provided to the IRS and OPR

If an authorized officer or employee of the IRS or OPR requests information or records regarding or in reference to a taxpayer, the tax preparer is required by law to comply with the request promptly unless he or she believes in good faith or on reasonable grounds that such records or information is privileged or that the request for, or effort to obtain, such record or information is of doubtful legality.

If the requested information is not in the possession of the tax professional or his or her client, the tax professional must promptly notify the requesting IRS or OPR personnel of that fact. In the case of requests from the IRS, the practitioner must make reasonable inquiries of the client regarding the identity of any person who has the records. The tax professional is not required to actually speak with anyone other than their client, but they must ask their client about the identity of any person who may have the records or information that was requested and then provide that information to the IRS.

A practitioner may not interfere, or attempt to interfere, with any proper and lawful effort by the IRS and its officers or employees or with the director of the Office of Professional Responsibility and his or her employees to obtain any record(s) or information unless the practitioner believes in good faith and on reasonable grounds that the record(s) or information is privileged.

As stated in §10.34(b) in regard to the submission of any documents that may be requested by the IRS or OPR, the tax professional cannot advise a client to submit any document to the IRS that falls under one or both of the following two categories:

➤ Frivolous.
➤ Contains or omits information in a manner demonstrating an intentional disregard of a rule or regulation unless the tax professional also advises the client to submit a document that evidences a good faith challenge to the rule or regulation.

Example: The IRS requests information about John Henry. Andres prepared Mr. Henry's return for the past two years; however, the year in question is prior to Mr. Henry becoming Andres' client. Andres has copies of Mr. Henry's tax return for the year in question, which contains the name, address, and identification number of the individual who prepared the return. Andres is required to provide the IRS with the information about the preparer listed on the return, but not the return itself. Andres needs to inform the client of the IRS request.
(Treasury Circular 230, §10.20, §10.34(b)).

Practice Before the IRS

"Practice before the IRS" constitutes all matters connected with a presentation to the IRS, or any of its officers or employees, related to a taxpayer's rights, privileges, or liabilities under the laws or regulations administered by the IRS. Such presentations include, but are not limited to, preparing documents, filing documents, and corresponding and communicating with the IRS. It also includes rendering oral and written advice with respect to any entity, transaction, plan, arrangement, or any matter that has a potential for tax avoidance or evasion; and representing a client at conferences, hearings, and meetings.

Individual Representation Rights

The following is a summary of the individuals who can practice before the IRS and their representation rights.

a. *Attorney*: Any attorney who is not currently under suspension or disbarment from practice before the Internal Revenue Service may do so by filing a written declaration stating that the individual is currently qualified as an attorney and is authorized to represent the party or parties.

b. *Certified public accountant* (CPA): Any certified public accountant who is not currently under suspension or disbarment from practice before the Internal Revenue Service may do so by filing a written declaration that the individual is qualified as a certified public accountant and is authorized to represent the party or parties.

c. *Enrolled agents*: Any individual enrolled as an agent pursuant to this part who is not currently under suspension or disbarment from practice before the Internal Revenue Service may practice before the Internal Revenue Service. (Enrolled agents take a three-part test and must pass each part).

d. ***Enrolled actuaries***: Any individual who is enrolled as an actuary by the Joint Board for the Enrollment of Actuaries pursuant to 29 U.S.C. 1242 who is not currently under suspension or disbarment from practice may do so by filing a written declaration stating that the individual is currently qualified as an enrolled actuary and is authorized to represent the party or parties on their behalf.

e. ***Enrolled retirement plan agents***: An individual enrolled as a retirement plan agent pursuant to this part who is not currently under suspension or disbarment from practice before the Internal Revenue Service may practice before the IRS.

f. ***Annual Filing Season Program Participants (AFSP)***: This voluntary program recognizes the efforts of return preparers who are not attorneys, certified public accountants, or enrolled agents. The IRS issues an Annual Filing Season Program Record of Completion to return preparers who obtain a certain number of continuing education hours in preparation for a specific tax year.

Tax Return Preparer

LTP believes that taxpayers should choose a tax return preparer who will be available for them in case the IRS examines their tax return. Most tax return preparers are professional, honest, and provide excellent customer service to their clients. However, dishonest, and unscrupulous tax return preparers do exist. The taxpayer should always check their return for errors to avoid penalties, along with financial and legal problems.

First, anybody who is paid to prepare tax returns should have complete understanding of tax matters and is required to have a PTIN.

A paid tax return preparer is primarily responsible for the overall accuracy of the taxpayer's return. By law, the paid tax preparer is required to sign the return and include their PTIN. Although the tax return preparer signs the return, the taxpayer is ultimately responsible for the accuracy of every item reported on the return.

The paid tax preparer is subject to Section 6694 and is responsible for the accuracy of the return. The individual who signs the return will be primarily responsible for all the positions on the return and/or claim for refund.

The Internal Revenue Service has also established ethical guidelines and practices. These guidelines, laws, and standard, in part, protect the *Taxpayer Bill of Rights* and are detailed in Circular 230, the consistent, definitive standard of tax professional responsibility that protects not only the taxpayer but the tax professional as well.

Everything the tax practitioner does, every choice he or she makes as a tax professional, affects not only him or herself but the professional's clients, coworkers, and firm as well. Decisions and judgments made in tax preparation are not always black and white. The paid tax preparer's first responsibility is to his or her clients, but one must still make decisions within the boundaries of the law. Issues are often not clearly defined and leave room for interpretation, and when making decisions or judgments as a professional tax preparer in such situations, you should take the following steps:

> ➢ Determine the nature of the issue in question.
> ➢ Obtain as much information and documentation from the client as possible.
> ➢ Research the issue thoroughly, documenting all findings, facts, and positions.
> ➢ Consider relevant case studies.
> ➢ Examine all possible solutions to the questions.

➤ Weigh the consequences of each solution and how each solution may affect all parties involved (the taxpayer, the preparer, and the firm).
➤ Inform the client of your position and explain the consequences of the available answers.
➤ Choose a solution that is legal, ethical, and actionable for all parties involved and comfortable for both you and your client.

LTP recommends that when the taxpayer is looking to hire a professional tax preparer, the taxpayers should keep in mind the following list.

1. Check the preparer's qualifications
2. Check the preparer's history
3. Ask about service fees
4. Ask to e-file the return
5. Make sure the preparer is available
6. Provide records and receipts
7. Never sign a blank check
8. Review your return before signing
9. Ensure the preparer signs and includes their PTIN
10. Report abusive tax preparers to the IRS
11. Visit the following link http://irs.treasury.gov/rpo/rpo.jsf to search for a tax professional in your area

> *Señor 1040 Says:* Privilege does not apply in a criminal matter unless the practitioner is an attorney.

Part 2 Review Questions

To obtain the maximum benefit from this chapter, LTP recommends that you complete each of the following questions, and then compare them to the answers with feedback that immediately follows. Under governing self-study standards, vendors are required to present review questions intermittently throughout each self-study course.

These questions and explanations are not part of the final examination and will not be graded by LTP.

DDPP2.1

A(n) _____ is any individual who has taken and passed a special three-part test and granted enrollment to practice before the IRS.

a. Attorney
b. Certified public accountant
c. Enrolled agent
d. Notary

DDPP2.2

A(n) _____ is any person who is a member in good standing of the bar of the highest court of any State, territory, or possession of the United States, including Commonwealth or the District of Columbia.

    a. Attorney
    b. Certified public account
    c. Enrolled agent
    d. Notary

DDPP2.3

Which of the following best describes the contents of Circular 230?

    a. Written regulations that govern those who represent taxpayers before the IRS.
    b. A document containing the statute and regulations detailing a tax professional's day and night job.
    c. A document containing statements and regulations detailing how to become a tax professional.
    d. A document containing the statute and regulations detailing the duties and obligations of the IRS.

DDPP2.4

What is the Office of Professional Responsibility authority (OPR)?

    a. The OPR oversees the Commissioner.
    b. The OPR oversees the United States Treasury.
    c. The OPR oversees the conduct of tax practice.
    d. The OPR oversees the unprofessional tax preparer.

DDPP2.5

Circular 230 provides a consistent standard for the tax professional to follow. Sometimes the choices made by the paid tax professional affect themselves and the taxpayer. The first responsibility of the paid tax preparer is to the client. When making a decision as a tax preparer, which guideline below should be followed?

    a. Determine the nature of the issue in question.
    b. Get as little information and documentation from the client as possible.
    c. Examine only one possible solution.
    d. Choose a solution that the client is not able to support.

DDPP2.6

Which of the following is the paid tax preparer's responsibility?

    a. Being primarily responsible for the overall substantive accuracy of the taxpayer's return.
    b. Signing the return and including their PTIN on it.
    c. Practicing due diligence in questioning and examining each piece of information.
    d. All the options are correct.

DDPP2.7
Noncompliance due diligence penalty can affect the employer of the tax preparer if the IRS or OPR finds that the employer failed to comply with the EITC due diligence requirements. Which of the following would not impact the firm's penalty?

    a. Revocation of e-file privileges
    b. Suspension
    c. Appeals process
    d. Protecting your firm's reputation

DDPP2.8
Which of the following is not a best practice?

    a. Communicate clearly with the client regarding the terms and conditions of the LTPA website
    b. Act fairly and with integrity
    c. Advise clients whether they may avoid accuracy-related penalties if the client acts in reliance on that person's advice
    d. Establish facts to arrive at a conclusion supported by those facts

DDPP2.9
Joseph is a tax preparer with limited representation rights. Which of the following scenario is Joseph unable to do?

    a. Joseph cannot represent his client in an appeals conference
    b. Joseph can only represent the clients he signed and prepared a tax return before a revenue agent
    c. Joseph can only represent clients he signed and prepared a tax return before an IRS customer service representative
    d. Joseph can only represent clients he signed and prepared a tax return before the IRS Taxpayer Advocate Service (TAS)

DDPP2.10
Which of the following does a paid tax return preparer need when preparing a tax return?

    a. ATIN
    b. PTIN
    c. ITIN
    d. ETIN

Part 2 Review Questions Answers

DDPP2.1
A(n) _____ is any individual who has taken and passed a special three-part test and granted enrollment to practice before the IRS.

    a. Attorney
    b. Certified public accountant
    c. Enrolled agent
    d. Notary

Feedback: Review section *Individual Representation Rights.*

DDPP2.2

A(n) _____ is any person who is a member in good standing of the bar of the highest court of any State, territory, or possession of the United States, including Commonwealth or the District of Columbia.

    a. Attorney
    b. Certified public account
    c. Enrolled agent
    d. Notary

Feedback: Review section *Individual Representation Rights*

DDPP2.3

Which of the following best describes the contents of Circular 230?

    a. Written regulations that govern those who represent taxpayers before the IRS.
    b. A document containing the statute and regulations detailing a tax professional's day and night job.
    c. A document containing statements and regulations detailing how to become a tax professional.
    d. A document containing the statute and regulations detailing the duties and obligations of the IRS.

Feedback: Review section *Rules Overseeing the Authority to Practice.*

DDPP2.4

What is the Office of Professional Responsibility authority (OPR)?

    a. The OPR oversees the Commissioner.
    b. The OPR oversees the United States Treasury.
    c. The OPR oversees the conduct of tax practice.
    d. The OPR oversees the unprofessional tax preparer.

Feedback: Review section *Rules Overseeing the Authority to Practice.*

DDPP2.5

Circular 230 provides a consistent standard for the tax professional to follow. Sometimes the choices made by the paid tax professional affect themselves and the taxpayer. The first responsibility of the paid tax preparer is to the client. When making a decision as a tax preparer, which guideline below should be followed?

    a. Determine the nature of the issue in question.
    b. Get as little information and documentation from the client as possible.
    c. Examine only one possible solution.
    d. Choose a solution that the client is not able to support.

Feedback: Review section *Rules Overseeing the Authority to Practice.*

DDPP2.6
Which of the following is the paid tax preparer's responsibility?

    a. Being primarily responsible for the overall substantive accuracy of the taxpayer's return.
    b. Signing the return and including their PTIN on it.
    c. Practicing due diligence in questioning and examining each piece of information.
    d. All the options.

Feedback: Review section *Best Practice Guidelines*.

DDPP2.7
Noncompliance due diligence penalty can affect the employer of the tax preparer if the IRS or OPR finds that the employer failed to comply with the EITC due diligence requirements. Which of the following would not impact the firm's penalty?

    a. Revocation of e-file privileges
    b. Suspension
    c. Appeals process
    d. Protecting your firm's reputation

Feedback: Review section *Best Practice Guidelines*.

DDPP2.8
Which of the following is not a best practice?

    a. Communicate clearly with the client regarding the terms and condition of the LTPA website
    b. Act fairly and with integrity
    c. Advise clients whether they may avoid accuracy-related penalties if the client acts in reliance on that person's advice
    d. Establish facts to arrive at a conclusion supported by those facts

Feedback: Review section *Best Practice Guidelines*.

DDPP2.9
Joseph is a tax preparer with limited representation rights. Which of the following scenario is Joseph unable to do?

    a. Joseph cannot represent his client in an appeals conference
    b. Joseph can only represent the clients he signed and prepared a tax return before a revenue agent
    c. Joseph can only represent clients he signed and prepared a tax return before an IRS customer service representative
    d. Joseph can only represent clients he signed and prepared a tax return before the IRS Taxpayer Advocate Service (TAS)

Feedback: Review section *Practice Before the IRS*.

DDPP2.10

Which of the following does a paid tax return preparer need when preparing a tax return?

    a. ATIN
    b. PTIN
    c. ITIN
    d. ETIN

Feedback: Review section *Tax Return Preparer*

Part 3 Responsibilities of the Tax Preparer

The paid tax preparer must understand the ethical responsibility to prepare accurate tax returns based on tax law and the information provided by the taxpayer.

OPR may propose censure, suspension, or disbarment of any practitioner from practice before the IRS if the individual shows to be incompetent or disreputable and/or fails to comply with any regulations found in Circular 230. OPR may impose a monetary penalty for an individual or their employer subject to Circular 230. The monetary penalty relates to activities the tax preparer associates with on behalf of the employer. The employer should have known what the employee was doing.

You can find the following explanations of tax professionals' responsibilities under Treasury Circular 230. This summary does not address all provisions of the regulations. The tax professional should read Circular 230 for a complete understanding of the duties and obligations of someone practicing before the IRS. Preparing a tax return is also considered practicing before the IRS.

Due Diligence

Tax professionals must exercise due diligence in preparing and filing tax returns and the correctness of their representation to their clients or the IRS. The tax professional can rely on another person's work if they are carefully engaged, supervised, trained, and evaluated, considering the nature of the relationship between the tax professional and that person. The tax professional generally may rely in good faith and without verification on information furnished by the client, but the tax professional cannot ignore other information furnished to them or which they know. The tax professional must make reasonable inquiries if any information furnished to them appears to be incorrect, incomplete, or inconsistent with other facts or assumptions (Treasury Circular 230, §10.22, §10.34(d)).

The tax professional could rely on the work product of another person if the individual used reasonable care in engaging, supervising, training, and evaluating that person, taking proper account of the nature of the relationship between the tax professional and the taxpayer.

The tax professional may also generally rely in good faith and without verification upon information furnished by their client, but the tax professional cannot ignore other information furnished to them or known by them. The tax professional must make reasonable inquiries if any information furnished to them appears to be incorrect, incomplete, or inconsistent with other facts or assumptions.

Competence

Tax professionals must have the necessary knowledge, skill, thoroughness, and preparation to engage in tax matters. If the tax professional is not competent in an area, they should consult a subject matter expert. When a tax professional consults with another individual, they must consider the requirements of Internal Revenue Code §7216 (Treasury Circular 230 §10.35).

Conflict of Interest

A conflict of interest exists when representing a client who is directly averse to another client of the paid tax professional. A conflict of interest also exists if there is a significant risk that representing a client will be materially limited by the tax professional responsibilities to another client, a former client, a third person, or their interests. When a conflict of interest exists, the tax professional may not represent a client in an IRS matter unless:

1. The tax professional reasonably believes that they can provide competent and diligent representation to all affected clients.
2. The law does not prohibit the tax professional's representation.
3. All affected clients give informed, written consent to the tax professional's representation. The tax professional must retain these consents for 36 months following the termination of the engagement and make them available to the IRS/OPR upon request (Treasury Circular 230, §10.29).

Tax Return Positions

Tax return positions are the strategies chosen when preparing a tax return. Tax preparers guide taxpayers in figuring out the proper positions for their return; it is the tax preparer's duty to perform due diligence and ensure the accuracy of the positions taken on the return and claim for refund. Good tax preparers will choose the positions that best help the taxpayer while complying with IRS guidelines.

The tax professional cannot sign a tax return or refund a claim or advise a client to take a position on a tax return, or refund claim that the tax professional knows (or should know) contains a position that (i) has no reasonable basis, (ii) is an unreasonable position as defined by Internal Revenue Code §6694(a)(2), or (iii) is a willful attempt to understate tax liability or a reckless or intentional disregard of rules or regulations.

On the other hand, an unreasonable position lacks substantial authority defined in IRC §6662, but it has a reasonable basis, and the taxpayer discloses the position. For Circular 230 disclosure, if the tax professional advised the client regarding a position, prepared, or signed the tax return, the tax professional must inform the client of any penalties that are reasonably likely to apply to the client with respect to the tax return position. The tax professional must then explain how to avoid the penalties through disclosure or not taking the position.

For purposes of Circular 230 disclosure, if the tax professional advises the client regarding a position or prepares or signs the tax return, the tax professional must inform the client of any penalties that will possibly apply to the client with respect to the tax return position, and how to avoid the penalties through disclosure (or, by not taking the position).

Written Tax Advice

In providing written advice concerning any federal tax matter, the tax professional must:

1. Base advice on reasonable assumptions.
2. Reasonably consider all relevant facts that a tax professional knows or should know.
3. Use reasonable efforts to identify and ascertain the relevant facts.

The tax professional cannot rely upon representations, statements, findings, or agreements that are unreasonable or known to be incorrect, inconsistent, or incomplete.

The tax professional must always consider the possibility of an IRS audit to a tax return or that a matter could raise an audit. When providing written advice, the tax professional may rely in good faith on the advice of another practitioner only if that advice is reasonable, considering all facts and circumstances. The tax professional cannot rely on the advice of a person they know, or should have known, is not competent to provide the advice, or has an unresolved conflict of interest as defined in §10.29 (Treasury Circular 230, §10.37).

Errors and Omissions

If the tax professional knows that a client has not complied with the U.S. revenue laws or has made an error in, or omission from, any return, affidavit, or other documents which the client submitted or executed under U.S. revenue laws, the tax professional must promptly inform the client of the noncompliance, error, or omission and advise the client regarding the consequences under the Code and regulations of the noncompliance, error, or omission. Depending on the facts and circumstances, the consequences of an error or omission could include (among other things) additional tax liability, civil penalties, interest, criminal penalties, and an extension of the statute of limitations (Treasury Circular 230, §10.21).

Handling Matters Promptly

The tax professional cannot unreasonably delay the prompt disposition of any matter before the Internal Revenue Service. This matter applies to responding to the tax professional's client and IRS personnel. The tax professional cannot advise a client to submit any document to the IRS for delaying or impeding the administration of the federal tax laws (Treasury Circular 230, §10.23, §10.34(b)).

Client Records

At the client's request, the tax professional must promptly return any client records necessary for the client to comply with their federal tax obligations, even if there is a dispute over fees. The tax professional may keep copies of these records. Suppose state law allows the tax professional to retain a client's records in the case of a fee dispute. In that case, the tax professional can only return the records attached to the client's return. Still, the tax professional must provide the client with reasonable access to review and copy any additional client records retained by the tax professional necessary for the client to comply with their federal tax obligations. The term "client records" includes all written or electronic materials provided by the client or a third party to the tax professional.

"Client records" also include any tax return or other document that the tax professional prepared and previously delivered to the client if that return or document is necessary for the client to comply with their current federal tax obligations. The tax professional is not required to provide a client with a copy of their work product. That is, any return, refund claim, or other documents that the tax professional prepared but has not yet delivered to the client if:

1. The tax professional is withholding the document pending the client's payment of fees related to the document.

2. The tax professional contract with the client requires the payment of those fees before delivery (Treasury Circular 230 §10.28).

Supervisory Responsibilities

If the tax professional has or shares principal authority and responsibility for overseeing the firm's tax practice, the tax professional must take reasonable steps to ensure that the tax professional firm has adequate procedures in place. These procedures should raise awareness and promote compliance with Circular 230 by the firm's members, associates, and employees. All such employees must comply with the regulations governing practice before the IRS (Treasury Circular 230, §10.36).

Personal Tax Compliance Responsibilities

The tax professional is responsible for ensuring the timely filing and payment of personal income tax returns and the tax returns for any entity over which the tax professional has, or shares, control. Failing to file 4 of the last 5 years' income tax returns, or 5 of the previous 7 quarters of employment/excise tax returns, is per se disreputable and incompetent conduct that can lead to sudden, indefinite suspension of the practitioner. The willful evasion of the assessment or payment of tax also violates Circular 230 regulations (Treasury Circular 230, §10.51(a)(6)).

Who Prepared the Return?

A tax return preparer is any person who prepares for compensation or employs one or more individuals to prepare all, or a substantial portion of the tax return or any claim for refund of tax. A signing tax return preparer is an individual tax return preparer responsible for the overall substantive accuracy of preparing such return or claim for refund.

A tax return preparer is any and all of the following:

➢ A preparer is any person who prepares all or a substantial portion of any tax return or claims for refund in exchange for compensation or employs one or more persons to prepare for payment.
➢ Any individual paid to prepare or assist with tax preparation of all or substantially all of a tax return or claim for refund must have a PTIN number and is subject to the duties and restrictions relating to practice in subpart B of Circular 230. Subpart B is §10.20 through §10.53. Anyone who prepares a return for compensation must have a PTIN.
➢ Any individual preparing or assisting others in preparing tax returns or claiming for refunds may appear as a witness for the taxpayer before the IRS or furnish information at the request of the IRS or any of the IRS officers or employees.
➢ Any individual preparing or assisting others to prepare all or a substantial portion of a document about any taxpayer's tax liability for compensation is subject to the duties and restrictions relating to practice in §10.20 through §10.53 (subpart B as well as subpart C) and §10.60 through §10.82.

A signing tax return preparer is the individual tax return preparer primarily responsible for the overall substantive accuracy of the preparation of such return or claim for refund. Even if someone else provides all the information and materials needed for the tax return, effectively "preparing" most of the return's material, the individual that inputs and arranges the material for the actual submission of the return or claim for refund is the person who must sign the return and thus claim responsibility for its accuracy. The person who needs to sign the return and claim responsibility for its accuracy is whoever decides the tax return's position.

A non-signing tax return preparer is any person who prepares all or a substantial portion of a return or claims for a refund but does not possess the primary responsibility for its accuracy. They were not individuals who input the information into the tax return or chose the tax return positions.

Whether or not an individual should be considered a non-signing or signing tax return preparer also depends on how much time the preparer spends advising the taxpayer. To be eligible to be a non-signing preparer, events that have occurred should represent less than 5% of the aggregated time incurred by the non-signing tax return preparer. You calculate the advice you give, whether written or oral, when given to the taxpayer and the signing tax preparer.

Example: An enrolled agent named Fiona hires Nick to do the literal inputting of W-2s, and other income documents, and other related materials into her preferred tax software. After Nick finishes, Fiona goes through the prepared material, ensures it is correct, and submits the return. Even though Nick spent more time on the return and was the one who put it all together, Fiona prepared the tax return because she was the one who checked its contents and performed the actual action of ensuring that the return was accurate. Therefore, Fiona must sign the return and thus claim responsibility for its accuracy. Even though Nick "prepared" the return by putting it together, Fiona checked and guaranteed its accuracy.

A person who renders tax advice on a position directly relevant to determining the existence, characterization, or amount of an entry on a return or claim for refund prepared the entry. The meaning of substantial portion is based upon whether the person knows or reasonably should know the tax characteristics of the schedule, entry, or other portion of a return or claim for refund. A single tax entry could constitute a considerable portion of the tax required to be shown on a return.

Example 1: Domingo is an attorney at ABC law firm; he provides legal advice to a large corporate taxpayer regarding a completed corporate transaction. The advice provided by Domingo is directly relevant to the determination of an entry on the taxpayer's return. Domingo, however, does not prepare any other portion of the taxpayer's return and is not signing the return. Domingo is a non-signing tax return preparer since his advice is limited to one entry on the tax return.

Example 2: The facts are the same as Example 1, except that Attorney Brittni provides supplemental advice to the corporate taxpayer on a phone call after completing the transaction. Brittni did not provide advice before the corporate transaction occurred with the primary intent to avoid being a tax return preparer. The time incurred on the supplemental advice by Brittni represents less than 5% of the aggregate amount of time spent by Brittni providing tax advice on the position. Brittni is not considered a tax return preparer.

Example 3: The facts are the same as Example 2, except that Attorney Brittni provides supplemental advice to the corporate taxpayer on a phone call after the transaction occurred with the primary intent to avoid being a tax return preparer. The time incurred on the supplemental advice by Brittni represents less than 5% of the aggregate amount of time spent by Brittni providing tax advice on the position. Brittni is not considered a tax return preparer.

Whether the schedule entry is a single-line entry or the entire schedule (A, B, K-1, etc.), or another entry on the tax return, the consideration is the substantial amount belonging to the single entry or the entire schedule. If the consideration is a significant portion of the return, then the individual responsible for the entry could be considered the signer of the tax return. The key is the amount of the entry. For example, Nick only entered Jesse's personal information and one W-2 into the tax return. Fernando completed Jesse's Schedule A, B, and C. Fernando would be the signer on the return since he entered a substantial portion of the return.

Any individual paid to prepare or assist with tax preparation of all or substantially all the tax returns or claims for refund must have a PTIN number and is subject to the duties and restrictions relating to practice in subpart B of Circular 230. Subpart B is §10.20 through §10.53.

Any individual preparing or assisting others to prepare a tax return or claims for a refund may appear as a witness for the taxpayer before the IRS. They can also furnish information at the request of the IRS or any of the IRS officers or employees.

Any individual who for compensation prepares, or assists in the preparation of, all or a substantial portion of a document pertaining to any taxpayer's tax liability is subject to the duties and restrictions relating to practice in §10.20 through §10.53 (subpart B as well as subpart C) and §10.60 through §10.82.

Example: Kristie is Maria's administrative assistant. Kristie collects information from Julie, Maria's client, to help Maria prepare the tax return. Maria signs the return. Kristie is not the paid preparer of Julie's tax return.

Factors to consider that make a substantial portion include:

1. The size and complexity of the item relative to the taxpayer's gross income
2. The size of the understatement attributable to the item compared to the taxpayer's reported tax liability

Example 1: Timothy prepares Form 8886, "*Reportable Transaction Disclosure Statement.*" He does not prepare the tax return or advise the taxpayer regarding the tax return position for the transaction to which Form 8886 relates. The preparation of Form 8886 is not directly relevant to the determination of the existence, characterization, or amount of an entry on a tax return or claim for a refund. Timothy is preparing Form 8886 to disclose a reportable transaction and not to prepare a substantial portion of the tax return and is not considered a tax return preparer under §6694.

Example 2: Vicente prepares a schedule for Jose's Form 1040, reporting $4,000 in dividend income, and gives Jose oral or written advice about his Schedule A, which results in a medical expense deduction totaling $5,000, but does not sign the return. Vicente is a non-signing tax return preparer because the aggregate total amount of the deduction is less than $10,000.

A tax refund claim includes a credit claim against any tax. A claim for refund also includes a claim for payment under sections 6420, 6421, or 6427.

Example 1: Jose received employment tax information from Maria, who prepares her recordkeeping. Jose did not render any tax advice to Maria or exercise any discretion or independent judgment on Maria's tax positions. Jose just processed the information that Maria gave to him. Jose signed the return as authorized by the client according to Form 8655, *Reporting Agent Authorization,* and filed Maria's return using the information supplied by Maria. Jose is a tax return preparer.

Example 2: Matthew rendered tax advice to Sharon on determining whether her workers are employees or independent contractors for federal tax purposes. Matthew received compensation for his advice and is the tax return preparer. The following individuals are not tax return preparers:

1. An official or employee of the Internal Revenue Service (IRS) performing official duties.
2. Any individual who provides tax assistance under the Volunteer Income Tax Assistance (VITA) program established by the IRS but the individual can only prepare returns for VITA.
3. Any organization sponsoring or administering a VITA program established by the IRS, but only concerning the sponsorship or administration.
4. An individual who provides tax counseling for the elderly under a program established under section 163 of the Revenue Act of 1978, but only concerning those returns prepared as part of that program.
5. An organization sponsoring or administering a program to provide tax counseling for the elderly established under section 163 of the Revenue Act of 1978, but only concerning that sponsorship or administration.
6. An individual who provides tax assistance as part of a qualified Low-Income Taxpayer Clinic (LITC) as defined by §7526, subject to the requirements, but only for the LITC tax returns.
7. Any organization that is a qualified LITC.
8. An individual providing just typing, reproduction, or other mechanical assistance in the preparation of a return or claim for a refund.
9. An individual preparing a return or claim for refund of a taxpayer, or an officer, a general partner, member, shareholder, or employee of a taxpayer, by whom the individual is regularly and continuously employed, compensated or in which the individual is a general partner.
10. An individual preparing a return or claim for a refund for a trust, estate, or other entity, of which the individual either is a fiduciary or is an officer, general partner, or employee of the fiduciary.
11. An individual preparing a claim for a refund for a taxpayer in response to:
    a. A notice of deficiency issued to the taxpayer.
    b. A waiver of restriction on assessment after initiating an audit of the taxpayer or another taxpayer if the audit determines the other taxpayer affects, directly or indirectly, the taxpayer's liability.
12. A person who prepares a return or claim for a refund for a taxpayer with no explicit or implicit agreement for compensation, even if the person receives an insubstantial gift, return service, or favor.

Part 3 Review Questions

To obtain the maximum benefit from this chapter, LTP recommends that you complete each of the following questions, and then compare them to the answers with feedback that immediately follows. Under governing self-study standards, vendors are required to present review questions intermittently throughout each self-study course.

These questions and explanations are not part of the final examination and will not be graded by LTP.

DDPP3.1

Fernando prepared Andres and Alberto's partnership return. Alberto sued Andres for misrepresentation of income for their partnership. Which of the partners can Fernando represent before the IRS?

    a. Fernando can represent them both since he knows the truth about both.
    b. Fernando cannot represent either one since it will be a conflict of interest.
    c. Fernando can represent either one if both have given him consent to do so.
    d. Fernando must keep the consent form when a disagreement is in place.

DDPP3.2

Tax return positions are the strategies chosen when preparing a tax return. To perform their task, what must a paid tax preparer do?

    a. Guide taxpayers in figuring out the proper positions for their return.
    b. Perform due diligence and ensure the accuracy of the positions taken on the return and claim for refund.
    c. Choose the positions that best help the taxpayer while still complying with IRS guidelines.
    d. All the options.

DDPP3.3

Which of the following due diligence should a tax preparer carry out?

    1. Prepare and file accurate tax returns.
    2. Rely on work of another individual.
    3. Ask additional questions.
    4. Understand tax positions.

    a. 1 and 2
    b. 1, 2, and 4
    c. 2, 3, and 4
    d. 1, 2, and 3

DDPP3.4

Which of the following representation rights automatically has an ending date?

    a. Form 8821
    b. Form 2848
    c. Third Party Designee
    d. AFTR Course

DDPP3.5

Alexandria is preparing Gloria's tax return. Gloria has a small house cleaning business. Which of these additional questions is not something Alexandria should ask Gloria to ensure she has the business?

    a. Gloria, do you have a business license?
    b. Gloria, do you have bank statements that show your earned income?
    c. Gloria, did you receive any 1099MISC Forms?
    d. Gloria, how many dependents do you have?

DDPP3.6
Ruth, an unenrolled preparer, wants to open her own tax preparation business and needs to know where to find guidelines and standards for her tax preparation business. Which of the following would be the best resource?

    a. California Tax Education Council Website
    b. Circular 230
    c. From her friend Jennifer who has just been sanctioned by the IRS
    d. From her insurance agent who is also a tax preparer

DDPP3.7
Which of the following is not considered the tax preparer?

    a. An official or employee of the Internal Revenue Service (IRS) performing official duties.
    b. An individual providing only typing, reproduction, or other mechanical assistance in the preparation of a return or claim for a refund.
    c. A person who prepares a return or claim for refund for a taxpayer with no explicit or implicit agreement for compensation, even if the person receives an insubstantial gift, return service, or favor.
    d. A person who inputs tax information prepared by the taxpayer, does not give tax advice to the client or exercise any discretion or independent judgment on any tax positions; he or she only inputs and reviews the information, signs, and submits the return.

DDPP3.8
Any individual or individuals who share principal authority will be subject to discipline for failing in of the following ways through willfulness, recklessness, or gross incompetence except which?

    a. The individual does not take reasonable steps to ensure the procedures of the firm are adequate.
    b. The individual does not take reasonable steps to ensure the firm's procedures are properly followed.
    c. The individual does not take a federal tax refresher course to stay current in federal tax law updates.
    d. The individual fails to take prompt action to correct any noncompliance despite knowing that one or more individuals associated with or employed by

DDPP3.9
Martha prepared Abel's 2022 tax return. Abel has decided not to have Martha prepare his tax return and asked for his tax records to be returned to him. Which of the following scenarios is correct with respect to Abel requesting his records from Martha?

    a. Martha may never return records to Abel even though he has requested them
    b. Martha and Abel or in a dispute over fees, so Martha can keep Abel's records
    c. Martha must promptly return to Abel his records, even if there is a dispute over fees
    d. Martha has three months to return Abel's records to him, once she has received the request

DDPP3.10

Maria prepared a tax return for Jose, who claimed to have 3 children. He was unable to remember all the children's birthdays and their social security numbers were written on paper. Which of the following is not an EITC due diligence requirement?

    a. Maria should ask additional questions and make sure the answers are documented and saved with the tax return.

    b. Maria should complete Form 8867 and make sure that the form is submitted electronically with the tax return

    c. Jose needs to mail his tax return in; Maria needs to make sure that Form 8867 is attached to the return being mailed

    d. Maria only needs to make sure that the tax return is completed

Part 3 Review Questions Answers

DDPP3.1

Fernando prepared Andres and Alberto's partnership return. Alberto sued Andres for misrepresentation of income for their partnership. Which of the partners can Fernando represent before the IRS?

    a. Fernando can represent them both since he knows the truth about both.

    b. Fernando cannot represent either one since it will be a conflict of interest.

    c. Fernando can represent either one if both have given him consent to do so.

    d. Fernando must keep the consent form when a disagreement is in place.

Feedback: Review section *Conflict of Interest*.

DDPP3.2

Tax return positions are the strategies chosen when preparing a tax return. To perform their task, what must a paid tax preparer do?

    a. Guide taxpayers in figuring out the proper positions for their return.

    b. Perform due diligence and ensure the accuracy of the positions taken on the return and claim for refund.

    c. Choose the positions that best help the taxpayer while still complying with IRS guidelines.

    d. All the options.

Feedback: Review section *Tax Return Positions*.

DDPP3.3

Which of the following due diligence should a tax preparer carry out?

    1. Prepare and file accurate tax returns.
    2. Rely on the work of another individual.
    3. Ask additional questions.
    4. Understand tax positions.

    a. 1 and 2

    b. 1, 2, and 4

    c. 2, 3, and 4

    d. 1, 2, and 3

Feedback: Review section *Who Prepared the Return?*

DDPP3.4
Which of the following representation rights automatically has an ending date?

    a. Form 8821
    b. Form 2848
    c. **Third Party Designee**
    d. AFTR Course

Feedback: Review section *Who Prepared the Return?*

DDPP3.5
Alexandria is preparing Gloria's tax return. Gloria has a small house cleaning business. Which of these additional questions is not something Alexandria should ask Gloria to ensure she has the business?

    a. Gloria, do you have a business license?
    b. Gloria, do you have bank statements that show your earned income?
    c. Gloria, did you receive any 1099MISC Forms?
    d. **Gloria, how many dependents do you have?**

Feedback: Review section *Who Prepared the Return?*

DDPP3.6
Ruth, an unenrolled preparer, wants to open her own tax preparation business and needs to know where to find guidelines and standards for her tax preparation business. Which of the following would be the best resource?

    a. California Tax Education Council Website
    b. **Circular 230**
    c. From her friend Jennifer who has just been sanctioned by the IRS
    d. From her insurance agent who is also a tax preparer

Feedback: Review section *Personal Tax Compliance Responsibilities*.

DDPP3.7
Which of the following is not considered the tax preparer?

    a. An official or employee of the Internal Revenue Service (IRS) performing official duties.
    b. An individual providing only typing, reproduction, or other mechanical assistance in the preparation of a return or claim for a refund.
    c. A person who prepares a return or claim for refund for a taxpayer with no explicit or implicit agreement for compensation, even if the person receives an insubstantial gift, return service, or favor.
    d. **A person who inputs tax information prepared by the taxpayer, does not give tax advice to the client or exercise any discretion or independent judgment on any tax positions; he or she only inputs and reviews the information, signs, and submits the return.**

Feedback: Review section *Who Prepared the Return?*

DDPP3.8
Any individual or individuals who share principal authority will be subject to discipline for failing in of the following ways through willfulness, recklessness, or gross incompetence except which?

    a. The individual does not take reasonable steps to ensure the procedures of the firm are adequate.
    b. The individual does not take reasonable steps to ensure the firm's procedures are properly followed.
    c. **The individual does not take a federal tax refresher course to stay current in federal tax law updates.**
    d. The individual fails to take prompt action to correct any noncompliance despite knowing that one or more individuals associated with or employed by

Feedback: Review section *Competence.*

DDPP3.9
Martha prepared Abel's 2022 tax return. Abel has decided not to have Martha prepare his tax return and asked for his tax records to be returned to him. Which of the following scenarios is correct with respect to Abel requesting his records from Martha?

    a. Martha may never return records to Abel even though he has requested them
    b. Martha and Abel or in a dispute over fees, so Martha can keep Abel's records
    c. **Martha must promptly return to Abel his records, even if there is a dispute over fees**
    d. Martha has three months to return Abel's records to him, once she has received the request

Feedback: Review section *Clients Records.*

DDPP3.10
Maria prepared a tax return for Jose, who claimed to have 3 children. He was unable to remember all the children's birthdays and their social security numbers were written on paper. Which of the following is not an EITC due diligence requirement?

    a. Maria should ask additional questions and make sure the answers are documented and saved with the tax return.
    b. Maria should complete Form 8867 and make sure that the form is submitted electronically with the tax return.
    c. Jose needs to mail his tax return in; Maria needs to make sure that Form 8867 is attached to the return being mailed.
    d. **Maria only needs to make sure that the tax return is completed.**

Feedback: Review section *Who Prepared the Return?*

Part 4 Preparer Penalties

The IRS has the authority to penalize the tax preparer for not being compliant with their due diligence in preparing a tax return with the following:

1. Earned Income Credit (EIC).
2. Child Tax Credit (CTC).
3. Additional Child Tax Credit (ACTC).
4. Other Dependent Credit (ODC).
5. American Opportunity Tax Credit (AOTC).
6. Head of Household Status

Although the ODC, is not refundable it is still a credit that one needs to ask questions about the dependent.

When completing Form 8867 the preparer should not just mark the question yes or no without asking the taxpayer. Don't assume that the questions are the same from year to year. Form 8867 is the form that determine in the tax preparer completed their due diligence in asking the appropriate questions. Compiling Taxpayers Information will guide you in identifying questions to help you determine if the taxpayer truly qualify for the credits and filing status. As a beginner preparer, you will soon find out that the taxpayer has learned to work the system. Your job is to ask and document the taxpayers' answers to your questions.

Failure to Furnish Tax Return Copy to Taxpayer

The penalty for the paid tax preparer is $50 for each failure to comply with IRC §6107 regarding furnishing a copy of a return or claim to a taxpayer. The maximum penalty imposed on any tax return preparer shall not exceed $27,000 (tax year 2022) in a calendar year. See IRC, §6695(a).

Failure to Sign Return

The penalty for each failure to sign a return or claim for refund as required by regulations is $50 for the paid tax preparer. The maximum penalty imposed on any tax return preparer shall not exceed $27,000 (tax year 2022) in a calendar year. See IRC, §6695(b).

A tax return is not considered to be valid unless the return has been signed. If the filing status is MFJ, both the taxpayer and spouse must sign the return. If the taxpayer and spouse have a representative sign the return for them, Form 2848 must be attached. If the taxpayer is filing a joint return, and he/she is the surviving spouse, the taxpayer must sign the return stating he/she is filing as the surviving spouse. The taxpayer and spouse (if filing jointly) must make sure to date the return and enter their occupation(s) and a daytime phone number. See Publication 501 and IRC §6695(b).

If the taxpayer received an identity protection PIN (IP PIN), he/she would enter it in the boxes. The tax professional does not enter it for the taxpayer. If the taxpayer has misplaced his/her IP PIN, the taxpayer should notify the IRS by telephone at 1-800-908-4490. The IP PIN is a 6-digit number.

When filing the return electronically, the return must still be signed using a personal identification number (PIN)—this is not the same number as the IP PIN. There are two ways to enter the PIN: self-select or practitioner PIN. The self-select PIN method allows the taxpayer and spouse (if filing jointly) to create their own PIN and enter it as their electronic signature. The practitioner PIN method allows the taxpayer to authorize the tax practitioner to generate or enter the PIN for the taxpayer(s). A PIN is a five-digit combination that can be any number except all zeros.

Señor 1040 Says: There is a difference between the electronically-filed PIN and the IP PIN. Do not mix up these numbers.

Preparers Failure to Furnish Identifying Number

The penalty for each failure to comply with IRC §6109(a)(4) regarding furnishing an identifying number on a return or claim is $50. The maximum penalty imposed on any tax return preparer shall not exceed $27,000 (tax year 2022) in a calendar year. See IRC §6695(c).

Preparer's Failure to Retain a Copy or List of Tax Return

The penalty is $50 for each failure to comply with IRC §6107(b) regarding retaining a copy or list of a return or claim. The maximum penalty imposed on any tax return preparer shall not exceed $27,000 in a return period. See IRC §6695(d). This list is what tax returns you completed for the current tax year. The preparer must maintain records for 4 years.

Preparers Filing Information Returns Incorrectly

If the tax professional is negligent or intentionally files incorrect information returns, the penalty is $50 per return or item on the return, with a maximum penalty of $27,000 (tax year 2022). See IRC §6695(e).

Preparer Endorses Others Checks

If the tax preparer endorses or negotiates any check payable to another person, the penalty is $545.00 per check. For 2023 the penalty is $560.00. See IRC §6695(f).

Failure to be Thorough in Due Diligence

If the tax preparer prepares an erroneous tax return for a head of household filing status and is claiming any of the following credits:

  - Additional Child Tax Credit (ACTC) and Child Tax Credit (CTC)
  - American Opportunity Credit (AOC)
  - Earned income Tax Credit (EITC)
  - Lifetime Learning Credit

See IRC §6695(g).

Preparer's Fraud and False Statements

Guilty of a felony and, upon conviction, a fine of not more than $100,000 ($500,000 in the case of a corporation), imprisonment of not more than three years, and are required to pay for the cost of prosecution. See IRC §7206.

Preparer's Fraudulent Returns, Statements, or Other Documents

Guilty of a misdemeanor and, upon conviction, a fine of not more than $10,000 ($50,000 in the case of a corporation), imprisonment of not more than one year. See IRC §7207.

Preparer's Disclosure or Use of Information of Client's Tax Return

Guilty of a misdemeanor for knowingly or recklessly disclosing information furnished about a tax return or using such information for any purpose other than preparing or assisting in the preparation of such return. Upon conviction, the tax preparer will receive a fine of not more than $1,000, imprisonment for not more than one year, or both as well as paying the costs of prosecution. See IRC §7216.

Preparer's Incompetence and Disreputable Conduct

The following is a summary of what is incompetence and disreputable conduct for which a practitioner may be sanctioned. The following was extracted from Circular 230 §10.51.

1. Conviction of any criminal offense under federal tax laws.
2. Conviction of any criminal offense involving dishonesty or breach of trust.
3. Conviction of any felony under federal or state law for which the conduct involved renders the practitioner unfit to practice before the IRS.
4. Giving false or misleading information or participating in any way in the giving of false or misleading information to the Department of the Treasury or any officer or employee.
5. Solicitation of employment as prohibited under section §10.30, the use of false or misleading representations with intent to deceive a client or prospective client to gain employment or insinuate that the practitioner can obtain special consideration with the IRS, or any officer or employee.
6. Willfully failing to make a federal tax return in violation of the federal tax laws or willfully evading or attempting to evade any assessment or payment of any federal tax.
7. Willfully assisting, counseling, encouraging a client or prospective client to violate any federal tax law, or knowingly counseling or suggesting to a client an illegal plan to evade paying federal tax.
8. Misappropriation of, or failure to remit properly or promptly, funds received from a client for the payment of taxes or other obligations due the United States.
9. Directly or indirectly attempting to influence or offer or agree to attempt to influence the official action of any officer or employee of the IRS using threats, false accusations, duress, or coercion, or any special inducement or promise of an advantage or by bestowing of any gift, favor, or item of value.
10. Disbarment or suspension from practice as an attorney, certified public accountant, public accountant, or actuary by any duly constituted authority of any state, territory, or possession of the United States, including a commonwealth or the District of Columbia, any federal court of record, or any federal agency, body, or board.

11. Knowingly aiding and abetting another person to practice before the IRS during a suspension, disbarment, or ineligibility of such other individual.
12. Contemptuous conduct in connection with practice before the IRS, including the use of abusive language, making false accusations or statements, knowing them to be false, or circulating or publishing malicious or libelous matter.
13. Giving a false opinion, knowingly recklessly or through gross incompetence including an opinion that is intentionally or recklessly misleading or engaging in a pattern of providing incompetent opinions on questions arising from federal tax laws.
14. Willfully failing to sign a tax return prepared by the practitioner when the practitioner's signature is required by federal tax laws unless the failure is due to reasonable cause and not due to neglect.
15. Willfully disclosing or otherwise using a tax return or tax return information in a manner not authorized by the IRC, contrary to the order of a court of competent jurisdiction or contrary to the order of an administrative law judge in a proceeding instituted under §10.60.
16. Willfully failing to file on magnetic or other electronic media a tax return prepared by the practitioner when the practitioner is required to do so by federal tax laws unless the failure is due to reasonable cause and not due to neglect.
17. Willfully preparing all or substantially all, or signing, a tax return or claim for refund when the practitioner does not possess a current or otherwise valid PTIN or other prescribed identifying number.
18. Willfully representing a taxpayer before an officer or employee of the IRS unless the practitioner is authorized to do so.

Depending on which of the above incompetence and disreputable conduct is how the penalty would be assessed. For example, if the preparer understated based on unreasonable position the penalty could be the greater of $250 or 50% of income obtained.

Preparers Understatement Due to Unreasonable Positions

If the preparer takes an unreasonable position for the tax return or claim for a refund, the penalty is $1,000 or 50% (whichever is greater). See IRC §6694(a).

Preparer's Understatement Due to Willful or Reckless Conduct

The penalty is the greater of $5,000 or 75% of the income derived by the tax return preparer with respect to the return or claim for refund. See IRC §6694(b).

Action to Enjoin Tax Return Preparers

A federal district court may enjoin a tax return preparer from engaging in certain proscribed conduct, or in extreme cases, from continuing to act as a tax return preparer altogether. See IRC §7407.

Action to Enjoin a Specified Conduct Related to Tax Shelters and Reportable Transactions

A federal district court may enjoin a person from engaging in certain proscribed conduct including any action, or failure to take action that is in violation of Circular 230. See IRC §7407.

Preparers Understatement of Tax Liability

If the tax preparer helps an individual or business entity to understate the tax liability, they could be assessed a penalty of $1,000 for individual; $10,000 for a corporate tax return. Penalties may be assessed for only once for documents involving to the same taxpayer and same tax period or event. See IRC §6701.

Preparers Disclosure or Use of Taxpayer Information

This penalty applies to disclosures or uses made on or after July 1, 2019. The tax preparer who uses or disclosure information from the taxpayer without permission will be penalized $250 for each tax return and up to $10,000 in a calendar year. For example, Watson gave his personal information to Chuck to prepare his tax return. Chuck is also an insurance agent. He added Watson's information to his insurance database, without Watson agreement.

If Chuck used Watson's information to commit identity theft, then the penalty is $1,000 for each use or disclosure and the maximum assessed is not greater than $50,000 in a calendar year. See IRC §6713.

How the IRS Calculates Penalties

The IRS may calculate tax preparer penalties based on the following:

1. Number of violations
2. Amount of regulations violated
3. Inflation rates
4. How many tax years involved in the penalties

Part 4 Review Questions

To obtain the maximum benefit from this chapter, LTP recommends that you complete each of the following questions, and then compare them to the answers with feedback that immediately follow. Under governing self-study standards, vendors are required to present review questions intermittently throughout each self-study course.

These questions and explanations are not part of the final examination and will not be graded by LTP.

DDPP4.1
Christina prepared Frank's tax return and failed to give him a copy of his return. Upon the discovery, she also realized that she did not provide copies to any of her clients during the 2021 tax season. Christina prepared 610 tax returns for the year. What could be her maximum penalty amount?

    a. $27,000
    b. $30,500
    c. $50 per return
    d. $2,500

DDPP4.2

Maribel prepared a tax return for Sergio. The IRS returned the tax return to Maribel because she did not sign the return. Maribel failed to sign 50 tax returns. What is the maximum amount of penalty that can be imposed upon a tax preparer for not signing their returns?

    a. $27,000
    b. $2,500
    c. $50 per return
    d. $2,750

DDPP4.3

Fernando was afraid of PTIN fraud, so he intentionally left off his PTIN on all tax returns he prepared. What could be his minimum penalty for not furnishing his identifying number?

    a. $27,500 per year
    b. No penalty
    c. $50 per return
    d. $2,500

DDPP4.4

Which of the following penalties could a tax preparer receive for not completing the due diligence requirements?

    a. $560 penalty per refundable credit for each failure to comply.
    b. $1,500 penalty for unreasonable position.
    c. $5,900 penalty for recklessness or intentional disregard of rules or regulations.
    d. $27,000 maximum penalty per tax period.

DDPP4.5

Helen prepared Samuel's tax return with an understatement of liability because she took an unreasonable position. Which of the following scenarios would best describe Helen's penalty?

    a. $545 for failure to disclose the understatement.
    b. 20% of the underpayment, reduced for those items for which there was adequate disclosure.
    c. Either $1,000 or 50% of the income derived by the understatement on Samuel's tax return, whichever is greater.
    d. $1,000 for the failure to furnish the tax shelter registration number.

DDPP4.6

Vicente prepared Esperanza's tax return and he forgot to ask her some questions to determine if Esperanza qualified for Earned Income Tax Credit (EITC). Which of the following best describe the EITC paid preparer requirement?

    1. Complete and maintain copies of all worksheets and additional questions asked
    2. Compute the credit incorrectly
    3. Knowledge of the taxpayers situation
    4. Make sure Form 8867 is completed and submitted with all EITC returns

    a. 1, 2, and 4
    b. 1, 3 and 4
    c. 3 only
    d. 1 and 4

DDPP4.7

The IRS audited Estrella's tax return and discovered that Areslia the tax preparer did not complete the due diligence requirement when preparing Estrella's tax return. The IRS also discovered that the position that Areslia took was unreasonable. What could be Areslia's minimum penalty?

a. $1,510
b. $510
c. $1,000
d. $5,000

DDPP4.8

A tax professional can be penalized $ _____ for each failure of EITC due diligence.

a. $50
b. $560
c. $1,000
d. No charge the taxpayer pays everything

DDPP4.9

Ruby was assigned an IP PIN from the IRS for identity protection. She is not sure if she brought the correct number to Rita to prepare her current year tax return. Ruby's IP number consists of how many digits?

a. Three
b. Five
c. Six
d. Seven

DDPP4.10

Which of the following IRC section deals with preparer penalties?

a. §6695
b. Both sections 6694 and 6695
c. §6694
d. Circular 230

Part 4 Review Questions Answers

DDPP4.1

Christina prepared Frank's tax return and failed to give him a copy of his return. Upon the discovery, she also realized that she did not provide copies to any of her clients during the 2021 tax season. Christina prepared 610 tax returns for the year. What could be her maximum penalty amount?

a. $27,000
b. $30,500
c. **$50 per return**
d. $2,500

Feedback: Review section *Failure to Furnish Tax Return Copy to Taxpayer.*

DDPP4.2

Maribel prepared a tax return for Sergio. The IRS returned the tax return to Maribel because she did not sign the return. Maribel failed to sign 50 tax returns. What is the maximum amount of penalty that can be imposed upon a tax preparer for not signing their returns?

    a. $27,000
    b. $2,500
    c. $50 per return
    d. $2,750

Feedback: Review section *Failure to Sign Return.*

DDPP4.3

Fernando was afraid of PTIN fraud, so he intentionally left off his PTIN on all tax returns he prepared. What could be his minimum penalty for not furnishing his identifying number?

    a. $27,000 per year
    b. No penalty
    c. $50 per return
    d. $2,500

Feedback: Review section *Failure to Furnish Identifying Number.*

DDPP4.4

Which of the following penalties could a tax preparer receive for not completing the due diligence requirements?

    a. $560 penalty per refundable credit for each failure to comply.
    b. $1,500 penalty for unreasonable position.
    c. $5,900 penalty for recklessness or intentional disregard of rules or regulations.
    d. $27,000 maximum penalty per tax period.

Feedback: Review Section *Penalties.*

DDPP4.5

Helen prepared Samuel's tax return with an understatement of liability because she took an unreasonable position. Which of the following scenarios would best describe Helen's penalty?

    a. $545 for failure to disclose the understatement.
    b. 20% of the underpayment, reduced for those items for which there was adequate disclosure.
    c. Either $1,000 or 50% of the income derived by the understatement on Samuel's tax return, whichever is greater.
    d. $1,000 for the failure to furnish the tax shelter registration number.

Feedback: Review Section *Penalties.*

DDPP4.6
Vicente prepared Esperanza's tax return and he forgot to ask her some questions to determine if Esperanza qualified for Earned Income Tax Credit (EITC). Which of the following best describe the EITC paid preparer requirement?

1. Complete and maintain copies of all worksheets and additional questions asked
2. Compute the credit incorrectly
3. Knowledge of the taxpayers situation
4. Make sure Form 8867 is completed and submitted with all EITC returns

   a. 1, 2, and 4
   b. 1, 3 and 4
   c. 3 only
   d. 1 and 4

Feedback: Review Section *Penalties*.

DDPP4.7
The IRS audited Estrella's tax return and discovered that Areslia the tax preparer did not complete the due diligence requirement when preparing Estrella's tax return. The IRS also discovered that the position that Areslia took was unreasonable. What could be Areslia's minimum penalty?

   a. $1,510
   b. $560
   c. $1,000
   d. $5,000

Feedback: Review Section *Penalties*.

DDPP4.8
A tax professional can be penalized $ _____ for each failure of due diligence.

   a. $50
   b. $560
   c. $1,000
   d. No charge the taxpayer pays everything

Feedback: Review Section *Penalties*.

DDPP4.9
Ruby was assigned an IP PIN from the IRS for identity protection. She is not sure if she brought the correct number to Rita to prepare her current year tax return. Ruby's IP number consists of how many digits?

   a. Three
   b. Five
   c. Six
   d. Seven

Feedback: Review Section *Penalties*.

DDPP4.10
Which of the following IRC section deals with preparer penalties?

    a. §6695
    b. Both sections 6694 and 6695
    c. §6694
    d. Circular 230

Feedback: Review Section *Penalties*.

Takeaways

Tax preparers must understand the ethical guidelines and practices established by the Internal Revenue Service provided in Circular 230. The Office of Professional Responsibility oversees the ethical guidelines and practices, and it also regulates practitioners' conduct and discipline. OPR also oversees the correct level of discipline to practitioners or imposes administrative proceeding to censure, suspend, or disbar practitioner from practicing before the IRS.

Tax preparers must recognize their rights, responsibilities, and representation limitations. We at LTP believe that everything a tax practitioner does—every choice one makes as a tax professional—affects not only themselves, but coworkers, the firm, and ultimately the taxpayer. We also believe that a paid tax preparer's first responsibility is to their client when making decisions and/or judgments about tax preparation.

TEST YOUR KNOWLEDGE!
Go online to take a practice quiz.

California Tax Preparer Due Diligence

Introduction

The California State Legislature established the California Tax Education Council (CTEC) to promote competent tax preparation within the State of California. California law requires anyone who prepares (or assists with the preparation of) tax returns for a fee, and is not an attorney, certified public accountant (CPA), or enrolled agent (EA) to register with CTEC.

Objectives

At the end of this lesson, the student will:

> ➢ Understand how to become a California Registered Tax Preparer (CRTP).
> ➢ Know the governing body for CRTPs
> ➢ Recognize who must register with CTEC
> ➢ Understand CRTP's responsibilities and sanctions/penalties

Table of Contents

Part 1 Tax Preparer Due Diligence and Penalties

California Registered Tax Preparer (CRTP)

California requires tax education for both new and experienced tax preparers. First time paid tax preparers must comply with 60 hours of qualifying tax education. Tax preparers who have completed the 60 hours must maintain their registration by completing a 20-hour course annually.

To register with CTEC, students must pass the 60-hour course with a score of 70% or better and:

1. Complete an online application https://www.ctec.org/App/Preparer/NewApplication/index.
2. Complete Live Scan and go through a background check review then receive notification of either an approval or denial sent via USPS within 1-2 weeks. If the student is denied, the denial letter will include the process to appeal.
3. Obtain or have a valid Personal Tax Identification Number (PTIN).
4. Purchase or have a valid tax preparer surety bond.
5. Complete online CTEC registration and submit payment.

For more information, go to CTEC.org.

LTP recommends that you start your application as soon as you start the course. The process could take a while depending on the background check.

CRTP Responsibilities and Sanctions/Fines

Per California Business and Professions Code §22253.2 and California Revenue and Taxation Code §19167, when a person prepares a tax return, for a fee, without the appropriate lawful designation, the Franchise Tax Board, pursuant to an agreement with the California Tax Education Council, will sanction the tax preparer in the following:

1. The amount of the penalty under the subdivision for the first failure to register is $2,500. This penalty shall be waived if proof of registration is provided to the Franchise Tax Board within ninety days from the date of notice of the penalty, which is mailed to the tax preparer.
2. The amount of the penalty for a failure to register, other than the first failure to register, is $5,000.

The Superior Court, in and for the county in which any person acts as a tax preparer in violation of the provisions of this statute, may, upon a petition by any person, issue an injunction or other appropriate order restraining the conduct.

Disclosure of Information

It is a misdemeanor under the California Business and Professions Code for anyone to disclose any information obtained in the business of preparing federal or state income tax returns or in assisting taxpayers to prepare their returns, unless the disclosure is:

Authorized with written consent of the taxpayer:

1. Authorized by law
2. Necessary to the preparation of the return
3. Pursuant to the court order

California and federal law provide for reciprocal exchange of information in the administration of tax laws. The Franchise Tax Board (FTB) and Internal Revenue Service (IRS) have a continuing program that informs each other of findings resulting from their examination of tax returns. To avoid duplication of efforts, the two agencies may agree that one of them will examine a taxpayer's return. Any improper disclosure or use of such information is a misdemeanor.

The California Civil Code provides rules and procedures regarding personal and confidential information in the files of state agencies. These rules are designed to ensure privacy of such information. It is a violation of California Business and Professional Code for any preparer to act in a negligent manner or intentionally disregard rules and regulations governing the preparation of income tax returns.

Tax preparers must include their EIN, SSN, or PTIN on all returns that they are paid to prepare. Preparers are required to give clients copies of their federal and state returns. Preparers must retain client records for four years from the date of completion or due date of the return, whichever is later. Law requires paid preparers to sign returns that they prepare for compensation.

California law requires anyone who prepares tax returns for a fee within the State of California and is not an exempt preparer to register annually as a tax preparer with the California Tax Education Council (CTEC). Exempt preparers in California are certified public accountants (CPAs), enrolled agents (EAs), and attorneys who are members of the State Bar of California.

Taxpayer Signature

All returns must be signed by the taxpayer and spouse in the space provided on the tax return. Requirements for signing with a power of attorney for a deceased taxpayer or for a surviving spouse are the same as on the federal return. If the taxpayer wishes to designate a power of attorney, they will use Form FTB 3520. The designee may sign the taxpayer's return, receive notices, and aid in tax-related issues for the taxpayer. If the power of attorney is for a married filing joint return, both spouses must sign Form FTB 3520. The taxpayer may also use Federal Form 2848 (power of attorney), handwritten authority documents, and general or durable power of attorney declarations.

Failure to Furnish Tax Return Copy to Taxpayer

Like the IRS, California has the same penalty. $50 per failure not to exceed $25,000 during any calendar year. This is for reasonable cause and not willful neglect. See R&TC §19167(a).

Preparers Failure to Furnish Identifying Number

Like the IRS, California has the same penalty. $50 per failure not to exceed $25,000 during any calendar year. This is for reasonable cause and not willful neglect. See R&TC §19167(b).

Preparer's Failure to Retain a Copy or List of Tax Return

Like the IRS, California has the same penalty. $50 per failure not to exceed $25,000 during any calendar year. This is for reasonable cause and not willful neglect. See R&TC §19167(d)(1) and (2).

Preparers Filing Information Returns Incorrectly

California has the same penalty. $50 per failure not to exceed $250,000 during any calendar year. For individuals with gross receipts of less than $5,000,000 the penalty will be $100,000, this is for reasonable cause and not willful neglect. Penalties could be more if the preparer is found to have intentional disregard depending on the type of information return. See R&TC §19183(a).

If the tax preparer corrects the failure to file correct information returns the reduction in penalty is $30 per failure and shall not exceed$150,000 during any calendar year. $50,000 for individuals with gross receipts or $5,000,000 or less. See R&TC §19183(a).

Preparer Endorses Taxpayers Checks

If the tax preparer endorses or negotiates any check payable to the taxpayer, the penalty is $250 per check. The tax preparer is not considered to have endorsed the taxpayers check if they are depositing into the taxpayers' account. See R&TC §19169, 20645.7.

Tax Preparer Due Diligence Penalty

Like the federal, California also has a penalty for the paid preparer for Due Diligence. Form 3596 *Paid Preparer's Due Diligence Checklist for California Earned Income Tax Credit (CalEITC)*. Tax preparer needs to ask the client all the pertaining questions on Form 3596. Assumption that the answers are the same every year, is not completing the form correctly. The penalty is $500 per penalty for each failure to comply.

Preparer's Fraud and False Statements

When a tax preparer completes a return or claim for a refund that permits the taxpayer to have an understatement based on an unreasonable position and the preparer knew about it. The penalty is the greater of $250 or %50% of income derived (or to be derived) by the tax preparer with respect to each return or claim. See R&TC §19166(a).

The preparer can avoid the penalty if the position is adequately disclosed and has a reasonable basis. The position is not disclosed and is not a tax shelter and there is substantial authority for the situation. The tax shelter position is defined in IRC Section 6662(d) or a reportable transaction under IRC Section 6011, and the preparer believes that the position is reasonable and more-likely-then not-correct.

Preparer's Fraudulent Returns, Statements, or Other Documents

When a preparer completes a return or claim for refund that results in the taxpayer's understatement based on an undisclosed reportable transaction, a listed transaction or a gross misstatement. The penalty is grater of $5,000 or 50% of the income derived or to be derived with respect to each return or claim.

A preparer is not considered to have recklessly or intentionally disregarded a rule or regulation if the position has a reasonable basis and is adequately disclosed. If a regulation is at issue, there must be a good faith challenge. If the position is contrary to a revenue ruling or notice, the substantial authority standard applies. The same rules of paying 15% and foiling a claim and suit in court apply. See R&TC §19166(a).

Tax Preparer Unreasonable Position

When a tax preparer completes a return or claim for refund that results in the taxpayer's understatement based on an unreasonable position, and the preparer knew or reasonably should have known of the unreasonable position, the penalty is $250 or 50% of the income derived by the tax preparer with respect to each return or claim, whichever is greater. The tax preparer could avoid the penalty if:

1. The position is adequately disclosed and has a reasonable basis
2. If the position is not disclosed and is not a tax shelter and there is substantial authority for the position
3. For a tax shelter position defined in IRC Section 662(d) or a reportable transaction under IRC Section 6011, if the preparer reasonably believes that the position is more likely-than-not correct.

If the preparer pays at least 15% of the penalty within 30 days of the bill and files a claim for refund, the preparer may file an action in court within 30 days of the claim denial or deemed denial.

If the tax preparer completes a return or claim for refund that results in the taxpayer's understatement based on an undisclosed reportable transaction, a listed transaction, or a gross misstatement, the penalty could be $1,000 or 50% of the income derived with respect to each return or claim. R&TC §19166(b)(2).

Preparer's Understatement Due to Willful or Reckless Conduct

If the understatement on the taxpayers' return is due to deliberate disregard of rules or regulations by the tax preparer's willful attempt to understate the liability or any careless intended disregard of the rules. The tax preparer could be fined the greater of $5,000 or 50% of the income derived with respect to each return of claim.

A preparer is not considered to have irresponsibly or deliberately disregarded a rule or regulation if the position has a reasonable basis and is adequately disclosed. If a regulation is at issue, there must be a good faith challenge. If the position is contrary to a revenue ruling or notice, the substantial authority standard applies. The same rules of paying 15% and foiling a claim and suit in court apply. See R&TC §19166(a).

Failure to File Electronically

If the tax preparer is subject to filing returns electronically and fails to file. The penalty is $50 pcr cach failurc. Exccptions to the rule are reasonable cause and not willful neglect. Reasonable cause could be that the taxpayer elected not to file electronically. See R&TC §19170.

Promotion of Abusive Tax Shelter

If the tax preparer engages in the organization of, or sale of any interest in, a partnership or other entity, an investment plan or arrangement, or any other plan or arrangement, and the preparer makes, furnishes, or cause another person to make or furnish:

1. A false or fraudulent tax benefits statement as to a material matter.
2. A gross valuation overstatement as to a material matter.

The penalty could be $1,000 or 100% of the gross income derived or will be derived by the person from the activity whichever is less.

Willful Misclassification of an Independent Contractor

It is unlawful for any person or employer to:

➢ Willfully misclassify an individual as an independent contractor.
➢ Charging an individual who has been willfully misclassified or make deductions from compensation for any purpose.

Violators could be subject to a civil penalty of not less than $5,000 and more than $15,000 per violation.

Part 1 Review Questions

To obtain the maximum benefit from this chapter, LTP recommends that you complete each of the following questions, and then compare them to the answers with feedback that immediately follow. Under governing self-study standards, vendors are required to present review questions intermittently throughout each self-study course.

These questions and explanations are not part of the final examination and will not be graded by

CDDPP1.1
A CTEC registered tax return preparer (CRTP) must meet which of the following requirements?

1. Must be 18-years-old
2. Must obtain a surety bond of $5,000
3. Must conduct business at any time
4. Must not make fraudulent statements

a. 1, 2, 3, and 4
b. 2, 3, and 4
c. 1 only
d. 1, 2 and 4

CDDPP1.2
Which of the following must a California paid tax preparer have?

1. Does not have to have a PTIN, only their CTEC number.
2. Must be an attorney, certified public accountant, enrolled agent, or registered tax return preparer; or another tax preparer who is registered with CTEC.
3. Is subject to the duties and restrictions relating to practice before the IRS.
4. Is subject to sanctions for violations of the regulations.

a. 1, 2, 3, and 4
b. 2, 3, and 4
c. 1 only
d. 3 and 4

CDDPP1.3

Which of the following organizations oversees the registration of CRTPs?

a. California Tax Education Council (CTEC)
b. Return Preparer Office (RPO)
c. Secretary of State (SOS)
d. Internal Revenue Service (IRS)

CDDPP1.4

Which of the following individuals must register with CTEC?

a. Enrolled agent
b. Attorney
c. Certified public accountant
d. An individual who prepares return for compensation and lives in California

CDDPP1.5

An individual in the state of California who prepares or assists with the preparation of a tax return:

1. Must have a PTIN
2. Must be an attorney, certified public accountant, enrolled agent, or registered tax return preparer; or other tax preparer who is registered with CTEC
3. Is subject to the duties and restrictions relating to practice before the IRS
4. Is subject to sanctions for violations of the regulations.

a. True
b. False

CDDPP1.6

Carol a California Registered Tax Preparer received a letter from the Office of Professional Responsibility (OPR). She is unsure why she received the letter since she lives in California. Carol believes that since she is a California preparer she is exempt from OPR. Which of the following would be a reason Carol would be receiving the letter?

1. Carol has been preparing fraudulent Schedule C returns with large refunds for her clients
2. Carol has not allowed EITC on tax return for those who do not qualify
3. Carol has been omitting income from the taxpayer's returns
4. Carol has been overstating expenses on the tax returns she has prepared

a. 2 only
b. 1, 3, & 4
c. 1 only
d. 3 and 4

CDDPP1.7
Which of the following agency(ies) oversee unenrolled paid tax preparers who live in California?

    a. California Tax Education Council (CTEC)
    b. Office of Professional Responsibility (OPR)
    c. Internal Revenue Service
    d. Both California Tax Education Council (CTEC) and Office of Professional Responsibility (OPR)

CDDPP1.8
Which of the following is a misdemeanor, under the California Business and Professional Code?

    a. Taxpayer consent to assist or prepare the tax return
    b. Taxpayer consent to disclose necessary information to prepare the tax return
    c. Taxpayer did not consent for tax preparer to share information with another company
    d. Taxpayer consent to obtain necessary information to complete the tax return

CDDPP1.9
Which of the following individual who prepares or assists with tax return preparation for a fee must register with CTEC?

    a. Certified public accountant
    b. Attorney
    c. Enrolled agent
    d. Anyone who is not an EA, CPA or attorney.

CDDPP1.10
Which of the following is not an exempt tax preparer in the State of California?

    a. A person enrolled to practice before the IRS
    b. Certified Public Accountant
    c. An individual who is an active member of the State bar of California
    d. A person who, for a fee, assists with or prepares tax returns

Part I Review Question Answers

CDDPP1.1
A CTEC registered tax return preparer (CRTP) must meet which of the following requirements?

    1. Must be 18-years-old
    2. Must obtain a surety bond of $5,000
    3. Must conduct business at any time
    4. Must not make fraudulent statements

    a. 1, 2, 3, & 4
    b. 2, 3, & 4
    c. 1 only
    d. 1, 2, & 4

Feedback: Review section *California Registered Tax Preparer (CRTP)*.

CDDPP1.2
Which of the following must a California paid tax preparer have?

1. Does not have to have a PTIN only their CTEC number
2. Must be an attorney, certified public accountant, enrolled agent, or registered tax return preparer; or other tax preparer who is registered with CTEC
3. Is subject to the duties and restrictions relating to practice before the IRS
4. Is subject to sanctions for violations of the regulations.

a. 1, 2, 3, and 4
b. 2, 3, and 4
c. 1 only
d. 3 and 4

Feedback: Review section *California Registered Tax Preparer (CRTP).*

CDDPP1.3
Which of the following organizations oversees the registration of CRTPs?

a. California Tax Education Council (CTEC)
b. Return Preparer Office (RPO)
c. Secretary of State (SOS)
d. Internal Revenue Service (IRS)

Feedback: Review section *California Registered Tax Preparer (CRTP).*

CDDPP1.4
CTEC requires which of the following to register?

a. Enrolled agent
b. Attorney
c. Certified public accountant
d. An individual who prepares return for compensation and lives in California

Feedback: Review section *California Registered Tax Preparer (CRTP).*

CDDPP1.5
An individual in the state of California who prepares or assists with the preparation of a tax return:

✓ Must have a PTIN;
✓ Must be an attorney, certified public accountant, enrolled agent, or registered tax return preparer; or other tax preparer who is registered with CTEC
✓ Is subject to the duties and restrictions relating to practice before the IRS; and
✓ Is subject to sanctions for violations of the regulations.

a. True
b. False

Feedback: Review section *California Registered Tax Preparer (CRTP).*

CDDPP1.6
Carol, a California Registered Tax Preparer received a letter from the Office of Professional Responsibility (OPR). She is unsure why she received the letter since she lives in California. Carol believes that since she is a California preparer, she is exempt from OPR. Which of the following would be a reason Carol would be receiving the letter?

1. Carol has been preparing fraudulent Schedule C returns with large refunds for her clients
2. Carol has not allowed EITC on tax return for those who do not qualify
3. Carol has been omitting income from the taxpayer's returns
4. Carol has been overstating expenses on the tax returns she has prepared

a. 2 only
b. 1, 3, & 4
c. 1 only
d. 3 & 4

Feedback: OPR oversees the conduct of tax practice. The oversight extends to all individuals who make a presentation to the IRS relating to a taxpayer's rights, privileges, or liabilities under laws or regulations administered by the IRS. This authority generally extends to any individual who interacts with federal tax administration in person, orally, in writing, or by the preparation and submission of documents. Preparing fraudulent returns, overstating expenses which lower the taxpayer's tax liability and understating income would all be a reason for the OPR to send Carol a letter.

Feedback: Review section *CRTP Responsibilities and Sanctions/Fines*.

CDDPP1.7
Which of the following agency(ies) oversee unenrolled paid tax preparers who live in California?

a. California Tax Education Council (CTEC)
b. Office of Professional Responsibility (OPR)
c. Internal Revenue Service
d. Both California Tax Education Council (CTEC) and Office of Professional Responsibility (OPR)

Feedback: Review section *CRTP Responsibilities and Sanctions/Fines*.

CDDPP1.8
Which of the following is a misdemeanor, under the California Business and Professional Code?

a. Taxpayer consent to assist or prepare the tax return
b. Taxpayer consent to disclose necessary information to prepare the tax return
c. Taxpayer did not consent for tax preparer to share information with another company
d. Taxpayer consent to obtain necessary information to complete the tax return

Feedback: Review section *CRTP Responsibilities and Sanctions/Fines*.

CDDPP1.9

Which of the following individual who prepares or assists with tax return preparation for a fee must register with CTEC?

    a. Certified public accountant
    b. Attorney
    c. Enrolled agent
    d. Anyone who is not an EA, CPA or attorney.

Feedback: Review section *California Registered Tax Preparer (CRTP)*.

CDDPP1.10

Which of the following is not an exempt tax preparer in the State of California?

    a. A person enrolled to practice before the IRS
    b. Certified Public Accountant
    c. An individual who is an active member of the State bar of California
    d. A person who, for a fee, assists with or prepares tax returns

Feedback: Review section *California Registered Tax Preparer (CRTP)*.

Takeaways

CTEC is the governing body for California Register Tax Preparers. The tax preparation industry has regulations to follow, which are found in Circular 230 and on the CTEC website. A beginning tax professional living in California must register with CTEC if he/she is not an enrolled agent, attorney, or certified public account. If he/she chooses not to register, the Franchise Tax Board (FTB) could impose the related fines.

Both federal and state have mandatory e-filing for all paid preparers. When e-filing a return, the paid tax preparer cannot just assume that once they hit the submit button (or transmit) that the return will automatically be accepted by the federal or state tax agency. The paid tax preparer should make sure they understand their due diligence when it comes to tax returns. Part of the responsibilities of the paid tax professional is to safeguard clients' information.

TEST YOUR KNOWLEDGE!
Go online to take a practice quiz.

Chapter 2 Compiling Taxpayer's Information

Introduction

This chapter explains the importance of interviewing the taxpayer. Each chapter segment will cover a section of Form 1040 with sample interview questions needed for the section discussed. The tax professional must understand the importance of knowledgeable questions to determine whether the taxpayer can claim certain credits. Interview questions should be documented along with the answers the taxpayer provided. Tax preparation, knowledge, and understanding are essential to a truthful tax return.

Just entering information into software does not prepare the tax return accurately. The saying is true: "garbage in, garbage out." Entering incorrect information so the taxpayer receives a higher refund is not the best situation for the tax practitioner or the client. This chapter provides a brief overview of current year forms and sample questions to determine the best accurate tax position for the taxpayer. Asking the taxpayer questions from the beginning gives the tax preparer truthful answers to complete the tax return.

This chapter will familiarize you with the most used forms. As you continue through the book, more information is added to the topics in this chapter. Our goal is to teach you a little more information at a time by building on the content. At the end of this course, you should be able to prepare a tax return containing Schedule 1, 2 & 3, and Schedule A.

Objectives

By the end of this chapter, the student will:

➢ Identify the various parts of Form 1040.
➢ Recognize items from each section.
➢ Understand the importance of asking questions to determine the best tax situation for the client.
➢ Remember questions from each section to create his/her own interviewing approach.

Resources

Form 1040	Publication 17	Instructions Form 1040
Schedule 1	Tax Topic 301, 303, 352	Eight Facts about Filing Status
Schedule 2		
Schedule 3		

Table of Contents

Part 1 Form 1040

In 2017, the Tax Cuts and Jobs Act changed Form 1040. The forms changed again in 2020. Most of the content on Form 1040 was divided in six (6) schedules for the 2018 tax year; for the 2022 tax year filing, there are three schedules.

Portion of Form 1040

The Following Sections are Found on the 2022 Form 1040:

- ➢ Filing Status
- ➢ General Information such as:
  - o Name
  - o Address
  - o Taxpayer Identification Number
- ➢ Standard Deduction Dependents
- ➢ Income
- ➢ Refund
- ➢ Amount You Owe
- ➢ Third Party Designee
- ➢ Sign Here
- ➢ Paid Preparer Use Only

Filing Status

Portion of Form 1040

There are five filing status options for the federal return:

- ➢ Single (S)
- ➢ Married filing jointly (MFJ)
- ➢ Married filing separately (MFS)
- ➢ Head of household (HOH)
- ➢ Qualifying Surviving Spouse (QSS), formerly known as Qualifying widow(er) (QW)

Filing status is determined on the last day of the tax year. A detailed explanation of filing status will be discussed in a later chapter. All individuals on the taxpayer's return must have a taxpayer identification number (TIN).

Interview Pointers

Below are sample questions to determine a taxpayer's correct filing status:

> ➢ Are you single?
> ➢ Are you legally married?
> ➢ Do you have children?
> ➢ Did the children live with you the entire year? If not, how long did the children live with you?
> ➢ How many months did the children live with you?
> ➢ What documentation do you have to prove the children lived with you?
> ➢ Does anyone else live in your house?
> ➢ Do you live with another taxpayer?

It is necessary that the tax professional determines the correct filing status by asking pertinent questions such as above.

General Information: Name, Address, and Taxpayer Identification Number

Gathering information from the taxpayer is vital to prepare an accurate tax return. Information collected verifies the taxpayer's identity and the taxpayer's spouse if filing jointly. The taxpayer will be glad you asked relevant questions to complete his or her tax return correctly. A straightforward interview process to gather a taxpayer's information makes tax return preparation easier. It also prevents misunderstanding between the tax preparer and taxpayer.

The following personal information is needed from the client:

> ➢ A current government-issued photo identification for the taxpayer and his or her spouse, if filing jointly.
> ➢ The taxpayer or spouse's SSN, ITIN, ATIN, or TIN. See the physical card and add to the taxpayer's electronic folder.
> ➢ The following information for each dependent, if applicable:
>   ○ SSN, ITIN, ATIN, or TIN.
>   ○ Date of birth.
>   ○ Current address.
>   ○ Income.
> ➢ The taxpayer's current address.
> ➢ The amount of total income earned for the year.

If the taxpayer is filing Married Filing Jointly, gather the information listed below from both the taxpayer and spouse to complete the return. Make sure to ask the following information:

> ➢ Name of taxpayer and spouse as it appears on the government-issued identification.
> ➢ Social Security numbers or taxpayer identification numbers for all individuals listed on the tax return.
> ➢ Date of birth (DOB) for everyone on the tax return.
> ➢ Date of death (DOD), if the taxpayer or spouse died during the tax year.

> ➤ Current Address (PO Box can be used). If the client uses a bank product, a physical address could be required. The address could be in a foreign country, but not for a bank product.

Señor 1040 Says: Remember, always ask for an official document to verify a client's DOB or DOD.

The names of the taxpayer and spouse (if applicable) must match the names on their Social Security cards, Adoption Tax Identification Numbers (ATIN), or Individual Tax Identification Numbers (ITIN). If the couple has recently married and has not filed the name change with the Social Security Administration, the current name on the Social Security card must be used. If not, the return could be rejected when filing electronically. Taxpayers who do not have a Social Security Number (SSN) should apply for an SSN or an ITIN. When filing a federal return, the Social Security Administration records are used to match all names, Social Security numbers, and dates of birth, for everyone on the tax return.

The exception to this is when a taxpayer is filing his or her tax return with an ITIN; in these cases, the SSN on the W-2 will not match.

When information is gathered, the tax preparer should make sure all W-2 forms match the taxpayer and spouse's Social Security numbers displayed on their Social Security cards. If not, the taxpayer must have the employer correct the tax document(s). Tax professionals need to ensure documents are accurate before filing the return.

Interview Pointers

Here are questions to ask regarding the taxpayers' personal information, which will help determine changes from the prior year return and the current year filing status.

> ➤ Did you bring your Social Security card(s)?
> ➤ Did any personal changes occur (divorce, marriage, new dependents, deaths, etc.)?
> ➤ Did your name change?
> ➤ Did you get married?
> ➤ Did you get divorced?
> ➤ Was there a death in the family? (Tax return related.)
> ➤ Did you have a job change?
> ➤ Did you have any births during the year? (Tax return related.)
> ➤ Do you want to contribute $3 to the Presidential Election Campaign Fund?

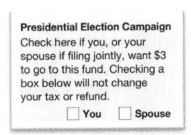

Portion of Form 1040

The Presidential Election Campaign Fund is intended to reduce a candidate's dependence on large contributions from individuals and groups. This aims to place candidates on an equal financial footing for the general election. The fund also helps pay for pediatric medical research. If the taxpayer wants $3 to go to the fund, check the box. If the taxpayer is filing a joint return, both taxpayers can have $3 each go to the fund. Checking the box does not affect the refund amount or the amount owed.

Standard Deduction

The standard deduction is based on the taxpayer's filing status. Each filing status matches a predetermined amount. That amount is subtracted from the taxpayer's total income resulting in the taxpayer's adjusted gross income. This line also reports the Itemized Deductions, which are amounts reported on Schedule A and will be described later. Itemized deduction amount is generally used when the taxpayer's deduction exceeds their standard deduction. The following factors determine an additional standard deduction allowable to certain taxpayers.

> ➤ Is the taxpayer considered age 65 or older?
> ➤ Is the taxpayer blind?
> ➤ Is the taxpayer claimed as a dependent on another individual's tax return?

Blind taxpayers and taxpayers over the age of 65 each have an additional exemption that can be claimed when filing status is determined.

Deduction amounts apply to most people and are for the current year's filing status.*

Filing Status and Standard Deduction	Tax Year 2021	Tax Year 2022	Tax Year 2023
Single	$12,550	$12,950	$13,850
Married Filing Jointly and Qualifying Widow(er)	$25,100	$25,900	$27,700
Married Filing Separately	$12,550	$12,950	$13,850
Head of Household	$18,800	$19,400	$20,800

*Do not use this chart if:

> ➤ The taxpayer was born before January 2, 1958.
> ➤ The taxpayer is blind.
> ➤ Someone else can claim the taxpayer or taxpayer's spouse as a dependent if filing status is MFJ.

Dependents

Basic information to collect is:

> ➤ Dependent(s) name (as it appears on the SSN, ATIN, or ITIN).
> ➤ DOB of the dependent(s).
> ➤ Relationship to taxpayer.

Note: If you prepare the tax return by hand, there is no place to enter the DOB (just remember that the dependent's age is important to calculate certain credits).

On the paper Form 1040, you will only see four lines for dependents. Mark the box on the left and follow the instructions to add an additional sheet for more dependents. When the return is prepared with software, the worksheet should be automatically generated. Make sure that the worksheet is attached to the tax return.

Dependents (see instructions):		(2) Social security number	(3) Relationship to you	(4) Check the box if qualifies for (see instructions):	
	(1) First name Last name			Child tax credit	Credit for other dependents
If more than four dependents, see instructions and check here ☐				☐	☐
				☐	☐
				☐	☐
				☐	☐

Portion of Form 1040

Interview Pointers

Here are questions to ask to determine if the taxpayer has qualifying dependents:

➢ Do you have any dependents?
➢ Did the dependents live with you?
➢ Did the dependents live with you the entire year?
➢ Do you have proof that the dependents live with you?
  o Lease agreement
  o School records
  o Medical records
➢ Do you have the dependents' SSN, ATIN, or ITIN documentation with you? If not, can you bring them in later so I can keep a copy for our records?
➢ What are the dependents' dates of birth?
➢ Can somebody else claim them as dependents?

Dependents will be studied in detail in a later chapter.

Income Form 1040, Lines 1 – 15

Portion of Form 1040

The tax information needed to complete this section includes all income for both the taxpayer and the spouse if Married Filing Jointly. Sources of income include:

➢ Form W-2 series
➢ Form 1099 series (G, DIV, INT, NEC, MISC., R, etc.)
➢ Social Security

Wage income is reported on Form 1040, line 1a. Other income Form 1040, line 1b - h. Interest is reported on Form 1040, line 2a and 2b. Qualified dividends are reported on Form 1040, line 3a and 3b. IRAs, pensions, and annuities are reported on Form 1040, line 4a - 5b. Social Security benefits are reported on Form 1040, line 6.

Income Recordkeeping

Both taxpayer and tax professional must keep copies of all Forms W-2, 1099 series, and other income documents with the client's tax return. If parents elect to claim their children's investment income, those forms should be kept as well, with the parents' tax return.

Interest earned as a beneficiary of an estate or trust is generally taxable income. Taxpayers should receive a Schedule K-1 for their portion of the interest. A copy of the Schedule K-1 should be kept with the tax return as well.

If the taxpayer is a U.S. citizen or resident alien, he or she must report income from sources outside the United States unless the income is exempt from U.S. law. All sources of income must be reported for all amounts of both earned and unearned income. See Publication 54.

Interview Pointers

Here are questions to determine the type of income the taxpayer received, and which tax form or schedule will be used to report the income:

➢ Did you receive a W-2 or W-2G?
➢ How many jobs did you have last year?
➢ Did you receive any income not reported on a W-2?
➢ Did you have any gambling or lottery winnings?
➢ Did you earn any interest or dividends?
  o Checking account
  o Savings account
➢ Did you have an investment broker?
  o Savings bonds and CDs
➢ Did you receive Social Security benefits or railroad retirement benefits?
➢ Did you receive a pension or annuity?
➢ Did you take a distribution from an IRA?
  o Roth or Traditional?
➢ Did you receive alimony income or separate maintenance payments? (Reported on Schedule 1, line 2a)
➢ Did you receive disability income?
➢ Did you receive rental income? File the Schedule E, and net income is reported on Schedule 1, line 5.

- ➤ Do you own a business? (When a taxpayer has a business, you must perform an extensive and thorough interview. This ensures the taxpayer reports all income, including cash payments received for work or services performed as well as all expenses. As a preparer, you must make sure you have the necessary knowledge of Schedule C to prepare the tax return correctly. Do your due diligence!)
- ➤ Did you receive Form 1099-NEC or Form 1099-MISC?
- ➤ Did you receive Form 1099-K?
- ➤ Did you receive an education scholarship? (Reported on Schedule 1, line 8r)
- ➤ Did you receive a refund from state taxes last year? (Reported on Schedule 1, line 1)
- ➤ Did you receive income from other sources such as prizes, jury duty pay, Schedule K-1, royalties, foreign income, etc.? (Reported on Schedule 1, line 8)
- ➤ Did you receive unemployment or paid family leave? (Reported on Schedule 1, line 7)
- ➤ Did you receive any other form of income whatsoever? (Reported on Schedule 1, line 8z)

More information on Schedule 1 will be found later in this chapter.

Form 1040, page 2, lines 16 - 33

This section reports information from other forms and schedules. Line 16 is the tax the individual will need to pay. This includes additional tax as well as the income tax. Line 33 reports the total payments made by the individual through withholding, estimated payments, or from credits.

Portion of Form 1040

Refund

Portion of Form 1040

On Form 1040, page 2, if the amount on line 33 is more than the amount on line 24, the taxpayer may receive a refund reported on line 34. If the taxpayer is receiving a refund and would like to have the refund deposited directly into a checking or savings account, enter the taxpayer's routing and account numbers on lines 35b and 35d. The account type (savings or checking) must be marked on line 35c.

A taxpayer must file Form 8888 if he or she would like to receive their refund by paper check or to have it deposited into up to three different accounts. Make sure to check the box at the end of line 35a to show that the form is attached. Not all software companies support this form; taxpayers wanting to file Form 8888 may need to file a paper return via mail.

Line 36 is used if the taxpayer wants the refund to be applied to their estimated payments for the following tax year.

Interview Pointers

These questions determine how the taxpayer will receive their refund:

> ➤ Do you want the refund to be directly deposited into your checking or savings account?
> ➤ Do you want a paper check from the IRS?
>   ○ If so, is the address on the tax return current?
> ➤ Would you like to have your refund applied to next year's estimated payments? (Normally, you would ask this question to self-employed taxpayers who are receiving a refund; this could lower the estimated payments.)

Amount Owed

Form 1040, page 2, line 37: Amount a taxpayer owes.

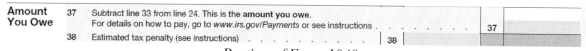

Portion of Form 1040

Form 1040, page 2, line 38: The amount of penalty for not paying enough tax during the year.

This is reported using Form 2210, which should be attached to the return after completion.

Interview Pointers

These questions determine how the taxpayer will pay their balance due.

> ➤ Do you want to mail your balance due to the IRS?
> ➤ Do you want to pay your balance due electronically?
> ➤ Do you want to pay your balance due with a credit card?

Third Party Designee

On Form 1040, page 2, the taxpayer would designate someone to discuss the tax return.

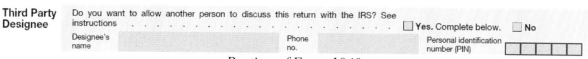

Portion of Form 1040

Checking the Yes box allows a third-party to talk on behalf of the taxpayer to provide certain information to the IRS. The authorization will automatically end no later than the filing due date for the current-year tax return (without extensions). For example, if the paid preparer is filing the tax return for tax year 2022, and the return is due on April 18, 2023, the authorization automatically expires on April 18, 2024.

A PIN (personal identification number) must be entered. PINs are not given or provided by any agency but are instead created by the third-party designee. However, whatever PIN is created must be kept and documented; this is what the IRS will ask for to verify they are talking to the correct third-party designee.

If the taxpayer marks the box No, then no one will be the taxpayer's designee.

The IRS may call the designee to answer any questions that arise during the processing of the return. The designee may perform the following actions:

➢ Give information that is missing from the return to the IRS.
➢ Call the IRS for information that is missing from the tax return.
➢ Upon request, receive copies of notices or transcripts related to the return.
➢ Respond to certain IRS notices about math errors and the preparation of the return.

When checking the box, authorization is limited to matters concerning the processing of the tax return.

The preparer would use Form 8821, *Tax Information Authorization,* if the taxpayer needed to authorize an individual or an organization to receive or inspect the taxpayer confidential tax return information but does not want to authorize an individual to represent the taxpayer before the IRS. If the taxpayer wanted to authorize an individual to receive or inspect their transcripts or confidential return information, but does not want to authorize an individual to represent the taxpayer before the IRS, use Form 4506T, *Request for Transcript of Tax Return.*

Interview Pointers

The following questions determine if the taxpayer wants to authorize a third-party designee. Make sure you thoroughly understand what a third-party designee's responsibilities are.

➢ Would you like the tax preparer to be able to talk to the IRS regarding this return?
➢ Would you like to have another individual talk to the IRS about your current year tax return?

Signing Form 1040

The taxpayer (and spouse if filing jointly) must sign the return in the section shown below from the second page of the Form 1040.

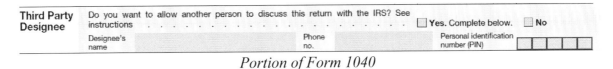

Portion of Form 1040

If either the taxpayer or spouse received an Identity Protection (IP) PIN from the IRS due to identity theft, the taxpayer must enter the number in the box provided. If both the taxpayer and spouse suffered from identity theft, only the taxpayer would enter the IP PIN. Make sure to enter the IP PIN on the correct line if the spouse or taxpayer or both had identity theft.

| If the IRS sent you an Identity Protection PIN, enter it here (see inst.) | |
| If the IRS sent your spouse an Identity Protection PIN, enter it here (see inst.) | |

Portion of Form 1040

Paid Preparer Use Only

Paid Preparer Use Only	Preparer's name	Preparer's signature	Date	PTIN	Check if: ☐ Self-employed
	Firm's name			Phone no.	
	Firm's address			Firm's EIN	

Go to *www.irs.gov/Form1040* for instructions and the latest information.

Form **1040** (2022)

Portion of Form 1040

Paid preparers must enter their PTIN, business name, business address, employer identification number (EIN), and business phone number. If the paid preparer is self-employed, he or she must check the box. The paid preparer must sign the return in the appropriate box; otherwise, the paid preparer could be charged a $50 penalty per return. This is a paid preparer penalty not a company penalty.

Form 1040-SR, for seniors.

Form **1040-SR** Department of the Treasury—Internal Revenue Service
U.S. Tax Return for Seniors 2022 OMB No. 1545-0074 IRS Use Only—Do not write or staple in this space.

Filing Status
Check only one box.
☐ Single ☐ Married filing jointly ☐ Married filing separately (MFS)
☐ Head of household (HOH) ☐ Qualifying surviving spouse (QSS)
If you checked the MFS box, enter the name of your spouse. If you checked the HOH or QSS box, enter the child's name if the qualifying person is a child but not your dependent:

Your first name and middle initial | Last name | Your social security number

If joint return, spouse's first name and middle initial | Last name | Spouse's social security number

Home address (number and street). If you have a P.O. box, see instructions. | Apt. no. | **Presidential Election Campaign**

City, town, or post office. If you have a foreign address, also complete spaces below. | State | ZIP code | Check here if you, or your spouse if filing jointly, want $3 to go to this fund. Checking a box below will not change your tax or refund.

Foreign country name | Foreign province/state/county | Foreign postal code | ☐ You ☐ Spouse

Digital Assets
At any time during 2022, did you: (a) receive (as a reward, award, or payment for property or services); or (b) sell, exchange, gift, or otherwise dispose of a digital asset (or a financial interest in a digital asset)? (See instructions.) . . . . . . ☐ Yes ☐ No

Standard Deduction
Someone can claim: ☐ You as a dependent ☐ Your spouse as a dependent
☐ Spouse itemizes on a separate return or you were a dual-status alien

Age/Blindness { You: ☐ Were born before January 2, 1958 ☐ Are blind
Spouse: ☐ Was born before January 2, 1958 ☐ Is blind

Portion of Form 1040-SR

The added benefit of Form 1040-SR is that it automatically calculates the higher standard deduction for seniors. Form 1040-SR is 4 pages instead of 2 for the regular Form 1040.

> *Señor 1040 Says:* Remember, the additional exemption amount is only for taxpayer and spouse and is automatically added to the standard deduction when using Form 1040-SR.

When a taxpayer files Married filing separate and one spouse itemizes deductions, the other taxpayer must itemize their deductions even if the standard deduction gives the taxpayer a better tax break.

Interview Pointers

These questions determine if the taxpayer should use the standard or itemized deduction. For questions relating to home ownership, be aware that a taxpayer may own their home and could be paid off. The other option is that the taxpayer purchased the house late in the year. (Itemized deductions will be covered in detail in a later chapter.)

> - Do you pay rent or own a home?
>   - If a home is owned:
>   - Did you pay mortgage interest?
>   - Did you pay real estate taxes (property taxes)?
>   - If a home was purchased in the current tax year:
>   - Must see the buyer's final closing statement
> - Did you have medical expenses?
> - Do you have medical insurance? (What the taxpayer pays out-of-pocket may be a deduction on Schedule A.)
> - Did you have debt from a mortgage or credit card canceled or forgiven by a commercial lender?
> - Did you live in an area that was affected by a presidentially-declared natural disaster?
>   - If yes, where and when?
> - Did you receive the First-Time Homebuyer Credit in 2008?
> - Did you make any charitable contributions last year?
>   - Were they cash or noncash?
>   - Do you have receipts? Can you bring them, so I can have a copy with your tax papers?
> - Did you receive Form 1095-A? (If so, the taxpayers' insurance premiums cannot be deducted on Schedule A.)
> - Do you have an exemption granted by the Marketplace? (If so, you need that number to complete the tax return.)
> - Did you take any higher education classes?
> - Did you pay someone to care for your children? (Only ask if there are dependents on the return).

Part 1 Review Questions

To obtain the maximum benefit from this chapter, LTP recommends that you complete each of the following questions, and then compare them to the answers with feedback that immediately follows. Under governing self-study standards, vendors are required to present review questions intermittently throughout each self-study course.

These questions and explanations are not part of the final examination and will not be graded by LTP.

CTIP1.1
Which of the following is not a section on Form 1040?

    a. Filing Status
    b. Dependents
    c. Income
    d. Educator Expense

CTIP1.2
To confirm the taxpayer's identity, which of the following does not need to be collected?

    a. Taxpayer expired government-issued photo identification.
    b. Documentation that confirms the taxpayer's current address.
    c. The tax preparer should verify the Social Security number(s) for everyone on the tax return.
    d. Date of birth.

CTIP1.3
When collecting information about dependents claimed on a tax return, what is the basic information that is needed to be asked?

    a. What is the dependent's nickname?
    b. What is the dependent's relationship to the taxpayer?
    c. What is the dependent's phone number?
    d. What is the dependent's school address?

CTIP1.4
Which of the following does not need to be entered in the "Paid Preparer Use Only" section?

    a. Preparer Tax Identification Number
    b. Business Name
    c. Business Address
    d. IP PIN

CTIP1.5
What is the added benefit for using the Form 1040-SR?

    a. The font size is automatically smaller.
    b. The higher standard deduction is automatically added.
    c. Paid preparers do not need to sign the return.
    d. There are 4 pages instead of 2 pages for Form 1040-SR.

CTIP1.6
Esther gave permission to Susan to check the box as her Third-party Designee. When will the authorization expire?

    a. April 15, 2022
    b. April 15, 2023
    c. April 15, 2024
    d. April 15, 2025

CTIP1.7
Maria has marked the box to be the third-party designee for her clients; she has not filed Form 8821 or Form 2848. As a third-party designee, which of the following can Maria not carry out?

   a.   Make payment arrangements for the taxpayer.
   b.   Call the IRS to obtain information regarding processing the taxpayer's return or the status of the return.
   c.   Respond to certain IRS notices that the taxpayer has shared with Maria about math errors, offsets, and return preparation.
   d.   Give the IRS any information that is missing from the return.

CTIP1.8
Todd would like to have Maggie receive his transcripts for 2022. Which form would Maggie use to receive Todd's IRS transcripts?

   a.   Form 8821
   b.   Form 4506-T
   c.   Form 2848
   d.   Form 1040

CTIP1.9
Which of the following is not reported in the Third-Party Designee section?

   a.   Designee's PTIN
   b.   Designee's Name
   c.   Designee's Phone Number
   d.   Designee's PIN

CTIP1.10
Which of the following is not reported in the "Paid Preparer Use Only" section?

   a.   PTIN
   b.   Business Name, address, and phone number
   c.   EFIN
   d.   EIN

Part 1 Review Questions Answers

CTIP1.1
Which of the following is not a section on Form 1040?

   a.   Filing Status
   b.   Dependents
   c.   Income
   d.   Educator Expense

Feedback: Review *the Following Sections are Found on the 2022 Form 1040.*

CTIP1.2

To confirm the taxpayer's identity, which of the following does not need to be collected?

a. **Taxpayer expired government-issued photo identification.**
b. Documentation that confirms the taxpayer's current address.
c. The tax preparer should verify the Social Security number(s) for everyone on the tax return.
d. Date of birth.

Feedback: Review section *General Information: Name, Address, and Identification Number.*

CTIP1.3

When collecting information about dependents claimed on a tax return, what is the basic information that is needed to be asked?

a. What is the dependent's nickname?
b. **What is the dependent's relationship to the taxpayer?**
c. What is the dependent's phone number?
d. What is the dependent's school address?

Feedback: Review section *Dependents.*

CTIP1.4

Which of the following does not need to be entered in the "Paid Preparer Use Only" section?

a. Preparer Tax Identification Number
b. Business Name
c. Business Address
d. **IP PIN**

Feedback: Review section *Signing Form 1040.*

CTIP1.5

What is the added benefit for using the Form 1040-SR?

a. The font size is automatically smaller.
b. **The higher standard deduction is automatically added.**
c. Paid preparers do not need to sign the return.
d. There are 4 pages instead of 2 pages for Form 1040-SR.

Feedback: Review section *Form 1040-SR for Seniors.*

CTIP1.6

Esther gave permission to Susan to check the box as her Third-party Designee. When will the authorization expire?

a. April 15, 2022
b. April 15, 2023
c. **April 15, 2024**
d. April 15, 2025

Feedback: Review section *Third Party Designee.*

CTIP1.7

Maria has marked the box to be the third-party designee for her clients; she has not filed Form 8821 or Form 2848. As a third-party designee, which of the following can Maria not carry out?

    a. Make payment arrangements for the taxpayer.
    b. Call the IRS to obtain information regarding processing the taxpayer's return or the status of the return.
    c. Respond to certain IRS notices that the taxpayer has shared with Maria about math errors, offsets, and return preparation.
    d. Give the IRS any information that is missing from the return.

Feedback: Review section *Third Party Designee.*

CTIP1.8

Todd would like to have Maggie receive his transcripts for 2022. Which form would Maggie use to receive Todd's IRS transcripts?

    a. Form 8821
    b. Form 4506-T
    c. Form 2848
    d. Form 1040

Feedback: Review section *Third Party Designee.*

CTIP1.9

Which of the following is not reported in the Third-Party Designee section?

    a. Designee's PTIN
    b. Designee's Name
    c. Designee's Phone Number
    d. Designee's PIN

Feedback: Review section *Third Party Designee.*

CTIP1.10

Which of the following is not reported in the "Paid Preparer Use Only" section?

    a. PTIN
    b. Business Name, address, and phone number
    c. EFIN
    d. EIN

Feedback: Review section *Paid Preparer Use Only.*

Part 2 Schedule 1, 2, & 3

Form 1040, Schedule 1, Part I

Schedule 1 reports additional income and adjustments to income. Each schedule's form, if used, is attached to Form 1040; however, not every schedule is used for each taxpayer. A change to Schedule 1 for 2022 is that other income now includes line 1 a - u. For 2021, all other income was reported on line 8.

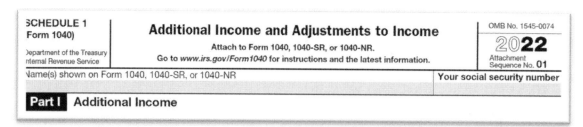

Portion of Schedule 1

Additional income consists of the following items:

➢ Taxable refunds.
➢ Alimony received.
➢ Schedule C income or loss.
➢ Form 4797 other gains or losses.
➢ Schedule E income.
➢ Schedule F income or loss.
➢ Unemployment and paid family leave.
➢ Sale of stocks or assets (if the taxpayer had a loss and not a gain on the sale report on line 4).
➢ Other income such as:
    o Net Operating loss
    o Gambling winnings
    o Cancelation of debt
    o Alaska Permanent Fund dividends
    o Jury duty pay
    o Hobby income
    o Wages earned while incarcerated
    o Etc…

Total income is the combination of all lines from Form 1040, Schedule 1, Part I. Some income reported on Schedule 1, line 3, 4, 5, and 6 could result in a negative number that is subtracted from the total income.

Form 1040, Schedule 1, Part II

Schedule 1 (Form 1040) 2022   Page **2**

Part II Adjustments to Income

Portion of Schedule 1

Adjusting one's income is not the same as filing Schedule A to itemize deductions; it is lowering the taxpayer's gross income to pay the least amount of tax, which consists of the following:
➢ Educator expense. Line 11
➢ Deductible part of self-employment tax. Line 15
➢ Alimony paid (if the agreement was signed prior to December 31, 2018). Line 19a
➢ Contributing to an IRA, SEP, SIMPLE, and other qualified plans. Line 20
➢ Student loan interest deduction.

Interview Pointers

To determine a taxpayer's adjusted gross income (AGI) on line 26, the following must be asked:

- ➢ Did you pay alimony or separate maintenance payments? (Only applicable if the agreement was signed prior to December 31, 2018).
- ➢ Were there any changes in your tax status from last year to this year?
- ➢ Do you have an IRA?
- ➢ What life changes did you have this year?
- ➢ If the W-2 is from a school district: "I see that you have a W-2 from a school district. What is your job title?"
  - ○ The answer will determine if the taxpayer(s) qualify for the educator expense.
- ➢ If the individual has more than one W-2: "I see that you have two different W-2s. Did you change jobs this year? If so, did you move? If so, how far is it from your old workplace to your new workplace?" (Due to TCJA this line is limited to certain taxpayers until 2026, more information later). Not all conformed this rule. Know if your state conformed or not.
- ➢ If the W-2 is from the armed forces: "I see that you have a W-2 from the armed forces. Are you full-time or in the reserves? Were you in a combat zone?"

Adjustments and Deductions

Adjustments and deductions are often confused as they appear to function very similarly. The differences between the two will be explained in full throughout the course; but for now, the main difference to know is that Adjustments are used to lower one's AGI before credit deductions are considered. This is important because credit deduction amounts will be calculated based on the taxpayer's AGI.

There are two ways to calculate deductions: "standard" and "itemized". "Standard deductions" are annually preset amounts the taxpayer will use to deduct from one's taxable income based on filing status. However, the taxpayer can also "itemize" their deductions by claiming Schedule A deductions, which will be covered in a later chapter. Taxpayers are typically free to either itemize their deductions or take the standard deduction amounts, and they are encouraged to calculate both and then choose which option will save them more money.

The government allows deductions, for various types of expenses, to help take the cost of maintaining your life into account when determining the amount of taxes that you owe. In other words, deductions exist to help make sure that you are being taxed on the amount of money you took home and keep after paying for all the expenses that come with life, rather than the total amount you were paid.

The taxpayer can choose to itemize deductions or use standard deductions to reduce their taxable income. Standard deductions are based on the taxpayer's filing status. Itemized deduction is generally used when the taxpayer's deduction exceeds their standard deduction. Subtracting applicable deductions from the taxpayer's total income becomes the taxpayer's adjusted gross income.

The tax to be paid is determined by the taxpayer's taxable income. Tax tables are also based on taxable income, as well. The current year's tax tables can be found in the Form 1040 Instruction on the IRS website. Schedule 2, page 1 is used to report any additional tax that must be declared.

Schedule 2 Additional Taxes

SCHEDULE 2 (Form 1040)	**Additional Taxes**	OMB No. 1545-0074
Department of the Treasury Internal Revenue Service	Attach to Form 1040, 1040-SR, or 1040-NR. Go to *www.irs.gov/Form1040* for instructions and the latest information.	**2022** Attachment Sequence No. **02**

Name(s) shown on Form 1040, 1040-SR, or 1040-NR | Your social security number

Part I — Tax

1	Alternative minimum tax. Attach Form 6251	1	
2	Excess advance premium tax credit repayment. Attach Form 8962	2	
3	Add lines 1 and 2. Enter here and on Form 1040, 1040-SR, or 1040-NR, line 17 . .	3	

Portion of Schedule 2

Schedule 2, Part 1 – Tax

Other Taxes are covered in detail in a later chapter. The type of additional tax is:

Line 1: Alternative minimum tax (AMT). Attach Form 6251.

Line 2: Excess advanced premium tax credit repayment. Attach Form 8962.

Line 3: Add lines 1 and 2.

Schedule 2 Part II – Other Taxes

Part II — Other Taxes

4	Self-employment tax. Attach Schedule SE	4	
5	Social security and Medicare tax on unreported tip income. Attach Form 4137	5	
6	Uncollected social security and Medicare tax on wages. Attach Form 8919	6	
7	Total additional social security and Medicare tax. Add lines 5 and 6	7	
8	Additional tax on IRAs or other tax-favored accounts. Attach Form 5329 if required. If not required, check here . . . . ☐	8	
9	Household employment taxes. Attach Schedule H	9	
10	Repayment of first-time homebuyer credit. Attach Form 5405 if required	10	
11	Additional Medicare Tax. Attach Form 8959	11	
12	Net investment income tax. Attach Form 8960	12	
13	Uncollected social security and Medicare or RRTA tax on tips or group-term life insurance from Form W-2, box 12	13	
14	Interest on tax due on installment income from the sale of certain residential lots and timeshares	14	
15	Interest on the deferred tax on gain from certain installment sales with a sales price over $150,000	15	
16	Recapture of low-income housing credit. Attach Form 8611	16	

(continued on page 2)

For Paperwork Reduction Act Notice, see your tax return instructions. Cat. No. 71478U Schedule 2 (Form 1040) 2022

Portion of Schedule 2

Line 4: Self-employment tax. Schedule SE should be attached.

Line 5: Unreported tip income, attach Form 4137.

Line 6: Uncollected social security and Medicare tax on wages, attach Form 8919.

Line 7: Total additional social security and Medicare tax from lines 5 and 6.

Line 8: Additional tax on IRAs and other qualified retirement plans are reported, attach Form 5329.

Line 9: Household employment tax is reported, attach Schedule H.

Line 10: First-time homebuyer credit repayment; Form 5405 is used to report this and should be attached.

Line 11: Additional Medicare Tax, attach Form 8959.

Line 12: Net investment income tax (NIIT), attach Form 8960.

Line 13: Uncollected social security and Medicare or RRTA tax on tips or group-term life insurance from box 12, Form W-2.

Line 14: Interest on tax due on installment income from the sale of certain residential lots and timeshares.

Line 15: Interest on the deferred tax on gain from certain installment sales with a sales price over $150,000.

Line 16: Recapture of low-income housing credit, attach Form 8611.

Interview Pointers

These questions determine if the taxpayer will be paying other taxes:

- ➢ Did your childcare provider come to your home to babysit?
  - ○ May need to file Schedule H.
- ➢ Did you withdraw money from your IRA or 401(k)? (Depending upon age and what the money was used for, it could result in an additional tax.)
  - ○ How much did you withdraw?
  - ○ What did you use it for?
- ➢ Did you have healthcare coverage for the entire year?
- ➢ Did you or your spouse receive Form 1095-A? (Did you purchase health insurance through an exchange?)
- ➢ Are you self-employed? (Ask this question if you are filing a Schedule C.)
  - ○ Did you receive Form 1099-MISC or NEC?
  - ○ Did you receive Form 1099-K?
- ➢ Did you or your spouse receive a first-time home buyer loan and are paying it back?
- ➢ Did you report all your tips to your employer? (Ask this question if you know the taxpayer is a server and there is an amount in box 7 of the W-2.)
- ➢ Do you have other additional taxes?
  - ○ Tax on a Health Savings Account (HSA)?
  - ○ Additional tax on HSA distributions?
  - ○ Recapture of a charitable contribution?

Schedule 3 Additional Credits and Payments

Schedule 3 is used to report nonrefundable credits, other payments, and refundable credits. Refundable credits are payments toward the taxpayer's tax liability; if the result is more than the tax, the excess is a refund to the taxpayer.

Form 1040, line 25 reports the amount of federal withholding from all income sources, such as W-2, Form 1099-R, unemployment compensation, etc. Earned income credit (EIC), the additional child tax credit, and the refundable portion of the American opportunity credit are reported on Form 1040, lines 27-29.

Schedule 3 Part I: Nonrefundable Credits

A nonrefundable credit is used to reduce the taxpayer's tax liability to zero. If the individual has more credits, they are not able to use them to lower the tax liability. The taxpayer forfeits the remaining credit. A nonrefundable credit can reduce the taxable income dollar for dollar. Nonrefundable credits will be covered in a later chapter. Some common nonrefundable credits are:

> Education credits.
> Foreign tax credit.
> Credit for child and dependent care expenses.
> Certain residential energy credits.
> Retirement savings contributions credit.

SCHEDULE 3 (Form 1040)	**Additional Credits and Payments**	OMB No. 1545-0074
Department of the Treasury Internal Revenue Service	Attach to Form 1040, 1040-SR, or 1040-NR. Go to *www.irs.gov/Form1040* for instructions and the latest information.	2022 Attachment Sequence No. 03
Name(s) shown on Form 1040, 1040-SR, or 1040-NR		Your social security number

Part I Nonrefundable Credits

1	Foreign tax credit. Attach Form 1116 if required	1
2	Credit for child and dependent care expenses from Form 2441, line 11. Attach Form 2441	2
3	Education credits from Form 8863, line 19	3
4	Retirement savings contributions credit. Attach Form 8880	4
5	Residential energy credits. Attach Form 5695	5
6	Other nonrefundable credits:	

Portion of Schedule 3

Schedule 3 Part II: Other Payments and Refundable Credits

A refundable credit can generate a larger refund than the amount of tax paid through withholdings or estimated tax payments throughout the year. Which means the taxpayer could get a refund from refundable credits that he or she qualifies for. Some common refundable credits are earned income tax credits, and new for tax year 2022, being prepared in 2023, is child and dependent care expenses, which was part of the American Rescue Plan Act (ARPA). The advanced child tax credit was not renewed for 2022.

Schedule 3 (Form 1040)

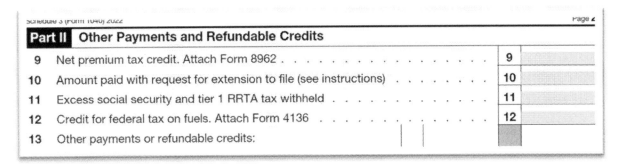

Part II	Other Payments and Refundable Credits		
9	Net premium tax credit. Attach Form 8962	9	
10	Amount paid with request for extension to file (see instructions)	10	
11	Excess social security and tier 1 RRTA tax withheld	11	
12	Credit for federal tax on fuels. Attach Form 4136	12	
13	Other payments or refundable credits:		

Portion of Schedule 3

Line 9: Net premium tax credit, attach Form 8962.

Line 10: Amount paid with extension request.

Line 11: Report excess social security and tier I railroad retirement benefits (SSA-1099).

Line 12: Used to report credit for federal tax on fuels used for a nontaxable purpose (for example, off-highway business use). Form 4136 is used to report this and must be attached.

Line 14: Add lines 13a - z. Total amount of payments or refundable credits.

Line 15: Add lines 9 - 12 and 14.

Other payments and refundable credits will be reviewed in a later chapter.

Interview Pointers

These questions could determine the taxpayer's total tax payments:

➢ Did you make any estimated payments during the tax year?
➢ Did you have last year's refund applied to the current tax year estimated payments?
➢ Did you take any higher education classes?
➢ Did you pay any money along with the request to file an extension? (Only ask if the taxpayer filed an extension.)

Señor 1040 Says: Make sure to do your due diligence for **all** tax returns with refundable credits.

Part 2 Review Questions

To obtain the maximum benefit from this chapter, LTP recommends that you complete each of the following questions, and then compare them to the answers with feedback that immediately follows. Under governing self-study standards, vendors are required to present review questions intermittently throughout each self-study course.

These questions and explanations are not part of the final examination and will not be graded by LTP.

CTIP2.1
Which of the following is not reported on Form 1040, Schedule 1, Part II?

a. Individual Retirement Account deduction
b. Taxable refunds
c. Educator expenses
d. Student loan interest

CTIP2.2
Which of the following is reported on Form 1040, Schedule 1, Part II?

a. Moving expenses for all taxpayers
b. Lifetime Learning credit
c. Educator expenses
d. Social Security benefits

CTIP2.3
Which of the following reports self-employment tax?

a. Schedule 2
b. Schedule C
c. Schedule 3
d. Schedule E

CTIP2.4
Which of the following is not reported on Form 1040, Schedule 2, Part I?

a. Additional Medicare Tax
b. Net Investment Income Tax
c. Early withdrawal of an IRA
d. Unreported Social Security and Medicare tax

CTIP2.5
Which of the following is not reported on Schedule 3?

a. Nonrefundable credits
b. Foreign Tax Credit
c. Refundable credits
d. First time homebuyer credit

CTIP2.6
Which of the following would report Residential energy credits?

a. Schedule 1, Part 1
b. Schedule 2, Part 2
c. Schedule 3, Part 2
d. Schedule 3, Part 1

CTIP2.7
Which of the following would report alternative minimum tax?

    a. Schedule 1, Part 1
    b. Schedule 1, Part 2
    c. Schedule 2, Part 2
    d. Schedule 2, Part 1

CTIP2.8
Which of the following would report Farm Income?

    a. Schedule 1, Part 2
    b. Schedule 1, Part 1
    c. Schedule 3, Part 2
    d. Schedule 3, Part 1

CTIP2.9
Which of the following would report student loan interest?

    a. Schedule 1, Part 2
    b. Schedule 1, Part 2
    c. Schedule 3, Part 2
    d. Schedule 3, Part 1

CTIP2.10
Which of the following would report household employment taxes?

    a. Schedule 1, Part 2
    b. Schedule 1, Part 2
    c. Schedule 2, Part 2
    d. Schedule 3, Part 1

Part 2 Review Questions Answers

CTIP2.1
Which of the following is not reported on Form 1040, Schedule 1, Part II?

    a. Individual Retirement Account deduction
    b. Taxable refunds
    c. Educator expenses
    d. Student loan interest

Feedback: Review section *Form 1040, Schedule I, Part I.*

CTIP2.2
Which of the following is reported on Form 1040, Schedule 1, Part II?

    a. Moving expenses for all taxpayers
    b. Lifetime Learning credit
    c. Educator expenses
    d. Social Security benefits

Feedback: Review section *Form 1040, Schedule I, Part II.*

CTIP2.3
Which of the following reports self-employment tax?

    a. Schedule 2
    b. Schedule C
    c. Schedule 3
    d. Schedule E

Feedback: Review section *Form 1040, Schedule I, Part I.*

CTIP2.4
Which of the following is not reported on Form 1040, Schedule 2, Part I?

    a. Additional Medicare Tax
    b. Net Investment Income Tax
    c. Early withdrawal of an IRA
    d. Unreported Social Security and Medicare tax

Feedback: Review section *Schedule 2, Part II – Other Taxes.*

CTIP2.5
Which of the following is not reported on Schedule 3?

    a. Nonrefundable credits
    b. Foreign Tax Credit
    c. Refundable credits
    d. First time homebuyer credit

Feedback: Review section *Schedule 3: Additional Credits and Payments.*

CTIP2.6
Which of the following would report Residential energy credits?

    a. Schedule 1, Part 1
    b. Schedule 2, Part 2
    c. Schedule 3, Part 2
    d. Schedule 3, Part 1

Feedback: Review section *Schedule 3, Part 1.*

CTIP2.7
Which of the following would report alternative minimum tax?

    a. Schedule 1, Part 1
    b. Schedule 1, Part 2
    c. Schedule 2, Part 2
    d. Schedule 2, Part 1

Feedback: Review section *Schedule 2, Part 1.*

CTIP2.8
Which of the following would report Farm Income?

    a. Schedule 1, Part 2
    b. Schedule 1, Part 1
    c. Schedule 3, Part 2
    d. Schedule 3, Part 1

Feedback: Review section *Schedule 1, Part 1.*

CTIP2.9
Which of the following would report student loan interest?

    a. Schedule 1, Part 2
    b. Schedule 1, Part 2
    c. Schedule 3, Part 2
    d. Schedule 3, Part 1

Feedback: Review section *Schedule 1, Part 2.*

CTIP2.10
Which of the following would report household employment taxes?

    a. Schedule 1, Part 2
    b. Schedule 1, Part 2
    c. Schedule 2, Part 2
    d. Schedule 3, Part 1

Feedback: Review section *Schedule 2, Part 2.*

Part 3 Filing the Federal Tax Return

Once the tax professional has gathered the required information and ensured its accuracy, it is time to file the return.

If a United States taxpayer has worldwide income, they need to file a tax return. Immigrants who are unauthorized to be or work in the United States need to file their taxes; the IRS even makes it very clear that the information provided for returns and filing are used for tax purposes only. The IRS does not share taxpayer information with any government immigration agency.

The Filing Process

To begin, gather information and materials from the taxpayer to complete an accurate return. The tax professional will need the following:

    ➤ Income sources such as Form W-2 or 1099 Series.
    ➤ Receipts, checks, or invoices for payments and expenses.
    ➤ Other statements that show other income received by the taxpayer (such as a statement reporting gambling winnings from a casino or interest from a bank).
    ➤ Current driver's license or other form of government-issued picture identification.
    ➤ Social Security card with SSN number or some other form of taxpayer ID.
    ➤ Full name, SSN, date of birth, or other equivalent of any dependents or spouse.

This is the bare minimum needed to begin the tax preparation process. There are many other components needed to complete the return. Some concepts have already been discussed. Others will be given throughout the course as you learn more in-depth tax law concepts.

How to Assemble a Federal Tax Return

When assembling the return to be mailed to the IRS, make sure the attachment sequence order shown in the upper right-hand corner is in numerical order starting with Form 1040. If the taxpayer must attach supporting statements, the preparer must arrange them in the same order as the schedules and attach them at the end of the return. When mailing the return, attach a copy of income such as Form(s) W-2, W-2G, and/or 1099-R to page 1 of Form 1040.

Portion of Schedule 2

Where to File a Paper Return

Based on where the taxpayer lives, the type of tax return and whether there is a refund or balance due determines where the taxpayer would send a paper return. It is more advantageous to file electronically. There are often separate mailing addresses for returns with enclosed payments and for returns without. Use the following link to find the correct address for mailing the federal return:

https://www.irs.gov/filing/where-to-file-addresses-for-taxpayers-and-tax-professionals-filing-form-1040

Electronic filing eliminates the need to mail in a physical paper return. This option is discussed further in the e-filing chapter.

See IRS section 6091.

When to File a Return

The IRS states that, for tax returns and payments, the tax return must meet the "timely mailing/timely paying" rule: taxes owed must be paid by April 15th or the next business day if the 15th falls on a weekend or legal holiday, even if the taxpayer has successfully filed for an extension of time.

How to File a Return

The following methods can be used to file a tax return:

➢ Electronic filing (e-file).
➢ Private delivery service: FedEx, UPS, etc.
➢ United States Postal Service.

If a tax professional prepares 11 or more returns, they must e-file all returns. Electronically-filed returns are given a postmark that includes the date and time of the return's electronic transmission.

Filing Deadlines

Individual Tax Returns: Forms 1040 and 1040NR (Non-Resident)

> ➢ The first deadline was April 18, 2023.
> ➢ April 18, 2023, for Maine and Massachusetts.
> ➢ The extended deadline is October 16, 2023.

Partnership Returns: Form 1065

> ➢ The first deadline is March 15, 2023.
> ➢ The extended deadline is September 15, 2023.

Trust and Estate Income Tax Returns: Form 1041

> ➢ The first deadline is April 18, 2023.
> ➢ The extended deadline is October 2, 2023.

Note the change: extensions for fiduciary returns now last five-and-a-half months instead of only five months.

C-corporation Returns: Form 1120

> ➢ The first deadline is April 18, 2023, for corporations; note the change of deadline.
> ➢ The extended deadline is October 16, 2023. Note the change of deadline; corporations are now permitted a six-month automatic extension.
> ➢ For corporations on a fiscal year other than the calendar year, the first deadline is the 15th day of the fourth month following the end of the corporation's fiscal year.
> ➢ EXCEPTION: for corporations with a fiscal year from July 1st to June 30th, the first deadline will remain September 15th (which is the 15th day of the third month following the end of the fiscal year) and the extended deadline will remain February 15th (five months after the first deadline) through the fiscal year ending on June 30, 2026.
> ➢ Starting with the fiscal year ending on June 30, 2017, the deadline moved to October 15th (the 15th day of the fourth month following the end of the tax year) and the extended deadline moved to March 15th (six months after the first deadline).

S-corporation Returns: Form 1120S

> ➢ The first deadline is March 15, 2023, for corporations.
> ➢ The extended deadline is September 15, 2023.

Foreign Bank Account Reports: FinCEN Form 114

> ➢ The first deadline is April 18, 2023; note the change of deadline.
> ➢ The extended deadline is October 16, 2023.

See IRS section 6072.

Part 3 Review Questions

To obtain the maximum benefit from this chapter, LTP recommends that you complete each of the following questions, and then compare them to the answers with feedback that immediately follows. Under governing self-study standards, vendors are required to present review questions intermittently throughout each self-study course.

These questions and explanations are not part of the final examination and will not be graded by LTP.

CTIP3.1
When assembling the tax return for the client, which is the best way to put the return together?

 a. Just staple everything together as it comes out of the printer.
 b. Use the sequence number that is found on the top right hand of all other forms except the 1040.
 c. Mail the state return with your federal return.
 d. Make sure the supporting documents are added at the end in sequential order.

CTIP3.2
Which method is not used to file a tax return?

 a. Electronic filing
 b. Private delivery service
 c. United States Post Office
 d. Fax the return to the local IRS Office

CTIP3.3
Which of the following is needed from the taxpayer to prepare their return?

 a. All income documents
 b. Determine taxpayer filing status
 c. Correct address for mailing the tax return
 d. Mail the payment due on October 15th

CTIP3.4
For tax year 2022 when is the individual tax return due?

 a. March 15, 2023
 b. February 12, 2023
 c. October 16, 2023
 d. April 18, 2023

CTIP3.5
Which of the following is not true about assembling the federal tax return?

 a. Make sure that the attachment sequence order that is shown in the upper right-hand corner is in numerical order starting with Form 1040
 b. If the taxpayer must attach supporting statements, arrange them in the same order as the schedules and attach them at the end of the return.
 c. Always attach a copy of the state tax return to the federal tax return.
 d. When mailing the return, attach a copy of Form(s) W-2, W-2G, and/or 1099-R to page 1 of the return.

CTIP3.6
Which of the following is not a method used to file a tax return?

a. Electronic filing (e-file)
b. Private delivery service (FedEx, UPS, etc.)
c. United States Postal Service
d. Email your tax return to efile.fed.taxreturn@irs.gov/

CTIP3.7
Which of the following are the correct due dates for individual tax returns (Form 1040 and 1040NR)?

a. First deadline is April 18, 2023, and the extended deadline is October 16, 2023.
b. First deadline is March 15, 2023, and the extended deadline is September 16, 2023.
c. First deadline is April 15, 2023, and the extended deadline is October 2, 2023.
d. First deadline is April 15, 2023, and the extended deadline is October 16, 2023.

CTIP3.8
Which of the following are the correct due dates for trusts and estate tax returns (Form 1041)?

a. First deadline is April 18, 2023, and the extended deadline is October 15, 2023.
b. First deadline is March 15, 2023, and the extended deadline is September 16, 2023.
c. First deadline is April 18, 2023, and the extended deadline is October 2, 2023.
d. First deadline is April 15, 2023, and the extended deadline is October 16, 2023.

CTIP3.9
Which of the following are the correct due dates for partnership returns (Form 1065)?

a. First deadline is April 15, 2023, and the extended deadline is October 15, 2023.
b. First deadline is March 15, 2023, and the extended deadline is September 16, 2023.
c. First deadline is April 15, 2023, and the extended deadline is October 2, 2023.
d. First deadline is April 15, 2023, and the extended deadline is October 16, 2023.

CTIP3.10
Which of the following are the correct due dates for C-corporation tax returns (Form 1120)?

a. First deadline is April 15, 2023, and the extended deadline is October 15, 2023.
b. First deadline is March 15, 2023, and the extended deadline is September 16, 2023.
c. First deadline is April 15, 2023, and the extended deadline is October 2, 2023.
d. First deadline is April 18, 2023, and the extended deadline is October 16, 2023.

Part 3 Review Questions Answers

CTIP3.1
When assembling the tax return for the client, which is the best way to put the return together?

a. Just staple everything together as it comes out of the printer.
b. **Use the sequence number that is found on the top right hand of all other forms except the 1040.**
c. Mail the state return with your federal return.
d. Make sure the supporting documents are added at the end in sequential order.

Feedback: Review section *How to Assemble a Federal Tax Return*.

CTIP3.2

Which method is not used to file a tax return?

    a. Electronic filing
    b. Private delivery service
    c. United States Post Office
    d. Fax the return to the local IRS Office

Feedback: Review section *How to File a Return*.

CTIP3.3

Which of the following is needed from the taxpayer to prepare their return?

    a. All income documents
    b. Determine taxpayer filing status
    c. Correct address for mailing the tax return
    d. Mail the payment due on October 15th

Feedback: Review section *The Filing Process*.

CTIP3.4

For tax year 2022 when is the individual tax return due?

    a. March 15, 2023
    b. February 12, 2023
    c. October 16, 2023
    d. April 18, 2023

Feedback: Review section *Filing Deadlines*.

CTIP3.5

Which of the following is not true about assembling the federal tax return?

    a. Make sure that the attachment sequence order that is shown in the upper right-hand corner is in numerical order starting with Form 1040
    b. If the taxpayer must attach supporting statements, arrange them in the same order as the schedules and attach them at the end of the return.
    c. Always attach a copy of the state tax return to the federal tax return.
    d. When mailing the return, attach a copy of Form(s) W-2, W-2G, and/or 1099-R to page 1 of the return.

Feedback: Review section *How to Assemble a Federal Tax Return*.

CTIP3.6

Which of the following is not a method used to file a tax return?

    a. Electronic filing (e-file)
    b. Private delivery service (FedEx, UPS, etc.)
    c. United States Postal Service
    d. Email your tax return to efile.fed.taxreturn@irs.gov/

Feedback: Review section *How to File a Return*.

CTIP3.7

Which of the following are the correct due dates for individual tax returns (Form 1040 and 1040NR)?

a. **First deadline is April 18, 2023, and the extended deadline is October 16, 2023.**
b. First deadline is March 15, 2023, and the extended deadline is September 16, 2023.
c. First deadline is April 15, 2023, and the extended deadline is October 2, 2023.
d. First deadline is April 15, 2023, and the extended deadline is October 16, 2023.

Feedback: Review section *Filing Deadlines*.

CTIP3.8

Which of the following are the correct due dates for trusts and estate tax returns (Form 1041)?

a. First deadline is April 18, 2023, and the extended deadline is October 15, 2023.
b. First deadline is March 15, 2023, and the extended deadline is September 16, 2023.
c. **First deadline is April 18, 2023, and the extended deadline is October 2, 2023.**
d. First deadline is April 15, 2023, and the extended deadline is October 16, 2023.

Feedback: Review section *Filing Deadlines*.

CTIP3.9

Which of the following are the correct due dates for partnership returns (Form 1065)?

a. First deadline is April 15, 2023, and the extended deadline is October 15, 2023.
b. **First deadline is March 15, 2023, and the extended deadline is September 16, 2023.**
c. First deadline is April 15, 2023, and the extended deadline is October 2, 2023.
d. First deadline is April 15, 2023, and the extended deadline is October 16, 2023.

Feedback: Review section *Filing Deadlines*.

CTIP3.10

Which of the following are the correct due dates for C-corporation tax returns (Form 1120)?

a. First deadline is April 15, 2023, and the extended deadline is October 15, 2023.
b. First deadline is March 15, 2023, and the extended deadline is September 16, 2023.
c. First deadline is April 15, 2023, and the extended deadline is October 2, 2023.
d. **First deadline is April 18, 2023, and the extended deadline is October 16, 2023.**

Feedback: Review section *Filing Deadlines*.

Part 4 What is an ITIN?

An ITIN is a tax processing number, issued by the IRS, for certain resident and nonresident aliens, their spouses, and their dependents. It is a nine-digit number beginning with the number 9. The ITIN range was expanded on April 13, 2011, to include "90" as the middle digits (70 to 88, 90-92, and 94-99) and is formatted like an SSN. The IRS started issuing ITINs in 1996 and required foreign individuals to use an ITIN as their unique identification number on federal tax returns. With ITINs, taxpayers can be effectively identified, and their tax returns processed efficiently.

ITINs play a critical role in the tax administration process and assist with the collection of taxes from foreign nationals, nonresident aliens, and others who have filing or payment obligations under U.S. tax law. Even when other institutions might use ITINs for other purposes, the IRS states that:

> ITINs are for federal tax reporting only and are not intended to serve any other purpose. IRS issues ITINs to help individuals comply with the U.S. tax laws, and to provide a means to efficiently process and account for tax returns and payments for those not eligible for social security numbers (SSNs).

Only individuals who have a valid filing requirement, a withholding requirement, or are filing a U.S. federal income tax return to claim a refund of over-withheld tax are eligible to receive an ITIN. The ITIN does not provide Social Security benefits, is not valid for identification outside of the tax system, and does not change immigration status. The ITIN holder enters their ITIN in the space provided for the SSN when completing and filing their federal income tax return.

Who needs an ITIN?

All tax returns (Form 1040), statements, and other related tax documents used to file a tax report require a taxpayer identification number (TIN). If an individual does not qualify for a Social Security number, then the individual must apply for an ITIN.

Individuals who may need an ITIN include:

➢ A nonresident alien individual eligible to obtain the benefits of a reduced rate of withholding under an income tax treaty.
➢ A nonresident alien not eligible for an SSN required to file a U.S. tax return or filing a U.S. tax return only to claim a refund.
➢ A nonresident alien not eligible for an SSN electing to file a joint tax return with a spouse who is a U.S. citizen or resident alien.
➢ A U.S. resident alien who files a U.S. tax return but is not eligible for an SSN.
➢ An alien individual, claimed as a spouse for an exemption on a U.S. tax return, who is not eligible for an SSN.
➢ An alien individual, who is not eligible for an SSN, claimed as a dependent on another person's U.S. tax return.
➢ A nonresident alien student, professor, or researcher filing a U.S. tax return or claiming an exception to the tax return filing requirement who is not eligible for an SSN.

Reason to Apply for an ITIN

A nonresident alien must apply for an ITIN to report earned income and claim the tax treaty benefits he or she qualifies for:

Box a. This box would be checked for certain nonresident aliens who must get an ITIN to claim certain tax treaty benefits whether they file a tax return or not. If box a is checked, then check box h as well. Enter on the dotted line next to box h the exceptions that relate to the taxpayer's situation. See Publication 901.

Box b. Nonresident alien filing a U.S. tax return.

Portion of Form W7

This category includes:

1. A nonresident alien who must file a U.S. tax return to report income directly or indirectly connected with the conduct of a trade or business in the United States.
2. A nonresident alien who is filing a U.S. tax return only to get a refund.

See Publication 519.

Box c. U.S. resident alien (based on the number of days present in the United States) filing a U.S. tax return.

Box c would be checked for a foreign individual living in the United States, who does not have permission to work from the USCIS and is ineligible for an SSN but may still have a filing requirement. See Publication 519.

Box d. Dependent of a U.S. citizen/resident alien.

Box d would be checked for an individual who can be claimed as a dependent on a U.S. tax return and is not eligible to get an SSN. Dependents of U.S. military personnel are exempt from the requirements of submitting original documents or certified copies of identifying documents, but a standard copy is required. A copy of the U.S. military ID is required, or the applicant must be applying from an overseas APO/FPO address. See Publications 501 and 519.

Box e. Spouse of a U.S. citizen/resident alien.

This category includes:

1. A resident or nonresident alien spouse who is not filing a U.S. tax return (including a joint return) and who is not eligible to get an SSN, but who as a spouse, is claimed as an exemption.
2. A resident or nonresident alien electing to file a U.S. tax return jointly with a spouse who is a U.S. citizen or resident alien.

A spouse or a person in the U.S. military is exempt from submitting original documents or certified copies of identifying documents, but a standard copy will be required. A copy of a U.S. military ID will be required, or the applicant must be applying from an overseas APO/FPO address. See Publications 501 and 519.

Box f. Nonresident alien student, professor, or researcher filing a U.S. tax return or *claiming an exception.*

Box f is checked if the individual applicant has not abandoned his/her residence in a foreign country and who is a bona fide student, professor, or researcher coming temporarily to the United States solely to attend classes at a recognized institution of education, to teach, or to perform research.

If this box is checked, complete lines 6c and 6g and provide a passport with a valid U.S. visa. If the applicant is present in the U.S. on a work-related visa (F-1, J-1, or M-1), but will not be employed (applicant's presence in the U.S. is study-related), attach a letter from the DSO (Designated School Official) or RO (Responsible Officer) instead of applying with the Social Security Administration (SSA) for an SSN. The letter must state clearly that the applicant will not be securing employment while in the U.S. and their presence here is solely study related. This letter can be submitted with the applicant's Form W-7 in lieu of the denial letter from the SSA. See Publications 519.

Box g. Dependent/spouse of a nonresident alien holding a U.S. visa.

Box g is checked when the individual can be claimed as a dependent or a spouse on a U.S. tax return and is unable or not eligible to get an SSN and has entered the U.S. with a nonresident alien who holds a U.S. visa. If this box is checked, be sure to include a copy of the visa with the W-7 application.

Box h. Other.

If box h is checked, it is because boxes a-g do not apply to the applicant. Be sure to describe in detail the reason for requesting an ITIN and attach all supporting documents.

Common Errors on Form W-7

Always make sure that you input the correct information; double check each document and Form W-7 for errors.

Name Mismatch

This is the number one reason ITIN applications are rejected. Make sure the W-7 applications have the same name that is on the tax return being submitted. If an individual is helping a taxpayer complete the Form W-7 application, make sure not to abbreviate the applicant's name, use initials, or leave off the second last name on the tax return or W-7 application. The IRS employee is trained to match the names with the tax return and the W-7 application.

W-2 Issues

Many ITIN holders use a different name with a Social Security number. When the W-7 application is submitted with a tax return, the names on the W-2s should match the application. The IRS wants to make sure that the W-2 income reported is the income the person earned. Remember the purpose of the ITIN is for foreign individuals to report their income. The tricky issue is to get the W-2 to match the legal name. Taxpayers who need an ITIN do not want to ask their employer to change their records for fear of being dismissed for submitting inaccurate information.

Date of Entry

Another common mistake is the date of entry line on the passport is empty. This does not allow the IRS employee to match the taxpayer's date of entry with beginning work history. For example, submit documents that establish when they began working and the type of work they have been doing; this will help the ITIN reviewer tie in the date entered and when work began. For certain dependents, a passport without a date of entry in not accepted as a stand-alone document. See Publication 1915.

Passport Rejection

The most common reason the IRS rejects passports is because they are not signed. The IRS will not accept an original passport that is not signed. Everyone entering the U.S. with a passport must sign it. Some countries do not allow children to sign passports, such as India; the IRS is still working on a solution to this.

Not Submitting Required Documents

Make sure that the required original identification documents or certified copies (if applicable) are submitted with Form W-7.

ITIN Tax Related Exceptions

Exception 1: Third Party Withholding on Passive Income

This exception may apply if the taxpayer is the recipient of partnership income, interest income, annuity income, rental income, or other passive income that is subject to third party withholding or covered by tax treaty benefits. To get an ITIN, the individual must include supporting documentation with Form W-7.

Supporting documentation is a letter or signed statement from the bank, financial institution, or withholding agent. It shows proof that the asset that generates income and belongs to the taxpayer is subject to IRS reporting requirements that take place in the current tax year.

Exception 2: Other Income

This exception may apply if:

1. Taxpayer is claiming the benefits of a U.S. income tax treaty with a foreign country and the taxpayer received any of the following:
    a. Wages, salary, compensation, and honoraria payments
    b. Scholarships, fellowships, and grants
    c. Gambling winnings

2. The taxpayer is receiving taxable scholarship, fellowship, or grant income, but not claiming the benefits of an income tax treaty.

Exception 3: Third Party Reporting of Mortgage Interest

If the ITIN applicant has a home mortgage loan on real property that they own in the United States, that is subject to third party reporting of mortgage interest. Information returns applicable to exception 3 may include Form 1098, *Mortgage Interest Statement.*

If the applicant is eligible to claim exception 3, the applicant must submit documentation showing evidence of a home mortgage loan. Evidence would include a copy of the contract or sale or similar documentation.

Exception 4: Third Party Withholding Dispositions by a Foreign Person of United States Real Property

This exception may apply if the individual is a party to a disposition of a U.S. real property interest by a foreign person, which is generally subject to withholding by the transferee or buyer (withholding agent). If the applicant uses this exception with their information return, one of the following may be included:

➢ Form 8288, *U.S. Withholding Tax Return Dispositions by Foreign Persons of U.S. Real Property Interests.*
➢ Form 8288-A, *Statement of Withholding on Dispositions by Foreign Persons of U.S. Real Property Interests.*
➢ Form 8288-B and a copy of the contract of the sale, *Application for Withholding Certificate for Dispositions by Foreign Persons of U.S. Real Property Interests.*

For the seller of the property, copies of Forms 8288 and 8288-A submitted by the buyer should be attached to Form W-7.

Exception 5: Reporting Obligations under Treasury Decision 9363(T. D. 9363)

This exception may apply if the taxpayer has an IRS reporting requirement under TD-9363 and is submitting Form W-7 with Form 13350.

If the applicant is eligible for this exception, Form 13350 should be submitted with the W-7 application, along with a letter from their employer on corporate letterhead stating they have been designated as the person responsible for ensuring compliance with IRS information reporting requirements.

Aliens

Determining if a taxpayer is a resident, nonresident, or dual-status alien dictate whether and how the taxpayer must file a return.

Resident Alien

The taxpayer is a resident alien of the United States for tax purposes if he/she meets either the "green card test" or the "substantial presence test" for the current calendar tax year. If the taxpayer has been a resident for the entire year, he/she must file a tax return following the same rules that apply to a U.S. citizen. See Publication 519.

Nonresident Alien

A nonresident alien is one who has not passed the green card test or the substantial presence test. Tax forms are different for the nonresident alien. For example, there are only 3 options for filing status on Form 1040NR: Single, Married Filing Separately, and Surviving spouse.

Dual-status Alien

Aliens who make a change from nonresident alien to resident alien or from resident alien to nonresident alien are considered a dual-status alien. Different rules apply for each part of the year the taxpayer is a nonresident or a resident alien.

Publication 519 will help in determining the taxpayer's alien status. This topic is not covered in depth in this textbook.

Tax Return Compliance

The IRS is enhancing compliance activities relating to certain credits, including the child tax credit. The changes will improve the ability of the IRS to review returns claiming this credit, including those returns utilizing ITINs for dependents. For example, additional residency information will be required on Schedule 8812, Child Tax Credit, to ensure eligibility criteria for the credit is met.

Information derived from the ITIN process will be better utilized in the refund verification process. New pre-refund screening filters were put in place to flag returns for audits that claim questionable refundable credits. Increased compliance resources will also be deployed to address questionable returns in this area. As part of these overall efforts, ITIN holders may be asked to revalidate their ITIN status as part of certain audits to help ensure the numbers are used appropriately.

Expiration of ITINs

An ITIN only needs to be renewed if it has expired and is needed on a U.S. federal tax return. If an ITIN has not been used on a tax return for the past 3 years, then the ITIN is expired.

The uniform policy applies to any ITIN, regardless of when it was issued. Only about a quarter of the 21 million ITINs issued since the program began in 1996 are being used on tax returns. The new policy will ensure that anyone who legitimately uses an ITIN for tax purposes can continue to do so, while at the same time expiring millions of unused ITINs.

Part 4 Review Questions

To obtain the maximum benefit from this chapter, LTP recommends that you complete each of the following questions, and then compare them to the answers with feedback that immediately follows. Under governing self-study standards, vendors are required to present review questions intermittently throughout each self-study course.

These questions and explanations are not part of the final examination and will not be graded by LTP.

CTIP4.1
Which of the required supporting documents for ITIN applications is a standalone document?

a. Passport
b. U.S. Citizenship and Immigration Services (USCIS) photo identification
c. National identification card
d. Foreign driver's license
e. Foreign voter's registration card

CTIP4.2
Which of the following is not a common error found when processing an application for an ITIN?

a. Name does not match the name on the tax return
b. Date of entry is not entered
c. Passport is not signed
d. W-2s match the name on the application

CTIP4.3
Which of the following is not a common error on Form W-7?

a. Name mismatch
b. No date of entry
c. Unsigned passports
d. Incomplete acceptance agent information

CTIP4.4
Preparers must determine how a taxpayer must file his/her file a tax return based on which of the following?

a. If taxpayer is a resident alien
b. If taxpayer is a nonresident alien
c. If taxpayer is a dual-status alien
d. All the options are correct

CTIP4.5
The taxpayer is a resident alien of the United States for tax purposes if he/she meets which of the following tests?

1. The "green card test"
2. The "Quarterly Test"
3. The "substantial presence test"

a. 1 only
b. 2 & 3 only
c. 3 only
d. 1 & 3

CTIP4.6

The taxpayer (or spouse) who does not have a Social Security number (SSN), should do which of the following?

    a. Do not file a tax return
    b. Leave the space blank
    c. Apply for an ATIN
    d. Apply for an SSN (if they qualify) or an ITIN

CTIP4.7

Which of the following individuals do not need an ITIN to file a tax return?

    a. Nonresident alien
    b. Taxpayer who does not qualify for an SSN
    c. Taxpayer who has an SSN
    d. Alien dependent not eligible for an SSN

CTIP4.8

Which of the following is not a common error found when processing an application for an ITIN?

    a. Name does not match the name on the tax return
    b. Date of entry is not entered
    c. Passport is not signed
    d. W-2s match the name on the application

CTIP4.9

Which government agency issues the ITIN?

    a. IRS
    b. FTB
    c. U.S. Treasury
    d. Secretary of State

CTIP4.10

Which of the following is not used to complete the application process of Form W-7 or W-7SP?

    a. Reason for applying
    b. Applicants' full name
    c. Applicants' mailing address
    d. Travel itinerary

Part 4 Review Questions Answers

CTIP4.1
Which of the required supporting documents for ITIN applications is a standalone document?

    a. Passport
    b. U.S. Citizenship and Immigration Services (USCIS) photo identification
    c. National identification card
    d. Foreign driver's license
    e. Foreign voter's registration card

Feedback: Review section *Documentation needed.*

CTIP4.2
Which of the following is not a common error found when processing an application for an ITIN?

    a. Name does not match the name on the tax return
    b. Date of entry is not entered
    c. Passport is not signed
    d. W-2s match the name on the application

Feedback: Review section *Common Errors on Form W-7.*

CTIP4.3
Which of the following is not a common error on Form W-7?

    a. Name mismatch
    b. No date of entry
    c. Unsigned passports
    d. Incomplete acceptance agent information

Feedback: Review section *Common Errors on Form W-7.*

CTIP4.4
Preparers must determine how a taxpayer must file his/her tax return based on which of the following?

    a. If taxpayer is a resident alien
    b. If taxpayer is a nonresident alien
    c. If taxpayer is a dual-status alien
    d. All the options are correct

Feedback: Review section *Aliens.*

CTIP4.5
The taxpayer is a resident alien of the United States for tax purposes if he/she meets which of the following tests?

1. The "green card test"
2. The "Quarterly Test"
3. The "substantial presence test"

a. 1 only
b. 2 & 3 only
c. 3 only
d. 1 & 3

Feedback: Review section *Aliens*.

CTIP4.6
The taxpayer (or spouse) who does not have a Social Security number (SSN), should do which of the following?

a. Do not file a tax return
b. Leave the space blank
c. Apply for an ATIN
d. Apply for an SSN (if they qualify) or an ITIN

Feedback: Review section *Reason to Apply for an ITIN*.

CTIP4.7
Which of the following individuals do not need an ITIN to file a tax return?

a. Nonresident alien
b. Taxpayer who does not qualify for an SSN
c. Taxpayer who has an SSN
d. Alien dependent not eligible for an SSN

Feedback: Review section *Who needs an ITIN?*

CTIP4.8
Which of the following is not a common error found when processing an application for an ITIN?

a. Name does not match the name on the tax return
b. Date of entry is not entered
c. Passport is not signed
d. W-2s match the name on the application

Feedback: Review section *Common Errors on Form W-7*.

CTIP4.9
Which government agency issues the ITIN?

    a. IRS
    b. FTB
    c. U.S. Treasury
    d. Secretary of State

Feedback: Review section *Who Needs an ITIN?*

CTIP4.10
Which of the following is not used to complete the application process of Form W-7 or W-7SP?

    a. Reason for applying
    b. Applicants' full name
    c. Applicants' mailing address
    d. Travel itinerary

Feedback: Review section *Reason to Apply for an ITIN.*

Takeaways

Knowing tax law and gathering the necessary information to satisfy the due diligence knowledge requirement is just the beginning of becoming a great tax preparer. What truly marks a successful career is applying this knowledge correctly to a tax return; this is the paramount responsibility of a tax professional.

Knowing the tax law and how to apply each law to each individual situation is the puzzle that the tax professional must solve for the rest of their career. Every situation is different, and the tax professional must learn how to put the pieces of the puzzle together to prepare an accurate tax return.

TEST YOUR KNOWLEDGE!
Go online to take a practice quiz.

California Compiling Taxpayer's Information

Introduction

The California tax return does not follow the federal return line-by-line, as established by the following:

> ➢ California subtracts the exemption amount from the tax owed.
> ➢ California did not conform to the Tax Cuts and Jobs Act (TCJA) with respect to not being able to claim an exemption for dependents.
> ➢ California begins by gathering the taxpayer's and spouse's personal information.
> ➢ If the couple's status is a registered domestic partner (RDP) or same sex married couple (SSMC), you will enter the spouse's information on Form 540.

The information needed to complete the state return is:

> ➢ First and last name as found on SSN or ITIN.
> ➢ Address (including city, state, and zip).
> ➢ Date of birth.
> ➢ Prior name (if the taxpayer or spouse filed a prior California return with a different last name).

California does not conform to most of the federal Tax Cuts and Jobs Act changes. A tax practitioner needs to understand state tax law to make sure that the taxpayer is receiving all the credits and paying the correct amount of tax.

Interview questions that were asked in the federal portion also will help with California tax law. Although, there will be interview questions for the state tax law that does not conform to the federal and to state specific content that is different from the federal.

Objectives

By the end of this chapter, the student will:

> ➢ Understand the difference between the federal and state calculation of personal exemptions.
> ➢ Know that the state's filing statuses differ from federal.
> ➢ Recognize the tax differences between the state and federal.

Resources

Form 540	Form 540 Booklet	California Tax Rates and Exemptions
Form 540 2EZ	Form 540 2EZ Booklet	

Table of Contents

Part 1 Form 540

While Form 1040 is used to file the federal tax return, California uses Form 540 to file the state return. There are differences between the federal and state forms.

One difference is Form 540 requests the taxpayer, spouse, or RDP's date(s) of birth and a prior name on the front page of the form. Another difference is the tax return has 5 sides. Before starting the California return, the taxpayer needs to complete the federal return.

The Franchise Tax Board (FTB) is the collection agency for the State of California. The mission of the FTB is to ensure that taxpayers file timely tax returns and pay the correct amount owed to the State of California.

The Following Sections are Found on Form 540

➢ Taxpayer and spouse information, (if applicable)
➢ Date of Birth
➢ Prior Name
➢ Principal Residence
➢ Filing Status

- ➢ Exemptions
- ➢ Taxable Income
- ➢ Tax
- ➢ Special Credits
- ➢ Other Taxes
- ➢ Payments
- ➢ Use Tax
- ➢ IRS Penalty
- ➢ Overpaid Tax/Tax Due
- ➢ Contributions
- ➢ Amount You Owe
- ➢ Interest and Penalties
- ➢ Refund and Direct Deposit
- ➢ Sign Here

Taxpayer and Spouse Information, (if applicable)

As with the federal, the state starts with the taxpayer's information and spouse if filing jointly. Information needed in this section is:

- ➢ First and last name
- ➢ Middle initial
- ➢ Suffix
- ➢ SSN or ITIN
- ➢ Address
- ➢ City, State, Zip
- ➢ Foreign country name, province, state, county
- ➢ Foreign postal code

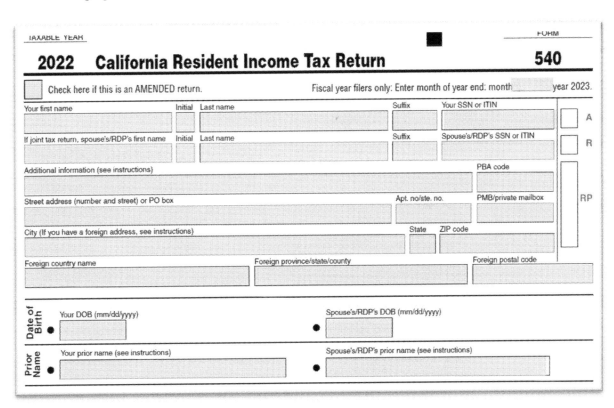

Portion of Form 540

Most common suffix are "SR", "JR", "III", "IV". Do not enter academic, professional, or honorary suffixes, such as CRTP (California Registered Tax Preparer), EA (enrolled agent), DR (doctor), CPA (certified public accountant), etc. Enter the taxpayer and spouse SSN or ITIN if filing jointly.

Additional information is "In-Care-Of" name and, if necessary, a different address for information only.

Foreign Address needs to be entered as it would be in the country the taxpayer lives in. Do not abbreviate the country name. For example, Canada (CA).

Date of Birth

The state requires the date of birth on the front page of the tax return. Enter date of birth for taxpayer and spouse if applicable.

Prior Name

If the taxpayer or spouse used a prior name in the prior year, enter the name used. Be aware that this question is especially needed if an RDP filing status is changed to MFJ filing status.

Filing Status

Line 1 through 5: Check only one box and enter the additional information if box 3 or 5 was checked. Filing status will be discussed in a later chapter.

California filing statuses are different from federal tax law. California filing status:

> ➢ Single.
> ➢ Married or Registered Domestic Partner (RDP) filing jointly.
> ➢ Married or Registered Domestic Partner (RDP) filing separately.
> ➢ Head of Household.
> ➢ Qualifying Surviving Spouse/RDP.

Unlike the federal form, California asks for the date of death next to box 5. Another difference with California is that if a joint tax return was filed on the federal return, then the taxpayer and spouse may file separately for California if either spouse was one of the following:

> ➢ An active member of the United States armed forces or any auxiliary military branch during 2022.
> ➢ A nonresident for the entire year and had no income from California sources during 2022.

However, if the taxpayer had no federal filing requirement, he or she should use the same filing status for the state return as the federal

Portion of Form 540

Interview Pointers

The following personal information is needed from the client:

➢ I see that you changed your filing status from RDP to MFJ. Did either of you have a name change?

Exemptions

California did not conform to some of the Tax Cuts and Jobs Act (TCJA). One difference is that exemptions are allowed for dependents. For this section, the tax professional will need the following information:

➢ Dependent(s) name (as it appears on the SSN, ATIN, or ITIN).
➢ Dependent(s) relationship to the taxpayer.

► For line 7, line 8, line 9, and line 10: Multiply the number you enter in the box by the pre-printed dollar amount for that line.

Whole dollars only

Exemptions

7 **Personal:** If you checked box 1, 3, or 4 above, enter 1 in the box. If you checked box 2 or 5, enter 2 in the box. If you checked the box on line 6, see instructions. ⦿ 7 ☐ X $140 = ⦿ $ ☐

8 **Blind:** If you (or your spouse/RDP) are visually impaired, enter 1; if both are visually impaired, enter 2. . . . . ⦿ 8 ☐ X $140 = ⦿ $ ☐

9 **Senior:** If you (or your spouse/RDP) are 65 or older, enter 1; if both are 65 or older, enter 2. See instructions. . . . . ● 9 ☐ X $140 = ⦿ $ ☐

Portion of Form 540

California returns calculate personal exemption amount prior to calculating the taxpayer's income.

Line 8: Blindness exemption. If this is the first year that the taxpayer or spouse is claiming an exemption for being blind, attach the doctor's statement to the back of Form 540 indicating who is blind: the taxpayer or the spouse or RDP. If the taxpayer is claimed as a dependent on another return, the taxpayer does not receive the additional amount.

Line 9: Senior exemption. California conforms to the federal tax law when the taxpayer's 65th birthday is January 1. If the taxpayer was over the age of 65 on December 31, 2021, the taxpayer and spouse would receive an additional credit. The additional credit cannot be claimed if the taxpayer is claimed as a dependent on another return.

Line 10: Dependent exemption. Although there are only four lines of the exemption section like the federal return, a preparer must still mark the box and follow the instructions to add an additional sheet for more dependents.

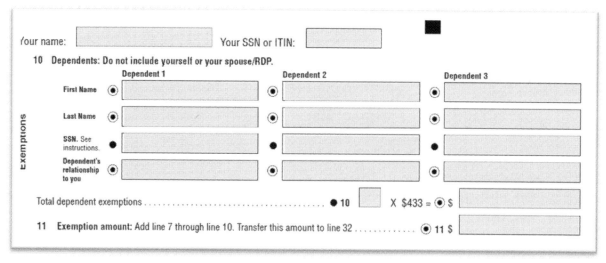

Portion of Form 540

Line 11: Exemption amount. Add lines 7-10 and enter the total dollar amount. This is the taxpayer's total amount of exemption.

Exemptions and dependents will be discussed in a later chapter.

Interview Pointers

The following personal information is needed from the client:

> ➤ Did the child live with you for the last 6 months of the year?
> ➤ Did you have a dependent that does not have an SSN or ITIN that could be your dependent? (This will be covered in a later chapter).
> ➤ Confirm the dependents are the same as on the federal.

Taxable Income

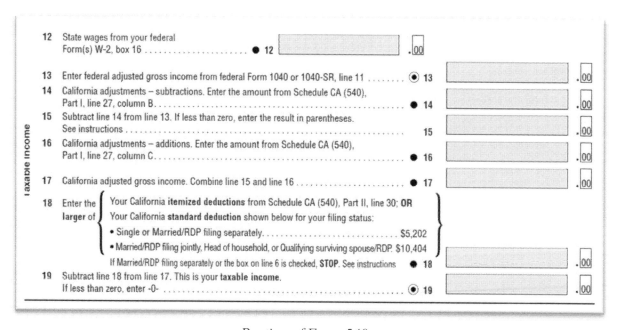

Portion of Form 540

California begins with the federal income and then adds or subtracts additional income based on California law.

Line 12: State wages. Enter the total amount of the state wages from all Form(s) W-2.

Line 13: Federal Adjusted Gross Income (AGI). Enter total from Form 1040, line 8b.

Line 14: California adjustments. Subtractions to income are reported on 540 Schedule CA and flow to line 14. Use 540 Schedule CA to calculate if necessary.

Line 15: Subtotal of taxes owed. Subtract line 14 from line 13 and enter the amount on line 15.

Line 16: California adjustments. Additions to income are reported on 540 Schedule CA, Column C and flows to line 16. Additions from adjustments to income on Schedule 1 that need to be added to California taxable income go here.

Line 17: California Adjusted Gross Income (AGI). Combine line 15 and line 16 to calculate the taxpayer's adjusted gross income and report it on Line 17.

Line 18: Report the total deduction amount on Line 18. Use either the California itemized deductions **or** the standard deduction. The taxpayer cannot calculate their deductions using both methods. He or she must use one or the other.

Line 19: Subtract Line 18 from Line 17 to calculate the taxpayer's taxable income amount and report it on Line 19.

Interview Pointers

If there are adjustments to income, make sure to complete 540 Schedule CA.

Tax

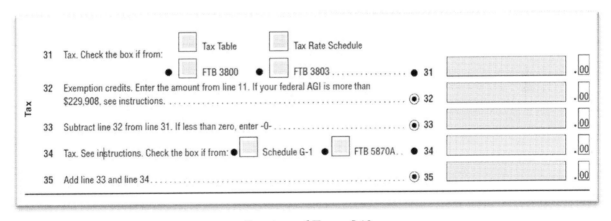

Portion of Form 540

Line 31: Tax. Check one of the boxes to report how the tax has been calculated up to this point. Check the "Tax Table" box if the predetermined table found in the 540 Instruction Booklet for taxpayers with less than $100,000 income was used. The "Tax Rate Schedule" is for taxpayers whose income is over $100,000. Form FTB 3800 is used when the parent will be claiming their child's unearned income. Form FTB 3803 is used when the parent elects to report their child's interest and dividends.

Line 32: Reports exemption credits. Exemption credits reduce the tax and are based on the amount of exemptions claimed. If the federal AGI is more than $212,288, find the instructions in the 540 Instruction Booklet on how to enter the correct amount on line 32.

Line 33: Subtract line 32 from line 31. IF the amount is less than zero, enter zero.

Line 34: Tax from Schedule G-1 and Form FTB 5870A is reported here. Schedule G-1 is used if the taxpayer was born before January 2, 1936, and had a qualified lump-sum distribution.

Line 35: Add lines 33 and 34.

Interview Pointers

Software may automatically mark the box for which method was used to calculate the tax. As a preparer you should double check that software marked the correct box.

Special Credits and Nonrefundable Credits

This section is equivalent to Form 1040, Schedule 3, Part 1. As with the federal form, nonrefundable credits will lower the tax to zero, but not below zero. A variety of California tax credits are available to reduce the tax if the taxpayer qualifies. If the taxpayer qualifies for any of the special credits, the form should be completed and attached to the return.

Line 40: Nonrefundable Child and Dependent Care Expenses Credit. If the taxpayer has child and dependent care expenses credit(s), he or she would report them on Form FTB 3506 (and attach the form to the return) and place the total amount on line 40.

Line 43 - 44: Additional special credits. Any additional special credits that a taxpayer qualifies for are reported here. The code associated with the special credits needs to be added in the "code box."

Portion of Form 540

Line 45: To claim more than 2 credits, Schedule P (540) must be attached.

Line 46: Nonrefundable renter's credit. Enter the appropriate renter's credit amount on line 46. The taxpayer would receive either $60 or $120.

Line 47: Add line 40 through 46 to get the total California Nonrefundable Credits and report it on line 47.

Line 48: Subtract line 47 from line 35 to get the remaining amount of tax liability after credits and deductions have been applied. If the total amount is less than zero, then enter zero because these are nonrefundable credits.

Interview Pointers

> ➢ Did you pay rent for at least the last 6 months of the year? Rent paid to parents is not deductible.

Other Taxes

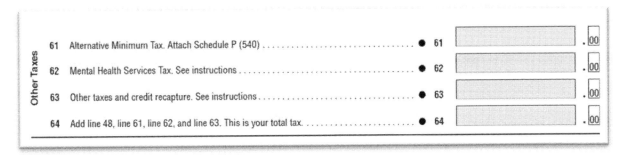

Portion of Form 540

Other taxes may include the following:

Line 61: Alternative minimum tax (AMT). Reported on Schedule P (540), the taxpayer may need to use this form if they itemized their deductions and claimed certain income and allowed deductions and credits. Individuals who benefit from the credits may need to pay an additional tax called AMT.

Line 62: Mental Health Services Tax. If the taxpayer's income is more than $1,000,000, he or she must pay an additional 1% tax called the "Mental Health Services Tax" based on their income on Form 540, line 19.

Line 63: Other taxes and credit recapture. If the taxpayer had an early distribution of a qualified retirement plan, which is reported on Form FTB 3805P, the additional tax is subject to 5% and is reported on line 63. Other taxes that might be recaptured on this line are:

> ➢ *New Employment Credit* (reported on Form FTB 3554).
> ➢ *Credit Carryover and Recapture Summary* (reported on Form FTB 3540).
> ➢ *California Competes Tax Credit* (reported on Form FTB 3531).

There are exceptions that apply to these credits.

Line 64: Add line 48, 61, 62 and 63, to reach taxpayer total tax.

Interview Pointers

If the client is new to you, ask these questions:

> ➢ Can I see last year's tax returns to see if you have any credits that will carry forward?

Payments

Payments made throughout the year via methods such as withholding or estimated payments are added up and subtracted from the tax owed listed on line 48 to arrive at the total remaining payment or refund.

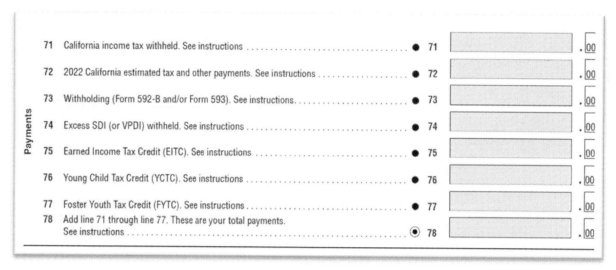

Portion of Form 540

Line 71: California income tax withheld. Enter the total amount of state income tax withheld from all sources of income on line 71.

The following taxes withheld are not included on line 71 as they are recorded elsewhere:

- ➢ City, local, or county tax withheld; tax withheld by other states.
- ➢ Non-consenting nonresident (NCNR) members tax from Schedule K-1 (568), line 15e.
- ➢ Withholding from Forms 592-B, *Resident and Nonresident Withholding Statement.*
- ➢ Form 593, *Real Estate Withholding Tax Statement.*

Line 72: 2022 CA estimated tax and other payments. Enter the total of any of the following:

- ➢ California estimated tax payments made using Form 540-ES (Estimated Payments), electronic funds withdrawal, Web Pay, or credit card.
- ➢ Overpayment from the taxpayer's 2022 California income tax return that was applied to 2023.
- ➢ Payment sent with Form 3519, *Payment for Automatic Extension for Individuals*; this is used to pay tax owed when filing for an extension.
- ➢ California estimated tax payments made on behalf of an estate, trust, or S-corporation are reported on Schedule K-1 (541) or Schedule K-1 (100S). These forms are beyond the scope of this course.

If the taxpayer and spouse/RDP paid estimated taxes but are filing separate returns, the taxpayer and spouse/RDP must determine which of them will claim the estimated payments on the separately filed returns. See Personal Income Tax Booklet 2022 on www.ftb.ca.gov, the official FTB website.

Line 73: Real estate withholdings. If a taxpayer sells income-producing property, the state will withhold 3 1/3% based on the total income. Report the total amount of California withholding from either of the following on this line:

➤ Form 593 – Residential Property
➤ Form 592-B – Business Property

Do not include federal tax withholding from the following:

➤ Form W-2, box 2
➤ Form W-2G, box 4
➤ Form 1099
➤ NCNR members tax from Schedule K-1 (568), line 15e

Line 74: Excess California SDI (State Disability Insurance) or VPDI (Voluntary Paid Disability Insurance) withheld. If you qualified for state disability insurance but had too much reported due to multiple jobs, report the excess withholding amount here.

Line 75: California Earned Income Tax Credit (CalEITC). Use Form 3514 to calculate the credit. If the taxpayer qualifies for the credit based on income, then attach the form to the return and enter the total credit amount on line 75.

Line 76: Young Child Tax Credit (YCTC). Enter your Young Child Tax Credit from form FTB 3514, line 28.

Line 77: Net Premium Assistance Subsidy (PAS)

Line 78: Add lines 71 through 76 to calculate the total state withholding payments and enter the amount on line 77.

Interview Pointers

If the client is new to you, ask these questions:

➤ Did you pay any estimated payments for the year?
➤ Did you sell property during the year? Did you receive Form 592-B or 593?

Use Tax

Taxpayers who purchase items through the Internet, over the phone, or via mail from out-of-state retailers and who are not charged sales or use tax may have to pay sales or use tax as a part of their California return. If the tax was not paid on the purchase, the end user must pay the tax to California when the purchased items are used in California. Use the tax worksheet found in Form 540 Booklet.

Portion of Form 540

Interview Pointers

➤ Did you purchase any product online and not pay sales tax?
➤ Did you purchase any product over the phone and not pay sales tax?

Individual Shared Responsibility (ISR) Penalty

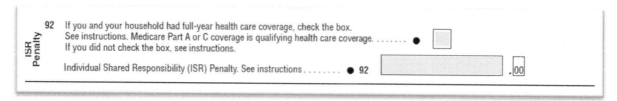

Portion of Form 540

If taxpayer and spouse or any dependents on the tax return did not have minimum essential coverage for the entire year, Form 3853 will be used to calculate the penalty.

Interview Pointers

> ➢ Did you have medical insurance for the entire year?
> ➢ Did everyone in your household and those you are claiming have medical insurance for the entire year?
> ➢ Did you have Medicare Part A or C? (Ask this question to someone over the age of 65).

Overpaid Tax or Tax Due

To avoid tax return processing delays, make sure all the lines are accurate. Ensure refunds or payments due are reported on the correct lines.

Portion of Form 540

Line 93: Payments balance. If line 78 is more than line 91, then subtract line 91 from line 78.

Line 94: Use Tax balance. If the amount on line 91 is more than the amount on line 78, then subtract the amount on line 78 from the amount on line 91.

Line 95: Payments after Individual Shared Responsibility Penalty. If line 93 is more than line 92, subtract line 92 from line 93.

Line 96: Individual Responsibility Shared Penalty Balance. If line 92 is more than line 93, then subtract line 93 from line 92.

Line 97: Overpaid tax. If line 95 is greater than line 65, subtract line 65 from 95, enter the total.

Your name:		Your SSN or ITIN:	■

98	Amount of line 97 you want applied to your **2023** estimated tax	● 98	.00
99	Overpaid tax available this year. Subtract line 98 from line 97	● 99	.00
100	Tax due. If line 95 is less than line 64, subtract line 95 from line 64	◉ 100	.00

Portion of Form 540

The state refund can be processed in several ways:

- ➤ Rolled over to the following year for the taxpayer's estimated payments.
- ➤ Directly deposited into the taxpayer's checking or savings account.
- ➤ Delivered as a check from the Franchise Tax Board (FTB) to the taxpayer.

California conforms to the split-refund option, a receiving method that allows the taxpayer to deposit the return into two separate accounts.

Line 98: Amount to be applied to next year's estimated tax. If taxpayer wants to roll over some or all the refund toward next year's tax liability, enter the determined amount on line 98.

Line 99: Overpaid tax available for a refund. If an amount less than the total amount of refund was inputted on line 98, then report the remaining refund amount on line 99.

Line 100: Tax due. If there is any remaining tax owed, report it on line 100. This is the total amount of tax owed by the taxpayer.

If taxpayers have a balance due on their tax return, they should mail Form FTB 3582 to the FTB with their payment for the full amount by the due date. If the taxpayers cannot pay the full amount, they should pay as much as they can when they mail in Form FTB 3582 to minimize additional charges. To request monthly payments, file Form FTB 3567, *Installment Agreement Request*. If the taxpayer fails to pay the tax liability by the April due date, a late payment penalty plus interest will accrue. The FTB may waive the late penalty assessment if the taxpayer can prove a reasonable cause.

Taxpayer can also pay their balance due electronically.

Form 3582: Payment Voucher

A taxpayer would use Form 3582 if there is a balance due and the tax return was filed electronically. The taxpayer can choose one of the following payment options:

- ➤ Web Pay; do not mail Form 3582 with this option.
- ➤ Credit card (a convenience fee is charged for the service); do not mail Form 3519 if this option is chosen.
- ➤ Check or money order; mail Form 3582 to use this option.

Form 3519: Extension Payment Voucher

If the taxpayer is filing an extension and making a payment, use Form 3519. The taxpayer would use Form 3519, *Automatic Extension for Individuals*, if both of the following apply:

➢ The taxpayer cannot file their tax return by the April due date.
➢ The taxpayer owes tax for the current tax year.

Contributions

This section covers voluntary contributions made on the tax form to certain organizations. These contributions will affect the taxpayer's amount of refund received and the amount a taxpayer may owe. Organizations that a taxpayer can donate to are listed in the image below.

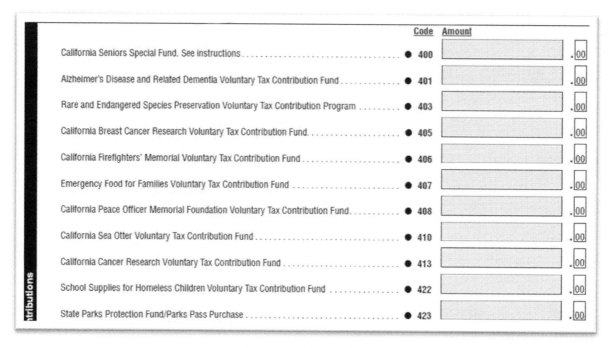

Portion of Form 540

Interview Pointers

➢ Did you want to contribute to any of these non-profits?

Amount Owed

Portion of Form 540

Line 111: Amount you owe. If the taxpayer does not have an amount on line 99, add line 94, 96, 100, and 110.

Individuals can pay the tax owed in different ways:

➢ Mail a check or money order to the FTB.
➢ Pay online at officialpayments.com with a credit card. Credit card fees may apply.
➢ Web Pay - make an Automated Clearing House (ACH) payment from a checking or savings account using the FTB's website.
➢ Electronic Funds Withdrawal via checking or savings account.

Interview Pointers

> ➢ How would you like to pay your balance due?

Line 114: Total Amount Due

If there is an amount on line 111, add lines 111, 112, and 113 and enter the result on line 114. If there is no entry on line 111, continue to line 115. California may, at its discretion, grant an extension of time to pay the tax due. If an extension is granted, interest is charged from the regular due date through the payment date using the rate charged for deficiencies. The California Franchise Tax Board accepts credit cards for payment of personal income tax, interest, and penalties.

Refund or No Amount Due

If the taxpayer receives a refund and would like the money directly deposited into a bank account, enter the taxpayer's bank account routing number and account number in the spaces shown in the following image.

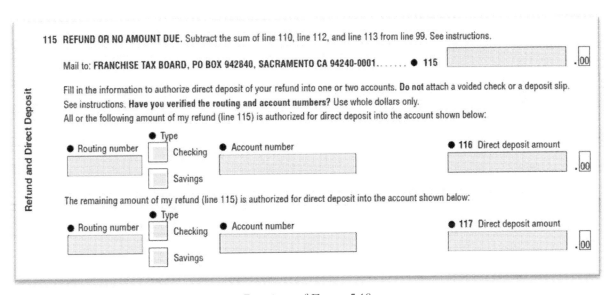

Portion of Form 540

Line 115: Refund or No Amount Due. Enter the total refund amount due the taxpayer. If the taxpayer does not qualify for any refund amount, leave this section (including lines 116 and 117) blank.

Lines 116 and 117: Direct deposit refund. The amount of refund due a taxpayer can be directly deposited into any existing bank accounts. Enter the taxpayer's bank routing and account number. Designate whether the account is a savings or checking account. The taxpayer can enter two different accounts if they would like.

Interview Pointers

> ➢ How would you like your refund sent to you?

Signature Section

The paid preparer enters their PTIN, business name, business address, FEIN (federal employer identification number), and business phone number in this section. The paid preparer must sign the return in the appropriate box; an unsigned tax return will be assessed a penalty. The taxpayer and spouse/RDP also need to sign and date the return. California conforms to the federal tax code regarding third-party designee responsibilities.

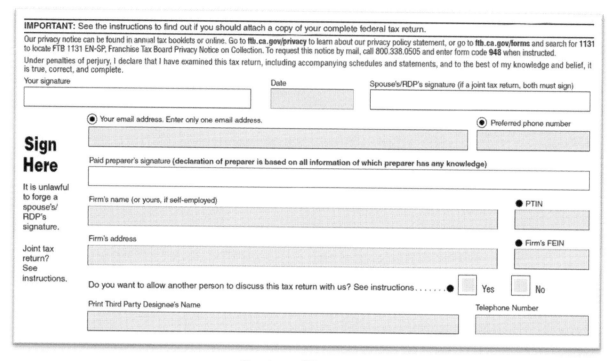

Portion of Form 540

Part 1 Review Questions

To obtain the maximum benefit from this chapter, LTP recommends that you complete each of the following questions, and then compare them to the answers with feedback that immediately follows. Under governing self-study standards, vendors are required to present review questions intermittently throughout each self-study course.

These questions and explanations are not part of the final examination and will not be graded by LTP.

CCTIP1.1
Which of the following is true about California Filing Status?

    a. California conforms with the federal filing status.
    b. California taxpayers can always file their taxes as married filing joint for federal and married filing separately for California.
    c. California taxpayers can file their taxes as Married/RDP filing jointly.
    d. California must always use their federal filing status.

CCTIP1.2
Which of the following exemptions could help the taxpayer?

    a. Blind
    b. Dependents
    c. Senior
    d. All of them

CCTIP1.3
Which of the following is not found in the "Special Credit" section on the California return?

    a. Nonrefundable renter's credit
    b. Nonrefundable child and dependent care expenses
    c. Alternative minimum tax
    d. Additional special credits

CCTIP1.4
California has a section called "Special Credits". What is the equivalent section on the federal return called?

    a. Other Taxes Section
    b. Tax and Credits Section, Schedule 3
    c. Payments Section
    d. Tax Section

CCTIP1.5
Which of the following reports the Nonrefundable Child and Dependent Care Expenses Credit?

    a. Form 3503
    b. Form 3502
    c. Form 3506
    d. Form 3507

CCTIP1.6
Which of the following is on the state return and not on the federal return?

    a. Exemptions
    b. Prior name
    c. Date of birth
    d. All of them

CCTIP1.7
California will withhold a certain amount of income based on the total income in which of the following scenarios?

    a. When a taxpayer sells their primary residence.
    b. When a taxpayer sells income-producing property.
    c. When a taxpayer purchases an income-producing property.
    d. When a taxpayer sells their primary residence for a loss.

CCTIP1.8
James is claiming 3 credits on his Form 540. Which of the following forms would he use?

    a. Schedule S
    b. Schedule P
    c. Schedule H
    d. Schedule R

CCTIP1.9
Elizabeth has a refund on her return. Which of the following ways could she receive her refund?

    a. Rolled over to the following year for estimated payments.
    b. Check by snail mail.
    c. Directly deposited into a savings or checking account.
    d. All of them.

CCTIP1.10
Which of the following are required to have minimum essential health coverage for the entire year?

    a. Taxpayer
    b. Spouse (if applicable)
    c. Dependent (if applicable)
    d. All of them

Part 1 Review Questions Answers

CCTIP1.1
Which of the following is true about California Filing Status?

    a. California conforms with the federal filing status.
    b. California taxpayers can always file their taxes as married filing joint for federal and married filing separately for California.
    c. California taxpayers can file their taxes as Married/RDP filing jointly.
    d. California must always use their federal filing status.

Feedback: Review section *Filing Status.*

CCTIP1.2
Which of the following exemptions could help the taxpayer?

    a. Blind
    b. Dependents
    c. Senior
    d. All of them

Feedback: Review section *Filing Status.*

CCTIP1.3

Which of the following is not found in the "Special Credit" section on the California return?

    a. Nonrefundable renter's credit
    b. Nonrefundable child and dependent care expenses
    c. Alternative minimum tax
    d. Additional special credits

Feedback: Review section *Special Credits*.

CCTIP1.4

California has a section called "Special Credits". What is the equivalent section on the federal return called?

    a. Other Taxes Section
    b. Tax and Credits Section, Schedule 3
    c. Payments Section
    d. Tax Section

Feedback: Review section *Special Credits and Nonrefundable Credits*.

CCTIP1.5

Which of the following reports the Nonrefundable Child and Dependent Care Expenses Credit?

    a. Form 3503
    b. Form 3502
    c. Form 3506
    d. Form 3507

Feedback: Review section *Special Credits and Nonrefundable Credits*.

CCTIP1.6

Which of the following is on the state return and not on the federal return?

    a. Exemptions
    b. Prior name
    c. Date of birth
    d. All of them

Feedback: Review section *Date of Birth, Prior Name and Exemptions*.

CCTIP1.7

California will withhold a certain amount of income based on the total income in which of the following scenarios?

    a. When a taxpayer sells their primary residence.
    b. When a taxpayer sells income-producing property.
    c. When a taxpayer purchases an income-producing property.
    d. When a taxpayer sells their primary residence for a loss.

Feedback: Review section *Payments*.

CCTIP1.8
James is claiming 3 credits on his Form 540. Which of the following forms would he use?

    a. Schedule S
    b. Schedule P
    c. Schedule H
    d. Schedule R

Feedback: Review section *Payments*.

CCTIP1.9
Elizabeth has a refund on her return. Which of the following ways could she receive her refund?

    a. Rolled over to the following year for estimated payments.
    b. Check by snail mail.
    c. Directly deposited into a savings or checking account.
    d. All of them.

Feedback: Review section *Overpaid Tax or Tax Due*.

CCTIP1.10
Which of the following are required to have minimum essential health coverage for the entire year?

    a. Taxpayer
    b. Spouse (if applicable)
    c. Dependent (if applicable)
    d. All of them

Feedback: Review section *Individual Shared Responsibility (ISR) Penalty*.

Part 2 Filing the California Tax Return

California has 2 forms that can be used to file a state tax return. The taxpayer may qualify to use Form 540 2EZ; otherwise one would use Form 540 to file. This part will discuss the difference between the two returns.

Which California Form to File

Unlike the federal tax changes from the Tax Cuts and Jobs Act (TCJA) where now only Form 1040 is used to file and claim income and expenses, California has two such forms: Form 540 2EZ and Form 540. Form 540 2EZ is the short form used for taxpayers who only have standard deductions.

Form 540 2EZ may be used in the following cases:

➢ Filing Status:
    ○ Single.
    ○ Married/RDP filing jointly.
    ○ Head of household.
    ○ Qualifying Surviving Spouse/RDP.
    ○ Dependents (zero to three allowed).

- Amount of Income:
  - $100,000 or less if single or head of household.
  - $200,000 or less if married, filing jointly, or a Qualifying Surviving Spouse/RDP.
- Sources of Income:
  - Wages, salaries, tips.
  - Taxable interest, dividends, pensions.
  - Capital gains from mutual funds (Form 1099-DIV, Box 2a).
  - Taxable scholarships and fellowship grants (only if reported on Form W-2).
  - U.S. Social Security benefits.
  - Tier 1 and 2 railroad retirement payments.
  - Unemployment compensation.
  - Paid family leave (reported on Form 1099G).
- No adjustments to income
- Standard deduction only
- Payments
  - Only withholding shown on Form(s) W-2 and 1099-R.
- Exemptions are:
  - Personal exemption credit.
  - Senior exemption credit.
  - Up to three exemptions.
- Credits
  - Nonrefundable renter's credit.
  - California earned income tax credit.

Tax is computed by using the 540 2EZ Table.

Form 540 2EZ cannot be used under the following circumstances:

- If the taxpayer or spouse filed a joint return.
- If the taxpayer or spouse has a dependent of their own.
- If the taxpayer is single with a total income that is less than or equal to $15,241.
- If the taxpayer is Married/RDP filing jointly or is a Qualifying Surviving Spouse/RDP with a total income less than or equal to $36,485.
- If the taxpayer is head of household with a total income of less than or equal to $30,841.
- If the taxpayer is required to use the modified standard deduction for dependents.

Form 540 may be used if any of the following apply or are present:

- Any filing status.
- Any number of dependents.
- Any amount of income.
- All sources of income.
- All adjustments to income.
- Using either the standard deduction or itemized deductions.
- If the taxpayer had payments such as:
  - Withholding from all income sources.
  - Estimated tax payments.
  - Payments made with an extension voucher.
  - Excess State Disability Insurance (SDI) or Voluntary Plan Disability Insurance (VPDI).
- Claiming any tax credits.
- Reporting other taxes.

If the taxpayer was a nonresident all year in the state of California, he or she would use Form 540NR.

Assembling a California Tax Return

Like the federal return, the FTB has an order for the forms to be attached together when mailing the return to the state. Form 540 has five pages, and all pages must be mailed to the state, even if there are no entries on the pages. To correctly assemble a California state tax return, the preparer must attach copy 2 of the various income documents to the front of the first page of the tax return. If the taxpayer is filing Form 540 or 540NR, he or she needs to include a copy of their federal return with the state return if the federal return contains Schedules A and B.

When a taxpayer mails the tax return to the FTB, the following items need to be attached to page 1 of the tax return. Do not staple the forms to the tax return; use paper clips.

1. All W-2's if filing MFJ for both taxpayer and spouse
2. All W-2G
3. 1099 Series
4. 592-B if applicable
5. 593 if applicable

The taxpayer may need to add supporting California Schedules and a copy of the other state, if the California return has multiple states.

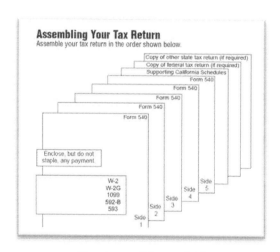

Portion of Form 540

There are situations in which the taxpayer must attach a copy of the federal return to the state return. If the taxpayer has certain forms or schedules attached to the federal return, then the federal return must be attached behind the state return. The following Form 1040 schedules require the federal Form 1040 or 1040-SR to be attached to the state tax return:

➢ Schedule A
➢ Schedule B
➢ Form 1040 Schedules 1, 2, and/or 3

If the taxpayer was not able to use Schedule A on the federal return due to phase outs, make sure you attach the federal Schedule A to the California return.

Filing the California Tax Return

As with the federal, make sure all the information on the state return has been collected, entered, and reviewed for accuracy. Then the tax return can be electronically filed.

Where to File a Paper Return

If a Californian taxpayer is requesting a refund or **not** enclosing a payment with their federal return, use this address to file a paper return:

> Department of Treasury
> Internal Revenue Service
> Ogden, UT
> 84201-0002

If a Californian taxpayer **is** enclosing a payment with their federal return, use this address:

> Internal Revenue Service
> PO Box 802501
> Cincinnati, OH
> 45280-2501

An individual taxpayer who is filing Form 1040-X (which is used to amend a tax return) would file their tax return with a refund, or zero balance, to the following address:

> Department of Treasury
> Internal Revenue Service
> Ogden, UT
> 84201-0052

An individual taxpayer who is filing Form 540, 540 2EZ, 540NR, or Schedule X (which is used to amend a tax return) would file their tax return with a refund, or zero balance, to the following address:

> Franchise Tax Board
> PO Box 942840
> Sacramento, CA
> 94240-0001

An individual taxpayer who is filing Form 540, 540 2EZ, 540NR, or Schedule X would file their tax return **with** a payment to a different address:

> Franchise Tax Board
> PO Box 942867
> Sacramento, CA
> 94267-0001

The best secure option is to electronically file, or e-file, the tax return. This eliminates the need to mail in a physical paper return and will receive an electronic receipt number. This option is discussed further in the e-filing chapter.

All other correspondence should be sent to this address:

> Franchise Tax Board
> PO Box 942840
> Sacramento, CA 94240-0040

Payment vouchers, such as estimated payments (540-ES), would be sent to this address:

> Franchise Tax Board
> PO Box 942867
> Sacramento, CA 94267-0008

Business returns without payment would be mailed to this address:

> Franchise Tax Board
> PO Box 942857
> Sacramento, CA 94257-0500

Business returns with payment or other correspondence regarding business returns would be mailed to this address:

> Franchise Tax Board
> PO Box 942857
> Sacramento, CA 94257-0501

Estates and trusts return without payment would be mailed to this address:

> Franchise Tax Board
> PO Box 942840
> Sacramento, CA 94240-0001

Estates and trusts return with payment would be mailed to this address:

> Franchise Tax Board
> PO Box 942867
> Sacramento, CA 94267-0001

Estates and trusts return with other correspondence use this address:

> Franchise Tax Board
> PO Box 942840
> Sacramento, CA 94240-0040

When filing personal and estates and trusts state estimated payments the address is:

> Franchise Tax Board
> PO Box 942867
> Sacramento, CA 94267-0008

When filing business state estimated payments the address is:

> Franchise Tax Board
> PO Box 942857
> Sacramento, CA 94257-0500

How to File a Return

California conforms to federal filing methods with tax returns.

California Tax Return Due Dates

For calendar-year taxpayers, Californians use the federal filing deadline of April 15th. Taxpayers that are traveling or residing abroad on the day of the tax filing deadline receive an automatic extension and have until June 15th to file. Interest will accrue on any unpaid balance from April 15th until the payment is completed. Residents traveling in another state are not considered to be abroad. Taxpayers must use Form 3519 and follow its instructions to pay the balance due.

If the taxpayer cannot file his or her California tax return by April 15, he or she will be allowed an automatic six-month extension without filing a written request, if the taxpayer is receiving a refund and the return is filed by October 15. To avoid late payment penalties and interest, 100% of the tax liability must be paid by April 15 using Form 3519. Remember, even with extensions, payment penalties are still applied, and interest is still accrued on the unpaid balance.

California conforms to the IRS for individual, business, and estates and trust, tax return due dates.

> ➢ The first deadline is April 18, 2023.
> ➢ The extended deadline is October 16, 2023.

Partnership Returns:

> ➢ The first deadline is March 15, 2023.
> ➢ The extended deadline is September 15, 2023.

Trust and Estate Income Tax Returns:

> ➢ The first deadline is April 18, 2023.
> ➢ The extended deadline is October 2, 2023.

S-corporation Returns:

> ➢ The first deadline is March 15, 2023, for corporations on a calendar year.
> ➢ The extended deadline is September 15, 2023.

Part 2 Review Questions

To obtain the maximum benefit from this chapter, LTP recommends that you complete each of the following questions, and then compare them to the answers with feedback that immediately follows. Under governing self-study standards, vendors are required to present review questions intermittently throughout each self-study course.

These questions and explanations are not part of the final examination and will not be graded by LTP.

CCTIP2.1
What is the due date for individual tax returns not including an extension?

    a. April 15, 2023
    b. April 17, 2023
    c. April 16, 2023
    d. April 18, 2023

CCTIP2.2
When should a taxpayer use Form 540 2EZ?

    a. Taxpayer had no adjustment to income.
    b. Taxpayer had 4 dependents to claim.
    c. Taxpayer had income of $100,100.
    d. Taxpayer will be filing Married/RDP with $38,685.

CCTIP2.3
When would the taxpayer use Form 540?

    a. Taxpayer had adjustment to income.
    b. Taxpayer had tax credits to claim.
    c. Taxpayer had excessive States Disability Insurance.
    d. All the answers are correct.

CCTIP2.4
When assembling the tax return, which form would require the federal return to be attached to the state?

    a. Form 540ES
    b. Schedule B
    c. Form 540NR
    d. Schedule S

CCTIP2.5
Which of the following can use Form 540 2EZ?

    a. Single taxpayer with less than $19,593 income.
    b. Head of Household with less than $22,556 income.
    c. Only have tax withholding from W-2's and 1099-R.
    d. Have a dependent.

CCTIP2.6
Mark purchases most of his supplies for his tax office online from out-of-state retailers. Which of the following would best describe what Mark will need to do?

    a. Mark will need to pay the Use Tax if he did not pay sales tax at the time of purchase.
    b. Mark does not need to pay the Use Tax, since he purchased the products over the phone.
    c. Mark will be charged a penalty for not paying sales tax at the time of purchase.
    d. Mark will need to return any unused supplies and then repurchase them to avoid paying the Use Tax.

CCTIP2.7

Charles wants to make a voluntary contribution to the California Sea Otter Fund. How will the contribution affect his refund?

    a. The contribution will lower his refund.
    b. The contribution will lower the amount owed.
    c. The contribution will not affect his refund.
    d. The contribution will not affect the balance due.

CCTIP2.8

Which of the following income sources are not eligible to use Form 540 2EZ?

    a. Wages, salaries, and tips
    b. Social Security Benefits
    c. Annuities
    d. Taxable Scholarships

CCTIP2.9

Which of the following is the correct order to assemble the state tax return?

    a. Attach all income documents to page 1 of Form 540 or 540 2EZ when mailing the tax return.
    b. Attach Form 1040, if the taxpayer is using Schedule A on the state return only.
    c. Attach Form 592-B every time a house is sold.
    d. Attach Form 3514 to all state returns.

CCTIP2.10

Which of the following PO Box would a taxpayer mail their individual state tax return with a zero balance?

    a. PO Box 942840
    b. PO Box 942867
    c. PO Box 942857
    d. PO Box 802501

Part 2 Review Questions Answers

CCTIP2.1

What is the due date for individual tax returns not including an extension?

    a. April 15, 2023
    b. April 17, 2023
    c. April 16, 2023
    d. April 18, 2023

Feedback: Review section *California Tax Return Due Dates.*

CCTIP2.2
When should a taxpayer use Form 540 2EZ?

a. Taxpayer had no adjustment to income.
b. Taxpayer had 4 dependents to claim.
c. Taxpayer had income of $100,100.
d. Taxpayer will be filing Married/RDP with $38,685.

Feedback: Review section *When to File the California Return*.

CCTIP2.3
When would the taxpayer use Form 540?

a. Taxpayer had adjustment to income.
b. Taxpayer had tax credits to claim.
c. Taxpayer had excessive States Disability Insurance.
d. All the answers are correct.

Feedback: Review section *Form 540 may be used in the following....*

CCTIP2.4
When assembling the tax return, which form would require the federal return to be attached to the state?

a. Form 540ES
b. Schedule B
c. Form 540NR
d. Schedule S

Feedback: Review section *Form 540 2EZ may be used in the following....*

CCTIP2.5
Which of the following can use Form 540 2EZ?

a. Single taxpayer with less than $19,593 income.
b. Head of Household with less than $22,556 income.
c. Only have tax withholding from W-2's and 1099-R.
d. Have a dependent of their own.

Feedback: Review section *Form 540 2EZ may be used in the following....*

CCTIP2.6
Mark purchases most of his supplies for his tax office online from out-of-state retailers. Which of the following would best describe what Mark will need to do?

a. Mark will need to pay the Use Tax if he did not pay sales tax at the time of purchase.
b. Mark does not need to pay the Use Tax, since he purchased the products over the phone.
c. Mark will be charged a penalty for not paying sales tax at the time of purchase.
d. Mark will need to return any unused supplies and then repurchase them to avoid paying the Use Tax.

Feedback: Review section *Use Tax*.

CCTIP2.7
Charles wants to make a voluntary contribution to the California Sea Otter Fund. How will the contribution affect his refund?

    a. **The contribution will lower his refund.**
    b. The contribution will lower the amount owed.
    c. The contribution will not affect his refund.
    d. The contribution will not affect the balance due.

Feedback: Review section *Contribution*.

CCTIP2.8
Which of the following income sources are not eligible to use Form 540 2EZ?

    a. Wages, salaries, and tips
    b. Social Security Benefits
    c. **Annuities**
    d. Taxable Scholarships

Feedback: Review section *Form 540 2EZ may be used in the following....*

CCTIP2.9
Which of the following is the correct order to assemble the state tax return?

    a. **Attach all income documents to page 1 of Form 540 or 540 2EZ when mailing the tax return.**
    b. Attach Form 1040, if the taxpayer is using Schedule A on the state return only.
    c. Attach Form 592-B every time a house is sold.
    d. Attach Form 3514 to all state returns.

Feedback: Review section *Assembling a California Tax Return*.

CCTIP2.10
Which of the following PO Box would a taxpayer mail their individual state tax return with a zero balance?

    a. **PO Box 942840**
    b. PO Box 942867
    c. PO Box 942857
    d. PO Box 802501

Feedback: Review section *Where to File a Paper Return*.

Part 3 Residency

Determining California Residency

When filing a state tax return, it is of vital importance to determine the residency of the taxpayer. An individual's residency status will determine such important factors as which credits are received and which tax rates will be applied, among others.

Señor 540 Says: The state of California adopts the position of assuming an individual is a resident until proven otherwise. Most of the guidelines provided here are likely to be used when attempting to prove non-residency.

Important Terms and Definitions

> Reside: To abide consistently or uninterruptedly in a specific dwelling place as a fixed, settled, or legal abode.
> Domiciled: The place where a taxpayer has voluntarily established him or herself and his or her family with the intent of establishing a home. Unlike most states, California marks a distinction between "reside" and "domiciled".

California defines a resident as any individual who fulfills the following:

> Resides in California for reasons other than a temporary or transitory purpose.
> Is domiciled in California, and only lives outside California for a temporary or transitory purpose (see "Meaning of Domicile" in FTB Publication 1031).

An individual domiciled in California who lives outside California for a temporary or transitory purpose remains a resident.

A *nonresident* is any individual who is not a resident. A *part-year resident* is any individual who is a California resident for part of the year and a nonresident for part of the year.

Form 540NR

Form 540NR is used in cases where the taxpayer resided in the state for only part of the tax year or was a nonresident who had California-sourced earned income.

Residency Requirements

Accurately determining the taxpayer's residency status is important to determining filing requirements. Residents of California are taxed on all income, including income from sources outside California (also known as *worldwide income*). California allows a credit for taxes paid to other states to prevent double taxation of income.

Part-year residents are taxed on all income earned in California and from income sources while a nonresident. Part-year residents file Form 540NR. Nonresidents are taxed only on income from Californian sources and file Form 540NR.

Form 540NR divides the total California income by the total worldwide income to calculate the California ratio. The taxpayer's residence is usually the place where he or she has the strongest ties; the taxpayer should compare ties to California with ties elsewhere. In using these factors, it is the strength of the ties, not just the number of ties, which determines residency.

The following factors are ties that need to be considered when determining an individual's residency status:

> ➢ Days spent in California versus outside of California.
> ➢ Location of spouse and children.
> ➢ Location of principal residence.
> ➢ Which state issued a taxpayer's driver's license.
> ➢ In which state a taxpayer's vehicles are registered.
> ➢ Where a taxpayer maintains professional licenses.
> ➢ Where a taxpayer is registered to vote.
> ➢ The location of the banks where a taxpayer's accounts are maintained.
> ➢ The location of a taxpayer's doctors, dentists, accountants, and attorneys.
> ➢ The location of a taxpayer's church, associations, or social and country clubs.
> ➢ The location of a taxpayer's real property and investments.
> ➢ The permanence of a taxpayer's work assignments in California.
> ➢ The location of social ties.

This is only a partial list; a complete list can be found in the "Meaning of Domicile" portion of FTB Publication 1031 from the FTB website. All factors must be considered in the taxpayer's situation to correctly identify the taxpayer's residency status.

Safe Harbor

Safe Harbor is a legal provision intended to reduce or eliminate liability in certain situations if certain conditions are met. If they are met, then the individual will be safe from the application of certain penalties. If an individual is penalized or charged while following these conditions, then he or she can legally challenge the penalties and have them dropped because he or she is protected from them under the Safe Harbor provision.

Individuals domiciled in California who reside outside of California under an employment-related contract for at least 546 consecutive days will safely be considered a nonresident under the Safe Harbor provision unless:

> ➢ The individual has intangible income exceeding $200,000 in any taxable year during which the employment-related contract is in effect.
> ➢ The principal purpose of the absence from California is to avoid personal tax.

The spouse or RDP of the individual covered by the safe harbor rule will also be considered a nonresident while accompanying the individual outside of California for at least 546 consecutive days.

Return visits to California that do not exceed a total of 45 days during any taxable year covered by the employment contract are considered *temporary*.

Individuals not covered by safe harbor determine their residency status based on their other facts and circumstances. The determination of residency status cannot be solely based on an individual's occupation, business, or vocation. Instead, all activities must be considered in the determination of a residency status.

For instance, residents of California who attend out-of-state schools do not automatically become nonresidents, nor nonresidents of California attending Californian schools automatically become residents. In these situations, individuals must determine their residency status based on their facts and circumstances.

Example 1: Gordon is a resident of Vermont who has moved across the country to attend a university in Southern California. He lives in California for the eight months that classes are in session and goes back home to Vermont during every school break. After attending school for two years, he applies to request in-state tuition and is denied, because he is not a permanent resident of California.

Example 2: Christopher attended university in Virginia for four years but did not fully complete his degree. He then moved back home and applied to attend a local California community college paying in-state tuition to finish the remainder of his needed courses. Seeing that his last listed university was in Virginia, the community college denied him in-state tuition. By filling out the right forms and providing the correct documentation, however, Christopher was able to successfully acquire in-state tuition as his attendance of a Virginian university was insufficient grounds to prove his lack of residency.

Even if the taxpayer had no income from California and they used a California address, they should file Form 540NR with all zeros to avoid getting a tax bill for not filing a California tax return even though it may not be required.

Example 1: Marty is a California resident and transferred to his employer's Germany office for a two-year work commitment. Marty visited California on his three-week vacation. Under the safe harbor rule, Marty is a nonresident for the two-year work assignment. The three-week vacation is considered a temporary visit because it did not exceed 45 days.

Example 2: Manolo and Abby are California residents. Abby agreed to work overseas for the next 20 months under an employment contract. Manolo and the children agreed to stay in Redding, California. During the 20-month assignment, Abby can be a nonresident under the safe harbor rule and potentially avoid penalties even though she came home for a month because it was still less than 45 days. Abby earned $80,000 for the year on her overseas trip, and Manolo earned $30,000 as a server. As a tax professional, you will have to figure out the best way for Abby and Manolo to file their tax return. See FTB Publication 1031 for more information.

Abby and Manolo would report their income in the following way if they filed a joint return using Form 540NR.

Joint Return	Total AGI Schedule CA (540NR) Column E	California AGI
Abby wages	$80,000	$40,000
Manolo wages	$30,000	$30,000
Total wages	$110,000	$70,000

Covenant not to Compete

California courts have held that a noncompete covenant in connection with the sale of a business is only enforceable to the extent it is reasonable and necessary. Covenants not to compete are generally void and unenforceable in the employment context under the law. California has exceptions to prohibition on noncompete. A noncompete could be enforceable:

➢ Against the seller of the business
➢ A former business partner
➢ A former business partner or a member of the LLC

Entering or Leaving California

If the taxpayer moved into or out of California during the tax year and has income attributable to California, the taxpayer would be considered a *part-year resident*. As a part-year resident, the taxpayer would file Form 540NR and may qualify for some California tax credits that would reduce the amount of California taxes owed.

Did Not Live in California

If the taxpayer did not reside in the state of California during the tax year but had income from a California source, the taxpayer is a nonresident of California and should file Form 540NR.

Part 3 Review Questions

To obtain the maximum benefit from this chapter, LTP recommends that you complete each of the following questions, and then compare them to the answers with feedback that immediately follows. Under governing self-study standards, vendors are required to present review questions intermittently throughout each self-study course.

These questions and explanations are not part of the final examination and will not be graded by LTP.

CCTIP3.1
Which scenario best describes how California residents are taxed on their income?

    a. Josue is a resident of California and worked in Arizona and California. Josue will pay tax only on his California income.
    b. Susan is a resident of California and is receiving pension income from New Mexico. Susan will pay California income tax on her pension from New Mexico.
    c. Esperanza is an Arizona resident and only has income from Arizona. California will tax Esperanza's Arizona income.
    d. Oliver is active military and a California resident. He has been stationed in Florida. Oliver will pay tax to Florida and California on his military income.

CCTIP3.2
Luis and Tiffany got married and moved to California and want to know how to file their tax return. Luis works for the local supermarket and Tiffany works for the local university. Based on the segment content, which of the following questions must be asked to determine how to file their tax return?

    1. What is their last name(s)?
    2. How long have they lived in California?
    3. Where are their income statements (for example, W-2, 1099-NEC, etc.)?
    4. Do they have a nonexpired government-issued photo identification to prove that they are who they say they are?
    5. Do they have any dependents?
    6. Will they be claiming moving expenses?

    a. 1, 2, 3, 4, and 5
    b. 2, 3, 4, 5, and 6
    c. 1, 3, and 5
    d. 2, 4, and 6

CCTIP3.3
Which of the following is not true about residency in California?

a. Live in California for other than a temporary or transitory purpose
b. Domiciled in California, but lives outside California for a temporary or transitory purpose
c. An individual domiciled in California who lives outside California for a temporary or transitory purpose remains a resident.
d. A *part-year resident* is any individual who is a California resident for part of the year and can choose to be treated as resident for the entire year.

CCTIP3.4
Which of the following factors does not need to be considered when determining an individual's residency status?

a. Days spent in California versus outside of California
b. Location of spouse and children
c. Location of principal residence
d. For which state is the taxpayer paying "use tax"

CCTIP3.5
Which of the following is not a temporary absence to meet the residency test?

a. Illness
b. Education
c. Vacation
d. Filing a joint return with their spouse

CCTIP3.6
California has a provision referred to as "Safe Harbor" that allows taxpayers who are domiciled in the state to be considered a nonresident following certain conditions. What is the amount of consecutive days the taxpayer needs to have?

a. 365
b. 450
c. 546
d. 120

CCTIP3.7
Which of the following are conditions that a noncompete could be enforceable?

a. Against the seller of the business.
b. A former business partner or a member of the LLC.
c. A former business partner.
d. All of them.

CCTIP3.8
Which scenario best describes how California will tax the individual as a part-year resident?

a. Juan moved into California and had income earned in California and New Mexico.
b. Susan lived the entire year in Alaska and moved to California January 1.
c. Bobby moved out of California and had no income.
d. Celia moved into California December 29.

CCTIP3.9
Which form is used for a part-year resident?

    a. Form 540NR
    b. Form 540
    c. Form 540 2EZ
    d. Form 540-SR

CCTIP3.10
Which individual would be considered a nonresident of California?

    a. Dana lives in New Mexico and receives a California pension.
    b. Joe, an active military member, is station in California, but is a resident of Alaska.
    c. Sean works in California, but resides in Oregon, and has an employment-related contract.
    d. Tracy lives in Fresno and works from home.

Part 3 Review Questions Answers

CCTIP3.1
Which scenario best describes how California residents are taxed on their income?

    a. Josue is a resident of California and worked in Arizona and California. Josue will pay tax only on his California income.
    b. Susan is a resident of California and is receiving pension income from New Mexico. Susan will pay California income tax on her pension from New Mexico.
    c. Esperanza is an Arizona resident and only has income from Arizona. California will tax Esperanza's Arizona income.
    d. Oliver is active military and a California resident. He has been stationed in Florida. Oliver will pay tax to Florida and California on his military income.

Feedback: Review section *Residency Requirements*.

CCTIP3.2
Luis and Tiffany got married and moved to California and want to know how to file their tax return. Luis works for the local supermarket and Tiffany works for the local university. Based on the segment content, which of the following questions must be asked to determine how to file their tax return?

    1. What is their last name(s)?
    2. How long have they lived in California?
    3. Where are their income statements (for example, W-2, 1099-NEC, etc.)?
    4. Do they have a nonexpired government-issued photo identification to prove that they are who they say they are?
    5. Do they have any dependents?
    6. Will they be claiming moving expenses?

    a. 1, 2, 3, 4, and 5
    b. 2, 3, 4, 5, and 6
    c. 1, 3, and 5
    d. 2, 4, and 6

Feedback: Review section *Residency Requirements*.

CCTIP3.3
Which of the following is not true about residency in California?

a. Live in California for other than a temporary or transitory purpose.
b. Domiciled in California, but lives outside California for a temporary or transitory purpose.
c. An individual domiciled in California who lives outside California for a temporary or transitory purpose remains a resident.
d. **A *part-year resident* is any individual who is a California resident for part of the year and can choose to be treated as resident for the entire year.**

Feedback: Review section *Residency Requirements*.

CCTIP3.4
Which of the following factors does not need to be considered when determining an individual's residency status?

a. Days spent in California versus outside of California
b. Location of spouse and children
c. Location of principal residence
d. **For which state is the taxpayer paying "use tax"**

Feedback: Review section *Residency Requirements*.

CCTIP3.5
Which of the following is not a temporary absence to meet the residency test?

a. Illness
b. Education
c. Vacation
d. **Filing a joint return with their spouse**

Feedback: Review section *Residency Requirements*.

CCTIP3.6
California has a provision referred to as "Safe Harbor" that allows taxpayers who are domiciled in the state to be considered a nonresident following certain conditions. What is the amount of consecutive days the taxpayer needs to have?

a. 365
b. 450
c. **546**
d. 120

Feedback: Review section *Safe Harbor*.

CCTIP3.7
Which of the following are conditions that a noncompete could be enforceable?

a. Against the seller of the business.
b. A former business partner or a member of the LLC.
c. A former business partner.
d. **All of them.**

Feedback: Review section *Covenant not to Compete*.

CCTIP3.8
Which scenario best describes how California will tax the individual as a part-year resident?

    a. Juan moved into California and had income earned in California and New Mexico.
    b. Susan lived the entire year in Alaska and moved to California January 1.
    c. Bobby moved out of California and had no income.
    d. Celia moved into California December 29.

Feedback: Review section *Entering or Leaving California*.

CCTIP3.9
Which form is used for a part-year resident?

    a. Form 540NR
    b. Form 540
    c. Form 540 2EZ
    d. Form 540-SR

Feedback: Review section *Entering or Leaving California*.

CCTIP3.10
Which individual would be considered a nonresident of California?

    a. Dana lives in New Mexico and receives a California pension.
    b. Joe, an active military member, is station in California, but is a resident of Alaska.
    c. Sean works in California, but resides in Oregon, and has an employment-related contract.
    d. Tracy lives in Fresno and works from home.

Feedback: Review section *Part 3*.

Takeaways

California generally conforms to federal tax law. A tax preparer should ask probing questions when gathering taxpayer's information. As a California tax professional, one must understand both federal and state law to prepare the tax returns.

TEST YOUR KNOWLEDGE!
Go online to take a practice quiz.

Chapter 3 Filing Status, Dependents, and Deductions

Introduction

The Tax Cuts and Jobs Act (TCJA) of 2017 impacts several areas of the tax law until 2025. This chapter describes how TCJA and recent changes have impacted the federal filing statuses, qualifying dependents, and the standard deduction. Filing status is determined on the last day of the year. This chapter will discuss the requirements to determine when a dependent is considered a qualifying dependent, who can claim the qualifying dependent, and how the IRS uses tie-breaker rules for individuals who qualify as a dependent for multiple taxpayers. The IRS has created an interactive tax assistant (ITA) to answer questions that can help you select the best course of action. Make sure to answer all the questions correctly. A tax professional must be aware of the consequences of determining dependents incorrectly—practice due diligence in all tax matters. Verifying the correct filing status and the qualifying dependents will determine the taxpayer's standard deduction.

Objectives

At the end of this chapter, the student will:

➢ Recognize how to determine the standard deduction.
➢ Understand who qualifies for the higher standard deduction.
➢ Explain the qualifying child test requirements.
➢ Identify the difference between a qualifying child and a qualifying relative.
➢ Describe the difference between custodial and noncustodial parents.
➢ List the five filing statuses.
➢ Recall the requirements for each filing status.
➢ Identify types of income to determine support.
➢ Recognize the requirements to claim a qualifying dependent.

Resources

Form 1040 Form 2120 Form 8332	Publication 17 Publication 501 Publication 555 Tax Topic 352, 851, 857, 858	Instructions Form 1040 Instructions Form 2120 Instructions Form 8332

Table of Contents

Part 1 Filing Status

At first glance filing status appears to be simple to determine; however, tax professionals must know, understand, and apply the requirements for each filing status. Choosing the correct filing status determines the filing requirements, deductions, correct tax, and taxpayer eligibility for certain credits and deductions. See Publication 17 and Publication 501.

The five federal filing statuses are:

1. Single (S)
2. Married filing jointly (MFJ)
3. Married filing separately (MFS)
4. Head of household (HOH)
5. Surviving spouse with a dependent child.

State law governs whether a taxpayer is married or legally separated under a divorce or separate maintenance decree when it comes to filing status. A taxpayer is generally considered unmarried for the whole year if, on the last day of the current tax year, the taxpayer is unmarried or legally separated from his/her spouse under a divorce or separate maintenance decree.

Under the Revenue Ruling 2013-17, same-sex couples will be treated as married for all federal tax purposes, including income, gifts, and estate taxes. The ruling applies to all federal tax provisions where marriage is a factor, including filing status, claiming a person and dependency exemptions, taking the standard deduction, employee benefits, contributing to an IRA, and claiming the earned income tax credit or child tax credit.

Single (S)

A taxpayer files as Single if, on the last day of the current tax year, the taxpayer is unmarried or legally separated from their spouse under a divorce or separate maintenance decree. Divorced taxpayers are unmarried the entire year if the divorce was finalized on, by, or before the last day of the year they are filing. If the divorce was strictly for tax purposes and the taxpayers remarry the following year, the couple will need to file a joint return for both tax years. State law governs whether a taxpayer is married or legally separated under a divorce or separate maintenance decree. The tax professional needs to know the individual state laws in which one works and prepares taxes.

When the taxpayer has annulled their marriage, they are considered unmarried, even if they file a joint tax return. The IRS may send the couple letters stating that their filing status is incorrect. In that circumstance, the taxpayers would amend their returns to Single or Head of Household, for all years that were filed incorrectly. Annulled means a legal action in which the marriage never existed in the eyes of the law.

A widow(er) may file Single if they were widowed before January 1st of the current tax year and did not remarry before the end of the same tax year. However, the taxpayer may qualify for a different filing status that might lower the tax liability further.

Married Filing Jointly (MFJ)

The taxpayer must file Married Filing Jointly (MFJ) if he or she meets any of the following criteria on December 31st of the tax year being filed:

➢ Taxpayers are married and filing a joint return even if one had no income or deductions.
➢ Taxpayers are living together in a common-law marriage that is recognized in the state where the taxpayers now live, or in the state where the common-law marriage began.
➢ Taxpayers are married and living apart but are not legally separated under a decree of divorce or separate maintenance.
➢ A spouse died during the tax year, and the taxpayer did not remarry before the end of the tax year.
➢ If a spouse died during the current tax year, and the taxpayer remarried before the end of the tax year, the taxpayer and his or her new spouse may file MFJ. A tax return must still be filed for the deceased spouse, and, in this instance, the decedents' filing status would be MFS for the tax year.

See Revenue Ruling 2013-17 above.

Community Property and Income

Community property states treat property acquired by a husband and wife after marriage as owned by them "in community." In other words, if a wife purchases property under her name before she is married, it is hers alone. If she purchases it after her marriage, then it is regarded as the property of both her and the spouse, even if the property is only under her name.

The community property states (Arizona, California, Idaho, Louisiana, Nevada, New Mexico, Texas, Washington, and Wisconsin) handle community property tax liability differently. When preparing state taxes for a community property state, the tax professional should research before preparing the tax return to ensure a complete understanding of the differences. Alaska is an equitable property state, and it allows couples to choose community property rules, a community property agreement, or community trust. Wisconsin divorce laws contain a presumption that all marital property must be equally divided between the divorcing spouses.

There are also exceptions to community property rules that the tax preparer must know. For example, property acquired before marriage or inherited by one spouse during the marriage is considered a separate property of that spouse. In Arizona, California, Nevada, New Mexico, Washington, and Wisconsin, any income from these separate properties is also considered separate income solely for that spouse. Therefore, if the spouses are filing separately, the income is not shared and reported on the owner's return. This is known as the "California Rule." Conversely, in Idaho, Louisiana, and Texas, income from separate properties is still considered community income; thus, if the spouses file separately, the income would be shared on their individual tax returns. This is known as the "Texas Rule."

According to §66 of the Internal Revenue Code (IRC), when spouses are living apart, the spouse who earned the income will keep it. Living apart entails the following:

➢ They are married to each other.
➢ They lived apart for an entire tax year.
➢ They did not file a joint return.
➢ One or both have earned income, none of which is transferred between them.

Individuals who meet all the above requirements must follow the rules below to cover the reporting of income on their separate returns:

➢ Earned income (other than trade, business, or partnership income) is treated as income of the spouse who rendered the personal services.
➢ Trade or business income is treated as the taxpayer's income unless the spouse substantially exercises control and management of the entire business.
➢ Community income derived from the separate property owned by one spouse is treated as the income of the owner.

All other community income is taxed in accordance with the applicable community property laws. See Code §897(a).

Innocent Spouse

Married taxpayers often choose to file a joint tax return due to the filing status's benefits. However, both taxpayers are jointly and individually responsible for any tax, interest, or penalty due on a joint tax return. Even after a couple is separated or divorced, a former spouse could be held responsible for amounts due on previously filed joint returns.

In this instance, the taxpayer might be able to claim that they are an "innocent spouse": an individual who was not aware of a position claimed on a tax return by their other half that resulted in liability for understatement of income filed on the joint return. In this situation, the innocent spouse can file for relief using Form 8857 to try to prove that they were not aware of the position on the return. The IRS will review the request for relief, come to a decision, and respond with their ruling. The taxpayer may appeal the decision if they find the ruling unacceptable.

To be eligible for the relief, the taxpayer must meet the following criteria:

➢ Must have filed a joint return with an erroneous understatement of tax responsibility relating directly to their spouse.
➢ Must have no knowledge of the error.
➢ The IRS identified the error and must agree that it is fair to relieve the taxpayer of the tax penalties.
➢ The taxpayer must apply for relief within two years of the IRS initial collections notice.

Example: Robert and Debbie were married and filed joint tax returns for 2021 and 2022. Debbie, usually let her husband handle the finances and tax preparation. She simply signed the tax return when Robert told her to, never questioning the man she thought she could implicitly trust. However, after finalizing their divorce on May 15, 2022, Debbie received a letter demanding penalties and interest from the IRS. Alarmed, Debbie found a tax preparer who helped her discover that her ex-husband Robert had illegally claimed business expenses on their personal 2021 and 2022 tax returns, causing significant penalties and interest to accrue for filing a fraudulent return. Based on her lack of knowledge, the tax preparer correctly advised her to file Form 8857 to apply for relief on the 2021 and 2022 tax returns.

Spousal Abandonment

"Spousal abandonment" and "innocent spouse" are two different tax implications. Spousal abandonment occurs when the abandoning spouse has left their family with no intention of returning or having responsibility for their family. In a legal context, failing to provide for a dependent, ailing spouse, or a minor child could be considered criminal spousal abandonment. Separation with no intent of reconciling is not spousal abandonment. Spousal abandonment often requires the abandoned spouse to file a separate return and receive all the unfavorable tax consequences that come with it. For example, the taxpayer must use the Tax Rate Schedule for married taxpayers filing separately. To mitigate such harsh treatment, Congress enacted provisions commonly referred to as the "abandoned spouse rules" which allow married taxpayers to file as Head of Household to bypass the tax consequences of married filing separately.

Married Filing Separately (MFS)

Married taxpayers, whether living together or apart, may choose to file Married Filing Separately (MFS) in the following circumstances:

> ➢ They want to be responsible for their own tax liability.
> ➢ If the MFS filing status results in the taxpayers paying less tax than filing jointly.

Taxpayers need to be advised that MFS filing status has limitations in deductions, adjustments, and credits.

Taxpayers who elect to file MFS must enter their spouse's full name and Social Security number or ITIN in the spaces provided and are also generally subject to the following special rules:

> ➢ Tax rates are generally higher.
> ➢ Must have lived apart the entire year to claim credit for the elderly or disabled.
> ➢ Unable to take certain credits.
> ➢ Capital loss deduction limited to $1,500.
> ➢ Must itemize deductions if spouse itemizes deductions.
> ➢ Individual retirement account (IRA) contributions are limited due to income amount.
> ➢ The interest can't be excluded from qualified U.S. savings bonds for higher education expenses.
> ➢ Alternative minimum tax is half of the allowed for MFJ.

See Publication 501.

If the taxpayers live in a community property state and file a separate return, the laws of the state in which the taxpayer reside governs whether they have community property income or separate property income for federal tax purposes. See Publication 555.

Head of Household (HOH)

The taxpayer must file Head of Household (HOH) if they meet any of the following criteria on December 31st of the tax year being filed:

> ➢ The taxpayer must be considered unmarried on the last day of the year.
> ➢ A qualifying child or relative lived in the home for more than half the year (there are exceptions for temporary absences). Children of divorced or separated parents, or parents who lived apart, can be claimed based on the residency test in most cases.

> ➤ The taxpayer paid for more than half the cost of keeping up the home for the tax year.

A married taxpayer could be considered as head of household if they maintain separate homes for more than the last 6 months of the year and a qualifying child lived with them. The filing status to choose on the tax return is Head of Household.

Keeping Up a Home

To qualify for the HOH filing status, a taxpayer must pay more than half of the cost for maintaining a household. Expenses can include rent, mortgage interest payments, repairs, real estate taxes, insurance, utilities, and food eaten in the house. Costs do not include clothing, education, medical treatment, vacations, life insurance, and the rental value of the home the taxpayer owns. Keeping up a house and monetary support will be discussed later in this chapter.

Suppose the taxpayer receives payments from Temporary Assistance for Needy Families (TANF) or other public assistance programs to pay rent or upkeep on the home. In that case, those payments cannot be included as money the taxpayer paid. However, they must be included in the total cost of keeping up the home to figure whether the taxpayer paid over half of the cost.

Señor 1040 Says: Remember, assistance given by TANF to pay for rent must be included in the total cost of keeping up a home.

Differences Between Filing Head of Household and Single

The difference between filing S and filing HOH is whether the unmarried taxpayer keeps up a home for a Qualifying Person. To qualify to register as Head of Household, there must first be a household to be the head of, and for there to be a household, there must first be a group of individuals that live together and are of qualifying relation to be considered a family unit. If these specifications do not apply to the taxpayer's living situation, the taxpayer must file Single.

A taxpayer would file Single rather than Head of Household in the following situations:

> ➤ The taxpayer lives alone. Although he is technically the head person in his home because he is the only person who lives there, there is no household to be the head of, and he thus must file Single.
> ➤ The taxpayer lives within a household but does not qualify to be its head. Whether it's because he doesn't provide a sufficient percentage of support or for another reason, although he is in a household, he is not its head and thus would file Single.
> ➤ If a taxpayer has a qualifying dependent but lives within a household without qualifying as Head of Household, they will file Single with a Dependent instead of Head of Household.

Example 1: Tyler lives alone in a suburban house, and no one else lives with him. He files Single because even though he is the "head" of his house, there is not a household or group of individuals living together of qualifying relation to be considered a family unit.

Example 2: Joseph and four of his friends live in a house they rent together and split all the living costs evenly amongst themselves. Assuming none of them are married or in a registered domestic partnership, they will all file Single since none provide more than 50% of support for the house to qualify as a Head of Household. The group does not possess sufficient qualifying relationships to be considered a family unit and cannot be considered a household; therefore, there is neither a head of household nor a household. All taxpayers must file Single.

Example 3: Barry and his son Don live with Barry's parents, Henry and Nora, who make $350,000 annually. Barry makes $27,840 a year as a part-time educational aide; he does not provide more than 50% percent of support for the household; yet does provide more than 50% of support for his son Don. Barry must file Single with a Dependent for the following reasons:

> ➤ He is a household member, but is not its head, because he provides too little support; thus, he would not file as Head of Household.
> ➤ He is unmarried and not in a registered domestic partnership; thus, he would file Single, even with a dependent.
> ➤ Don is Barry's qualifying dependent because Don is Barry's child, and Barry provides more than 50% of Don's support; thus, he would file Single with a dependent.

Surviving Spouse with Dependent Child

The taxpayer can file as a Surviving Spouse (SS) with Dependent Child if they meet any of the following criteria on December 31st of the tax year being filed:

> ➤ The taxpayer was entitled to file a joint return with their spouse for the tax year in which the spouse died (whether the taxpayer filed a joint return or not).
> ➤ The taxpayer did not remarry before the end of the tax year.
> ➤ The taxpayer has a dependent child who qualifies as their dependent for the tax year.
> ➤ The taxpayer paid more than half the cost of keeping up a home that was the main home for the taxpayer and the dependent child for the entire year.

For the tax year in which the spouse died, the taxpayer can file MFJ or QSS. If the taxpayer still meets the requirements, the taxpayer will file as QSS with a dependent child for the next two years. If the taxpayer has not remarried and still has a qualifying dependent child living with them after the two years, the taxpayer's filing status would change to HOH.

Example: John's wife died in 2020, and John has not remarried and has continued to keep up a home with his qualifying children, Riley and Galvan. For tax year 2020, John filed MFJ. In 2021 and 2022, he would qualify to file as Surviving Spouse if Riley and Galvan are still qualifying dependents. Starting in tax year 2023, however, if John still has qualifying children and has not remarried, he would not be able to file as a QSS with dependent children and would instead qualify to file as HOH.

Determining the Correct Federal Filing Status

The following scenarios are based on the information you have been studying so far. Determine the best answer for each question.

1. James, age 19, works full time, and his W-2 shows $17,000 in box 1. He claims that his 14-year-old sister lived with him all year long. He tells you that his mother and brother have lived in the same household all year long. His mother's income is $32,000. James wants to claim his sister as his dependent. Which scenario best describes James' filing status based on the information provided?

a. James will file Single and claim his sister as a dependent.
b. James will file Single with no dependents.
c. James will file Head of Household and claim his sister as a dependent.
d. James does not have to file a tax return because his mother will claim him as a dependent.

Feedback: James cannot claim his sister since his mother lives in the same home, and she has the higher income. James is not a dependent on his mother's return since his income is $17,000. James will file Single with no dependents.

2. Linda, age 56, works full time and her W-2 shows $27,000 in box 1. She tells you that her 22-year-old daughter, Julie, was a full-time student until she graduated in June. Julie lived with her until November when she got married to Todd. Linda wants to claim Julie as her dependent. Linda tells you that Julie and Todd filed a joint return to receive their federal withholding, and their total income was less than $6,000. Which scenario best describes Linda's filing status based on the information provided?

a. Linda will file Head of Household without Julie as her dependent.
b. Linda will file Head of Household and claim Julie as her dependent.
c. Linda will file Single with no dependents.
d. Linda will file Single with Julie as her dependent.

Feedback: Linda can claim Julie as her dependent since Julie meets the residency requirements, the relationship requirements, and the joint return test. Therefore, Linda's filing status would be Head of Household, and Linda will claim Julie as her dependent.

3. Javier, age 45, and Janice, age 42, support Javier's uncle, Chris, who does not live with them. Javier gives Chris $500 per month for support. Which of the following questions must you ask Javier to determine if Chris is their dependent?

1. How much and what kind of income did Chris receive?
2. Can any other taxpayer claim Chris as a dependent?
3. Do you have documentation that shows your support?
4. Does Chris have any dependents?

a. All the questions must be asked
b. 3 and 4
c. 1 and 2
d. 1, 2, and 3

Feedback: To make sure the taxpayer can claim a relative as a dependent, the tax professional must ask specific questions to determine if the relative is a Qualifying Relative. All the questions need to be asked. The following Qualifying Relative Checklist can help you determine a member of the household test:

➤ Your child, stepchild, foster child, or a descendant of any of them (for example, your grandchild). (A legally adopted child is considered your child.)
➤ Your brother, sister, half-brother, half-sister, stepbrother, or stepsister.
➤ Your father, mother, grandparent, or other direct ancestors, but not foster parent.
➤ Your stepfather or stepmother.
➤ A son or daughter of your brother or sister.
➤ A son or daughter of your half-brother or half-sister.
➤ A brother or sister of your father or mother.

> ➢ Your son-in-law, daughter-in-law, father-in-law, mother-in-law, brother-in-law, or sister-in-law.
> ➢ Any of these relationships that were established by marriage aren't ended by death or divorce.

4. Jonathan, age 37, wants to claim his mother as a dependent on his tax return. His mother receives Social Security benefits of $22,000. Jonathan's W-2 box 1 shows $22,000. Based on the information provided, which scenario best describes Jonathan's filing status?

    a. Jonathan will file Single and claim his mother as a dependent.
    b. Jonathan will file Single with no dependents.
    c. Jonathan will file Head of Household and claim his mother as a dependent.
    d. Jonathan does not have to file a tax return because his mother will claim him as a dependent.

Feedback: Jonathan cannot claim his mother since he did not provide more than 50% of her support due to his mother's Social Security benefits. Jonathan will file Single with no dependents.

5. Mia, age 28, has a son Bobby, age 6. They have lived all year with Mia's mother. Mia has a full-time job and is a full-time student. Box 1 of her W-2 shows $19,000. Mia's mother, Billie, wants to claim Bobby as her dependent. Billie's W-2 has $12,000 in box 1. Mia provides all the support for Bobby. Which scenario best describes Mia's filing status based on the information provided?

    a. Mia will file Single with no dependent.
    b. Billie will file Head of Household and claim Bobby.
    c. Mia will file Head of Household and claim Bobby as her dependent.
    d. Billie will file Head of Household and claim Mia and Bobby as her dependents, since they live with her.

Feedback: Billie is unable to claim either Mia or Bobby since Mia makes more than Billie does. Mia can file Head of Household since she provides 100% of Bobby's support. Billie is not able to claim Mia or Bobby since she made less income than Mia. Mia will file Head of Household and claim Bobby as her dependent.

6. Esperanza, age 19, is a full-time student and has a part-time job. Esperanza and her daughter Elissa, age 3, live with Esperanza's parents. Her W-2 box 1 shows $4,000 in income. Esperanza's parents' combined income is $75,000. Both Esperanza and Elissa are on her parents' medical insurance. Which scenario best describes Esperanza's filing status based on the information provided?

    a. Esperanza will file Single with no dependent.
    b. Esperanza will file Single, as a dependent, on another return, with no dependent.
    c. Esperanza will file Head of Household and claim Elissa as a dependent.
    d. Esperanza will file Single and claim Elissa as a dependent.

Feedback: Esperanza and Elissa are both dependents on Esperanza's parents' tax return because her parents provided the majority of support for both Esperanza and her daughter. Because Esperanza only earned $4,000 on her W-2, which is below the dependent exemption threshold, she's filing a tax return to receive her federal tax withholding back (if applicable). Esperanza will file Single, as a dependent, on another return with no dependent.

7. Colton and Brittney are legally married. They have a separation agreement and have been living apart since November 2021. They filed a joint return for 2021. Brittney's earned income is $46,000 and her daughter Mika lives with her 100% of the time. Colton's earned income is $31,000. Colton wants to claim Mika as his dependent for the tax year 2023. Based on the information provided, which scenario best describes what must happen for Colton to be able to claim Mika?

    a. Colton can file Head of Household and claim Mika since she is his daughter.
    b. Brittney must sign Form 8332 to allow Colton to claim Mika.
    c. Mika can choose which parent she wants to claim her.
    d. Brittney will file Head of Household and claim Mika since her income is higher than Colton's, and Mika has lived with her 100% of the time.

Feedback: Colton will not be able to claim Mika unless Brittney signs Form 8332. Mika has lived with Brittney 100% of the time, and Brittney's earned income is more than Colton's. Tie-breaker rules could also help determine filing status and who can claim Mika. Colton must have Brittney sign Form 8332 to be able to claim Mika. Apply the following rules to determine which person can claim the child as a qualifying child:

    ➢ If the parents file jointly, both will claim the child as a qualifying child.
    ➢ If only one taxpayer is the child's parent, the child is the qualifying child of the parent.
    ➢ If the parents do not file a joint return, the IRS will treat the child as a qualifying child of the parent whom the child lived with for the longest time during the year. Children who live with each parent an equal amount of time are qualifying children for both parents. The IRS then treats them as qualifying children of the parent with the highest AGI for the year.
    ➢ If no parent can claim the child as a qualifying child, the child is the qualifying child of the person with the highest AGI for the year.
    ➢ If a parent can claim the child as a qualifying child and no parent claims the child, the child is the qualifying child of the person with the highest AGI for the year.

8. Pedro and Celeste are legally married and have two children. Celeste does not want to pay Pedro's back taxes and self-employment tax. Pedro has his own business. Celeste owned the house before their marriage (they do not live in a community property state). Celeste's W-2 box 1 shows $150,000. Pedro's gross income from his Schedule C is $15,000. Which scenario best describes Pedro and Celeste's filing status based on the information provided?

    a. Pedro should file as Head of Household with the two children, and Celeste should file Single.
    b. Celeste should file as Head of Household with the two children, and Pedro should file Single.
    c. Pedro and Celeste should file Married Filing Separately and then decide who claims the children and the deductions.
    d. Pedro and Celeste don't have to file a tax return since they can't decide how to file.

Feedback: A married taxpayer may choose MFS if any of the following applies:

    ➢ If they are married, living together, or apart.
    ➢ If they want to be responsible for their tax liability.
    ➢ If it results in less tax than they would owe on a joint return; however, let taxpayers know that MFS filing status has severe limitations in deductions, adjustments, and credits.

Pedro and Celeste should file Married Filing Separately and then decide who claims the children and the deductions.

9. Peter, age 21, and his son Paul lived with his parents the entire year. His W-2 box 1 shows $4,050. Peter is a full-time student. Peter would like to file on his own and claim his son, Paul. Peter and his son are both on his parents' medical insurance. His parents, Roberto and Melissa, have a combined income of $175,000. Which scenario best describes Peter's filing status based on the information provided?

   a. Peter will file Single and be a dependent on his parents' return.
   b. Peter will file Single and be a dependent on another return and claim Paul as a dependent.
   c. Roberto and Melissa will file Married Filing Joint and claim Peter and Paul as dependents.
   d. Peter will file Single on his return and declare he is a dependent on another return, and Roberto and Melissa will file Married Filing Joint and claim Peter and Paul as their dependents.

Feedback: The taxpayer should pay more than half of the cost of keeping up a home for the year, but Peter has not provided more than 50% for his or Paul's support, which means he cannot claim Paul as his dependent. Peter will file Single on his return and declare he is a dependent on another return, and Roberto and Melissa will file Married Filing Joint and claim Peter and Paul as their dependents.

10. Fernando and Tabitha are legally married (Tabitha has an ITIN) they have three children with SSNs. Tabitha is a stay-at-home mom, and Fernando's W-2 box 1 shows $29,000. Fernando and his family live with his brother Charles. Which scenario best describes Fernando and Tabitha's filing status based on the information provided?

   a. Fernando and Tabitha will file Married Filing Jointly and claim all three children as dependents.
   b. Fernando will file as Head of Household and claim Tabitha and his three children as dependents.
   c. Fernando will file single and let Charles claim the others as dependent.
   d. Charles will claim Fernando and his family as dependents since they all live with him.

Feedback: Even though Tabitha has an ITIN, this does not eliminate her from the tax return. Fernando and Tabitha are legally married, and Fernando and Tabitha are not dependents on Charles' tax return just because the family lives there. Similarly, since neither Fernando and Tabitha nor Charles provide more than 50% of support for each other, neither would claim the other as a dependent. Fernando and Tabitha will file Married Filing Jointly and claim all their children as dependents.

Exemptions and Suspensions

The Tax Cuts and Jobs Act in 2017 suspended the personal exemption for tax years **2018 to 2025**. Though there may not be a filing requirement for the federal portion of a return currently, a taxpayer might still have a filing requirement for the state and, in the future, potentially for the federal return as well.

Similar to a deduction, a personal exemption reduces the amount of income used to compute tax liability. Unlike tax deductions, an exemption is simply a set amount of reduction given on the return. The taxpayer can generally claim an exemption for himself, his or her spouse, and any qualifying dependents. The total amount of reduction provided from any personal exemptions before the tax year 2017 goes on Form 1040, line 42, and Form 1040A, line 26. Form 1040EZ, line 5, is the sum of the total standard deduction amount added to the personal exemption amount.

Rules for Dependent Exemptions

➢ The taxpayer cannot claim any dependents if they file a joint return or if they could be claimed as a dependent by another taxpayer.
➢ The taxpayer cannot claim a married person who files a joint return as a dependent unless the joint return is only a claim for a refund.
➢ The taxpayer cannot claim a person as a dependent unless the individual is a U.S. citizen, a U.S. resident, a U.S. national, or a resident of Canada or Mexico for some part of the year; there are exceptions to this rule, but they are beyond the scope of this course.
➢ A taxpayer cannot claim a person as a dependent unless that person is their qualifying child or qualifying relative.

The taxpayer is allowed one exemption for each person claimed on the tax return. The taxpayer can claim an exemption for a dependent even if they file a tax return.

Part 1 Review Questions

To obtain the maximum benefit from this chapter, LTP recommends that you complete all questions and then compare them to the answers with feedback that immediately follow. Under governing self-study standards, vendors are required to present review questions intermittently throughout each self-study course.

These questions and explanations are not part of the final examination and will not be graded by LTP.

FSDDP1.1
On which date is the taxpayer's filing status determined?

    a. October 31
    b. December 31
    c. January 1
    d. April 15

FSDDP1.2
Which of the following is not a federal filing status?

    a. Single
    b. Married filing separately
    c. Head of household
    d. Married filing single

FSDDP1.3
Which of the following best describes community property?

    a. All property acquired by a husband or wife while domiciled in a common law state.
    b. All property acquired by a husband or wife while domiciled in a community property state.
    c. All property acquired by a husband or wife while domiciled in a separate property state.
    d. All property acquired by a husband or wife while domiciled in a joint property territory.

FSDDP1.4
A federal tax return needs to be filed by all the following except:

    a. Individuals in general
    b. Dependents
    c. Self-employed persons
    d. Anyone over the age of 65

FSDDP1.5
Jeff's filing status is married filing separately. Which of the following does not apply to Jeff?

    a. Must itemize deductions if the spouse itemizes.
    b. Cannot claim student loan interest.
    c. Can claim the EITC (earned income tax credit).
    d. Cannot take the child and dependent care credit or expenses.

FSDDP1.6
Which of the following would allow Gunther to file as head of household?

    a. Gunther maintained a home for himself all year.
    b. Gunther's mother did not live with the taxpayer, but Gunther paid 100% of her living expense.
    c. Gunther is the noncustodial parent of Hunter.
    d. Gunther's dependents did not live with him the entire year.

FSDDP1.7
Carina needs to determine her filing status. Which of the following would allow Carina to file as head of household?

    1. Carina maintained a home for herself all year.
    2. Carina's mother did not live with her but then she paid 100% of her mother's living expense.
    3. Carina is the noncustodial parent and unable to claim their dependent.
    4. Carina's dependents did not live with her the entire year.

    a. 1, 2, and 4
    b. 2 only
    c. 2 and 3
    d. 4 only

FSDDP1.8
Which of the following is not one of the requirements for the federal single filing status?

a. Is unmarried on the last day of the year.
b. Is legally separated by divorce or separate maintenance decree.
c. Does not qualify for another filing status.
d. Spouse died during the tax year, and taxpayer did not remarry before the end of the current tax year.

FSDDP1.9
Wendy is filing single. Which of the following is not one of the requirements to use the single filing status?

1. Is unmarried on the last day of the year.
2. Is legally separated by divorce or separate maintenance decree.
3. Does not qualify for another filing status.
4. Spouse died during the tax year, and taxpayer did not remarry before the end of the current tax year.

a. 1, 2, and 3
b. 4 only
c. 1 and 3
d. 2, 3, and 4

FSDDP1.10
Victoria's filing status is married filing separately. Which of the following does not apply to a married filing separately taxpayer?

1. Must itemize deductions if the spouse itemizes.
2. Cannot claim student loan interest.
3. Can claim EIC.
4. Cannot take the child and dependent care credit or expenses.

a. 3 only
b. 1, 2, and 4
c. 1 and 3
d. 2 and 4

Part 1 Review Questions Answers

FSDDP1.1
On which date is the taxpayer's filing status determined?

a. October 31
b. December 31
c. January 1
d. April 15

Feedback: Review section *Filing Status*.

FSDDP1.2
Which of the following is not a federal filing status?

    a. Single
    b. Married filing separately
    c. Head of household
    d. Married filing single

Feedback: Review section *Filing Status*.

FSDDP1.3
Which of the following best describes community property?

    a. All property acquired by a husband or wife while domiciled in a common law state.
    b. All property acquired by a husband or wife while domiciled in a community property state.
    c. All property acquired by a husband or wife while domiciled in a separate property state.
    d. All property acquired by a husband or wife while domiciled in a joint property territory.

Feedback: Review section *Community Property and Income*.

FSDDP1.4
A federal tax return needs to be filed by all the following except:

    a. Individuals in general
    b. Dependents
    c. Self-employed persons
    d. Anyone over the age of 65

Feedback: Review section *Filing Status*.

FSDDP1.5
Jeff's filing status is married filing separately. Which of the following does not apply to Jeff?

    a. Must itemize deductions if the spouse itemizes.
    b. Cannot claim student loan interest.
    c. Can claim the EITC (earned income tax credit).
    d. Cannot take the child and dependent care credit or expenses.

Feedback: Review section *Married Filing Separately*.

FSDDP1.6
Which of the following would allow Gunther to file as head of household?

    a. Gunther maintained a home for himself all year.
    b. Gunther's mother did not live with the taxpayer, but Gunther paid 100% of her living expense.
    c. Gunther is the noncustodial parent of Hunter.
    d. Gunther's dependents did not live with him the entire year.

Feedback: Review section *Head of Household*.

FSDDP1.7
Carina needs to determine her filing status. Which of the following would allow Carina to file as head of household?

1. Carina maintained a home for herself all year.
2. Carina's mother did not live with her but then she paid 100% of her mother's living expense.
3. Carina is the noncustodial parent and unable to claim their dependent.
4. Carina's dependents did not live with her the entire year.

a. 1, 2, and 4
b. 2 only
c. 2 and 3
d. 4 only

Feedback: Review section *Head of Household.*

FSDDP1.8
Which of the following is not one of the requirements for the federal single filing status?

a. Is unmarried on the last day of the year.
b. Is legally separated by divorce or separate maintenance decree.
c. Does not qualify for another filing status.
d. Spouse died during the tax year, and taxpayer did not remarry before the end of the current tax year.

Feedback: Review section *Filing Status.*

FSDDP1.9
Wendy is filing single. Which of the following is not one of the requirements to use the single filing status?

1. Is unmarried on the last day of the year.
2. Is legally separated by divorce or separate maintenance decree.
3. Does not qualify for another filing status.
4. Spouse died during the tax year, and taxpayer did not remarry before the end of the current tax year.

a. 1, 2, and 3
b. 4 only
c. 1 and 3
d. 2, 3, and 4

Feedback: Review section *Single.*

FSDDP1.10
Victoria's filing status is married filing separately. Which of the following does not apply to a married filing separately taxpayer?

1. Must itemize deductions if the spouse itemizes.
2. Cannot claim student loan interest.
3. Can claim EIC.
4. Cannot take the child and dependent care credit or expenses.

a. **3 only**
b. 1, 2, and 4
c. 1 and 3
d. 2 and 4

Feedback: Review section *Filing Status.*

Part 2 Member of Household or Relationship Test

To meet this test, either of the following must be true:

> ➤ The person lived with the taxpayer all year as a member of the taxpayer's household.
> ➤ If the person did not live with the taxpayer all year, then they must be related to the taxpayer in one of the ways listed in the next section of the chapter.

If the person was the taxpayer's spouse at any time during the year, that person cannot be the taxpayer's qualifying relative.

Relatives Who Do Not Need to Live with the Taxpayer to be Considered a Member of Their Household or Meet the Relationship Test

A person related to the taxpayer in any of the following ways does not have to live with the taxpayer all year as a member of the taxpayer's household to meet this test:

> ➤ The taxpayer's child, stepchild, eligible foster child, or any descendant thereof (e.g., a grandchild).
> ➤ The taxpayer's brother, sister, half-brother, half-sister, stepbrother, or stepsister.
> ➤ The taxpayer's father, mother, grandparent, any other direct ancestor, or stepfather or stepmother, but **not** a foster parent.
> ➤ A son or daughter of the taxpayer's brother, sister, half-brother, or half-sister.
> ➤ A brother or sister of the taxpayer's father or mother.
> ➤ The taxpayer's son-in-law, daughter-in-law, father-in-law, mother-in-law, brother-in-law, or sister-in-law.

Relationships that are established by marriage do not end by death or divorce.

Adopted Child

An adopted child is always treated as the taxpayer's own child. The term "adopted child" includes a child who was lawfully placed with the taxpayer for legal adoption.

Joint Return

If the taxpayer files a joint return, the qualifying relative does not have to be related to the spouse who provides support. For example, Sal and Julie are married, and Julie's uncle received more than half of his support from Sal. Julie's uncle could be Sal's qualifying relative, even though he does not live with Sal. However, if Sal and Julie file separate tax returns, Julie's uncle is a qualifying relative only if he lives with Sal all year as a member of Sal and Julie's household.

Temporary Absence

A qualifying relative is considered to have lived with the taxpayer as a member of the taxpayer's household during periods of time when either the taxpayer or spouse is absent due to specific circumstances such as:

> ➢ Illness
> ➢ Education
> ➢ Business
> ➢ Vacation
> ➢ Military service

Even if the person has been placed in a nursing home to receive medical care for an indefinite period, the absence can be considered temporary.

Death or Birth

A person who died during the year would meet the test if they lived with the taxpayer as a household member until their death. The same is true if a child was born and lived with the taxpayer during the year.

Local Law Violated

A person does not meet the member of the household test if the relationship between the taxpayer and that person violates local law at any time during the year.

Example: Roberto's girlfriend Alicia lived with him as a member of his household all year. However, Roberto's relationship with Alicia violates the state's laws where he lives because she was married to someone else. Therefore, Alicia does not meet the household member or the relationship test, and Roberto cannot claim her as a dependent.

Cousin

A cousin is a descendant of a brother or a sister of the taxpayer's mother or father. If the cousin lives with the taxpayer all year as a member of the taxpayer's household, the cousin can meet the member of household relationship test.

Gross Income Test

To meet this test, a person's gross income must be less than $4,400. "Gross income" is any and all non-tax-exempt revenue that comes in the form of money, property, or services, including gross receipts (sales) from rental property, specific scholarships and fellowship grants, all taxable unemployment compensation, and a partner's share of the gross (not net) income from a partnership. Certain Social Security benefits that are tax-exempt income are not considered gross income. See Publication 501.

Disabled Dependent Working at a Sheltered Workshop

For the purposes of the gross income test, gross income does not include income received for services provided at a sheltered workshop by an individual who is permanently and totally disabled at any time during the year. Some conditions apply; the availability of medical care at the workshop must be the main reason for the individual's presence there, and the income must come solely from activities at the workshop that are incidental to medical care. A "sheltered workshop" is a school that does the following:

➤ Provides special instruction or training designated to alleviate the individual's disability.
➤ It is operated by specific tax-exempt organizations or by a state, U.S. possession, political subdivision of a state or possession of the U.S., or the District of Columbia.

Qualifying Relative Support Test

The taxpayer determines whether they have provided more than half of a relative's total support by using the taxpayer's contribution to their support with the entire amount of support the person received from all sources. These amounts include any support the relative provided from their funds. A taxpayer's funds are not a means of support unless used exclusively for this purpose. See Worksheet 1 in Publication 501.

Example: Robin is retired and lives with her adult son, Ryan. She has received $2,400 in Social Security benefits and $300 in interest. Robin paid $2,000 for lodging and $400 for recreation and has $300 in her savings account. Even though Robin received a total of $2,700, she only spent $2,400 for her support, and Ryan spent more than $2,400 for his mother's support and received no other help, so Ryan has provided more than half of Robin's support.

The individual total support includes tax-exempt income, savings, and borrowed amounts. These are examples of tax-exempt income: Certain Social Security benefits, welfare benefits, nontaxable life insurance proceeds, armed forces family allotments, nontaxable pensions, and tax-exempt interest.

Calculated yearly support when paid.

The taxpayer cannot use support paid in 2021 for 2022, and a taxpayer's support is still calculated on a calendar year even if they use a fiscal-year accounting method.

Armed Forces Dependency Allotments

If the government contributes a certain amount of support and the taxpayer has a portion of their income taken out of their wages, the total amount is half of their support. If the taxpayer uses part of the income to support individuals other than the ones the taxpayer has previously claimed, those individuals may qualify as dependents. See Publication 501.

Example: Doug is in the Armed Forces. He authorizes an allotment to his widowed mother, Debbie, and she uses it to support herself and her brother, Doug's uncle. If the portion that Doug gives her is more than half of their support, Doug can claim Debbie and his uncle as dependents.

Military housing allowances that are tax-exempt are treated as dependency allotments when figuring the support test.

Tax-Exempt Income

Calculating a person's total support includes tax-exempt income, savings, and borrowed amounts used to support the qualifying relative. Though tax-exempt income consists of all the following, we are only emphasizing the first two, which are the most common:

➤ Certain Social Security benefits.
➤ Welfare benefits.

- ➢ Nontaxable life insurance proceeds.
- ➢ Armed forces family allotments.
- ➢ Nontaxable pensions.
- ➢ Tax-exempt interest.

Example: Danelle is Jose's brother's daughter (Jose's niece), and she lives with Jose. Danelle has taken out a student loan of $2,500 to pay her college tuition, and Jose has provided $2,000 for Danelle's support. Jose cannot claim an exemption for Danelle because, due to her student loan, he has not provided more than half of her support.

Social Security Benefits for Determining Support

If a husband and wife each received benefits paid by one check made out to both, the total amount is divided equally between each spouse and counted as having provided support for each of them, unless they can show otherwise. If a child receives Social Security benefits and uses them toward his or her support, it is support provided by the child.

Support Provided by the State (Welfare, Food Stamps, Housing, and others)

Benefits provided by the state to a needy person are amounts provided by the state. However, payments based on the recipients' needs will not be used entirely for their support if they do not use part of the support payments.

Payments received for the support of a foster child from a child placement agency are considered support provided by the agency, not the foster parents. In the same way, payments received for the support of a foster child from a state or county agency are considered support provided by the state or county, not the foster parents.

The taxpayer must pay more than half of the cost of an individual's support to claim them as a qualifying relative. Expenses can include rent, mortgage interest payments, repairs, real estate taxes, utilities, insurance, and food eaten in the home. Costs do not include clothing, education, medical treatment, vacations, life insurance, or the rental value of the house the taxpayer owns.

Suppose the taxpayer receives payments from Temporary Assistance for Needy Families (TANF) or any other public assistance programs to help him or her pay rent or pay for upkeep on the home. In that case, those payments are not money the taxpayer paid. (As of this printing the Treasury has proposed regulations to allow the TANF money to be included as part of the taxpayer's support). However, taxpayer must include the payments in the total cost of keeping up the home to figure who paid over half of the cost-of-living expenses.

Example: Tammy spent $700 of her own money and $300 of her TANF support to pay for the upkeep of the home she and her dependents live in for the entire year. The $300 she received from TANF does not count as support from Tammy to any of her dependents, but it does count toward the total upkeep amount ($1,000) used to determine the head of household filing status and claimant strength.

Use the following blank worksheet to determine if the dependent is a qualifying relative of the taxpayer's household for the two upcoming examples. When interviewing clients and asking support questions, LTP sees that most clients give a monthly amount, so the tax preparer would need to clarify if the numbers given were monthly or annually. In the scenarios below, the calculated numbers are annual amounts.

Example 1: Scenario

Mary Vega (age 37) and her daughter, Sierra (age 9), lived with Mary's aunt all year. Using the following information, determine if Mary paid more than half of their support. If the total amount paid by Mary is less than the amount paid by her aunt, Mary and her daughter are qualifying relatives of her aunt.

Expenses paid by Mary:		Expenses paid by Mary's aunt:	
Electric	$2,149	Mortgage interest	$3,202
Water	$480	Property taxes	$798
Repairs	$1,500	Food eaten in the house	$600
Food eaten in the house	$2,600	Property insurance	$280
Telephone	$576		

Cost of Keeping a Household

	Amount Paid by Taxpayer	Total Costs
Property taxes	$_____	$_____
Mortgage interest expense	$_____	$_____
Rent	$_____	$_____
Utility charges	$_____	$_____
Repairs/maintenance	$_____	$_____
Property insurance	$_____	$_____
Food consumed on the premises	$_____	$_____
Other household expenses	$_____	$_____
TOTALS	$_____	$_____
Subtract total amount taxpayer paid		(_____)
Amount others paid		$_____

Example 1: Answers

Cost of Keeping a Household

	Amount Paid by Taxpayer (Mary)	Total Costs
Property taxes	$_____	$798____
Mortgage interest expense	$_____	$3,202__
Rent	$_____	$_____
Utility charges	$3,205____	$3,205__
Repairs/maintenance	$1,500____	$1,500__
Property insurance	$_____	$280____
Food consumed on the premises	$2,600____	$3,200__
Other household expenses	$_____	$_____
TOTALS	**$7,305____**	**$12,185__**
Minus total amount taxpayer paid		**($7,305)__**
Amount others paid		**$4,880__**

If the total amount paid by Mary is more than the amount paid by her aunt, Mary meets the requirement of paying more than half the cost of keeping up the home.

Mary paid more than 50% of her support; therefore, she would not be claimed as a qualifying relative on her aunt's tax return.

Example 2: Scenario

Steven Renwick (age 27) and his cousin, Sasha Sweet (age 21), lived together all year. Use the following information to determine if Steven can claim Sasha as a dependent. Sasha receives $550 per month from TANF to help pay rent.

Expenses paid by Steven (taxpayer)		Expenses paid by Sasha	
Electric	$1,200	Rent	$6,600
Food eaten in the home	$6,100	Repairs	$661
Telephone	$800	Food eaten in the home	$965
Water	$325		
Renters insurance	$1,200		

Cost of Keeping a Household

	Amount Paid by Taxpayer	Total Costs
Property taxes	$	$
Mortgage interest expense	$	$
Rent	$	$
Utility charges	$	$
Repairs/maintenance	$	$
Property insurance	$	$
Food consumed on the premises	$	$
Other household expenses	$	$
TOTALS	**$**	**$**
Minus total amount taxpayer paid		( )
Amount others paid		$

Example 2: Answers

Cost of Keeping a Household

	Amount Paid by Taxpayer (Steven)	Total Costs
Property taxes	$	$
Mortgage interest expense	$	$
Rent	$	$6,600
Utility charges	$2,325	$2,325
Repairs/maintenance	$	$661
Property insurance	$	$
Food consumed on the premises	$6,100	$965
Other household expenses	$1,200	$
TOTALS	**$9,625**	**$10,551**
Minus total amount taxpayer paid		**($9,625)**
Amount others paid		**$926**

Steven paid more than 50% of Sasha's support; he can claim Sasha as a qualifying relative.

Total Support

When calculating to determine total support for a qualifying relative, the following items are not included in the calculation:

➤ Federal, state, and local income taxes paid by the individual out of their personal income.
➤ Social Security and Medicare tax paid individually.
➤ Life insurance premiums.
➤ Funeral expenses.
➤ Scholarships received by the student's relative or child.
➤ Survivors' and Dependents' Educational Assistance payments are used for the support of the child.

Total support does include food, lodging, clothing, education, medical and dental care, recreation, transportation, and other daily provisions.

Multiple Support Agreement (Form 2120)

Generally, the taxpayer must provide more than half of a qualifying relative's total support during the calendar year. However, if two or more people provided support but any person provided more than half of the individual's full support, the taxpayers may be able to file Form 2120, *Multiple Support Agreement*. A multiple support agreement is a document signed by the various taxpayers providing support that states which of the individuals will claim the qualifying relative as a dependent. The agreement identifies the taxpayers who agreed not to claim the exemption and must be attached to the return of the taxpayer claiming the exemption.

Each member of such a group, including whichever individual claiming the exemption, must provide more than 10% of the support. To qualify for claiming the dependency exemption, the individual must also obtain the consent of the other members of the support group. The group does not have to file signed consents with the IRS; however, they must be kept with the taxpayer's records and be available as proof of eligibility to claim the person as a dependent.

Members of the group may decide who is entitled to the dependency exemption on a year-by-year basis. They do not have to allocate the exemption to the taxpayer providing the most support; however, the person claiming the exemption must provide a total of more than 10%. The members of the group must collectively contribute with more than 50%. Again, the group cannot claim someone as a collective; only one individual can claim the qualifying child or relative.

Example: Carlos, Lydia, Ernest, and Caroline provided full support for their mother, Emma. Carlos provided 45%, Lydia provided 35%, and Ernest and Caroline provided 10% each. Since Caroline and Ernest give only 10% of the support (not more than 10% as required), neither can claim an exemption for Emma, nor do they have to sign the statement. Only Lydia and Carlos qualify to claim an exemption for Emma. Whoever does not claim the exemption must sign Form 2120 or a similar statement agreeing not to take Emma as a qualifying relative.

Deceased Taxpayers

The general filing requirements that apply to other taxpayers also apply to a decedent (someone who has died). Write the word "Deceased," the decedent's name, and the date of death across the top of the return. Only report the items of income that the decedent actually or constructively received before he died. Likewise, only deduct the expenses the decedent paid before his death. Claim the total exemption amount if the decedent was the taxpayer's dependent prior to death.

Should a personal representative be appointed (an executor, administrator, or anyone who oversees the decedent's property), that person should sign the return. If the spouse acts as the personal representative, write "filed as surviving spouse" in the signature location. If someone other than the spouse claims a refund for a decedent, the representative should file Form 1310,

Statement of Person Claiming Refund Due to a Deceased Taxpayer, with the return. Either way, a final return for the decedent must be filed.

Allowances for a Surviving Spouse

If the taxpayer's spouse died during the current tax year and the taxpayer does not remarry in the year of death, the surviving spouse may file a joint return.

Inherited Property

The property the taxpayer received as a gift, bequest, or inheritance is not included as income and is not taxable. However, if the inherited property produces income such as interest or rent, that income is taxable.

Income in Respect of the Decedent

Income in respect of the decedent includes all gross income that the decedent had a right to receive and was not includable in the decedent's final return. If the estate acquires the right to receive revenue from the decedent, the income is reported in the decedent's estate's return (Form 1041) by tax year received rather than in the decedent's final return. Should payment not be reported on Form 1041, the person to whom the estate properly distributes the income will have to do so. However, if someone acquires the direct right to the income without going through the estate, then that person will have to report the income.

Deductions in Respect of the Decedent

Decedent deductions can include items such as business expenses, interest, taxes, or income-producing expenses for which the decedent was liable but that were not deductible on the decedent's final tax return. The decedent's estate can pay and deduct these items in the same year. If the estate is not liable for the expenses, the individual who acquired the decedent's property due to death is subject to tax liability. Life insurance received is generally not a taxable event.

Part 2 Review Questions

To obtain the maximum benefit from this chapter, LTP recommends that you complete each of the following questions, and then compare them to the answers with feedback that immediately follow. Under governing self-study standards, vendors are required to present review questions intermittently throughout each self-study course.

These questions and explanations are not part of the final examination and will not be graded by LTP.

FSDDP2.1

James is filing head of household for the current tax year. Which person related to James must live with him the entire tax year for the head of household filing status?

   a. Peyton, his daughter, is away at college as a full-time student.
   b. Fernando, his cousin, lives with him and is a full-time student at the local junior college.
   c. Taylor, his mother who lives in her home and James supports 100%.
   d. Ezra, who is his grandson by marriage and is a full-time student he supports.

FSDDP2.2
Which scenario best describes the treatment of an adopted child?

    a. Manny and Victoria adopted her niece's son at birth, and Victoria passed away and Manny is still considered the father of the adopted child.
    b. Joel and Susan are godparents for Joel's cousin Joshua. Joshua has lived with them the entire year.
    c. Andres and Stephanie are filing married filing joint and still live with Stephanie's parents.
    d. Josue and Sandra support his daughter, Sydney, who lives with her mother, and Josue would like to claim Sydney as their dependent.

FSDDP2.3
Mercedes is a disabled individual and a qualifying relative of her sister Mary. Which of the following is not included in Mercedes' gross income test to determine if Mercedes is Mary's qualifying dependent?

    a. Child away at school, working part time.
    b. Disabled dependent working at a sheltered workshop.
    c. Mary's Social Security benefits.
    d. Taxpayer who babysits.

FSDDP2.4
Lisa and Larry were married with two qualifying dependents, and Larry died in August of 2021. What would be Lisa's best filing status for 2021?

    a. Head of household
    b. Single
    c. Married filing jointly
    d. Surviving Spouse with Dependent Child

FSDDP2.5
Ted is single, 18-years-old, and a full-time student. He works part-time and lives at home with his parents year-round. His W-2 shows $4,000 in box 1. Can Ted's parents claim him as a dependent on their tax return?

    a. Yes
    b. No

FSDDP2.6
Which of the following is not a temporary absence to meet the residency test?

    a. Illness
    b. Education
    c. Vacation
    d. Filing a joint return with their spouse

FSDDP2.7
Which of the following is not used to calculate the dependent's total personal support?

a. Social Security benefits
b. Welfare benefits
c. Nontaxable pensions
d. Money the dependent received from taxpayer

FSDDP2.8
Which of the following is not tax-exempt income?

a. Specific Social Security Benefits
b. TANF benefits
c. Tax-exempt interest
d. Interest earned on a savings account

FSDDP2.9
Which of the following is not used to determine total support?

a. Life insurance payments
b. Funeral expenses
c. Food and lodging
d. Individually paid Social Security and Medicare payments

FSDDP2.10
Which of the following best describes an adopted child?

a. An adopted child is always treated as a stepchild.
b. An adopted child is treated as a niece or nephew.
c. An adopted child is always treated as the taxpayer's own child.
d. An adopted child includes a foster child that is placed in the taxpayer's residence.

Part 2 Review Question Answers

FSDDP2.1
James is filing head of household for the current tax year. Which person related to James must live with him the entire tax year for the head of household filing status?

a. Peyton, his daughter, is away at college as a full-time student.
b. **Fernando, his cousin, lives with him and is a full-time student at the local junior college.**
c. Taylor, his mother who lives in her home and James supports 100%.
d. Ezra, who is his grandson by marriage and is a full-time student he supports.

Feedback: Review section *Cousin.*

FSDDP2.2
Which scenario best describes the treatment of an adopted child?

    a. Manny and Victoria adopted her niece's son at birth, and Victoria passed away and Manny is still considered the father of the adopted child.
    b. Joel and Susan are godparents for Joel's cousin Joshua. Joshua has lived with them the entire year.
    c. Andres and Stephanie are filing married filing joint and still live with Stephanie's parents.
    d. Josue and Sandra support his daughter, Sydney, who lives with her mother, and Josue would like to claim Sydney as their dependent.

Feedback: Review section *Adopted Child.*

FSDDP2.3
Mercedes is a disabled individual and a qualifying relative of her sister Mary. Which of the following is not included in Mercedes' gross income test to determine if Mercedes is Mary's qualifying dependent?

    a. Child away at school, working part time.
    b. Disabled dependent working at a sheltered workshop.
    c. Mary's Social Security benefits.
    d. Taxpayer who babysits.

Feedback: Review section *Disabled Dependent Working at a Sheltered Workshop.*

FSDDP2.4
Lisa and Larry were married with two qualifying dependents, and Larry died in August of 2021. What would be Lisa's best filing status for 2021?

    a. Head of household
    b. Single
    c. Married filing jointly
    d. Surviving Spouse with dependent child

Feedback: Review section *Allowance for a Surviving Spouse.*

FSDDP2.5
Ted is single, 18-years-old, and a full-time student. He works part-time and lives at home with his parents year-round. His W-2 shows $4,000 in box 1. Can Ted's parents claim him as a dependent on their tax return?

    a. Yes
    b. No

Feedback: Review section *Gross Income Test.*

FSDDP2.6
Which of the following is not a temporary absence to meet the residency test?

    a. Illness
    b. Education
    c. Vacation
    d. **Filing a joint return with their spouse**

Feedback: Review section *Temporary Absence.*

FSDDP2.7
Which of the following is not used to calculate the dependent's total personal support?

    a. Social Security benefits
    b. Welfare benefits
    c. Nontaxable pensions
    d. **Money the dependent received from taxpayer**

Feedback: Review section *Tax-Exempt Income.*

FSDDP2.8
Which of the following is not tax-exempt income?

    a. Specific Social Security benefits
    b. TANF benefits
    c. Tax-exempt interest
    d. **Interest earned on a savings account**

Feedback: Review section *Tax-Exempt Income.*

FSDDP2.9
Which of the following is not used to determine total support?

    a. Life insurance payments
    b. Funeral expenses
    c. **Food and lodging**
    d. Individually paid Social Security and Medicare payments

Feedback: Review section *Total Support.*

FSDDP2.10
Which of the following best describes an adopted child?

    a. An adopted child is always treated as a stepchild.
    b. An adopted child is treated as a niece or nephew.
    c. **An adopted child is always treated as the taxpayer's own child.**
    d. An adopted child includes a foster child that is placed in the taxpayer's residence.

Feedback: Review section *Adopted Child.*

Part 3 Dependent Filing Requirements

If a parent (or someone else) can claim a person as a dependent, and if any of the situations listed below apply, the dependent must file a return. Income that qualifies as "unearned income" includes taxable interest, dividends, capital gains, unemployment compensation, taxable Social Security, pensions, annuities, and distributions of unearned income from a trust. Income that qualifies as "earned income" includes wages, tips, taxable scholarships, and fellowship grants.

The term "dependent" is defined as a qualifying child or relative, which will be explained below.

Caution: If gross income is $4,400 or more, generally, the taxpayer cannot be claimed as a dependent unless the taxpayer is under age 19 or a full-time student under the age of 24.

For lodging, it is the fair rental value of the lodging. Expenses that are not directly related to any one member of a household, such as food, must be divided between the total members of the family. For example, the food bill for the year was $17,600. There are four household members, so divide $17,600 by $4,400 per member of the household.

Dependent Exemptions

A taxpayer can claim a qualifying child or a qualifying relative as a dependent if the following three tests are met:

> ➢ Dependent taxpayer test.
> ➢ Joint return test.
> ➢ Citizen or resident test.

Dependent Taxpayer Test

Should the taxpayer be claimed as a dependent by another person, the taxpayer cannot claim anyone else as a dependent on their own. Even if the taxpayer has a qualifying child or a relative, the taxpayer still cannot claim that individual as a dependent.

If the taxpayer is filing a joint return and the spouse and somebody claim her as a dependent by someone else, they cannot claim any dependents on their joint return.

Dependency Rules

Children of Parents Who Live Apart, Divorce, or Separate

In most cases, a child will be treated as the dependent of the custodial parent. A child will be treated as the qualifying child of his or her noncustodial parent if all the following apply:

1. The parents were any of the following:
   a. Divorced or legally separated under a decree of divorce or separate maintenance,
   b. Separated under a written separation agreement,
   c. Living apart for the last six months of the year, whether married or not;
2. The child received over half of the support for the year from the parents;
3. The child is in the custody of one or both parents for more than half of the year;

4. If either of the following is true:
    a. The custodial parent signed a written declaration stating that the custodial parent will not claim the child as a dependent for the current year, and the noncustodial parent attaches the written declaration to his or her return.
    b. A pre-1985 decree of divorce, separate maintenance, or written separation agreement, which applies to 2022, states that the noncustodial parent can claim the child as a dependent and will provide at least $600 for the support of the child during the year.

If all four of the above statements are true, the noncustodial parent can only do the following:

➢ Claim the child as a dependent.
➢ Claim the child as a qualifying child for the child tax credit or the credit for other dependents.

Custodial vs. Noncustodial Parent

If the parents divorced or separated during the year and if the child lived with both parents before the separation, the "custodial parent" is the parent with whom the child lived for the greater part of the year.

A child is treated as living with a parent for a night if the child sleeps as follows:

➢ At the parent's home, whether the parent is present or not.
➢ In the company of the parent when the child does not sleep at a parent's house (for example, going on vacation).

The rule for divorced or separated parents also applies to parents who never married and lived apart for the last six months of the year.

If the child lived with each parent for an equal number of nights, the parent with the higher adjusted gross income (AGI) is the custodial parent. If the child is emancipated under state law, the child is treated as having not lived with either parent.

Written Declaration Form 8332

The custodial parent should use Form 8332 to make the written declaration to release the exemption to the noncustodial parent. If the custodial parent has more than one dependent, a separate form should be used for each child. The exemption can have the following conditions:

➢ Be released for one year.
➢ Have specified years (for example, alternate years).
➢ Be designated for all future years, as specified in the declaration.
➢ Can revoke the release from the noncustodial parent.

If the custodial parent released his or her claim to the exemption for the child for any future year, Form 8332 must be attached to each year that the taxpayer can claim the exemption. If the return is filed electronically, Form 8332 should be filed with the tax return. Tax professionals should keep copies of Form 8332 for their records.

Señor 1040 Says: The household of the divorced or separated parent, whom a court order has given legal and physical custody, is the child's principal place of residency. Ask the taxpayer questions about adding a qualifying dependent who is not a newborn baby.

Tie-Breaker Rules

The following rules apply to determine which parent will claim the qualifying child:

> ➤ If both claimants are the parents and file a joint return, they can claim the child as a qualifying child. Even if there are other qualified claimants, the child cannot be the qualifying child of another person.
> ➤ If only one claimant is the child's parent, the child will be the parent's qualifying child.
> ➤ If both claimants are parents and do not file a joint return, the IRS will treat the child as a qualifying child of the parent with whom the child lived the longest during the year.
> ➤ If one of the above does not resolve the dispute, then the IRS will treat the child as the qualifying child of the claimant with the highest AGI for the year. Also, use this rule as a tiebreaker in the following instances:
>> o If the child lived with each of his two parents for the same amount of time.
>> o If no parent can claim the child as a qualifying child.
>> o If a parent can claim the child as a qualifying child, but no parent claims the child.

Qualifying Relative

There are four tests that must be met for a person to be a qualifying relative:

1. Not a qualifying child test.
2. Member of household or relationship test.
3. Gross income test.
4. Support test.

Unlike a qualifying child, a qualifying relative can be any age, and there is no age test for a qualifying relative. A child is not the taxpayer's qualifying relative if the child is the taxpayer's qualifying child or the qualifying child of anyone else.

Not a Qualifying Child Test

A child who is not the qualifying child of another taxpayer could qualify as the taxpayer's qualifying relative if:

1. The child's parent is not required to file an income tax return, or
2. The child's parent only files a return to get a refund.

Child in Canada or Mexico

A child living in a foreign country cannot be claimed as a dependent unless the child is a U.S. citizen, U.S. resident alien, or U.S. national. By not living in the household, the taxpayer could claim their child for a qualifying dependent credit if the child fails the residency test. However, a taxpayer may claim their child as a dependent if the child lives in Canada or Mexico, even if the child is not a U.S. citizen, resident alien, or national.

Qualifying Child

There are five tests that must be met for a child to be considered a qualifying dependent of the taxpayer. Do not confuse these tests with the Dependent Exemptions qualifications. The five tests are:

1. Relationship
2. Age
3. Residency
4. Support
5. Joint Return

Relationship Test

To meet this test, a child must be the taxpayer's:

- son or daughter,
- stepchild,
- eligible foster child,
- brother or sister,
- half-brother or half-sister,
- stepbrother or stepsister,
- or a descendant of any of these (for example, the taxpayer's grandchild).

An adopted child is always the taxpayer's child. The term "adopted child" includes one lawfully placed with the taxpayer for legal adoption.

A foster child is an individual who is placed with the taxpayer by an authorized placement agency or by judgment, decree, or other order of any court of competent jurisdiction.

The Adopted Child Exception

Taxpayer is a U.S. citizen and legally adopted a child who is not a U.S. citizen or U.S. national. The child lived with the taxpayer all year, as a member of the household, he will meet the citizen test. Children lawfully placed with the taxpayer for legal adoption also meet the requirement.

Exceptions for Stillborn Children and Children Born Alive

A child born or who died during the year is considered to have lived with the taxpayer the entire year while alive. The same is true if the child lived with the taxpayer all year except for any required hospital stay following birth.

The taxpayer cannot claim a stillborn child as a dependent but may claim an exemption for a child born alive during the year but died shortly after, even if the child only lived for a moment. State or local law must treat the child as having been born alive.

There must be proof of a live birth shown by an official document, such as a birth certificate. To be a dependent, the child must be a qualifying child or relative and meet all the other tests.

Kidnapped Children

A kidnapped child can meet the residency test if the following statements are factual:

> ➢ Law enforcement authorities presumed someone kidnapped the child, not a member of the taxpayer's family or the child's family.
> ➢ The child lived with the taxpayer more than half of the time before the date of the kidnapping.
> ➢ On the child's return, the child lived with the taxpayer more than half of the portion of the year following the date of the child's return to home.

This treatment applies until the child returns; however, the last year you can treat the child as such is the earlier of the two following situations:

> ➢ The year there is a determination that the child is dead.
> ➢ The year the child would have reached age 18.

Age Test

To meet this test, a child must be one of the following:

> ➢ Under the age of 19 at the end of the year.
> ➢ A student under the age of 24 at the end of the year.
> ➢ Younger than the taxpayer or spouse if filing a joint return.
> ➢ Permanently and totally disabled at any time during the year, regardless of age.

Example 1: Mr. and Mrs. Swift have Jonathon, Mr. Swift's brother, living with them. Jonathon, age 23, is a full-time student. Mr. and Mrs. Swift are both 21-years-old. Even though he is a student, Jonathon cannot be their dependent since he is older than both.

Example 2: Mr. and Mrs. Swift have Jonathon, Mr. Swift's brother, living with them. Jonathon, age 23, is a full-time student. Mr. and Mrs. Swift are both 25-years-old. If Jonathon meets all the other tests, he can be their dependent since he is younger than both.

Residency Test

Additional Qualifying Child Rules

Dependents must also meet the following conditions to qualify as a child of a taxpayer:

> ➢ The child must have lived with the taxpayer for more than half of the year, though some exceptions may apply.
> ➢ The child must not have provided more than half of their support for the year.
> ➢ If the child meets the rules to be a qualifying child of more than one person, the taxpayer must be the person most entitled to claim the child as a qualifying child. This information is explained in full in "Special Rules for a Qualifying Child of More Than One Person" below.

Special Rules for a Qualifying Child of More Than One Person

Sometimes, a child meets the relationship, age, residency, and support tests to be a qualifying child for more than one person. Even if an individual is a qualifying child of several people, only one claimant (a person attempting to claim something) can claim the child as their qualifying child.

If a taxpayer and one or more others have the same qualifying child, it is up to everyone involved to decide who will claim the child as a qualifying child. The individual can claim the following tax benefits based on the qualifying child (provided the taxpayer is eligible for each one):

➢ Child tax credit.
➢ HOH filing status (if applicable).
➢ Child and dependent care expenses.
➢ Earned income credit.

When one parent claims the child, other taxpayers do not share the tax benefits. Since you cannot divide the benefits between taxpayers, it is not uncommon for the parents to decide who will claim the qualifying child. If two or more taxpayers attempt to claim the child, the IRS will determine who will be able to claim the child based on the Tie-breaker Rules. (Tie-breaker Rules are discussed later in this chapter).

Qualifying Relative

Meet the following conditions to be considered a qualifying relative:

➢ The person cannot be the taxpayer's qualifying child or anyone else's qualifying child.
➢ The person must be only one of these things:
  o Be related to the taxpayer in one of the ways listed under "Relatives Who Do Not Need to live with the taxpayer."
  o Live with the taxpayer all year as a member of their household. This relationship must not violate local law.
➢ The person's gross income for the year must be less than $4,400. Exceptions apply.
➢ The taxpayer must provide more than half of the person's total support for the year. Exceptions apply.

Citizen and Residency Tests

The taxpayer's child must have lived with the taxpayer for more than half of the year to meet these tests. Additionally, the taxpayer cannot claim a person as a dependent unless that person is a U.S. citizen, U.S. resident, U.S. national, or a resident of Canada or Mexico. However, there are exceptions to these requirements for a group of adopted children, temporary absences, children born or died during the year, kidnapped children, and children of divorced or separated parents.

A Child's Citizenship and Place of Residence

Generally, you determine a child's citizenship and residency by the citizenship and residence of their parents. If the taxpayer was a U.S. citizen when their child was born, the child might be a U.S. citizen even if the other parent was a nonresident alien and the child was born in a foreign country. If so, the child meets the citizen test.

Students brought to this country under a qualified international education exchange program and placed in American homes temporarily are generally not U.S. residents and will not meet the test. The taxpayer cannot claim them as a dependent. See Publication 526.

A U.S. national is an individual who owes their allegiance to the United States. U.S. nationals include American Samoans and Northern Mariana Islanders who became U.S. nationals instead of U.S. citizens.

The taxpayer's home can be any location where they regularly live, and the taxpayer does not need a traditional home. For example, if a child lived with the taxpayer for more than half of the year in one or more homeless shelters, the child meets the residency test.

Full-Time Student

Taxpayers may receive additional deductions for qualifying costs to dependents who are full-time students. A full-time student is a student who enrolls for the number of hours or courses the school considers to be full-time attendance.

To qualify as a student, the taxpayer's dependent must be one of the following during some part of each of any five calendar months of the year (the five calendar months do not need to be consecutive):

> ➤ A full-time student at a school with regular teaching staff, course of study, and regularly enrolled student body at the school.
> ➤ A student taking a full-time, on-farm training course given by a school as described above or by a state, county, or local government agency.

A "school" can be an elementary school, junior or senior high school, college, university, or a technical, trade, or mechanical school for the full-time student deduction. However, on-the-job training courses, correspondence schools, or online schools are not qualifying schools.

Vocational high school students who work on "co-op" jobs in the private industry as part of a school's classroom study course and practical training are considered full-time students for the deduction.

Temporary Absence Exceptions

The taxpayer's child lived with them during periods of time when one or both are temporarily absent due to any of the following:

> ➤ Illness
> ➤ Education
> ➤ Business
> ➤ Vacation
> ➤ Military service
> ➤ Detention in a juvenile facility

One must assume that the child will return home after the temporary absence.

Joint Return Test

Generally, the taxpayer cannot claim a married person as a dependent when filing a joint return. The joint return test does not apply if the dependent and the spouse file a joint return to claim a refund.

Example 1: April, age 17, is married to Joe, age 18, and they live with April's parents. Both April and Joe have some earned income but are not required to file a return, and the only reason they file a joint return is to get the refund on the taxes withheld. If they meet all the other tests, April's parents may be able to claim them as dependents.

Example 2: Aaron, age 18, lived with his parents while his wife was in the military. His parents supported him. His wife Mackenzie earned $25,000 for the year. Aaron and Mackenzie will file a joint return. Aaron cannot be a dependent on his parents' return because he and his wife filed jointly, and Mackenzie's income is too high.

Permanently and Totally Disabled

The taxpayer's child is permanently and totally disabled if both apply:

- ➢ The child cannot engage in any substantial gainful activity due to a physical or mental condition.
- ➢ The condition is determined by a physician that the child's disability will last or can be expected to last continuously for at least a year or could lead to death.

Support Tests to be a Qualifying Child

Determine the total amount of support that a taxpayer provides for a proposed dependent before the taxpayer can claim a qualifying child or qualifying relative. Full support includes amounts spent to provide food, lodging, clothing, education, medical and dental care, recreation, transportation, and similar necessities. Generally, the amount of an item of support is the amount of the expense incurred by providing the item.

To meet the support test successfully, the child cannot have provided more than half of his or her support for the year. This test is different from the support test to be a qualifying relative. "Keeping Up a Home" will be discussed in the next section. If a child receives a scholarship, and the student is full-time, the scholarship does not count toward determining the child's support.

Foster Care Payments and Expenses

Payments received from a placement agency for the child's support are considered support provided by the agency. If the agency is state- or county-based, provided payments are considered support from the state or county for the child.

Joint Return Test to be a Qualifying Child

The child cannot file a joint return for the year to meet this test. The exception to this rule is if the taxpayer's child and the spouse are not required to file a tax return but decide to file a joint return solely to claim a refund.

Part 3 Review Questions

To obtain the maximum benefit from this chapter, LTP recommends that you complete each of the following questions, and then compare them to the answers with feedback that immediately follow. Under governing self-study standards, vendors are required to present review questions intermittently throughout each self-study course.

These questions and explanations are not part of the final examination and will not be graded by LTP.

FSDDP3.1
Perla is 65 years old, and her income is $12,600. She claims she has a qualifying dependent living with her. Which of the following questions is best to ask to determine her filing status?

1. How is the qualifying dependent related to you?
2. How old is the qualifying child?
3. How much income did the qualifying dependent earn?
4. Can the child be a qualifying child of another taxpayer?

    a. 1 and 4
    b. 2 and 3
    c. 1, 2, and 4
    d. 1, 2, 3, and 4

FSDDP3.2
Which of the following temporary absences will not allow the taxpayer to claim the qualifying child or qualifying relative as a dependent?

    a. Illness
    b. Education
    c. Military service
    d. Dependent of another taxpayer

FSDDP3.3
Tyler, age 27, is single and lives with his parents Sharon and Rory. Tyler was unable to work due to a temporary medical condition. He received $4,250 for a speaking engagement. Can Sharon and Rory claim Tyler as a dependent?

    a. Yes
    b. No

FSDDP3.4
Trini is single, 18-years-old, and a full-time student. She works part-time and lives at home with her parents. Her W-2 shows $4,000 in box 1. Can Trini's parents claim her as a dependent on their tax return?

    a. Yes
    b. No

FSDDP3.5
Alma must meet five tests to claim Freddy as a dependent. Which of the following is not one of the tests?

    a. Residency
    b. Relationship
    c. Disability Test
    d. Joint Return Test

FSDDP3.6
Which scenario describes custodial parent?

    a. Ezra lives with his dad 300 days a year, and only sees his mother on school holidays.
    b. David and Maria have joint custody of their children.
    c. Cara and her daughter Joyce live with her parents, and Joyce is on her grandparent's insurance.
    d. Eli is 18 years old and has a full-time job and still lives with his parents.

FSDDP3.7
Danelle is the noncustodial parent and would like to claim her children on her current year tax return. What does Jake need to do so Danelle can claim the children?

    a. Jake would need to file first by filing Form 1040 and claim the children.
    b. Jake would need to sign Form 8332 and give the form to Danelle to file with her tax return.
    c. Jake would need to rev Form 8332 and give the form to his tax preparer.
    d. Jake would still be able to claim his children even if Danelle does.

FSDDP3.8
Which of the following best describes foster care payments?

    a. Income to the foster parents
    b. Support for the foster child
    c. Support for the taxpayer
    d. Income for the foster child

FSDDP3.9
Which of the following is not a test to meet the qualifying relative rule?

    a. Not a qualifying child test
    b. Member of the household
    c. Member of the relationship test
    d. Age test

FSDDP3.10
Armando's daughter was kidnapped at the age of 6. Armando can claim his daughter until she turns _____ or until the year there is a determination that the child is dead.

    a. 18
    b. 20
    c. 17
    d. 14

Part 3 Review Questions Answers

FSDDP3.1

Perla is 65 years old, and her income is $12,600. She claims she has a qualifying dependent living with her. Which of the following questions is best to ask to determine her filing status?

1. How is the qualifying dependent related to you?
2. How old is the qualifying child?
3. How much income did the qualifying dependent earn?
4. Can the child be a qualifying child of another taxpayer?

    a. 1 and 4
    b. 2 and 3
    c. 1, 2, and 4
    d. 1, 2, 3, and 4

Feedback: Review section *Qualifying Child.*

FSDDP3.2

Which of the following temporary absences will not allow the taxpayer to claim the qualifying child or qualifying relative as a dependent?

    a. Illness
    b. Education
    c. Military service
    d. Dependent of another taxpayer

Feedback: Review section *Temporary Absence Exceptions.*

FSDDP3.3

Tyler, age 27, is single and lives with his parents Sharon and Rory. Tyler was unable to work due to a temporary medical condition. He received $4,250 for a speaking engagement. Can Sharon and Rory claim Tyler as a dependent?

    a. Yes
    b. No

Feedback: Review section *Qualifying Child.*

FSDDP3.4

Trini is single, 18-years-old, and a full-time student. She works part-time and lives at home with her parents. Her W-2 shows $4,000 in box 1. Can Trini's parents claim her as a dependent on their tax return?

    a. Yes
    b. No

Feedback: Review section *Qualifying Child.*

FSDDP3.5
Alma must meet five tests to claim Freddy as a dependent. Which of the following is not one of the tests?

    a. Residency
    b. Relationship
    c. Disability Test
    d. Joint Return Test

Feedback: Review section *Qualifying Child.*

FSDDP3.6
Which scenario describes custodial parent?

    a. Ezra lives with his dad 300 days a year, and only sees his mother on school holidays.
    b. David and Maria have joint custody of their children.
    c. Cara and her daughter Joyce live with her parents, and Joyce is on her grandparents' insurance.
    d. Eli is 18 years old and has a full-time job and still lives with his parents.

Feedback: Review section *Custodial vs. Noncustodial Parent.*

FSDDP3.7
Danelle is the noncustodial parent and would like to claim her children on her current year tax return. What does Jake need to do so Danelle can claim the children?

    a. Jake would need to file first by filing Form 1040 and claim the children.
    b. Jake would need to sign Form 8332 and give the form to Danelle to file with her tax return.
    c. Jake would need to revoke Form 8332 and give the form to his tax preparer.
    d. Jake would still be able to claim his children even if Danelle does.

Feedback: Review section *Written Declaration Form 8332.*

FSDDP3.8
Which of the following best describes foster care payments?

    a. Income to the foster parents
    b. Support for the foster child
    c. Support for the taxpayer
    d. Income for the foster child

Feedback: Review section *Foster Care Payment and Expenses.*

FSDDP3.9
Which of the following is not a test to meet the qualifying relative rule?

    a. Not a qualifying child test
    b. Member of the household
    c. Member of the relationship test
    d. Age test

Feedback: Review section *Age Test.*

FSDDP3.10
Armando's daughter was kidnapped at the age of 6. Armando can claim his daughter until she turns____ or until the year there is a determination that the child is dead.

    a. 18
    b. 20
    c. 17
    d. 14

Feedback: Review section Kidnapped Children.

Part 4 Deductions

There are two types of deductions available to taxpayers: standard or itemized deductions. The total amount is subtracted from the taxpayer's adjusted gross income to reduce the taxpayer's tax liability. Taxpayers must choose the one that is best for them. As a tax professional they should use the one that reduces the taxpayer's taxable liability the most.

Itemized deductions are a variety of personal expenses designated clearly as itemized deductions to help taxpayers lower their tax liability. The standard deduction is a pre-determined dollar amount based on the taxpayer's filing status. Standard deductions do not require taxpayers to save receipts for actual personal expenses such as medical bills, charitable contributions, and certain deductible taxes.

The standard deduction is not always an option for every taxpayer. In cases like these (for example, if the taxpayer's standard deduction amount is zero), it is best to check if itemizing deductions would benefit the taxpayer. Taxpayers are required to itemize deductions in the following:

> ➤ A taxpayer is married, filing a separate return, and their spouse itemizes deductions.
> ➤ The taxpayer is filing a tax return for a short tax year because of a change in his or her annual accounting period.
> ➤ The taxpayer is a nonresident or dual-status alien during the year. The taxpayer is a dual-status alien if both a nonresident and a resident alien during the year. Suppose the nonresident alien is married to a U.S. citizen or resident alien at the end of the year. In that case, the nonresident alien or the resident alien can choose to be treated as a U.S. resident.

Itemized deductions are discussed further in another chapter. See Publication 519.

Standard Deductions

The Standard deduction amount varies depending on the taxpayer's filing status. Standard deduction is a set dollar amount that reduces the taxable income. Other factors used to determine the amount of the allowable standard deduction are:

> ➤ Taxpayer is age 65 or older
> ➤ Taxpayer is blind

Standard Deduction for Most People

These deduction amounts apply to most people and are for the current year's filing status.*

Filing Status and Standard Deduction	Tax Year 2021	Tax Year 2022	Tax Year 2023
Single	$12,550	$12,950	$13,850
Married Filing Jointly and Qualifying Surviving Spouse	$25,100	$25,900	$27,700
Married Filing Separately	$12,550	$12,950	$13,850
Head of Household	$18,800	$19,400	$20,800

*Do not use this chart if:

- ➢ The taxpayer was born before January 2, 1958.
- ➢ The taxpayer is blind.
- ➢ Someone else can claim the taxpayer or taxpayer's spouse as a dependent if filing status is MFJ.

Example 1: Tax year 2022, Lilly is 26 years old, never married, and does not have children or other dependents. Lilly's filing status will be Single. Use the above chart. Her standard deduction will be $12,950.

Example 2: Using example 1 with these changes: Lilly is married and a joint return. They will use the standard deduction. Their standard deduction will be $25,900.

Example 3: Using example 2 with these changes: Lilly and her husband had a son born during the tax year. Lilly and her husband have decided to file separate tax returns. Since they are still married and living together, they must use the MFS filing status. As per the chart, Lilly's standard deduction will be $12,950.

Example 4: Using example 2 with these changes: Lilly and her husband divorced during the tax year. Lilly has sole custody of her son and will file using the Head of Household filing status. Her standard deduction is $19,400.

Standard Deduction for Age 65 and Older or Blind

A higher standard deduction is allowed for taxpayers aged 65 or older by the end of the tax year. A taxpayer is age 65 on their 65th birthday and the date immediately beforehand.

Example: Frank turned 65 on January 1, 2023, he is considered 65 on the day before his birthday, December 31, 2022. Frank is considered 65 for the entire tax year. Frank qualifies for the standard deduction amount for the 65 or older taxpayer.

A higher standard deduction is also allowed for taxpayers who are considered blind on the last day of the year. If the taxpayer is partially blind, they must get an official statement from a licensed eye physician (either an optometrist or an ophthalmologist). The note should state that the taxpayer's field of vision is not more than twenty degrees or that the taxpayer cannot see better than 20/200 in their best eye, even with glasses or contact lenses.

If the examining physician determines that the eye condition will never improve beyond its limits, the physician must include this fact in their statement. Suppose you correct the vision beyond these limits solely using contact lenses that can only be worn briefly due to pain, infection, or ulcers. In that case, the taxpayer can take the higher standard deduction for which they otherwise qualify. Keep the doctor's statement with the rest of the taxpayer's records.

The higher standard deduction is also allowed for the spouse of a taxpayer who is age 65 or older or blind under the following circumstances:

> ➤ The taxpayer and their spouse file a joint tax return.
> ➤ The taxpayer filed a separate return, the spouse had no gross income, and another taxpayer could not claim an exemption for the spouse.

If the taxpayer is a dependent on another tax return and was born before January 2, 1958, or is blind, multiply the amount of the additional standard deduction by $1,700 if that taxpayer is Single. If taxpayers are married, multiply the amount of the other standard deduction by $1,350.

2022 Standard Deduction Worksheet for People Born Before January 2, 1958, or Blind

Check the correct number of boxes below, then proceed to the chart.

1. Taxpayer   Born before January 2, 1958 ☐   Blind ☐
2. Spouse, if claiming exemption   Born before January 2, 1958 ☐   Blind ☐

Total number of boxes checked

If filing status is:	And at the end of 2022 you were….	Standard Deduction is:
Single	1	$14,700
	2	$16,450
Married Filing Jointly	1	$27,300
	2	$28,700
	3	$30,100
	4	$31,500
Married Filing Separately	1	$14,350
	2	$15,750
	3	$17,150
	4	$18,550
Surviving Spouse	1	$27,300
	2	$28,700
Head of Household	1	$21,150
	2	$22,900

Señor 1040 Says: If the taxpayer is MFS and their spouse itemizes or is a dual-status alien, the taxpayer **cannot** take the standard deduction. The taxpayer *must* itemize their deductions.

Example 1: For the tax year 2022, David and his wife Nancy are both over age 65. They are required to file a tax return and will file MFJ. Neither is blind, so they will use the standard deduction.

Standard deduction for MFJ taxpayers:	$25,900
Additional standard deduction for MFJ, 65+	$ 2,800 ($1,400 × 2)
Total standard deduction:	$28,700

Example 2: The scenario is the same as example 1 but with one change: Nancy is legally blind. The couple will file MFJ and use the standard deduction.

Standard deduction for MFJ taxpayers:	$25,900
Additional standard deduction for MFJ, blind	$ 1,400
Additional standard deduction for MFJ, 65+	$ 2,800 ($1,400 × 2)
Total standard deduction:	$30,100

Example 3: Tax year 2022, Nancy's husband David, died two years ago. Nancy is over age 65, legally blind, and must file a return. Nancy will file Single and use the standard deduction with the additional standard deductions for being blind and over 65. She is not married or a dependent.

Standard deduction for single taxpayers:	$ 12,950
Additional standard deduction for blind	$ 2,800
Total standard deduction:	$ 16,450

Standard Deduction for Dependents

The standard deduction amount is limited if the taxpayer is a dependent on another return. The dependent's standard deduction amount will either be a). $1,150; or b). the taxpayer's earned income amount for the year, plus $400 if it does not exceed the regular standard deduction, whichever is greater. If the taxpayer is 65 or older or blind, they may still be eligible for a higher standard deduction even if claimed as a dependent.

Earned income consists of salaries, wages, tips, professional fees, and all other monetary amounts received for any work the taxpayer performed. Include scholarships or fellowship grants in the gross income to calculate the standard deduction correctly. For more information on what qualifies as a scholarship or fellowship grant. See Publication 970.

2022 Standard Deduction Worksheet for Dependents

This worksheet is used only if someone else can claim the taxpayer or spouse as a dependent if filing MFJ.

1. Enter the taxpayer's earned income (defined below). If none, enter a zero.	1. $
2. Additional amount	2. $400
3. Add lines 1 and 2	3. $
4. Minimum standard deduction	4. $1,150
5. Enter the larger of line 3 or line 4	5. $

6. Enter the amount shown below for taxpayer's filing status.
    Single or MFS: $12,950
    MFJ: $25,900
    Head of Household: $19,400
	6. $

7. Standard deduction a. Enter the smaller of line 5 or line 6. If born after January 1, 1958, and not blind, stop here. This is the standard deduction. Otherwise, go to line 7b.	7a. $
b. If born before January 2, 1958, or blind, multiply $1,750 ($1,400 if married) by the number in.	7b. $
c. Add lines 7a and 7b. Enter the total here and on Form 1040 or Form 1040-SR, line 12a.	7c. $

Earned income includes wages, salaries, tips, professional fees, and other compensation received for personal services performed. Also included is the amount received as a taxable scholarship or fellowship grant.

Part 4 Review Questions

To obtain the maximum benefit from this chapter, LTP recommends that you complete each of the following questions, and then compare them to the answers with feedback that immediately follow. Under governing self-study standards, vendors are required to present review questions intermittently throughout each self-study course.

These questions and explanations are not part of the final examination and will not be graded by LTP.

FSDDP4.1
Which of the following best describes standard deduction?

    a. Standard deduction is a yearly pre-determined dollar amount.
    b. Standard deduction includes certain expenses that require the taxpayer to save receipts to determine the amount he or she can deduct.
    c. Standard deduction is the amount of the taxpayer's charitable contribution.
    d. Standard deduction is only for taxpayers who are married.

FSDDP4.2

Samuel, filing single, is 64 years old and is legally blind. What would be his standard deduction for tax year 2022 (prepared in 2023)?

a. $12,950
b. $16,450
c. $19,400
d. $14,700

FSDDP4.3

For tax year 2022 (prepared in 2023) what is the federal standard deduction for Maria who is filing head of household?

a. $14,700
b. $21,150
c. $15,750
d. $19,400

FSDDP4.4

If the taxpayer is _____ on Jan 1, 2023, they are _____ for tax year 2022.

a. 65/65
b. 65/66
c. 64/65
d. 66/65

FSDDP4.5

What is the federal standard deduction for a taxpayer who is filing married filing separately for tax year 2022?

a. $12,950
b. $19,400
c. $25,900
d. $16,450

FSDDP4.6

What is the federal standard deduction for a taxpayer who is filing as a qualifying surviving spouse for tax year 2022?

a. $19,400
b. $25,900
c. $16,450
d. 12,950

FSDDP4.7

When a dependent file their 2022 tax return what is their standard deduction limitation?

a. $900
b. $400
c. The greater of $1,000 plus $350
d. The greater of $1,150 or the taxpayer's earned income for the year plus $400 not to exceed the standard deduction

FSDDP4.8
What is the federal standard deduction for a taxpayer who is filing single for tax year 2022?

    a. $19,400
    b. $27,300
    c. $12,950
    d. $21,150

FSDDP4.9
What is the 2022 federal standard deduction for a taxpayer filing head of household over 65 and blind?

    a. $19,400
    b. $27,300
    c. $22,900
    d. $21,150

FSDDP4.10
Which of the following best describes standard deduction?

    a. Standard deduction is not limited to age and filing status.
    b. Standard deduction is not limited to the amount of deductions one can have.
    c. Standard deduction is a set dollar amount that is determined yearly.
    d. Standard deductions can only be used by single taxpayers.

Part 4 Review Questions Answers

FSDDP4.1
Which of the following best describes standard deduction?

    a. Standard deduction is a yearly pre-determined dollar amount.
    b. Standard deduction includes certain expenses that require the taxpayer to save receipts to determine the amount he or she can deduct.
    c. Standard deduction is the amount of the taxpayer's charitable contribution.
    d. Standard deduction is only for taxpayers who are married.

Feedback: Review section *Part I: Deductions*.

FSDDP4.2
Samuel, filing single, is 64 years old and is legally blind. What would be his standard deduction for tax year 2022 (prepared in 2023)?

    a. $12,950
    b. $16,450
    c. $19,400
    d. $14,700

Feedback: Review section *Standard Deduction for Age 65 and Older or Blind*.

FSDDP4.3

For tax year 2022 (prepared in 2023) what is the federal standard deduction for Maria who is filing head of household?

    a. $14,700
    b. $21,150
    c. $15,750
    d. $19,400

Feedback: Review section *Standard Deduction for Age 65 and Older or Blind*.

FSDDP4.4

If the taxpayer is _____ on Jan 1, 2023, the individual is _____ for tax year 2022.

    a. 65/65
    b. 65/66
    c. 64/65
    d. 66/65

Feedback: Review section *Standard Deduction for Age 65 and Older or Blind*.

FSDDP4.5

What is the federal standard deduction for a taxpayer who is filing married filing separately for tax year 2022?

    a. $12,950
    b. $19,400
    c. $25,900
    d. $16,450

Feedback: Review section *Standard Deduction for Most People*.

FSDDP4.6

What is the federal standard deduction for a taxpayer who is filing as a qualifying surviving spouse for tax year 2022?

    a. $19,400
    b. $25,900
    c. $16,450
    d. $12,950

Feedback: Review section *Standard Deduction for Most People*.

FSDDP4.7

When a dependent files their 2022 tax return, what is their standard deduction limitation?

    a. $900
    b. $400
    c. The greater of $1,150 plus $350
    d. The greater of $1,150 or the taxpayer's earned income for the year plus $400 not to exceed the standard deduction

Feedback: Review section *Standard Deduction for Most People*.

FSDDP4.8
What is the federal standard deduction for a taxpayer who is filing single for tax year 2022?

    a. $19,400
    b. $27,300
    c. $12,950
    d. $21,150

Feedback: Review section *Standard Deduction for Most People.*

FSDDP4.9
What is the 2022 federal standard deduction for a taxpayer filing head of household over 65 and blind?

    a. $19,400
    b. $27,300
    c. $22,900
    d. $21,150

Feedback: Review section *Standard Deduction for Age 65 and Older or Blind.*

FSDDP4.10
Which of the following best describes standard deduction?

    a. Standard deduction is not limited to age and filing status.
    b. Standard deduction is not limited to the amount of deductions one can have.
    c. Standard deduction is a set dollar amount that is determined yearly.
    d. Standard deductions can only be used by single taxpayers.

Feedback: Review section *Standard Deductions.*

Takeaways

The tax professional must understand filing statuses and ask questions that will determine the correct filing status for their client. Some clients might tell the tax professional their filing status is Head of Household because a friend told them so. However, the tax preparer's responsibility is to perform a thorough interview and complete the paid tax preparer's Due Diligence Form 8867. A taxpayer's filing status determines the taxpayer's tax liability and many tax credits, so make sure to claim the correct filing status.

Tax Topic 303 has a checklist of the most common errors on a tax return. "What is My Filing Status?" is on the list. The IRS has created an interactive tax assistant to answer questions relating to determining filing status. "What was your marital status on the last day of the year?" is the first question in the interactive tax assistant (ITA). Be aware of the consequences of preparing tax returns incorrectly. Make sure you do your due diligence and get it right.

It is important to understand how to determine a qualifying child or a qualifying relative to prepare an accurate tax return. Knowledge of tax law is imperative; the tax professional cannot rely on software to prepare an accurate tax return. Ensure the taxpayer qualifies as the taxpayer's dependent by understanding the rules for a qualifying child and a qualifying relative. Knowledge of the taxpayer's situation is crucial in preparing correct tax returns. If the IRS audits a tax preparer, your excuse better not be that you did not ask the taxpayer enough questions.

TEST YOUR KNOWLEDGE!
Go online to take a practice quiz.

California Filing Status, Dependents, and Deductions

Introduction

California did not conform to most changes in the federal Tax Cuts and Jobs Act. Consequently, as a California tax preparer, you must make sure your software allows for the personal exemptions as required to complete the California state return.

As you have already seen, filing statuses can get very complicated at the Federal level. Unfortunately, it gets even more complicated when you include filing statuses at the state level as well. As previously indicated, state law governs many aspects of filing status. For example, whether a taxpayer is married or legally separated under a divorce or separate maintenance decree. It is important for California tax preparers to know the state laws to prepare returns as truthfully and efficiently as possible.

Objectives

At the end of this chapter, the student will:

- ➢ Recognize how California determines residency.
- ➢ List the differences of how exemptions are calculated at the state and federal level.
- ➢ Recite the California filing statuses.
- ➢ Identify the differences between the Federal and California filing statuses.
- ➢ Understand how an RDP will file their tax returns.

Resources

FTB Form 540	FTB Publication 737	Instructions Form 540
FTB 540 Booklets	FTB Publication 1051A	540 Schedule CA
California Tax Rates and	FTB Publication 1540	Instructions
Exemptions	540 Schedule CA	FTB Publication 1032

Table of Contents

Part 1 Filing Status

California Filing Status

Despite the numerous differences, there are many ways that California law conforms to Federal law when determining filing statuses. Taxpayers normally use the same filing status they used on their federal return on their state return. The California filing statuses are:

1. Single
2. Married/RDP Filing Jointly
3. Married Filing Separately
4. Head of Household
5. Surviving Spouse with qualifying dependent

As with all rules, however, there are exceptions. Suppose a taxpayer does not meet federal filing requirements. In that case, they must use the filing status on their California return that they would use on the federal return if the taxpayer had a filing requirement. Additionally, California has a sixth filing status called a Registered Domestic Partnership (RDP). The following sections will explain RDPs, the many differences for the five main filing statuses, and California's filing status as a community property state and how that affects a couple's tax return.

Single and Head of Household

For unmarried taxpayers in California, there are two primary filing statuses: Single and Head of Household.

Single (S)

The taxpayer must file Single (S) if he or she meets any of the following criteria on December 31st of the tax year:

➢ The taxpayer is neither married nor a Registered Domestic Partner (RDP).
➢ The taxpayer is legally separated under a decree of divorce or separate maintenance.
➢ The taxpayer is claiming no dependents and does not provide more than 50% of support for anyone other than him or herself.
➢ The taxpayer is widowed without dependents before January 1 and did not remarry or enter another registered domestic partnership during that year.

Head of Household (HOH)

The taxpayer is entitled to file Head of Household status only if all the following apply:

➢ The taxpayer was unmarried, met the requirements to be considered unmarried, or not in a registered domestic partnership on the last day of the year.
➢ The taxpayer paid more than one-half the cost of keeping up the home for the year.

> ➤ The taxpayer's home was the main home of the taxpayer and one specific relative which, by law, qualifies the taxpayer for Head of Household.
> ➤ The taxpayer was not a nonresident alien at any time during the year.

Filing Jointly

For the state return, filing as married and filing as a registered domestic partner are the same filing status. The taxpayer would file Married/RDP filing joint if they meet the following criteria on December 31 of the tax year:

> ➤ The RDP or taxpayer's spouse died in 2022, and taxpayer did not remarry or enter another registered domestic partnership in 2022.
> ➤ The taxpayer's spouse or RDP died in 2023 before filing a 2022 return.

Filing Federal and State Returns

Married taxpayers who file a joint federal income tax return may file separate California returns if one of the following applies:

> ➤ One of the taxpayers was an active-duty member of either the U.S. Armed Forces or any auxiliary military branch during the tax year.
> ➤ One of the taxpayers was a non-resident for the entire year and had no income from Californian sources during the tax year.

If the taxpayer or spouse meets either of the above requirements. They may file Married filing separately (MFS) for their California return on Form 540NR, *California Nonresident or Part-Year Resident Income Tax Return*. Registered Domestic Partners would file two individual returns as single on the federal return unless one of the partners qualifies to file as Head of Household.

Qualifying Surviving Spouse/RDP with Dependent

If the taxpayer's spouse died during the current year, they may still qualify to file a joint return. All five of the following must apply:

> ➤ The spouse/RDP died in 2021 or 2022 and the surviving spouse has not remarried or entered into another RDP during 2022.
> ➤ The taxpayer has a child, stepchild, or adopted child being claimed by the taxpayer for 2022, except if:
>   - Child had gross income of $4,400 or more
>   - Child filed a joint return
>   - Taxpayer cannot be a dependent on another return
> ➤ The child lived in the taxpayer's home for all of 2022. Temporary absences still apply.
> ➤ The taxpayer paid over half the cost of keeping up the home
> ➤ Taxpayer could have filed a joint return in the year of death.

Filing Separate

The following is true if a taxpayer files Married/RDP filing separately:

> ➤ Community property rules apply to the allocation of income.

➢ The taxpayer may not claim a personal exemption credit for the RDP even if the RDP had no income, is not filing a return, and is not claimed as a dependent on another person's tax return.

➢ Taxpayer may be able to file as Head of Household if their child lived with them, and they lived apart from their RDP during the entirety of the last six months of the year.

Marriage and Registered Domestic Partnerships

Since many states have different laws governing the situations in which a couple may marry, federal law complies to the state and local law in handling the issue of legal marriages. Suppose the marriage conforms to both state and local laws (in both the jurisdiction in which the ceremony was performed and the taxpayer's location). In that case, it is considered a legal marriage. Common-law marriages are only permitted if a couple lives together for the prescribed period in a state that recognizes them. After this period, the married individuals must proclaim themselves married. If the marriage violates state or local law, it is not legal.

California does not recognize common-law marriages. California does recognize the union of a person legally married in another state who moves to California if the marriage would be legal in California. It also recognizes those individuals who have filed as *Married Filing Jointly* on the federal return in a common-law marriage.

Example: A taxpayer lives together with his girlfriend in Texas for six years before moving to California. The state of Texas recognizes common-law marriage after five years. If the couple had deemed themselves to be married in Texas before they moved to California and filed a Married Filing Jointly (MFJ) federal return, California would recognize the marriage.

Registered Domestic Partnerships (RDP)

A registered domestic partnership (RDP) is a type of formal legal contract in California that can be entered into by two people. Many couples choose it because it provides all the legal benefits of marriage at the state level without the potential baggage of marriage. A drawback, however, is that at the federal level RDPs are not recognized and thus do not provide any federal legal benefits provided by marriage. Under California law, registered domestic partnerships are available to all same-sex couples if both individuals are at least 18 years of age and some heterosexual couples if at least one partner is at least 62 years of age.

Registering as an RDP

In California, two individuals can register to become domestic partners if both individuals file a *Declaration of Domestic Partnership* with the Secretary of State and meet the following requirements:

➢ Both individuals are members of the same sex, at least 18 years of age, and capable of consenting to the domestic partnership.

➢ If the registering couple is heterosexual, one or both individuals must be over 62. They meet the eligibility criteria under Title II of the Social Security Act as defined in 42 USC §402(a) for old-age insurance benefits or must meet the eligibility criteria under Title XVI of the Social Security Act as defined in 42 USC §1381 for aged individuals.

➢ Both individuals have an ordinary residence, although both names do not have to be on the lease or title to the home under Family Code §297(c). Both individuals need to have a common address.

> ➢ Neither party is married to someone else, nor are they a member of another domestic partnership that has not yet been terminated, dissolved, or deemed a nullity. They are also not related to each other by blood in a way that would prevent them from being married in California.
> ➢ Both individuals consent to California jurisdiction of the superior courts in all matters relating to the legal status of their domestic partnership (See California Family Code §297).

Registration means that couples may be permitted to make medical decisions for one another and hold titles to property as community property. However, RDP couples must file their California return as Married/RDP filing jointly or Married/RDP filing separately.

RDP Termination

Terminating a registered domestic partnership is like a divorce proceeding for a marriage. It ends the partnership and returns the partners to separate individuals. Upon termination, the partners no longer have the rights, protections, benefits, obligations, and responsibilities as RDPs under the law. The termination process will divide the community property and the partners obligations to each other. Once the termination is effective, it may not be undone except in limited circumstances by order of the Superior Court.

Interstate Classifications

Managing the differences between the state and federal laws can be complicated. Unfortunately, it becomes even more difficult when you encounter situations that require you to take the rules of other states into account as well.

Domestic partnerships registered in another state will have the same rights and benefits as California RDPs if the other state has domestic partnership rules that are "substantially equivalent" to California's.

> A legal union of two persons of the same sex, other than a marriage, that was formed in another jurisdiction and that is substantially equivalent to a California domestic partnership… shall be recognized as a valid domestic partnership in this state regardless of whether it bears the name of domestic partnership (Family Code §299.2).

Filing as Married/RDP Filing Jointly

In California, married couples, and registered domestic partners (RDPs) must submit all files as married or RDP in taxable years beginning or after January 1, 2007. The law requires domestic partnerships registered with the Secretary of State, as of the close of the taxable year, to file using the same rules for married couples even though they cannot do so at the federal level since federal law does not recognize register domestic partnerships.

When doing tax planning, the tax professional should complete two separate projection calculations: one for federal and one for California.

Dependents

California law conforms to federal law when determining dependency. The taxpayer should claim the same dependents on the federal and state return. The taxpayer must calculate their allowable standard deduction on the *California Standard Deduction Worksheet for Dependents*.

Deceased Taxpayer

The final state return for a deceased taxpayer is due on April 15th of the calendar year after the death occurred. For example, if a person passes away in 2022, their final tax return would be due on April 15th, 2023, regardless of when they died in 2022. California conforms to the federal when deceased taxpayer returns are due.

An estate or trust is filed within three-and-a-half months after terminating or closing the estate or trust, just as the federal return. For example, when closing an estate or trust on March 1st, the return would be due the three-and-a-half months after the end of March on the 31st, not three-and-a-half months after March 1st.

Exemptions

California exemptions are nonrefundable tax credits that reduce tax liability. California allows an additional exemption credit for seniors age 65 and over and another credit for being blind. The exemption credit for each taxpayer, spouse, senior, and blind taxpayer or spouse is $140 each (2022). The dependent credit is $433 each. Review these numbers in the chart below:

Single, Married/RDP Filing Separately, and Head of Household	$140.00
Married/RDP Filing Jointly and Surviving Spouse with qualifying dependent	$280.00
Blind	$140.00
Age 65 or Older	$140.00
Dependent (each)	$433.00

California did not conform to the TCJA by adding the exemption amount to the standard deduction or by having a phase-out for personal exemptions. California still phases out personal exemptions for taxpayers with adjusted gross income (AGI) over the following:

Single or Married/RDP Filing Separately	$229,908
Married/RDP Filing Jointly and Surviving Spouse	$459,821
Head of Household	$344,867

To calculate the reduction, use the *AGI Limitation Worksheet* located in the *California Personal Income Tax Booklet*.

Deductions

Taxpayers have the option to itemize on their California returns even if they did not itemize on the federal return. Taxpayers have the option to lower the amount of tax they will owe by choosing between whichever deduction option will give them the largest deduction amount: itemized deductions or standard deductions. California conforms to federal standards regarding Married Filing Separately returns; if the taxpayer itemizes deductions, the spouse must also itemize.

The standard deduction amounts for 2022 are:

Single	$5,202
Married/RDP Filing Jointly	$10,404
Married/RDP Filing Separately	$5,202
Head of Household	$10,404
Qualifying Surviving Spouse/RDP	$10,404

Do not use these amounts if a parent (or someone else) claims the taxpayer as a dependent on their tax return.

California standard deduction amounts are less than the federal amounts. For that reason, it may be to the taxpayer's advantage to itemize on the California return even though he or she did not itemize on the federal return. The minimum standard deduction for dependents is $1,150.

Señor 540 Says: California standard deduction for head of household is the same as MFJ/RDP and requires more detailed information to confirm that the taxpayer qualifies for the head of

California and Prenuptial Agreements

California law states that a written prenuptial agreement, signed by both individuals in contemplation of marriage, becomes automatically effective once the two individuals marry. Agreements must have a valid consent that an individual has the mental ability to consent, and the consent cannot be the result of fraud, inappropriate influence, or mistake.

Part 1 Review Questions

To obtain the maximum benefit from this chapter, LTP recommends that you complete each of the following questions, and then compare them to the answers with feedback that immediately follow. Under governing self-study standards, vendors are required to present review questions intermittently throughout each self-study course.

These questions and explanations are not part of the final examination and will not be graded by LTP.

CFSDDP1.1
Which of the following is not included when determining support for a dependent? Remember that California law conforms to the federal law when determining dependency.

a. Fair rental value of lodging.
b. Social Security benefits added to savings accounts.
c. Life insurance premiums.
d. Mortgage payments on lodging facilities.

CFSDDP1.2

Jim Planter, age 65 as of January 1 of the current year, filed a joint return with his wife, Rita, age 50. Mary, their 21-year-old daughter, was a full-time student at a college until her graduation on June 2 of the current year. Rita's niece lived with them and had no income, and Jim and Rita treated her as their own child. How many exemptions should the Planters claim on their current-year tax return?

a. Two
b. Three
c. Four
d. Five

CFSDDP1.3

When are California tax returns for deceased individuals due?

1. April 15.
2. California conforms to the federal return due date.
3. California Estate tax returns need to be filed within three-and-a-half months of the date of death.
4. The deceased taxpayer does not have to file because the taxpayer is dead.

a. 1 and 4
b. 2 and 3
c. 1, 2, and 3
d. 4 only

CFSDDP1.4

Which filing status is unique to California?

a. Single
b. Married/RDP filing joint
c. Head of household
d. Surviving Spouse with qualifying dependent

CFSDDP1.5

California has adopted the rule for tax purposes when using the term "spouse" it will also refers to which of the following?

a. California RDP unless stated otherwise
b. California head of household
c. California surviving spouse
d. California single taxpayer

CFSDDP1.6

California has adopted the rule for tax purposes that when using the term "spouse" it will also refer to which of the following?

a. California RDP unless stated otherwise
b. California head of household
c. California surviving spouse
d. California single taxpayer

CFSDDP1.7
California conforms to federal law when determining a(n) _____.

    a. qualified dependent
    b. unemployment benefit
    c. Earned Income Tax Credit
    d. Social Security benefit

CFSDDP1.8
Shelly and Ben separated in February of 2022. Shelly wants to file head of household with their dependents. Shelly has 100% legal custody and the children have lived with her the entire year. What would be the California head of household standard deduction amount for Shelly for 2022?

    a. $5,202
    b. $7,569
    c. $9,606
    d. $10,404

CFSDDP1.9
Which of the following is a California filing status?

    a. Single
    b. Married/RDP Filing Joint
    c. Head of household
    d. All the answers

CFSDDP1.10
Grace has 2 children. What is her 2022 California personal exemption amount?

    a. $998
    b. $1,006
    c. $140
    d. $866

Part 1 Review Questions Answers

CFSDDP1.1
Which of the following is not included when determining support for a dependent? Remember that California law conforms to the federal law when determining dependency.

    a. Fair rental value of lodging.
    b. Social Security benefits added to savings accounts.
    c. Life insurance premiums.
    d. Mortgage payments on lodging facilities.

Feedback: Review section *Standard Deduction for Most People*.

CFSDDP1.2
Jim Planter, age 65 as of January 1 of the current year, filed a joint return with his wife, Rita, age 50. Mary, their 21-year-old daughter, was a full-time student at a college until her graduation on June 2 of the current year. Rita's niece lived with them and had no income, and Jim and Rita treated her as their own child. How many exemptions should the Planters claim on their current-year tax return?

    a. Two
    b. Three
    c. Four
    d. Five

Feedback: Review section *Standard Deduction for Most People*.

CFSDDP1.3
When are California tax returns for deceased individuals due?

    1. April 15.
    2. California conforms to the federal return due date.
    3. California Estate tax returns need to be filed within three-and-a-half months of the date of death.
    4. The deceased taxpayer does not have to file because the taxpayer is dead.

    a. 1 and 4
    b. 2 and 3
    c. 1, 2, and 3
    d. 4 only

Feedback: Review section *Standard Deduction for Most People*.

CFSDDP1.4
Which filing status is unique to California?

    a. Single
    b. Married/RDP filing joint
    c. Head of household
    d. Surviving Spouse with qualifying dependent

Feedback: Review section *Filing Jointly*.

CFSDDP1.5
California has adopted the rule for tax purposes when using the term "spouse" it will also refers to which of the following?

    a. California RDP unless stated otherwise
    b. California head of household
    c. California surviving spouse
    d. California single taxpayer

Feedback: Review section *Filing Jointly*.

CFSDDP1.6

California has adopted the rule for tax purposes that when using the term "spouse" it will also refer to which of the following?

    a. California RDP unless stated otherwise
    b. California head of household
    c. California surviving spouse
    d. California single taxpayer

Feedback: Review section *Filing Federal and State Returns*.

CFSDDP1.7

California conforms to federal law when determining a(n) _____.

    a. qualified dependent
    b. unemployment benefit
    c. Earned Income Tax Credit
    d. Social Security benefit

Feedback: Review section *Dependents*.

CFSDDP1.8

Shelly and Ben separated in February of 2022. Shelly wants to file head of household with their dependents. Shelly has 100% legal custody and the children have lived with her the entire year. What would be the California head of household standard deduction amount for Shelly for 2022?

    a. $5,202
    b. $7,569
    c. $9,606
    d. $10,404

Feedback: Review section *Exemptions*.

CFSDDP1.9

Which of the following is a California filing status?

    a. Single
    b. Married/RDP Filing Joint
    c. Head of household
    d. All the answers

Feedback: Review section *California Filing Status*.

CFSDDP1.10

Grace has 2 children. What is her 2022 California personal exemption amount?

    a. $998
    b. $1,006
    c. $140
    d. $866

Feedback: Review section *Exemptions*.

Part 2 Community Property and Income

Community property rules are state regulations that determine ownership of items purchased by married individuals prior to marriage and during marriage. California is a community property state, and so are Arizona, New Mexico, Texas, Washington, Idaho, Nevada, Louisiana, and Wisconsin. Just because they are a community property state, this does not mean that the other state laws mirror California; every state has its laws regarding community property.

Community Property and Separate Property

Community property is anything the husband and wife acquired during the marriage while domiciled in a community property state. For California tax purposes, community property rules for spouses also apply to RDPs. Community property is all property that does not fall within the definition of separate property. For this section, separate property means:

> Separate property is all property owned separately by the husband or wife before marriage. It is also property acquired separately after marriage by the husband or wife as a gift, devise, bequest or inheritance. Separate property may be acquired during marriage by purchase with separate funds by exchanging the separate property or in accordance with a pre- or post-nuptial agreement.

Community property rules that apply to spouses also apply to RDPs registered in California for tax purposes. If an RDP elects to file a separate tax return, they must use the Married filing separately filing status.

Community Property

Community property is the total of property acquired and earnings received by the following:

➢ By a married or RDP couple while domiciled in a community property state.
➢ By a married or RDP couple that is not separate property.

Each RDP owns one-half of all community property. In 2010, the IRS ruled that California's RDPs must report one-half of community income on their federal tax returns.

Separate Property

California defines separate property as:

➢ All property is owned separately by an individual and/or an RDP before entering the relationship.
➢ All property is acquired separately after entering into a registered domestic partnership, such as gifts, inheritances, and property purchased with separate funds.
➢ Money earned while domiciled in a separate property state.
➢ All property declared separate property in a valid agreement entered before or after registration of the partnership.

Community Property Income

In a state like California, community property income means that one-half of all income earned by one spouse belongs to and is taxable to the other spouse.

Income is not community property income if the following is true:

> ➤ The taxpayer and spouse live together in a state that is not a community property state.
> ➤ The taxpayer and spouse live separately for the entire tax year with no immediate intention of reconciliation.

Señor 540 Says: If the taxpayer and spouse live together, it may be in their best interest to file jointly on their California return. Filing a separate state tax return could require the spouse to file and claim their community property share of the person's California-sourced income, resulting in two MFS returns versus one MFJ.

Community Property When Filing a Separate Return

If the taxpayer filed MFS/RDP, they must follow community property rules for the division of income and deductions and must evenly divide the value of the community property and its income between them. The taxpayer and their spouse must each report their half of the community income, their respective individual incomes, and the other spouse's half of the community income on each of their separate returns.

Taxable income, exemptions, and deductions might differ if the taxpayer filed Married filing separately instead of MFJ on the federal return. Some differences may also apply to the California return.

Example: Sydney and Peggy are registered domestic partners and residents of California. On June 30, Peggy and Sydney physically separated with no likelihood for reconciliation. From January 1 to June 30, Peggy earned $30,000, and Sydney earned $10,000. From July 1 to December 31, Peggy earned an additional $30,000, and Sydney made $0. Peggy and Sydney have decided to file separate California returns. Peggy will report $5,000 of Sydney's income on her current year's tax return, and Sydney will report $15,000 on this year's tax return. Though they are physically separated, they have not yet legally ended their RDP. They must still follow community property rules for the income division and report the other's half of the community income on each of their separate returns.

Exemption Credit Phase-out

Exemption credits reduce the taxpayer's tax liability. Depending on the filing status, the exemption credits could be limited. When applying the phase-out amount, use the $6 or $12 amount to each exemption credit but don't reduce the credit below zero. If the personal exemption credit is less than the phase-out amount, do not apply the excess against a dependent exemption credit.

Part 2 Review Questions

To obtain the maximum benefit from this chapter, LTP recommends that you complete each of the following questions, and then compare them to the answers with feedback that immediately follow. Under governing self-study standards, vendors are required to present review questions intermittently throughout each self-study course.

These questions and explanations are not part of the final examination and will not be graded by LTP.

CFSDDP2.1
In a community property state like California, one-half of all income earned by one spouse belongs to and is taxable to the other spouse. This is called Community Property income. Which of the following is correct about separate property as defined by California?

a. All property owned separately by an individual and/or an RDP before entering in the relationship.
b. All property acquired separately after entering in a registered domestic partnership, such as gifts, inheritances, and property purchased with separate funds.
c. Money earned while domiciled in a separate property state.
d. All property declared separate property in a valid agreement entered before or after registration of the partnership.
e. All the options are correct.

CFSDDP2.2
Which of the following best describes California tax law?

a. California is a common law state
b. California is a community property state
c. California is a separate property state
d. California is a joint property territory

CFSDDP2.3
Which of the following states is a community property state?

a. Oregon
b. Kansas
c. Louisiana
d. New Hampshire

CFSDDP2.4
If the taxpayer is married and lives in a _____, when the taxpayer receives a distribution, one-half belongs to the spouse.

a. community property state
b. common law state
c. common territory
d. community property territory

CFSDDP2.5
Which of the following best describes community property?

a. All property acquired by a husband or wife while domiciled in a common law state.
b. All property acquired by a husband or wife while domiciled in a community property state.
c. All property acquired by a husband or wife while domiciled in a separate property state.
d. All property acquired by a husband or wife while domiciled in a joint property territory.

CFSDDP2.6
Which of the following does not describe separate property?

 a. Property owned separately by the husband or wife before marriage.
 b. Property purchased with separate property funds.
 c. Money earned while domiciled in a separate property state.
 d. Property that was purchased together as husband and wife.

CFSDDP2.7
Which of the following best describes California tax law?

 a. California is a common law state.
 b. California is a community property state.
 c. California is a separate property state.
 d. California is a joint property territory.

Part 2 Review Question Answers

CFSDDP2.1
In a community property state like California, one-half of all income earned by one spouse belongs to and is taxable to the other spouse. This is called Community Property income. Which of the following is correct about separate property as defined by California?

 a. All property owned separately by an individual and/or an RDP before entering in the relationship.
 b. All property acquired separately after entering in a registered domestic partnership, such as gifts, inheritances, and property purchased with separate funds.
 c. Money earned while domiciled in a separate property state.
 d. All property declared separate property in a valid agreement entered before or after registration of the partnership.
 e. All the options are correct.

Feedback: Review section *Community Property and Income*.

CFSDDP2.2
Which of the following best describes California tax law?

 a. California is a common law state
 b. California is a community property state
 c. California is a separate property state
 d. California is a joint property territory

Feedback: Review section *Community Property and Income*.

CFSDDP2.3
Which of the following states is a community property state?

 a. Oregon
 b. Kansas
 c. Louisiana
 d. New Hampshire

Feedback: Review section *Community Property and Income*.

CFSDDP2.4
If the taxpayer is married and lives in a _____ , when the taxpayer receives a distribution, one-half belongs to the spouse.

    a. community property state
    b. common law state
    c. common territory
    d. community property territory

Feedback: Review section *Community Property and Income.*

CFSDDP2.5
Which of the following best describes community property?

    a. All property acquired by a husband or wife while domiciled in a common law state.
    b. All property acquired by a husband or wife while domiciled in a community property state.
    c. All property acquired by a husband or wife while domiciled in a separate property state.
    d. All property acquired by a husband or wife while domiciled in a joint property territory.

Feedback: Review section *Community Property and Income.*

CFSDDP2.6
Which of the following does not describe separate property?

    a. Property owned separately by the husband or wife before marriage.
    b. Property purchased with separate property funds.
    c. Money earned while domiciled in a separate property state.
    d. Property that was purchased together as husband and wife.

Feedback: Review section *Community Property and Income.*

CFSDDP2.7
Which of the following best describes California tax law?

    a. California is a common law state.
    b. California is a community property state.
    c. California is a separate property state.
    d. California is a joint property territory.

Feedback: Review section *Community Property and Income.*

Takeaways

Apart from these exceptions, California generally conforms with federal tax law for dependent and exemption credits; the California tax preparer must be sure to know it well.

When compared to federal tax law, California tax law has additional filing statuses that can result in the need to prepare multiple returns. If the client is considered married or an RDP in California, then the couple must file a MFJ/RDP or MFS/RDP tax return to meet state requirements before filing two separate returns to meet the federal requirements.

TEST YOUR KNOWLEDGE!
Go online to take a practice quiz.

Chapter 4 Income

Introduction

This chapter covers Form 1040, lines 1 – 7, and Part I on Schedule 1, *Additional Income and Adjustments to Income*. Also covered are the common taxable and nontaxable income types. A tax professional must identify the different types of taxable income, tax-exempt income, and other income included in Schedule 1, line 10, and know how to determine the taxable income percentage for Social Security benefits.

The IRS has the authority to tax all income from all sources. Including compensation for services, gains from property dispositions, interest and dividends, rent and royalties, pensions and annuities, gambling winnings, and even illegal activities. A person's income is collectively referred to as "worldwide income." However, not all money or property is taxable or subject to tax.

Most interest or dividends are taxable income if the interest is credited to the taxpayer's account and the taxpayer can withdraw the money. This chapter also discusses the exceptions to interest and dividends, including those which are not taxable income.

Objectives

At the end of this chapter, the student will:

➢ Explain "worldwide income."
➢ Understand where to report wages and other compensation.
➢ Differentiate earned vs. unearned income.
➢ Identify where income is reported.
➢ Identify the different types of interest income.
➢ Recognize which tax forms report interest income.
➢ Recite which dividends are reported as interest.
➢ Understand the different types of savings bonds.
➢ Explain where to report dividend income.
➢ Understand when Schedule B is required to be filed with the tax return.
➢ Indicate how to report interest and dividend income on the tax return.

Resources

Form W-2	Schedule B	Instructions Schedule B
Form W-2G	Schedule D	Instructions for Schedule D
Form 1040	Publication 15-B	Instructions Form W-2
Form 1099-B	Publication 17	Instructions Form W-2G
Form 1099-DIV	Publication 505	Instructions Form 1040
Form 1099-G	Publication 514	Instructions Form 1099-B
Form 1099-INT	Publication 523	Instructions Form 1099-DIV
Form 1099-OID	Publication 525	Instructions Form 1099-INT
Form 1099-Q	Publication 531	Instructions Form 1099-OID

Form 1099-R	Publication 544	Instructions Form 1099-Q
Form RRB-1099	Publication 550	Instructions Form 1099-R
Form SSA-1099	Publication 551	Instructions RRB-1099
Form 5329	Publication 554	Instructions Form SSA-1099
Form 6252	Publication 575	Instructions Form 4070
Form 8606	Publication 590 A & B	Instructions Form 4797
Form 8615	Publication 915	Instructions Form 5329
Form 8814	Publication 929	Instructions Form 6252
Form 8815	Publication 939	Instructions Form 8606
Form 8818	Publication 1244 (which includes	Instructions Form 8615
Form 8949	Form 4070 and 4070A)	Instructions Form 8814
Form 8960	Publication 4078	Instructions Form 8815
	Tax Topics 403, 404, 409, 411,	Instructions Form 8818
	412, 413, 417, 418, 419, 420, 421,	Instructions Form 8949
	451, 553, 557, 558, 703	Instructions Form 8960

Table of Contents

Part 1 Form W-4 and Form W-2

A tax professional needs to understand the importance of Form W-4, *Employee's Withholding Certificate*. Form W-4 is the IRS document that an employee completes for their employer to determine how much should be withheld from the employee's paycheck for federal income taxes and sent to the IRS. Accurately completing the W-4 will avoid overpaying taxes or having a balance due come tax time. Many taxpayers do not understand the form and want to have as much income on their paycheck. Not accurately calculating the W-4 is an issue for the taxpayer.

The IRS has created an online tax withholding estimator to help taxpayers determine their withholding is enough. The IRS wants the taxpayer to "pay as you go." This is to determine that the taxpayer pays enough withholding. To use the estimator online, gather the following needed documents.

1. Most recent paycheck(s), if filing jointly; need both taxpayer and spouse.
2. Income from other sources, if applicable.
3. Have the most recent tax return handy.

The estimator is only as accurate as the information that is entered. Below is the link to the estimator. https://www.irs.gov/individuals/tax-withholding-estimator.

Tax Withholding

Income tax is withheld from employee compensation; the amount of income tax the employer withholds is based on two factors:

➢ The amount one earns in each payroll period.
➢ he information provided to the employer when the employee completes Form W-4.

The withholding counts toward paying the annual income calculated tax bill when the taxpayer files their current year tax return. Prior to the current W-4 version, taxpayers were allowed to claim personal allowances. The more allowances claimed, the less an employer would withhold from the taxpayer's paycheck. Allowances were tied to personal and dependent exemptions claimed on the tax form. Due to the Tax Cuts and Jobs Act (TCJA), personal exemptions have been suspended until 2025. TCJA is federal law, and some states did not conform to TCJA.

To declare a filing status, the employee would mark one of the boxes in Step 1(c). If steps 2-4 apply to the taxpayer, then the individual would complete the steps; otherwise, continue to step 5.

Step 2 is used if the taxpayer has multiple jobs simultaneously or the taxpayer and spouse have jobs.

Step 3 is used if the taxpayer and spouse claim the child tax credit and have a qualifying other dependent. To qualify for child tax credit, the taxpayer must have a qualifying dependent child under the age of 17 as of December 31 who has lived with the taxpayer for over half of the year. Other tax credits can also be used in this step to reach a more accurate credit allowance.

Step 4 is used when the taxpayer has other income that would affect their W-2 withholding. This includes interest earned and dividend distributions. If the taxpayer claims itemized deductions, and/or extra withholding deducted from each pay period, this action could influence the withholding amount.

Form W-4, Prior to TCJA

The *Employee's Withholding Allowance Certificate* included four types of information that an employer would use to figure out the taxpayer's withholding. Some payroll companies (private or commercial) still use the old system to calculate tax withholding. The following would apply to the prior Form W-4:

1. Whether to withhold at the single rate or at the lower married rate.
2. How many withholding allowances does the taxpayer claim; each allowance reduces the amount withheld.
3. Whether the taxpayer wants an additional amount withheld.
4. Whether the taxpayer is claiming an exemption from withholding in 2022.

The taxpayer must complete Form W-4 to determine the amount of withholding to claim. It is the taxpayer's responsibility to determine the correct withholding.

The taxpayer should annually evaluate his or her Form W-4 and provide employer(s) with a new Form W-4 as needed. If the taxpayer wants to withhold from pensions or annuities, use Form W-4P.

In most situations, the tax withheld from the taxpayer's pay will be close to the tax figured on the return if one of the following applies:

➢ The taxpayer accurately completes Form W-4.
➢ The taxpayer changes Form W-4 when their tax situation changes.

The worksheets provided with the W-4 do not account for all possible situations, and thus the taxpayer may not have the correct amount withheld. This is most likely to happen in the following situations:

1. The taxpayer is married, and the taxpayer and spouse work.
2. The taxpayer has more than one job at a time.
3. The taxpayer has nonwage income such as interest, dividends, alimony, unemployment compensation, or self-employment income, rental income, or capital gains.
4. The taxpayer could owe additional tax amounts if they are reporting self-employment income or household employment income.
5. The taxpayer had tax withholdings from an obsolete Form W-4 for a substantial part of the year.
6. The taxpayer works only part of the year.
7. The taxpayer has changed the number of withholding allowances during the year.

If the taxpayer has income from two or more jobs at the same time, the allowances could be claimed on one W-4 and split the allowances between the jobs. Withholding will usually be more accurate when all allowances are claimed on Form W-4 for the highest-paying job and zero allowances are claimed on the others.

If the taxpayer and the spouse are employed and expect to file a joint return, they should figure out withholding allowance using their combined income, adjustments, deductions, exemptions, and credits. They can divide their total allowances any way they want, but they cannot claim an allowance the other spouse has claimed. See Publication 505.

Form W-4

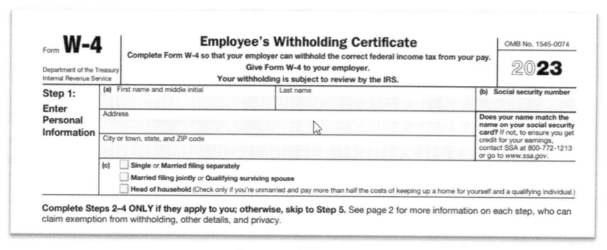

Portion of Form W-4

Exemption from Withholding

If a taxpayer had no tax liability in the previous year and fully expects to have no tax liability in the coming year, one can write "Exempt" on Form W-4 in the space below Step 4(c). Then complete Steps 1(a), 1(b), and 5. Do not complete any other steps. If the taxpayer claims exemption from withholding, the exemption applies only to income tax and not to Social Security or Medicare tax.

The taxpayer may claim an exemption for the current tax year if the following apply:

➤ The taxpayer had a right to a refund of all federal income tax withheld because the taxpayer had no tax liability the previous year.
➤ The taxpayer expects a refund of all federal income tax withheld because the individual expects to have no tax liability for the current year.

The employer must send the IRS a copy of the taxpayer's Form W-4 if the taxpayer claims to be exempt from withholding and if the taxpayer's pay is expected to usually be more than $200 a week. If the taxpayer does not qualify for the exemption, the IRS will send the taxpayer and the taxpayer's employer a written notice.

If the taxpayer claims to be exempt on Form W-4 but the situation changes so that he or she must pay income tax after all, the taxpayer must file a new Form W-4 within 10 days of the change. If the taxpayer claims to be exempt in 2023 but expects to owe income tax for 2024, the taxpayer should file a new Form W-4 as soon as possible. An exemption is valid for one year. The taxpayer must provide the employer with a new Form W-4 yearly by February 15th of each year to continue the exemption.

The taxpayer is required to complete and file a new Form W-4 with the employer within 10 days in the following cases:

➤ The taxpayer was claiming to be married and becomes divorced.
➤ An event occurs that decreases the number of withholding allowances the taxpayer can claim.

Señor 1040 Says: Students are not automatically exempt from tax withholding.

If the taxpayer wishes to change his or her W-4 during the year, the employer must put the new Form W-4 into effect no later than the start of the first payroll period ending on or after the 30th day after the taxpayer turned in the new Form W-4. If the taxpayer's change is for the next year, the new form will not take place until the next year.

Household Workers Withholding

If a taxpayer paid an employee $2,400 or more in cash wages for 2022, the taxpayer must report and pay Social Security and Medicare taxes on all the wages. A household worker is an employee who performs household work in a private home, local college club, or local fraternity or sorority chapter. Tax is withheld only if the taxpayer has asked the employer to do so. If the taxpayer does not have enough tax withheld, the individual must make estimated payments. To be able to file the appropriate forms to have the taxes withheld, the employer of the household worker must obtain an employer identification number by submitting a SS-4 EIN Application to the IRS. The taxpayer needs to employ an individual that can legally work in the United States. The employee needs to complete Form I-9, and the employer needs to verify the information and give the employee a W-2.

A taxpayer who is an employee should receive a Form W-2 from their employer(s) that shows the wages the taxpayer earned in exchange for services performed. A W-2 is the tax form generated by employers that details the employees' earnings and government withholdings for a given tax year. A tax year's W-2 should be distributed to the employees by the end of the first month after the tax year ends; for example, W-2s for tax year 2022 should have been delivered by January 31, 2023. A taxpayer will receive a W-2 from each employer he or she is employed by and should give each W-2 they have received to the individual preparing the tax return. Most taxpayers will only receive one W-2; it is possible to receive more than one if a taxpayer has worked multiple jobs during a given tax year. If employees notice an error on their Form W-2, they should notify their employer and request a corrected Form W-2 before filing their taxes.

Tax professionals use the information provided on a W-2 to determine the client's earned income for the year. The total amount of wages is reported on Form 1040, line 1. Wages include salaries, vacation allowances, bonuses, commissions, and fringe benefits. Compensation includes everything received in payment for personal services.

How to Read the W-2

Below is a W-2 that an employee receives from his employer. It is important for the tax professional to know what is reported on each line of the W-2 so that he or she will know how to use the information provided in the form when preparing the employee's tax return.

Copy of Form W-2

The Lettered Boxes of Form W-2

Box a: Employee's Social Security Number

The Social Security number should match the number shown on the employee's Social Security card. If the Social Security number is incorrect, the employee should notify the employer and request a corrected Form W-2.

> Note: ITINs are not replacements for Social Security numbers. ITINs are only available to resident and nonresident aliens ineligible for U.S. employment that need identification for tax purposes. Under normal circumstances, ITIN holders cannot receive a W-2 because they lack an SSN, but it is possible for an ITIN holder to receive a W-2 using an unlawful SSN. When entering the W-2 information into software for these clients, make sure that the SSN does not auto-populate into box a, because this is where the ITIN number needs to go.

Box b: Employer Identification Number (EIN)

This box shows the employer identification number (EIN) assigned to the employer by the IRS. EINs consist of two digits and a dash followed by seven more digits, as seen in this example: 00-0000000.

Box c: Employer's Name, Address, and ZIP Code

This entry should be the same as the information shown on the employer's Form 941, 941-SS, 943, 944, CT-1 or Form 1040, Schedule H.

Box d: Control Number

Though it is often left blank, this box can be used by employers to distinguish between individual W-2s whenever needed. For example, if an employer has multiple employees with the same first and last names, they can distinguish between them using control numbers.

Boxes e and f: Employee's Name and Address

The taxpayer's name should match the name shown on the Social Security card (first, middle, and last). The taxpayer's name may be different if the taxpayer has recently married, divorced, or had a name change of any kind. The taxpayer's address should include the number, street, apartment and suite number, or a P.O. Box number if mail is not delivered to a physical address.

The Numbered Boxes of Form W-2

Box 1: Wages, Tips, and Other Compensation

Shows the total taxable wages, tips, and other compensation paid to the employee during the year before any payroll deductions or tax withholdings were subtracted.

The following items are included in the total amount provided in box 1:

> ➢ Total wages and bonuses (including signing bonuses, prizes, and awards) paid to employees during the year.
> ➢ Total noncash payments, including certain fringe benefits.
> ➢ Total tips reported by the employee to the employer; allocated tips are not reported in this box.
> ➢ Certain employee business expense reimbursements.
> ➢ An S corporation's cost of accident and health insurance premiums for a shareholder with 2% or more of the company.
> ➢ If the employee chooses cash for certain taxable benefits from a section 125 cafeteria plan.
> ➢ Employee contributions to an Archer MSA.
> ➢ Contributions to an Archer MSA from an employer if included in the employee's income.
> ➢ Employer contributions for qualified long-term care services to the extent that such coverage is provided through flexible spending plans or similar arrangements.
> ➢ The taxable portion of the cost of group-term insurance of more than $50,000.
> ➢ Unless excludable under an education assistance program, payments for non-job-related education expenses or for payments under a nonaccountable plan.
> ➢ The amount included as wages because the employer paid the employee's share of Social Security and Medicare taxes.
> ➢ Designated Roth contributions made under a section 401(k) plan, a section 403(b) salary reduction agreement, or a governmental section 457(b) plan.
> ➢ Distributions to an employee or former employee from a nonqualified deferred compensation plan (NQDC) or a nongovernmental section 457(b) plan.
> ➢ Amounts included as income under an NQDC (nonqualified deferred compensation) plan because of section 409A.
> ➢ Amounts includable in income under section 457(f) because the amounts are no longer subject to a substantial risk of forfeiture.
> ➢ Payments to statutory employees who are subject to Social Security and Medicare taxes but are not subject to federal income tax withholding must be shown in box 1 as "other compensation."
> ➢ Cost of current insurance protection under a compensatory split-dollar life insurance arrangement.

- ➤ Employee contributions to a health savings account (HSA).
- ➤ Employer's contributions to an HSA if included in the employee's income.
- ➤ Nonqualified moving expenses and expense reimbursement.
- ➤ Payments made to former employees while on active duty in the armed forces or other uniformed services.
- ➤ All other compensation, including certain scholarships and fellowship grants; other compensation includes taxable amounts paid to the employee from which federal income tax was not withheld. An employer may use another Form W-2 to show an employee's compensation apart from their earned wages based on their bookkeeping practices.

Box 2 through Box 11

Box 2: Federal Income Tax Withheld

Shows the total federal income tax withheld from the employee's wages for the year. Parachute payments include compensation for certain covered employees and are taxed at 20%, including the 20% excise tax withheld on excess parachute payments.

If the taxpayer claims itemized deductions, and/or extra withholding deducted from each pay period, this action could influence the withholding amount.

Box 3: Social Security Wages

Shows the total amount of non-tip wages used to figure out the taxpayer's Social Security pay-in and pay-out amounts. The total of boxes 3 and 7 cannot exceed the Social Security yearly pay-in limit of $147,000.00.

Box 4: Social Security Tax Withheld

Shows the total employee Social Security tax withholding, which is determined by multiplying the taxing percentage (6.2%) against the Social Security wage limit of $147,000.00 for 2022. The Social Security Administration sets the Social Security wage limit every year and can also change the taxed percentage, though they rarely do. For 2023, the Social Security wage limit of $160,200.00.

Box 5: Medicare Wages and Tips

The wages and tips subject to Medicare tax are determined using the same method as the Social Security tax in boxes 3 and 7 except that there is no wage base limit for Medicare tax.

Box 6: Medicare Tax Withheld

This box shows the total employee Medicare tax withheld. The tax withholding percentage is 1.45%. Medicare tax withholdings are determined from the employee's total income amount in box 1.

Example: Ryan's total wages for 2022 were $150,000.00; thus, this is the amount reported in box 1. Because $150,000.00 exceeds the 2022 Social Security yearly pay-in limit, $147,000.00 will be the amount shown in box 3. Box 4 is determined by multiplying the amount in box 3 by the taxing percentage of 6.2%, meaning the amount shown in box 4 is $9,114.00. Since the wages and tips subject to Medicare tax have no wage base limit, the amount reported in box 5 will simply be Ryan's total wages for 2022 ($150,000.00), the same as in box 1. Determine box 6 by multiplying the amount in box 5 by the Medicare tax withholding percentage of 1.45%, meaning the amount shown in box 6 will be $2,175. Thus, the amounts reported in the boxes will appear as follows:

Box 1: $150,000.00
Box 3: $147,000.00
Box 4: $9,114.00
Box 5: $150,000.00
Box 6: $2,175.00

Federal Insurance Contributions Act (FICA) is the money taken out of workers' paychecks to pay the Social Security retirement income and Medicare. The employer and employee portion of the Social Security and Medicare tax is also referred to as FICA. The amount of FICA payments depends on the taxpayer's income. Consider the following scenarios:

Alberto earns $50,000 for tax year 2022, so his FICA contributions would be $3,825. In this case, $3,100 is his Social Security portion and $725 for Medicare.

$50,000 X 6.2% = $3,100 $50,000 X 1.45% = $725 $3,100 + $725 = $3,825

Ezra earns $250,000 for tax year 2022; he would pay $13,189. He would pay 6.2% on the first $147,000 for Social Security ($9,114.00), then 1.45% on the first $250,000 earned for Medicare ($3,625) and the additional 0.9% for earning $50,000, which is $450.

$$\$147,000 \times 6.2\% = \$9,114.00$$
$$\$250,000 \times 1.45\% = \$3,625$$
$$\$50,000 \times 0.9\% = \$450$$
$$\$9,114 + \$3,625 + \$450 = \$12,464$$

Alberto earns $50,000 for tax year 2023, so his FICA contributions would be $3,825. In this case, $3,100 is his Social Security portion and $725 for Medicare.

$50,000 X 6.2% = $3,100 $50,000 X 1.45% = $725 $3,100 + $725 = $3,825

Ezra earns $250,000 for tax year 2023; he would pay $14,007.40. He would pay 6.2% on the first $160,200 for Social Security ($9,932.40), then 1.45% on the first $250,000 earned for Medicare ($3,625) and the additional 0.9% for earning $50,000, which is $450.

$$\$160,200 \times 6.2\% = \$9,932.40$$
$$\$250,000 \times 1.45\% = \$3,625$$
$$\$50,000 \times 0.9\% = \$450$$
$$\$9,932.40 + \$3,625 + \$450 = \$14,007.40$$

Box 7: Social Security Tips

This box shows the tips the employee reported to the employer, which is not included in box 3. The combined amount of boxes 3 and 7 is used to figure Social Security tax and should exceed the maximum yearly Social Security wage base limit.

Box 8: Allocated Tips

Shows allocated tips paid to the employee. Allocated tips will be discussed later in this chapter. The amount in box 8 is not included in the amounts in boxes 1, 3, 5, or 7.

Box 9: Verification Code

If the employer participates in the W-2 Verification Code, the code numbers are in this box. Apart from this, box 9 will be left blank.

Box 10: Dependent Care Benefits

Shows the total amount paid for dependent-care benefits under a dependent-care assistance program (section 129) paid for or paid by the employer for the employee. This amount could also include the fair market value (FMV) of employer-provided or employer-sponsored day-care facilities and the amounts paid or incurred in a section 125 cafeteria plan. All amounts paid or earned are reported in this box, regardless of employee forfeitures, including those exceeding the $6,000 exclusion.

Box 11: Nonqualified Plans

The purpose of box 11 is for the SSA to determine if any part of the amount reported in boxes 1, 3, or 5 was earned in a prior year. The SSA uses this information to verify that it has properly applied the Social Security earnings test and paid the correct amount of benefits. Box 11 shows a distribution to an employee from a nonqualified plan or a nongovernmental section 457 plan, and this amount is also reported in box 1.

Box 12: Codes

Box 12 consists of "sub-boxes" 12a, 12b, 12c, and 12d

Though sometimes left completely blank, these boxes are used as needed when certain, infrequent items are reported to the taxpayer by their employer for tax purposes. Each "sub-box" consists of a small space followed by a line and a larger space. If used, the employer will place a letter in the small place that designates one of the codes explained below, with the code's corresponding amount placed in the larger space. Which "sub-box" a code is placed in and what order they are shown is arbitrary. No more than four codes can be entered in box 12. Box 12 has 4 sub-boxes that are used to report the following income. If the employer only needs to report one item, enter it in box a. Only four items are reported on one W-2; if more than four items are reported, then an additional W-2 must be used. The following are the codes that must be reported in box 12.

> **Code A:** Uncollected Social Security or RRTA tax on tips. The employee's Social Security or Railroad Retirement Tax Act (RRTA) tax on all the employee's tips that the employer could not collect because the employee did not have enough funds to deduct the tax. This amount is not included in box 4.

Code B: Uncollected Medicare tax on tips (but not Additional Medicare Tax). Shows the employee's Medicare tax or RRTA Medicare tax on tips that the employer could not collect because the employee did not have enough funds from which to deduct the tax. This amount is not included in the total shown in box 6.

Code C: Taxable cost of group-term life insurance over $50,000. Shows the taxable cost of group-term life insurance coverage over $50,000 provided to the employee (including a former employee). This amount is included in boxes 1 and 3 up to the Social Security wage limit.

Code D: Elective deferrals to a section 401(k) cash or deferred arrangement. Shows deferrals under a SIMPLE retirement account part of section 401(k) arrangement.

Code E: Elective deferrals under a section 403(b) salary reduction agreement.

Code F: Elective deferrals under a section 408(k)(6) salary reduction SEP.

Code G: Elective deferrals and employer contributions (including non-elective deferrals) to any governmental or nongovernmental section 457(b) deferred compensation plan.

Code H: Elective deferrals to a section 501(c)(18)(D) tax-exempt organization plan.

Code J: Nontaxable sick pay (information only not included in box 1, 3, and 5).

Code K: 20% excise tax on excess golden parachute payments.

Code L: Business expense reimbursements under an accountable plan are excluded from the employee's gross income.

Code M: Uncollected Social Security or RRTA tax on the cost of group-term life insurance over $50,000 (former employees only).

Code N: Uncollected Medicare tax on the taxable cost of group-term life insurance over $50,000 (former employees only).

Code P: Excludable moving expense reimbursements paid directly to a member of the U.S. Armed Forces employee. The amount for moving expense reimbursement is not included in boxes 1, 3, or 5. For tax years 2018 through 2025, these reimbursements have been suspended for all other moving taxpayers.

Code Q: Nontaxable combat pay.

Code R: Employer contributions to an Archer MSA. The tax professional must use Form 8853 to report the amount and attach the form to the return.

Code S: Employee salary reduction contributions under a section 408(p) SIMPLE (not included in box 1).

Code T: Adoption benefits (not included in box 1). If Code T is used, complete Form 8839 to determine which benefits are taxable and nontaxable.

Code V: Income from the exercise of nonstatutory stock options(s) are included in boxes 1, 3 (up to the Social Security wage base).

Code W: Employer contributions to a health savings account (HSA) including amounts contributed using a section 125 cafeteria plan. Form 8889 reports the amount and is attached to the client's return.

Code Y: Deferrals under a section 409A nonqualified deferred compensation plan.

Code Z: Income under section 409A on a nonqualified deferred compensation plan that fails to satisfy section 409A is shown here. This amount is included in box 1 and is subject to an additional 20% tax plus interest.

Code AA: Designated Roth contributions under a section 401(k) plan.

Code BB: Designated Roth contributions under a section 403(b) plan.

Code DD: Cost of employer-sponsored health coverage. The amount reported with this code is nontaxable.

Code EE: Designated Roth contribution under a governmental section 457(b) plan. This amount does not apply to contributions under a tax-exempt organization 457(b) plan.

Code FF: Permitted benefits under a Qualified Small Employer Health Reimbursement Arrangement (QSEHRA).

Code GG: Income from qualified equity grants under section 83(i).

Code HH: Aggregate deferrals under section 83(i) elections as of the close of the calendar year.

Box 13: Statutory Employee, Retirement Plan, and Third-Party Sick Pay

If the retirement plan box is checked, special limits may apply to the amount of traditional IRA contributions that can be deducted. See Publication 590.

Statutory Employee

This box is checked for statutory employees whose earnings are subject to Social Security and Medicare taxes but are not subject to federal income tax withholding. Do not check this box for common-law employees. There are workers who are independent contractors under the common-law rules but are treated as employees by statute. The following are considered statutory employees:

➢ A driver who is an agent or is paid on commission and distributes beverages (other than milk), meat, vegetables, fruit, bakery products, or who picks up and delivers laundry or dry cleaning.
➢ A full-time life insurance sales agent whose principal business activity (primarily for one life insurance company) is selling life insurance, annuity contracts, or both.
➢ An individual working from home on materials or goods that his/her employer supplied, which must be returned to the employer or to an employer's representative if the employer furnished specifications on how to do the work.

> ➢ A full-time traveling or city salesperson who works on the employer's behalf and turns in orders to the employer from wholesalers, retailers, contractors, and operators of hotels, restaurants, or other similar establishments. The goods sold must be merchandise for resale or supplies for use in the buyers' business operations. The work performed for the employer must be the salesperson's principal business activity.

See Publication 15-A, section 1.

Retirement Plan

This box is checked if the employee was an "active participant" (for any part of the year) in any of the following:

> ➢ A qualified pension, profit-sharing, or stock bonus plan described in section 401(a), including a 401(k) plan.
> ➢ An annuity plan described in section 403(a).
> ➢ An annuity contract or custodial account described in section 403(b).
> ➢ A simplified employee pension (SEP) plan described in section 408(k).
> ➢ A SIMPLE retirement account described in section 408(p).
> ➢ A trust described in section 501(c)(18).
> ➢ A plan for federal, state, or local government employees or by an agency or instrumentality thereof, other than a section 457(b) plan.

An employee is an active participant if covered by:

> ➢ A defined benefit plan for any tax year in which one is eligible to participate.
> ➢ A defined contribution plan for any tax year that employer or employee contributions (or forfeitures) are added to their individual account.

Third-Party Sick Pay

This box will be checked only if a third-party sick-pay provider's program covers the individual. Sick pay can include short- and long-term benefits. See Publication 15-A.

Box 14: Other.

Employers use this box to report information such as state disability insurance taxes withheld, union dues, uniform payments health, 100% of a vehicle's annual lease paid in the employees income.

Box 15 through Box 20

State and local income tax information. Research is needed depending on the state you live in or preparing a tax return for your individual state (if applicable).

If the employee has an error on their Form W-2, he or she should notify the employer and request a corrected Form W-2. As a tax professional you should not prepare the return until the Form W-2 is corrected.

Part 1 Review Questions

To obtain the maximum benefit from this chapter, LTP recommends that you complete each of the following questions, and then compare them to the answers with feedback that immediately follow. Under governing self-study standards, vendors are required to present review questions intermittently throughout each self-study course.

These questions and explanations are not part of the final examination and will not be graded by LTP.

IP1.1
When should the taxpayer receive their W-2s?

    a. W-2s should be postmarked by January 31, 2023.
    b. W-2s should be in the taxpayer's possession by January 31, 2023.
    c. W-2s should be in the taxpayer's possession by February 1, 2023.
    d. W-2s need to be emailed to all employees by January 31, 2023.

IP1.2
Which of the following is not reported in box 1 of the W-2?

    a. Box 1 reports total wages.
    b. Box 1 reports allocated tips.
    c. Box 1 reports all compensation.
    d. Box 1 reports noncash payments.

IP1.3
Which circumstance does not require a taxpayer to change their W-4 within 10 days?

    a. Daniel divorced his wife in March and has been filing separate tax returns for the past 2 years.
    b. Jake and Danelle had a new baby in February.
    c. Karina began supporting her mother in January.
    d. Gigi and David got married in May.

IP1.4
Which of the following is the reporting tool for Form 1040, line 1?

    a. W-4
    b. W-7
    c. W-2
    d. I-9

IP1.5
The employer provided group-term life insurance that exceeds _____ coverage is reported to the employee as income.

    a. $50,000
    b. $25,000
    c. $5,000
    d. $2,500

IP1.6
Which individual is not a statutory employee?

a. An individual who delivers milk and is paid on commission.
b. An individual who delivers beverages and is paid on commission.
c. An individual who delivers bakery products and is paid on commission.
d. An individual who delivers fruit and is paid on commission.

IP1.7
Which of the following best describes an active participant in a retirement plan?

a. Parent contributed to their daughter's a 408(k).
b. Participant contributed to a SIMPLE plan.
c. Parent contributed to their son's 529 plan.
d. Participant did not contribute during the current calendar year.

IP1.8
The employee's W-4 needs to be changed within _____ days if the taxpayer's situation changes for either of the following reasons:

1. The taxpayer was claiming married and becomes divorced
2. Any event occurs that decreases the number of withholding allowances the taxpayer is allowed

a. 10
b. 100
c. 15
d. 5

IP1.9
If the taxpayer is an employee, the taxpayer receives a Form _____ showing the wages they received in exchange for their services.

a. 1040
b. W-2
c. 1099-G
d. 1099-R

IP1.10
Who makes the decision regarding the amount of tax withholding?

a. Employer
b. Taxpayer
c. Withholding not required
d. The amount of payroll

Part 1 Review Questions Answers

IP1.1
When should the taxpayer receive their W-2s?

   a. W-2s should be postmarked by January 31, 2023.
   b. W-2s should be in the taxpayer's possession by January 31, 2023.
   c. W-2s should be in the taxpayer's possession by February 1, 2023.
   d. W-2s need to be emailed to all employees by January 31, 2023.

Feedback: Review section *Form W-2.*

IP1.2
Which of the following is not reported in box 1 of the W-2?

   a. Box 1 reports total wages.
   b. Box 1 reports allocated tips.
   c. Box 1 reports all compensation.
   d. Box 1 reports noncash payments.

Feedback: Review section *Box 1: Wages, Tips, and Other Compensation.*

IP1.3
Which circumstance does not require a taxpayer to change their W-4 within 10 days?

   a. Daniel divorced his wife in March and has been filing separate tax returns for the past 2 years.
   b. Jake and Danelle had a new baby in February.
   c. Karina began supporting her mother in January.
   d. Gigi and David got married in May.

Feedback: Review section *Exemption from Withholding.*

IP1.4
Which of the following is the reporting tool for Form 1040, line 1?

   a. W-4
   b. W-7
   c. W-2
   d. I-9

Feedback: Review section *How to Read the W-2.*

IP1.5
The employer provided group-term life insurance that exceeds _____ coverage is reported to the employee as income.

   a. $50,000
   b. $25,000
   c. $5,000
   d. $2,500

Feedback: Review section *Box 1: Wages, Tips, and Other Compensation.*

IP1.6
Which individual is not a statutory employee?

    a. An individual who delivers milk and is paid on commission.
    b. An individual who delivers beverages and is paid on commission.
    c. An individual who delivers bakery products and is paid on commission.
    d. An individual who delivers fruit and is paid on commission.

Feedback: Review section *Box 13, Statutory Employee, Retirement Plans and Third-Party Sick Pay.*

IP1.7
Which of the following best describes an active participant in a retirement plan?

    a. Parent contributed to their daughter's a 408(k).
    b. Participant contributed to a SIMPLE plan.
    c. Parent contributed to their son's 529 plan.
    d. Participant did not contribute during the current calendar year.

Feedback: Review section *Retirement Plan.*

IP1.8
The employee's W-4 needs to be changed within _____ days if the taxpayer's situation changes for either of the following reasons:

    1. The taxpayer was claiming married and becomes divorced
    2. Any event occurs that decreases the number of withholding allowances the taxpayer is allowed

    a. 10
    b. 100
    c. 15
    d. 5

Feedback: Review section *Exemption from Withholding.*

IP1.9
If the taxpayer is an employee, the taxpayer receives a Form _____ showing the wages they received in exchange for their services.

    a. 1040
    b. W-2
    c. 1099-G
    d. 1099-R

Feedback: Review section *How to Read the W-2.*

IP1.10
Who makes the decision regarding the amount of tax withholding?

    a. Employer
    b. Taxpayer
    c. Withholding not required
    d. The amount of payroll

Feedback: Review section *Tax Withholding.*

Part 2 Income

The IRS has the authority to tax all income from however the source is acquired. This includes compensation for services, gains from dispositions of property, interest and dividends, rent and royalties, pensions and annuities, gambling winnings, and even illegal activities. All such income a person receives is collectively referred to as "worldwide income." However, not all money or property is taxable or subject to tax. Most clients will probably only have employer-provided income reported on a W-2. This is only one type of income.

There are two major types of income: *earned income* and *unearned income*. Earned income is revenue the taxpayer received for working and includes the following types of income:

➤ Wages, salaries, tips, and other types of taxable employee pay.
➤ Net earnings from self-employment.
➤ Gross income received as a statutory employee.
➤ Union strike benefits.
➤ Long-term disability benefits received prior to reaching the minimum retirement age.

Unearned income is any amount received indirectly and not as a direct repayment of any services rendered or work provided. Unearned income includes:

➤ Interest and dividends.
➤ Pensions and annuities.
➤ Social Security and railroad retirement benefits (including disability benefits).
➤ Alimony and child support.
➤ Welfare benefits.
➤ Workers' compensation benefits.
➤ Unemployment compensation.
➤ Income while an inmate.
➤ Workfare payments (review Publication 596 for a definition).

Form 1040, lines 1a - z

The following picture shows which income form is used to report income. All income is reported based on the tax form the taxpayer receives and the form used to report it.

Portion of Form 1040

Line 1a: Total Amount from Form(s) W-2, box 1.

If the taxpayer is an employee, the taxpayer would receive Form W-2 showing the wages earned in exchange for services performed. A W-2 is a tax form created by employers to detail earnings and government withholdings for a given tax year. The W-2 should be distributed to the employees by January 31, 2023, for 2022 tax year. The tax professional uses the W-2 to determine the client's earned income for the year. A taxpayer may receive multiple W-2s to if they worked more than one job during the year.

Line 1a of Form 1040 reports the total amount of wages earned. Wages include salaries, vacation allowances, bonuses, commissions, and fringe benefits, and compensation includes everything received in payment for personal services.

Line 1b: Household employee wages not reported on Form(s) W-2.

Report wages that are not reported on Form W-2 for household employees. See Publication 926.

Line 1c: Tip Income not reported on line 1a.

Report tip income that was not reported on Form 1040, line 1a.

Line 1d: Medicaid Waiver Payments not reported on Form(s) W-2.

Report any Medicaid waiver payments that were received and was included in earned income to claim refundable credits.

Line 1e: Taxable Dependent Care Benefits from Form 2441, line 26.

Report the taxable dependent care benefits that is reported on Form 2441, line 26. Make sure to complete Form 2441 first.

Line 1f: Employer-provided adoption benefits from Form 8839, line 26.

Report the total amount of adoption benefits that were paid by the employer. Employer-provided benefits should be in box 12 on the W-2, with code T.

Line 1g: Wages from Form 8919, line 6.

Report wages that are reported on Form 8919, line 6.

Line 1h: Other Earned Income.

Report the following income types:

1. Excess elective deferrals over $20,500, excluding catch-up amounts. The SIMPLE plan limit is $14,000. If the plan is a 403(b) the maximum is $23,500. See Publication 571.
2. Disability pensions shown on Form 1099-R.
3. Corrective distributions from a retirement plan shown on Form 1099-R of excess elective deferrals and contributions, plus earnings.

Line 1i: Nontaxable Combat Pay election.

Report the nontaxable combat pay that was used to calculate the earned income credit.

Line 1z: Add lines 1a through 1h.

Add all the lines together.

Line 2a – 6b

Portion of Form 1040

Form 1099-INT

This form is given by banks or investment companies to inform the taxpayer of their interest earned. Interest is generally reported on Form 1099-INT or a substitute statement. Form 1099-INT shows the interest earned for the year but is not attached to the tax return. Some interest is not reported on Form 1099-INT, yet it must still be reported on the tax return. For example, when Samantha received interest from the partnership she is a member of, her interest would be reported to her on the Schedule K-1 that she received. A substitute statement can come from an individual payer and not a large institution and must contain all the information found on Form 1099-INT.

	VOID		CORRECTED			

PAYER'S name, street address, city or town, state or province, country, ZIP or foreign postal code, and telephone no.	Payer's RTN (optional)	OMB No. 1545-0112	**Interest Income**
		Form **1099-INT**	
	1 Interest income	(Rev. January 2022)	
		For calendar year	
	$	20 ____	
	2 Early withdrawal penalty		**Copy 1**
PAYER'S TIN	RECIPIENT'S TIN	$	**For State Tax Department**
		3 Interest on U.S. Savings Bonds and Treasury obligations	
		$	
RECIPIENT'S name	**4** Federal income tax withheld	**5** Investment expenses	
	$	$	
	6 Foreign tax paid	**7** Foreign country or U.S. possession	
Street address (including apt. no.)	$		
	8 Tax-exempt interest	**9** Specified private activity bond interest	
City or town, state or province, country, and ZIP or foreign postal code	$	$	
	10 Market discount	**11** Bond premium	
FATCA filing requirement	$	$	
	12 Bond premium on Treasury obligations	**13** Bond premium on tax-exempt bond	
☐	$	$	
Account number (see instructions)	**14** Tax-exempt and tax credit bond CUSIP no.	**15** State | **16** State identification no.	**17** State tax withheld $ $
Form **1099-INT** (Rev. 1-2022)	www.irs.gov/Form1099INT	Department of the Treasury - Internal Revenue Service	

Form 1099-INT

As with any form reported with the taxpayer's name, address, and taxpayer identification number (TIN), make sure the information is correct.

Box 1: Reports interest income paid to the recipient not included in box 3. Form 1099-INT is issued for interest earned of $10 or more.

Box 2: Reports interest or principal that was forfeited because of an early withdrawal penalty. Do not reduce the amount in box 1 by the forfeited amount. Form 1040, Schedule 1, line 18 reports Box 2 since will adjust the taxpayer's tax liability.

Box 3: Reports interest from U.S. Savings Bonds and Treasury obligations (another word used for bonds). For taxable covered securities and acquired at a premium, see Box 12. The amount in this box may or may not be taxable. Review Publication 550.

Box 4: Reports federal income tax withheld. If the taxpayer does not receive a TIN (taxpayer identification number), the payer is required to withhold at a 24% rate on the amount in box 1.

Box 5: Investment expenses for a single-class real estate mortgage investment conduit (REMIC) only. Also, include the amount in box 1.

Box 6: Reports foreign taxes paid.

Box 7: Shows the foreign country or U.S. possession taxes paid.

Box 8: Shows tax-exempt interest paid to the person's account during the calendar year. This amount may be subject to backup withholding.

Box 9: This box shows the Specified Private Activity bond interest. Specified Private Activity Bonds are defined in section 141 and issued after Aug 7, 1986.

Box 10: This box shows the value of a taxable or tax-exempt covered security acquired with a market discount, but only if the taxpayer made an election under section 1278(b) to include the market discount in income as it accrues. The taxpayer must notify the payer of the election in writing [certain restrictions apply, see Regulations section 1.6045-1(n)(5)].

Box 11: Bond premium. A taxable covered security other than a U.S. Treasury obligation acquired at a premium.

Box 12: For a U.S. Treasury obligation that is a covered security. This box shows the amount of premium amortization allocable to the interest payment(s).

Box 13: Bond Premiums on Tax-Exempt Bonds. If you report a tax-exempt covered security acquired at a premium, the amount entered is the bond premium amortization that is allocable to the interest paid during the year.

Box 14: Tax-Exempt and Tax Credit Bond CUSIP Number. The CUSIP is entered for single bonds or accounts containing a single bond.

Box 15-17: State's information. These boxes designate where the taxpayer lives as well as any state in which the taxpayer may have earned the income.

Señor 1040 Says: Make sure that the year on Form 1099-INT is the year that you are preparing the tax return for. It is important to verify the year on all documents that report income to the taxpayer to ensure that the income being reported is for the correct tax year.

When to Report Interest Income

Interest income is reported based on the accounting method the taxpayer is using to report his or her income. If taxpayers use the cash method, they generally report their interest income in the year in which it was actually or constructively received. Use the special rules to report the discount on certain debt instruments such as U.S. savings bonds and original issue discount (OID).

Taxpayers should always keep a list showing their sources of income. For example, all Forms 1099-INT and Forms 1099-DIV should be kept with their yearly tax return. If parents elect to claim the investment income of their child, those forms should be kept with their tax returns as well. Interest earned as a beneficiary of an estate or trust is generally taxable income. Taxpayers should receive a Schedule K-1 for their portion of the interest. A copy of the Schedule K-1 should be kept with the tax return as well.

Constructively Received

Interest is constructively received when it is credited to the taxpayer's account or made available to the taxpayer; the taxpayer does not need to have physical possession of the money. The taxpayer is considered to have received interest, dividends, or other earnings from any deposit, bank accounts, savings, loans, similar financial institution, or life insurance policy when the income has been credited to the taxpayer's account and is able to be withdrawn.

Income is constructively received on the deposit or account if the taxpayer does any of the following:

> ➢ Makes multiple withdrawals in even amounts.
> ➢ Makes the withdrawal, with prior notice.
> ➢ Withdraws the earnings in portions or all at once.
> ➢ Receives an early withdrawal or redemption with a penalty due to the payable interest at maturity.

The accrual method reports income earned, whether it was received or not. Interest is earned over the life term of the debt instrument. With coupon bonds, interest is taxable the year the coupon becomes due and payable; it does not matter when the coupon payment is mailed. See Publication 550.

Backup Withholding

Interest income is generally not subject to regular withholding, but it may be subject to the backup withholding rate of 24% in the following situations:

> ➢ The taxpayer did not give the income provider his or her TIN (taxpayer identification number) in the required manner.
> ➢ The IRS notifies the income provider that the TIN is incorrect.
> ➢ The taxpayer is required to certify that he or she is not subject to backup withholding but fails to do so.
> ➢ The IRS notifies the income provider to start withholding on interest and dividends because the taxpayer has underreported interest or dividends on the taxpayer's tax return.

There are civil and criminal penalties for giving false information to avoid backup withholding. The civil penalty is $500. If the taxpayer willfully falsified information, he or she may be subject to criminal penalties including fines and/or imprisonment. If backup withholding is deducted from the interest income, the income provider, (or payer), must give the taxpayer Form 1099-INT to indicate the amount that was withheld.

Accounts and Payee-Identifying Numbers

Banks and other financial institutions pay certain kinds of income when an account or an investment has been opened. When opening the account, the individual is required by federal law to provide his or her SSN to any financial institution or individual who needs the information to make a return, statement, or any other form of document. For instance, when opening a joint account, the primary SSN must be provided.

Example: Gina and her son, Trenton, opened a joint account with Trenton's birthday money. Trenton's SSN would be given to the bank, and his name would appear on the account first. If the primary SSN is not given to the payer, the account holder (Trenton) would have to pay a $50 penalty for each incident.

Truncating

A payer identification number is any number issued by a government agency for the purpose of identification, including Social Security numbers (SSN), individual tax identification numbers (ITIN), employer identification numbers (EIN), taxpayer identification numbers (TIN), and adoption identification numbers (ATIN). Anyone issuing documents containing taxpayer identification information may truncate payee-identifying numbers by replacing the first 5 numbers of payer identification numbers with an X or * (XXX-XX-0000 or ***-**-1111, for example). This can be done on payee statements such as Forms 1097, 1098, 1099, 3921, 9322, and 5498, but it may not be done on Form W-2G.

Number and Certification

For new accounts paying interest or dividends, the payer will give the taxpayer Form W-9: Request for Taxpayer Identification. The taxpayer must certify under penalty of perjury that the SSN or EIN are correct, and they are not subject to backup withholding.

If the taxpayer neglects to make this certification, backup withholding will begin immediately on the taxpayer's new account or investment. If the taxpayer has been notified that backup withholding will be deducted from their income due to not providing an SSN or EIN, the taxpayer can stop the withholding by giving the information to the payer. A payer is the one who administers the account, such as the bank.

Line 2a Tax-Exempt Interest

Certain types of interest income are tax-exempt and are reported on Form 1040, line 2a. Interest paid by state and local governments are exempt from federal taxation but may be taxable at the state level. The fact that this interest is tax-exempt does not mean that it is not reported; tax-exempt interest must be reported. Tax-exempt interest is included when determining how much Social Security could be taxable to the taxpayer and spouse.

Taxpayers are required to use Schedule B if any of the following are true:

> ➤ The taxpayer received over $1,500 of taxable interest or ordinary dividends.
> ➤ The taxpayer received interest from a seller-financed mortgage and the buyer used the property as a personal residence.
> ➤ The taxpayer received interest or ordinary dividends.
> ➤ The taxpayer had a financial interest in, or signature authority over, a financial account in a foreign trust.
> ➤ The taxpayer accrued interest from a bond.
> ➤ The taxpayer is reducing the interest income on a bond by the amortizable bond premium.
> ➤ The taxpayer is reporting original issue discount (OID) in an amount less than the amount on Form 1099-OID.
> ➤ The taxpayer is claiming the exclusion of interest from U.S. savings bonds series EE, or I issued after 1989.

Government Bonds

A government bond is a debt security issued by the government to support government spending. This section will give an overview of the most common federal government bonds. If the taxpayer purchases a government bond for a discount when interest has been defaulted or when interest has accrued and has not been paid, the transaction is considered as "trading a bond flat." The defaulted or unpaid interest is not income and is not taxable to the taxpayer. When an interest payment is received, it reduces the capital of the remaining cost of the bond. Interest that accrues after the date of purchase is taxable interest for the year received or accrued.

Interest for a bond can be reported in one of two ways. First, the taxpayer can elect to pay the interest as it is accrued. In this case, the taxpayer would pay taxes on the interest each year. Taxpayers who use the accrual basis must report interest as it accrues. They cannot postpone reporting interest until they receive it or until the bonds mature. The second option is the cash method in which taxes on the savings bonds are paid when they are redeemed or when the bond has matured. If this option is selected, the taxpayer would report all the interest in the year the bond is redeemed.

Series EE and Series E Bonds

Series EE and series E bonds are issued at a discount and sold for less than the face value of the bond. The buyer makes money by holding them to the bond's maturity date, at which point the face value is paid to the taxpayer. Series EE bonds were first offered in January 1980 and have a 30-year maturity period. Before July 1980, series E bonds were issued. The original 10-year maturity period of series E has been extended to 40 years for bonds issued before December 1965 and to 30 years for bonds issued after November 1965. Both paper series EE and E bonds were issued at a discount. Electronic bonds are issued at face value. Paper savings bonds are no longer sold at financial institutions. Owners of paper series EE bonds can convert them to electronic bonds. These converted electronic bonds do not retain the denomination listed on the paper certificate but are posted at their purchase price with accrued interest.

Series H and HH Bonds

Series H and HH bonds are issued at face value. Interest is paid twice a year and must be reported when received. Series H bonds have a maturity period of 30 years. Series HH bonds were first offered in 1980 and were last offered in August 2004. Series H bonds are treated the same way as series HH. Series HH bonds mature at 20 years. The last series H bonds matured in 2009, and the last series HH bonds will mature in 2024.

Series I Bonds

Series I bonds were first offered in 1998. These are inflation-indexed bonds issued at their face amount with a maturity period of 30 years. The face value plus all accrued interest is payable at maturity.

If the taxpayer uses the cash method of reporting income, he or she can report the interest on his or her series EE, series E, and series I bonds using one of the following two methods:

> ➤ Method 1: Postpone reporting the interest earned until either the year in which the bonds were cashed or disposed of, or the year the bonds mature, whichever is earliest.
> ➤ Method 2: Choose to report the increase in redemption value as interest earned each year.

The taxpayer must use the same method for all series EE, series E, and series I bonds they own. If method 2 is not used, method 1 must be used. If the taxpayer wants to change from method 1 to method 2, the taxpayer does not need the permission of the IRS. However, if the taxpayer wants to change from method 2 to method 1, permission must be requested by attaching a statement with the following information to the tax return for the year of the change:

> ➤ "131" printed or typed at the top of the statement.
> ➤ The taxpayer's name and Social Security number written beneath "131."
> ➤ The year the change was requested (beginning and ending dates).
> ➤ Identification and information from the savings bonds for which the change is being requested.

- The statement includes the following:
  - All interest received on any bonds acquired during or after the year of change when it is realized upon disposition, redemption, or final maturity, whichever is earliest.
  - All interest on the bonds acquired before the year of the change when the interest is realized upon disposition, redemption, or final maturity; whichever is earliest, with the exception of interest already reported in prior years.

Taxpayers may file an automatic extension on their tax returns to give them more time to file the paperwork. On the statement, the following should be typed: "Filed pursuant to section 301.9100-2(b)." To qualify for the extension, the original tax return should have been filed by the required due date (normally April 15th) based on the type of tax return being filed. Review Publication 550.

Señor 1040 Says: Interest on U.S. savings bonds is exempt from state and local taxes. Form 1099-INT will indicate the amount of interest that is earned for U.S. savings bonds in box 3.

Municipal Bonds

State and local governments issue municipal bonds to provide funding for capital improvement projects. Municipal bonds are not taxable by the federal government. Not all states or localities tax municipal bond interest income. Some states and localities tax all municipal bond interest, while others tax municipal bond interest income from other states or localities only.

A mortgage revenue bond (MRB) is issued by a local housing authority to finance mortgages for qualifying taxpayers. Those who qualify are normally first-time homebuyers with low income. Investors often prefer these bonds since they are tax-free and are secured by the monthly mortgage payments. Every state has MRBs, and they are limited by the minimum state issuance. The home's purchase price cannot exceed a certain percentage of the area's average purchase price.

State or Local Government Obligations

Interest received on a state or local government obligation is generally not taxable. The issuer should tell the receiver if the interest is taxable or not and then give the receiver a periodic statement showing the tax treatment of the obligation. If the obligation was invested through a trust, a fund, or other organization, that issuer should provide that information.

Even if the interest may not be subject to income tax, the receiver may have to report capital gains or losses when the obligation is sold.

Line 2b Taxable Interest

Interest is a cost created by those who lend money (lenders) that is charged to the people they lent money to (borrowers). A taxpayer will pay interest whenever he or she borrows money and will earn money whenever he or she lends or deposits money, such as into a bank account.

Certain interest is taxable income if it is credited to the taxpayer's account and can be withdrawn. Interest is typically not calculated based on the original amount of borrowed money (called the principal) but is instead usually determined by multiplying a predetermined percentage point by the total amount of money currently owed to the lender by the borrower. For example, John borrowed $5,000 at a 5% interest rate. Although his principal was $5,000, after making several payments, he now owes $4,365, making his interest payment for the month 5% of $4,365, or $218.25.

Taxable Interest

Taxable interest is reported using Schedule B and includes interest received from bank accounts, loans made to others, and interest from other sources. The taxpayer could be the payer or the recipient of the interest. Examples of sources of interest are as follows:

  ➢ Banks.
  ➢ Credit unions.
  ➢ Government entities (federal and state).
  ➢ Certificates of deposit (CDs).
  ➢ Life insurance.
  ➢ Installment sales.

U.S. Obligations

Interest on U.S. obligations (U.S. Treasury bills, notes, or bonds) is taxable at the federal level, but exempt from taxation in most states. Make sure to know if your state taxes the interest.

Interest and Community Property States

If a taxpayer lives in a community property state and receives an interest or dividend distribution, one-half of the distribution is considered to be received by each spouse. If the taxpayer and spouse file MFS, each must report one-half of the distribution on their separate returns. If the distribution is not considered community property under state law, each taxpayer must report his or her separate distributions.

Example: Johanna and Jacob are filing MFS, and they have a joint money market account. Under certain states law, half the income belongs to Johanna and the other half belongs to Jacob. Each would report half of the income.

Foreign Accounts and Trust Requirements

In a global economy, many people in the United States have foreign financial accounts. The law requires owners of foreign financial accounts to report their accounts to the U.S. Treasury Department, even if the accounts don't generate any taxable income. Account owners need to report accounts by the April due date following the calendar year that they own a foreign financial account.

The U.S. government requires individuals to report foreign financial accounts because foreign financial institutions may not be subject to the same reporting requirements as domestic ones.

Reporting Requirements

The Bank Secrecy Act requires a U.S. taxpayer who owns a foreign bank account, brokerage account, mutual fund, unit trust, or other financial account to file a *Report of Foreign Bank and Financial Accounts (FBAR)* if the taxpayer has any of the following:

1. Financial interest in, signature authority, or other authority over one or more accounts in a foreign country, and
2. The aggregate value of all foreign financial accounts exceeds $10,000 at any time during the calendar year.

A U.S. person is a citizen or resident of the United States or any domestic legal entity such as a partnership, corporation, limited liability company, estate, or trust. A foreign country includes any area outside the United States or outside the following U.S. territories and possessions:

➢ Northern Mariana Islands
➢ District of Columbia
➢ American Samoa
➢ Guam
➢ Puerto Rico
➢ United States Virgin Islands
➢ Trust Territories of the Pacific Islands
➢ Indian lands, as defined in the Indian Gaming Regulatory Act

How to Report

Taxpayers required to report their foreign accounts should file the FBAR electronically using the BSA E-Filing System. The FBAR is due April 15. If April 15 falls on a Saturday, Sunday, or legal holiday, the FBAR is due the next business day. Taxpayers don't file the FBAR with individual, business, trust, or estate tax returns.

If two people jointly own a foreign financial account or if several people each own a partial interest in an account, then each person has a financial interest in that account. Each person must report the entire value of the account on an FBAR.

Spouses do not need to file a separate FBAR if they complete and sign Form 114a, Record of Authorization to Electronically File FBARs, and:

1. All reportable financial accounts are jointly owned with the filing spouse, and
2. The filing spouse reports the jointly owned accounts on a timely-filed FBAR.

Otherwise, both spouses must file separate FBARs, and each spouse must report the entire value of the jointly owned accounts. The e-filing system will not allow both spouses' signatures on the same electronic form. Spouses need to complete Form 114a to designate which one will file the FBAR. The Form 114a is not submitted with the FBAR; it should be kept with other financial and tax records.

Generally, a child is responsible for filing their own FBAR. If a child can't file their own FBAR for any reason, such as age, the child's parent or guardian must file it for them. If the child can't sign their FBAR, a parent or guardian must sign it.

How to Calculate the Greatest Account Value of Foreign Financial Accounts

Those filing the FBAR need to reasonably figure and report the greatest value of currency or non-monetary assets in their accounts during the calendar year. The taxpayer may rely on their periodic account statements if the statements fairly show the greatest account value during the year.

Taxpayers figure the greatest value in the currency of the account, then convert that value into U.S. dollars using the exchange rate on the last day of the calendar year. The taxpayer may use another valid exchange rate and give the source of the rate, if there's no Treasury Financial Management Service rate available. For example, someone would typically value an account located in Mexico in pesos. The taxpayer would figure the greatest value of the account in pesos and then convert it into U.S. dollars. See IRS FBAR Reference Guide for more information.

Personal Loans

A personal loan that a taxpayer is collecting interest on is a taxable event. For example, Samuel purchased a house for his cousin Samantha and is charging her 2.5% interest on the price of the house. Samuel will need to create an amortization schedule to track that he is getting paid and reporting the interest earned from Samantha. Samantha is able to report the interest paid to Samuel on her Form 1040, Schedule A, if she is able to itemize. See Publication 550. Itemized deductions are discussed in Itemized Deductions.

Part 2 Review Questions

To obtain the maximum benefit from this chapter, LTP recommends that you complete each of the following questions, and then compare them to the answers with feedback that immediately follow. Under governing self-study standards, vendors are required to present review questions intermittently throughout each self-study course.

These questions and explanations are not part of the final examination and will not be graded by LTP.

IP2.1
Which of the following is not the best description of constructively received income?

a. Amanda received an interest payment on December 31 but did not put it into the bank until Jan 2.
b. Andres earned money from his employer for the prior year. He did not pick the money up until the following year.
c. Karina received an early penalty withdrawal that was substantially less than what she would have earned if she left the money in the account until maturity.
d. Kevin had some bond payments credited to his account on January 1. He did not withhold the payment until April 15.

IP2.2
Where would interest earned be reported on Form 1099INT?

a. Box 1
b. Box 2
c. Box 4
d. Box 8

IP2.3
Where would exempt interest earned be reported on Form 1099INT?

   a. Box 1
   b. Box 2
   c. Box 6
   d. Box 8

IP2.4
Which of the following best describes how U.S. obligations are taxed?

   a. U.S. obligations are taxed on the federal and state.
   b. U.S. obligations are not taxed on the federal and state.
   c. U.S. obligations are taxed on the federal return and may not be taxable on the state return.
   d. U.S. obligations are not taxed on the federal but are taxed by the state.

IP2.5
Josie has an annuity contract that was sold prior to the maturity rate. Which of the following best describes her situation?

   a. Josie will have no tax consequence.
   b. Josie will have to pay tax on the accumulated interest.
   c. Josie will receive a new annuity contract.
   d. Josie will need to purchase an insurance contract for her protection.

IP2.6
Kay and Mark are married and live in a community property state. They want to file their returns separately. How would they report their $1,000 earned interest?

   a. Kay would report 100% of the interest since her name is first.
   b. Mark would report 100% of the interest since his name is first.
   c. Since Mark's name is first, he would report 60%, and Kay would report 40%.
   d. Each would report 50% on their tax return.

IP2.7
Which of the following does the individual taxpayer need to do regarding federal tax-exempt interest?

   a. Report the interest and pay tax.
   b. Report the interest and pay no tax.
   c. Does not need to report the interest.
   d. Report the interest only on the state return.

IP2.8
Original issue discount (OID) is a form for which of the following?

   a. Interest
   b. Dividend
   c. Non-dividend distribution
   d. Nontaxable interest

IP2.9
Which of the following is not a government debt security?

    a. Series EE and E bonds
    b. Series I bonds
    c. Series H bonds
    d. Series A bonds

IP2.10
Which of the following is the way to report the interest earned on a bond?

    a. Pay quarterly as interest accrues.
    b. Pay monthly as interest accrues.
    c. Pay yearly as interest accrues.
    d. Pay yearly on July 1 as interest accrues.

IP2.11
Which of the following is the way to report the interest earned on a bond?

    a. Pay quarterly as interest accrues.
    b. Pay monthly as interest accrues.
    c. Pay when the bonds have been redeemed.
    d. Pay yearly on July 1 as interest accrues.

Part 2 Review Questions Answers

IP2.1
Which of the following is not the best description of constructively received income?

    a. Amanda received an interest payment on December 31 but did not put it into the bank until Jan 2.
    b. Andres earned money from his employer for the prior year. He did not pick the money up until the following year.
    c. Karina received an early penalty withdrawal that was substantially less than what she would have earned if she left the money in the account until maturity.
    d. Kevin had some bond payments credited to his account on January 1. He did not withhold the payment until April 15.

Feedback: Review section *Constructively Received.*

IP2.2
Where would interest earned be reported on Form 1099INT?

    a. Box 1
    b. Box 2
    c. Box 4
    d. Box 8

Feedback: Review section *Form 1099-INT.*

IP2.3

Where would exempt interest earned be reported on Form 1099INT?

    a. Box 1
    b. Box 2
    c. Box 6
    d. Box 8

Feedback: Review section *Form 1099-INT.*

IP2.4

Which of the following best describes how U.S. obligations are taxed?

    a. U.S. obligations are taxed on the federal and state.
    b. U.S. obligations are not taxed on the federal and state.
    c. U.S. obligations are taxed on the federal return and may not be taxable on the state return.
    d. U.S. obligations are not taxed on the federal but are taxed by the state.

Feedback: Review section *U.S. Obligations.*

IP2.5

Josie has an annuity contract that was sold prior to the maturity rate. Which of the following best describes her situation?

    a. Josie will have no tax consequence.
    b. Josie will have to pay tax on the accumulated interest.
    c. Josie will receive a new annuity contract.
    d. Josie will need to purchase an insurance contract for her protection.

Feedback: Review section *Miscellaneous Types of Interest.*

IP2.6

Kay and Mark are married and live in a community property state. They want to file their returns separately. How would they report their $1,000 earned interest?

    a. Kay would report 100% of the interest since her name is first.
    b. Mark would report 100% of the interest since his name is first.
    c. Since Mark's name is first, he would report 60%, and Kay would report 40%.
    d. Each would report 50% on their tax return.

Feedback: Review section *Interest and Community Property States.*

IP2.7

Which of the following does the individual taxpayer need to do regarding federal tax-exempt interest?

    a. Report the interest and pay tax.
    b. Report the interest and pay no tax.
    c. Does not need to report the interest.
    d. Report the interest only on the state return.

Feedback: Review section *Tax-Exempt Interest.*

IP2.8
Original issue discount (OID) is a form for which of the following?

    a. Interest
    b. Dividend
    c. Non-dividend distribution
    d. Nontaxable interest

Feedback: Review section *When to Report Interest Income.*

IP2.9
Which of the following is not a government debt security?

    a. Series EE and E bonds
    b. Series I bonds
    c. Series H bonds
    d. Series A bonds

Feedback: Review section *Government Bonds.*

IP2.10
Which of the following is the way to report the interest earned on a bond?

    a. Pay quarterly as interest accrues.
    b. Pay monthly as interest accrues.
    c. Pay yearly as interest accrues.
    d. Pay yearly on July 1 as interest accrues.

Feedback: Review section *Government Bonds.*

IP2.11
Which of the following is the way to report the interest earned on a bond?

    a. Pay quarterly as interest accrues.
    b. Pay monthly as interest accrues.
    c. Pay when the bonds have been redeemed.
    d. Pay yearly on July 1 as interest accrues.

Feedback: Review section *Government Bonds*

Part 3 Dividends

Dividends are a share of the profits generated by a company that can be paid in money, stock, stock rights, other property, or services; they can also be paid by a corporation, mutual fund, partnership, estate, trust, or association that is taxed as a corporation. Distributions are benefits from a closely held entity such as the S-corporation, Partnership, Limited Liability Company, and Trusts.

Dividends can be paid in the form of additional stock, which is sometimes referred to as a reinvested dividend. These are fully taxable to the recipient and must be reported, although some amounts reported as dividends may be taxed at different rates.

Form 1099-DIV: Reporting Dividend Income

Form 1099-DIV

As with all forms, make sure the taxpayer's name, address, and TIN are correct. The following is just for informational purposes about what each box on the Form 1099-DIV reports. The most common entries on Form 1099-DIV are: Box 1a, 1b, 2a, 3, 5, 7, and 11.

Box 1a, Total ordinary dividends: Included are money market funds, net short-term capital gains from mutual funds, and other distributions on stock. Reinvested dividends and section 404(k) dividends paid directly from the corporation are taxable. Report this amount on Form 1040, page 2, line 3b.

Box 1b, Qualified dividends: Shows the portion in box 1a that meets the IRS criteria for a lower capital gains tax rate.

Box 2a, Total (long-term) capital gain distributions: Shows total capital gain distributions from a regulated investment company or real estate investment trust. Amount shown in box 2a is reported on Schedule D, line 13.

Box 2b, Unrecaptured section 1250 gain: From certain depreciable real property. This box shows the amount in box 2a that is unrecaptured section 1250 gain from depreciable property.

Box 2c, Section 1202 gain: Shows any amount in box 2a that is a section 1202 gain from certain small business stocks.

Box 2d, Collectibles (28%) gain: Shows any amount included in box 2a that has a 28% rate gain from sales or exchanges of collectibles. Apart from this fact, this concept is beyond the scope of this course.

Box 3, Nondividend distributions: Nondividend distributions are shown here, if determinable.

Box 4, Federal income tax withheld: This box shows the amount of federal income tax withheld. Federal taxes are usually withheld when backup withholding is required.

Box 5, Section 199A Dividends: Shows the section 199A dividends paid to the taxpayer. This amount is included in box 1a.

Box 6, Investment Expenses: Shows the taxpayer's reported pro rata share of certain amounts deductible by a non-public offering from a regulated investment company (RIC) in computing the taxable income. Do not include any investment expense in box 1b.

Box 7, Foreign tax paid: Shows foreign tax paid on dividends and other distributions on stock. Report this amount in U.S. dollars.

Box 8, Foreign country or U.S. possession: Lists the foreign country or U.S. possession to which the foreign taxes were paid. There should be no entry if the investment company paid the tax for the funds.

Box 9, Cash liquidation distributions: Shows cash distributed as part of a liquidation.

Box 10, Noncash liquidation distributions: Shows noncash distributions made as part of a liquidation. Place the fair market value as of the date of distribution.

Box 11, Exempt-interest dividends: Shows exempt-interest dividends paid during the calendar year from a mutual fund or other regulated investment company. Include specified private activity bond interest in box 11.

Box 12, Specified private activity bond interest dividends: This box shows exempt-interest dividends paid by a RIC on specified private activity bonds to the extent that the dividends are attributable to interest on bonds received by the RIC.

Box 13-15, State Boxes: Shows state information depending upon the state the taxpayer lives in.

Dividends and other distributions that earn $10 or more are reported to the taxpayer on Form 1099-DIV by the payee. If the taxpayer's ordinary dividends are more than $1,500, the taxpayer would complete Schedule B, Part III, in addition to receiving Form 1099-DIV. Ordinary dividends stated in box 1a are reported on Form 1040, line 3b. Qualified dividends are reported on line 3a of Form 1040. The amount reported on 1b is a portion of the amount shown in box 1a.

Form 1040, line 3a, Qualified Dividends

Qualified dividends are taxed at the capital gains rate for the taxpayer. Qualified dividends are included with ordinary dividends on Form 1040, page 2, line 3b. Qualified dividends are shown in box 1b of Form 1099-DIV. The rates are 0, 15 or 20% based on taxpayer's income.

0% Qualifying Dividends Tax Rate for tax year 2022

$0 to $41,675	Single or married filing separately
$0 to $83,350	Married filing jointly or Qualifying Surviving Spouse
$0 to $55,800	Head of household

0% Qualifying Dividends Tax Rate for tax year 2023

$0 to $44,625	Single or married filing separately
$0 to $89,250	Married filing jointly or Qualifying Surviving Spouse
$0 to $59,750	Head of household

15% Qualifying Dividends Tax Rate for tax year 2022

$41,676 to $459,750   Single
$41,676 to $258,600   Married filing separately
$83,351 to $ 517,200   Married filing jointly or Qualifying Surviving Spouse
$55,801 to $488,500   Head of household

15% Qualifying Dividends Tax Rate for tax year 2023

$44,626 to $492,300   Single
$44,626 to $276,900   Married filing separately
$89,251 to $ 553,850   Married filing jointly or Qualifying Surviving Spouse
$59,751 to $523,050   Head of household

20% Qualifying Dividends Tax Rate for 2022

$459,750 or more   Single
$258,601 or more   Married filing separately
$517,201 or more   Married filing jointly or Qualifying Surviving Spouse
$488,501 or more   Head of household

20% Qualifying Dividends Tax Rate for 2023

$492,300 or more   Single
$276,900 or more   Married filing separately
$553,850 or more   Married filing jointly or Qualifying Surviving Spouse
$523,050 or more   Head of household

Form 1040, line 3b, Ordinary Dividends

Ordinary dividends are the most common type of dividend distributions and are taxed as ordinary income (as are mutual fund dividends) at the same tax rate as wages and other ordinary income of the taxpayer. All dividends are considered ordinary unless they are specifically classified as qualified dividends. Dividends received from common or preferred stock are considered ordinary dividends and are reported in box 1a of Form 1099-DIV. Ordinary dividends received on common or preferred stock can be reinvested and taxed as ordinary income.

Dividends That Are Really Interest

Certain distributions that are often reported as "dividends" are actually interest income. The taxpayer will report as interest any received dividends from deposits, or shared accounts, from the following sources:

> ➢ Credit unions.
> ➢ Cooperative banks.
> ➢ Domestic building and loan associations.
> ➢ Federal savings and loan associations.
> ➢ Mutual savings banks.

These dividends will be reported as interest in box 1 of Form 1099-INT. Generally, amounts received from money market funds are dividends and should not be reported as interest.

Dividends Used to Buy More Stock

The corporation in which the taxpayer owns stock may have a dividend reinvestment plan. This plan allows the taxpayer to choose whether to use the dividends to purchase more shares of stock or receive the dividends in cash. If the reinvestment plan is chosen, the taxpayer still reports the dividends as income.

The taxpayer may choose to use dividends to purchase additional shares of stock if the corporation has such a plan. The plan is called a "dividend reinvestment plan." If the taxpayer chooses to have the dividends reinvested, the taxpayer is still required to report the dividends as income in the year they are received. The amount of the dividend is then considered part of the purchase price of the stock. Taxpayers should be reminded to keep records of reinvested dividends to help establish an accurate cost basis for their stocks at the time of purchase. "Reinvested dividend" is not a tax term; it is a phrase that is used by investors to refer to dividends earned by reinvesting dividend distributions to purchase more stock instead of receiving money.

Money Market Funds

Income received from money market funds is considered dividend income. Money market funds are a kind of mutual fund and should not be confused with money market accounts that one may get at the local bank, which report the income earned as interest, not dividends. A mutual fund is a regulated investment company generally created by "pooling" funds of investors to allow them to take advantage of a diversity of investments and professional management.

A distribution received from a mutual fund may be an ordinary dividend, a capital gain distribution, an exempt-interest dividend, a nontaxable return of capital, or a combination of two or more of these types of distributions. The fund company reports the distributions on Form 1099-DIV or a similar statement that indicates the type of distributions received.

If a mutual fund or another regulated investment company declares a dividend, including any exempt-interest dividend or capital gain distribution in the last quarter of the tax year, the dividend is considered paid in the year that the dividend was declared.

Capital Gains Distributions

Capital gains distributions (CGD) received as part of dividends from a mutual fund or real estate investment trusts (REIT) are taxed on Schedule D. These distributions are found in box 2a of Form 1099-DIV. These dividends should be considered long-term regardless of the length of time the taxpayer owned the share in the regulated investment companies more commonly known as real estate investment trusts.

Capital gains distributions are paid to the taxpayer by brokerage firms, mutual funds, and investment trusts. The capital gains distributions from mutual funds are long-term capital gains regardless of how long the taxpayer owned the stock. Distributions of net-realized short-term capital gains are reported on Form 1099-DIV as ordinary dividends.

Nontaxable Dividends

Nontaxable dividends are a return of a shareholder's original investment. These distributions are not treated the same as ordinary dividends or capital gain distributions. Nondividend distributions reduce the taxpayer's basis in the stock. Return of capital distributions are not taxable until the taxpayer's remaining basis (investment) is reduced to zero. The basis of the stock has been reduced to zero when the taxpayer receives a distribution, and then it is reported as a capital gain. The holding period determines the reporting of short-term or long-term capital gain.

Return of Capital

A return of capital is a distribution that is not paid out of the earnings and profits of a corporation. It is a return of the taxpayer's investment in the stock of the company. The taxpayer will receive Form 1099-DIV or another statement from the corporation showing what part of the distribution is a return of capital. If the taxpayer does not receive such a statement, he will report the distribution as an ordinary dividend.

Liquidating Distributions

Liquidating distributions, also known as liquidating dividends, are distributions received during a partial or complete liquidation of a corporation. These distributions are, at least in part, one form of a "return of capital" and may be paid in two or more installments.

Any liquidating dividend received is not taxable until the basis of the stock has been recovered. However, the basis of the stock, which earned the right to the dividends, must be reduced by the amount of the dividends. After the basis of the stock is reduced to zero, the liquidating dividend must be reported as a capital gain.

Exempt-Interest Dividends

Exempt-interest dividends received from a regulated investment company or mutual fund are not included in taxable income. Exempt-interest dividends are reported on Form 1099-DIV, box 10. The taxpayer should receive a notice from the mutual fund giving information concerning the dividends the taxpayer received. The exempt-interest dividends should be shown on the return (if the taxpayer is required to file) as tax-exempt interest on line 2a of Form 1040.

Specified private activity bonds that have paid tax-exempt interest may be subject to alternative minimum tax. The exempt-interest dividends subject to alternative minimum tax should be shown on Form 1099-DIV, box 12.

Dividends on Insurance Policies

Insurance policy dividends that the insurer keeps and uses to pay premiums are not taxable. However, the taxpayer must report the interest that is paid or credited on dividends left with the insurance company as taxable income.

Dividends on Veterans' Insurance Policies

Dividends received on veterans' insurance policies and ones that were left with the Department of Veterans Affairs are not taxable.

Patronage Dividends

Patronage dividends received as money from a cooperative organization are included as income. Do not include the following patronage dividends as income:

➢ Property bought for personal use.
➢ Capital assets or depreciable property bought for use in business. If the dividend is more than the adjusted basis of the asset, it is reported as excess income.

Form 1040, line 4: IRA Distributions

Any money received from a traditional IRA is a distribution and must be reported as income in the year it was received. On Form 1040, report the nontaxable distribution on line 4 and report the taxable distributions on line 4b. Distributions from a traditional IRA are taxed as ordinary income. Not all distributions will be taxable if the taxpayer made nondeductible contributions. Complete Form 8606 to report the taxable and nontaxable portions of the IRA distribution.

The following distributions are not subject to the early withdrawal penalty:

➢ A rollover from one IRA to another.
➢ Tax-free withdrawals of contributions.
➢ The return of nondeductible contributions.

These funds will be reported as received, but the taxable portion will be reduced or eliminated.

Normal IRA distributions are usually fully taxable because contributions to the IRA account were fully tax-deferred when they were originally contributed. Form 5329, *Additional Taxes on Qualified Plans*, is not required if the early withdrawal penalty is the only reason for using the form. This penalty is in addition to any tax due on the distributions, though some exceptions to it exist.

Form 1040, line 5a and Line 5b, Pensions and Annuities

A distribution is a payment received by taxpayers from their pension or annuity. If taxpayers contributed "after-tax" dollars to their pension or annuity plan, they could exclude part of each annuity payment from income as a recovery of their cost. This tax-free part of the payment is figured when their annuity starts and remains the same each year, even if the amount of the payment changes. Pension is a contract for a fixed sum to be paid regularly following retirement from service. The rest of each payment is taxable. If the taxpayer wants to have taxes withheld from their pensions or annuities, they will use W-4P. The tax-free portion of the payment is calculated using one of the following methods:

General Rule

This method is generally used to determine the tax-free treatment of pension and annuity income from nonqualified plans.

The taxpayer must use the general rule if:

1. The taxpayer receives pension and annuity payments from a nonqualified plan (such as a private annuity, a purchased commercial annuity, or a nonqualified employee plan).

2. The taxpayer is age 75 or older on the annuity starting date, and the annuity payments are guaranteed for at least five years.

Simplified Method

Using the simplified method, the taxpayer will figure the tax-free part of each monthly annuity payment by dividing the cost by the total number of expected monthly payments. For an annuity that is payable for the life of the annuitant, this number is based on the annuitant's age on the annuity starting date and is determined from a table. For any other annuity, this is the number of monthly annuity payments under the contract. If the taxpayer received a pension or annuity payment from a qualified plan, and he/she is not able to use the general rule, the taxpayer must use the simplified method.

Guaranteed Payments

The annuity contract provides guaranteed payments based on the investment amount and may be payable even if the taxpayer and the survivor annuitants do not live to receive the minimum payment.

Form 1040, line 6a: Social Security Benefits

The Social Security system was designed to provide supplemental monthly benefits to taxpayers who contributed to the system. It is indexed for inflation, provides Medicare benefits, disability, and certain death insurance, and is reported on Form SSA-1099 based on the amount listed in Box 5 of W-2. Taxpayers also have the option to have federal taxes withheld from Social Security. See IRC Sec 86 and Publication 915.

When a taxpayer has Social Security from other countries, such as Canada, that income could be taxable in the United States. Remember the IRS rule "gross income means all income from whatever source derived." However, if the social security was not taxed in Canada, it may not be taxable in the United States. See IRC Sec 61(a).

Social Security benefits are not taxable if income does not exceed these base amounts:

➢ $25,000: If Single, Head of Household, or Qualifying widow(er).
➢ $25,000: If Married Filing Separately and he or she lived apart from spouse the entire year.
➢ $32,000: If Married Filing Jointly.
➢ $0: If Married Filing Separately and lived with spouse at some time during the year.

Form 1040, line 6b: Taxable Amount

50% taxable: If the income plus half of the Social Security benefits is more than the above stated base amounts, up to half of the benefits must be included as taxable income. The following are base amounts for the applicable filing statuses:

➢ $25,000–$34,000: Single, Head of Household, Qualifying widow(er), and Married Filing Separately and lived apart from spouse
➢ $32,000–$44,000: Married Filing Jointly
➢ $0: Married Filing Separately and lived with spouse

85% taxable: For taxpayers who file MFS and live with their spouse, 85% of their benefits will always be taxable. If the income plus half the benefits is more than the following adjusted base amounts, up to 85% of the benefits must be included as taxable income.

> ➤ $34,000: Single, Head of Household, or Qualifying widow(er)
> ➤ $34,000: Married Filing Separately and lived apart from spouse for entire year
> ➤ $44,000: Married Filing Jointly
> ➤ $0: Married Filing Separately and lived with spouse at any time during the tax year

Most taxpayers assume they will not be taxed if their income falls below the base amount, but they fail to include tax-exempt interest or half of their Social Security income when determining the amount.

Example: Napoleon and Ilene file a joint return. Both are over the age of 65 and have received Social Security benefits during the current tax year. In January, Napoleon's Form SSA-1099 showed benefits of $7,500 in box 5. Ilene's Form SSA-1099 showed a net benefit of $3,500 in box 5. Napoleon received a taxable pension of $20,800 and interest income of $500, which was tax exempt. Their benefits are not taxable for the current year because their income is not more than the base amount of $32,000.

Any benefit repayments made during the current year would be subtracted from the gross benefits received. It does not matter whether the repayment was for a benefit received in the current year or in an earlier year; it only matters what year the repayment was received.

Social Security and Equivalent Railroad Retirement Benefits (Tier 1)

The taxpayer should receive Form SSA-1099 from the SSA, which reports the total amount of Social Security benefits paid in box 3. Box 4 of the form shows the amount of any benefits that were repaid from a prior year. Railroad retirement benefits that should be treated as Social Security benefits are reported on Form RRB-1099.

Railroad Retirement Benefits

Railroad Retirement Benefits (RRB) is a benefits program that began before Social Security; its recipients are not covered under Social Security because they receive more money than they would have under the SSA. Tier 1 benefits are reported to the taxpayer on Form RRB 1099, are equivalent to Social Security benefits, and they are treated as such. Tier 1 benefits are reported to the IRS on Form 1040, Line 6b.

Tier 2 benefits are above the Social Security equivalent and are treated like pensions, allowing retirees to receive both tier 1 and tier 2 benefits. As with other pensions, the "cost" they invested is recovered tax-free. It is usually necessary to use the simplified method to figure the taxable portion of tier 2 benefits. To use the *Simplified Method Worksheet*, the tax preparer must know the age of the taxpayer, how many payments were received in the tax year, and how much has been recovered tax-free since 1986. When the taxpayer has recovered his or her cost, the entire tier 2 benefit becomes taxable.

The difference between Form RRB 1099 for tier 1 and tier 2 is that the form for tier 1 is known simply as Form RRB 1099. Tier 2 is a retirement; therefore, it has the letter "R" following the 1099 (Form RRB 1099-R).

Repayment of COVID-19 Related Distributions from Retirement Accounts and Form 8915-F

Form 8915-F was turned into a forever form in 2022. This means Form 8915-F will not become 8915-G for 2023, as it will remain 8915-F. As you see in the picture below, there are four different boxes to correlate the disaster to the year the disaster will be claimed on the return.

Portion of Form 8915-F

For tax year 2022, there is a total of 88 major disasters throughout the U.S. per FEMA (Federal Emergency Management Agency).

Part 3 Review Questions

To obtain the maximum benefit from this chapter, LTP recommends that you complete each of the following questions, and then compare them to the answers with feedback that immediately follow. Under governing self-study standards, vendors are required to present review questions intermittently throughout each self-study course.

These questions and explanations are not part of the final examination and will not be graded by LTP.

IP3.1
Which of the following is a form of dividend income?

    a. Qualified dividends
    b. Dividends from a credit union
    c. Dividends from mutual funds
    d. Dividends from a partnership

IP3.2
Which of the following is a form of dividend income?

    a. Ordinary dividends
    b. Dividends from a credit union
    c. Reinvested dividends
    d. Dividends from a partnership

IP3.3
Jacob's daughter Peyton inherited some money from her great grandma. Peyton's interest earned this year was $2,210. Which of the following is the best answer for the scenario?

    a. Peyton will file her own tax return since the amount earned is more than $2,200.
    b. Jacob can file Form 8814 and report Peyton's earned interest.
    c. Jacob and Peyton need to decide which is the lowest tax consequence for the two of them and that is who files the interest earned.
    d. Peyton does not need to file a return since it is lower than her filing requirements.

IP3.4
Ordinary dividend income is taxed at what rate?

    a. The taxpayer's ordinary income tax rate
    b. 15%
    c. 25%
    d. 10% penalty plus the ordinary rate of the taxpayer

IP3.5
Capital gain distributions from a mutual fund occur when the fund company has liquidated a portion of the stock. Where is the distribution found on Form 1099-DIV?

    a. Box 2
    b. Box 2a
    c. Box 1
    d. Box 4

IP3.6
Which of the following best describes the difference between ordinary and qualified dividends?

    a. The way they are taxed
    b. There is no difference
    c. The names are different
    d. Ordinary dividends are taxed at 15%

IP3.7
Which of the following best describes reinvested dividends?

    a. Allows the taxpayer to buy more shares of stock in the corporation
    b. Allows the taxpayer to sell more shares of stock in the corporation
    c. Allows the taxpayer to buy more dividends of the corporation
    d. Allows the taxpayer to sell shares to their family

IP3.8
Which of the following is reported to the taxpayer as a dividend but is actually interest?

    a. Dividends received through a partnership
    b. Capital gain distribution
    c. Credit union dividends
    d. Interest on a CD

IP3.9

Which of the following best describes the shareholder's return of their original investment?

    a. Nondividend distribution
    b. Reinvested dividends
    c. Nominee income
    d. Capital gain

IP3.10

Which of the following best describes liquidating dividends?

    a. Distributions received during a partial or complete liquidation of a corporation
    b. Distributions received during a partial or complete liquidation of a trust
    c. Distributions received during a partial or complete liquidation of a partnership
    d. Distributions received during a partial or complete liquidation of an MFJ return

Part 3 Review Questions Answers

IP3.1

Which of the following is a form of dividend income?

    a. Qualified dividends
    b. Dividends from a credit union
    c. Dividends from mutual funds
    d. Dividends from a partnership

Feedback: Review section *Dividend Income.*

IP3.2

Which of the following is a form of dividend income?

    a. Ordinary dividends
    b. Dividends from a credit union
    c. Reinvested dividends
    d. Dividends from a partnership

Feedback: Review section *Dividend Income.*

IP3.3

Jacob's daughter Peyton inherited some money from her great grandma. Peyton's interest earned this year was $2,210. Which of the following is the best answer for the scenario?

    a. Peyton will file her own tax return since the amount earned is more than $2,200.
    b. Jacob can file Form 8814 and report Peyton's earned interest.
    c. Jacob and Peyton need to decide which is the lowest tax consequence for the two of them and that is who files the interest earned.
    d. Peyton does not need to file a return since it is lower than her filing requirements.

Feedback: Review section *Child's Interest and Dividend Income.*

IP3.4
Ordinary dividend income is taxed at what rate?

    a. **The taxpayer's ordinary income tax rate**
    b. 15%
    c. 25%
    d. 10% penalty plus the ordinary rate of the taxpayer

Feedback: Review section *Form 1040, line 3, Ordinary Dividends.*

IP3.5
Capital gain distributions from a mutual fund occur when the fund company has liquidated a portion of the stock. Where is the distribution found on Form 1099-DIV?

    a. Box 2
    b. **Box 2a**
    c. Box 1
    d. Box 4

Feedback: Review section *Capital Gains Distribution.*

IP3.6
Which of the following best describes the difference between ordinary and qualified dividends?

    a. **The way they are taxed**
    b. There is no difference
    c. The names are different
    d. Ordinary dividends are taxed at 15%

Feedback: Review section *Form 1040, line 3, Ordinary Dividends.*

IP3.7
Which of the following best describes reinvested dividends?

    a. **Allows the taxpayer to buy more shares of stock in the corporation**
    b. Allows the taxpayer to sell more shares of stock in the corporation
    c. Allows the taxpayer to buy more dividends of the corporation
    d. Allows the taxpayer to sell shares to their family

Feedback: Review section *Dividends Used to Buy More Stock.*

IP3.8
Which of the following is reported to the taxpayer as a dividend but is actually interest?

    a. Dividends received through a partnership
    b. Capital gain distribution
    c. **Credit union dividends**
    d. Interest on a CD

Feedback: Review section *Dividends That Are Really Interest.*

IP3.9

Which of the following best describes the shareholder's return of their original investment?

    a. Nondividend distribution
    b. Reinvested dividends
    c. Nominee income
    d. Capital gain

Feedback: Review section *Nontaxable Dividends.*

IP3.10

Which of the following best describes liquidating dividends?

    a. Distributions received during a partial or complete liquidation of a corporation
    b. Distributions received during a partial or complete liquidation of a trust
    c. Distributions received during a partial or complete liquidation of a partnership
    d. Distributions received during a partial or complete liquidation of an MFJ return

Feedback: Review section *Liquidating Dividends.*

Part 4 Schedule 1: Additional Income

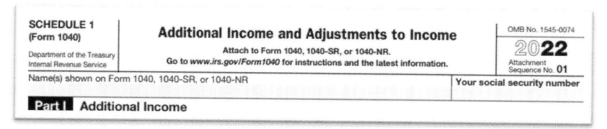

Portion of 2022 Schedule 1

Schedule 1, line 1: Taxable Refunds

If a taxpayer claims state income taxes were paid as an itemized deduction in the prior tax year, he or she must report the state income tax refund (part of the state taxes claimed in the previous year) as income in the year it was received. If the state income tax refund is taxable, report it on Form 1040, Schedule 1, line 1. Tax refunds are reported to the taxpayer on Form 1099-G, not to be confused with unemployment, which is also reported on the same form number. The state sends Form 1099-G to all refund recipients by January 31st of the current year.

To understand how a state income tax refund may be taxable, the tax professional must understand the "tax benefit rule," which states the following:

> If a taxpayer recovers an amount that was deducted or credited against tax in a previous year, the recovery must be included in income to the extent that the deduction or credit reduced the tax liability in the earlier year. However, if no tax benefit was derived from a prior year deduction or credit, the recovery does not have to be included as income.

Recovery of Items Previously Deducted

A recovery is a return of an amount the taxpayer deducted or took a credit for in a prior year. The most common recoveries are state tax refunds, reimbursements, and rebates of deductions itemized on Form 1040, Schedule A. The taxpayer may also have recoveries of nonitemized deductions (such as payments on previously deducted bad debts) and recoveries of items for which the taxpayer previously claimed a tax credit. Taxpayers who used a deduction or credit to reduce their tax liability in the previous year must include those reductions as income on their current tax return.

Schedule 1, line 2: Alimony Received

Alimony is a payment or series of payments to a spouse or former spouse required under a divorce or separation instrument that must meet certain requirements. Alimony payments are deductible by the payer and are includable as income by the recipient. Alimony received should be reported on Form 1040, Schedule 1, line 2. Alimony paid should be deducted as an adjustment on Form 1040, Schedule 1, line 19. The Tax Cuts and Jobs Act changed the alimony rule; alimony will no longer be an adjustment to income or a source of income if the divorce or separation agreement was completed after December 31, 2018.

Payments are alimony or separate maintenance if *all* the following are true:

> ➤ Payments are required by a divorce or separation agreement.
> ➤ The taxpayer and the recipient spouse do not file a joint return.
> ➤ Payments are in cash (including checks or money orders).
> ➤ Payments are not designated in the instrument as "not alimony."
> ➤ Spouses are legally separated under a decree of divorce or separate maintenance agreement and are not members of the same household.
> ➤ Payments are not required after the death of the recipient spouse.
> ➤ Payments are not designated as child support.

The following are not considered alimony or separate maintenance payments.

> ➤ Payments designated as child support.
> ➤ A noncash property settlement, such as giving the spouse the house.
> ➤ Payments that are the spouse's part of community property income.
> ➤ Payments used for property upkeep of the alimony payer's house.
> ➤ Use of property and voluntary payments not required by the written decree.

These payments are neither deductible by the payer nor includable in income by the recipient.

There are different rules for payments under a pre-1985 instrument and those rules were revised in 2004. See Publication 504 *Divorced or Separated Individuals.*

Payments made by cash, check, or money order for the taxpayer's spouse's medical expenses, rent, utilities, mortgage, taxes, tuition, etc., are considered third-party payments. If the payments are made on behalf of the taxpayer's spouse under the terms of the divorce or separation agreement, they may be considered alimony.

If the payer must pay all mortgage payments (both principal and interest) on a jointly owned home and if the payments otherwise qualify, he or she may deduct one-half of the payments as alimony payments. The spouse will report one-half as alimony received.

The deductibility of real estate taxes and insurance depend on how the title is held. Additional research may be needed to determine how to handle the taxpayer's situation.

Example: In November 1984, Kael and Braxton executed a written separation agreement. In February 1985, a decree of divorce was substituted for the written separation agreement. The decree of divorce did not change the terms for the alimony that Kael had to pay Braxton because it is treated as having executed before 1985 since the terms of the alimony are still the same as the original agreement made in 1984. Alimony payments under this decree are not subject to the rules for payments under instruments after 1984.

Alimony Recapture

If the amount of alimony paid by the taxpayer decreases or terminates within the first three calendar years, the payments could be subject to the recapture rule. If the taxpayer is subject to the rule, the individual will include a portion of the previously deducted alimony payments as income in the third year. The spouse would then be entitled to deduct previously included alimony that was received as income in the same year. The three-year period begins with the first calendar year in which the payer makes a qualifying alimony payment under a decree of divorce or separate maintenance or a written separation agreement. See Publication 504 and IRC Sec 85.

Qualified Domestic Relations Order (QDRO)

Qualified Domestic Relations Order (QDRO) is a written decree for a retirement plan to pay child support, alimony, or marital property rights to one of the following: spouse, former spouse, child, or dependent. QDRO contains detailed information such as the participant and alternate payee's name, last known mailing address, and the amount or percentage of the benefit's to be paid to the beneficiary(s).

If the benefit is not available in plan, a QDRO cannot award an amount or form of benefit. For a spouse or former spouse who receives a QDRO benefit from a retirement plan, the payments received are taxed as if the participant received the money directly from the plan. A spouse or former spouse may be able to do a tax-free rollover as if they were employee. A QDRO distribution paid to a child or other dependent is taxed to the plan participant.

Schedule 1, line 3: Business Income or Loss

Use Schedule C for business income if an individual operated a business as a sole proprietor. An activity will qualify as a business if the primary purpose for engaging in such activity is for income or profit and if the proprietor is continually and regularly involved in such activity. Schedule C will be discussed in a later chapter.

Schedule 1, line 4: Other Gains or Losses

Use Schedule D to report capital gains and losses. Use Form 4797 to report other capital gains and losses not reported on Schedule D, line 13. Use Schedule D to figure out the overall gain and loss from transactions reported on Form 8949 and to report gain from Form 2439 or 622 or Part I of Form 4797. Capital gains and losses will be discussed in a later chapter.

Schedule 1, line 5: Rental Income Form 1040

To report income or loss from rental real estate, royalties, partnerships, S corporations, estates, trusts, and residual interests in Real Estate Mortgage Investment Conduits (REMICs), use Schedule E. Rental income is any payment received for the use or occupation of real estate or personal property. Payment received by the taxpayer is reportable. Schedule E will be discussed in a later chapter.

Schedule 1, line 6: Farm Income or Loss

Schedule F would be used to report farm income or loss. Schedule F will be discussed in a later chapter.

Schedule 1, line 7: Unemployment Compensation

Unemployment compensation is taxable, and the taxpayer may elect to have taxes withheld for income tax purposes. To make this choice, the taxpayer must complete Form W-4V, *Voluntary Withholding Request*. The recipient of unemployment compensation will receive Form 1099-G to report the income.

If the taxpayer had to repay unemployment compensation for a prior year because they received unemployment while employed, he or she would subtract the total amount repaid for the year from the total amount received and enter the difference on Form 1040, Schedule 1, line 7. On the dotted line, next to the entry on the tax return, write "Repaid" and enter the amount repaid.

Paid Medical Family Leave

Paid family leave is an element of a state disability insurance program, and workers covered by State Disability Insurance (SDI) could be covered for this benefit. The maximum claim is six weeks; this is reported as unemployment on the individual's tax return. In some states, paid family leave and unemployment could be reported on separate forms. Be aware of how the individual state reports the two programs. Both are considered a form of unemployment compensation that must be reported on Form 1040, Schedule 1, line 7.

Señor 1040 Says: A good tax professional may have to add the totals of paid family leave with unemployment to report the correct amount of unemployment.

Schedule 1, line 8a – 8z: Other Income

Use Form 1040, Schedule 1, line 8, to report any income not reported on the previous lines of the tax return or schedules. If necessary, attach a statement to give the required details concerning the income. The type of income should be identified on the dotted line.

Income that is not reported on line 8:

1. Self-employment

2. Notary public income
3. Income reported on Form 1099-MISC
4. Income reported on Form 1099-NEC, unless it is NOT self-employment income, such as a hobby
5. Form 1099-K

Examples of Other Income reported on line 8 are:

➢ Net operating loss (8a).
➢ Gambling winnings, including the lottery and raffles (8b).
➢ Form 1099-C, *Cancellation of Debt* (8c).
➢ Foreign income exclusion from Form 2555 (8d).
➢ Archer MSAs and Long-term Care Insurance Contracts Form 8853 (8e).
➢ Health Savings Account distributions, Form 8889 (8f).
➢ Alaska Permanent Fund dividend (8g).
➢ Jury duty pay (8h).
➢ Prizes and awards (8i).
➢ Activity not for profit income (8j).
➢ Stock options (8k).
➢ Income from the rental of personal property if taxpayer engaged in the rental for profit but was not in the business of renting such property (8l).
➢ Olympic and Paralympic medal and USOC prize money (8m).
➢ Section 951(a) inclusion (8n).
➢ Section 951A(a) inclusion (8o). Attach Form 8992.
➢ Section 461(l) excess business loss adjustments (8p).
➢ Taxable distributions from an ABLE account (8q).
➢ Scholarships and fellowship grants not reported on W-2 (8r).
➢ Nontaxable amount of Medicaid waiver payments included on Form 1040, line 1a or 1d (8s).
➢ Pension or annuity from a nonqualified deferred compensation plan or a nongovernmental section 457 plan (8t).
➢ Wages earned while incarcerated (8u).
➢ Other income, such as bartering (8z).

See Publication 525 *Taxable and Nontaxable Income*.

Señor 1040 Says: Form 1099-NEC, *Nonemployee Compensation,* is reported on line 8 unless it is not self-employment income.

Line 8a, Net Operating Loss

When a taxpayer is taking a net operating loss (NOL) from an earlier year, it would be reported Schedule 1, line 8(a). An NOL is a loss so enter the amount in parentheses as a negative number. See Publication 536, *Net Operating Losses (NOLs) for Individuals, Estates, and Trusts*.

Line 8b, Gambling Winnings

Form W-2G now is an evergreen form, by just having to add the last 2 digits for the filing year. Form W-2G would be given to a taxpayer when winnings are $1,200 or more from a bingo game or slot machine. Keno winnings are more than $1,500 and for a poker tournament the amount is $5,000. Winnings from all other gambling wagers or buy-in would be reduced at the option of the payer, if the wager is $600 or more, and at least 300 times the amount of the wager and if the winnings are subject to federal income tax withholding. Gambling winnings include lotteries, lump-sum payment from the sale of a right to receive future lottery payments, bingo, slot machines, keno and poker, etc. Winnings are subject to federal income tax. Gambling losses are no more than the taxpayers' winnings and are reported on Schedule A, line 16.

There are two types of withholding on gambling winnings: regular gambling withholding and backup withholding.

Regular gambling is withheld at a flat 24% rate from certain kinds of gambling. Gambling winnings of more than $5,000 (not including the wager) from the following sources are subject to income tax withholding:

1. Any sweepstakes, wagering pools (including payments made to winners of poker tournaments), or lotteries.
2. Any other winnings if the proceeds are at least 300 times the amount of the bet.
3. Wagering on horse and dog races.

Regular gambling withholdings are calculated on the total amount of gross proceeds (winnings minus the amount wagered). Generally, the 24% withholding is not withheld from bingo, keno, or slot machines. It does not matter how the taxpayer is paid for the winnings; payments could be in cash, in property, or as an annuity. Winnings not paid in cash are considered at their fair market value. The taxpayer may have to provide the payer his or her Social Security number to avoid withholding.

Gambling winnings are reported to the taxpayer by the gambling organization (such as a casino) on Form W-2G, which shows both the amount won and withheld. The tax withheld (box 4) is reported with all other federal income tax withholding on Form 1040, page 2, line 25. "Backup" withholding on gambling winnings occurs when the payee does not give the payer his or her Social Security number. The withholding rate will be 24% and applies to winnings more than $600.

If the winner is not a U.S. citizen their withholding could be 30%, and they would receive Form 1042-S, *Foreign Person's U.S. Source Income Subject to Withholding.*

Form W-2G

Line 8c, Cancellation of Debt

A debt is any amount owed to the lender; this includes, but is not limited to, stated principal, stated interest, fees, penalties, administrative costs, and fines. If a taxpayer's debt is canceled or forgiven, the canceled amount would generally be included as income. The amount of canceled debt can be all, or part, of the total amount owed. For a lending transaction, the taxpayer is required to report only the stated principal. If the cancellation of a debt is a gift, it would not be included as income. If a federal government agency, financial institution, or credit union forgives or cancels a debt of $600 or more, the taxpayer should receive a Form 1099-C *Cancellation of Debt*. The amount to be included as income is listed in box 2 of Form 1099-C.

If the forgiven or canceled debt includes interest, the amount considered interest would be listed in box 3 and can only be included as income if it would have been deductible on the taxpayer's tax return.

The taxpayer should not include a canceled debt as income in the following situations:

➤ The debt is canceled in a bankruptcy case under Title 11 of the U.S. Code. See Publication 908, *Bankruptcy Tax Guide*.
➤ The debt is canceled when the taxpayer is insolvent. However, this does not apply to the extent the debt exceeds the amount by which the taxpayer is insolvent.
➤ The debt is qualified farm debt and is canceled by a qualified person. See chapter 3 of Publication 225, *Farmer's Tax Guide*.
➤ The debt is qualified real property business debt. See Publication 468, *Canceled Debts, Foreclosures, Repossessions and Abandonments (For Individuals)*.

> ➤ The debt is qualified principal residence indebtedness.

If the taxpayer has included a canceled debt amount in their income and later pays the debt off, the taxpayer may be able to file an amended return for a refund. The statute of limitations for filing would apply.

There may be terms in the following section that you are not familiar with; research to become familiar with them.

Depending upon the actual date of the discharge, a debt is deemed canceled on the date one of the following identifiable events occur:

> ➤ A discharge in bankruptcy under Title 11 of the U.S. Code. There are certain discharges in bankruptcy that are not required to be reported.
> ➤ A cancellation or extinguishment making the debt unenforceable in a receivership, foreclosure, or similar federal non-bankruptcy or state court proceeding.
> ➤ A cancellation or extinguishment when the statute of limitations for collecting the debt expires, or when the statutory period for filing a claim or beginning a deficiency judgment proceeding expires. Expiration of the statute of limitations is an identifiable event only when the debtor's affirmative statute of limitations defense is upheld in a final judgment or decision of a court and the appeal period has expired.
> ➤ A cancellation or extinguishment when the creditor elects the foreclosure remedies, which by law extinguishes or bars the creditor's right to collect the debt. This event applies to a mortgage lender or holder who is barred by local law from pursuing debt collection after a "power of sale" in the mortgage or deed of trust is exercised.
> ➤ A cancellation or extinguishment making the debt unenforceable under a probate or similar proceeding.
> ➤ A discharge of indebtedness under an agreement between the creditor and the debtor to cancel the debt at less than full consideration, for example, short sales.
> ➤ A discharge of indebtedness because of a decision or a defined policy of the creditor to discontinue collection activity and cancel the debt. A creditor's defined policy can be in writing or an established business practice of the creditor. A creditor's established practice to stop collection activity and abandon a debt when a particular nonpayment period expires is a defined policy.
> ➤ The expiration of nonpayment testing period. This event occurs when the creditor has not received a payment on the debt during the testing period. The testing period is a 36-month period ending on December 31, plus any time when the creditor was precluded from collection activity by a stay in bankruptcy or similar bar under state or local law. The creditor can rebut the occurrence of this identifiable event if:
>   - o The creditor (or a third-party collection agency on behalf of the creditor) has engaged in significant bona fide collection activity during the 12-month period ending on December 31.
>   - o Facts and circumstances that exist on January 31 following the end of the 36-month period indicate that the debt was canceled. Significant bona fide collection activity does not include nominal or ministerial collection action, such as an automated mailing. Facts and circumstances indicating that a debt was not canceled include the existence of a lien relating to the debt (up to the value of the security) or the sale of the debt by the creditor.
> ➤ Other actual discharge before identifiable event.

Form 1099-C

Canceled debt is income to the taxpayer, since the recipient received a benefit without paying for it. The taxpayer would receive Form 1099-C to report the taxable event. There are some exceptions that apply. Form 1099-C has become an evergreen form, by just having to add the last 2 digits for the filing year.

Form 1099-C

Box 1, Date of identifiable event: The date shown is the date the debt was canceled.

Box 2, Amount of debt discharged: Shows the amount of the canceled debt. The amount of the canceled debt cannot be greater than the total debt or less than any amount the lender receives in satisfaction of the debt by means of agreement, foreclosure sale, and a short sale that partially satisfied the debt.

Box 3, Interest, if included in box 2: The lender would show any interest that is included in the canceled debt in box 2.

Box 4, Debt description: Shows a description of the origin of the debt (such as if it's from a student loan, mortgage, or credit card expenditure). Be as specific as possible. The lender must include a property description when filing Form 1099-C and 1099-A.

Box 5, Check here if the debtor was personally liable for repayment of the debt: If the taxpayer (debtor) was personally liable for repayment of the debt at the time it was canceled, then an X will be in the box.

Box 6, Identifiable event code: This code shows the nature of the identifiable event.

Box 7, Fair market value (FMV) of property: Generally, the gross foreclosure bid price is the FMV. If an abandonment or voluntary conveyance to the lender in lieu of foreclosure occurred, enter the appraised value of the property.

Who Must File Form 1099-C?

➢ A section 581 or 591(a) financial institution, which could be a domestic bank, trust company, building and loan, or savings and loan association.

- ➢ A credit union.
- ➢ Any of the following or subunits thereof and its successor:
  - o Federal Deposit Insurance Corporation.
  - o National Credit Union Administration.
  - o Any other federal executive agency, including government corporations.
  - o Any military department.
  - o U.S. Postal Service.
  - o Postal Rate Commission.
- ➢ Any corporation that is a subsidiary, financial institution, or credit union are subject to supervision and examination by a federal or state regulatory agency.
- ➢ A federal government agency including:
  - o A department.
  - o An agency.
  - o A court or court administrative office.
  - o An instrumentality in the judicial or legislative branch of the government.
- ➢ Any organization whose trade or business is significantly lending money, such as a finance or credit card company.

If the debt is owned by more than one creditor, each creditor that is defined under "Who must file" above must issue a Form 1099-C if the debt is more than $600. A creditor will be deemed to have met its filing requirements if a lead bank, fund administrator, or other designee of the creditor complies on its behalf. Debt owned by a partnership is treated as being owned by all the partners and must follow the rules for multiple creditors.

If the taxpayer is insolvent, they may qualify to use Form 982 to discharge indebtedness that can be excluded as gross income. See IRC Section 108.

Health Savings Accounts (HSAs) Form 8889 (8f).

Generally, medical expenses that have been paid during the year are not reimbursed by the plan until the taxpayer has met the deductible. The taxpayer may receive a tax-free distribution from the HSA to pay or reimburse for qualified medical expenses after the taxpayer has established an HSA. Distributions received for any other reason are subject to an additional 20% tax.

Alaska Permanent Fund Dividends line 8g

The Alaska Permanent Fund is a dividend that is paid to all qualifying residents of Alaska. The dividend is based upon a five-year average of the Permanent Fund's performance, which depends on the stock market and other factors. The dividend is taxable on the recipients' federal tax returns.

Activity Not Engaged in for Profit line 8j

Income received through activities from which the taxpayer does not expect to make a profit (such as money made from a hobby) must be reported on Form 1040, Schedule 1, line 8. Deductions for the business or investment activity cannot offset other income. To determine if the taxpayer is carrying on an activity for profit, you must consider the following factors:

- ➢ The taxpayer carries on the activity in a businesslike manner.
- ➢ The time and effort put into the activity indicate the taxpayer intended to make a profit.

- ➢ Losses are due to circumstances beyond the taxpayer's control.
- ➢ Methods of operation were changed to improve profitability.
- ➢ The taxpayer or the taxpayer's advisor(s) have the knowledge needed to carry on the activity as a successful business.
- ➢ The taxpayer was successful in making a profit in similar activities in the past.
- ➢ The activity makes a profit in some years.
- ➢ The taxpayer can expect to make a future profit from the appreciation of the assets used in the activity.
- ➢ The taxpayer depends on the income for his or her livelihood.

An activity is presumed to be carried on for profit if it produced a profit in at least three of the last five years, including the current year. Activities that consist of breeding, training, showing, or racing horses are presumed to be carried on for profit if they produced a profit in at least two of the last seven years. The activity must be substantially the same for each year within the period, and the taxpayer has a profit when the gross income from the activity exceeds the deductions.

Hobby Income

Hobby income is one example of an activity not for profit; however, a hobby can become a business. The ability to claim losses on a hobby have been suspended until 2026 due to the Tax Cuts and Jobs Act (TCJA). To show the IRS that an activity is a business, the taxpayer should maintain the following:

- ➢ Comprehensive recordkeeping.
- ➢ A separate business checking account for the income.
- ➢ Separate credit cards for business and personal purchases.
- ➢ Logbook(s) to keep records of business and personal use of such items as computers, charter boats, camcorders, etc.
- ➢ Required licenses, insurance, certifications, etc.
- ➢ If operated from home, keeping a separate phone line for business use.
- ➢ An attempt to make a profit.
- ➢ Research on market trends or technology related to the taxpayer's business.
- ➢ If the taxpayer has employees, the taxpayer must file forms to report employment taxes (Review Publication 15, r, *Employer's Tax Guide* for more info). Employment taxes include the following items:
  - o Social Security and Medicare.
  - o Federal income tax withholding.
  - o Federal unemployment (FUTA) tax.

Not for profit income could include income from a hobby or rental income from tangible property; both are reported on Form 1040, Schedule 1, line 8. See Publication 527 and IRC Sec 183.

Line 8k, Stock Options

There are three kinds of stock options:

- ➢ Incentive stock options.
- ➢ Employee stock purchase plan options.
- ➢ Non-statutory (non-qualified) stock options.

The employer must report excess of the fair market value (FMV) of the stock received, and will be reported in box 12 with the code *V*. For more information about employee stock options, see Internal Revenue Code (IRC) section 1.83-7, §421, §422, and §423 and related regulations.

Part 4 Review Questions

To obtain the maximum benefit from this chapter, LTP recommends that you complete each of the following questions, and then compare them to the answers with feedback that immediately follow. Under governing self-study standards, vendors are required to present review questions intermittently throughout each self-study course.

These questions and explanations are not part of the final examination and will not be graded by LTP.

IP4.1
What is the maximum taxable amount of Social Security?

   a. 85%
   b. 35%
   c. 10%
   d. 25%

IP4.2
Which of the following could be a taxable event, if a credit was taken in the prior tax year?

   a. Repayment of a personal loan
   b. State income tax paid
   c. Real estate tax payments
   d. Bad debt

IP4.3
Which of the following income is taxable?

   a. Workers' compensation
   b. Welfare and other public assistance benefits
   c. Veterans' benefits
   d. Alimony (prior to December 31, 2018)

IP4.4
Which of the following is taxable on the federal return?

   a. Unemployment
   b. Paid family leave
   c. Child support
   d. Unemployment and paid family leave

IP4.5
Alaska Permanent Fund is reported on which line?

   a. Is not reported.
   b. Is reported on Schedule 1, line 8e.
   c. Is reported on Schedule 1, line 8f.
   d. Is reported on Schedule 1, line 8g.

IP4.6

Sophia won a $21,000 jackpot from Wild Bill's in Atlantic City. She did not provide her SSN to the casino. What would the casino do before it pays Sophia her money?

    a. Withhold 21%
    b. Withhold 25%
    c. Withhold 30%
    d. Withhold 24%

IP4.7

Which of the following is the reporting tool for a prior year state refund to the taxpayer?

    a. Form 1099-INT
    b. Form 1099-DIV
    c. Form 1099-R
    d. Form 1099-G

IP4.8

Which of the following federal gambling winnings is subject to income tax withholding?

    a. Bingo
    b. Keno
    c. Slot machines
    d. Sweepstakes of more than $5,000

IP4.9

Which of the following reports gambling winnings?

    a. Form W-2
    b. Form W-2G
    c. Form W-4
    d. Form W-7SP

IP4.10

Which of the following are not Employee Stock Options?

    a. Incentive stock options
    b. Employee stock purchase plan options
    c. Non-statutory (non-qualified) stock options
    d. Qualified Domestic Relations Order

Part 4 Review Questions Answers

IP4.1

What is the maximum taxable amount of Social Security?

    a. 85%
    b. 35%
    c. 10%
    d. 25%

Feedback: Review section *Line 5b: How Much Is Taxable?* Under Schedule 1.

IP4.2

Which of the following could be a taxable event, if a credit was taken in the prior tax year?

a. Repayment of a personal loan
b. State income tax paid
c. Real estate tax payments
d. Bad debt

Feedback: Review section *Schedule 1, line 1: Taxable Refunds*.

IP4.3

Which of the following income is taxable?

a. Workers' compensation
b. Welfare and other public assistance benefits
c. Veterans' benefits
d. Alimony (prior to December 31, 2018)

Feedback: Review section *Schedule 1, line 2: Alimony Received*.

IP4.4

Which of the following is taxable on the federal return?

a. Unemployment
b. Paid family leave
c. Child support
d. Unemployment and paid family leave

Feedback: Review section *Schedule 1, line 7: Unemployment Compensation*.

IP4.5

Alaska Permanent Fund is reported on which line?

a. Is not reported.
b. Is reported on Schedule 1, line 8e
c. Is reported on Schedule 1, line 8f
d. Is reported on Schedule 1, line 8g

Feedback: Review section *Alaska Permanent Fund Dividends line 8g*.

IP4.6

Sophia won a $21,000 jackpot from Wild Bill's in Atlantic City. She did not provide her SSN to the casino. What would the casino do before it pays Sophia her money?

a. Withhold 21%
b. Withhold 25%
c. Withhold 30%
d. Withhold 24%

Feedback: Review section *Line 8b, Gambling Winnings*.

IP4.7
Which of the following is the reporting tool for a prior year state refund to the taxpayer?

    a. Form 1099-INT
    b. Form 1099-DIV
    c. Form 1099-R
    d. Form 1099-G

Feedback: Review section *Schedule 1, line 7: Unemployment Compensation.*

IP4.8
Which of the following federal gambling winnings is subject to income tax withholding?

    a. Bingo
    b. Keno
    c. Slot machines
    d. Sweepstakes of more than $5,000

Feedback: Review section *Line 8b, Gambling Winnings.*

IP4.9
Which of the following reports gambling winnings?

    a. Form W-2
    b. Form W-2G
    c. Form W-4
    d. Form W-7SP

Feedback: Review section *Line 8b, Gambling Winnings.*

IP4.10
Which of the following are not Employee Stock Options?

    a. Incentive stock options
    b. Employee stock purchase plan options
    c. Non-statutory (non-qualified) stock options
    d. Qualified Domestic Relations Order

Feedback: Review section *Line 8j, Employees Stock Options.*

Part 5 Other Taxable Income

Taxable income is more than just earned wages; it can include overlooked sources. Some of these taxable income types will be reported on a W-2, but others may be reported to the taxpayer on a 1099-MISC or 1099-NEC. This section covers the most common type of other taxable income.

Advance Commission and Other Earnings

If the cash-method is used and the taxpayer received an advance commission, that amount is included as income in the year received. If the taxpayer repays unearned commission in the same year it was received, then reduce the amount included by the repayment. If the repayment is in a later year, then the taxpayer would deduct the repayment on Schedule A as an itemized deduction.

Prepaid income, in most cases, is included as compensation in the year the taxpayer received the income. If the taxpayer is on the accrual method of accounting, the income is reported when it is earned in the performance of the services. See Publication 525.

Back Pay

If a taxpayer receives a settlement or judgment for back pay, it is included in their income. Back pay is treated as wages in the year paid, not the year it was supposed to have been paid. If a settlement was reached in 2021 for pay that should have been given in 2018, and the back pay is received in 2022, the back pay is reported as income for tax year 2022, not 2021 or 2018. Taxpayer could receive one of the following:

➢ Form W-2
➢ Form 1099-INT
➢ Form 1099-MISC or 1099-NEC

Payments made to the taxpayer for damages, unpaid life insurance premiums, and unpaid health insurance premiums are reported to the taxpayer on Form W-2. There are special rules on how to report these wages to the Social Security Administration, and those guidelines are not covered in this course. See https://www.dol.gov/general/topic/wages/backpay.

Bartering

Bartering is an exchange of property or services. Goods and services acquired through bartering must be included as income at the value they held when they were received. Taxpayer should use Form 1099-B to report the exchange of services or property received. See Publication 525.

Employee Achievement Awards

Employee achievement awards received for outstanding work are included in the employee's income and should be reported on the W-2. These include prizes such as vacation trips for meeting sales goals. If the prize or reward received is a good or service, include the fair market value of the goods and services in the income. If the employee receives tangible personal property as an award for length of service or a safety achievement, then the value of the award is generally excluded from income unless the compensation is cash, a gift certificate, or some equivalent item. The amount that can be excluded is limited to no more than $1,600 ($400 for awards that are non-qualified plans) or the employer's cost of the award if less than the maximum. See Publication 525.

Government Cost-of-Living Allowances

Cost-of-living allowances are generally included in income if the employee was a federal civilian or a federal court employee. Allowances and differentials that increase basic pay as an incentive for taking a less desirable position is included as compensation and must be included in income. See Publication 516 for tax treatments.

Relocation for Temporary Work Assignment

If an employee is away from his regular place of work on a temporary work assignment, certain travel expenses that are reimbursed or paid directly by the employer with an accountable plan may be excluded from wages. Generally, a temporary work assignment is in one location and lasts for one year or less.

Scholarship Prizes

If a scholarship was won in a contest and not used for education purposes, they are not considered a scholarship. The prize amounts are reported as income on Form 1040, Schedule 1, line 8i. See Publication 525.

Severance Pay

When an employee receives a severance package, any payment for the cancellation of the employment contract is included in the employee's income. A severance package is considered wages and is subject to Social Security and Medicare taxes. See Publication 525.

Sick Pay

Pay received from an employer while the employee is sick or injured is part of the employee's salary or wages. Taxpayers must include sick pay benefits in their income that are received from any of the following sources:

> ➢ A welfare fund.
> ➢ A state sickness or disability fund.
> ➢ An association of employers or employees.
> ➢ An insurance company if the employer paid for the plan.
> ➢ Railroad sick pay.

If the employee paid the premiums on an accident or health insurance policy, the benefits received under the policy are not taxable.

Sick pay is intended to replace regular wages while an employee is unable to work due to injury or illness. Payments received from the employer or an agent of the employer that qualify as sick pay must have federal withholding, just as any other wage compensation. Payments under a plan in which the employer does not participate (i.e., the taxpayer paid all the premiums) are not considered sick pay and are not taxable.

Sick pay does not include any of the following payments:

> ➢ Disability retirement payments.
> ➢ Workers' compensation.
> ➢ Payments to public employees as workers' compensation.
> ➢ Medical expense payments.
> ➢ Payments unrelated to absences from work.
> ➢ Black lung benefit payments.

Señor 1040 Says: Do not report any amounts as income that were reimbursed for medical expenses that were incurred after the plan was established.

See Publication 525 and IRC Sec 61(a)(1).

Tips

All received tips are income, subject to federal income tax, and must be reported to employers regardless of whether they were received directly or indirectly. There are several ways an individual could receive tips such as tip-splitting pool, a tip-pooling arrangement, or some other method. Noncash tips, such as tickets, passes, or other items of value, are also reported to the employer. The market value of the item is counted as income and subject to tax, although the taxpayer does not pay Social Security or Medicare taxes on them. The IRS states that all tips received from customers must be included as income regardless of what an employer considers to be a tip; an employer's characterization of a payment as a "tip" is not determinative for withholding purposes.

Employees who receive tips should keep daily records of the tips received. A daily report will help the employee when it comes to filing his or her tax return. Employees should do the following:

➢ Report tips accurately to their employer.
➢ Report all tips accurately on their tax return.
➢ Keep a daily report of tips received and those paid out.
➢ Provide their tip income report if their tax return is ever audited.

If the server paid out tips, that amount should be documented on Publication 1244. The amount paid out is not reported on the payer's tax return and then subtracted out. There are two ways to keep a daily tip log. Employees should:

➢ Write information about their tips in a tip diary.
➢ Keep copies of documents that show tips.

Señor 1040 Says: The taxpayer can use Publication 1244 to track their daily tips totals and amount reported to their employer. Taxpayer can download the publication @ https://www.irs.gov/forms-pubs/about-publication-1244

This daily record should be kept with tax and other personal records. The daily tip report should include:

➢ The date and time of work.
➢ Cash tips received directly from customers or other employees.
➢ Credit and debit card charges that customers paid directly to the employer.
➢ Total tips paid out to other employees through tip pools or tip splitting.
➢ The value of noncash tips received, such as tickets, passes, etc.

If more than $20 worth of tips are received per month from one employer, they must be reported to the taxpayer's employer on Form 4070: *Employee's Report of Tips to Employer.* The employer will withhold Social Security, Medicare, federal taxes, and state taxes from the employee's reported tips based on the total amount of the employee's regular wages and reported tips. Form 4070 should be filed with the employer no later than the 10th of each month. If the 10th of the month falls on a Saturday, Sunday, or legal holiday, the due date to report tips becomes the next business day.

Tips not reported to the employer are still required to be reported as income on Form 1040. If the taxpayer fails to report tips, the taxpayer may be subject to a penalty equal to 50% of the Social Security and Medicare taxes or railroad retirement tax owed on unreported tips. This penalty amount is an addition tax owed, although the taxpayer could try to avoid the penalty by attaching a statement to the return showing the reasonable cause for not reporting the tips. Taxpayer would use Form 4137: *Social Security Tax on Unreported Tip Income*, to report unreported tips to the IRS.

Do not include service charges in the tip diary. Service charges that are added to the customer's bill and paid to the employee are treated as wages, not tips. The absence of any of the following factors creates doubt as to whether a payment is a tip and indicates that the payment may be a service charge:

➢ The payment must be made free from obligation.
➢ The customer must have an unrestricted right to determine the amount.
➢ The payment should not be subject to discussion or defined by employer policy.
➢ The customer has the right to determine who receives the payment.

Example: Fish 'n' Chips for You specifies that an 18% service charge will be added to bills with parties of six or more. Julio's bill included the service charge for food and beverages for the party of eight he served. Under these circumstances, Julio did not have the unrestricted right to determine the amount of payment because it was dictated by Fish 'n' Chips for You. The 18% charge is not a tip; it is distributed to the employees as wages. Julio would not include that amount in his tip diary.

Employees who work in an establishment that must allocate tips to its employees or who fail to earn or report an amount of tips that is equal to at least 8% of the total amount of their gross receipts are subject to "allocated tips." In this case, the employer will assign them (or "allocate") additional tips to ensure they reach the 8% minimum. Allocated tips are calculated by adding the tips reported by all employees from food and drink sales (this does not include carryout sales or sales with a service charge of 10% or more). The employee's share is then determined using the sales based on hours worked.

Allocated tips are shown separately in box 8 of Form W-2 and are reported as wages on Form 1040, line 1c. Social Security and Medicare taxes have not been taken out of allocated tips, but are still subject to them, they must be reported on Form 4137: *Social Security Tax on Unreported Tip Income.* Employers must also report them by filing Form 8027: *Employer's Annual Information Return of Tip Income and Allocated Tips.* The purpose of Form 4137 is to calculate the Social Security and Medicare tax on tips that were not reported to the taxpayer's employer. Once calculated, report the amount of unreported Social Security and Medicare tax on Form 1040, Schedule 2, line 5. See Publication 525.

Disability Income

Disability income is the amount paid to an employee under the employee or employer's insurance or pension plan (under some plans, employees can also contribute) while the employee is absent from work due to a disability. Disability income reported as wages on Form W-2 is taxable, but income attributable to employee contributions would not be taxable. If the employee pays for the entire cost of the accident or health plan, he or she should not include any amount received as income. If the premiums of a health or accident plan were paid through a cafeteria plan, and the amount of the premium was not included as taxable income, then it is assumed that the employer paid the premiums, and the disability benefits are taxable.

If a taxpayer retires using disability payments before reaching the minimum retirement age of 59½, the payments will be treated as wages until the taxpayer reaches the minimum retirement age. Once a taxpayer is over the age of 59½, their disability payments will be taxed as a pension and not as regular income. Tax professionals should not confuse disability income (which may be taxable) with workers' compensation (which may not be taxable) for those who are injured at work.

> *Señor 1040 Says*: The minimum retirement age is 59½ or the age at which the taxpayer could first receive an annuity or pension if he or she was not disabled. The taxpayer must report all his or her taxable disability payments until the taxpayer reaches the minimum retirement age.

Clergy

Clergy are the formal leaders within certain religious groups. The roles and functions of clergy members vary amongst different religious traditions, but these usually involve presiding over specific ceremonies and teaching religious doctrines and practices.

If the taxpayer is a member of the clergy, offerings and fees received for marriages, baptisms, funerals, masses, etc., are included as income in addition to his salary. If the offering is made to the religious institution, it is not taxable to the member of the clergy. If he is a member of a religious organization, and if he gives his outside earnings to the organization, he must still include the earnings in his income. However, he may be entitled to a charitable contribution deduction for the amount he paid to the organization.

Special rules for housing allowances apply to members of the clergy. Under these rules, the taxpayer does not include in his income the rental value of a home (including utilities), or a housing allowance provided to him as a part of his pay. However, the exclusion cannot be more than the least of the following amounts:

➢ The exact amount used to provide or rent a home.
➢ The fair market rental value of the home (including furnishings, utilities, etc.).
➢ The amount officially designated (in advance of payment) as a rental or housing allowance.
➢ An amount that represents reasonable pay for services.

The home or allowance must be provided as compensation for the taxpayer's duties as an ordained, licensed, or commissioned minister. However, the rental value of the home or the housing allowance as earnings from self-employment is included on Schedule SE (Form 1040), *Self-Employment Tax.* See Publication 517.

Part 5 Review Questions

To obtain the maximum benefit from this chapter, LTP recommends that you complete each of the following questions, and then compare them to the answers with feedback that immediately follow. Under governing self-study standards, vendors are required to present review questions intermittently throughout each self-study course.

These questions and explanations are not part of the final examination and will not be graded by LTP.

IP5.1

Reverend Alex performs marriages and is paid from the offering for the performance. Are the offerings taxable to Alex?

    a. Yes, they are because all offerings are taxable.
    b. No, they are not, because it was given from the church members and not the offerings.
    c. Yes, they are because he performed the marriage and was given the offering.
    d. No, they are not, because he is a clergyman.

IP5.2

Which of the following is taxable income?

    a. Workers' compensation
    b. Welfare benefits
    c. Veterans' benefits
    d. Disability reported on Form W-2

IP5.3

Tips received totaling more than _____ per month, per employee, must be reported to the employer on Form 4070.

    a. $5.00
    b. $10.00
    c. $15.00
    d. $20.00

IP5.4

Allocated tips are tips the employer assigns to the employee for reporting daily tips less than ___ of their total gross receipts.

    a. 8%
    b. 10%
    c. 15%
    d. 12%

IP5.5

Which of the following is **not** reported on Schedule 1, line 8?

    a. Hobby income
    b. Awards
    c. Gambling winnings
    d. Tip income

IP5.6

Wages are reported on Form 1040, line 7. Wages do not include:

a. Salaries
b. Vacation allowances
c. Disability payments
d. Commissions

IP5.7

Manuel received sick-pay from his employer that was considered wages. Which of the following would not be included in the employee's wages?

1. A welfare fund.
2. A state sickness or disability fund.
3. Health insurance policy where employee paid premiums.
4. An insurance company, if the employer paid for the plan.

a. 3 only
b. 4 only
c. 1, 2, and 4
d. 3 and 4

IP5.8

Alimony received is reported on Schedule 1, line _____.

a. Schedule 1, line 2a
b. Schedule 1, line 2b
c. Schedule 1, line 1
d. Schedule 1, line 8

IP5.9

Francisco has all the following income sources. Which of the following is not a type of compensation income?

1. Salaries
2. Workers' compensation
3. Vacation allowances
4. Bonuses

a. 1, 2, and 3
b. 3 and 4
c. 2 only
d. 1, 2, 3, and 4

IP5.10

Bartering is a form of income and the _____ needs to be included in income.

a. trade value
b. fair market value
c. lowest item value
d. highest item value

IP5.11

Pedro was released from his employment contract. He was given a severance package from his prior employer. What will Pedro need to do with his severance package?

1. Report the entire amount as income.
2. Report only the amount he saved as income.
3. Report only the increase from his wages as income.
4. Report the amount that he used for purchasing gifts.

    a. 1, 2, and 4
    b. 1 only
    c. 4 only
    d. 2, 3, and 4

Part 5 Review Questions Answers

IP5.1

Reverend Alex performs marriages and is paid from the offering for the performance. Are the offerings taxable to Alex?

    a. Yes, they are because all offerings are taxable.
    b. No, they are not, because it was given from the church members and not the offerings.
    c. Yes, they are because he performed the marriage and was given the offering.
    d. No, they are not, because he is a clergyman.

Feedback: Review section *Clergy.*

IP5.2

Which of the following is taxable income?

    a. Workers' compensation
    b. Welfare benefits
    c. Veterans' benefits
    d. Disability reported on Form W-2

Feedback: Review section *Disability Income.*

IP5.3

Tips received totaling more than _____ per month, per employee, must be reported to the employer on Form 4070.

    a. $5.00
    b. $10.00
    c. $15.00
    d. $20.00

Feedback: Review section *Tips.*

IP5.4
Allocated tips are tips the employer assigns to the employee for reporting daily tips less than ___ of their total gross receipts.

   a. 8%
   b. 10%
   c. 15%
   d. 12%

Feedback: Review section *Tips.*

IP5.5
Which of the following is **not** reported on Schedule 1, line 8?

   a. Hobby income
   b. Awards
   c. Gambling winnings
   d. Tip income

Feedback: Review section *Tips.*

IP5.6
Wages are reported on Form 1040, line 7. Wages do not include:

   a. Salaries
   b. Vacation allowances
   c. Disability payments
   d. Commissions

Feedback: Review section *Disability Income.*

IP5.7
Manuel received sick pay from his employer that was considered wages. Which of the following would not be included in the employee's wages?

   1. A welfare fund.
   2. A state sickness or disability fund.
   3. Health insurance policy where employee paid premiums.
   4. An insurance company, if the employer paid for the plan.

   a. 3 only
   b. 4 only
   c. 1, 2, and 4
   d. 3 and 4

Feedback: Review section *Sick Pay.*

IP5.8

Alimony received is reported on Schedule 1, line _____.

    a. Schedule 1, line 2a
    b. Schedule 1, line 2b
    c. Schedule 1, line 1
    d. Schedule 1, line 8

Feedback: Review section *Schedule 1, line 2: Alimony Received.*

IP5.9

Francisco has all the following income sources. Which of the following is not a type of compensation income?

    1. Salaries
    2. Workers' compensation
    3. Vacation allowances
    4. Bonuses

    a. 1, 2, and 3
    b. 3 and 4
    c. 2 only
    d. 1, 2, 3, and 4

Feedback: Review section *Disability Income.*

IP5.10

Bartering is a form of income and the _____ needs to be included in income.

    a. trade value
    b. fair market value
    c. lowest item value
    d. highest item value

Feedback: Review section *Bartering.*

IP5.11

Pedro was released from his employment contract. He was given a severance package from his prior employer. What will Pedro need to do with his severance package?

    1. Report the entire amount as income.
    2. Report only the amount he saved as income.
    3. Report only the increase from his wages as income.
    4. Report the amount that he used for purchasing gifts.

    a. 1, 2, and 4
    b. 1 only
    c. 4 only
    d. 2, 3, and 4

Feedback: Review section *Severance Pay.*

Part 6 Fringe Benefits

A fringe benefit is any benefit provided by an employer to individuals in addition to their normal compensation. A person who performs services for the employer does not have to be an employee; he or she can be an independent contractor, partner, or director. The employer is the provider of the fringe benefit if it is provided for services performed for the employer, and the person who performs services for the employer is the recipient of the fringe benefit.

Fringe benefits received from an employer are considered compensation. They are taxable and must be included in income unless tax law specifically excludes the benefits, or the taxpayer paid fair market value for the benefit (in which it would no longer be a provision from the employer or a fringe benefit). The employer usually determines the amount of the fringe benefits and includes this amount in the employee's W-2. The total value of the fringe benefits should be shown in box 12. The employer is the provider of the benefit even if a customer of the employer provided the services. The employee who profits from the fringe benefit reports the provision as income.

Employers can report noncash fringe benefits in box 1 of the W-2 (with a notation in box 14) using one of the two following accounting periods:

> ➤ The general rule, under which benefits are reported for a full calendar year (January 1st through December 31st).
> ➤ The special accounting period rule, under which benefits provided during the last two months of the calendar year (or any shorter period) are treated as being paid during the following calendar year.

Example 1: Smith's Enterprises has provided Frank Jones and Courtney Keys noncash fringe benefits since 2020 and reports some of them to the IRS using the special accounting period rule. To report the value of those provided benefits on their W-2s, Smith's Enterprises will count November and December of 2021 and January through October of 2022 as one calendar year.

Employers do not have to use the same accounting period for each fringe benefit they provide, but they must use whichever accounting period they choose for every person who receives the benefit. The employee must use the same accounting period as the employer to report taxable noncash fringe benefits.

Example 2: Smith's Enterprises provided employee discounts and athletic facilities as fringe benefits to both Frank Jones and Courtney Keys. The company can report each fringe benefit using a different accounting rule, but no matter which rule they use for each benefit, the fringe benefit must be reported the same way for both Frank and Courtney. In other words, the company can report the employee discounts using the general rule and the athletic facilities using the special accounting period rule, but they cannot report athletic facilities under the general rule for Courtney and then report them under the special accounting period rule for Frank.

Cafeteria Plans

Cafeteria plans are a type of benefit package consisting of fringe benefits; most are written flexible spending arrangement plans that allow employees to choose between receiving cash or taxable benefits instead of certain qualified benefits that are excluded from wages. Generally, a cafeteria plan does not include any plan that offers a benefit that defers pay, but a cafeteria plan can include a qualified 401(k) plan as a benefit. Qualified benefits under a cafeteria plan can include the following:

> ➤ Accident and health benefits (but not Archer medical savings accounts or long-term care insurance).
> ➤ Adoption assistance.
> ➤ Dependent care assistance.
> ➤ Group-term life insurance coverage.
> ➤ Health savings accounts (HSAs). Distributions from an HSA may be used to pay eligible long-term care insurance premiums or qualified long-term care services in addition to unreimbursed medical expenses.

Excluded fringe benefits are not subject to federal income tax withholding; in most cases, they are not subject to Social Security, Medicare, or federal unemployment tax (FUTA) and aren't reported on Form W-2. A cafeteria plan cannot include the following benefits:

> ➤ Archer medical savings accounts (MSAs).
> ➤ Athletic facilities.
> ➤ *De minimis* (minimal) benefits.
> ➤ Educational assistance (including scholarships or fellowships; see Publication 970, *Tax Benefits for Education*).
> ➤ Employee discounts.
> ➤ Employer-provided cell phones.
> ➤ Lodging on the business premises.
> ➤ Meals.
> ➤ No-additional-cost services.
> ➤ Retirement planning services.
> ➤ Transportation (commuting) benefits.
> ➤ Tuition reduction.
> ➤ Working condition benefits.

The following are some of the possible fringe benefits that can be included under the cafeteria plan.

Adoption Assistance

Adoption assistance is considered a benefit when it meets the following requirements:

> ➤ The plan must benefit the employees who qualify under the rules set up by the employer, and the rules cannot give special treatment or perks to highly compensated employees or their dependents.
> ➤ The plan does not pay more than 5% of its payments during the year to shareholders, owners, their spouses, or their dependents.
> ➤ The employer gives reasonable notice of the adoption plan to all eligible employees.
> ➤ Employees provide substantiation that the payments or the reimbursements are used for qualifying expenses.

A highly compensated employee is an employee who meets either of the following tests:

> ➤ The employee was a 5% owner at any time during the year or the preceding year.
> ➤ The employee received more than $130,000 in pay for the preceding year.

The second test listed above can be disregarded if the employee was not in the top 20% of the employees' pay ranking for the preceding year. All payments or reimbursements made under the adoption assistance program is excluded from wages subject to federal income tax withholding.

All qualifying adoption assistance expenses paid or reimbursed by the employer is reported in box 12 of the employee's Form W-2. Code T is used to identify the amount of the nonrefundable credit. Nonrefundable credits lower the taxpayer's tax liability. See Publication 15-B and IRC Sec 137.

Dependent Care Assistance

If the employer provides dependent care assistance under a qualified plan, the taxpayer may be able to exclude the amount from income. Dependent care benefits include the following:

> ➤ Amounts the employer paid directly to the care provider.
> ➤ The fair market value of the care in a day-care facility provided or sponsored by the employer.

The amounts paid are reported on Form W-2, box 10. To claim the exclusion, the taxpayer would complete Part III of Form 2441: *Child and Dependent Care Expenses*. See Publication 503.

 Señor 1040 Says: Individuals who provide childcare in their own home are considered self-employed and should report their income on Schedule C. If the childcare is provided in the child's home, they are considered employees and should receive a W-2 from the child's parent or guardian, who should report the caretaker's income on Schedule H.

Group-Term Life Insurance

Generally, group-term life insurance coverage provided by an employer (current or former) to employees is not included as income up to the cost of $50,000 after being reduced by any amount the employee paid toward the purchase of the insurance.

If the coverage is worth more than $50,000, the employee must include the amount of money that the employer-provided insurance is costing the employer as the employee's personal income. If the employer provided more than $50,000 of coverage, the includable amount is reported as part of the employee's wages in boxes 1, 3, and 5 of Form W-2. It is also shown separately in box 12 with code C on the W-2. Life insurance coverage should meet the following conditions:

> ➤ The employer provided a general death benefit that is not included in income.
> ➤ The employer provided it to a group of employees (usually 10 or more).
> ➤ The employer provided an amount of insurance to each employee based on a formula that prevents individual selection.
> ➤ The employer provided the insurance under a policy that was directly or indirectly carried. Even if the employer did not pay any of the cost, the employer is considered to carry it since the employer arranged for payment of its cost by the employees and charged at least one employee less than, and one employee more than, the cost of their insurance.

Group-term life insurance that is payable on the death of the employee, employee's spouse, or dependent, and with a payment amount of less than $2,000, is considered a *de minimis* benefit.

The following types of insurance plans are not group-term insurance:

> ➢ Insurance that does not provide general death benefits such as travel insurance or only provides accidental death benefits.
> ➢ Life insurance on the life of the employee's spouse or dependent.
> ➢ Insurance provided under a policy that provides a permanent benefit (an economic value that extends more than 1 year unless certain requirements are met). See Internal Revenue Code (IRC) section 1.79-1 for more information.

Health Savings Accounts (HSAs)

A Health Savings Account (HSA) is a form of pretax savings account set up to help set aside money to pay for future medical costs. If the taxpayer is an eligible individual, HSA contributions can be made by the employer, the taxpayer, or any of the taxpayer's family members. Medical expenses must not be reimbursable by the insurance or other sources, Taxpayer must be covered by a High Deductible Health Plan (HDHP) and not covered by another health plan.

Contributions made by the employer are not included in income. Distributions from the HSA that are used to pay for qualified medical expenses are included in income. Contributions to the account are used to pay current or future medical expenses of the account owner, spouse, and any qualified dependent.

Contributions by a partnership to a bona fide partner's HSA are not considered to be contributions by an employer. The contributions are treated as a distribution and are not included in the partner's gross income.

If the contributions by the partnership are for the partner's services rendered, they are treated as guaranteed payments that are included in the partner's gross income.

Contributions by an S corporation to a 2% shareholder-employee's HSA for services rendered are treated as guaranteed payments and are included in the shareholder-employee's gross income. The shareholder-employee may deduct the contribution made to the shareholder-employee's HSA. See Publication 969.

Holiday Gifts

If the employer provides nominal-value holiday gifts such as a turkey or ham, they do not have to be included in the employees' income. If the employer gives the employee cash, a gift certificate, or a similar item that can be exchanged for cash, the gift is compensation and must be included in the employee's income.

Transportation

If an employer provides a qualified transportation fringe benefit, a certain amount may be excluded from income. Providing any of the below can be a qualified transportation fringe benefit:

> ➢ A transit pass.
> ➢ Qualified parking.
> ➢ Transportation in a commuter highway vehicle (must seat at least 6 adults) between the taxpayer's home and workplace.

Cash reimbursements by an employer for these expenses under a bona fide reimbursement arrangement are also excludable. However, cash reimbursement for a transit pass is excludable only if a voucher or similar item that can be exchanged only for a transit pass is not readily available for direct distribution to the taxpayer.

The exclusion for commuter highway vehicle transportation and transit passes fringe benefits cannot be more than a total of $280 a month, regardless of the total value of both benefits.

The exclusion for the qualified parking fringe benefit cannot be more than $280 a month, regardless of its value. For benefits with a value higher than the limit, the excess must be included as income. If the benefits have a value that is more than these limits, the excess is included as income. See IRC Sec 132(f).

Other Fringe Benefits

The following fringe benefits are not included under the cafeteria plan.

Athletic Facilities

The value of an employee's on-site use of a gym or another athletic facility operated by the employer can be excluded from the employee's income. The gym must be primarily used by employees, their spouses, and their dependent children. However, if the employer pays for a fitness program provided to the employee that is off-site at a hotel or athletic club, the value of the program is included as income. Some exceptions apply.

De Minimis Fringe Benefits

If an employer provides its employees with a product or service, and the cost of it is so small that it would be unreasonable for the employer to account for it, the value is not included in the employee's income. These are *de minimis* fringe benefits. Generally, the value of these benefits, such as discounts at company cafeterias, cab fares when working overtime, and company picnics, are not included in the employee's income.

While many of the *de minimis* fringe benefits are typically not included in an employee's gross income, in most circumstances, the employer is allowed a deduction for costs incurred. Any cash benefit or its equivalent (such as the use of a company credit card) cannot be excluded as a *de minimis* benefit under any circumstance.

Educational Assistance

If the taxpayer received educational assistance benefits from his or her employer under a qualified educational assistance program, up to $5,250 of eligible assistance can be excluded yearly, in which case it would not be included on the W-2 or be a part of a return. However, if the education was not work-related or if the taxpayer is a highly compensated employee, the assistance from the employer may be taxable. See Publication 970.

An employee who meets either of the following tests is a highly compensated employee:

➢ The employee was a 5% owner at any time during the year or the preceding year.
➢ The employee received more than $130,000 in pay for the preceding year.

The second test listed above can be ignored if the employee was not in the top 20% of the employees' pay ranking for the preceding year. All payments or reimbursements made under the adoption assistance program must be excluded from wages subject to federal income tax withholding.

A student in a degree-program can exclude amounts received from a qualified scholarship or fellowship. Excludable income from a qualified scholarship or fellowship is any amount received that is used for the following:

> ➢ Tuition and fees to enroll at or attend an eligible educational institution.
> ➢ Fees, books, and equipment required for courses at the eligible educational institution.

Payments received for services required as a condition of receiving a scholarship or fellowship grant must be included in the taxpayer's income, even if the services are required of all students for the degree. Amounts used for room and board do not qualify for the exclusion. This includes amounts received for teaching and research. Include these payments on Form 1040, line 1.

Employee Discounts

The exclusion applies to a price reduction given to the employee for property or services offered to the customer in the ordinary course of the line of business. The discount does not apply to discounts given on real property or discounts on personal property of a kind commonly held for investment, such as stocks and bonds.

Employer-Provided Cell Phones

The value of an employer-provided cell phone that is provided primarily for non-compensatory business reasons is excludable from an employee's income as a working condition. Personal use of an employer-provided cell phone is excludable from an employee's income as a *de minimis* fringe benefit.

Employer-Provided Lodging and Meals

Do not include the value of meals and lodging the employer provided at no charge to the taxpayer and the taxpayer's family as income, if the following conditions are met:

The meals are:

> ➢ Furnished on the business premises of the employer.
> ➢ Furnished for the convenience of the employer.

The lodging is:

> ➢ Furnished on the business premises of the employer.
> ➢ Furnished for the convenience of the employer.
> ➢ A condition of employment for the employee.

No-Additional-Cost Services

The value of services received from one's employer for free, at no cost, or for a reduced price is not included in the taxpayer's income. If the employer offers the same service for sale to customers in the ordinary course of the business and does not have a substantial additional cost to provide the employee with the same service.

No-additional-cost services are excess capacity services, such as tickets for airlines, buses, or trains, hotel rooms, or telephone services provided for free or at a reduced price to employees working in that line of service.

Example: Amanda is employed as a flight attendant for a company that owns both an airline and a hotel chain. The employer allows Amanda to take free personal flights if there is an unoccupied seat and to stay in any of the company's hotels for free if there is an unoccupied room. What would and wouldn't be included as income?

Explanation: The value of the personal flight isn't included in her income because there is no cost involved in letting her take a seat that would have remained unoccupied anyway. However, if the company allowed Amanda to reserve her seat, then the value of the ticket would be included as income because the company can no longer sell that seat and has lost the potential revenue that they could have gained from it. However, this potential loss or gain isn't a factor with the hotel room; since Amanda does not work in the hotel side of the business, the value of the hotel room would be included as income either way.

Nontaxable Income

Although it may seem like taxes are collected on all income, there are several types of income that are exempt from taxation because of the nature of the reason behind the payment.

Child Support

Taxpayers who receive child support payments do not report the payments as income. Payments designed to be child support should be defined in legal documents such as divorce or separation agreements or the child custody paperwork.

Workers' Compensation

Amounts received as workers' compensation for an occupational sickness or injury are fully exempt from tax if they are paid under a workers' compensation act or some similar statute. The exemption also applies to the taxpayer's survivors. This exception does not apply to retirement plan benefits received based on age, length of service, or prior contributions to the plan, even if the taxpayer retired because of an occupational sickness or injury.

If the taxpayer returns to work after qualifying for workers' compensation, payments received while assigned to light duties are taxable. Report these payments as wages on line 1 of Form 1040.

Income paid under a statute that provides benefits only to employees with service-connected disabilities could be considered workers' compensation or disability for pension. The rest is taxable as annuity or pension income. If a taxpayer dies and his or her survivor benefits from the pension, the workers' compensation remains exempt from tax.

Welfare and Other Public Assistance Benefits

Benefit payments made by a public welfare fund to individuals with disabilities (such as blindness) should not be included as income. Welfare or public assistance payments from a state fund for the victims of a crime should not be included in the victims' income. Do not deduct medical expenses that are reimbursed by such a fund. Any welfare payments obtained fraudulently are not tax-exempt and must be included as income.

Veterans' Benefits

Veterans' benefits paid under any law, regulation, or administrative practice administered by the Department of Veterans Affairs (VA) should not be included as income.

For veterans and their families, the following benefits are not taxable:

- ➢ Education, training, and subsistence allowances.
- ➢ Disability compensation and pension payments for disabilities paid either to veterans or their families.
- ➢ Grants for homes designed for wheelchair living.
- ➢ Grants for motor vehicles for veterans who lost their sight or the use of their limbs.
- ➢ Veterans' insurance proceeds and dividends paid either to veterans or to their beneficiaries, including the proceeds of a veteran's endowment policy paid before death.
- ➢ Interest on insurance dividends left on deposit with Veterans Affairs.
- ➢ Benefits under a dependent-care assistance program.
- ➢ The death gratuity paid to a survivor of a member of the armed forces who died after September 10, 2001.
- ➢ Payments made under the compensated work therapy program.
- ➢ Any bonus payment by a state or political subdivision because of services in a combat zone.

How to Read the Tax Tables

Tax tables are charts that show how much tax is charged per income amount for each of the federal filing statuses. Tax tables apply to income that is less than $100,000 and each filing status has a separate table. If the taxpayer's income is over $100,000, then the tax is calculated differently.

To read the tax table, you must find the income range your client's income amount falls between and then look along the line until you come to your client's filing status. If a client's income is the exact amount of one of the ranges, always round up and use the higher tax amount. Tax tables are found in the Form 1040 Instructions. Tax tables can also be accessed through the IRS website.

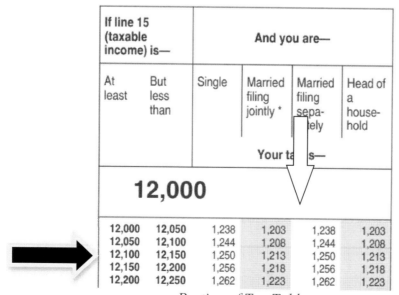

Portion of Tax Table

The tax tables are not used by the following:

➤ Estates or trusts.
➤ Individuals claiming the exclusion for foreign tax credits.
➤ Taxpayers who file a short-period return.
➤ Taxpayers whose income exceeds $100,000.

Part 6 Review Questions

To obtain the maximum benefit from this chapter, LTP recommends that you complete each of the following questions, and then compare them to the answers with feedback that immediately follow. Under governing self-study standards, vendors are required to present review questions intermittently throughout each self-study course.

These questions and explanations are not part of the final examination and will not be graded by LTP.

IP6.1
Which of the following best describes fringe benefits?

a. Employer provided an employee birthday lunch.
b. Employer provided a plaque for continuous service to their faithful employees.
c. Employer provided airfare for their employees to work at a different location for 3 days.
d. Employer provided benefits to their employees in addition to their normal compensation.

IP6.2
Which of the following is not included in a Cafeteria plan?

a. Archer medical savings account
b. Adoption assistance
c. Group-term life insurance
d. Dependent care assistance

IP6.3
Which of the following is nontaxable income?

a. Child support
b. Social Security benefits
c. Fringe benefits
d. Earned income

IP6.4
A cafeteria plan including a_____ allows employees to choose between receiving cash or taxable benefits.

a. Flexible spending arrangement
b. Flexible spending agreement
c. Flexible adoption arrangement
d. Flexible spending alignment

IP6.5
Which *de minimis* benefit is included in the employee's wages?

    a. A transit pass
    b. Group Term Life Insurance
    c. Holiday ham and turkey
    d. Tickets to see the Super Bowl

IP6.6
Group-term life insurance that is payable on death of an employee, employee spouse or dependent that is less than _____is considered a *de minimis* benefit.

    a. $5,000
    b. $2,500
    c. $2,000
    d. $900

IP6.7
Which of the following is nontaxable on the federal tax return?

    a. Child support
    b. Unemployment income
    c. Paid medical family leave
    d. Social Security benefits

IP6.8
When disability income is reported on Form W-2 the amount is _____.

    a. not taxable
    b. taxable
    c. the same as workers' compensation
    d. the same as Social Security benefits

IP6.9
Which *de minimis* benefit is included in the employee's wages?

    a. Gift card for $500
    b. Holiday cash bonus for $250
    c. Holiday ham and turkey
    d. Group term life insurance

IP6.10
Veronica received educational assistance benefits from her employer under the qualified educational assistance program. Veronica's employer can exclude up to____of eligible benefits from her wages.

    a. $5,000
    b. $5,250
    c. $5,500
    d. $5,750

Part 6 Review Questions Answers

IP6.1
Which of the following best describes fringe benefits?

    a. Employer provided an employee birthday lunch.
    b. Employer provided a plaque for continuous service to their faithful employees.
    c. Employer provided airfare for their employees to work at a different location for 3 days.
    d. Employer provided benefits to their employees in addition to their normal compensation.

Feedback: Review section *Fringe Benefits.*

IP6.2
Which of the following is not included in a Cafeteria plan?

    a. Archer medical savings account
    b. Adoption assistance
    c. Group-term life insurance
    d. Dependent care assistance

Feedback: Review section *Cafeteria Plan.*

IP6.3
Which of the following is nontaxable income?

    a. Child support
    b. Social Security benefits
    c. Fringe benefits
    d. Earned income

Feedback: Review section *Nontaxable Income.*

IP6.4
A cafeteria plan including a_____ allows employees to choose between receiving cash or taxable benefits.

    a. Flexible spending arrangement
    b. Flexible spending agreement
    c. Flexible adoption arrangement
    d. Flexible spending alignment

Feedback: Review section *Cafeteria Plans.*

IP6.5
Which *de minimis* benefit is included in the employee's wages?

    a. A transit pass
    b. Group Term Life Insurance
    c. Holiday ham and turkey
    d. Tickets to see the Super Bowl

Feedback: Review section *Nontaxable Income.*

IP6.6

Group-term life insurance that is payable on death of an employee, employee spouse or dependent that is less than_____is considered a *de minimis* benefit.

    a. $5,000
    b. $2,500
    c. $2,000
    d. $900

Feedback: Review section *Fringe Benefits.*

IP6.7

Which of the following is nontaxable on the federal tax return?

    a. Child support
    b. Unemployment income
    c. Paid medical family leave
    d. Social Security benefits

Feedback: Review section *Nontaxable Income.*

IP6.8

When disability income is reported on Form W-2 the amount is _____.

    a. not taxable
    b. taxable
    c. the same as workers' compensation
    d. the same as Social Security benefits

Feedback: Review section *Nontaxable Income.*

IP6.9

Which *de minimis* benefit is included in the employee's wages?

    a. Gift card for $500
    b. Holiday cash bonus for $250
    c. Holiday ham and turkey
    d. Tickets to see the Super Bowl

Feedback: Review section *Fringe Benefits.*

IP6.10

Veronica received educational assistance benefits from her employer under the qualified educational assistance program. Veronica's employer can exclude up to____of eligible benefits from her wages.

    a. $5,000
    b. $5,250
    c. $5,500
    d. $5,750

Feedback: Review section *Other Fringe Benefits.*

Takeaways

Gross income, or "worldwide income," includes all income received from any source earned. Covered in this chapter was the most common types of income earned or unearned. Later chapters will go in depth with the most common income that is reported on Schedule A, B, C, E, and F.

If the taxpayer repays an amount that was included in an earlier year as income, the taxpayer may be able to deduct the amount repaid from income for the year in which it was repaid. If the amount repaid is more than $3,000, the taxpayer may be able to take a credit against the tax for the year in which it was repaid. This credit is taken on Schedule A. Schedule A will be discussed in a later chapter. Generally, the taxpayer can claim a deduction or credit only if the repayment qualifies as an expense or loss incurred in the taxpayer's business or in a for-profit transaction.

Any individual with taxable compensation may be eligible to contribute to a traditional IRA. The individual may be able to contribute to a Roth IRA, establish a new traditional IRA, or fund the new IRA with funds transferred from either another traditional IRA or an employer-sponsored qualified retirement plan. In the taxable year in which an individual turns 72, the taxpayer cannot make future contributions to a traditional IRA.

TEST YOUR KNOWLEDGE!
Go online to take a practice quiz.

California Income and the 540 Schedule CA

Introduction

Although California does not conform to certain provisions of the Internal Revenue Code, it does conform in the following ways:

➢ The "general rule."
➢ The "simplified general rule," or the "safe harbor method."
➢ IRA rollovers.
➢ Roth IRAs.
➢ Archer MSAs.
➢ Coverdell ESAs.
➢ Current-year IRA deductions.
➢ Lump-sum credits received by federal employees.

Any interest or dividends can be taxable income if they are credited to the taxpayer's account and can be withdrawn. This chapter will cover the safe harbor rule and show which interest and dividends are not taxable income and which expenses can be deducted on the taxpayer's Schedule A if the taxpayer itemizes.

Objectives

At the end of this chapter, the student will:

➢ Explain how California taxes "worldwide income."
➢ Understand when military income is taxable.
➢ Define a *subtraction* on 540 Schedule CA.
➢ Describe an *additional income* on 540 Schedule CA.
➢ Understand how California taxes interest income.
➢ Define when California conforms to taxing dividend income.
➢ Know which municipal bonds are taxable in California.

Resources

Form 540	FTB 989	Instructions 540 Schedule CA
540 Schedule CA	FTB Publication 1001	Instructions Form 540
FTB Form 593-I	FTB 1004	Instructions Form 593-I
FTB Form 593-C	FTB Publication 1005	Instructions Form 593-C
FTB 593-E Booklet	FTB Publication 1017	Instructions Form 3805-E
FTB Form 3805-E	FTB Publication 1032	Instructions Schedule D (540 or 540NR)
Form 3800	FTB Publication 1004	
Form 3803	FTB Publication 1016	Instructions Form 3800
	FTB Publication 1017	Instructions Form 3803
	Schedule D (540 or 540NR)	

Table of Contents

Part 1 How to Read the State Items on the W-2.

While the federal portion of the W-2 consists of boxes a-f and 1-14, boxes 15-20 are reserved for information needed to report state and local wages and withholdings.

Copy of Form W-2

Box 15. *Employer's state ID Number.* This box shows the employer's state EIN identification number. This ID number is also administered by the Employment Development Department (EDD), but it is not the same number found in box b; that is the employer's federal EIN number.

Box 16. *State wages, tips, etc.* This box shows the amount of state wages the taxpayer earned.

Box 17. *State income tax.* This box shows the amount of state income tax withheld from the taxpayer's state wages.

Box 18. *Local wages, tips, etc.* This box reports local wages or tips the taxpayer has earned. This box is typically not used in California.

Box 19. *Local income tax.* This box reports the local income tax such as CASDI or VPDI. Although some employers enter the amount in box 14. This box is typically not used in California.

Box 20. *Locality name.* This box reports the locality of the local income tax. For example, if San Francisco has a higher minimum wage than the rest of the state, it would be indicated in this box. This box is typically not used in California.

Income

California differs from federal law when determining taxable income, but it conforms when it comes to taxing it. California defines gross income as "all income from whatever source derived." California did not conform with the TCJA and still allows the deduction of the greater of itemized or standard deductions as well as the use of personal exemptions that lower an individual's tax liability.

The image below shows lines 12-19 of Form 540, which are used to determine the taxable amount of the AGI at the state level. To determine California income, the tax professional begins by entering the state wages reported on the W-2 into line 12 of the Form 540 and the adjusted gross income from the federal return into line 13. To calculate California's adjusted gross income (AGI), the federal AGI is the starting point then California adds or subtracts income according to state law.

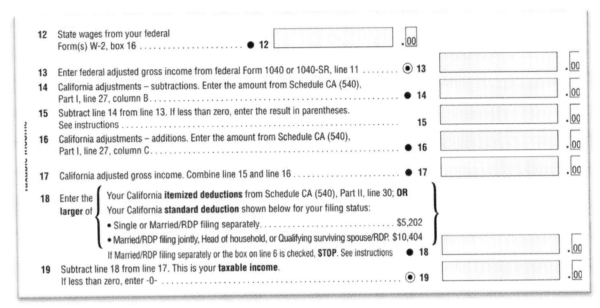

Portion of Form 540

540 Schedule CA, Part 1 Income Adjustment Schedule

The purpose of 540 Schedule CA is for the California resident taxpayer to adjust his or her federal AGI and federal itemized deductions based on California law to determine the tax liability at the state level. Due to the TCJA, Part II of 540 Schedule CA was revamped to reflect the federal form changes.

In column A, enter the taxpayer's federal amount from Federal Form 1040, lines 1-5, and Federal Form 1040, Schedule 1, lines 10-21. Column B and column C are used to make the necessary additions and subtractions from the federal return. All amounts are entered as positive numbers unless the instructions say otherwise.

Portion of 540 Schedule CA

Wages, Salaries, tips, etc. Line 1

Normally, adjustments are not made to this line. The taxpayer may need an adjustment if they received any of the following types of income:

> ➢ Active military pay has special rules for military taxpayers. See FTB Form 1032.
> ➢ Combat zones pay for active military personnel can be nontaxable on the federal return, but for certain combat zones, California does not conform. Tax professionals in this situation will need to do more research to ensure the preparation of an accurate return. See FTB Form 1032.
> ➢ California excludes sick pay received under the Federal Insurance Contributions Act and Railroad Retirement Act from income. Enter the amount of sick pay received in column B that is included in column A.
> ➢ Ride-sharing fringe benefit differences. On line 7, on column B, enter the amount of ride-sharing benefits that were received and included as federal income.
> ➢ Exclusion for compensation from exercising a California qualified stock option (CQSO): to claim the exclusion the taxpayer must meet the following conditions:
>> o Earned income is $40,000 or less from the corporation granting the CQSO.
>> o The market value of the options granted is less than $100,000.
>> o The total number of shares must be 1,000 or less.
>> o The corporation issuing the stock must designate that the stock issued is a CQSO at the time of the granted option.
> ➢ Employer health savings account (HSA) contributions: enter the amount from the employer HSA contribution from federal Form W-2, box 12, code *W* on line 7, column C.
> ➢ Income exclusions for supplementary payments for in-home supportive services (IHSS): supplementary payment is equal to the sales tax paid plus any increase in the federal payroll withholding paid due to the supplementary payment.

If an active military taxpayer is stationed in California, but joined the service in another state, that state is the servicemember's residency. For example, Jason joined the armed services in Texas and is stationed in San Diego. His W-2 will have TX in box 15. He would file a California return as a nonresident. More research may be needed on this subject.

Doug is an active military taxpayer and joined the Navy in California and is stationed in Nevada. He would file a California return as a nonresident since he is active military. Since Nevada is a state with no income tax, he does not file a Nevada tax return.

Taxable Interest, Line 2

Most interest income taxable by federal standards is taxable by the state of California. Enter interest received from the following sources in column B of 540 Schedule CA:

> ➢ Interest from U.S. savings bonds unless from series EE; U.S. savings bonds issued after 1989 that qualified for the Education Savings Bond Program exclusion.
> ➢ U.S. Treasury bills, notes, and bonds.
> ➢ All other bonds or obligations of the United States and its territories.
> ➢ Interest from Ottoman Turkish Empire settlement payments.
> ➢ Interest income from children under the age of 19 or students under the age of 24 that was included on the child's federal tax return and reported on the California return by the parent.

Enter any tax-exempt interest that was reported on Form 1040 into column C of the 540 Schedule CA:

> ➤ Federal exempt-interest dividends from other states, their municipal obligations, or from mutual funds that do not meet the 50% rule. The 50% rule is certain mutual funds pay exempt-interest dividends. If the mutual fund has at least 50% of the assets invested in tax-exempt U.S. obligations/and or in California or its municipal obligations, that dividend amount is exempt from California tax.
> ➤ Non-California state bonds.
> ➤ Non-California municipal bonds issued by a county, city, town, or other local government unit outside of the state of California.
> ➤ Obligations of the District of Columbia issued after December 27, 1973.
> ➤ Non-California bonds if the interest was passed through to the taxpayer from an S corporation, trust, partnership, or limited liability company (LLC).
> ➤ Interest or other earnings from a health savings account (HSA) is not treated as taxed deferred; interest or earnings in an HSA are taxable in the year earned.
> ➤ Interest on any bond or other obligation issued by the government of American Samoa.
> ➤ Interest income from children under the age of 19 or students under the age of 24 that was included on the parent's federal tax return and reported on the California tax return by the child.

No entry is made in column B or C if the taxpayer earned interest on any or all of the following:

> ➤ Federal National Mortgage Association (Fannie Mae) Bonds.
> ➤ Government National Mortgage Association (Ginnie Mae) Bonds.
> ➤ Federal Home Loan Mortgage Corporation (FHLMC) securities.
> ➤ Grants paid to low-income individuals.

Ordinary Dividends, Line 3

Usually, no difference exists between the amount of dividends reported in column A and the amount that California law requires to be reported. Dividends derived from other states and their municipal obligations are taxed in California.

The following dividends obtained in the current year are entered in column C:

> ➤ Controlled foreign corporation (CFC) dividends.
> ➤ Regulated investment company (RIC) capital gains.
> ➤ Distributions of pre-1987 earnings from an S corporation.
> ➤ Dividend income from children under the age of 19 or students under the age of 24 that were excluded on either the parent's or child's federal tax return and reported on the California tax return by whomever did not report it on the federal.

The following child earned dividends obtained would be reported on column B:

> ➤ Noncash patronage dividends from farmers' cooperatives or mutual associations.
> ➤ A controlled foreign corporation.
> ➤ Distributions of pre-1987 earnings from S corporations.
> ➤ Undistributed capital gains for regulated investment company (RIC) shareholders.

Enter the dividend amount in column B if the taxpayer received dividend income from children under the age of 19 or from students under the age of 24 that was included on the parent's or child's federal tax return and reported on the California tax return by the opposite taxpayer. See FTB Publication 1001.

IRA Distributions, Line 4

California conforms to certain provisions of the Internal Revenue Code related to pension plans and deferred compensation. Federal law prohibits the states from taxing the retirement income of nonresidents. If the taxpayer has an IRA basis and was a prior nonresident, taxpayer may have to restate the California basis. See Publication 1005.

If the taxpayer received an early distribution from a qualified retirement plan and the taxpayer reported additional tax on the federal return, the individual may have to use Form 3805P to report the additional tax on line 63 of the California return as well. California and federal laws are generally the same when it comes to the tax on early distributions. However, California does not conform to all federal exceptions to the additional tax on an early distribution. California does not tax the excess contributions to a traditional IRA, Roth IRA, Coverdell ESA, Archer MSA, or excess accumulation in a qualified plan. The additional tax is 2.5% on the part of the distribution that is includable in income.

Form 3805P must be filed if the taxpayer has received any of the following:

1. Received an early taxable distribution from a qualified retirement plan and a distribution code other than 2, 3, or 4 is shown in box 7 of federal Form 1099-R.
2. Owes tax on early distributions from an IRA, some other qualified retirement plan, an annuity, or a modified endowment contract, and there is an exception code in box 7 of Form 1099-R. See Instructions Form 1099-R for more information.
3. Owes a tax because the taxpayer received distributions from a Coverdell ESA in excess of the educational costs; if this is true, complete Form 3805P, Part II.
4. Received taxable distributions from an Archer MSA. This penalty is 12.5%.
5. Meet an exception to the tax on early distributions, and distribution code 2, 3, or 4 is *not* shown or is incorrect on federal Form 1099-R.

The taxpayer does not have to file Form FTB 3805P if the following are true:

➤ The taxable portion of the distribution was rolled over into another qualified plan within 60 days of receipt on the year received.
➤ The taxpayer received an early distribution and had a distribution code 2, 3, or 4 shown on federal Form 1099-R.

California conforms to the exceptions for a penalty on an early withdrawal from retirement plans for reservists while serving on active duty for at least 180 days after September 11, 2001; as well as for public safety employees after separation from service after age 50, if distributions were made after August 17, 2006. When filing a joint return, each spouse or RDP must file a separate form FTB 3805P for taxes attributable to his or her distribution from a qualified retirement plan.

A qualified retirement plan includes:

➤ A qualified pension, profit-sharing, or stock bonus plan.
➤ A Keogh retirement plan (outside the scope of this course).
➤ A qualified cash or deferred arrangement (CODA) as described in IRC section 401(k).
➤ A qualified annuity plan.

> ➤ A tax-shelter annuity contract.
> ➤ An individual retirement plan or account.

See Instructions Form 3805P.

Pensions and Annuities, Line 5

Normally there are no adjustments needed for IRAs, pensions, or annuities because California conforms to federal tax law regarding them. California does tax these items; however, their penalty for early withdrawal is only 2.5%, but for early distribution from a SIMPLE the penalty is 6%. There are also differences between federal and state law regarding self-employment pensions, although this is beyond the scope of this course.

Social Security Benefits, Line 6

California excludes Social Security benefits or equivalent tier 1 railroad retirement benefits from taxable income. The taxable amount of Social Security benefits or equivalent tier 1 benefits are entered on column A. An adjustment would be made on 540 Schedule CA on Line 6b of Part 1, column B, for the amount that was taxed on the federal return.

Capital Gain or Loss, Line 7

California taxes all capital gains as regular income and does not conform with federal. It does not recognize the distinction between short-term and long-term capital gains. Depending on the taxpayer's California tax bracket, their capital gains tax could be 1% to 13.3%.

540 Schedule CA, Part 2 Additional Income

The following section is equivalent to the Federal Form 1040, Schedule 1, Part 1.

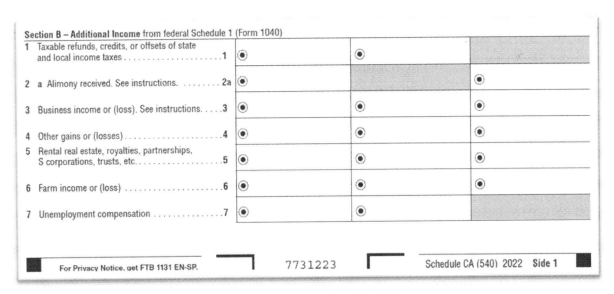

Portion of 540 Schedule CA

Section B, line 1: Taxable Refunds, Credits, or Offsets of State and Local Income Taxes.

If the taxpayer received a refund in the prior year for the California return, then the taxpayer would not report it as income on the state return for the current tax year. Enter the amount received on line 10, column B, 540 Schedule CA.

Section B, line 2a: Alimony Received.

California conforms to federal law regarding alimony as income to the taxpayer. California did not conform to the new rules of TCJA for alimony. An RDP may be able to receive alimony in the state of California, but the couple cannot report that alimony on the federal return. If the taxpayer is a nonresident and receives alimony from a resident of California, the nonresident reports the income on Line 11, column C.

Section B, line 3: Business Income or Loss.

Federal business income or loss that need to be adjusted due to California and federal law differences are:

- ➢ Depreciation methods.
- ➢ Special credits.
- ➢ Accelerated write-offs.

As a result, the recovery period or basis used to figure California depreciation may be different from the amount used for federal purposes. The adjustment differences are figured on FTB Form 3885A: *Depreciation and Amortization Adjustments*. More research will be needed to complete the adjustments. See FTB 3801 and FTB 3885A.

Section B, line 4: Other Gains or Losses.

California taxes long- and short-term capital gains as regular income. Generally, no adjustments are made. California's basis of an asset may be different due to the differences between California and federal laws. The capital gains tax rate for an individual in California is the same rate as their income bracket. If differences exist, the calculations are made on 540 Schedule D: *California Capital Gain or Loss Adjustment*. See FTB Publication 1001.

Normally, no adjustments are needed. However, if the basis of the taxpayer's assets for California differs from the federal due to differences between California and federal law. Adjustments are made for the taxpayer on Schedule D-1: *Sales of Business Property*.

Section B, line 5: Rental Real Estate, Royalties, Partnerships, S Corporations, Trusts, etc.

Federal income or loss adjustments are usually reported in column A. The adjustments are necessary because of the differences between California and federal law relating to depreciation methods, special credits, and accelerated write-offs. California law does not conform to federal law for material participation in rental real estate activities. For more information, see FTB Form 3801.

Section B, line 6: Farm Income or Loss.

Adjustments are generally necessary since California and federal law differ on depreciation methods, special credits, and accelerated write-offs. As a result, the recovery period or basis on the California return may be different than the federal, and adjustments are made on column B and column C, line 3.

Use FTB Form 3801 to figure the total adjustment if the taxpayer has one of the following:

- ➢ One or more passive activities that produced a loss.

➤ One or more passive activities that produce a loss and any nonpassive activity report on federal Schedule F (Form 1040), *Profit or Loss from Farming.*

Use FTB Form 3885A to figure the total adjustment for line 18 if the taxpayer has both of the following:

➤ Nonpassive activities only that produced either gains, losses, or combination of gains and losses. If the taxpayer has more than one passive activity.
➤ Passive activities that produce gains. If the taxpayer has more than one passive activity.

Line 7: Unemployment Compensation.

Unemployment compensation and paid family leave payments are not taxable income for California. Enter the amount shown in column A on column B.

Line 8: Other Income.

California does not tax winnings from the California lottery. Enter the California amount only in column B. Gambling winnings from other states, are taxable in California. If the gambling winnings are reduced on the federal return, then the gambling losses must be subtracted on the California return on 540 Schedule CA, Part II, line 16, column A for federal itemized deductions.

Distributions from a health savings account (HSA) for unqualified medical expenses are not taxable in California.

Income that has been exempted from federal law by a tax treaty on Form 1040, Schedule 1 may be excluded from California if it specifically excludes the income for state purposes.

Part 1 Review Questions

To obtain the maximum benefit from this chapter, LTP recommends that you complete each of the following questions, and then compare them to the answers with feedback that immediately follow. Under governing self-study standards, vendors are required to present review questions intermittently throughout each self-study course.

These questions and explanations are not part of the final examination and will not be graded by LTP.

CIP1.1
When gathering information off the state boxes on Form W-2, where is the state income tax found?

a. Box 15
b. Box 16
c. Box 17
d. Box 18

CIP1.2

When gathering information off the state boxes on the W-2, where is the state income reported?

a. Box 15
b. Box 16
c. Box 17
d. Box 18

CIP1.3

Where should CASDI or VPDI be reported?

a. Box 14
b. Box 16
c. Box 18
d. Box 19

CIP1.4

What is the purpose of 540 Schedule CA?

a. Adjust the state return.
b. Adjust the federal Schedule A
c. Adjust the federal return
d. Adjust the federal itemized deductions

CIP1.5

Which of the following obligations is nontaxable on the federal but is taxable on the state return?

a. Interest on Non-California State municipal obligations
b. Dividends on Non-California State municipal obligations
c. Interest of U.S. obligations
d. Military wages

CIP1.6

Which of the following is entered on column C of the California 540 Schedule CA, line 8a?

a. Interest of U.S. obligations
b. Dividends of U.S. obligations
c. Social Security benefits
d. Interest on Non-California state Municipal obligations

CIP1.7

Which of the following is not an FTB form?

a. Form 540 2EZ
b. 540 Schedule CA
c. Form 540
d. Form 1040

CIP1.8

The purpose of 540 Schedule CA is for the California resident taxpayer to____.

    a. increase exemptions based on California law
    b. adjust their federal adjusted gross income
    c. increase the taxpayer's tax refund
    d. decrease the taxpayer's tax refund

CIP1.9

On 540 Schedule CA, no entry is made on column B or C if the taxpayer earned interest on which of the following?

    a. U.S. Treasury bills, notes, and bonds
    b. Federal National Mortgage Association Bonds
    c. Interest from Ottoman Turkish Empire Settlement Payments
    d. Non-California state bonds

CIP1.10

Which of the following is the reporting tool for column A, line 2?

    a. Form 1099-INT
    b. Form 1099-DIV
    c. Form 1099-R
    d. Form 1099-G

Part 1 Review Questions Answers

CIP1.1

When gathering information off the state boxes on Form W-2, where is the state income tax found?

    a. Box 15
    b. Box 16
    c. Box 17
    d. Box 18

Feedback: Review section *How to Read the State Items on the W-2.*

CIP1.2

When gathering information off the state boxes on the W-2, where is the state income reported?

    a. Box 15
    b. Box 16
    c. Box 17
    d. Box 18

Feedback: Review section *How to Read the State Items on the W-2.*

CIP1.3
Where should CASDI or VPDI be reported?

    a. Box 14
    b. Box 16
    c. Box 18
    d. Box 19

Feedback: Review section *540 Schedule CA, Part 1 Income Adjustment Schedule.*

CIP1.4
What is the purpose of 540 Schedule CA?

    a. Adjust the state return.
    b. Adjust the federal Schedule A
    c. Adjust the federal return
    d. Adjust the federal itemized deductions

Feedback: Review section *540 Schedule CA, Part 1 Income Adjustment Schedule.*

CIP1.5
Which of the following obligations is nontaxable on the federal but is taxable on the state return?

    a. Interest on Non-California State municipal obligations
    b. Dividends on Non-California State municipal obligations
    c. Interest of U.S. obligations
    d. Military wages

Feedback: Review section *Taxable Interest, Line 2.*

CIP1.6
Which of the following is entered on column C of the California 540 Schedule CA, line 8a?

    a. Interest of U.S. obligations
    b. Dividends of U.S. obligations
    c. Social Security benefits
    d. Interest on Non-California state Municipal obligations

Feedback: Review section *Taxable Interest, Line 2.*

CIP1.7
Which of the following is not an FTB form?

    a. Form 540 2EZ
    b. 540 Schedule CA
    c. Form 540
    d. Form 1040

Feedback: Review section *How to Read the State Items on the W-2.*

CIP1.8
The purpose of 540 Schedule CA is for the California resident taxpayer to___.

    a. increase exemptions based on California law
    b. adjust their federal adjusted gross income
    c. increase the taxpayer's tax refund
    d. decrease the taxpayer's tax refund

Feedback: Review section *540 Schedule CA, Part 1 Income Adjustment Schedule.*

CIP1.9
On 540 Schedule CA, no entry is made on column B or C if the taxpayer earned interest on which of the following?

    a. U.S. Treasury bills, notes, and bonds
    b. Federal National Mortgage Association Bonds
    c. Interest from Ottoman Turkish Empire Settlement Payments
    d. Non-California state bonds

Feedback: Review section *Ordinary Dividends.*

CIP1.10
Which of the following is the reporting tool for column A, line 2?

    a. Form 1099-INT
    b. Form 1099-DIV
    c. Form 1099-R
    d. Form 1099-G

Feedback: Review section *Taxable Interest.*

Part 2 Other Income

California does not always conform to federal tax law. This part gives a brief overview of other taxable income for California and explains if the state conforms or does not conform to federal tax law.

Health Savings Account

California does not conform to federal legislation for contributions to an HSA account. Contributions made by the employer on behalf of the employee are excluded from W-2 wages. Distributions not used for qualified medical expenses are taxable on the federal return but are not taxable on the California return. Interest and other earnings of an HSA are excluded from federal gross income; California does not conform, and the HSA earnings are taxable in the year earned. A rollover from an MSA to an HSA constitutes distributions and is subject to state income tax plus the additional 10% California rollover penalty tax. Any distribution from an IRA to an HSA must be added to AGI on the tax return and would be subject to an additional 2.5% tax since this distribution is considered a premature distribution. The total tax rate will become 12.5% after the 10% additional penalty and the 2.5% penalty for an early distribution have both been applied.

After December 31, 2007, contributions to an MSA for the taxpayer cannot be made. If the taxpayer was an active participant before January 1, 2008, and an active MSA participant after December 31, 2007, and covered by an HDHP of an MSA participant employer, they are eligible to have an MSA.

Early Distributions

California law conforms to federal law, with the exception that the early withdrawal penalty is 2.5%. Use FTB Form 3805P: *Additional Taxes on Qualified Plans (Including IRAs) and Other Tax-Favored Accounts*, to figure the additional tax. California does not conform to the one-time rollover from an IRA to an HSA. The taxpayer is liable for the 2.5% additional tax.

Military Pay

Taxpayers stationed in California who possess domiciles outside of California are considered nonresidents, and California will not tax their military pay. However, nonmilitary pay earned by the taxpayer or spouse will be subject to state income tax with no regard as to the domicile. If the taxpayer's domicile is in California, and he or she is stationed inside the state of California, the taxpayer is a resident of California and his or her military pay, along with all other income (what is termed *worldwide income*), is taxable by California.

If the taxpayer's domicile is in California, and he or she is stationed outside the state, any military pay received while stationed outside of California would not be taxed by California. However, any other California-sourced income is subject to California tax. See FTB Publication 1032.

Military Pension

If the taxpayer is a California resident, military pension is taxable by California, regardless of where the service was performed. What matters is where income is received, not where it was earned.

Fringe Benefits

Under federal law and the provisions administered by the Employment Development Department (EDD), qualified transportation benefits are excluded from gross income. There are no monthly limits for the exclusion of the benefits, and California's definitions are more expansive.

For example, California law provides income exclusion for compensation, or the fair market value of other benefits received for participating in a California ride-sharing arrangement such as the following:

- ➢ Subsidized parking.
- ➢ Commuting in a third-party vanpool.
- ➢ Using private commuter buses.
- ➢ Subscription taxi pools.
- ➢ Monthly transit passes provided for employees or their dependents.

Enter the amount of the ride-sharing fringe benefits received and include the amount as federal income on 540 Schedule CA, line 1, column B.

Sick Pay

Sick pay received under the Federal Insurance Contributions Act and Railroad Act is excluded from income. Enter qualifying sick pay as federal income on Schedule CA (540 or 540NR), line 1, column B.

Income of a Child

Any child 18-years-old or younger and any student under the age of 24 at the end of 2022 that has investment income over $2,300 must use Form FTB 3800 to determine the child's tax. Include only income taxed by California on this form. Also include investment income that was not taxed on the child's federal tax return but is taxable under California law. The child's investment income could be taxed at the parent's rate if the parent's rate is higher than the child's rate and any of the following apply:

> ➤ The child is 18 years or younger or a student under the age of 24 (as of the end of 2022, children born on January 1, 2005, are 18, and children born on January 1, 1999, are 24).
> ➤ The child had investment income of more than $2,300 that was taxable in California.
> ➤ At least one parent was alive at the end of 2022.
> ➤ The children were 18 at the end of 2022 and didn't earn income equaling more than half of their support.

Election to Claim Child's Unearned Income on Parent's Return

Parents may elect to report their child's unearned income from interest and dividends on their California income tax return by completing FTB Form 3803. If the taxpayers make this selection, the child will not have to file a return. The taxpayers may report their child's income on their California income tax return even if they do not do so on their federal income tax return.

The taxpayer may make this election if the child meets all the following conditions:

> ➤ The child was under the age of 19 or was a student under the age of 24 at the end of 2022.
> ➤ The child is required to file a 2022 return.
> ➤ The child had income only from interest and dividends.
> ➤ The child had gross income for 2022 that was less than $11,000.
> ➤ The child made no estimated tax payments for 2022.
> ➤ No overpayment of tax shown on his or her 2021 return was applied to the child's 2022 estimated taxes.
> ➤ The child had no state income tax withheld from income or backup withholding.

If all these conditions are satisfied, the child is treated as having no gross income and is not required to file a tax return; California Form 3803 (comparable to federal Form 8814) is attached to the parent's return. For the parent to report his or her child's unearned income, the child's adjusted gross income would be reported on Form 540, Line 17. If the parent reported the unearned income on the federal return but not on the state return, an adjustment would be made on 540 Schedule CA column B or C, using line 8 to include the calculations from FTB 3803. For more information, see Instructions for 540 Schedule CA.

Foreign Income

California does not conform to the federal tax treaties and other worldwide income adjustments. California taxes all income. The tax professional needs to prepare an accurate tax return by doing the research on which income needs to be added to the 540 Schedule CA.

How to Read the California Tax Tables

Instead of writing out the filing status, California uses numbers associated with the filing statuses. Number 1 is for the Single taxpayer. Number 2 is for Married/RDP Filing Jointly.

Number 3 is for Married/RDP filing separately. Number 4 is for Head of Household. Number 5 is for Surviving Spouse.

Tax tables are based on taxable income. Tax tables apply to income that is less than $100,000 and each filing status has a separate table. If the taxpayer's income is over $100,000, then the tax is calculated differently. The tax tables are used by individual taxpayers but not by the following:

➢ Estates or trusts.
➢ Individuals claiming the exclusion for foreign tax credit.
➢ Taxpayers who file a short period return.
➢ Taxpayers whose income exceeds $100,000.

When reading the tax table, the first column is the taxable income found on Form 540, line 31. To read the tax table, find the income that is between the two numbers. For example, Mr. & Mrs. Yellow file a joint return, and their taxable income is $13,101. First find the $13,051-$13,150 taxable income amount in the tax table charts. Then, find the filing status column and read down the column. The amount shown in the taxable income line and filing status is $131. This amount is entered on line 31 of Form 540. Check the box that is labeled "Tax Table". Most software will do this automatically. If the taxpayer qualifies for the 540 2EZ you would not use this tax table; Form 540 2EZ has a separate tax table.

Tax Rates

The California tax tables must be used with all California returns unless the taxable income exceeds $100,000, in which case the taxpayer will need to complete a worksheet to calculate the tax liability. Nonresidents and part-year residents are taxed using the same table or schedule as residents. However, the tax computation (via the 540NR) is done according to the ratio of California source income versus income from all sources. The California AGI for nonresidents and part-year residents includes the following:

➢ All items of AGI (regardless of their source) for any period the taxpayer was a resident of the state.
➢ Income items attributable to California sources; these are taxed for any period the taxpayer was a resident of the state.

If Your Taxable Income Is ...		The Tax For Filing Status		
At Least	But Not Over	1 Or 3 Is	2 Or 5 Is	4 Is
12,951	13,050	175	130	130
13,051	13,150	177	131	131
13,151	13,250	179	132	132
13,251	13,350	181	133	133
13.351	13.450	183	134	134

Portion of California Tax Table

Part 2 Review Questions

To obtain the maximum benefit from this chapter, LTP recommends that you complete each of the following questions, and then compare them to the answers with feedback that immediately follow. Under governing self-study standards, vendors are required to present review questions intermittently throughout each self-study course.

These questions and explanations are not part of the final examination and will not be graded by LTP.

CIP2.1
California conforms to federal law when it comes to military pension income.

a. True
b. False

CIP2.2
Santos, age 50, took an early distribution from his retirement account. What would his additional California tax be?

a. 6%
b. 2.5%
c. 12.5%
d. 9%

CIP2.3
Which of the following is reported on 540 Schedule CA, line 2, column C, in the year received?

a. Interest
b. Regulated investment company capital gains
c. Reinvested dividends
d. Income

CIP2.4
If the parents claimed their child's income on the federal return, which of the following state forms must be used?

a. Form 3800
b. Form 3803
c. Form 3506
d. Form 540A

CIP2.5
When calculating the California tax when is the exemption amount subtracted?

a. Before the tax is calculated from the tax table
b. After the tax is calculated from the tax table
c. After the special credits are calculated
d. Before the taxable income is calculated

CIP2.6
California allows the employer to provide certain fringe benefits to their employees. Which of the following is not considered to be a fringe benefit for California?

    a. Social Security benefits
    b. IRA distributions
    c. Wages from a foreign country
    d. Winning the Nevada Lottery

CIP2.7
Under California law, any distribution from an IRA to an HSA would be subject to a _____ additional tax under the rules for premature distributions.

    a. 9.3% (.093%)
    b. 3.2% (.032%)
    c. 10% (.10%)
    d. 2.5% (.025%)

CIP2.8
When there are differences between the taxable federal and state amounts for an IRA distribution, which of the following FTB publication would be helpful for more research?

    a. FTB Publication 1034A-9
    b. FTB PIT 540
    c. FTB Publication 1001
    d. FTB Publication 1005

CIP2.9
Jose worked in Texas before moving and becoming a resident of California. He receives a monthly pension from his prior Texas employer. How will Jose be taxed on his pension?

    a. Jose will be taxed 100% in California and 100% in Texas
    b. Jose will be taxed 100% in California
    c. Jose will be taxed 50% in California and 50% in Texas
    d. Jose will be taxed 100% in Texas

CIP2.10
Out-of-state pensions received by California residents are_____.

    a. non-taxable
    b. 100% taxable
    c. prohibited
    d. 50% taxable

Part 2 Review Questions Answers

CIP2.1
California conforms to federal law when it comes to military pension income.

    a. True
    b. False

Feedback: Review section *Military Pension.*

CIP2.2
Santos, age 50, took an early distribution from his retirement account. What would his additional California tax be?

    a. 6%
    b. 2.5%
    c. 12.5%
    d. 9%

Feedback: Review section *Premature Distributions.*

CIP2.3
Which of the following is reported on 540 Schedule CA, line 2, column C, in the year received?

    a. Interest
    b. Regulated investment company capital gains
    c. Reinvested dividends
    d. Income

Feedback: Review section *Line 2: Taxable Interest.*

CIP2.4
If the parents claimed their child's income on the federal return, which of the following state forms must be used?

    a. Form 3800
    b. Form 3803
    c. Form 3506
    d. Form 540A

Feedback: Review section *Income of a Child.*

CIP2.5
When calculating the California tax when is the exemption amount subtracted?

    a. Before the tax is calculated from the tax table
    b. After the tax is calculated from the tax table
    c. After the special credits are calculated
    d. Before the taxable income is calculated

Feedback: Review section *How to Read the California Tax Tables.*

CIP2.6
California allows the employer to provide certain fringe benefits to their employees. Which of the following is not considered to be a fringe benefit for California?

    a. Subsidized parking
    b. Commuting in a third-party vanpool
    c. Private commuter bus
    d. Claiming their child's income.

Feedback: Review section *Income of a Child.*

CIP2.7
Under California law, any distribution from an IRA to an HSA would be subject to a _____ additional tax under the rules for premature distributions.

    a. 9.3% (.093%)
    b. 3.2% (.032%)
    c. 10% (.10%)
    d. 2.5% (.025%)

Feedback: Review section *Health Savings Account.*

CIP2.8
When there are differences between the taxable federal and state amounts for an IRA distribution, which of the following FTB publication would be helpful for more research?
    a. FTB Publication 1034A-9
    b. FTB PIT 540
    c. FTB Publication 1001
    d. FTB Publication 1005

Feedback: Review section *IRA Distributions*

CIP2.9
Jose worked in Texas before moving and becoming a resident of California. He receives a monthly pension from his prior Texas employer. How will Jose be taxed on his pension?

    a. Jose will be taxed 100% in California and 100% in Texas
    b. Jose will be taxed 100% in California
    c. Jose will be taxed 50% in California and 50% in Texas
    d. Jose will be taxed 100% in Texas

Feedback: Review section *Military Pension.*

CIP2.10
Out-of-state pensions received by California residents are _____.

    a. non-taxable
    b. 100% taxable
    c. prohibited
    d. 50% taxable

Feedback: Review section *Military Pension.*

Takeaways

California gross income is all income the taxpayer received in the form of money, goods, property, and services from all sources that are not exempt from tax. Gross income does not include any adjustments or deductions. California adjusted gross income is the federal adjusted gross income from all sources reduced or increased by all California income adjustments.

California's treatment of pensions, annuities, and IRAs is generally the same as the federal. There are some differences between California and federal law that may cause the amount of the taxpayer's California distribution income to be different than the amount reported on the federal return. Remember: always complete the federal return before completing the state return.

Interest received by a taxpayer or credited to the taxpayer must be included in gross income. Interest income includes interest on bank accounts, loans, notes, corporate bonds, and U.S. savings bonds. Interest income received from obligations from other states, territories, or possessions of the United States is generally exempt from taxation. Dividends are distributions of property made by a corporation to its shareholders out of its earnings and profits. The American Taxpayer Relief Act of 2012 raised the top marginal federal tax rate on dividends to 20%, up from 15%. For taxpayers whose ordinary income is taxed below 25%, dividends will be subject to a 0% rate.

The reduction of a previously reported capital gain is a capital loss subject to the same limitations as other capital losses. California law generally follows federal law with respect to basis. To report sales or exchanges of property other than capital assets, including the sale or exchange used in a trade or business and involuntary conversions (other than casualties and thefts), use California Schedule D-1, *Sales of Business Property*. California does not have a special capital gain tax rate. California basis may be different from the federal return based on the differences in the federal and state law, which will affect the gain or loss on a disposition.

TEST YOUR KNOWLEDGE!
Go online to take a practice quiz.

Chapter 5 Adjustments to Income

Introduction

Students will learn how various expenses affect the taxpayer's income to get to their adjusted gross income (AGI). The Tax Cuts and Jobs Act (TCJA) has impacted adjustments at the federal level and some states did not conform to the TCJA. The nonconforming state will have differences on the state return if applicable. For returns prior to TCJA, the tax professional may need to do more research to file a correct return. TCJA mandates affect the Schedule A, which will be discussed in a later chapter.

Objectives

At the end of this lesson, the student will:

- ➢ Understand how an adjustment to income can decrease the taxpayer's AGI.
- ➢ Explain the differences between the education credits.
- ➢ Define who qualifies to use Form 2106.
- ➢ Know the different types of Health Savings Account.

Resources

Form 1040	Publication 17	Instructions Form 1040
Form 1098-E	Publication 504	Instructions Form 1098-E
Form 2106	Publication 521	Instructions Form 2106
Form 3903	Publication 560	Instructions Form 3903
Form 8889	Publication 969	Instructions Form 8889
Form 8917	Publication 4334	Instructions Form 8917
Schedule SE	Tax Topics 450, 451, 452,	Instructions Schedule SE
Schedule 1	455, 456, 458	

Table of Contents

Part 1 Adjustments to Income

Adjustments are certain expenses that directly reduce the taxpayer's total income and are known as "above the line" tax deductions in the industry. Adjustments reduce total income to arrive at the adjusted gross income (AGI), the total income from all sources minus any adjustments to income. Adjustments are calculated and reported using Form 1040, Schedule 1, lines 11 – 24z.

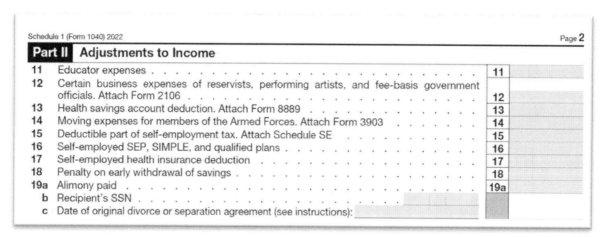

Portion of Schedule 1

Changes Made by the Tax Cuts and Jobs Act

Due to the Tax Cuts and Jobs Act (TCJA), adjustments have been suspended from December 31, 2017, to December 31, 2025. Not all states conformed to the TCJA.

The TCJA eliminated Form 1040A and 1040EZ from 2018 to 2025. Here are some adjustments that will be discussed:

> ➢ Educator expenses.
> ➢ IRA deductions.
> ➢ Student loan interest deductions.
> ➢ Tuition and fees.

Educator Expenses

If the taxpayer was an eligible educator, they can deduct up to $300 of qualified expenses paid in 2022. An eligible educator is a teacher for kindergarten through 12th grade or an instructor, counselor, principal, or aide who works in a school for at least 900 hours during a school year. If the taxpayer and spouse are filing jointly and eligible educators, the maximum deduction is $600. Neither spouse may deduct more than $300 of qualified expenses on line 11 of Form 1040, Schedule 1. The PATH act made this adjustment permanent.

Qualified expenses include ordinary and necessary expenses paid in connection with books, supplies, equipment (including computer equipment, software, and services), and other materials used in their classroom. An ordinary expense is common and accepted in the taxpayer's education field, and a necessary expense is helpful and appropriate for the taxpayer's profession as an educator. An expense does not have to be required to be considered necessary.

Qualified expenses do not include homeschooling expenses or nonathletic supplies for health or physical education courses. The income adjustment amount must be reduced if the educator has any of the following:

➢ Excludable interest on qualified U.S. savings bonds series EE and I are reported on Form 8815.
➢ Any distribution from a qualified tuition program that was excluded from income.
➢ Any tax-free withdrawals from Coverdell education savings account(s).
➢ Any reimbursements received for expenses not reported in box 1 of the W-2.

Form 2106: Unreimbursed Employee Business Expense

Due to the suspension of Form 2106 for tax years 2018 through 2025, most employees cannot use the form. Individuals who can still file Form 2106 include Armed Forces reservists, qualified performing artists, fee-basis state or local government officials, or individuals with a disability claiming impairment-related work expenses. These individuals may qualify to deduct unreimbursed employee business expenses as an adjustment to gross income. This happens by calculating the adjustment using Form 2106 and then flowing the calculated amount to Form 1040, Schedule 1, line 12. To qualify, the taxpayer must meet the following requirements:

1. During the tax year, performing artists performed for at least two employers.
2. The taxpayer received at least $200 from each of at least two of these employers.
3. The taxpayer's related performing arts business expenses are more than 10% of the gross income from the performance of those services.
4. The taxpayer's adjusted gross income is not more than $16,000 before deducting these business expenses.

If the taxpayer meets all the above requirements, the taxpayer should complete Form 2106. If the taxpayer is married, they must file a joint return to claim the adjustment unless they lived apart during the tax year. When filing jointly, the couple must figure out requirements 1, 2, and 3 separately for each of them. However, requirement 4 applies to their combined AGI. If all the requirements are met, the amount on Form 2106, line 10, is entered on Form 1040, Schedule 1, line 12.

Armed Forces Reservists

If the taxpayer is a member of the U.S. military's reserve, National Guard, or a member of the Public Health Service Reserve Corps, the expense for traveling more than 100 miles from their main home is deductible. The deductible expenses are limited to the federal per diem rates for the city the taxpayer is traveling to.

Armed Forces reservists are members of a reserve component of the following organizations:

➢ The United States Army, Navy, Marine Corps, or Air Force.
➢ The Coast Guard Reserve.
➢ The Army National Guard of the United States.
➢ The Air National Guard of the United States.
➢ The Reserve Corps of the Public Health Service.

Fee-Basis State or Local Government Official

Fee-basis state or local government officials qualify if they are employed by a state or a political subdivision of a state and are compensated in whole or in part on a fee basis. Under the Fair Labor Standards Act (FLSA), a "fee-basis" is defined as follows:

Administrative and professional employees may be paid on a fee basis. An employee will be considered to be paid on a "fee basis" within the meaning of these regulations if the employee is paid an agreed upon sum for a single job regardless of the time required for its completion. These payments resemble piecework payments with the important distinction that generally a "fee" is paid for the kind of job that is unique rather than for a series of jobs repeated an indefinite number of times and for which payment on an identical basis is made over and over again. Payments based on the number of hours or days worked and not on the accomplishment of a given task are not considered payments on a fee basis (Section 541.605).

Health Savings Accounts

Health savings accounts contributions from both the employer and the employee are reported on Form 8889 and can be claimed as an adjustment to income on Form 1040, Schedule 1, line 13. Distributions made from the HSA that were paid for qualifying medical expenses are excludable from income. If the maximum possible amount of the HSA were contributed, then that amount would become taxable on the tax return.

A health savings account (HSA) is a tax-exempt trust or custodial account that is set up with a qualified HSA trustee to pay or reimburse certain incurred medical expenses. While this account is always paired with a medical insurance plan, an HSA is not health insurance. What separates this type of account from a regular savings account is the tax advantages that come with it. The taxpayer will receive a tax form stating the exact amount deposited into the account at the end of the year, and that amount is tax-deductible.

To qualify to contribute to an HSA as an eligible individual, the taxpayer must meet the following requirements:

➢ As explained further in the chapter, have a high-deductible health plan (HDHP).
➢ Have no other health coverage except permitted coverage.
➢ Not be enrolled in Medicare.
➢ Not be claimed as a dependent on another return.

Anyone can contribute to the plan for the taxpayer, and no permission or authorization from the IRS is necessary to establish an HSA. When an HSA is set up, the taxpayer will have to work with a qualified HSA trustee, which can be a bank, an insurance company, or anyone already approved by the IRS to be a trustee of individual retirement accounts (IRAs) or Archer medical savings accounts (MSA). The HSA can be established through a trustee that is not a health plan provider.

Last-Month Rule

If the taxpayer is an eligible individual on the first day of the last month of the taxpayer's tax year, they are considered an eligible individual for the entire year. The taxpayer must remain an eligible individual during the tax year. For most taxpayers, this would be January 1st through December 31st, meaning the last-month rule would go into effect as of December 1st. If the taxpayer fails to be eligible other than becoming disabled or deceased, the taxpayer's contributions made during the tax year will become taxable. This amount is also subject to a 10% additional tax.

2022 HSA Contribution Limits with an HDHP:

Type of Coverage	Contribution Limit
Self-only	$3,650
Family	$7,300

2023 HSA Contribution Limits with an HDHP:

Type of Coverage	Contribution Limit
Self-only	$3,850
Family	$7,750

2022 Annual Deductible Limits:

Type of Coverage	Minimum Annual Deduction	Maximum Annual Deduction
Self-only	$1,400	$7,050
Family	$2,800	$14,100

2023 Annual Deductible Limits:

Type of Coverage	Minimum Annual Deduction	Maximum Annual Deduction
Self-only	$1,500	$7,050
Family	$3,000	$14,100

The maximum annual out-of-pocket limit does not apply to deductibles and expenses for out-of-network services if the plan uses a network of providers. Only deductibles and out-of-pocket expenses for services within the network should be used to figure out whether the limit is reached.

Contributions to an HSA

Contributions made to the HSA on behalf of the employee by the employer are not included in the taxpayer's income. An employer's contributions to an employee's account using a salary reduction through a cafeteria plan are treated as an employer contribution. All contributions are reported on Form 8889 and must be filed with Form 1040.

Distributions from an HSA

Generally, medical expenses that have been paid for during the year are not reimbursed by the plan until the taxpayer has met the deductible. The taxpayer may receive a tax-free distribution from the HSA to pay for or reimburse qualified medical expenses after the taxpayer has established an HSA. Distributions received for any other reason are subject to an additional tax.

The Three Primary Types of HSAs

1. High-Deductible Health Plan (HDHP)

An HDHP has:

> ➢ A higher annual deductible than typical health plans.
> ➢ A maximum limit on the total yearly deductible amount and out-of-pocket medical expenses.

An HDHP can provide preventive care and other benefits with no deductible or deductible below the annual minimum. Preventive care can include the following:

> ➢ Routine exams and periodic health evaluations
> ➢ Routine prenatal and well-childcare
> ➢ Child and adult immunizations
> ➢ Stop-smoking programs
> ➢ Weight-loss programs

See IRS Notice 2019-45 for more preventive specific chronic conditions listed as preventive care. https://www.irs.gov/pub/irs-drop/n-19-45.pdf

2. Archer Medical Savings Accounts (MSAs)

Archer MSAs are an IRA-type savings account for use when the taxpayer has medical expenses. They were created to help self-employed individuals and employees of certain small employers meet the medical costs of the account holder, the account holder's spouse, or the account holder's dependent(s). MSAs can be used when the taxpayer has low-cost health insurance with a high-deductible health plan (HDHP). MSA contributions are tax-deductible.

The portion of the medical expense not covered by insurance can be withdrawn tax-free from the MSA. The participant cannot pay their insurance premiums using funds in the MSA. Taxpayers who use Medicare, which counts as health insurance, cannot use any MSA they may have unless it is a Medicare MSA. If the taxpayer has no medical expenses in one year, the contributions remain in the account to be used in the future. The maximum the taxpayer can contribute is 65% of the health-plan deductible for individuals (self-only plan) and 75% for families.

3. Health Flexible Spending Arrangements (FSAs)

A health FSA is usually funded through voluntary salary reduction and reimbursing employees for medical expenses. An FSA is not reported on the tax return, and the salary-reduction contribution limit is $2,850. Regardless of the amount contributed, the taxpayer can receive tax-free distribution amount used to pay for qualified medical expenses. Self-employed individuals do not qualify for this reduction.

Part 1 Review Questions

To obtain the maximum benefit from this chapter, LTP recommends that you complete each of the following questions and then compare them to the answers with feedback immediately following. Under governing self-study standards, vendors must present review questions intermittently throughout each self-study course.

These questions and explanations are not part of the final examination and will not be graded by LTP.

ATIP1.1
Which of the following is not an adjustment to income?

   a. Educator expense
   b. Early penalty withdrawal
   c. Alimony
   d. Itemized deductions

ATIP1.2
Julie is a junior high school teacher, and she spent $1,200 for her classroom. What would be the total of her qualified educator expense?

   a. $1,200
   b. $1,450
   c. $300
   d. $500

ATIP1.3
What is the 2022 HSA Family Contribution limit with a High-Deductible Health Plan?

   a. $3,650
   b. $7,300
   c. $7,350
   d. $7,050

ATIP1.4
The Archer MSA has some great benefits. Which of the following is not a benefit of the Archer MSA?

   a. The interest or other earnings on the asset in the Archer MSA are tax-free.
   b. The taxpayer can claim a tax deduction for contributions even if they do not itemize their deductions on Form 1040.
   c. The contributions cannot remain in the Archer MSA from year to year.
   d. All the answers are correct.

ATIP1.5
Heather just became a 3rd grade teacher. How many hours per year does Heather need to work to qualify for the educator expense?

   a. 250
   b. 500
   c. 900
   d. 1,200

ATIP1.6
Joaquin, a qualifying 7th grade teacher, purchased items for his classroom and wants to know which of the following qualify for the educator expenses.

   1. Crayons for his classroom for art projects.
   2. Computer software about social studies for students to create reports.
   3. Science textbooks that are not provided by the school and needed for research.
   4. Paper supplies for his personal use

a. 1, 2, and 3
b. 4 only
c. 1 and 3
d. 1 and 2

ATIP1.7
Which of the following does not define a performing artist?

a. Performed services in the performing arts as an employee for at least two employers during the tax year.
b. Received wages of $200 or more per employer from at least two employers.
c. Had allowable business expenses attributable to more than 10% of gross income from the performing arts.
d. Had adjusted gross income of $36,000 or more before deducting expenses as a performing artist.

ATIP1.8
Fernando teaches tax law at two different community colleges and has employee business expenses not covered by his employers. Which of the following individuals can no longer claim employee business expenses?

1. Armed Forces reservist
2. Qualified performing artist
3. Fee-basis state or local government official
4. Individuals with a disability claiming impairment-related work expenses
5. Teacher and correctional officers.

a. 1, 3, & 5
b. 2 & 4
c. 3, 4, & 5
d. 5

Part 1 Review Questions Answers

ATIP1.1
Which of the following is not an adjustment to income?

a. Educator expense
b. Early penalty withdrawal
c. Alimony
d. Itemized deductions

Feedback: Review section *Adjustments to Income*.

ATIP1.2
Julie is a junior high school teacher, and she spent $1,200 for her classroom. What would be the total of her qualified educator expense?

a. $1,200
b. $1,450
c. $300
d. $500

Feedback: Review section *Educator Expenses.*

ATIP1.3
What is the 2022 HSA Family Contribution limit with a High-Deductible Health Plan?

    a. $3,650
    b. $7,300
    c. $7,350
    d. $7,050

Feedback: Review section *Health Savings Account.*

ATIP1.4
The Archer MSA has some great benefits. Which of the following is not a benefit of the Archer MSA?

    a. The interest or other earnings on the asset in the Archer MSA are tax-free.
    b. The taxpayer can claim a tax deduction for contributions even if they do not itemize their deductions on Form 1040.
    c. The contributions cannot remain in the Archer MSA from year to year.
    d. All the answers are correct.

Feedback: Review section *Health Savings Account.*

ATIP1.5
Heather just became a 3rd grade teacher. How many hours per year does Heather need to work to qualify for the educator expense?

    a. 250
    b. 500
    c. 900
    d. 1,200

Feedback: Review section *Educator Expenses.*

ATIP1.6
Joaquin, a qualifying 7th grade teacher, purchased items for his classroom and wants to know which of the following qualify for the educator expenses.

    1. Crayons for his classroom for art projects.
    2. Computer software about social studies for students to create reports.
    3. Science textbooks that are not provided by the school and needed for research.
    4. Paper supplies for personal use.

    a. 1, 2, and 3
    b. 4 only
    c. 1 and 3
    d. 1 and 2

Feedback: Review section *Educator Expenses.*

ATIP1.7
Which of the following does not define a performing artist?
   a. Performed services in the performing arts as an employee for at least two employers during the tax year.
   b. Received wages of $200 or more per employer from at least two employers.
   c. Had allowable business expenses attributable to more than 10% of gross income from the performing arts.
   d. Had adjusted gross income of $36,000 or more before deducting expenses as a performing artist.

Feedback: Review section *Form 2106: Unreimbursed Emplyee Business Expense.*

ATIP1.8
Fernando teaches tax law at two different community colleges and has employee business expenses not covered by his employers. Which of the following individuals can no longer claim employee business expenses?

   1. Armed Forces reservist
   2. Qualified performing artist
   3. Fee-basis state or local government official
   4. Individuals with a disability claiming impairment-related work expenses
   5. Teacher and correctional officers.

   a. 1, 3, & 5
   b. 2 & 4
   c. 3, 4, & 5
   d. 5

Feedback: Review section *Form 2106: Unreimbursed Emplyee Business Expense.*

Part 2 Other Adjustments to Income

This part covers other adjustments that have been changed due to the Tax Cuts and Jobs Act. The two with the most changes are moving expenses and alimony.

Form 3903: Moving Expenses

Under some circumstances, moving expenses can be claimed as adjustments to income. Moving expenses are reported on Form 1040, Schedule 1, line 14. Complete and attach Form 3903, *Moving Expenses*, to the tax return to claim this adjustment. The taxpayer does not have to itemize deductions to claim the adjustment. Although the Tax Cuts and Jobs Act has made several changes to moving expenses, it is still important for the tax professional to know how moving expense adjustments worked before and after the TCJA.

Moving Expenses Before the TCJA

To claim moving expenses as adjustments to income, the taxpayer must meet the following requirements:

   ➢ The move is closely related to the start of work.
   ➢ The taxpayer meets the distance test.
   ➢ The taxpayer meets the time test.

Señor 1040 Says: Recordkeeping is vital to maintaining an accurate record of expenses for a move. The taxpayer should save receipts, bills, canceled checks, credit card statements, and mileage logs to correctly report the amount of moving expense.

Before the Tax Cuts and Jobs Act was enacted, moving expenses were claimed based on whether the move was made in conjunction with the taxpayer's job or business. The distance between the old home and the new workplace must be at least 50 miles more than the old home to the old workplace. Also, if the taxpayer did not have any reimbursed moving expenses, they could report the expenses in the year they were incurred or when they were paid in full. The following moving expenses could be claimed as adjustments to income before the TCJA:

➢ The cost of packing and moving household goods and personal effects.
➢ The cost of storing and insuring household goods once 30 days have passed.
➢ The cost of connecting and disconnecting utilities.
➢ The cost of one trip, including lodging but not meals, to the new home.
➢ The cost of tolls and parking fees.

The taxpayer would first report the moving expenses on Form 3903 and then on line 14 of Form 1040, Schedule 1. If the taxpayer had reimbursed moving expenses under an *accountable plan*, the expenses would be reported on the taxpayer's Form W-2 in box 12 and designated with code *P*. Reimbursed expenses reported with code *P* do not have to be reported on the tax return. If taxpayers were reimbursed for the moving expenses, they cannot double-dip and claim moving expenses as adjustments to income on their tax return.

To be considered an accountable plan, the employer's reimbursement or allowance arrangement must include the following rules:

➢ The expenses must have a business connection, which means the taxpayer must have paid or incurred deductible expenses while performing services as an employee.
➢ The taxpayer must adequately account to the employer for these expenses within a reasonable time.
➢ The taxpayer must return any excess reimbursement or allowance within a reasonable time.

Example: Donald lives in Seattle, WA, and accepted a job in Portland, ME. Donald's new employer reimbursed him using their accountable plan for his travel expenses from Seattle to Portland. Donald's employer would report the reimbursement with code *P* on his W-2, box 12.

Distance Test

The distance between a job's location and the taxpayer's main home is the shortest of the most traveled routes between them. The distance test considers only the location of the former home, and it does not account for the location of any new home. If the taxpayer had more than one job during the year, only use the "main job" location to calculate the distance for this test. To determine which job was the "main job," examine the following factors:

➢ The total time spent at each job.
➢ The amount of work completed at each job.
➢ The amount of money earned at each job.

Whichever job had the highest or the majority of the above is the main job.

Time Test

The taxpayer must also meet a time test to qualify for moving expenses. According to the time test, if a taxpayer moves to another location and claims it was job-related, they must work in the new location for at least 39 weeks during the first 12 months of their stay to claim the moving expenses as adjustments to income.

The taxpayer would need to work 39 weeks out of 52 weeks after the move to calculate full-time work as an employee.

Moving Expenses During the TCJA

One of the many changes made by the TCJA was to suspend adjustments for moving expenses with one exception: Active Armed Forces who have a military order to move or permanently change their station can claim moving expenses if they meet the normal qualifications. For 2022 the standard mileage rate is 18 cents per mile from January to June and 22 cents per mile from July - December. For 2023 the mileage rate is 22 cents per mile. If the taxpayer has made multiple moves in one tax year, then a different Form 3903 will be used for each move.

A permanent station change can be any of the following:

➤ A move from the taxpayer's current home to their first post of duty.
➤ A move from one permanent post to another.
➤ A move from the taxpayer's last permanent post to a new home in the United States. The move must occur within one year of the end of active duty or within the allowable period designated by the Joint Travel Regulations, which is beyond the scope of this course.

Penalty on Early Withdrawal of Savings

If a taxpayer withdraws money from a savings program and incurs a penalty, the penalty is an allowable adjustment to gross income. This penalty is reported to the taxpayer on Form 1099-INT or Form 1099-OID. The bank or other private institution imposes the early withdrawal penalty. Report the early withdrawal penalty on Form 1040, Schedule 1, line 18, as an adjustment to income.

Alimony Paid

Alimony is a payment or a series of payments to a spouse or former spouse required under a divorce or under a separation agreement that meets certain requirements. Any alimony a taxpayer receives should be reported on Form 1040, Schedule 1, line 2a. The amount of alimony paid should be reported on Form 1040, Schedule 1, line 19a, as an adjustment to income. The paying spouse must report the recipient's Social Security number on line 19b. Not all payments received from a spouse are considered alimony. For a description of what is considered alimony, see Publication 504.

The term "divorce or separation instrument" refers to the following:

➤ A decree of divorce or separate maintenance or a "written instrument incident" (see IRS Publication 504) to that decree.
➤ A written separation agreement.

➢ A decree or a type of court order requiring a spouse to make payments for the support or maintenance of the other spouse.

Payments that are not alimony include:

➢ Child support
➢ Noncash property settlements
➢ Payments that are the taxpayer's spouse's part of community income
➢ Payments to keep up the payer's property
➢ Use of the payer's property
➢ Noncash property settlements, whether in lump sum or installments
➢ Voluntary payments

Divorce Agreement Post 2018

Alimony will no longer be an adjustment to income or a source of income if the divorce or separation agreement is completed after December 31, 2018. The new law applies if an agreement was executed on or before December 31, 2018, and then modified after that date. The new law applies if the modification does these two things:

➢ It changes the terms of the alimony or separate maintenance payments.
➢ It says explicitly that alimony or separate maintenance payments are not deductible by the payer spouse or includable in the income of the receiving spouse.

Agreements executed on or before December 31, 2018, follow the previous rules. If an agreement was modified after January 1, 2019, the new agreement should state that they are following the 2018 laws if the modifications didn't change what's described above.

Community property laws may not apply to an item of community property income, and special rules may apply to community property states.

Example: Kathy and Lloyd live in Arizona and are a married couple. Kathy's father passed away in 1995. Her mother sold her country residence and moved in town to be closer to friends and church. Her mother had a trust and passed away in 2019. Kathy was a beneficiary of the trust and received $75,000 as an inheritance. Since Kathy and Lloyd live in a community property state, she would need to put her inherited money in a separate bank account to preserve her inheritance. If the money was deposited into a joint account, then the inheritance becomes both of theirs. See Publication 504.

Individual Retirement Account (IRA) Deduction

Taxpayers may participate in a personal savings plan that offers tax advantages to set aside money for retirement or education expenses. This personal savings plan is known as an individual retirement account or IRA. There are different types of IRAs: traditional, Roth, SIMPLE, or education.

It is necessary to understand the difference between a contribution and a deduction. Contributions are amounts paid to a taxpayer's plan, whereas deductions are the actual amount the taxpayer may reduce their taxable income.

Individuals who have not reached the age of 72 with taxable compensation may contribute to an IRA (with certain other conditions). Compensation for IRA purposes includes wages, salaries, commissions, tips, professional fees, bonuses, and other amounts received for personal services. Also included are taxable alimony and separate maintenance payments.

The deductible amount of the IRA contributions may be limited depending on the following two factors:

> ➢ If the taxpayer or spouse had an employer-provided pension plan.
> ➢ The amount of the modified adjusted gross income.

The maximum a single taxpayer can contribute is either $6,000 or the taxpayer's taxable compensation, whichever is lowest. If the taxpayers are married and only one spouse has taxable compensation, the maximum contribution the couple can make is $12,000. The maximum that can be contributed to one account is $6,000. If the married spouses have compensation more than $6,000 each, they both may contribute $6,000.

If the taxpayer is 50-years-old or older, they may make a "catch-up" contribution to their IRA account in the amount of $1,000. Taxpayers may not contribute more than $7,000 to their IRA account during the tax year. Contributions must be in the form of money, and property cannot be contributed to an IRA.

Suppose a taxpayer contributes more than $6,000 ($7,000 if age 50 or older) in one year to an IRA. In that case, the taxpayer will be penalized with a tax on the excess contribution and earnings each year until the taxpayer withdraws the excess contribution. This penalty is not limited to the year the excess contribution is made. The excess contributions must be reported on Form 5329, *Additional Taxes Attributable to IRAs, Other Qualified Retirement Plans, Annuities, Modified Endowment Contracts, and MSAs*, Part II.

For tax year 2023 the contribution amount is $6,500 ($7,500 age 50 and over).

In addition to adjusting the taxpayer's gross income, interest earned on a traditional IRA account is accumulated tax-deferred until it is withdrawn, thus benefiting the taxpayer.

Spousal IRA

A nonworking spouse can contribute to a traditional IRA the same amounts as a working individual: $6,000 or $7,000 if older than 50.

Form 1098-E: Qualified Student Loans

Student loan providers will send Form 1098-E to their borrowers who have $600 or more interest. For the taxpayer to report their student loan interest, one of the following must apply:

> ➢ The loan has been subsidized, guaranteed, financed, or otherwise treated as a student loan under a federal, state, or local government program or a postsecondary education institution.
> ➢ The loan is certified by the borrower as a student loan incurred solely to pay qualified higher education expenses.

Reading Form 1098-E

2023 Form 1098-E

Box 1: The interest received by the taxpayer for their student loan is shown here, including capitalized interest, as well as loan origination fees.

Box 2: This box is checked if box 1 has loan origination fees and/or capitalized interest that, for some reason, were not included in box 1.

Academic Period

An academic period includes a semester, trimester, quarter, or other study period (such as a summer school session) as reasonably determined by an educational institution. In the case of an educational institution that uses credit hours or clock hours and does not have academic terms, each payment period can be treated as an academic period.

Student Loan Interest Deduction

Taxpayers with education loans can claim up to $2,500 of education loan interest paid in 2022 as adjustments to income. Although prior-year student loan interest was reported on line 33 of Form 1040 or line 18 of Form 1040A, the deduction is now taken as an adjustment to income on Form 1040, Schedule 1, line 21. The adjustment is allowed on qualifying loans for the taxpayer's benefit or the taxpayer's spouse or dependent when the debt was incurred. The adjustment phases out at incomes of $85,000 ($175,000 for MFJ). MFS individuals are unable to adjust student loan interest. If more than $600 were paid in interest on the student loan, Form 1098-E would be received.

The person for whom the expenses were paid must have been an eligible student; however, a loan is not a qualified student loan if both of the following are true:

➢ Any of the proceeds were used for other purposes.
➢ The loan was from either a related person, a person who borrowed the proceeds under a qualified employer plan, or a contract purchased under such a plan.

An eligible student is a person who meets the following conditions:

> ➢ Was enrolled in a degree, certificate, or another program (including a studying abroad program approved for credit by the institution the student is registered with), leading to a recognized education credential at an eligible education institution.
> ➢ They carried at least half of the normal full-time workload for the course of study the student is pursuing.

See Publication 970, *Tax Benefits for Education*.

Part 2 Review Questions

To obtain the maximum benefit from this chapter, LTP recommends that you complete each of the following questions and then compare them to the answers with feedback that immediately follow. Under governing self-study standards, vendors must present review questions intermittently throughout each self-study course.

These questions and explanations are not part of the final examination and will not be graded by LTP.

ATIP2.1
Before TCJA was written into law, which taxpayer could claim moving expenses?

a. Daniel, an electrician, moved to Idaho for a new job.
b. Dennis, who retired and moved to Florida.
c. Danelle moved to attend the state university.
d. Debbie has lived in the same town and recently got married and moved in with her spouse.

ATIP2.2
Which individual can claim moving expenses after TCJA?

a. David is an active military electrician moving to Idaho for a new job.
b. Damon retired and moved to Florida.
c. Diana, who moved to attend the university.
d. Domingo, who recently got married and moved in with his spouse.

ATIP2.3
Sergio and Faith got divorced on January 2, 2020. Sergio needs to pay Faith alimony of $1,500 per month. Which scenario best describes how to claim their alimony?

a. Sergio will claim the adjustment, and Faith will claim the alimony as income.
b. Sergio will not claim the adjustment, and Faith does not claim the alimony as income.
c. Faith will claim the adjustment, and Sergio will claim the alimony as income.
d. Faith will not claim the adjustment, and Sergio cannot claim the adjustment to income.

ATIP2.4
Conner is an employee and wants to know if he can deduct moving expenses. Which of the following time tests must Conner meet to deduct moving expense prior to TCJA?

    a. Conner must work full-time for at least 39 weeks during the first 12 months.
    b. Conner must work at least part-time for at least 39 weeks during the first 12 months.
    c. Conner must work full-time for at least 21 weeks during the first 6 months.
    d. Conner must work at least part-time for the first year.

ATIP2.5
Which of the following can claim moving expenses during TCJA?

    a. Bonita who moved from Florida to California for her new job.
    b. Diego who moved from California to Nevada for Navy training.
    c. Roberto who moved into a new house in the same city.
    d. Vicente who purchased a new house 100 miles away.

ATIP2.6
Rita graduated from the local university five years ago. Which form would she receive so she can claim her student loan interest?

    a. Form 1098-T
    b. Form 1098
    c. Form 1098-E
    d. Form 1099-A

ATIP2.7
Which of the following scenarios best describes when Gilbert can claim his student loan?

    a. A non-guaranteed student loan program subsidizes Gilbert's student loan.
    b. Gilbert's student loan is guaranteed as a student loan solely to pay higher education expenses.
    c. Gilbert does not attend a qualifying higher education school.
    d. Gilbert attends a private high school, and his parents took out a loan on their house.

Part 2 Review Questions Answers

ATIP2.1
Before TCJA was written into law, which taxpayer could claim moving expenses?

    a. Daniel, an electrician, moved to Idaho for a new job.
    b. Dennis, who retired and moved to Florida.
    c. Danelle moved to attend the state university.
    d. Debbie has lived in the same town and recently got married and moved in with her spouse.

Feedback: Review section *Form 2106: Unreimbursed Employee Expense.*

ATIP2.2
Which individual can claim moving expenses after TCJA?

a. **David is an active military electrician moving to Idaho for a new job.**
b. Damon retired and moved to Florida.
c. Diana, who moved to attend the university.
d. Domingo, who recently got married and moved in with his spouse.

Feedback: Review section *Armed Forces Reservist.*

ATIP2.3
Sergio and Faith got divorced on January 2, 2020. Sergio needs to pay Faith alimony of $1,500 per month. Which scenario best describes how to claim their alimony?

a. Sergio will claim the adjustment, and Faith will claim the alimony as income.
b. **Sergio will not claim the adjustment, and Faith does not claim the alimony as income.**
c. Faith will claim the adjustment, and Sergio will claim the alimony as income.
d. Faith will not be able to claim the adjustment, and Sergio cannot claim the alimony payment as an adjustment to income.

Feedback: Review section *Alimony Paid.*

ATIP2.4
Conner is an employee and wants to know if he can deduct moving expenses. Which of the following time tests must Conner meet to deduct moving expense prior to TCJA?

a. **Conner must work full-time for at least 39 weeks during the first 12 months.**
b. Conner must work at least part-time for at least 39 weeks during the first 12 months.
c. Conner must work full-time for at least 21 weeks during the first 6 months.
d. Conner must work at least part-time for the first year.

Feedback: Review section *Moving Expenses Before the TCJA.*

ATIP2.5
Which of the following can claim moving expenses during TCJA?

a. Bonita who moved from Florida to California for her new job.
b. **Diego who moved from California to Nevada for Navy training.**
c. Roberto who moved into a new house in the same city.
d. Vicente who purchased a new house 100 miles away.

Feedback: Review section *Moving Expenses During the TCJA.*

ATIP2.6
Rita graduated from the local university five years ago. Which form would she receive so she can claim her student loan interest?

a. Form 1098-T
b. Form 1098
c. **Form 1098-E**
d. Form 1099-A

Feedback: Review section *Reading Form 1098-E.*

ATIP2.7
Which of the following scenarios best describes when Gilbert can claim his student loan?

a. A non-guaranteed student loan program subsidizes Gilbert's student loan.
b. Gilbert's student loan is guaranteed as a student loan solely to pay higher education expenses.
c. Gilbert does not attend a qualifying higher education school.
d. Gilbert attends a private high school, and his parents took out a loan on their house.

Feedback: Review section *Which Expenses Qualify for Tuition and Fee Deductions?*

Part 3 Self-Employment Adjustments

Self-employed taxpayers must pay both the employer and employee portions of the Medicare and Social Security taxes. Since the self-employed person pays the entire amount, the taxpayer will make an adjustment to income equal to one-half of the total self-employment tax. This tax is figured on Schedule SE, and the adjustment is then carried to Form 1040, Schedule 1, line 15. If the taxpayer has W-2 wages, the taxpayer's net self-employment earnings are combined with their wages when determining the earning limit for the self-employment tax.

Self-Employment Tax

Self-employment tax does not apply to income earned as a shareholder of an S corporation or as a limited partner of a partnership (except for guaranteed payments). Self-employment tax is calculated on Schedule SE and must be paid if the following apply:

➢ Net earnings for the year from self-employment (excluding income as a church employee) were $400 or more.
➢ Church-employee income for the year is more than $108.28.

The self-employment tax rules apply even if the taxpayer receives Social Security and Medicare benefits. Special rules apply to workers who perform in-home services for elderly or disabled individuals. Caregivers are typically classified as employees of the individuals they provide care for. Self-employed individuals may have to make estimated quarterly payments to the IRS. See IRC Section 6017 and Schedule SE Instructions.

Self-Employment Retirement Plans

This line item for adjustments is for self-employed taxpayers who provide retirement plans for themselves and their employees.

The plans that can be deducted on this line are as follows:

➢ Simplified Employee Pension (SEP) plans.
➢ Savings Incentive Match Plan for Employees (SIMPLE).
➢ Qualified plans, including HR (10) or Keogh plans, which are beyond this course's scope.

SEP (Simplified Employee Pension)

A business of any size may establish a specific type of traditional IRA for their employees called a Simplified Employee Pension (SEP), also referred to as a SEP-IRA. A self-employed individual is also eligible to participate in this plan. There are three basic steps in starting a SEP:

➢ Must have a formal written agreement to provide benefits to all eligible employees.
➢ Must give each eligible employee certain information.
➢ A SEP-IRA must be set up for each employee.

The formal written agreement must state that the employer will benefit all eligible employees under the SEP. The employer may adopt an IRS-provided model by filing Form 5305-SEP. Professional advice should be sought when setting up the SEP. Form 5305-SEP cannot be filed if any of the following apply:

➢ The company already has a qualified retirement plan other than a SEP.
➢ The company has eligible employees whose IRAs have not been set up.
➢ The company uses the service of leased employees who are not common-law employees.
➢ The company is a member of one of the following trades or businesses:
  o An affiliated service group as described in section 414(m).
  o A controlled group of corporations as described in section 414(b).
  o A trade or business under common control as described in section 414(c).
➢ The company does not pay the cost of the SEP contributions.

The contributions are made to IRAs (SEP-IRAs) of the eligible participants in that plan. Interest accumulates tax-free until the participant begins to make withdrawals. Contribution limits are based on net profits.

A taxpayer is eligible for a SEP if they meet the following requirements:

➢ Has reached age 21.
➢ Has worked for the employer for at least 3 of the past five years.
➢ Has received at least $600 in compensation from the employer during each of the last three tax years.

The least of the following amounts is the maximum amount that an employer may annually contribute to an employee's IRA:

➢ $61,000 (for 2022).
➢ $66,000 (for 2023).
➢ 25% of the employee's compensation, or 20% for the self-employed taxpayer.

Contributions made by the employer are not reported as income by the employee, nor can they be deducted as an IRA contribution. Excess contributions are included in the employee's income for the year and are treated as contributions. Do not include SEP contributions on the employee's Form W-2 unless the contributions are pre-tax contributions.

Example: Susan Plant earned $21,000 in 2022. Because the maximum employer contribution for 2022 is 25% of the employee's compensation, the employer can contribute $5,250 to her SEP-IRA (25% x $21,000).

SIMPLE Retirement Plan

A SIMPLE retirement plan is a tax-favored retirement plan that certain small employers (including self-employed individuals) can set up to benefit their employees.

A SIMPLE plan can be established for any employee who received at least $5,000 in compensation during the two years before the current calendar year and is reasonably expected to receive at least $5,000 during the current calendar year. Self-employed individuals are also eligible. The plan may also use less restrictive guidelines, but it may not use more stringent ones.

The employee's elective deferrals from salary reduction are limited to $14,000; or $17,000 (an additional $3,000) if age 50 or older (for 2022). For 2023 the limit is $15,500. Salary-reduction contributions are not treated as catch-up contributions. The employer can match employee deferrals dollar-for-dollar up to 3% of the employee's compensation.

SIMPLE IRA

A SIMPLE IRA is a plan that uses separate IRA accounts for each eligible employee. A SIMPLE plan is a written agreement (salary-reduction agreement) between the taxpayer and their employer that allows the taxpayer to choose to do either of the following:

 ➢ Reduce the taxpayer's compensation by a certain percentage each pay period.
 ➢ Have the employer contribute the salary reductions to a SIMPLE IRA on the taxpayer's behalf. These contributions are called "salary-reduction contributions."

All contributions under a SIMPLE IRA plan must be made to SIMPLE IRAs and not to any other type of IRA. The SIMPLE IRA can be an individual retirement account or an individual retirement annuity. In addition to salary reduction contributions, the employer must make either matching contributions or non-elective contributions. The taxpayer is eligible to participate in their employer's SIMPLE plan if the taxpayer meets the following requirements:

 ➢ They received compensation from their employer two years before the current year.
 ➢ They are reasonably expected to receive at least $5,000 in compensation during the calendar year in which contributions were made.

The difference between the SIMPLE retirement plan and the SIMPLE IRA is that the retirement plan is part of a 401(k) plan, and the IRA plan uses individual IRAs for each employee. See Publication 560.

Self-Employed Health Insurance Deductions

Self-employed taxpayers can claim (as adjustments to income on Form 1040, Schedule 1, line 17) 100% of the amount paid in 2022 for medical insurance and qualified long-term care insurance for the taxpayer and the taxpayer's family if any of the following apply:

 ➢ The taxpayer is a self-employed individual.
 ➢ The taxpayer is a general partner (or limited partner receiving guaranteed payments) in a partnership.
 ➢ The shareholder owns more than 2% of the outstanding stock of an S corporation.

Premiums are not deductible any month that the taxpayer or spouse was eligible to participate in an employer-subsidized health plan. The earned income also limits the deduction. Schedule C would be the net profit minus the SE tax deduction (Schedule 2, line 4) and SEP deductions (Schedule 1, line 16). Self-employed individuals must have a net profit for the year to deduct their paid premiums as adjustments to income.

The self-employed health insurance deduction should be calculated using the *Worksheet for the Health Insurance Deduction* found in Publication 535.

If any of the following exceptions apply, the above worksheet cannot be used:

➤ The taxpayer had more than one source of income subject to self-employment.
➤ The taxpayer filed Form 2555.
➤ The taxpayer included their qualified long-term care insurance to calculate the deduction.

Part 3 Review Questions

To obtain the maximum benefit from this chapter, LTP recommends that you complete each of the following questions and then compare them to the answers with feedback that immediately follow. Under governing self-study standards, vendors must present review questions intermittently throughout each self-study course.

These questions and explanations are not part of the final examination and will not be graded by LTP.

ATIP3.1
Which of the following is not a self-employment retirement plan?

a. Simplified Employee Pension (SEP) plan
b. Savings Incentive Match Plan for Employers (SIMPLE)
c. HR 10 or Keogh plan
d. 401(k) plan

ATIP3.2
Which of the following is an adjustment to income?

a. Moving expense for everyone except active military
b. Qualified tuition expense
c. Employee health insurance
d. Deductible part of self-employment

ATIP3.3
Which of the following reports self-employed health insurance?

a. Schedule A
b. Schedule SE
c. Schedule 1, Part II
d. Schedule C

ATIP3.4

Self-employment tax applies to everyone who has net earnings of_____ or more.

    a. $600
    b. $400
    c. $1,200
    d. $2,100

Part 3 Review Questions Answers

ATIP3.1

Which of the following is not a self-employment retirement plan?

    a. Simplified Employee Pension (SEP) plan
    b. Savings Incentive Match Plan for Employers (SIMPLE)
    c. HR 10 or Keogh plan
    d. 401(k) plan

Feedback: Review section *Self-Employment Retirement Plans.*

ATIP3.2

Which of the following is an adjustment to income?

    a. Moving expense for everyone except active military
    b. Qualified tuition expense
    c. Employee health insurance
    d. Deductible part of self-employment

Feedback: Review section *Self-Employment Tax.*

ATIP3.3

Which of the following reports self-employed health insurance?

    a. Schedule A
    b. Schedule SE
    c. Schedule 1, Part II
    d. Schedule C

Feedback: Review section *Self-Employment Health Insurance Deductions.*

ATIP3.4

Self-employment tax applies to everyone who has net earnings of_____ or more.

    a. $600
    b. $400
    c. $1,200
    d. $2,100

Feedback: Review section *Self-Employment Tax.*

Takeaways

Taxpayers can take various "deductions" directly on the tax return. These "deductions," however, are not itemized or standardized deductions (discussed later) but are instead called adjustments to income since they "adjust" the taxpayer's gross income. The adjustments are also referred to as "above the line," which appears above the tax form for adjusted gross income.

An HSA is a health savings account set up exclusively for paying the qualified medical expenses of the account beneficiary or the account beneficiary's spouse or dependents. Other adjustments to income that can be claimed are deductible parts of self-employment tax, IRA deductions, self-employed health insurance, and student loan interest of more than $600 and less than $2,500.

TEST YOUR KNOWLEDGE!
Go online to take a practice quiz.

California Adjustments to Income

Introduction

This chapter will teach which adjustments need to be made to California income and enter it on 540 Schedule CA. First, you will review a few items from Part I, Section A, *Income*. Then, you will review Part I, section B, *Adjustments to Income*. The chapter will conclude by presenting a few items from Part II, Adjustments to Federal Itemized Deductions.

Objectives

At the end of this lesson, the student will be able to do the following:

➢ Identify the California adjustments to income.
➢ Understand which federal adjustments are subtracted from California income.
➢ Know which federal adjustments are added to California income.

Resources

540 Schedule CA	FTB Publication 1001	Instructions 540 Schedule CA

Table of Contents

Part 1 California Adjustments

The purpose of the 540 Schedule CA is to help California resident taxpayers adjust both their federal adjusted gross income and their federal itemized deductions to reconcile the differences between how income is taxed by federal and state tax law. Federal information is put into Column A following the same line items as the federal return, which forms the basis of the California return. Column B is where any subtractions required by state law are reported. For example, suppose an entry is taxed at the federal level but not the state. In that case, the line amount in Column A is copied into Column B, canceling out the amount and subtracting it from the total state tax liability.

On the other hand, Column C is where any additions required by state law are added to the total amount of state taxable income. For example, suppose an item was not taxed on the federal return but is taxable at the state level. In that case, the taxable amount is put into Column C, adding it to the total state tax liability.

540 Schedule CA

California has several adjustments to income. To arrive at the state's adjusted gross income, California starts with the federal AGI and:

- ➤ subtracts income that is not taxable by California.
- ➤ adds income that is taxable by California.

The most common subtractions from federal AGI are allowed on page 1 of Form 540. Suppose the taxpayer has subtractions not listed on Form 540 or any addition to income. In that case, they must be listed on California 540 Schedule CA, *California Adjustments—Residents*, which is an attachment to Form 540. Part-year or nonresidents must use the specific 540NR Schedule CA. California adjustments consist of certain taxable income on the federal return which are not taxable on the California return.

Section A – Income

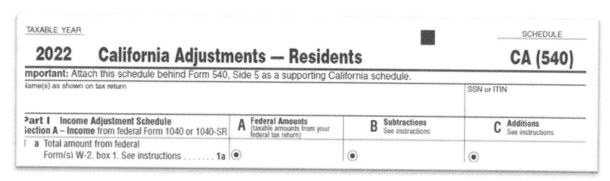

Portion of 540 Schedule CA

Wages (Section A, line 1, a-z)

540 Schedule CA follows the income section of Form 1040. Line 1 is the same on both forms. If there are subtractions or additions to income, the tax preparer should know where to enter them in the correct column.

California Taxable Interest and Dividends Income (Section A, lines 2 and 3)

California does not tax interest earned from U.S. savings bonds or U.S. Treasury bills, notes, bonds, or bonds and obligations of U.S. territories and government agencies exempted explicitly by federal law. Municipal or state bond interest received from other states by a California resident is taxed by California.

IRA Distributions, Pensions, and Annuities (Section A, lines 4 and 5)

Normally, no adjustments are needed for IRAs, pensions, or annuities because California conforms to the federal tax law. California does tax these items; however, their penalty for early withdrawal is only 2.5%. But for early distribution from a SIMPLE, the penalty is 6%. There are also differences between federal and state law regarding self-employment pensions. See FTB Instructions Form 3805P.

Social Security Benefits (Section A, line 6)

California does not tax Social Security benefits or equivalent Tier 1 railroad retirement benefits from taxable income. Claim the benefit amount of these adjustments to income in Column B, line 6.

Section B – Additional Income

Section B – Additional Income Continued	A Federal Amounts (taxable amounts from your federal tax return)	B Subtractions See instructions	C Additions See instructions
9 a Total other income. Add lines 8a through 8z. 9a			
b1 Disaster loss deduction from form FTB 3805V.. 9b1			
b2 NOL deduction from form FTB 3805V 9b2			
b3 NOL from form FTB 3805Z, 3807, or 3809 .. 9b3			
10 Total. Combine Section A, line 1z through line 7, and Section B, line 1 through line 7, and line 9a in column A. Add Section A, line 1z through line 7, and Section B, line 1 through line 7, line 9a, and line 9b1 through line 9b3 in column B (as applicable). See instructions................10			

Portion of 540 Schedule CA

Taxable Refunds, Credits, or Offsets of State and Local Income Taxes (Section B, line 1)

Federal law includes the state income tax refund as income, and California excludes the state income tax refund from income. Enter the state income tax refund amount included in federal income on Schedule CA 540, section B, line 1, column B.

Alimony Received (Section B, line 2a)

No entry is made unless the taxpayer was a nonresident and received alimony that was not included in the federal amount in Column A; enter the alimony on Column C – Additions.
Business Income or Loss (Section B, line 3)

This section will be covered in the Schedule C chapter.

Other Gains or Losses (Section B, line 4)

This section will be covered in the Capital Gains and Losses chapter.

Rental Real Estate, Royalties, Partnerships, S Corporations, Trusts, etc. (Schedule B, line 5)

This section will be covered in the Schedule E chapter.

Farm Income (Schedule B, line 6)

This section will be covered in the Schedule F chapter.

Unemployment Compensation (Section B, line 7)

California does not tax unemployment compensation; however, unemployment is taxable on the federal return. Claim the adjustment to income on 540 Schedule CA, section B, line 7, column B.

California Lottery Winnings (Section B, line 8b)

Only California lottery winnings are not taxable. All other gambling winnings, including lottery winnings from other states, are fully taxable, and no adjustment would be made. An adjustment must be made for California lottery winnings but not for any Indian Gaming Casinos.

Section C - Adjustments to Income

Portion of 540 Schedule CA

Educator Expenses (Section C, line 11)

California does not conform to federal law. To claim this adjustment to income, enter the $300 educator expense from Form 1040, Schedule 1, line 11 to 540 Schedule CA, section C, column B, line 11.

Certain Business Expenses (Section C, Line 12)

California conforms to federal law in the tax treatment of reservists, performing artists, and fee-basis government officials. Suppose the taxpayer is claiming a depreciation deduction on Form 2106. In that case, an adjustment may have been made in column B or column C. If the federal depreciation is more than the state depreciation, enter the difference in column B. If the federal depreciation is less, enter the difference in column C of 540 Schedule CA.

Health Savings Account (Section C, line 13)

California does not allow a deduction for a contribution to an HSA account. Transfer the amount from column A to column B, section C, line 13 of 540 Schedule CA.

Moving Expenses (Section C, line 14)

California does not conform to federal law regarding the suspension of the deduction for moving expenses, except for members of the Armed Forces on active duty. Non-military and military taxpayers would use Form FTB 3913 to report the expenses.

Alimony Paid (Section C, line 19a)

California did not conform to the TCJA regarding alimony and separate maintenance payments for the payor. Alimony payments that are made to a recipient are deductible if *all* the following conditions are met:

> ➤ The payments were made in cash, checks, or money orders.
> ➤ The divorce or separation instrument does not explicitly state that the payment is not considered alimony.
> ➤ The taxpayer and former spouse are not members of the same household.
> ➤ There is no liability to make any payment after the death of the spouse or former spouse.
> ➤ The payment is not treated as child support.

Alimony payments paid by a nonresident alien that was not taken on the federal return are a deduction on the California return. Enter the amount of paid alimony in column A, line 19a. Taxpayer needs to enter the alimony recipient's SSN and last name. Column C of 540 Schedule CA is used to claim the amount as an adjustment.

IRA Deduction (Section C, line 20)

This section will be covered in the Other Taxes and Taxpayer Penalties chapter.

Student Loan Interest (Section C, line 21)

Federal law allows a deduction for student loan interest and has eliminated the 60-month limitation. California will allow a deduction only on the interest required to be paid on student loans for the first 60 months. California also has a different phase-out amount of the deduction. Use the worksheet included in 540 Schedule CA to calculate the California adjustment. Enter the amount of the federal deduction not allowed for California in 540 Schedule CA, section C, line 21, column B. For more information, see FTB Publication 1032.

Archer MSA Deduction (Section C, line 23)

If the taxpayer uses federal Form 8853, the taxpayer has a taxable event on their California return. The income is reported on FTB 3805P. California does not recognize Health Savings Account (HSAs); the rollover from an Archer MSA to an HSA is included in the taxpayer's California income.

Part 1 Review Questions

To obtain the maximum benefit from this chapter, LTP recommends that you complete each of the following questions and then compare them to the answers with feedback that immediately follow. Under governing self-study standards, vendors must present review questions intermittently throughout each self-study course.

These questions and explanations are not part of the final examination and will not be graded by LTP.

CATIP1.1
California does not conform to which of the following adjustments to income?

    a. Educator expenses.
    b. The business expense of reservists.
    c. The business expense of performing artists.
    d. The business expense of fee-basis government officials.

CATIP1.2
Which of the following adjustments to income does California conform to?

    a. Student loan interest paid within 60 months.
    b. Health Savings Account deduction.
    c. Educator expenses deduction.
    d. Moving expense deduction for reservists.

CATIP1.3
Javier paid alimony to his spouse. Where would he report the amount of alimony paid?

    a. 540 Schedule CA line 19a
    b. 540 Schedule CA line 19b
    c. 540 Schedule CA line 20
    d. 540 Schedule CA line 17

CATIP1.4
Alimony payments are deductible by the_____.

    a. recipient
    b. payor
    c. employer
    d. employer's family member

CATIP1.5
Susie received alimony from Joe and needs to know which of the following is considered alimony.

    1. Child support
    2. Payments to an ex-spouse
    3. Both child support and payments to the ex-spouse
    4. Noncash payment settlements

a. 1, 3, and 4
b. 2 only
c. 3 only
d. 2 and 4

Part 1 Review Questions Answers

CATIP1.1
California does not conform to which of the following adjustments to income?

a. Educator expenses.
b. The business expense of reservists.
c. The business expense of performing artists.
d. The business expense of fee-basis government officials.

Feedback: Review *Section C – Adjustments to Income.*

CATIP1.2
Which of the following adjustments to income does California conform to?

a. Student loan interest paid within 60 months.
b. Health Savings Account deduction.
c. Educator expenses deduction.
d. Moving expense deduction for reservists.

Feedback: Review *Section C – Adjustments to Income.*

CATIP1.3
Javier paid alimony to his spouse. Where would he report the amount of alimony paid?

a. 540 Schedule CA line 19a
b. 540 Schedule CA line 19b
c. 540 Schedule CA line 20
d. 540 Schedule CA line 17

Feedback: Review *Section C – Adjustments to Income.*

CATIP1.4
Alimony payments are deductible by the_____.

a. recipient
b. payor
c. employer
d. employer's family member

Feedback: Review *Section C – Adjustments to Income.*

CATIP1.5

Susie received alimony from Joe and needs to know which of the following is considered alimony.

1. Child support
2. Payments to an ex-spouse
3. Both child support and payments to the ex-spouse
4. Noncash payment settlements

a. 1, 3, and 4
b. 2 only
c. 3 only
d. 2 and 4

Feedback: Review *Section C – Adjustments to Income.*

Takeaways

California does not always conform to federal tax law. When the state does not conform, the adjustments are made to income on 540 Schedule CA. When California law does conform, no adjustments are necessary on 540 Schedule CA.

TEST YOUR KNOWLEDGE!
Go online to take a practice quiz.

Chapter 6 Other Taxes and Taxpayer Penalties

Introduction

This chapter provides an overview of taxes reported on Schedule 2. Some common other taxes that a tax preparer will see are:

- ➢ Alternative Minimum Tax (AMT)
- ➢ Additional taxes on IRAs
- ➢ Additional Medicare Tax
- ➢ Additional tax on IRAs
- ➢ Excess Social Security tax
- ➢ Household employment taxes
- ➢ Net investment income tax (NIIT)
- ➢ Self-employment tax (will be covered in a later chapter)
- ➢ Unreported tip income

Objectives

At the end of this chapter, the student will:

- ➢ Complete Form 1040, Schedule 2.
- ➢ Explain when a taxpayer must repay the Premium Tax Credit.
- ➢ Understand the taxability of excess Social Security.
- ➢ Identify when a taxpayer must pay an additional tax on IRAs.
- ➢ Clarify when to use Schedule H.

Resources

Form 1040	Publication 17	Instructions Form 1040
Form 4137	Publication 334	Instructions Form 4137
Form 5329	Publication 560	Instructions Form 5329
Form 5405	Publication 575	Instructions Form 5405
Form 6251	Publication 590-B	Instructions Form 6251
Form 8919	Publication 594	Instructions Form 8919
Form 8959	Publication 721	Instructions Form 8959
Form 8962	Publication 939	Instructions Form 8962
Form 8965	Publication 974	Instructions Form 8965
Schedule 2	Tax Topic 410, 554, 556,	Instructions Schedule 2
Schedule H	557, 558, 560, 561, 611,	Instructions for Schedule H
Schedule SE	612, 653	Instructions for Schedule SE

Table of Contents

Part 1 Additional Taxes from Schedule 2

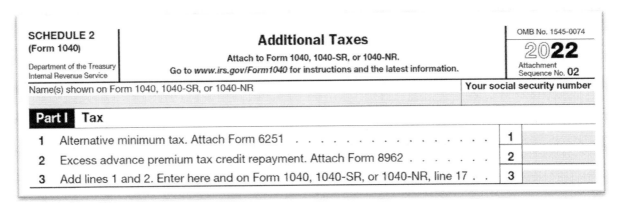

Portion of Schedule 2

Line 1 Alternative Minimum Tax (Form 6251)

The alternative minimum tax (AMT) applies to taxpayers who qualify for certain deductions under tax law. The additional tax is on preference items, which is normally tax-free income or a high amount of itemized deductions. If the taxpayer has deducted preference items and their income exceeds a certain amount, AMT recalculates income tax after adding tax preference items back into the adjusted gross income. As the name suggests, the AMT is the minimum tax possible so that taxpayers cannot go without paying taxes, despite whatever exclusions, credits, or deductions may have been taken. If an adequate amount of a taxpayer's income is from the preference items, and that income exceeds the preset amounts discussed below, they will have to pay AMT even if they had otherwise lowered their tax liability below zero. Form 6251 calculates the AMT and reported on Schedule 2, line 1. AMT could offset personal and business taxes.

AMT is determined based on taxpayer's income. If a taxpayer with an excess amount of deductions received an amount of income that exceeds $75,900 (2022) (for Single and Head of Household), and $118,100 (2022) (for Qualifying Widow(er) or Married Filing Jointly), and $59,050 (for taxpayers filing separately), then the AMT will be triggered and applied. The 2022 AMT rate was 26% on the first $206,100 worth of income. If the taxpayer's income exceeds $199,900, the tax rate is 28%. Married Filing Separate taxpayers' AMT threshold is $103,050. For 2023, the AMT amount is $81,300 for singles and $126,500 for married couples. The 2023 begins to phase out as a single filer at $578,150 and for married jointly $1,079,800.

AMT is calculated using Alternative Minimum Tax Income (AMTI) instead of the adjusted gross income (AGI). If the AMTI amount is zero, then the taxpayer would use their AGI to calculate the AMT after reducing the AGI amount by their itemized or standard deduction and qualified business income deduction. AMTI cannot be reduced by the standard deduction or the net qualified disaster loss that increased the standard deduction. This amount will be added back into the AMT calculation later. For 2022 the AMTI excess is $206,100 for all taxpayers. For 2023 the AMTI is $220,700 for all taxpayers, except the married filing separately, and that excess is $110,350.

The following taxpayers must file Form 6251:

1. If line 7 on Form 6251 is greater than line 10.
2. Taxpayer claimed a general business credit, and either line 6 or 25 in Part I of Form 3800 is more than zero.
3. Taxpayer claimed the qualified electric vehicle credit on Form 8834, using the personal part of the alternative fuel vehicle refueling property credit on Form 8911 or the prior year minimum tax on Form 8801.
4. The total of lines 2c through 3 on Form 6251 is negative and line 7 is greater than line 10, if lines 2c through 3 were not taken into account.

The exemption begins to phase out when an individual income reaches $539,600 and $1,079,800 for married filing joint taxpayers. See Instructions Form 6251.

Taxpayers who need to file Form 8801, *Credit for Prior Year Minimum Tax*, could be an individual, estates or trust. This form is used when the taxpayer has a credit carryforward to the next year. The taxpayer had claimed a qualified vehicle credit that was unallowed. Another cause could be the AMT liability and adjustments or preferences that were not an exclusion item. See IRC Code Section 53.

Line 2 Excess Advanced Premium Tax Credit (Form 8962)

Although there is no penalty for not having health insurance, if the taxpayer purchased health care through the Marketplace, the individual must complete Form 8962 to calculate if they need to repay the premium tax credit repayment.

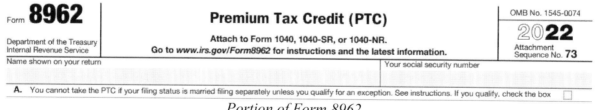

Portion of Form 8962

Using Form 8962, the Premium Tax Credit (PTC) is a credit that can help individuals and their families pay for their health insurance if they have enrolled in a qualified health plan through the Marketplace. The Marketplace is an exchange for those who need qualified health care to purchase qualifying plans, and a taxpayer may be able to claim the Premium Tax Credit if an individual and their tax family (as defined below) enrolled through the Marketplace for a qualified health plan. For more information, see Publication 974 and Instructions Form 8962. The Premium Tax Credit is reported on both Form 1040 and Form 1040NR.

Terms to know for PTC purposes:

- ➤ **Tax Family**: Tax family comprises taxpayer and/or spouse and qualifying individual(s). Family's size is the number of qualifying individuals claimed on the tax return unless the taxpayer and spouse are claimed as a dependent on another tax return.
- ➤ **Household Income**: Household income is the modified gross income of the taxpayer and spouse if filing joint. Add the modified AGI of everyone claimed as a dependent and required to file a tax return due to threshold. Household income does not include the modified AGI of dependents who file return just to receive their refund.
- ➤ **Modified AGI**: Modified AGI is the AGI plus specific income not subject to tax. That income is foreign earned income, tax-exempt interest, and the portion of nontaxable Social Security benefits.
- ➤ **Coverage Family**: The coverage family includes all individuals in the tax family who are enrolled in a qualified health plan and are not eligible for minimum essential coverage (MEC) beyond the coverage in the individual market. Individuals included in the coverage family may change from month to month. If an individual in the tax family is not enrolled in a qualified health plan or is enrolled in a qualified health plan but is eligible for minimum essential coverage, they are not included in the coverage family. The Premium Tax Credit is available to pay the coverage of those included in the coverage family.
- ➤ **Monthly Credit Amount**: The amount of tax credit for a month. The PTC for the year is the sum of all monthly credit amounts. The monthly credit amount is the least of the following:
  - o The enrollment premiums for the month for one or more qualified health plans in which any individual in the tax family was enrolled.
  - o The applicable, monthly amount of the Second Lowest Cost Silver Plan (SLCSP) premium after the monthly contribution amount has been subtracted.
  - o To qualify for the monthly credit amount, at least one tax family member must be enrolled in a qualified health plan on the first day of the month. The monthly credit will not apply if the tax family was not enrolled in a qualified health plan on the 1st of the month. See Instructions Form 8962.
- ➤ **Enrollment Premiums**: Total monthly premiums for one or more qualified health plans that any tax family member enrolled in. Form 1095-A reports the enrollment premiums. The tax professional should ask to see all forms related to health coverage.
- ➤ **Applicable Second Lowest Cost Silver Plan (SLCSP)**: The Second Lowest Cost Silver Plan is, as the name suggests, the plan in the silver category (discussed further in the "Marketplace Plan Levels" Section) that costs the second least. It is not the cheapest but the second-cheapest plan. It is important to know the premium of the SLCSP offered in your area, because that premium is one of the things used to calculate the PTC. The SLCSP premium is a different premium than the enrollment premium described above.
- ➤ **Monthly Contribution Amount**: The monthly contribution is also one of the things used to calculate the Premium Tax Credit amount. The monthly contribution is the amount of income that taxpayers are responsible to pay as their monthly premiums.
- ➤ **Qualified Health Plan**: A qualified health insurance plan purchased through the Marketplace. Catastrophic health plans and stand-alone dental plans purchased through the Marketplace, as well as all plans purchased through Small Business Health Options Programs, are not qualified health plans.

Minimum Essential Coverage (MEC)

Minimum essential coverage includes government-sponsored programs, eligible employer-sponsored plans, individual market plans, and any other coverage that the Department of Health and Human Services designates as minimum essential coverage:

- Health plans offered in the individual market.
- Grandfathered health plans.
- Government-sponsored programs.
- Employer-sponsored plans.
- Other health coverage plans designated as minimum essential coverage by the Department of Health and Human Services.

Señor 1040 Says: Minimum essential coverage does not include coverage consisting solely of excepted benefits. Excepted benefits include stand-alone vision and dental plans (except pediatric dental coverage), workers' compensation coverage, and coverage limited to a specified disease or illness. A taxpayer may have any of these types of coverage and still qualify for the PTC on their qualified health plan.

The Individual Shared Responsibility Provision requires the taxpayer and each family member to do one of the following:

- Have qualifying health coverage.
- Qualify for a health coverage exemption.
- Make a shared responsibility payment when filing their federal income tax return.

Many people already have minimum essential coverage and do not have to do anything more than maintain the coverage and report their coverage when they file their tax return. If the taxpayer is covered by any of the following types of plans, they are considered covered under the health care law and will not pay a penalty or get a health coverage exemption:

- Any Marketplace plan or any individual insurance plan already established.
- Any job-based plan, including retiree plans and COBRA coverage.
- Medicare Part A or Part C.
- Most Medicaid coverage.
- The Children's Health Insurance Program (CHIP).
- Most individual health plans bought outside the Marketplace, including "grandfathered" plans (not all plans sold outside the Marketplace qualify as minimum essential coverage).
- Dependents under the age of 24 who are covered under a parent's plan.
- Self-funded health coverage offered to students by universities for plan or policy years that started on or before Dec. 31, 2014. Taxpayer should check with the university to confirm their plan is minimum essential coverage.
- Health coverage for Peace Corps volunteers.
- Certain types of veteran's health coverage through the Department of Veterans Affairs.
- Department of Defense Nonappropriated Fund Health Benefits Program.
- Refugee Medical Assistance.
- State high-risk pools for plan or policy years that started on or before December 31, 2014. Taxpayer should check with the high-risk pool to confirm their plan is minimum essential coverage.

For a more detailed list of types of plans that may or may not be a minimum essential coverage. See Instructions Form 8965, *Health Coverage Exemptions*.

Marketplace Plan Levels

The ACA requires that all new policies, including those plans that are sold on the exchange (except stand-alone dental, vision, and long-term care plans), comply with one of the four benefit categories set up by the Patient Protection and Affordable Care Act (PPACA). PPACA established four levels of coverage based on the concept of "actuarial value," which is the share of health care expenses the plan covers for a typical group of enrollees. As plans increase in actuarial value, they would cover a greater share of enrollee's medical expenses overall, though the details could vary across different plans. The levels of coverage provided for in the PPACA are central to the coverage that individuals will get and how each will ultimately perceive the effects of the health reform law.

The four Marketplace levels are:

Bronze	60%
Silver	70%
Gold	80%
Platinum	90%

The ACA provides reduced cost sharing for enrollees who select a plan from the silver tier in the federal or state marketplace. The cost-sharing reductions are achieved by requiring insurers to create variants of each standard silver plan, with each variant meeting a successively higher actuarial value. The federal government reimburses insurance companies for the loss of profit resulting from reducing costs for their customers. The reimbursement is known as a "subsidy."

Employer-sponsored Coverage

If the taxpayer and other family members had the opportunity to enroll in a plan that is offered by their employer for 2023, the taxpayer is considered eligible for MEC. Even if the offer of coverage met a minimum standard of affordability and provided a minimum level of benefits." The coverage offered by an employer is generally considered affordable for the taxpayer and qualifying family members allowed to enroll in the coverage. Share of the annual cost for self-only coverage, which is sometimes referred to as the employee required contribution, is not more than 9.78% of household income.

Example: Don was eligible to enroll in his employer's coverage for 2023 but instead applied for coverage in a qualified health plan through the Marketplace. Don provided accurate information about his employer's coverage to the Marketplace, and the Marketplace determined that the offer of coverage was not affordable, and that Don was eligible for APTC. Don enrolled in the qualified health plan for 2023. Don got a new job with employer coverage that he could have enrolled in as of September 1, 2023, but chose not to. Don did not return to the Marketplace to determine if he was eligible for APTC for the months September through December 2023, and remained enrolled in the qualified health plan. Don is not considered eligible for employer-sponsored coverage for the months January through August of 2023 because he gave accurate information to the Marketplace about the availability of employer coverage, and the Marketplace determined that he was eligible for APTC for coverage in a qualified health plan. The Marketplace determination does not apply, however, for the months September through December of 2023. This is because Don did not provide information to the Marketplace about his new employer's offer of coverage. Whether Don is considered eligible for employer-sponsored coverage and ineligible for the PTC for the months September through December of 2023 is determined under the eligibility rules described under Employer-Sponsored Plans. If taxpayer cannot get benefits under an employer-sponsored plan until after a waiting period has expired, taxpayer is not treated as being eligible for that coverage during the waiting period. See Publication 974.

Advance Payments of the Premium Tax Credit

If the taxpayer purchased insurance through the Health Insurance Marketplace, they may be eligible for an Advanced Premium Tax Credit (APTC) to help pay for the insurance coverage. Receiving too little or too much in advance will affect the taxpayer's refund or balance due. To avoid owing a balance, the taxpayer should contact the insurance provider to report changes in income or family size to the Marketplace as soon as possible.

If the taxpayer and family members are enrolled in Marketplace coverage, Form 1095-A should be received from the Marketplace with the months of coverage and the amounts of APTC paid. If the taxpayer received a Form 1095-A showing APTC, Form 8962 must be filed, even if the taxpayer is not otherwise required to file. The taxpayer's Premium Tax Credit is determined by reference to the premium amount for the second lowest cost silver plan offered by an exchange in the rating area where the taxpayer resides.

The Premium Tax Credit is limited to the amount of premium paid for the chosen plan. The credit may be payable in advance, with the payments going directly to the insurance company. A taxpayer who is eligible for an advanced assistance payment may decline it and receive the full amount of the credit on the tax return. Eligibility and the amount of the credit itself are affected by the family size and household income. A married couple must file a joint return to claim the credit. If a married couple files Married Filing Separately, they are not eligible for the credit. If taxpayers file separately because they are victims of domestic abuse, then see Notice 2014-23 for the criteria.

A taxpayer is allowed an advanceable and refundable credit to help subsidize the purchase of health insurance. The taxpayer must have household income of at least 100% but not more than 400% of the federal poverty line for their family size. The taxpayer must not receive health insurance under an employer-sponsored plan (including COBRA) or certain government plans such as Medicare.

Individuals purchasing health insurance through the Marketplace may choose to receive the credit in advance. With this choice, the government would make payments to the health insurance provider for the taxpayer. The difference between the advanced credit and the allowable credit may be claimed or paid when the taxpayer files their current tax return.

Household income means an amount equal to the sum of the following items:

➢ The taxpayer's Modified Adjusted Gross Income (MAGI).
➢ The MAGI of all other individuals who are both of the following:
   o Counted in family size.
   o Required to file an income tax return for the year under IRC §1 without regard to the exception for a child whose parents elect to use IRC §1(g)(7).

Remember, Modified Adjusted Gross Income (MAGI) is adjusted gross income, plus all the following:

➢ The amount excluded under IRC §911, *Foreign-Earned Income Exclusion.*
➢ Tax-exempt interest income.
➢ The excluded portion of Social Security benefits.

Excess Advanced Premium Tax Credit Repayment

The Premium Tax Credit helps pay health insurance premiums that were purchased through the Health Insurance Marketplace. If the advanced payments of this credit were made for coverage for the taxpayer, spouse, or dependents, Form 8962 would be used. If the advanced payments were more than the Premium Tax Credit, the taxpayer has an excess to be repaid, which is reported on Schedule 2, line 46, and added to their tax liability, meaning that paying their taxes will also repay that excess. An additional tax liability could be caused by the taxpayer or spouse having an increase in income and not reporting the change to the Marketplace. If the advanced payments exceed the credit allowed, the income tax liability imposed for the tax year is increased by the difference.

Shared Policy Allocation

For any month during the year the taxpayer, spouse, or dependents did not have minimum essential coverage and do not have a coverage exemption, the taxpayer may need to make an individual shared responsibility payment on the tax return. The annual payment amount is either a percentage of taxpayer's household income or a flat dollar amount, whichever is greater. The national average premium is capped for a bronze level health plan on the Marketplace.

Part 1 Review Questions

To obtain the maximum benefit from this chapter, LTP recommends that you complete each of the following questions, and then compare them to the answers with feedback that immediately follow. Under governing self-study standards, vendors are required to present review questions intermittently throughout each self-study course.

These questions and explanations are not part of the final examination and will not be graded by LTP.

OTTPP1.1
Betty is subject to alternative minimum tax (AMT). Which form is used to calculate her AMT?

    a.   Form 6251
    b.   Form 4868
    c.   Form 8863
    d.   Form 8801

OTTPP1.2
A taxpayer may qualify for an exemption to claim the exclusion from the "shared responsibility." Which form would the taxpayer use to report the exclusion?

    a.   Form 8611
    b.   Form 8965
    c.   Form 8828
    d.   Form 8834

OTTPP1.3
Which of the following is not true about Form 8962, *Premium Tax Credit*?

a. It's a credit that can help individuals and their families pay for their health insurance.
b. Reported on Schedule 2, line 2, and calculated using Form 8962.
c. It's a credit that provides health insurance for the taxpayer and his/her family.
d. Taxpayer may be able to claim the premium tax credit if an individual and his or her tax family enrolled through the Marketplace for a qualified health plan.

OTTP1.4
Which of the following is not true about the Advance Premium Tax Credit (APTC)?

a. Helps pay for the insurance coverage.
b. Receiving too little or too much in advance will affect the taxpayer's refund or balance due.
c. To avoid a balance due, report changes in income or family size to the Marketplace as soon as possible.
d. The Advance Premium Tax Credit is considered a refundable credit.

OTTPP1.5
What is the alternative minimum tax (AMT) exemption amount for married filing jointly?

a. $75,900
b. $118,100
c. $59,050
d. $578,150

OTTPP1.6
What is the alternative minimum tax (AMT) exemption amount for married filing separately?

a. $75,900
b. $118,100
c. $59,050
d. $578,150

OTTPP1.7
Which of the following taxpayers would not use Form 8801, *Credit for Prior Year Minimum Tax*?

a. Individual
b. Estate
c. Trust
d. Partnership

Part 1 Review Questions Answers

OTTPP1.1
Betty is subject to alternative minimum tax (AMT). Which form is used to calculate her AMT?

a. Form 6251
b. Form 4868
c. Form 8863
d. Form 8801

Feedback: Review section *Line 1 Alternative Minimum Tax.*

OTTPP1.2
A taxpayer may qualify for an exemption to claim the exclusion from the "shared responsibility." Which form would the taxpayer use to report the exclusion?

    a. Form 8611
    b. Form 8965
    c. Form 8828
    d. Form 8834

Feedback: Review section *Shared Policy Allocation.*

OTTPP1.3
Which of the following is not true about Form 8962, *Premium Tax Credit*?

    a. It's a credit that can help individuals and their families pay for their health insurance.
    b. Reported on Schedule 2, line 2, and calculated using Form 8962.
    c. It's a credit that provides health insurance for the taxpayer and his/her family.
    d. Taxpayer may be able to claim the premium tax credit if an individual and his or her tax family enrolled through the Marketplace for a qualified health plan.

Feedback: Review section *Line 2, Form 8962: Premium Tax Credit.*

OTTPP1.4
Which of the following is not true about the Advance Premium Tax Credit (APTC)?

    a. Helps pay for the insurance coverage.
    b. Receiving too little or too much in advance will affect the taxpayer's refund or balance due.
    c. To avoid a balance due, report changes in income or family size to the Marketplace as soon as possible.
    d. The Advance Premium Tax Credit is considered a refundable credit.

Feedback: Review section *Advance Payments of the Premium Tax Credit.*

OTTPP1.5
What is the alternative minimum tax (AMT) exemption amount for married filing jointly?

    a. $75,900
    b. $118,100
    c. $59,050
    d. $578,150

Feedback: Review section *Line 1 Alternative Minimum Tax.*

OTTPP1.6
What is the alternative minimum tax (AMT) exemption amount for married filing separately?

    a. $75,900
    b. $118,100
    c. $59,050
    d. $578,150

Feedback: Review section *Line 1 Alternative Minimum Tax.*

OTTPP1.7
Which of the following taxpayers would not use Form 8801, *Credit for Prior Year Minimum Tax?*

a. Individual
b. Estate
c. Trust
d. Partnership

Feedback: Review section *Line 1 Alternative Minimum Tax.*

Part 2 Taxes for Self-Employed

The self-employed individual pays both the employer and the employee tax. This part will discuss which taxes the self-employed individual must pay, as well as how to pay their Social Security and Medicare tax. Other taxes are reported on Part II of Schedule 2.

Part II	Other Taxes	
4	Self-employment tax. Attach Schedule SE	4
5	Social security and Medicare tax on unreported tip income. Attach Form 4137	5
6	Uncollected social security and Medicare tax on wages. Attach Form 8919	6
7	Total additional social security and Medicare tax. Add lines 5 and 6	7

Portion of Schedule 2

Line 4 Self-Employment tax. Attach Schedule SE

This will be covered in "*Federal Schedule C*" chapter.

Line 5 Social Security and Medicare Tax on Unreported Tip Income (Form 4137)

Form 4137 is used to calculate the Social Security and Medicare tax on tips not reported to the taxpayer's employer. Unreported tips were covered in Chapter 4, "Federal Income."

Line 6 Uncollected Social Security and Medicare Tax (Form 8919)

If the taxpayer was an employee but was treated as an independent contractor by the employer, Form 8919, *Uncollected Social Security and Medicare Tax on Wages*, is used to figure and report the taxpayer's share of uncollected Social Security and Medicare taxes due on compensation. Filing this form ensures that the Social Security and Medicare taxes will be credited to the correct Social Security record.

Line 8 Additional Tax on IRAs and Other Tax-Favored Accounts

The calculated amount from Form 5329 is reported on Line 8 of the Schedule 2. Form 5329 is used to report additional taxes on the following items:

➤ Early distributions from an IRA.

- ➢ Early distributions from qualified retirement plans.
- ➢ Excess contributions made to an IRA and other accounts such as:
  - ○ Archer MSA
  - ○ Health savings account
  - ○ ABLE Account
  - ○ Coverdell education savings account.
- ➢ Taxpayer did not tax their required minimum distribution.

The additional tax on an early distribution is included in the taxpayer's gross income and is an additional 10%, although there are some exceptions to the rule. The additional 10% tax on an early withdrawal does not apply to any of the following:

- ➢ A qualified disaster distribution.
- ➢ A qualified HSA funding distribution from an IRA.
- ➢ A distribution from a traditional or SIMPLE IRA that was converted to a Roth IRA.
- ➢ An in-plan Roth rollover.
- ➢ A distribution of certain excess IRA contributions.

Required Minimum Distributions

IRA custodians, trustees or the IRA issuer are required to provide IRA owners with an RMD statement indicating the need to take the distribution. The taxpayer needs to withdraw the amount by April 1st of the year after turning 72. Failing to withdraw the RMD by the deadline may result in owing an additional tax of 50% of the excess accumulation. The taxpayer can request a waiver of the fee from the IRS with reasonable cause by including a letter of explanation with Form 5329 with the tax return.

Excess accumulation relating to traditional IRA, Simplified Employee Pensions (SEP), Savings Incentive Match Plans for Employees of Small Employers (SIMPLE), and beneficiary Individual Retirement Accounts (IRAs) is defined as an amount remaining in the IRA because of an account owner or beneficiary failing to satisfy an RMD.

Line 9 Household Employment Taxes

Taxpayers who employ household workers may be required to pay and withhold employment taxes from their employees. Employment taxes include Social Security tax, Medicare tax, federal unemployment tax, federal income tax withholding, and state employment taxes. To determine if the worker is self-employed, the worker must provide their own tools and offer services to the general public in an independent business.

Some examples of household workers include: babysitters, caretakers, cleaning people, domestic workers, drivers, health aides, housekeepers, maids, nannies, private nurses, private chefs, and yard workers. A worker who performs childcare services in their home is generally not the taxpayer's employee. Household workers are not considered to be the taxpayer's employees but are instead considered self-employed if their services are offered to the general public in an independent business.

Example: Melchior has made an agreement with Jess to care for his lawn. Melchior runs a lawn care business and offers his services to the general public. Melchior provides his own tools and supplies, and he hires and pays his employees. Neither Melchior nor his employees are Jess's household employees.

Form 1040, Schedule H, *Household Employment Taxes*, must be used to report household employment taxes if the taxpayer pays any of the following wages to the employee:

> ➢ Social Security and Medicare wages of $2,400 or more.
> ➢ Federal Unemployment Tax Act (FUTA) wages.
> ➢ Wages from which federal income taxes were withheld.

If the taxpayer pays more than $2,400 in a calendar year to a household employee, the taxpayer must pay Social Security and Medicare taxes for that employee and withhold (or pay) the employee's portion of those taxes.

The taxpayer, who is the employer, is not required to withhold federal income taxes for household employees unless the employee asks to have withholdings taken out and the employer agrees to withhold. The employer must have their employee(s) complete Form W-4, *Employee's Withholding Allowance Certificate*. As with the other employment taxes, withheld federal income taxes may be reported on Schedule H. Schedule H is reported on Form 1040, Schedule 2, line 9. Schedule H can be a standalone form if the taxpayer is not filing a yearly tax return. If a paid tax preparer completed the form for the taxpayer, then they would complete the Paid Preparer Use Only section on Schedule H.

Line 10 First-Time Homebuyer Credit Repayment (Form 5405)

If the taxpayer purchased their primary residence in 2008 and qualified for the first-time homebuyer credit, the taxpayer needs to repay the credit that was received on the 2008 tax return. The credit that was received in 2008 was an interest-free loan to the taxpayer and is to be repaid over a 15-year period. If the taxpayer purchased a home prior to April 8, 2008, and did not own another main home for 36 months prior to the date of purchase and received the credit, repayment of the loan is required.

If the taxpayer sold or converted the main home prior to repayment of the first-time homebuyer credit, the remaining portion of the loan must be repaid in the year the taxpayer sells or converts the property. This repayment is reported using Form 5405 on Form 1040, Schedule 2, line 10.

Example: In June 2008, Watson purchased his primary home. Watson moved out and converted his home to a rental in 2022; Watson will have to repay the remaining portion of the first-time homebuyer credit on his 2022 tax return because he sold it before the end of the 15-year repayment period.

Line 11 Additional Medicare Tax (Form 8959)

The taxpayer may be subject to a 0.9% additional Medicare tax that applies to Medicare wages, railroad retirement act compensation, and self-employment income over the filing status threshold. This tax is an employee tax, not an employer tax. The employer is responsible for withholding the additional tax once the taxpayer's compensation exceeds $200,000 (regardless of filing status) in a calendar year. The taxpayer cannot request their employer to stop the withholding of the additional tax. If the taxpayer has wages as well as self-employment income, the threshold is reduced on the self-employment income, but not below zero.

Filing Status	Threshold Amount
Married Filing Jointly	$250,000
Married Filing Separately	$125,000
Single	$200,000
Head of Household	$200,000
Surviving Spouse with Qualifying Child	$200,000

The above threshold amounts are not indexed for inflation.

Example: Terri, a single filer, has $130,000 in self-employment income and $0 in wages. Terri is not liable for the Additional Medicare Tax and does not have to file Form 8959.

Example: George and Jean are married and filing a joint return. George has $190,000 in wages and Jean has $150,000 in compensation subject to railroad retirement taxes. Neither George nor Jean has wages or compensation that exceed $200,000 because their employers do not combine the wages and railroad retirement compensation to determine whether they are more than the $250,000 threshold for a joint return. George and Jean are not liable for the additional tax.

Example: Carl, a single filer, has $220,000 in self-employment income and $0 in wages. Carl must file Form 8959 as he is liable to pay the additional Medicare Tax on $20,000 of his $220,000 income ($220,000 minus the threshold of $200,000).

Line 12 Net Investment Income Tax (NIIT)

Reported using Form 8960, NIIT is a 3.8% tax on the lesser of net investment income or the excess of the taxpayer's modified adjusted gross income amount that is over the filing status threshold. NIIT generally includes income and gain from passive activities. For the purposes of the NIIT, a passive activity, as defined by §469 of the Internal Revenue Code, includes rental activity whether the taxpayer materially participated or not. The activity must also be a trade or business as defined under §162 of the Internal Revenue Code and be non-passive before the income can be excluded from NIIT. Individuals who have NIIT and modified adjusted gross income (MAGI) over the following thresholds will owe 3.8%:

Filing Status	Threshold Amount
Married filing jointly	$250,000
Married filing separately	$125,000
Single	$200,000
Head of Household (with qualifying person)	$200,000
Surviving spouse with dependent child	$250,000

Taxpayers should be aware that these threshold amounts are not indexed for inflation. If an individual is exempt from Medicare taxes, they may still be subject to NIIT if the taxpayer's modified adjusted gross income is over the thresholds.

NIIT includes gross income from interest, dividends, capital gains, rental and royalty income, and annuities, unless they are derived from the ordinary course of a trade or business that is:

1. Not a passive activity,
2. A trade or business of financial instruments or commodities.

The net investment income tax will not apply to any amount of gain that is excluded from gross income for regular income tax purposes. The pre-existing statutory exclusion in IRC §121 exempts the first $250,000 (or $500,000 in the case of a married couple filing jointly) of gain recognized on the sale of a principal residence from gross income for regular income tax purposes and, thus, from the NIIT. For more information on NIIT, go to www.irs.gov and see the FAQs for the NIIT.

The following gains are examples of items that are taken into consideration when computing NIIT:

➢ Gains from sale of stocks, bonds, and mutual funds.
➢ Capital gain distributions from mutual funds.
➢ Gain from the sale of investment real estate, including the gain on the sale of a second home that is not the taxpayer's primary residence.
➢ A gain from the sale of interest in partnerships and S corporations (to the extent that the partner or shareholder was a passive owner).

Distributions are considered when determining the modified adjusted gross income threshold. Distributions from a nonqualified retirement plan are included in net investment income. Form 8960 will be filed if the taxpayer has net investment income tax. For more information, refer to IRS Regulation Sections 1.1411-1 through 1.1411-10.

The Alaska Permanent Fund is a dividend that is paid to all qualifying residents of Alaska. The dividend is based upon a five-year average of the Permanent Fund's performance, which is based on the stock market and other factors. The dividend is taxable on the recipients' federal tax returns.

Additional Taxes

The following are other taxes reported on Form 1040, Schedule 2, line 17:

➢ Form 8611   *Recapture of Low-Income Housing Credit*
➢ Form 8828   *Recapture of Federal Mortgage Subsidy*
➢ Form 8853   *Archer MSAs and Long-Term Care Insurance Contracts*
➢ Form 4255   *Recapture of Investment Credit*
➢ Form 8889   *Health Savings Account*

Line 18 Total Additional Taxes

Add the amounts of 17a - z and report the total on line 18. This is the total amount of Additional Taxes. Report this amount on Form 1040, line 23, to add the amount toward the taxpayer's total tax liability.

Line 20 Net Tax Liability Installment

This line reports the amount calculated from Form 965-A. See Instructions Form 965-A.

Kiddie Tax (Form 8615)

Although the Form 8615 is not included on Schedule 2 as an additional tax, it is an additional tax to the parent. If the parent claims their child's unearned income, the child will not file a tax return. Claiming the child's unearned income would change the parents' tax liability and could affect the taxpayers' adjusted gross income (AGI). The election is made annually. The parent can claim their child's unearned income if the child meets the following conditions:

1. The child had $2,300 or more of unearned income.
2. The child is required to file a tax return.
3. The child either:
   a. Was under age 18 at the end of 2022.
   b. Was age 18 at the end of 2022 and didn't have earned income that was more than half of their support.

  c. Was a full-time student at least age 19 and under age 24 at the end of 2022 and did not have earned income that was more than half of their support.
4. At least one of the child's parents was alive at the end of 2022.
5. The child does not need to file a joint return for 2022.

A "child" regarding the kiddie tax rules includes legally adopted children and stepchildren. These rules apply whether the child is or is not a dependent. If neither of the child's parents were living at the end of the year, none of the rules apply.

Support includes all amounts spent to provide the child with food, lodging, clothing, education, medical and dental care, recreation, transportation, and similar necessities. To calculate the child's support, count support provided by parents and their child, and others who support the child. Scholarship received by the child is not considered support if the child is a full-time student.

The Setting Every Community Up for Retirement Act (SECURE ACT) of 2019 repealed the TCJA changes made for Kiddie Tax. For tax year 2020 and beyond, the law reverts the kiddie tax back to the parent's marginal tax rate. See Publication 919 and IRC Section 1(g).

Part 2 Review Questions

To obtain the maximum benefit from this chapter, LTP recommends that you complete each of the following questions, and then compare them to the answers with feedback that immediately follow. Under governing self-study standards, vendors are required to present review questions intermittently throughout each self-study course.

These questions and explanations are not part of the final examination and will not be graded by LTP.

OTTPP2.1
Cesar pays Rosa $200 weekly to clean his house. Rosa does not live with Cesar, but she does clean other individuals' houses as well. Which of the following scenarios best describes Cesar's tax responsibility?

  a. Cesar is required to withhold employment taxes for Rosa.
  b. Cesar is required to pay withholding taxes for Rosa.
  c. Cesar is not required to withhold employment taxes for Rosa.
  d. Cesar is not required to pay or withhold employment taxes for Rosa.

OTTPP2.2
Which of the following taxpayers would report other taxes on Schedule 2, line 1?

  a. Yesenia, who earned $75,000 as gross wages.
  b. Paul, who earned $12,000 as gross wages and $75,000 from self-employment.
  c. Jim, who earned $10,000 in interest and $360,000 as gross wages.
  d. Kathy, who only had Social Security benefits.

OTTPP2.3

Ezekiel, a single filer, has $220,000 in self-employment income and $0 in wages. Ezekiel must file Form 8959 as he is liable to pay the .9% Additional Medicare Tax. What is the Additional Medicare Tax threshold amount for single taxpayers?

 a. $230,000
 b. $250,000
 c. $200,000
 d. $125,000

OTTPP2.4

Jerimiah, a single filer, has $420,000 in self-employment income and $0 in wages. Jerimiah must file Form 8959 as he is liable to pay the .9% Additional Medicare Tax. What is the Additional Medicare Tax threshold amount for single taxpayers?

 a. $230,000
 b. $250,000
 c. $200,000
 d. $125,000

OTTPP2.5

Esther is 4 years old and lives with her parents. They would like to claim the income that she earned while being a movie star for a local television station. The earned income was $2,310.45. Which of the following would describe what Esther and her parents need to do?

 a. Esther's parents should not claim her earned income.
 b. Esther would need to file her own tax return as a dependent on another return.
 c. Esther does not need to file since she is under the reporting amount.
 d. Esther cannot be claimed as a dependent on her parents' return.

OTTPP2.6

Stephen would like to include his son Richard's interest and dividend income (including capital gain distributions) on his personal tax return. Which of the following would not allow Stephen to report the income?

 a. Richard is 18 years old.
 b. Richard's gross income is $7,500.
 c. Richard had income only from interest and dividends.
 d. Richard is 22 years old and a part-time student.

Part 2 Review Question Answers

OTTPP2.1

Cesar pays Rosa $200 weekly to clean his house. Rosa does not live with Cesar, but she does clean other individuals' houses as well. Which of the following scenarios best describes Cesar's tax responsibility?

 a. Cesar is required to withhold employment taxes for Rosa.
 b. Cesar is required to pay withholding taxes for Rosa.
 c. Cesar is not required to withhold employment taxes for Rosa.
 d. Cesar is not required to pay or withhold employment taxes for Rosa.

Feedback: Review section *Line 7a – Household Employment Taxes.*

OTTPP2.2
Which of the following taxpayers would report other taxes on Schedule 2, Line 1?

    a. Yesenia, who earned $75,000 as gross wages.
    b. Paul, who earned $12,000 as gross wages and $75,000 from self-employment.
    c. Jim, who earned $10,000 in interest and $360,000 as gross wages.
    d. Kathy, who only had Social Security benefits.

Feedback: Review section *Line 8: Taxes from Other IRS Forms.*

OTTPP2.3
Ezekiel, a single filer, has $220,000 in self-employment income and $0 in wages. Ezekiel must file Form 8959 as he is liable to pay the .9% Additional Medicare Tax. What is the Additional Medicare Tax threshold amount for single taxpayers?

    a. $230,000
    b. $250,000
    c. $200,000
    d. $125,000

Feedback: Review section *Form 8959: Additional Medicare Tax.*

OTTPP2.4
Jerimiah, is married filing separately, has $420,000 in self-employment income and $0 in wages. Jerimiah must file Form 8959 as he is liable to pay the .9% Additional Medicare Tax. What is the Additional Medicare Tax threshold amount for married filing separately?

    a. $230,000
    b. $250,000
    c. $200,000
    d. $125,000

Feedback: Review section *Form 8959: Additional Medicare Tax.*

OTTPP2.5
Esther is 4 years old and lives with her parents. They would like to claim the income that she earned while being a movie star on the local television station. The earned income was $2,310.45. Which of the following would describe what Esther and her parents need to do?

    a. Esther's parents should not claim her earned income.
    b. Esther would need to file her own tax return as a dependent on another return.
    c. Esther does not need to file since she is under the reporting amount.
    d. Esther cannot be claimed as a dependent on her parents' return.

Feedback: Review section *Kiddie Tax.*

OTTPP2.6

Stephen would like to include his son Richard's interest and dividend income (including capital gain distributions) on his personal tax return. Which of the following would not allow Stephen to report the income?

    a. Richard is 18 years old.
    b. Richard's gross income is $7,500.
    c. Richard had income only from interest and dividends.
    d. Richard is 22 years old and a part-time student.

Feedback: Review section *Kiddie Tax.*

Part 3 Taxpayer Penalties

Penalties and Interest Charges

Preparer penalties are enforced by the IRS under Revenue Code §6694, and in §6695 "*Understatement of taxpayer's liability by tax return preparer,*", "*Other assessable penalties with respect to the preparation of tax returns for other persons.*" These due diligence penalties affect both the taxpayer and the tax preparer. Tax professionals can also receive penalties based on how they prepare their clients' returns. Preparer penalties were discussed in Chapter 1.

The tax law imposes penalties to ensure that all taxpayers pay their taxes. If taxpayers underpay their tax due to fraud, they may be subject to a civil fraud penalty. In those cases, the taxpayer may be subject to a criminal prosecution.

Penalties are treated as additions to taxes and are not deductible for federal income tax purposes. Taxpayers can receive penalties based on their filed tax return or not filing a return. Due diligence is the responsibility of both the taxpayer and the tax professional. Penalties and interest for a taxpayer could be assessed for not filing a tax return or filing an incorrect return. An incorrect return could be when the taxpayer understates their income and overstates their expenses.

If the taxpayer and tax professional prepare a tax return with an understatement of tax liability, both could be taking a frivolous stance where there is no credible possibility the tax return would survive an audit. In this case, the penalty would be the greater of $1,000 or 50% of the income derived by the tax return preparer with respect to the tax return. The tax preparer may face a penalty of $5,000 or 50% of the income derived by the tax return if the attempt to understate the tax liability is intentional (IRC, §6695(a)).

If an individual owes taxes, the IRS will calculate penalties and interest on the amount owed. Penalties are calculated on the balance due. There are several separate types of penalties:

    ➢ Failure-to-file.
    ➢ Failure-to-pay.
    ➢ Failure to pay proper estimated tax.
    ➢ Dishonored check.

The interest accrues until the tax owed is paid in full. A late-payment penalty may be charged as well, but if the taxpayer shows a reasonable cause for not paying on time, they may be able to abate these penalties. The taxpayer must still make a good effort to properly estimate and pay the tax due on the due date.

Failure-to-File Penalty

The penalty for failing to file a return by the due date is 5% of the amount of tax due if the failure is for not more than one month, with an additional 5% for each additional month or fraction thereof, but not exceeding 25% in total of the tax. The failure-to-pay penalty reduces it for any month in which both penalties apply. However, if the return is more than 60 days late, the penalty will not be less than $435 or 100% of the tax balance, whichever is less. The taxpayer will not have to pay the penalty if they show reasonable cause for not filing on time.

If the taxpayer files an extension, the tax is still due on the filing date, normally April 15th. A tax professional needs to understand and tell their clients that they owe the tax and that penalties and interest will accrue on the unpaid tax. A taxpayer can apply for an installment agreement. See 26 U.S. Code Section 6651 and 26 Code of Federal Regulations section 301.665-1.

Failure-to-Pay Penalty

The IRS will calculate the Failure-to-Pay based on how late the tax return is from the due date and how much unpaid tax is due. This penalty cannot be more than 25% of the unpaid tax. The taxpayer will not have to pay the fine if they show a good reason for not paying the tax on time. Add the failure-to-pay penalty to interest charges on late payments. The monthly or partial month rate is half the usual rate—25% instead of 50%—if an installment agreement is in effect for the month.

When the IRS issues an intent to levy, the tax rate increases to 1% if the taxpayer does not pay the amount in 10 days of the notice. When the IRS issues a notice and demands immediate payment, the rate will increase to 1% at the start of the first month, beginning after the notice and demand are issued. See 26 U.S. Code Section 6651 and 26 Code of Federal Regulations section 301.665-1.

Combined Penalties

If both the failure-to-file penalty and the failure-to-pay penalty apply in any month, the 5% (or 15%) failure-to-file penalty is reduced by the failure-to-pay penalty. However, if the taxpayer filed the return more than 60 days after the due date or extended due date, the minimum penalty is the smaller of $435 (for tax returns for 2020, 2021, and 2022) or 100% of the unpaid tax.

Underpayment of Estimated Tax by Individuals Penalty

The IRS incurs that all income is on the "pay as you go." In other words self-employed taxpayers should make quarterly estimated payments. Taxpayers that owe additional tax payments for tax year 2022 may need to pay estimated payments for 2023 tax year.

The taxpayer may owe a penalty if the total of the withholding was timely filed but the estimated payments, did not equal the smaller of:

1. 90% of the tax owed on the 2023 tax return.
2. 100% of the taxpayer 2022 tax. The tax return covers a 12-month period.

The penalty is figured on Form 2210 or Form 2210-F for farmers or fishermen. See Instructions Form 2210 and Publication 505.

Dishonored Check

If the taxpayer writes a check to pay for the amount due and the check bounces (dishonored), the IRS may impose a penalty. A penalty will be assessed as well if the taxpayer does not have enough funds in the bank account to pay the balance due. The penalty is whichever is less: 2% of the amount of the check or $25 if the check is less than $1,250. See *IRC §6695(f)*.

If the taxpayer is required to make a payment by Electronic Funds Transfer (EFT) and makes the payment by another means, the penalty is 10% of the amount paid via non-EFT. Reasonable cause and not willful neglect could be an exception.

Paying or Receiving Interest

If taxpayers have a balance due on their current year tax return or owe taxes to the IRS for prior years and fail to pay the amount due by the due date, interest will be owed on the unpaid balance. Taxpayers cannot deduct the interest paid to the IRS on their return. When the taxpayer receives interest on a delayed refund or an amended return, that amount is considered earned income in the year received.

Information Reporting Penalties

If an individual files information returns and does not file them timely, they could receive penalties. An information return is used more in business, such as filing W-2s or 1099s. The IRS charges penalties based on the due date of the information return. For example, Diego prepares W-2s for his business client's company. For tax year 2023 up to 30 days late the penalty is $50 per information return or payee statement; 31 days through August 1, the penalty is $110 per return or statement. After August 1 or not filed, the penalty amount is $280 per item. If the taxpayer or Diego are intentionally disregarding the payment dates, the penalty amount is $580 per failure to file. For tax year 2024, the amounts are $60, $120, $310, and $630 per failure to file.

Filing Late

Taxpayers who do not file their returns by the due date (including extensions) could be assessed to pay a failure-to-file penalty. The penalty is based on the tax owed by the due date (without regard to extensions). The penalty is usually ½% of the balance due for each month or part of a month that a return is late, but not more than 25%. See IRC code 6651.

Late-Filed Return with a Refund

If the taxpayer was due a refund but did not file a return, the taxpayer generally must file within three years from the date the original return was due. If the taxpayer files the return late, more than 60 days after the due date or extended due date, the minimum penalty is the smaller of $135 or 100% of the unpaid tax.

If the taxpayer could show reasonable cause for not filing a timely return, the penalty may not be assessed.

Reduced Refund

The taxpayer's refund may be reduced by an additional tax liability that has been assessed. A refund may also be reduced for owed past-due child support, debts to another federal agency, delinquent student loans, or state tax.

Penalty for Failure to Disclose Foreign Income

Penalties for failure to disclose a foreign bank account report (FBAR) can be criminal or civil. Criminal penalties would be charged if the taxpayer fails to report an asset or have an underpayment of tax. If the taxpayer is required to file Form 8938 by the due date, the penalty would be $10,000 or up to $50,000 depending on circumstances.

In addition to the penalty for failure to file Form 8938, the IRS could assess an additional penalty under IRC §6662 for failure to report the income attributable to an undisclosed foreign financial asset. The maximum additional penalty for not filing Form 8938 is $50,000. See Instructions Form 8938.

First-Time Abate Policy

The IRS has a policy for penalty relief called First Time Abate (FTA). The FTA penalty relief option for failure-to-file, and failure-to-pay penalties, under certain conditions, does not apply if the taxpayer has not filed all returns and paid or arranged to pay all tax currently due. The taxpayer is considered current with an open installment agreement and if the current installment payments are up to date.

Penalties are imposed on taxpayers who file late and who fail to timely pay the tax in full. The late penalty is 5% of the unpaid taxes for each month or part of a month that the return is late, up to 25%. To reward past tax compliance and promote future tax compliance, the IRS waives these penalties for taxpayers who have demonstrated full compliance over the prior three years.

Failure to Supply Social Security Number

If the taxpayer does not include a Social Security number (SSN) or the SSN of another person where required on a return, statement, or other document, the taxpayer will be subject to a penalty of $50 for each failure. The taxpayer may also be subject to the penalty of $50 if he or she does not give his or her SSN to another person when it is required on a return, statement, or other document. The taxpayer will not have to pay the penalty if he or she is able to show that the failure was due to reasonable cause and not willful neglect.

Example: Lauren has a bank account that earns interest. Lauren must give her SSN to the bank. The number must be shown on Form 1099-INT or other statement the bank sends Lauren. If Lauren does not give the bank her SSN, she will be subject to the $50 penalty. Lauren could also be subject to "backup" withholding of income tax.

Failure to Furnish Correct Payee Statements

Any person who does not provide an individual with a complete and correct copy of an information return (payee statement) by the due date is subject to a penalty of $250 for each statement. If any failure is corrected within 30 days of the due date, the penalty could be $50. See IRC Code 6722.

Interest Charges

April 15 is normally the deadline for taxpayers to file and pay any amount due on their individual return. Interest is generally charged on the unpaid tax from the due date until the amount is paid in full. If the taxpayer does not make the balance due, the IRS will charge a late-payment penalty. The taxpayer may have to pay the penalty for understating income, understating a reportable transaction, or filing an erroneous claim for a refund or credit. There are two kinds of penalties regarding understating a reportable transaction: civil and criminal.

The taxpayer may have to pay the penalty if the individual substantially understates the tax, files a frivolous return, or fails to supply a Social Security number. If the taxpayer provides fraudulent information on the tax return, the individual may pay a civil fraud penalty.

Criminal Penalties

The taxpayer may be brought to trial for criminal prosecution for the following actions:

➢ Tax evasion.
➢ Willful failure to file a return, supply information, or pay any tax due.
➢ Fraud and false statements.
➢ Preparing and filing a fraudulent return.
➢ Identity theft.

A taxpayer convicted of criminal fraud is subject to a fine of up to $100,000 or imprisonment of up to 5 years, or both, together with the cost of the prosecution. For more information, see code section 7201.

Tax Evasion

Tax evasion is illegally avoiding paying taxes, failing to report, or reporting income and expenses erroneously. The government imposes strict and serious penalties for tax evasion. The following are some common contradictions that the IRS looks for to validate tax evasion:

➢ Understatement of income.
➢ Claiming fictitious or improper deductions.
➢ Accounting irregularities.
➢ Allocation of income.
➢ Acts and conduct of the taxpayer.

Fraud and Tax Evasion

If the taxpayer's failure to file is due to fraud, the maximum fine is $250,000 for individuals and $500,000 for corporations. For fraud and tax avoidance, the individual could be jailed for up to five years.

Tax Avoidance

Tax avoidance is different from tax evasion. Tax avoidance is using legal methods to minimize the amount of income tax owed by a taxpayer or business. What distinguishes tax avoidance from tax evasion is the intent of the taxpayer. The intent to evade tax occurs when a taxpayer knowingly misrepresents the facts. The intent is a state of mind. A taxpayer's intent is judged by others, and others judge a taxpayer's intent.

Negligence or Disregard

The term "Negligence" is a failure to make a reasonable attempt to comply with the tax law or to exercise ordinary and reasonable care in preparing a return. Negligence also includes a failure to keep adequate books and records. The taxpayer will not have to pay a negligence penalty if they have a reasonable basis for the position taken. "Disregard" includes any careless, reckless, or intentional disregard of rules or regulations. Negligence or ignorance of the law does not constitute fraud.

Civil, Criminal, and Fraud Penalties

If the taxpayer does not file the tax return and pay the tax by the due date, he or she may have to pay a penalty. The law provides penalties for failure to file returns or pay taxes as required.

If IRS examiners find strong evidence of fraud, they will refer the case to the Criminal Investigation Division (CID) for prosecution. They can impose both civil sanctions and criminal prosecution.

Joint Return

The fraud penalty on a joint return may not apply to a spouse unless some part of the underpayment is due to the spouse's fraud. The spouse may need to file a separate return.

Section 7201 provides that "any person who willfully attempts in any manner to evade or defeat any tax imposed by this title or the payment thereof shall, in addition to other penalties provided by law, be guilty of a felony." In addition to criminal penalties, any person can be guilty of a felony and upon conviction thereof, shall be fined not more than $100,000 or imprisoned not more than 5 years, or both, and the individual will pay for the cost of prosecution.

Adequate Disclosure

The taxpayer can avoid the penalty for disregarding rules or regulations if the taxpayer adequately disclosed a position that has at least a reasonable basis on the return. The exception will not apply if the taxpayer did not keep adequate books or the item relates to a tax shelter.

Substantial Understatement of Income Tax Penalty

The taxpayer understates the tax if the tax shown on the tax return is less than the correct tax. The understatement is substantial if it is more than the larger of 10% of the correct tax or $5,000.

However, reduce the amount of understatement to the extent the understatement is due to:

> ➤ Substantial authority.
> ➤ Adequate disclosure and a reasonable basis.

Whether there is or was substantial authority for the tax treatment of an item depends on the facts and circumstances—consider the court opinions, Treasury regulations, revenue rulings, revenue procedures, and notices. Announcements issued by the IRS and published in the Internal Revenue Bulletin that involve the same or similar circumstances as the taxpayer will also be considered.

Filing Erroneous Claim for Refund or Credit

The taxpayer might have to pay the penalty if they filed for an erroneous claim for refund or credit in their tax return. The penalty is 20% of the excess amount of the claim unless the taxpayer can show a rational basis for the claim. See code section 6676(b).

Frivolous Tax Return Penalty

The taxpayer may have to pay a penalty of $5,000 for filing a "frivolous return." A frivolous return does not include enough information to figure out the correct tax or contains information clearly showing that the tax reported is substantially incorrect.

The taxpayer would have to pay the penalty if they filed this kind of return due to a need to delay or interfere with the administration of federal income tax laws. This action includes altering or striking out the preprinted language above the space provided for the taxpayer's signature. This penalty is added to any other penalty that is provided by law.

Part 3 Review Questions

To obtain the maximum benefit from this chapter, LTP recommends that you complete each of the following questions, and then compare them to the answers with feedback that immediately follow. Under governing self-study standards, vendors are required to present review questions intermittently throughout each self-study course.

These questions and explanations are not part of the final examination and will not be graded by LTP.

OTTPP3.1
Which of the following is not an individual penalty?

    a. Failure-to-file
    b. Dishonored check
    c. First Time Abate
    d. Failure-to-pay

OTTPP3.2
Hamilton has filed fraudulent tax returns resulting in underpayment of tax due. Hamilton has been charged with civil fraud. Which additional penalty could Hamilton pay for the fraudulent underpayment?

    a. Additional penalty of 75% of the underpayment.
    b. Additional penalty of 100% of the underpayment.
    c. Additional penalty of 50% of the underpayment.
    d. Additional penalty of 25% of the underpayment.

OTTPP3.3
The taxpayer may owe a penalty if the total of their withholding and his or her timely filed estimated payments, sometimes called quarterlies, did not equal the smaller of what?

    a. 100% of the taxpayer 2020 tax.
    b. 95% of the tax owed on their 2022 tax return.
    c. 90% of the tax owed on his or her 2021 tax return.
    d. No penalty on underpaid estimated payments.

OTTPP3.4

A frivolous return does not include enough information to figure out the correct tax or contains information clearly showing that the tax reported is substantially incorrect. The taxpayer may have to pay a penalty of how much for filing a "frivolous return"?

    a. $1,000
    b. $5,000
    c. 5% of balance due
    d. $570

OTTPP3.5

The taxpayer might have to pay the penalty if they filed for an erroneous claim for refund or credit in their tax return. The penalty is what percent of the excess amount of the claim?

    a. 10%
    b. 20%
    c. 25%
    d. 50%

Part 3 Review Question Answers

OTTPP3.1

Which of the following is not an individual penalty?

    a. Failure-to-file
    b. Dishonored check
    c. **First Time Abate**
    d. Failure-to-pay

Feedback: Review section *Taxpayer Penalties.*

OTTPP3.2

Hamilton has filed fraudulent tax returns resulting in underpayment of tax due. Hamilton has been charged with civil fraud. Which additional penalty could Hamilton pay for the fraudulent underpayment?

    a. **Additional penalty of 75% of the underpayment.**
    b. Additional penalty of 100% of the underpayment.
    c. Additional penalty of 50% of the underpayment.
    d. Additional penalty of 25% of the underpayment.

Feedback: Review section *Taxpayer Penalties.*

OTTPP3.3

The taxpayer may owe a penalty if the total of their withholding and his or her timely filed estimated payments, sometimes called quarterlies, did not equal the smaller of what?

    a. 100% of the taxpayer 2020 tax.
    b. 95% of the tax owed on their 2022 tax return.
    c. **90% of the tax owed on his or her 2021 tax return.**
    d. No penalty on underpaid estimated payments.

Feedback: Review section *Taxpayer Penalties.*

OTTPP3.4

A frivolous return does not include enough information to figure out the correct tax or contains information clearly showing that the tax reported is substantially incorrect. The taxpayer may have to pay a penalty of how much for filing a "frivolous return"?

    a. $1,000
    b. $5,000
    c. 5% of balance due
    d. $570

Feedback: Review section *Taxpayer Penalties.*

OTTPP3.5

The taxpayer might have to pay the penalty if they filed for an erroneous claim for refund or credit in their tax return. The penalty is what percent of the excess amount of the claim?

    a. 10%
    b. 20%
    c. 25%
    d. 50%

Feedback: Review section *Taxpayer Penalties.*

Takeaways

"Other taxes" consist of different types of taxes. Some taxes have forms that are attached to the Form 1040, while others are reported on Form 1040, Schedule 2. The IRS has expanded Schedule 2 by detailing certain additional taxes, which have their own line on Schedule 2. For example, on page 2 of Schedule 2, line 17 is for additional tax items such as Health Savings Account, Archer Medical Savings Account, and recapturing deductible credits.

AMT is a separate tax that is added to the income tax. Under tax law, certain deductions could give taxpayers a beneficial treatment for those who qualify for the tax deduction. The purpose of the minimum tax credit is to prevent the double taxation of deferral preference adjustments. AMT is a tax imposed in addition to the regular income tax to recapture the reductions resulting from the use of special tax relief provisions of the tax law. The repayment of the Premium Tax Credit is based on the amount of the premium paid and the taxpayer's income.

TEST YOUR KNOWLEDGE!
Go online to take a practice quiz.

California Other Taxes and Taxpayer Penalties

Introduction

The Franchise Tax Board (FTB) is the California government agency responsible for collecting state personal income taxes. The revenues FTB collects are placed in the state's general fund to help pay for items such as roads, parks, law enforcement, and schools. California's state income tax system is based on the principle of voluntary compliance. Voluntary compliance is a system of taxation that relies on individual citizens to properly report their income, calculate their tax liability, and file their tax returns timely.

State personal income tax, like federal income tax, is a tax imposed on wages, tips, interest, dividends, pensions, capital gains, and other types of income. First imposed in 1936, state personal income tax is the largest single source of revenue in California. Personal income tax is based on the amount of taxable income that people receive annually. Taxable income is less than total income, due to tax deductions.

This chapter gives an overview of other California taxes and penalties that a taxpayer might be responsible for. California may have different taxes and penalties.

Objectives

At the end of this lesson, the student will:

> ➢ Understand the California AMT.
> ➢ Recognize when the taxpayer will need to pay mental health services tax.
> ➢ Clarify when the additional tax on IRAs might apply.
> ➢ Know the difference between federal and state determination of who is a Household employees.

Resources

Form 540	FTB Publication 1001	Instructions Form 540
FTB Form 3510	FTB Publication 1005	Instructions Form 3510
FTB Form 3805P	Form DE 1HW (EDD)	Instructions Form 3805P
540 Schedule CA	EDD Publication DE 8829	Instructions 540 Schedule CA
Schedule P		Instructions Schedule P

Table of Contents

Part 1 Other Taxes on Form 540

Like the federal, California has additional taxes. Some of the taxes are the same as the federal such as alternative minimum tax (AMT), additional tax on IRA distributions, and Archer Medical Savings Plan. One tax that is state only is the Mental Health Services Tax.

Line 61 Alternative Minimum Tax

California's AMT is similar to the federal AMT. The purpose of the AMT is to make sure that taxpayers do not use various tax incentives to pay little or no California income tax. As with the federal version, whether a taxpayer is subject to AMT is based on their 2022 income. If the California taxpayer exemption amount on their federal return exceeds the amounts from Form 1040, line 24 the taxpayer may be subject to AMT.

If the taxpayer's federal adjusted gross income is less than the amount of the individual's filing status, then no AMT is required. If the taxpayer's AGI and itemized deductions are greater than, AMT might be owed. For tax year 2022 the NOL suspension has been repealed. See Instructions Schedule P (540) and Instructions Form 540.

Señor 1040 Says: If the taxpayer paid AMT in a prior year, they may be able to claim a credit for the AMT paid. The prior year credit must be applied before any current year credit can be used to reduce regular tax below the AMT.

The AMT rate for C corporations is 6.65%. California allows small businesses to exempt $40,000 up to $150,000 from AMTI. Small businesses in California are companies that are independently owned and operated with 100 or fewer employees and the average annual gross income is $10 million or less.

Line 62 Mental Health Services Tax

The mental health service tax is paid by individual taxpayers whose taxable income is more than $1 million. The employers are not responsible for paying the employees mental health service tax. If the taxpayer's taxable income is more than $1 million, the taxpayer is subject to paying the tax, which is 1% of every dollar of taxable income after $1,000,000. For example, April made $1,100,000 in 2022, so she would pay an additional tax of .01 on the $100,000 of taxable income that she made after her first million.

$$\begin{array}{r} \$1,100,000 \\ - \$1,000,000 \\ \hline \$100,000 \times 1\% = \$1,000 \end{array}$$

Line 63 Other Taxes and Credit Recapture

If the taxpayer received an early distribution of a qualified retirement plan and was required to report additional tax on the federal tax return, the taxpayer may be required to report additional tax on their California return. California conforms to federal law for income received under Internal Revenue Code section 409A on a Nonqualified Deferred Compensation (NQDC) plan, discounted stock options, and stock appreciation rights. If the taxpayer used any of the following forms, the additional tax will be reported on Form 540, line 63.

- ➤ FTB 3531, *California Competes Tax Credit*
- ➤ FTB 3540, *Credit Carryover and Recapture Summary*
- ➤ FTB 3554, *New Employment Credit*

Additional Tax on IRAs

If the taxpayer received an early distribution from a qualified retirement plan and the taxpayer reported additional tax on the federal return, the individual may have to use Form 3805P to report the additional tax on line 63 of the California return as well. California and federal laws are generally the same when it comes to the tax on early distributions. However, California does not conform to all federal exceptions to the additional tax on an early distribution. California does not tax the excess contributions to a traditional IRA, Roth IRA, Coverdell ESA, Archer MSA, or excess accumulation in a qualified plan. The additional tax is 2.5% on the part of the distribution that is includable in income.

Form 3805P must be filed if any of the following apply to the taxpayer:

6. Received an early taxable distribution from a qualified retirement plan and a distribution code other than 2, 3, or 4 is shown in box 7 of federal Form 1099-R.
7. Owes tax on early distributions from an IRA, some other qualified retirement plan, an annuity, or a modified endowment contract, and there is an exception code in box 7 of Form 1099-R. See Instructions Form 1099-R for more information.
8. Owes a tax because the taxpayer received distributions from a Coverdell ESA in excess of the educational costs; if this is true, complete Form 3805P, Part II.

9. Received taxable distributions from an Archer MSA. This penalty is 12.5%.
10. Meet an exception to the tax on early distributions, and distribution code 2, 3, or 4 is *not* shown or is incorrect on federal Form 1099-R.

The taxpayer does not have to file Form FTB 3805P if any of the following are true:

➢ The taxable portion of the distribution was rolled over into another qualified plan within 60 days of receipt on the year received.
➢ The taxpayer received an early distribution from the plan but met an exception to the tax (distribution code 2, 3, or 4 must be correctly shown on federal Form 1099-R).

California conforms to the exceptions for a penalty on an early withdrawal from retirement plans for reservists while serving on active duty for at least 180 days after September 11, 2001; as well as for public safety employees after separation from service after age 50, if distributions were made after August 17, 2006. When filing a joint return, each spouse or RDP must file a separate form FTB 3805P for taxes attributable to his or her distribution from a qualified retirement plan.

A qualified retirement plan includes:

➢ A qualified pension, profit-sharing, or stock bonus plan.
➢ A Keogh retirement plan (outside the scope of this course).
➢ A qualified cash or deferred arrangement (CODA) as described in IRC section 401(k).
➢ A qualified annuity plan.
➢ A tax-shelter annuity contract.
➢ An individual retirement plan or account.

For more information, see Instructions Form 3805P.

California Achieving a Better Life Experience (ABLE)

The California ABLE program sets up trust accounts like an IRA that exclusively pays for qualified disability expenses for a designated beneficiary. California's ABLE program did not conform to the changes made by the TCJA. California conforms to the federal income tax treatment of the ABLE program as of January 1, 2016. Family and friends may contribute up to $17,000 a year for the account.

Archer Medical Savings Account

California conforms to federal law regarding contributions and deductions for those taxpayers who filed federal Form 8853. California is different regarding the amount of the additional tax on MSA distributions that are not used for qualified medical expenses. The additional tax is 12.5%. California does not have a separate form, so report the additional tax on FTB Form 3805P, lines 9 and 10. California does not conform to rollovers from an MSA to a health savings account (HSA) being treated as a tax-free distribution. When completing federal Form 8853, if there is an amount in Line 6b due to an MSA rollover to an HSA, the amount must be reported on FTB Form 3805P, lines 9 and 10. This may result in an additional penalty as well because California does not allow MSAs to convert to HSAs. See Instructions FTB 3805P. See R&TC Section 17215.

California conforms to the Medicare Advantage MSA Distributions.

Household Employees

If the taxpayer controls the hours of a worker in their home, California does not consider the worker to be an independent contractor.

Example 1: Manuel, Miquel's gardener, has a written contract with Miquel to mow and weed his front lawn two times a month. Because Miquel does not control his hours, Manuel would be an independent contractor.

Example 2: Matt schedules Michael's days and time of work to mow and weed his front yard. Michael is Matt's employee because he determines Michael's hours to mow and weed his yard.

A California taxpayer must register with the Employment Development Department (EDD) within 15 days after he or she has (in a calendar quarter) paid $750.00 or more in cash wages to one or more employees who worked in their home. Cash wages include payment for services by check or cash. Once the employer meets the $750 cash wage limit, all cash and noncash payments are wages. The amount of employee wages paid in a calendar quarter will determine the taxes the employer is required to pay.

Household employees must register with the EDD and report household employees by filing Form DE 1HW, *Registration Form for Employers of Household Workers*, when the taxpayer employs one or more individuals and pays cash wages between $750 and $999.99 in a calendar quarter. Household employers must also file Form DE 34, *Report of New Employee(s)*, for each new employee within 20 days of hiring. Household employers who pay less than $20,000 in wages per year may elect to pay taxes annually by checking the "yes" box in Item I on Form DE 1HW or, if previously registered with the EDD, may complete Form DE 89, *Employer of Household Worker Election*. For more information, see the EDD Publication DE 8829.

Kiddie Tax

California did not conform to the TCJA regarding Kiddie Tax. For 2022, the first $1,150 of a child's unearned income qualifies as their standard deduction, the next $1,150 is taxed at the child's income tax rate. Income above $2,300 is taxed at the parent's tax bracket. For 2023, the first $1,250 of a child's unearned income qualifies as their standard deduction. The next $1,250 is taxed at the child's rate. The amount above $2,500 is taxed at the parent's rate.

Use Tax

The California Department of Tax and Fee Administration (CDTFA) administers California's sales and use taxes, fuel taxes, and other tax and fee programs including the Electronic Waste Recycling (eWaste) Fee, California Tire Fee, alcoholic beverage tax, and cigarette and tobacco products taxes.

If sales tax is not charged on online purchases, taxpayers are required by the FTB to report the unpaid sales tax and pay it on the return. This is referred to as the "use tax". Some taxpayers are required to report business purchases as well. "Use taxes" for business purposes that have not been paid must be reported on Form 540, line 91, if the following apply to the taxpayer:

> ➤ Has a California seller's permit.
> ➤ Does not hold a California seller's permit but receives at least $100,000 in gross receipts.
> ➤ Is otherwise required to register with the state Board of Equalization for Sales or Use Tax purposes.

Failure to report and pay the use tax may result in the assessment of interest, penalties, and fees.

Example: Barbara purchased a television for $2,000 from an out-of-state retailer that did not collect use tax. Barbara must use the *Use Tax Worksheet* to calculate the use tax due on the price of the television, since the price of the television is $1,000 or more.

Sales tax applies to tangible property; for example, clothing, appliances, toys, and furniture. The seller is responsible for the payment of sales tax to CDTFA, but the retailer may charge and collect tax reimbursement from its customer. When sales tax does not apply, the law requires use tax to be paid on items purchased for use in California. Use tax is owed on Internet or mail-order purchases from out-of-state retailers. Use tax is owed by the person purchasing the property for use in California when the out-of-state retailer does not collect the California tax.

The Lookup Table is used to estimate the use tax for personal items that have been purchased for personal use online.

Cost Recovery Fee

The FTB collects and files enforcement cost on delinquent accounts.

Mandatory Health Insurance Penalty

Californians are required to have minimum essential coverage (MEC) health insurance. MEC is the same requirement as the federal. Unlike the federal the state will penalize the taxpayer and family members for not having insurance. If the taxpayer purchased insurance through the Marketplace, they would receive Form 3849. The taxpayer could have an Individual Shared Responsibility Penalty if they do not have health insurance. There are exemptions to claim if the taxpayer qualifies. The exemptions follow the federal exemptions. The penalty is the larger of $800 per adult and $400 per child or a percentage based on income that exceeds the filing threshold.

On March 11, 2021, the American Rescue Plan Act increased the federal Premium Tax Credit for taxpayers. By receiving additional federal subsidies, many taxpayers no longer qualify for the state subsidy they received and therefore must pay this amount back with their tax return. Taxpayers who purchased insurance through Covered California will receive Form FTB 3895. All taxpayers no matter their filing requirement will need to complete a tax return and pay the amount due if they have one.

Moving out of California

If the taxpayer is a nonresident and has a distribution from a retirement plan, that income is not taxable to the individual. If the taxpayer received income for performance of services in California, then that amount is taxable in California. For example, Joe is an Oregon resident and had a temporary work assignment in California. He received four months of California income from his employer in Oregon; his retirement distribution will be taxable.

Moving into California

California does not allow a step up in basis for annual contributions made as a nonresident. The years that are affected or 1982 to 1986. These are the years that California did not conform to federal laws.

Part 1 Review Questions

To obtain the maximum benefit from this chapter, LTP recommends that you complete each of the following questions, and then compare them to the answers with feedback that immediately follow. Under governing self-study standards, vendors are required to present review questions intermittently throughout each self-study course.

These questions and explanations are not part of the final examination and will not be graded by LTP.

COTTPP1.1
Melchior employs California household employees and pays them less than $20,000. Which of the following may Melchior elect to do?

    a. Pay taxes annually.
    b. Pay taxes quarterly.
    c. Pay taxes daily.
    d. Pay taxes monthly.

COTTPP1.2
Yenny, age 45, withdrew money from her 401(k), and on her Form 1099-R, the code in box 7 was 1. Which of the following forms would Yenny use to report the additional tax on her distribution?

    a. Form 540
    b. Form 3805P
    c. Form DE 1HW
    d. Form DE 89

COTTPP1.3
Martin's adjusted gross wages for the current tax year are $1,200,250. Martin does not claim dependents or itemize his deductions on his federal return. Which of the following other taxes would Martin have to pay?

    a. Mental health services tax
    b. Alternative minimum tax
    c. Additional tax on his IRA
    d. Household employee wages

COTTPP1.4
Isabel will use which of the following California forms to report an early withdrawal from her IRA?

    a. Form 3805P
    b. Schedule S
    c. 540 Schedule P
    d. 540 Schedule CA

COTTPP1.5
What is the California percentage of the additional tax on a Medical Savings Account (MSA) if the money was not used to pay medical bills?

    a. 2.9%
    b. 12.5%
    c. 5%
    d. 0%

Part 1 Review Question Answers

COTTPP1.1
Melchior employs California household employees and pays them less than $20,000. Which of the following may Melchior elect to do?

    a. Pay taxes annually.
    b. Pay taxes quarterly.
    c. Pay taxes daily.
    d. Pay taxes monthly.

Feedback: Review section *Household Employees.*

COTTPP1.2
Yenny, age 45, withdrew money from her 401(k), and on her Form 1099-R, the code in box 7 was 1. Which of the following forms would Yenny use to report the additional tax on her distribution?

    a. Form 540
    b. Form 3805P
    c. Form DE 1HW
    d. Form DE 89

Feedback: Review section *Additional Tax on IRAs.*

COTTPP1.3
Martin's adjusted gross wages for the current tax year are $1,200,250. Martin does not claim dependents or itemize his deductions on his federal return. Which of the following other taxes would Martin have to pay?

    a. Mental health services tax
    b. Alternative minimum tax
    c. Additional tax on his IRA
    d. Household employee wages

Feedback: Review section *Line 62 Mental Health Service Tax.*

COTTPP1.4
Isabel will use which of the following California forms to report an early withdrawal from her IRA?

    a. Form 3805P
    b. Schedule S
    c. 540 Schedule P
    d. 540 Schedule CA

Feedback: Review section *Additional Tax on IRAs.*

COTTPP1.5

What is the California percentage of the additional tax on a Medical Savings Account (MSA) if the money was not used to pay medical bills?

    a. 2.9%
    b. 12.5%
    c. 5%
    d. 0%

Feedback: Review section *Archer Medical Saving Account.*

Part 2 Interest and Penalties

If a taxpayer does not have enough withholding and owes more than $1,000, then an interest charge and penalty could be applied for not paying enough tax throughout the year. These penalties and charges are reported on lines 112 and 113.

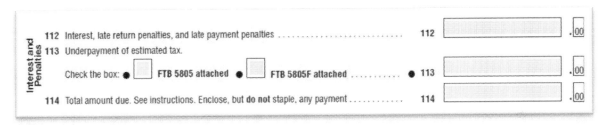

Portion of Form 540

If the taxpayer files their 2022 tax return after October 16, 2023, penalty and interest will be charged. The total penalty is 25% of the balanced due. Interest compounds daily, and the interest rate is adjusted twice a year. Interest and penalties are entered on line 112, and an underpayment of estimated taxes is reported on line 113.

Line 112: Interest, late return penalties, and late payment penalties. Interest and penalties will be charged on any late filing or payment received after the due date of the return. If other penalties are not paid within 15 days, interest will be charged from the date of the notice. The taxpayer will receive a letter with the stated amount of money owed.

Line 113: Underpayment of estimated tax. Check the box for either Form 5805 (Individual taxpayers) or Form 5805F (Farmers and Fishermen). The taxpayer may pay an estimated payment penalty.

The taxpayer may be subject to underpayment of estimated tax if any the following are true:

> The withholding and credits are less than 90% of the current tax year liability.
> Withholding and credits are less than 100% of the prior year tax liability (110% if AGI is more than $150,000 or $75,000 if married or RDP filing separately).
> The taxpayer did not pay enough through withholding to keep the amount owed under $500 ($250 if married or RDP filing separately).
> Taxpayer did not make the required estimated tax payments for 2022.

Like the federal, the state could calculate the interest and penalty and send the taxpayer the bill.

Individual Electronic Payment Requirement

Taxpayer who has a tax liability greater than $80,000 or makes estimated payments that exceeds $20,000 must pay their tax electronically. See R&TC §19011.5.

Mandatory e-Pay for Individuals

When a taxpayer has an estimated payment of over $20,000 or a tax liability over $80,000, an electronic payment is required. Fiduciaries, estates, and trusts are not required to make electronic payments. See R&TC §19011.5.

Electronic Funds Transfer (EFT) Penalty

If the taxpayer is required to pay their balance due electronically and chooses to pay with other means, they are subject to 10% of the amount paid not through EFT. Reasonable cause and willful neglect are exceptions to the rule. See R&TC §19011(c).

Late Payment Penalty for Failure to File a Return

The penalty for unpaid tax, also referred to as underpayment, is 5% of the unpaid tax after allowing the taxpayer to make timely payments up to 25% maximum. If the late payment is due to fraud, then the amount is 15% with a maximum of 75%. See R&TC §19131.

Failure to Pay Tax and Late Payment Penalty

R&TC §19132 states that if a taxpayer fails to pay the amount owed by the due date penalties are not enforced if in the same tax year the total of §19131 and §19133 are equal to or greater than the penalty. The penalty is 5% of the unpaid tax plus .05% of 1% for every month up to 40 months of late filing. The penalty will not exceed 25% of the total unpaid tax.

A preparer is not considered to have recklessly or intentionally disregarded a rule or regulation if the position has a reasonable basis and is adequately disclosed. If a regulation is at issue, there must be a good faith challenge. If the position is contrary to a revenue ruling or notice, the substantial authority standard applies.

Failure to Provide Requested Information

Taxpayer who failed to file a tax return and where requested to provide their tax information and did not will be assessed 25% of the total liability. Reasonable cause and willful neglect are exceptions to the rule. See R&TC §19133.

Demand to File a Tax Return

Taxpayer who received the "notice and demand" requests the taxpayer to file a tax return or explain why there is no filing requirement. The penalty amount is 25% of the total tax amount due. Payments and credits are not including in the claim. See R&TC §19133.

Dishonored Payments (Bounced Checks)

Taxpayer who bounces a check or an electronic payment, such as EFT or credit cards, that was returned due to insufficient funds will be charged 2% of the insufficient amount. If the check is less than $1,250, the penalty is $25 or the amount of the check, whichever is less. Reasonable cause and willful neglect are exceptions to the rule. See R&TC §19134.

Accuracy Related Penalty

Any underpayment shown on a tax return that is attributable to negligence or disregard of rules and regulations are subject to 20% of the underpayment of tax and 40% unless certain exceptions apply. See R&TC §19164.

Underpayment of Estimated Tax

Taxpayer who fails to pay their required estimated tax will be charged a penalty. The penalty is figured by applying the underpayment rate discussed in §19521 to the amount of the underpayment for the estimated tax period. There is an exception in California if the taxpayer's situation conforms to the Safe Harbors under IRC §6654. Underpayment created or increased by any provision of law that is chaptered during and operative for the taxable year of the underpayment. See §17053.80(g) or 23623(g).

Taxpayer Noneconomic Substance Transaction Understatement (NEST) Penalty

If the taxpayer has understated their income in California this is referred to as *Noneconomic Substance Transaction Understatement.* This penalty is 40% of the understatement and 20% of the understatement if the income was adequately disclosed.

First Time Abatement

Federal allows a first-time abatement of penalties; California did not conform.

Part 2 Review Questions

To obtain the maximum benefit from this chapter, LTP recommends that you complete each of the following questions, and then compare them to the answers with feedback that immediately follow. Under governing self-study standards, vendors are required to present review questions intermittently throughout each self-study course.

These questions and explanations are not part of the final examination and will not be graded by LTP.

COTTPP2.1
When a taxpayer has an estimated payment of over _____ or on the original return the tax liability is over $80,000 an electronic payment is required. Fiduciaries, estates, and trusts are not required to make electronic payments.

    a. $20,000
    b. $30,000
    c. $25,000
    d. $15,000

COTTPP2.2
Federal law allows a first-time abatement of tax penalties. Does California conform?

    a. California did not conform.
    b. California did confirm.
    c. California agreed to partially conform.
    d. California chose to follow federal law.

COTTPP2.3

Samantha's withholding did not cover the balance due. What amount would make Samantha pay a penalty and interest charge?

a. $500
b. $900
c. $1,000
d. $0

COTTPP2.4

What is the penalty for late payment of California tax?

a. 15%
b. 5%
c. 7%
d. 10%

COTTPP2.5

A California taxpayer who is required to file a return, but fails to do so by the due date may be subject to which penalty?

a. 5% of the tax due up to 25%
b. 10% of the tax due up to 35%
c. $100 per every $100 due
d. 5% of the tax due per month

Part 2 Review Questions Answers

COTTPP2.1

When a taxpayer has an estimated payment of over _____ or on the original return the tax liability is over $80,000 an electronic payment is required. Fiduciaries, estates, and trusts are not required to make electronic payments.

a. $20,000
b. $30,000
c. $25,000
d. $15,000

Feedback: Review section *Mandatory e-Pay for Individuals*.

COTTPP2.2

Federal law allows a first-time abatement of tax penalties. Does California conform?

a. California did not conform.
b. California did confirm.
c. California agreed to partially conform.
d. California chose to follow federal law.

Feedback: Review section *First Time Abatement*.

COTTPP2.3

Samantha's withholding did not cover the balance due. What amount would make Samantha pay a penalty and interest charge?

    a. $500
    b. $900
    c. $1,000
    d. $0

Feedback: Review section *Interest and Penalties.*

COTTPP2.4

What is the penalty for late payment of California tax?

    a. 15%
    b. 5%
    c. 7%
    d. 10%

Feedback: Review section *Late Payment Penalty for Failure to File a Return?*

COTTPP2.5

A California taxpayer who is required to file a return, but fails to do so by the due date may be subject to which penalty?

    a. 5% of the tax due up to 25%
    b. 10% of the tax due up to 35%
    c. $100 per every $100 due
    d. 5% of the tax due per month

Feedback: Review section *Late Payment Penalty for Failure to File a Return.*

Takeaways

There are some major differences between California and federal laws regarding other taxes. A California tax preparer must understand when the state conforms to a particular federal other tax. When the state does not conform, the tax preparer must make an adjustment on 540 Schedule CA.

TEST YOUR KNOWLEDGE!
Go online to take a practice quiz.

Chapter 7 Payments and Tax Credits

Introduction

Unlike a deduction, which reduces the income subject to taxation, credits directly reduce the taxpayer's tax liability to zero. Depending on the type of credit, the amount will reduce the tax liability below zero, resulting in a refund for the taxpayer. There are two types of credits: refundable and nonrefundable. The refundable credits reduce the tax liability below zero, resulting in a refund. tax credits reduce the taxpayer's tax liability to zero. In some instances, after reducing the tax liability to zero, the remaining amount will be a carryover to the next year until the full amount is used. Not all the nonrefundable credits can be carryover.

Objectives

At the end of this chapter, the student will:

➢ Explain how a nonrefundable credit affects the taxpayer's tax liability.
➢ Name the refundable credits.
➢ Recognize the Earned Income Credit (EIC) qualifications.
➢ Identify who qualifies for the additional child tax credit.
➢ Know the rules for the refundable portion of the American opportunity credit (AOC).
➢ Recognize when a dependent qualifies for the Other Dependent Credit (ODC).

Resources

Form 1040	Publication 17	Instructions Form 1040
Form 1098-T	Publication 503	Instructions Form 1098-T
Form 1116	Publication 505	Instructions Form 1116
Form 2441	Publication 514	Instructions Form 2441
Form 8396	Publication 524	Instructions Form 8396
Form 8801	Publication 596	Instructions Form 8801
Form 8812	Publication 972	Instructions Form 8812
Form 8863	Publication 4933	Instructions Form 8863
Form 8867	Publication 4935	Instructions Form 8867
Form 8880	Tax Topic 601, 602, 607, 608, 610	Instructions Form 8880
Form 8959	Schedule 3	Instructions Form 8959
Schedule EIC	Instructions Schedule 3	Instructions Schedule EIC
Schedule R		Instructions Schedule R

Table of Contents

Part 1 Nonrefundable Credits

Nonrefundable credits reduce the taxpayer's income tax. The credits are computed based on the order found on Form 1040, Schedule 3, Part I.

Foreign Tax Credit

The foreign tax credit intends to reduce the double tax burden that could occur to a foreign source of income taxed by the foreign country and the United States. Generally, the credit for foreign taxes paid or accrued to a foreign country or U.S. possession will qualify for the tax credit reported on Form 1040, Schedule 3, line 1. If the taxpayer claims a foreign tax credit using Schedule 3, Form 1116, *Foreign Tax Credit*, it must be attached to the tax return. The other way that the taxpayer could claim the credit is as an itemized deduction on Schedule A under "other taxes."

Do not complete Form 1116 if the taxpayer qualifies for any of the following:

> ➢ All foreign gross income is from interest and dividends and reported on Form 1099-INT, 1099-DIV, or Schedule K-1.
> ➢ Total foreign taxes were not more than $300 ($600 if married filing jointly).
> ➢ All foreign source gross income was "passive category income."

SCHEDULE 3 (Form 1040)	**Additional Credits and Payments**	OMB No. 1545-0074
Department of the Treasury Internal Revenue Service	Attach to Form 1040, 1040-SR, or 1040-NR. Go to *www.irs.gov/Form1040* for instructions and the latest information.	2022 Attachment Sequence No. 03

Name(s) shown on Form 1040, 1040-SR, or 1040-NR | Your social security number

Part I Nonrefundable Credits

1 Foreign tax credit. Attach Form 1116 if required . . . . | **1**

2 Credit for child and dependent care expenses from Form 2441, line 11. Attach Form 2441 . . . . | **2**

3 Education credits from Form 8863, line 19 . . . . | **3**

4 Retirement savings contributions credit. Attach Form 8880 . . . . | **4**

5 Residential energy credits. Attach Form 5695 . . . . | **5**

6 Other nonrefundable credits:

a General business credit. Attach Form 3800 . . . . | **6a**

b Credit for prior year minimum tax. Attach Form 8801 . . . . | **6b**

c Adoption credit. Attach Form 8839 . . . . | **6c**

d Credit for the elderly or disabled. Attach Schedule R . . . . . | **6d**

e Alternative motor vehicle credit. Attach Form 8910 . . . . . | **6e**

f Qualified plug-in motor vehicle credit. Attach Form 8936 . . . | **6f**

g Mortgage interest credit. Attach Form 8396 . . . . | **6g**

h District of Columbia first-time homebuyer credit. Attach Form 8859 | **6h**

i Qualified electric vehicle credit. Attach Form 8834 . . . . . | **6i**

j Alternative fuel vehicle refueling property credit. Attach Form 8911 | **6j**

k Credit to holders of tax credit bonds. Attach Form 8912 . . . | **6k**

l Amount on Form 8978, line 14. See instructions . . . . . . | **6l**

z Other nonrefundable credits. List type and amount: _____ | **6z**

7 Total other nonrefundable credits. Add lines 6a through 6z . . . . | **7**

8 Add lines 1 through 5 and 7. Enter here and on Form 1040, 1040-SR, or 1040-NR, line 20 . . . . | **8**

(continued on page 2)

For Paperwork Reduction Act Notice, see your tax return instructions. | Cat. No. 71480G | Schedule 3 (Form 1040) 2022

Schedule 3

Form 2441: Child and Dependent Care

Dependent care benefits are payments the employer paid directly to either the taxpayer or the care provider for taking care of the qualifying dependent(s) while the taxpayer worked. Dependent care benefits are pre-taxed contributions made based on the fair market value of care in a daycare facility provided by or sponsored by the employer under a Flexible Spending Arrangement (FSA).

"Care" is the cost of attending a facility to qualifying individual(s) outside the taxpayer's home. It does not include food, lodging, education, clothing, or entertainment. If a dependent care facility provides the care, the center must meet all the applicable state and local regulations. A dependent care facility is a place that offers care for more than six individuals who do not live there and receives a fee, payment, or grant for providing those services for any individual. Include the cost of a day camp, but not the cost of an overnight camp, summer school, or tutoring program.

The taxpayer can take a nonrefundable credit of up to 35% of the qualifying expenses for the care of a qualified dependent when the expenditures are work-related. The percentage of credit goes down as income goes up, with 20% of eligible expenses as the least amount allowed. Expenses are limited to $3,000 for one child and $6,000 for two or more qualified dependents. Child and dependent care are reported on Form 2441 and flow to Form 1040, Schedule 3, line 2.

403
©2023 Latino Tax Pro

A qualifying person is:

➢ A qualifying child under 13 and claimed as a dependent. If a child turns 13 during the tax year, you can still prorate their care for the portion of the year the child was not 13.
➢ A disabled spouse who wasn't physically or mentally able to care for him or herself.
➢ Any disabled person who wasn't physically or mentally able to care for him or herself and whom the taxpayer can claim as a dependent unless one of the following is true:
  ○ The disabled individual had a gross income of $4,400 or more.
  ○ The disabled individual filed a joint return.
  ○ The disabled individual or spouse, if filing a joint tax return, could be claimed as a dependent on another individual's 2022 tax return.

To be able to claim the child and dependent care expenses, the taxpayer must meet all the following requirements:

➢ The care must be for one or more qualifying persons who are identified on Form 2441.
➢ If filing a joint return, the taxpayer (and spouse if filing a joint return) must have earned income during the year.
➢ The taxpayer must pay child and dependent care expenses to allow the taxpayer and spouse to work, or look for work.
➢ The taxpayer must make payments for child and dependent care to someone who cannot be claimed as a dependent on the taxpayer's return.
➢ The filing status may be Single, Head of Household, or Surviving spouse with a dependent child. If married, they must file a joint return (unless an exception applies).
➢ The taxpayer must fill out Form 2441 to identify the provider's name, TIN, the cost of care, and the address of the location where the care was provided and attach the form to their tax return.
➢ If the taxpayer excludes or deducts dependent care benefits provided by a dependent care benefit plan, the total amount excluded or deducted must be less than the dollar limit for qualifying expenses ($3,000 per child up to $6,000).

Below is the portion of the current chart used to calculate the child and dependent care credit. Calculate the credit amount by multiplying the percentage on the right against the credit's monetary limit ($3,000-$6,000) and which percentage, based on the taxpayer(s) combined income. For tax year 2022, the income increase was part of the American Rescue Plan Act. The percentage is 35% to 20%. The following is just a snapshot of certain portions of the percentage chart.

Income	Percentage
$0 – $15,000	35%
$23,001 – $25,000	30%
$33,001 – $35,000	25%
$43,001 – No limit	20%

For example, a taxpayer and his spouse each made $50,000 for a combined income of $100,000, and they paid $8,500 for childcare for one child. Because they paid $8,500 for childcare and only for one child, they will be allowed to use $3,000 of that expense to calculate their credit amount. This is because that is the credit limit no matter how much they paid for childcare. Because their combined income was under $125,000, they will calculate their credit amount using the 20% section from the chart. Therefore, the 20% deduction is calculated as follows: $3,000 × .20 = $600. Their credit amount is $600.

If all other details were the same, but they had only spent $2,000 on childcare, their credit amount would be 20% of that two thousand, not three. This is because they did not spend enough to reach the credit limit, meaning their credit amount would be $1,000 ($2,000 × .20 = $400).

Child of Divorced or Separated Parents

In addition to meeting the qualifying person requirements, additional rules apply in the case of divorced or separated parents. The parent who has physical custody of the child for the more significant portion of the year is the only parent who can claim the credit, regardless of how much support the other parent provides or if the dependency exemption is released.

Earned Income Test

The taxpayer and spouse (if filing jointly) must have earned income to claim the credit. Earned income includes wages, salary, tips, other taxable employee compensation, and net earnings from self-employment. A loss from self-employment reduces income. If the taxpayer has nontaxable combat pay not included in earned income, they may include the income to calculate the child and dependent credit. If both the taxpayer and spouse have nontaxable combat pay, both will have to make the election. A good tax professional should calculate the credit both ways for the taxpayer and see which results in the higher credit amount.

> *Señor 1040 Says*: Remember Child and Dependent Care Expenses are a different credit than the Additional Child Tax Credit.

Work-Related Expense Requirement

Child and dependent care expenses must be work-related to qualify for the credit. You can consider work-related expenses only if the following are true:

> ➤ Dependent care allows the taxpayer(s) to work or look for work.
> ➤ The expenses are for a qualifying person's care.

Example 1: Darlene works during the day, and her spouse, Craig, works at night and sleeps while Darlene is working. Their five-year-old son, Trevor, goes to daycare so Craig can sleep. Their expenses are work-related because the care allows Craig to sleep to perform his job adequately.

Example 2: Darlene and Craig get a babysitter on Craig's night off, so they can go out to eat and spend some time together. This expense is not work-related because the care is not directly facilitating Darlene or Craig's ability to work or look for work.

Married Taxpayer Filing Separately

Usually, married couples file a joint return to take the child and dependent care credit. However, if the taxpayer and spouse are legally separated or living apart, they may still take the credit. If the following apply, the taxpayer would be able to claim the credit:

➢ The taxpayer's home was the qualifying individual's home for more than half the year.
➢ The taxpayer paid more than half the cost of home upkeep for the year.
➢ The taxpayer's spouse did not live in their home during the last six months of the year.

Rules for Students' Spouses Who Are Not Able to Care for Themselves

A married couple is treated as having earned income for any month that one was a full-time student or attended a school during any five months of the tax year (the months do not have to be consecutive) or is physically or mentally disabled or unable to care for themself. This definition of "school" does not include night school or a correspondence school.

If the taxpayer or spouse was a full-time student for at least five months or was disabled, they are considered to have earned an income of $250 per month (or $500 if more than one qualifying person was cared for during the tax year). This is done to help taxpayers who have little-to-no earned income qualify for the Child and Dependent Care Credit, because credits can only be claimed if the taxpayer or spouse has earned income.

Employer Dependent Care Assistance

If the employer provides dependent care benefits excluded from income (such as those received under a cafeteria plan), the taxpayer must subtract that amount from the applicable dollar limit of the Child and Dependent Care Credit. Dependent care benefits include the following:

➢ Amounts the employer paid directly to the taxpayer or the taxpayer's provider while the taxpayer worked.
➢ The fair market value of care in a daycare facility provided or sponsored by the employer.
➢ Pre-tax contributions made under a dependent flexible spending arrangement.

Box 10 reports dependent care benefits on the taxpayer's W-2. If a partner received benefits, they would appear in box 13 on the K-1, Form 1065 with code O.

The amount excluded from income is limited to the smallest of the following:

➢ The total amount of dependent care benefits received during the year.
➢ The total amount of qualified expenses incurred during the year.
➢ The taxpayer's earned income.
➢ The spouse's earned income.
➢ $5,000 or $2,500 if married filing separately.

Señor 1040 Says: Make sure to always check if there is an amount in box 10 of the W-2 for Dependent Care Payments.

If dependent care assistance exceeds the amount paid for dependent care, the excess amount becomes income to the taxpayer and is reported on line 1 of Form 1040. The letters "DCB" (dependent care benefit) should be written on the dotted line in the space before the entry block for line 1.

The taxpayer can also pay for the care provided in the home with the dependent care benefits. The taxpayer may have to withhold taxes (FICA and FUTA) for the dependent care provider if dependent care is in the taxpayer's home. The taxpayer is not required to withhold taxes if the dependent care provider is self-employed.

Due to the COVID-19 pandemic, the Taxpayer Certainty and Disaster Relief Act of 2020 allows Cafeteria Plans to permit a carryover of unused dependent care benefits funds. Unused dependent care for 2020 and 2021 are combined and would be carried forward to 2022. See Notice 2021-15.

Expenses Not for Care

Care expenses do not include the taxpayer's money for food, lodging, clothing, education, or entertainment. Expenses for a child in nursery school, preschool, or similar programs for children below the kindergarten level are considered expenses for care. Expenses to attend kindergarten or higher schooling are not expenses for childcare. In certain situations, expenses for before- or after-school care are expenses for care; there are exceptions. Do not use the summer school and tutoring programs as dependent care expenses. The cost of sending the dependent to an overnight camp is not considered work-related; however, the cost of a day camp might be a work-related expense.

Payments to Relatives or Dependents

Payments made to relatives for dependent care, which enable the taxpayer to work when the relative lives in the taxpayer's home, and not a dependent. However, if any of the following apply, the payments cannot be counted as payment for dependent care:

➢ The individual is claimed as the taxpayer's dependent (or spouse filing jointly).
➢ The child was under 19 at the end of the year, even if they were not the taxpayer's dependent.
➢ The person was the taxpayer's spouse during the year.
➢ The parent of the qualifying person if the qualifying person is the child, and under age 13.

Dependent Care Provider Information

The following information is needed to complete Form 2441 regarding the individual or organization that provides care for the qualifying person:

➢ The individual or organization provider's name.
➢ The individual or organization provider's address.
➢ The individual or organization provider's identification number (EIN or SSN).

The taxpayer should show due diligence by keeping and maintaining the provider's completed Form W-10, *Dependent Care Provider's Identification and Certification*. The taxpayer could supply a statement from the employer if the employer's dependent care plan is the provider. The statement could be a year of end invoice that provides the above information needed.

Señor 1040 Says: Encourage the taxpayer to maintain records in relation to their childcare provider and store the documents with their tax returns.

Tax Tip: If the dependent care provider cares for the dependent in the taxpayer's home, the provider may be considered a household employee. As a tax professional, ask questions about dependent care and document your questions and answers from the taxpayer.

Form 8863: Education Credits

Education credits are available for taxpayers who pay expenses for postsecondary education. To claim the education credit, the student must receive Form 1098-T from the student's school and provide that form to the tax preparer. The two education credits are the American opportunity credit (AOC) and the lifetime learning credit; both are reported on Form 8863, *Education Credits*. Lifetime learning is a nonrefundable credit, and the American opportunity is a partially refundable credit. The student must meet the following requirements to be eligible for the education credits:

➤ Qualified education expenses were for higher education.
➤ Paid qualifying education expenses for the eligible student.
➤ The student is either taxpayer, spouse, or a qualifying dependent.

Tax Tip: If the qualifying dependent pays their own tuition, it is considered paid by the taxpayer.

American Opportunity Credit (AOC)

The American opportunity credit (AOC) is a credit of up to $2,500, up to 40% of which may be refundable. Base the credit on 100% of the first $2,000 and 25% of the next $2,000. To qualify for the AOC, the taxpayer's MAGI must be less than $180,000 for taxpayers filing MFJ and $90,000 for all others.

Qualified expenses include tuition and fees for enrollment at an eligible post-secondary program and expenses for books, supplies, and equipment needed for a course of study, whether or not the student purchases the materials from the education institution. The student must carry at least half the normal full-time workload for the course of study the student enrolled in. The student must also be free of federal or state felony offenses consisting of the possession or distribution of a controlled substance. The refundable portion of the education credit is reported on Form 8863, line 8, and reported on Form 1040, page 2, line 29.

For example, Donna and Doug are first-year students at an eligible post-secondary program. They must have certain books and other reading materials to use in their mandatory first-year classes. Doug bought his books directly from a friend, and Donna purchased hers at the college bookstore. Although Donna and Doug purchased their books through different avenues, the cost of both purchases is qualifying education expenses since books qualify for the American opportunity credit.

The American opportunity credit can be claimed for a student who has not completed their first four years of postsecondary education determined by the post-secondary program. The student qualifications to claim AOC is all the following:

➤ The student did not complete the first 4 years of postsecondary education.
➤ For at least one academic period beginning in 2022, the student:
   o Was enrolled in a program that leads to a degree, certificate, or other recognized credential.
   o Carried at least one-half of the normal full-time workload for their course of study.
➤ The student did not have a felony conviction for possessing or distributing a controlled substance.

Tax Tip: When interviewing the taxpayer to determine if they qualify for the American opportunity credit, be sure to ask the following questions:

➤ Did the student receive Form 1098-T?
➤ Has the American opportunity credit been claimed for this student for four tax years before 2022?
➤ Was the student enrolled at least half-time for at least one academic period that began (or treated as begun) in 2022 at an eligible education institution in a program leading toward a postsecondary degree, certificate, or other recognized postsecondary education credential?
➤ Did the student complete the first four years of postsecondary education before 2022?
➤ Was the student convicted of a felony for possession or distribution of a controlled substance before the end of 2022?

Asking and documenting these questions are part of the tax professional's due diligence.

Lifetime Learning Credit

The lifetime learning credit is available at any time for the taxpayer, the taxpayer's spouse, or the taxpayer's dependent. The maximum allowed credit is $2,000 per tax return. Qualified expenses include tuition and fees required for enrollment at an eligible post-secondary program. Expenses incurred to acquire or improve the taxpayer's job skills are eligible expenses.

An expense related to a course that involves sports, games, or hobbies is not a qualified expense unless it is part of the student's degree program. Taxpayers must reduce their qualified expense by any education assistance from the post-secondary program, scholarships, or amounts to compute the lifetime learning credit.

The lifetime learning credit is not based on the student's workload. Expenses for graduate-level courses are eligible. The amount of credit a taxpayer can claim does not increase based on the number of students for whom the taxpayer paid qualified expenses. The student does not have to be enrolled at least half-time in the course of study to be eligible for the credit. The nonrefundable portion of the education credits is reported on Form 8863, line 19, and is carried to Form 1040, Schedule 3, line 3. To qualify for the lifetime learning credit, the taxpayer's modified adjusted gross income (MAGI) should be less than $180,000 for taxpayers filing MFJ or less than $90,000 for all others.

Remember, modified adjusted gross income (MAGI) is adjusted gross income, plus all the following:

➤ The amount excluded under IRC §911, *Foreign-Earned Income Exclusion.*
   o Foreign housing exclusion
   o Foreign housing deduction
➤ Exclusion of income for residents of American Samoa and Puerto Rico.

Double Benefit Not Allowed

The taxpayer cannot do any of the following:

> ➤ Deduct higher education expenses on their income tax return and claim an education credit based on the same expenses.
> ➤ Claim more than one credit based on the same qualified education expenses.
> ➤ Claim a credit based on expenses paid with tax-free scholarship, grant, or employer-provided education assistance.
> ➤ Claim a credit based on the same expenses used to figure the tax-free portion of a distribution from a Coverdell education savings account (ESA) or a qualified tuition program (QTP).

Adjustment to Qualified Education Expenses

If taxpayers pay qualified education expenses with certain tax-free funds, they cannot claim a credit for those amounts. Taxpayers must reduce the qualified education expense by the amount of any tax-free education assistance.

Tax-free education assistance includes the following:

> ➤ The tax-free parts of scholarships and fellowships.
> ➤ The tax-free portion of Pell grants.
> ➤ Employer-provided education assistance.
> ➤ Veterans' education assistance.
> ➤ Received other nontaxable (tax-free) payments (other than gifts or inheritances) as educational assistance.

Scholarships and Fellowships

A scholarship is generally an amount paid or allowed for the benefit of a student attending a post-secondary program. The student may be either an undergraduate or a graduate student. A fellowship is paid for the benefit of an individual to aid in the pursuit of study or research. How the student pays for their expenses with the fellowship money determines the taxable portion. A scholarship or fellowship qualifies as tax-free if the following conditions are met:

> ➤ The fellowship or scholarship does not exceed qualifying expenses.
> ➤ The funds are not designated for other purposes such as room and board and cannot be used for qualified education expenses.
> ➤ It does not represent payment for teaching, research, or other services required as a condition for receiving the scholarship.

Señor 1040 Says: When a student receives a scholarship, make sure that it is not taxable to the student. Do research on how the funds were used by the student. If they were not used for qualifying expenses, the funds could be taxable to the student.

Who Claims the Expenses?

If there are qualified education expenses for the taxpayer's dependent for a year, the taxpayer can claim an education credit for the dependent's expenses for the current year. For the taxpayer to claim an education credit for their dependent's expenses, the student must be their dependent. The taxpayer does this by listing the dependent's name and other required information on Form 1040.

Expenses Paid by the Dependent

If the taxpayer claims an exemption on their tax return for an eligible student who is the taxpayer's dependent, expenses paid or deemed paid by the dependent are as if the taxpayer paid them. Include these expenses when figuring the amount of the taxpayer's education credit.

Expenses Paid by the Taxpayer

If the taxpayer claimed an exemption for a dependent who is an eligible student, only the taxpayer could include any expenses paid when figuring the amount of the education credit. If neither the taxpayer nor anyone else claims an exemption for the dependent, the dependent can include any expenses paid when figuring the education credit.

Expenses Paid by Others

Someone other than the taxpayer, the taxpayer's spouse, or the taxpayer's dependent (such as a relative or former spouse) may make a payment directly to an eligible post-secondary program to pay for an eligible student's qualified education expenses. In this case, treat the student as receiving the payment from the other person and, in turn, paying the college. The taxpayer paid the expenses if they claimed an exemption on their return for the student.

Example: In 2022, Laura Hardy directly pays the college for her grandson's qualified education expenses. Thomas is treated as receiving the money as a gift from his grandmother and, in turn, paying his qualified education expenses himself. Unless someone else claims Thomas's exemption, only Thomas can use the payment to claim the education credit. If Thomas's parents claim an exemption for Thomas, they may be able to use the expenses to claim an education credit. If anyone else claims an exemption for Thomas, Thomas cannot claim an education credit.

Academic Period

An academic period includes a semester, trimester, quarter, or another period of study determined by the college or university.

Eligible Education

An eligible post-secondary program is any college, university, vocational school, or other postsecondary educational institution eligible to participate in a student aid program administered by the Department of Education. It includes virtually all accredited, public, nonprofit, and proprietary (privately owned profit-making) postsecondary colleges. The education institution should tell the taxpayer if it is an eligible college or university. Certain colleges and universities outside the United States also participate in the U.S. Department of Education's Federal Student Aid (FSA) programs.

Certain colleges and universities outside the United States also participate in the U.S. Department of Education's Federal Student Aid (FSA) programs. You can find a list of these foreign schools on the Department of Education's website at www.fafsa.ed.gov/index.htm. Click "Find my school codes," complete the two items on the first page, click "Next," and then follow the remaining instructions to search for a foreign school.

Be aware that not all eligible education institutions treat certain Coverdell education savings accounts (529 Plans) the same way, nor do they consider the same things when determining if a scholarship or fellowship grant is not taxable. To determine if you can use the Coverdell education savings account for the college, university, vocational school, or another postsecondary education institute, the school in question must participate in a student aid program administered by the U.S. Department of Education. The education institution can be an accredited public, nonprofit, or proprietary postsecondary institution. Beginning in 2018, this includes any private, religious, or public school for kindergarten through 12th grade as determined by state law. To determine if scholarships and fellowship grants are tax-free, the education institution must maintain a regular facility and curriculum and normally have a regularly enrolled body of students where it carries on its educational activities.

Claiming Credits for More than One Eligible Student

The taxpayer can claim only one credit (per student) for each eligible student but can claim different credits for different students. A taxpayer who pays qualified education expenses for more than one student and each dependent qualifies for different credits; this is acceptable.

Form 8863, Part III, must be completed for each individual claiming education credits on the tax return before completing Part I and Part II. Form 1098-T must be given to the tax preparer; making sure to receive the form is part of the tax professional's due diligence.

Form 1098-T

To help figure the education credit reported on Form 8863, the student should receive Form 1098-T from their school. Generally, an eligible education institution (such as a college or university) must send Form 1098-T (or an acceptable substitute) to each enrolled student by January 31st of each year. An institution reports payments received (box 1) or billed (box 2) for qualified education expenses. Form 1098-T should provide other information from the school, including adjustments made for prior years, the amount of scholarships, grants, reimbursements, or refunds provided, and whether the student was enrolled at least half-time or was a graduate student.

The eligible educational institution may ask for a completed Form W-9S, *Request for Student's or Borrower's Taxpayer Identification Number and Certification*, or some similar statement to obtain the student's name, address, and taxpayer identification number.

All filers of Form 1098-T may truncate the student's identification number on payee statements. When completing the tax return, you must use the institution's EIN. Tax preparers should review their clients' Form 1098-T and keep a copy in each taxpayer's file.

Box 1: The school enters the amount of qualified tuition and related expenses from all sources during the calendar year here. The amount in box 1 is the total amount received by the taxpayer minus any reimbursements or refunds made during the tax year. Do not reduce this amount by scholarships or grants (reported separately in box 5).

Box 2: Reserved.

Box 3: Reserved.

Box 4: Adjustments made for a prior year. Enter reimbursements or refunds of qualified tuition and expenses made in 2023 related to payments received for any prior year after 2002. See Instructions Form 1098-T.

Box 5: This box shows the total amount received for scholarships or grants administered and processed during the calendar year. Remember, if the amount in box 5 is larger than the amount in box 1, do not claim the education credit for the taxpayer.

Box 6: Adjustments to Scholarships or Grants for a prior year. Enter the amount of any reduction reported for any prior year after 2002.

Box 7: If this box is checked, the amount in box 1 or 2 includes amounts the taxpayer paid before the end of the current year for the next year's tuition.

Box 8: A checkmark in this box indicates that the student was at least a half-time student during any academic period that began during the tax year. Although each university determines who and what is considered a "part-time student," the part-time student workload must be equal to or exceed the standards established by the Department of Education under the Higher Education Act.

Box 9: If this box is checked, the taxpayer is a graduate student. A graduate student must be enrolled in a program or programs leading to a graduate-level degree, graduate-level certificate, or another recognized graduate-level educational credential.

Box 10: If the insurer of the qualified tuition and related expenses made reimbursements to the student, enter the amount here.

Some eligible educational institutions combine all fees for an academic period into one amount. The student should contact the school if the student does not receive or have access to a statement showing amounts for qualified education expenses and personal expenses. The institution must provide this information to the taxpayer and report the amount paid or billed for qualified education expenses on Form 1098-T.

Tuition Payments Statement

When an eligible education institution provides a reduction in tuition to an employee of the institution or a spouse or dependent child of an employee, the amount of the reduction may or may not be taxable. If taxable, the employee receives a payment and, in turn, paid the educational institution on behalf of the student.

Form 8880: Retirement Savings Contributions Credit

The Retirement Savings Contributions Credit is based on the first $2,000 contributed to IRAs, 401(k)s, and certain other retirement plans. Use Form 8880, *Credit for Qualified Retirement Savings Contributions*, to calculate the credit. The taxpayer can contribute until the tax return's due date; filing an extension does not change the due date for making these contributions. This credit reduces the taxpayer's income tax dollar-for-dollar and is reported on Form 1040, Schedule 3, line 4. To claim this credit for 2022, the taxpayer's MAGI must be less than $34,000 if Single or MFS, $51,000 if filing Head of household, or $68,000 if married filing jointly or Surviving spouse with qualifying dependent. Report this credit on Form 1040, Schedule 3, line 4. If a taxpayer claims the credit, attach Form 8880 to Form 1040. The 2023 numbers for single and MFS filing status is not more than $36,500. For HOH $54,750, and MFJ and SS is $73,000.

Form 5695: Residential Energy Credits

If taxpayers made energy-saving improvements to their main home in the United States, they might be able to claim the residential energy efficient property credit and report it on Form 1040, Schedule 3, line 5. The credit and its ability to carry forward any portion are still available from 2022 to 2032. The following residential energy efficient property credits are available for the 2022 tax year if the taxpayer made such improvements to the main home located in the United States:

- ➢ Qualified solar electric property costs.
- ➢ Qualified solar water heating property costs.
- ➢ Qualified small wind energy property costs.
- ➢ Qualified geothermal heat pump property costs.
- ➢ Qualified biomass fuel property costs.

If the taxpayer is a condominium owner or a tenant-stockholder in a cooperative housing corporation and has paid their proportionate share of the cost, the taxpayer could qualify for the credit. There is a 30% credit for installing qualified solar water-heating property, qualified solar electric property, geothermal heat pumps, and small wind-energy property. The credit applies for property placed in service for 2022 and 2032.

Energy efficient home improvement credit reported on Part II of Form 5695 may be able to take a credit equal to the sum of:

1. 10% of the amount paid or incurred by the taxpayer for qualified energy efficiency improvements installed during such taxable year, and
2. any residential energy property expenditures paid or incurred by the taxpayer during such taxable year.

The credit is limited to the following:

➢ A total of $500 for all tax years after 2005.
➢ A combined credit limit of $200 for windows.

Any subsidized energy financing cannot be used to figure the energy credit. See Instructions Form 5695.

Part 1 Review Questions

To obtain the maximum benefit from this chapter, LTP recommends that you complete each of the following questions and then compare them to the answers with feedback that immediately follow. Under governing self-study standards, vendors must present review questions intermittently throughout each self-study course.

These questions and explanations are not part of the final examination and will not be graded by LTP.

PTC1.1
Jerry has three qualifying children for the federal dependent care expense. What is the maximum amount Jerry can claim?

a. $3,000
b. $1,500
c. $6,000
d. No limit

PTC1.2
Tiffany has two children: Hunter, age 12, and Suzy, age 11. At what age will Tiffany be unable to claim the child and dependent care expense?

a. 12
b. 13
c. 14
d. 18

PTC1.3
Jenny files married filing separately. How much will she be able to claim for her education credit?

a. $0
b. $4,000
c. $1,500
d. $3,000

PTC1.4

Doug and his wife Brittney are full-time students at a qualifying school. For tax purposes, they have earned income if they are full-time students for how many months?

a. 12
b. 7
c. 5
d. 4

PTC1.5

Which of the following is a nonrefundable tax credit?

a. Lifetime learning credit
b. Earned Income Tax Credit
c. Additional Child Tax Credit
d. Federal income tax withheld

PTC1.6

Angel will claim the American opportunity credit for 2022. Which federal form will he use to report the credit?

a. Form 8855
b. Form 8863
c. Form 1116
d. Schedule D

PTC1.7

Brasilia will be filing MFS. Which of the following deductions will she be unable to claim?

a. Education credit
b. Loss on capital gain of $1,500 or more
c. IRA contribution
d. Brasilia can claim all the credits

PTC1.8

Arturo had some college expenses and wants to apply for the American opportunity credit. Which of the following expenses must Arturo exclude on Form 8863?

a. Tuition and fees to enroll or attend an educational institution
b. Amounts used for room and board
c. Course fees and books
d. Supplies and equipment required for courses at the educational institution
e. Arturo can include all these expenses

PTC1.9

Andrew is in his second year of college and a full-time student. Andrew qualifies for the American opportunity credit. What is the maximum qualified education expense Andrew can claim?

a. $1,500
b. $2,500
c. $5,000
d. $7,500

PTC1.10

Callie has 3 children and needs to know what information she needs to bring to complete Form 2441 for her current year tax return. Which of the following would Callie not bring to complete Federal Form 2441?

    a. The provider's name
    b. The provider's address
    c. The provider's identification number (EIN or SSN)
    d. The provider's age

Part 1 Review Questions Answers

PTC1.1

Jerry has three qualifying children for the federal dependent care expense. What is the maximum amount Jerry can claim?

    a. $3,000
    b. $1,500
    c. $6,000
    d. No limit

Feedback: Review section *Form 2441: Child and Dependent Care.*

PTC1.2

Tiffany has two children: Hunter, age 12, and Suzy, age 11. At what age will Tiffany be unable to claim the child and dependent care expense?

    a. 12
    b. 13
    c. 14
    d. 18

Feedback: Review section *Form 2441: Child and Dependent Care.*

PTC1.3

Jenny files married filing separately. How much will she be able to claim for her education credit?

    a. $0
    b. $4,000
    c. $1,500
    d. $3,000

Feedback: Review section *Form 8863: Education Credits.*

PTC1.4

Doug and his wife Brittney are full-time students at a qualifying school. For tax purposes, they earned income if they are full-time students for how many months?

    a. 12
    b. 7
    c. 5
    d. 4

Feedback: Review section *Form 8863: Education Credits.*

PTC1.5

Which of the following is a nonrefundable tax credit?

    a. Lifetime learning credit
    b. Earned Income Tax Credit
    c. Additional Child Tax Credit
    d. Federal income tax withheld

Feedback: Review section *Part 1: Nonrefundable Credits.*

PTC1.6

Angel will claim the American opportunity credit for 2022. Which federal form will he use to report the credit?

    a. Form 8855
    b. Form 8863
    c. Form 1116
    d. Schedule D

Feedback: Review section *Part 1: Nonrefundable Credits.*

PTC1.7

Brasilia will be filing MFS. Which of the following deductions will she be unable to claim?

    a. Education credit
    b. Loss on capital gain of $1,500 or more
    c. IRA contribution
    d. Brasilia can claim all the credits

Feedback: Review section *Part 1: Nonrefundable Credits.*

PTC1.8

Arturo had some college expenses and wants to apply for the American opportunity credit. Which of the following expenses must Arturo exclude on Form 8863?

    a. Tuition and fees to enroll or attend an educational institution
    b. Amounts used for room and board
    c. Course fees and books
    d. Supplies and equipment required for courses at the educational institution
    e. Arturo can include all these expenses

Feedback: Review section *Part 1: Nonrefundable Credits.*

PTC1.9

Andrew is in his second year of college and a full-time student. Andrew qualifies for the American opportunity credit. What is the maximum qualified education expense Andrew can claim?

    a. $1,500
    b. $2,500
    c. $5,000
    d. $7,500

Feedback: Review section *Part 1: Nonrefundable Credits.*

PTC1.10

Callie has 3 children and needs to know what information she needs to bring to complete Form 2441 for her current year tax return. Which of the following would Callie not bring to complete Federal Form 2441?

    a. The provider's name
    b. The provider's address
    c. The provider's identification number (EIN or SSN)
    d. The provider's age

Feedback: Review section *Part 1: Nonrefundable Credits.*

Part 2 Other Nonrefundable Credits

Line 6 a-z report other current nonrefundable credits on Form 1040, Schedule 3. LTP has chosen to cover those that are the most common credits.

Line 6b: Credit for prior year minimum tax; attach Form 8801.

Line 6c: Adoption credit; attach Form 8839.

Adoption Credit or Exclusion

The maximum adoption credit amount a taxpayer can receive from their employer for 2022 is $14,890. Suppose the taxpayer's modified adjusted gross income (MAGI) is between $223,410 and $263,4100; in that case, the credit may be reduced based on income. A taxpayer can use the adoption credit for foreign and domestic adoptions in most circumstances. Some states have determined that if a child has special needs, the taxpayer may receive the maximum amount of the credit unless they claimed some expenses in a prior year. Tax credit phaseout for 2023 is $239,230 and ends at $279,230.

Line 6d: Credit for the Elderly or Disabled

Schedule R: Credit for the Elderly or Disabled

The Credit for the Elderly or Disabled is a nonrefundable credit based on the taxpayer's filing status, age, and income. A person is permanently and totally disabled if the taxpayer cannot engage in any substantial gainful activity due to a physical or mental condition or if a qualified physician determined that the condition has lasted or can be expected to last continuously for at least a year or until death. If the taxpayer is under 65, a physician's statement must be attached to the tax return. The statement must certify that the taxpayer was permanently and totally disabled on the date of retirement.

The base amount is reduced by most nontaxable pension and Social Security benefits and by half of the AGI that exceeds the base amount. To claim this credit, the taxpayer must meet the following criteria:

➢ Be age 65 or older by the end of the tax year.
➢ Meet the following conditions if under the age of 65 at the end of the tax year:
   o Retired on permanent and total disability: they must have been permanently and totally disabled on or before January 1, 1976, or January 1, 1977, if the taxpayer retired before 1977.
   o Received taxable disability benefits in the current tax year.
   o Have not reached the employer's mandatory retirement age (when the employer's retirement program requires an employee to retire) on or before January 1 of the tax year in question.

If the taxpayer is under the age of 65, they must have a physician's statement certifying that they were permanently and totally disabled on the date of retirement. Do not file the statement with the taxpayer's Form 1040; however, the taxpayer must keep it for their records. The instructions for Schedule R include a template statement taxpayers can provide to their physicians to complete and keep for their records. The taxpayer's income cannot exceed the limits listed below to qualify for the credit, so many taxpayers will not be able to take advantage of it.

> *Señor 1040 Says:* Be aware that when preparing a Schedule R to determine a taxpayer's eligibility for the elderly or disabled credit, the Social Security income must be considered as well even though it is not taxable.

Income Limits for Schedule R

If the taxpayer's income exceeds the following limits, the taxpayer cannot claim the credit.

If filing status is:	The taxpayer cannot take the credit if the amount from Form 1040, or Form 1040-SR, line 11, is:	Or the taxpayer received:
Single, Head of Household, or Surviving spouse with qualifying dependent	$17,500 or more	$5,000 or more of nontaxable Social Security or other nontaxable pensions, annuities, or disability income
Married Filing Jointly if only one spouse qualifies for the credit	$20,000 or more	$5,000 or more of nontaxable Social Security or other nontaxable pensions, annuities, or disability income
Married Filing Jointly if both spouses qualify for the credit	$25,000 or more	$7,500 or more of nontaxable Social Security or other nontaxable pensions, annuities, or disability income
Married Filing Separately and the taxpayer did not live with spouse any time during the year	$12,500 or more	$3,750 or more of nontaxable Social Security or other nontaxable pensions, annuities, or disability income

Example 1. Adam retired on disability as a salesperson, and he now works as a daycare provider assistant earning minimum wage. Although he does different work, Adam is a daycare provider assistant on ordinary terms for minimum wage. Thus, he cannot take the credit because he is engaged in a substantial gainful activity.

Example 2. Jess retired on disability and took a job with a former employer on a trial basis. The trial period lasted for some time, during which Jess was paid at a rate equal to minimum wage. Due to Jess's disability, he performed light-duty of a nonproductive, make-work nature. Unless the activity is both substantial and gainful, Jess is not engaged in a substantial, gainful activity. The activity was gainful because Jess's payment was at or above the minimum wage rate. However, the activity was not substantial because the duties were of a nonproductive, make-work nature. More information is needed to determine if Jess can engage in a substantial gainful activity.

How to Calculate the Credit

If the taxpayer checked box 6, the total amount entered on line 11 would be $5,000. If the taxpayer checked boxes 2, 4, or 9, then enter the total amount of disability income received. If the taxpayer checked box 5, enter the total amount of disability income received from the taxpayer and spouse on line 11.

Line 6f: Qualified plug-in motor vehicle credit; attach Form 8936

2-Wheeled Plug-in Electric Vehicle

The taxpayer could qualify for purchasing a qualified 2-wheeled electric vehicle that was acquired before 2022 and:

➢ Can go 45+ miles per hour.

> ➤ Is propelled by an electric motor that the battery is not less than 2.5 kilowatt hours and can be recharged.
> ➤ Is manufactured primarily for use on public streets, roads, and highways.
> ➤ Has a gross vehicle weight of less than 14,000 pounds.
> ➤ Other certain additional requirements. See Instructions Form 8936.

Qualified 4-Wheel Plug-in Electric Drive Motor Vehicle (EV)

The taxpayer could receive credit for purchasing a 4-wheel vehicle (placed in service before 2023), with gross weight of less than 14,000 pounds and the battery with at least 4 kilowatt hours and is rechargeable. The electric motor must draw electricity from a rechargeable battery with not less than 4 kilowatt hours. The vehicle must be manufactured primarily to be used on public streets, roads, and highways. The owner is the only one that can claim the credit. If the vehicle is leased, only the lessor and not the lessee is able to claim the credit. The vehicle must be used primarily in the United States and the final assembly of the car must occur in North America. See IRC Code Section 30D.

Line 6g: Mortgage interest credit; attach Form 8396.

Form 8396: Mortgage Interest Credit

If the taxpayer has claimed the following credits:

> ➤ Credit for the elderly or the disabled
> ➤ Credit for alternative motor vehicle credit
> ➤ Qualified plug-in electric drive motor vehicle credit

These credits need to be calculated prior to the mortgage interest credit.

Taxpayers claim the mortgage interest credit if a state, local governmental unit, or agency under a qualified mortgage credit certificate program issues them a Mortgage Credit Certificate (MCC). If the mortgage is equal to or smaller than the certified indebtedness amount (known as the loan) shown on the MCC, multiply the certified credit rate shown on the MCC by all interest paid on the mortgage during the year.

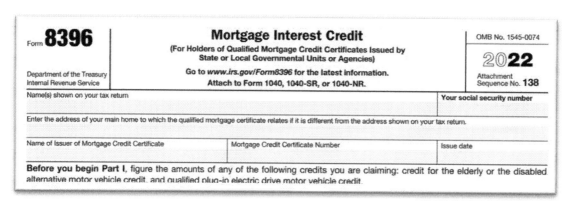

Portion of Form 8396

If the mortgage amount is larger than the certified indebtedness amount shown on the MCC, multiply the certified credit percentage rate shown on the MCC by the interest allocated to the certified indebtedness amount shown on the MCC to calculate the credit.

Señor 1040 Says: Certificates issued by the Federal Housing Administration, Department of Veterans Affairs, and Farmers Home Administration (as well as Homestead Staff Exemption Certificates) do not qualify for the credit.

The home to which the certificate relates must be the taxpayer's primary residence, and the home must be within the jurisdiction of the governmental agency that issued the certificate. The taxpayer could not claim the credit if the interest were paid to a related party. If the taxpayer refinances the mortgage, be aware that the certificates must be reissued to the taxpayer and meet all the following conditions:

> ➢ The owner and the property cannot change.
> ➢ The new certificate must entirely replace the existing certificate. The holder cannot retain any portion of the outstanding balance of the previous certificate.
> ➢ The certified indebtedness on the new certificate cannot exceed the outstanding balance shown on the certificate.
> ➢ The credit rate of the new certificate cannot exceed the credit rate of the old certificate.
> ➢ The new certificate cannot result in a larger amount on line 3 than would otherwise have been allowable under the previous certificate for any tax year.

The taxpayer may have an unused mortgage credit to carry forward up to the next three tax years or until they use it completely, whichever comes first. They have to use the current year's credit before using any carryforward credits. If using the carryforward credits from more than one year, begin with the carryforward credit from the earliest prior year (i.e., 2020 before 2019, 2019 before 2018). If the certificate credit is more than 20%, do not carry forward amounts over $2,000. To complete Form 8396, *Mortgage Interest Credit*, see the form's instructions.

Figure the current year credit and carry any excess forward to the next year on Form 8396, *Mortgage Interest Credit*, and attach Form 8396 to Form 1040. On Form 8396, be sure to include any credit carried forward from the prior three tax years. Use the current-year credit before prior-year credits are applied. Include the credit in the total amount of other credits reported on Schedule 3, line 6; check box c and write in "Form 8396" to show which nonrefundable credit was included on that line. The tax professional should keep a copy of the MCC in the taxpayer's files, as the IRS may want to see the certificate at a future point in time.

Form 1098, *Mortgage Interest Statement*, is required to include the amount of the outstanding principal, the loan origination date, and the property's address. The owner of an inherited property may not treat the property as having a different basis than was reported by the state for estate tax purposes. IRC §6035 requires estates that file an estate tax return to issue payee statements listing the property's value reported on the estate tax return to all persons inheriting property from the estate. These changes apply to all estate tax returns filed after February 29, 2016. For more information, see Notice 2015-57 and IRC §6035.

If the taxpayer purchased and sold the home within nine years, the homeowner may recapture some credit. In this case, one must file Form 8828, *Recapture of Federal Mortgage Subsidy*; you must do more research on this topic.

Form 1098-MA

If the taxpayer has received mortgage assistance payments allocated from the Housing Finance Agency Innovation Fund for the Hardest Hit Housing Markets (HFA Hardest Hit Fund) or the Emergency Homeowner's Loan Program, report the amount paid by the homeowner and the assistance payments on Form 1098-MA.

☐ VOID ☐ CORRECTED		
FILER'S name, street address, city, state, ZIP code, and telephone no.	OMB No. 1545-2221	**Mortgage Assistance Payments**
	Form **1098-MA** (Rev. September 2019) For calendar year 20___	
FILER'S TIN HOMEOWNER'S TIN	**1.** Total State HFA and homeowner mortgage payments $	**Copy A** For **Internal Revenue Service Center**
HOMEOWNER'S name	**2.** State HFA mortgage assistance payments $	For Privacy Act and Paperwork Reduction Act Notice, see
Street address (including apt. no.) (optional)	**3.** Homeowner mortgage payments $	the **current General Instructions for Certain Information Returns.**
City, state, and ZIP code (optional)		
Account number (optional)		

Form **1098-MA** (Rev. 9-2019)   Cat. No. 58017D   www.irs.gov/Form1098MA   Department of the Treasury - Internal Revenue Service

Do Not Cut or Separate Forms on This Page — Do Not Cut or Separate Forms on This Page

Señor 1040 Says: Do not confuse Mortgage Interest Credit with Mortgage Assistance Payments. They are not the same credit.

Child Tax Credits Schedule 8812

The child tax credit (CTC) is a nonrefundable credit for taxpayers who have a qualifying child. For tax year 2022, the credit reverted to $2,000 per child under the age of 17. The refundable portion is $1,500.

The maximum phaseout amounts are $400,000 for married taxpayers filing a joint return and all others is $200,000. The taxpayer's tax liability and modified AGI limits the child tax credit. If the child were not issued a valid Social Security number, they would not qualify the taxpayer for either credit. This credit is reported on Form 1040, line 19.

To be a qualifying child for the child tax credit, the child must be a citizen, national, or resident of the United States. Qualifying child must have an SSN for the taxpayer to claim the child for the Child Tax Credit and/or the Advanced child tax credit. If the dependent does not qualify for the child tax credit, the taxpayer cannot include that dependent in the calculation for the credit. However, the dependent may still qualify for the Other Dependent Credit (ODC).

The Additional Child Tax Credit (ACTC) is a refundable credit available for taxpayers with qualifying children. Use Schedule 8812, Parts II-III to calculate the additional child tax credit. This credit is reported on Form 1040, line 27 and Schedule 3 should be completed.

Qualifying Child for Child Tax Credit

For a child to qualify for the child tax credit, they must meet the following conditions:

➢ The child is the son, daughter, stepchild, eligible foster child, brother, sister, stepbrother, stepsister, half-brother, half-sister, or a descendant of any of these.
➢ The child did not provide over half of their support.
➢ The child lived with the taxpayer for more than half of 2022.
➢ The child is claimed as a dependent on the taxpayer's return.
➢ The child does not file a joint return for the year or only files to claim a refund of withheld income tax or if the dependent paid estimated payments.
➢ The child was a U.S. citizen, U.S. national, U.S. resident alien, or adopted by a U.S. citizen, U.S. national, or U.S. resident alien.

Qualifying Person for the ODC

An individual qualifies for the Other Dependent Credit (ODC) if they meet the following conditions:

➢ The taxpayer claims the qualifying dependent on their tax return.
➢ The dependent is ineligible for the CTC or the ACTC.
➢ The dependent was a U.S. citizen, U.S. national, U.S. resident alien, or adopted by a U.S. citizen, U.S. national, or U.S. resident alien.
➢ They have a TIN on or before the due date of the 2022 tax return.
➢ The maximum phaseout amounts are $400,000 for married taxpayers filing a joint return and all others are $200,000.

Example: Levi is claiming his 10-year-old nephew Fernando, who lives in Mexico and qualifies as Levi's dependent. Because Fernando is not a U.S. citizen, U.S. national, or a U.S. resident alien, Levi cannot use Fernando to claim the Other Dependent Credit (ODC) unless Levi adopts him, and Fernando comes to live with Levi in the United States.

Improperly Claiming the CTC, ODC, or ACTC

If the taxpayer has claimed any of these credits in error, they may be prohibited from claiming these credits for two years. If the error is determined to be fraud, they may be prohibited from claiming the credit for 10 years. The taxpayer may also have to pay penalties and interest. If the tax preparer committed the error and the IRS determines that the error was intentional, the tax preparer will be charged penalties and interest and may be prohibited from preparing returns for as long as the IRS decides it is appropriate. ODC has been added to both the due diligence questionnaire and part III of Form 8862, *Information to Claim Certain Credits After Disallowance*.

Part 2 Review Questions

To obtain the maximum benefit from this chapter, LTP recommends that you complete each of the following questions and then compare them to the answers with feedback that immediately follow. Under governing self-study standards, vendors are required to present review questions intermittently throughout each self-study course.

These questions and explanations are not part of the final examination and will not be graded by LTP.

PTC2.1
Which of the following is a nonrefundable credit?

  a. American opportunity act
  b. Mortgage Interest Credit
  c. Earned income tax credit
  d. Residential energy credit

PTC2.2
Olivia is single and wants to know if she qualifies for the Credit for the Elderly or Disabled. To qualify for the credit, Olivia's adjusted gross income cannot be more than _____ to qualify.

  a. $17,000
  b. $17,500
  c. $20,000
  d. $25,000

PTC2.3

What is the maximum amount of daycare expenses that can be claimed on Form 2441?

  a. $3,000
  b. $6,000
  c. No limit
  d. $4,500

PTC2.4
Russel is a single dad and has three children between the ages of 7 – 17. He has another child who lives in Mexico, but claims that he lives with him. IRS determined that he filed a fraudulent tax return. Which of the following could happen to Russel?

  1. Russel could be prohibited from claiming credits for two years.
  2. Russel could be prohibited from claiming credits for ten years.
  3. Russel will be charged penalties and interest.
  4. Russel could be prohibited from claiming credits for eight years.
  5. Russel will have to file Form 8862 for two years.
  6. Russel will have to file Form 8862 for ten years.

  a. 1, 3 & 5
  b. 1 – 4
  c. 1, 2, 3, 5 & 6
  d. 2, 4, & 6

PTC2.5
Jane has 3 children who qualify for the child tax credit. Jane was not able to claim the entire $3,000 child tax credit because of her tax liability. Jane was able to claimed $2,500 of the child tax credit. What is her maximum additional child tax credit she can claim if she meets all the requirements?

  a. $3,000
  b. $250
  c. She cannot claim any additional child tax credit
  d. $500

PTC2.6
Which of the following is a condition to qualify for the Mortgage Interest Credit?

a. Owner and property cannot change.
b. Owner can never refinance the property.
c. Owner must live in the house for at least 10 years.
d. Owner must have unused credit to apply.

PTC2.7
Norman wants to know if he qualifies to use Schedule R. What income amount will allow Norman to qualify for the credit?

a. $17,000
b. $18,000
c. $17,500
d. $18,500

PTC2.8

Which of the following is a requirement of a 2-wheeled plug-in electric vehicle?

a. Maximum speed is 45 mph.
b. Must be less than 14,000 pounds.
c. Is not street legal.
d. Can be a hybrid vehicle.

PTC2.9
Which of the following is a requirement of a 4-wheeled plug-in electric vehicle?

a. Minimum speed is 45 mph.
b. Must be less than 15,000 pounds.
c. Must have a rechargeable battery.
d. Kilowatt must be 6 hours or more.

PTC2.10
Which of the following would qualify for the other dependent credit?

1. Francisca is ineligible to qualify for the advanced child tax credit.
2. Diego lives in the U.S. but does not have a taxpayer identification number.
3. Gloria is a U.S. citizen living in Mexico.
4. Veronica claims her daughter as a dependent.

a. 1 and 4
b. 1, 2, and 4
c. 2
d. 3 and 4

Part 2 Review Questions Answers

PTC2.1
Which of the following is a nonrefundable credit?

   a. American opportunity act
   b. Mortgage Interest Credit
   c. Earned income tax credit
   d. Residential energy credit

Feedback: Review section *Part 2: Other Nonrefundable Credits*.

PTC2.2
Olivia is single and wants to know if she qualifies for the Credit for the Elderly or Disabled. To qualify for the credit, Olivia's adjusted gross income cannot be more than_____to qualify.

   a. $17,000
   b. $17,500
   c. $20,000
   d. $25,000

Feedback: Review section *Schedule R: Credit for the Elderly or Disabled*.

PTC2.3

What is the maximum amount of daycare expenses that can be claimed on Form 2441?

   a. $3,000
   b. $6,000
   c. No limit
   d. $4,500

Feedback: Review section *Part 2: Other Nonrefundable Credits*.

PTC2.4
Russel is a single dad and has three children between the ages of 7 – 17. He has another child who lives in Mexico, but claims that he lives with him. IRS determined that he filed a fraudulent tax return. Which of the following could happen to Russel?

     1. Russel could be prohibited from claiming credits for two years.
     2. Russel could be prohibited from claiming credits for ten years.
     3. Russel will be charged penalties and interest.
     4. Russel could be prohibited from claiming credits for eight years.
     5. Russel will have to file Form 8862 for two years.
     6. Russel will have to file Form 8862 for ten years.

   a. 1, 3, & 5
   b. 1 – 4
   c. 1, 2, 3, 5, & 6
   d. 2, 4, & 6

Feedback: Review section *Part 2: Other Nonrefundable Credits*.

PTC2.5

Jane has 3 children who qualify for the child tax credit. Jane was not able to claim the entire $3,000 child tax credit because of her tax liability. Jane was able to claimed $2,500 of the child tax credit. What is her maximum additional child tax credit she can claim if she meets all the requirements?

    a. $3,000
    b. $250
    c. She cannot claim any additional child tax credit
    d. $500

Feedback: Review section *Part 2: Other Nonrefundable Credits.*

PTC2.6

Which of the following is a condition to qualify for the Mortgage Interest Credit?

    a. Owner and property cannot change.
    b. Owner can never refinance the property.
    c. Owner must live in the house for at least 10 years.
    d. Owner must have unused credit to apply.

Feedback: Review section *Part 2: Other Nonrefundable Credits.*

PTC2.7

Norman wants to know if he qualifies to use Schedule R. What income amount will allow Norman to qualify for the credit?

    a. $17,000
    b. $18,000
    c. $17,500
    d. $18,500

Feedback: Review section *Part 2: Other Nonrefundable Credits.*

PTC2.8

Which of the following is a requirement of a 2-wheeled plug-in electric vehicle?

    a. Maximum speed is 45 mph.
    b. Must be less than 14,000 pounds.
    c. Is not street legal.
    d. Can be a hybrid vehicle.

Feedback: Review section *Part 2: Other Nonrefundable Credits.*

PTC2.9

Which of the following is a requirement of a 4-wheeled plug-in electric vehicle?

    a. Minimum speed is 45 mph.
    b. Must be less than 15,000 pounds.
    c. Must have a rechargeable battery.
    d. Kilowatt must be 6 hours or more.

Feedback: Review section *Part 2: Other Nonrefundable Credits.*

PTC2.10

Which of the following would qualify for the other dependent credit?

1. Francisca is ineligible to qualify for the advanced child tax credit.
2. Diego lives in the U.S. but does not have a taxpayer identification number.
3. Gloria is a U.S. citizen living in Mexico.
4. Veronica claims her daughter as a dependent.

   a. 1 and 4
   b. 1, 2, and 4
   c. 2
   d. 3 and 4

Feedback: Review section *Part 2: Other Nonrefundable Credits.*

Part 3 Payments and Refundable Tax Credits

In the tax industry, the term "refundable credit" refers to a credit that allows the taxpayer to lower their tax liability dollar-for-dollar to zero and below, resulting in a refund. When the refundable credit exceeds the amount of taxes owed, it could result in a tax refund.

A refundable tax credit is a tax credit that is treated as a payment and can be refunded to the taxpayer by the IRS. Refundable tax credits offset certain taxes that are normally not reduced. The credits can create a federal tax refund higher than the amount of money a person had withheld during the year. Refundable tax credits are applied toward a person's tax obligation, and the overpayment could be refunded back to the individual. Withholding for federal income taxes and estimated taxes could be refundable, since they are prepayments toward a person's annual tax liability that can be refunded to the taxpayer if withholding was overpaid.

Federal Income Tax Withheld

Form 1040, page 2, line 25, reports the federal income tax withheld from all income reported by forms such as the W-2, W-2G, 1099-R, 1099-NEC, SSA-1099, and Schedule K. The amount of tax withheld is on Form W-2 in box 2 and on the Form 1099 series in box 4. If the taxpayer had federal tax withheld from Social Security benefits, it is in box 6 of Form SSA-1099. If the taxpayer had additional Medicare tax withheld by their employer, that amount shows on Form 1040, Schedule 2, line 11. Calculate the additional Medicare tax on Form 8959 and attach it to the return.

Estimated Tax Payments

Form 1040, page 2, line 26, reports any estimated tax payments made in the current tax year and any overpayments applied from the prior year's tax return. If a taxpayer and their spouse have divorced during the current tax year and made estimated payments together, enter the former spouse's SSN in the space provided on the front of Form 1040. The taxpayer should attach a statement to Form 1040 explaining that the divorced couple made the payments together; that statement should also contain proof of payments, the name, and SSN of the individual making the payments.

Estimated tax payments are also referred to as quarterlies since the payments are due in four equal payments. If the due dates fall on a Saturday, Sunday, or a legal holiday, estimated payments are due on the next business day. Estimated payments are due on the following dates:

➤ April 15th
➤ June 15th
➤ September 15th
➤ January 15th (of the following year)

Amount Overpaid

The taxpayer can receive their overpayment as a paper check from the U.S. Treasury Department or through a direct deposit from the U.S. Treasury Department into a checking or savings account. After filing the tax return electronically, the taxpayer can go to www.irs.gov and click "Where's My Refund?" to receive information that is available about their return within 24 hours after it has been electronically accepted by the IRS. If the overpayment amount is different than what the taxpayer was expecting, the taxpayer should receive an explanation from the IRS within two weeks after depositing the refund.

Form 1040, page 2, line 34, states if there was an overpayment of current-year taxes and indicates how the taxpayer would like to receive the overpayment refund. Enter on Line 35a the desired refund amount the taxpayer wants. They can select a portion of that amount as a refund and forward the rest as estimated tax payments for the following tax year. Use line 36 to enter the desired estimated payments. The taxpayer can also elect to carry forward their entire refund amount. If the taxpayer wants to carry out overpayments to the following year, enter the amount they would like to have applied on Form 1040, line 36. Suppose a couple filed MFJ, and a taxpayer's spouse wants the overpayment applied to her account. In that case, the refund amount splits to the taxpayer's account and the spouse's separate account. The taxpayer can include up to three bank accounts on Part I in Form 8888. Use Part II to purchase U.S. Series I Savings Bonds.

Tax Tip: The IRS will allow the taxpayer to have their direct deposit split between multiple accounts, but not all software supports the use of Form 8888 to do so.

Example: Pat made estimated payments for the current tax year of $11,000 and overpaid her quarterlies by $4,500. Pat wants $2,000 refunded, so enter $2,000 on Line 36. Pat would like the remaining $2,500 applied to next year's estimated payments, so enter the $2,500 amount on Line 35a.

If the taxpayer wants to deposit the entire overpayment directly, submit a valid routing number and account number. A routing number is a nine-digit number that indicates which financial institute receives the direct deposit refund. The account number is specific to the taxpayer. The first two digits of the routing number must be 01 through 12 or 21 through 32. Some financial institutions have a separate routing number for direct deposits. If there is no entry on Form 1040, Page 2, line 35b or line 35d, the taxpayer will receive a paper check.

The routing number on a deposit slip may differ from the routing number on the bottom of a personal check. If the tax preparer is entering the numbers from the bottom of the check, make sure you do not enter the check number when entering the account number. On Form 1040, be sure to indicate whether the account is a checking or savings account.

ROBERT SAMPLE
JOAN SAMPLE
123 MAIN ST.
PORTLAND, ME 04101

9999

~~11/30/2011~~
Date

Pay to the
Order of *Sample Check* | $ 158.00

one hundred and fifty eight ———— 00/100 🔒 ▤

Dollars

TD Bank
America's Most Convenient Bank®

For *SAMPLE*

Joan Sample

⑆123454321⑆ ⑈0123454321⑈ 9999

Routing Number   Account Number

If any of the following happen, the financial institution rejects the direct deposit, and the IRS sends a paper check to the taxpayer instead:

➢ Any numbers or letters on lines 35b or 35d are crossed out, or some type of correction material (such as correction tape or white-out) has been used.
➢ The taxpayer's financial institution(s) will not allow a joint return to be deposited to an individual account; The U.S. Treasury Department is not responsible if the financial institution rejects the direct deposit.
➢ Three direct deposits have already been made to that account.
➢ The name on the account does not match the name on the tax refund.
➢ The name on the account is not the same as on the tax return.

Señor 1040 Says: The IRS is not responsible for a lost refund if the account information is entered incorrectly. The taxpayer is responsible for making sure that his or her routing number and account number are accurate, and that the financial institution will accept the direct deposit.

Returns with Refunds

When individual taxpayers have an overpayment on their current-year tax return, they have several options for receiving the overpayment:

➢ They can apply the overpayment to next year's estimated tax return.
➢ They can receive a paper check.
➢ They can receive a direct deposit.
➢ They can divide the refund amount into different bank accounts.

Direct Deposit

Taxpayers may have refunds deposited into their checking or savings accounts. The tax professional must have the taxpayer's account number, routing number, and the financial institution's name to directly deposit the refund. The information is found at the bottom of the taxpayer's check. Be careful not to include the check number.

Form 8888, *Allocation of Refund*, allows the taxpayer to split and deposit refunds into multiple accounts. A qualified account can be a checking or savings account or other accounts such as a money market account or an IRA. The taxpayer should not try to deposit money into an account not in their name directly. This form is limited to three accounts and can also be used to purchase U.S. Series I Savings Bonds.

Direct Deposit Limits

The IRS has imposed a limit of three direct deposits that can be electronically deposited into a single financial account or loaded on a pre-paid debit card. Any further deposits will be converted to a paper check and mailed to the taxpayer within four weeks. Taxpayers will receive a notification via mailed letter that their account has exceeded the direct deposit limit.

The IRS has imposed this direct deposit limit to prevent criminals from obtaining multiple refunds. The new limitations also protect taxpayers from tax preparers who illegally obtain their tax preparation fees by using Form 8888 to split the refund into multiple accounts. Tax preparers who do this are subject to a fine.

Señor 1040 Says: The IRS will send refunds under $1 only if requested in writing.

If the taxpayer files a joint return and either the taxpayer or the spouse has an offset of bad debt to pay, the other spouse may be an injured spouse. If the IRS took one spouse's refund to pay the other spouse's tax liability, the injured spouse would file Form 8379 to see if they meet the conditions to get their portion of the refund back from the IRS.

Amount Paid with a Request for Extension

If the taxpayer used Form 4868 to file an extension and is making a payment, report the payment amount with the extension on Form 1040, Schedule 3, line 10. Do not include the taxpayer's fees when the individual pays by debit or with credit card.

Señor 1040 Says: If the taxpayer itemizes his deductions and paid by credit or with debit card, the convenience fees are no longer a deduction on Schedule A.

Excess Social Security or Railroad Retirement Tax Withheld

When a taxpayer has more than one employer, it is possible that the employers withhold too much for Social Security or Railroad Retirement Tax Act (RRTA) benefits. If that is the case, the taxpayer may claim the excess payment on Form 1040, Schedule 3, line 11, as a refundable credit. If, however, one employer withholds too much tax for Social Security or Railroad Retirement Tax Act, the employer makes the adjustment for the employee. Even if the employer does not refund the extra withholding to the employee, the taxpayer cannot adjust their income tax form but must instead file Form 843 to claim the refund.

The taxpayer is entitled to the credit if they had more than one employer and exceeded the withholding limits for 2022 of $147,000 in wages subject to Social Security and tier 1 RRTA withholding taxes of $9,114.00 or less. For 2023, the amount will be $160,200 to Social Security and tier 1 RRTA withholding taxes of $9,932.40 or less. All wages are subject to Medicare tax withholding.

Earned Income Credit (EIC)

The earned income credit (EIC), also referred to as earned income tax credit (EITC), is a refundable tax credit for low-to-moderate-income working individuals and families. When the EIC exceeds the amount of taxes owed, it results in a refundable credit. Report the EIC on Form 1040, page 2, line 27.

Twenty-eight states and the District of Columbia have an EITC program. Most use federal eligibility rules, and their version of the credit parallels major elements of the federal structure. In most states and localities, the credit is refundable (as is federal), although, in a few areas, the EITC is used only to offset taxes owed. For more information, go to www.irs.gov/eitc. The taxpayer must have earned income during the tax year to be eligible for the earned income tax credit. If a married couple is filing a joint return, and only one spouse worked, both could still meet the earned income requirement.

Remember, earned income is revenue the taxpayer received for working and includes the following types of income:

> ➢ Wages, salaries, tips, and other types of taxable employee pay.
> ➢ Net earnings from self-employment.
> ➢ Gross income received as a statutory employee.
> ➢ Union strike benefits.
> ➢ Long-term disability benefits received before reaching the minimum retirement age.

Unearned income includes the following:

> ➢ Interest and dividends.
> ➢ Pensions and annuities.
> ➢ Social Security and railroad retirement benefits (including disability benefits).
> ➢ Alimony and child support.
> ➢ Welfare benefits.
> ➢ Workers' compensation benefits.
> ➢ Unemployment compensation.
> ➢ Income while an inmate.
> ➢ Workfare payments (see Publication 596).

A taxpayer and their spouse, if filing jointly, must have a valid SSN to qualify for the earned income tax credit. If the SSN says, "Not valid for employment," and if the SSN was issued so the taxpayer or spouse could receive aid from a federally-funded program, they do not qualify to receive earned income credit. If the SSN says, "Valid for work only with INS authorization," or "Valid only with DHS authorization," then the SSN is valid, but only if the authorization has not expired.

Community Property

Taxpayers who live in a community property state could qualify for Head of Household if the couple has lived apart for at least the last six months of the year. A taxpayer's earned income for EIC does not include any amount earned by their spouse, even though income belongs to the spouse under the state's community property laws and is not earned income for EIC purposes. The taxpayer, however, must include it with all their earned income on the federal tax return. The same rules apply to taxpayers living in Nevada, Washington, and California who are Registered Domestic Partners (RDP's).

The IRS may ask the taxpayer to provide additional documentation to prove that the qualifying dependents belong to the taxpayer. The IRS might ask for the following documents:

➢ Birth certificate
➢ School records
➢ Medical records

During the initial interview, tax professionals should inform their clients what they might need if the IRS audits their claim for EIC. If a taxpayer receives an audit letter, the letter will include the taxpayer's name, address, telephone number, and the name of the IRS employee responsible for the taxpayer's audit. This process will delay the client's refund. If the taxpayer is found to fraudulently claim the EIC, the taxpayer will be denied the credit for the current tax year and for the next nine years after that.

Minister's Housing

The housing allowance provided to a minister as part of the minister's pay is generally not subject to income tax. Still, net earnings from self-employment include this pay; therefore, it is earned income for EIC.

Earned Income Rules

To qualify for EIC, the taxpayer's adjusted gross income (AGI) must be below a certain amount, and the taxpayer (and spouse if married filing jointly) must meet the following requirements:

➢ Have a valid Social Security number (if filing MFJ, the spouse must also have a valid SSN).
➢ Have earned income from employment or self-employment income.
➢ Not file as Married filing separately (MFS).
➢ File MFJ as a U.S. citizen, as a resident alien all year, or as a nonresident alien married to a U.S. citizen.
➢ Not file Form 2555 or Form 2555-EZ.
➢ Not have investment income over $10,300.
➢ Have a qualifying child who meets the four dependent tests (age, relationship, residency, and joint return; see "Qualifying Child" below).
    o Be at least age 25 and under age 65 at the end of the year.
    o Live in the United States for more than half the year.
    o Not qualify as a dependent of another person.
➢ The 2022 AGI must be less than:
    o $53,057 ($59,187 MFJ) with three or more qualifying children.
    o $49,399 ($55,529 MFJ) with two qualifying children.
    o $43,492 ($49,662 MFJ) with one qualifying child.
    o $16,480 ($22,610 MFJ) with no qualifying children.

Valid Social Security Number

The qualifying child must have a valid Social Security number (SSN) issued by the Social Security Administration (SSA) unless a child died in the same year they were born. Social Security cards with the legend "not valid for employment" are issued to aliens who are not eligible to work in the United States but who need an SSN so they can get a federally funded benefit such as Medicaid. Suppose the immigration status of a taxpayer or spouse has changed to U.S. citizen or permanent resident. In that case, the taxpayer should ask the SSA for a new Social Security card without the legend. If the SSN says, "valid for work only with INS authorization or DHS authorization," this is considered a valid SSN, and the taxpayer may qualify for the credit. Taxpayers with an ITIN do not qualify for EIC.

Uniform Definition of a Qualifying Child

The Working Families Tax Relief Act of 2004, amended in 2008, added the joint return test and standardized the definition of a qualifying child for the five child-related tax benefits. The tax law also defined exceptions and special rules for dependents with a disability, children of divorced parents, and adopted children (always treated as the taxpayer's child), including a child lawfully placed with the taxpayer for adoption.

Taxpayers that have missing or kidnapped children that a non-family member abducted may still claim the child. The IRS treats a kidnapped child as living with the taxpayer for more than half of the year if the child lived with the taxpayer for more than half of the part of the year before the date of the kidnapping, even if that length of time does not amount to half of a year. For example, if they kidnap a child on March 1, the parent can still claim the child if they lived with the taxpayer for at least half of the two months (January and February) preceding the date of the kidnapping.

Although there are five tests to claim a dependent, a qualifying child must meet only four of the dependent tests to qualify for the EIC:

> ➤ Relationship
> ➤ Age
> ➤ Residency
> ➤ Joint return

To review these tests' rules and guidelines, please refer to "The Filing Status, Dependents, and Deductions" Chapter.

Foster Child

To receive the EIC, a person is the taxpayer's foster child if the child is placed with the taxpayer by a judgment, decree, other order of any court of competent jurisdiction, or by an authorized placement agency such as a state or local government agency, a tax-exempt organization licensed by a state, an Indian tribal government, or an organization authorized by an Indian tribal government to place Indian children.

Example: Allison, who is 12 years old, was placed in the taxpayer's care two years ago by an authorized agency responsible for placing children in foster homes. Allison is the taxpayer's eligible foster child because she was placed there by an authorized licensed agency.

A Qualifying Child of More than One Person

Sometimes a child meets the rules to be a qualifying child of more than one person. However, only one person can use a qualifying child to claim the EIC. If two eligible taxpayers have the same qualifying child, they can decide who will take all the following related tax benefits:

> ➢ The child's exemption.
> ➢ The child tax credit.
> ➢ Head of Household filing status.
> ➢ The credit for child and dependent care expenses.
> ➢ The exclusion for dependent care benefits.
> ➢ The Earned Income Credit.

Only one taxpayer can claim these benefits, and they must claim either all of them or none of them. Do not divide the benefits between the two competing taxpayers. The tie-breaker rule applies if the taxpayer and the other person(s) cannot agree and if more than one person claims the EIC or other benefits using the same child. However, the tie-breaker rule does not apply if the other person is the taxpayer's spouse and files a joint return.

If the taxpayer and someone else have the same qualifying child, but the other person cannot claim the EIC because the taxpayer is not eligible or because their earned income or AGI was too high, the child is a qualifying child for the taxpayer. Suppose a taxpayer's EIC is denied because the qualifying child is treated as the qualifying child of another person for the current tax year. In that case, one may claim the EIC if there is another, separate qualifying child. However, the taxpayer cannot take the EIC using the qualifying child that another individual claimed.

Example: Pedro has two children, Nora from his first marriage to Darla and a son named Francisco from his current spouse Martha. Even if Pedro and Darla agree to let Darla claim the EIC for Nora, Pedro can still claim the EIC for his son Francisco, and Pedro is not prohibited from claiming Francisco simply because he chose to give up his claim to Nora.

Tiebreaker rules

The tie-breaker rules covered in *Chapter 4 Income* also apply to the EIC.

Example: 25-year-old Jeannie and her five-year-old son, Billy, lived with Jeannie's mother, Sarah, all year. Jeannie is unmarried, and her AGI is $8,100. Her only source of income was from a part-time job. Sarah's AGI was $20,000 from her job. Billy's father did not live with Billy or Jeannie. Billy is a qualifying child of both Jeannie and Sarah since he meets the relationship, age, residency, and joint return tests. Jeannie and Sarah must decide who will claim Billy as their dependent. If Jeannie does not claim Billy as a qualifying child for the EIC or Head of household filing status, Jeannie's mother can claim Billy as a qualifying child for each of those tax benefits for which she qualifies. Remember that the dependent test for support does not apply to the EIC.

Special Rule for Divorced or Separated Parents

The special rules covered in Chapter 4 that apply to divorced or separated parents trying to claim an exemption for a dependent do not apply to the EIC. For more information, see Publication 501 and Publication 596.

The Taxpayer as a Qualifying Child of Another Person

To review how to determine if a taxpayer is a qualifying child of another person, refer to Income Chapter in this textbook. If the taxpayer (or spouse filing a joint return) is a qualifying child of another person, the taxpayer or spouse cannot claim the EIC. This rule is true even if the person for whom the taxpayer or spouse is a qualifying child does not claim the EIC or meet all the rules to claim the EIC. Write "No" beside line 64a (Form 1040) to show that the taxpayer does not qualify.

Example: Max and his daughter, Letty, lived with Max's mother all year. Max is 22-years-old and attended a trade school full time. Max had a part-time job, earned $5,100, and had no other income. Because Max meets the relationship, age, and residency tests, he is a qualifying child of his mother, and she can claim the EIC if she meets all the other requirements. Because the taxpayer is his mother's qualifying child, he cannot claim the EIC for his daughter.

EIC for Taxpayers without Qualifying Children

Taxpayers who do not have qualifying children may also be eligible for the EIC. To be eligible for the EIC, the taxpayer must meet the following conditions:

- ➢ The taxpayer must be at least 25 years old and under the age of 65 at the end of 2022. If the taxpayer is filing a joint return; however, it is not required that both the taxpayer and the spouse meet the age requirement.
- ➢ The taxpayer must not be dependent on another person.
- ➢ The taxpayer must not be the qualifying child of another person.
- ➢ The taxpayers must have resided in the United States for more than half of the year.
- ➢ Maximum income should be more than $21,430 or $27,380 if married filing jointly.

Schedule EIC Worksheets

Taxpayers eligible for the EIC with qualifying children must complete Schedule EIC. Schedule EIC requires including the child's name, Social Security number, year of birth, the number of months lived in the home located in the United States, and the child's relationship to the taxpayer. Schedule EIC must be attached to the taxpayer's Form 1040. The taxpayer's income must be less than the threshold amounts to qualify for EIC. Worksheets are available to help with the calculations of the EIC and completing the EIC worksheets is essential to determining the amount of credit a taxpayer may claim on their return. The completed worksheet should be placed in the client's file and not be attached to the federal tax return. The IRS has the EIC worksheets on its website. If the taxpayer is self-employed, the taxpayer must complete EIC Worksheet B, found in Instructions Form 1040. All other taxpayers would figure their earned income by using Worksheet A of the Form 1040 Instructions.

EIC Disallowed

There are circumstances when the IRS does not allow the EIC. Some of the most common reasons for disallowance of the EIC include:

> ➢ Claiming a child who does not meet all the qualifying child tests.
> ➢ The Social Security numbers are mismatched or incorrect.
>> ○ Example: A couple is married during the current tax year, and they file their tax return under the spouse's married name; however, the wife did not change her name with the Social Security Administration, so her Social Security number is assigned with her maiden name listed, making the information on the return incorrect.
> ➢ Filing as Single or Head of Household when the taxpayer is married.
> ➢ Over- or underreporting income.

If the taxpayer's EIC has been denied or reduced for any year after 1996 for any reason other than a mathematical error, the taxpayer will have to complete Form 8862, *Information to Claim Earned Income Credit after Disallowance,* and attach it to their tax return. When interviewing the taxpayer, the tax preparer should ask if the taxpayer has ever received a notice from the IRS or filed Form 8862 in any year after 1996. If the taxpayer has received a notice that the EIC was denied or reduced from a previous tax year, the preparer should complete Form 8862 to claim the credit again if the taxpayer is eligible.

The purpose of Form 8862 is to claim the EIC after it has been disallowed or reduced in an earlier year. Form 8862 must be attached to the tax return if all the following apply:

> ➢ The EIC was reduced or disallowed for any reason other than a mathematical or clerical error for a year after 1996.
> ➢ The taxpayer wants to claim the EIC and meet all the requirements.

The taxpayer must attach Schedule EIC and Form 8862 to the return if the taxpayer has any qualifying children. The taxpayer may be asked for additional information before a refund is issued. If the IRS contacts the taxpayer to request additional information, and the taxpayer does not provide the necessary information or documentation, the taxpayer will receive a statutory notice of deficiency from the IRS. The notice explains that an adjustment will be assessed unless the taxpayer files a petition in the tax court within 90 days. If the taxpayer fails to reply to the IRS or file a petition within 90 days, the IRS will deny their petition for the EIC and assess to determine how much tax they might owe.

EIC Taxpayer Penalties

The IRS may penalize the taxpayer if it determines that the taxpayer has been negligent or has disregarded rules or regulations relating to the EIC. The taxpayer may be prohibited from claiming EIC for the next two years if they are found negligent. If the taxpayer has fraudulently claimed the credit, the taxpayer will be prohibited from claiming the credit for the next 10 years.

The tax preparer may be assessed penalties for not performing their due diligence.

Example: Brittni claimed the EIC on the 2022 tax return that she filed in February 2023. The IRS determined that she was not entitled to the EIC due to fraud. She received a statutory notice of deficiency in September 2023, explaining the adjustment amount that would be assessed unless she filed a petition in the tax court within 90 days. The IRS determined that Brittni did not file her petition, and she was prohibited from claiming the EIC on her return, for 10 years, until 2033. In that year, she will need to complete and attach Form 8862 to her return to claim the credit again.

Claiming a Child in Error

The most common error is claiming a child that is not a qualifying child and does not meet the tests. The knowledge requirement for paid tax preparers states that the preparer must apply a reasonable standard (as defined by Circular 230 and the Form 8867 Instructions) to the information received from the client. If the information provided by the client appears to be incorrect, incomplete, or inconsistent, then the paid preparer must make additional inquiries of the client until they are satisfied that they have gathered the correct and complete information.

Example 1: Cindy tells Jack, her tax preparer, that she is 22 years old and has two sons, aged 10 and 11. Jack may need to ask Cindy the following questions:

> ➤ Are these Cindy's biological children, foster sons, or adopted sons?
> ➤ Was Cindy ever married to the children's father?
> ➤ Were the children placed in Cindy's home for adoption or as foster children?
> ➤ Did the father live with Cindy?
> ➤ How long have the children lived with Cindy?
> ➤ Does Cindy have any records to prove that the children lived with her, such as school or medical records?

Example 2: Maria tells Andres, her tax preparer, that last year she filed Single and claimed the EIC for her child, but that this year she has two children to claim for EIC. Andres may need to ask Maria the following questions:

> ➤ You claimed one child last year. What changed?
> ➤ How many months did the children live with you?
> ➤ Do you have any records to prove the children living with you, such as school or medical records?

Nontaxable Combat Pay Election for EIC

Nontaxable combat pay for armed forces members is only considered earned income for the EIC if they elect to include nontaxable combat pay in earned income to increase or decrease the EIC. Figure the credit with and without the nontaxable combat pay before making the election. If the taxpayer makes the election, they must include all nontaxable combat pay as earned income. Examples of nontaxable military pay are combat pay, basic allowance for housing (BAH), and the basic allowance for subsistence (BAS). Combat pay is reported on Form W-2 in box 12 with code Q.

Part 3 Review Questions

To obtain the maximum benefit from this chapter, LTP recommends that you complete each of the following questions and then compare them to the answers with feedback that immediately follow. Under governing self-study standards, vendors are required to present review questions intermittently throughout each self-study course.

These questions and explanations are not part of the final examination and will not be graded by LTP.

PTC3.1
Refundable credits are considered payments toward the taxpayer's liability. Which of the following does not lower the taxpayer's liability?

    a. Earned Income Tax Credit
    b. Excess CASDI
    c. Additional Child Tax Credit
    d. American Opportunity Credit

PTC3.2
Estimated payments are due in four equal payments. Which of the following is not a due date for estimated tax payments?

    a. April 15th
    b. September 15th
    c. June 15th
    d. December 15th

PTC3.3
Which of the following is a refundable tax credit?

    a. Lifetime learning credit
    b. Child tax credit
    c. Retirement savings contribution credit
    d. Additional child tax credit

PTC3.4
Which of the following could qualify the taxpayer for EIC?

    a. 6-year-old with an ITIN
    b. 12-year-old with an SSN and lives in Mexico
    c. 30-year-old and partially disabled
    d. A 23-year-old full-time student attending a qualifying college

PTC3.5
Which taxpayer would not qualify for EIC?

a. Dependent with a valid ITIN
b. Cannot file MFS
c. Investment income under $3,400
d. Have earned income

PTC3.6
Which taxpayer could qualify for EIC?

a. 68-year-old single with an income of $10,395
b. MFJ with two children and an income of $59,292
c. MFJ with three children, an income of $19,589, and qualifying children do not live with the taxpayer
d. HH with one child, age 23, and going to school full-time, with an income of $17,422

PTC3.7
Which form allows a taxpayer to split their refund into multiple bank accounts?

a. Form 8812
b. Form 8962
c. Form 8888
d. Form 1040

PTC3.8
Which payment method is not used to receive a refund from the IRS?

a. Receive a paper check.
b. Receive the refund via direct deposited into the taxpayer's checking account.
c. Receive the refund into multiple accounts.
d. Apply the overpayment to the next year's estimated payments.

PTC3.9
Which form allows the taxpayer to file an extension?

a. Form 4868
b. Form 8962
c. Form 8812
d. Form 8888

PTC3.10
What does Form 843 report?

1. Excess Social Security.
2. Excess Railroad Retirement.
3. Taxes paid.
4. Earned Income Credit.
5. Filing and Extension

a. 1, 2, and 5
b. 1, 2, and 3
c. 1 and 2
d. 3, 4, and 5

Part 3 Review Questions Answers

PTC3.1

Refundable credits are considered payments toward the taxpayer's liability. Which of the following does not lower the taxpayer's liability?

a. Earned Income Tax Credit
b. Excess CASDI
c. Additional Child Tax Credit
d. American Opportunity Credit

Feedback: Review section *Part 3: Refundable Tax Credits and Payments*.

PTC3.2

Estimated payments are due in four equal payments. Which of the following is not a due date for estimated tax payments?

a. April 15th
b. September 15th
c. June 15th
d. December 15th

Feedback: Review section *Estimated Tax Payments*.

PTC3.3

Which of the following is a refundable tax credit?

a. Lifetime learning credit
b. Child tax credit
c. Retirement savings contribution credit
d. Additional child tax credit

Feedback: Review section *Child and Dependent Credits*.

PTC3.4

Which of the following could qualify the taxpayer for EIC?

a. 6-year-old with an ITIN
b. 12-year-old with an SSN and lives in Mexico
c. 30-year-old and partially disabled
d. A 23-year-old full-time student attending a qualifying college

Feedback: Review section *Qualifying Child for Child Tax Credit*.

PTC3.5
Which taxpayer would not qualify for EIC?

    a. Dependent with a valid ITIN
    b. Cannot file MFS
    c. Investment income under $3,400
    d. Have earned income

Feedback: Review section *Child and Dependent Credits.*

PTC3.6
Which taxpayer could qualify for EIC?

    a. 68-year-old single with an income of $10,395
    b. MFJ with two children and an income of $59,292
    c. MFJ with three children, an income of $19,589, and qualifying children do not live with the taxpayer
    d. HH with one child, age 23, and going to school full-time, with an income of $17,422

Feedback: Review section *Earned Income Rules.*

PTC3.7
Which form allows a taxpayer to split their refund into multiple bank accounts?

    a. Form 8812
    b. Form 8962
    c. Form 8888
    d. Form 1040

Feedback: Review section *Direct Deposit.*

PTC3.8
Which payment method is not used to receive a refund from the IRS?

    a. Receive a paper check.
    b. Receive the refund via direct deposited into the taxpayer's checking account.
    c. Receive the refund into multiple accounts.
    d. Apply the overpayment to the next year's estimated payments.

Feedback: Review section *Direct Deposit.*

PTC3.9
Which form allows the taxpayer to file an extension?

    a. Form 4868
    b. Form 8962
    c. Form 8812
    d. Form 8888

Feedback: Review section *Amount Paid with a Request for Extension.*

PTC3.10
What does Form 843 report?

 1. Excess Social Security.
 2. Excess Railroad Retirement.
 3. Taxes paid.
 4. Earned Income Credit.
 5. Filing and Extension

a. 1, 2, and 5
b. 1, 2, and 3
c. 1 and 2
d. 3, 4, and 5

Feedback: Review section *Excess Social Security or Railroad Retirement Tax Withheld.*

Takeaways

A tax credit reduces the amount of tax the taxpayer is liable for. Unlike a deduction, which reduces the amount of income subject to tax, a tax credit directly reduces the taxpayer's liability. A tax credit is a sum deducted from the total amount a taxpayer owes. There are two categories of tax credits: nonrefundable and refundable.

There are a variety of credits and deductions for the taxpayer. This lesson covered a few credits that allow taxpayers to lower their tax liability to zero and below and possibly receive a refund from the credits. A refundable credit is a tax credit treated as a payment and can thus be refunded to the taxpayer by the IRS. Refundable credits can help offset certain types of taxes that normally cannot be reduced and can even produce a federal refund.

TEST YOUR KNOWLEDGE!
Go online to take a practice quiz.

California Payments and Tax Credits

Introduction

Although various California tax credits are available to help taxpayers reduce their tax liability, California does not conform to all the credits that are claimed on the federal return. This chapter will cover FTB Form 540, lines 40-48, and California refers to this section as "Special Credits." A tax preparer is responsible for ensuring (to the best of their knowledge) that the taxpayer is filing a true and accurate return by asking the client detailed questions and doing as much research and documentation as necessary.

Objectives

At the end of this lesson, the student will:

> ➤ Determine how to calculate the taxes paid to another state for both resident and non-resident taxpayers.
> ➤ Identify which taxpayers qualify for the renter's credit.
> ➤ Understand the different special credits.
> ➤ Know how to calculate child and dependent care expenses.
> ➤ Realize the differences between a nonrefundable and refundable credit.
> ➤ Recognize the earned income tax qualifications.

Resources

Form 540	Publication 1001 California Tax Rates and Exemption Table	Instructions Form 540
Form 3506		Instructions Form 3506
Form 3510		Instructions Form 3510
Form 3514		Instructions Form 3514
Form 3596		Instructions Form 3596
Schedule S		Instructions Schedule S

Table of Contents

Part 1 Child and Dependent Care Expense and Other Credits

Taxpayers whose federal AGI is $100,000 or less and who qualify for the federal credit for child and dependent care on federal Form 2441 could also qualify for the nonrefundable California Child and Dependent Care Expense Credit. The California credit is either 50%, 43%, or 34% of the federal credit, which means the federal amounts must be determined before the preparer can figure the California credit on FTB Form 3506. Therefore, the taxpayer must complete federal Form 2441 to claim the California credit, even if the credit was not claimed on the federal tax return. The child and dependent care must be provided in California to qualify for the credit.

The taxpayer income needs to be $40,000 or less to claim 50% of the childcare. 43% is for income $40,001 but not over $70,000. 34% is for taxpayers whose income is $70,001 but not over $100,000. Taxpayers who make more than $100,000 are unable to claim the California childcare credit.

The qualifications required to claim the Child and Dependent Care Expense Credit in California differ from federal law in the following ways:

> ➢ Care can only be provided in California.
> ➢ Nonresidents must have earned wages or self-employment income earned in California.
> ➢ The credit is a percentage of the federal credit.
> ➢ RDPs may file a joint return and claim the credit.

For California purposes, the following are considered dependent care benefits that are reported in box 10 of the taxpayer's W-2:

> ➢ Employer benefits paid directly to either the taxpayer or their care provider to care for a qualifying person(s) while the taxpayer or spouse worked.
> ➢ Employer provided daycare facilities.
> ➢ Generally deducted from the salary.

As on the federal form, if the spouse or RDP were a student or disabled, the taxpayer would be able to claim $250 (or $500 if the taxpayer has more than two qualifying children) as actual earned income. If both the taxpayer and the spouse or RDP were students in the same month, they would claim $250 each for that month (or those months, if several) as their actual earned income.

Nonrefundable Child and Dependent Care Expense Credit Code 232

To qualify for the nonrefundable credit the child must be under the age of 13. A dependent that is physically and/or mentally incapable of caring for themselves would also qualify. Care must be provided in California for qualifying individuals. The federal adjusted gross income is less than $100,000. FTB Form 3506 is attached to Form 540.

However, to qualify according to California law, the child must be a citizen or national of the U.S. or a resident of the U.S., Canada, or Mexico.

Special Credits

California residents have a variety of additional special tax credits available to them that are identified by codes. If the taxpayer can claim more than two credits, use Schedule P (540) and attach it to the tax return. Many claimed credits are income-limited, also known as "Tentative Minimum Tax" (TMT). Special credits include the following:

- ➢ Code 163: Credit for the Senior Head of Household.
- ➢ Code 170: Credit for Joint Custody Head of Household.
- ➢ Code 173: Credit for the Dependent Parent.
- ➢ Code 197: Credit for the Child Adoption Costs.

Credit for Senior Head of Household

Taxpayer may claim Code 163 if:

- ➢ Taxpayer was 65 years or older on December 31 for current tax year.
- ➢ Taxpayer qualified for head of household in 2020 or 2021 by providing a household for qualifying person who passed away during 2020 or 2021.
- ➢ Taxpayers AGI is not over $89,931 for 2022.

If taxpayer turned 65 on January 1, 2023, the individual is 65 on December 31, 2022.

Credit for Joint Custody Head of Household Code 170

This credit cannot be claimed if the taxpayer is using the following filing statuses:

- ➢ Married/RDP Filing Jointly.
- ➢ Head of Household.
- ➢ Surviving Spouse.

The credit is claimed if the taxpayer is unmarried or married/RDP filing separately at the end of 2022; and has provided more than one-half of the household expenses for the taxpayer's home, which also served as the primary home for the dependent child, stepchild, or grandchild for at least 146 days, but not more than 219 days of the taxable year, or it will no longer be considered joint custody. Additionally, the custody arrangement must be part of a decree of dissolution or legal separation or a written agreement between the parents where the proceedings have begun, but a decree of dissolution or legal separation has not been completed. The credit amount equals 30% of the net tax found on Form 540, line 43 or 44, but only up to $556.

Credit for Dependent Parent Code 173

To be able to claim this credit the taxpayer's filing status cannot be single, head of household, qualifying surviving spouse/RDP, or married/RDP filing jointly. This credit is only claimed if the following apply:

> ➤ Taxpayer's was married/or an RDP at the end of the current tax year and filed as married/RDP filing separately.
> ➤ Taxpayer's spouse/RDP was not a member of the taxpayer's household during the last 6-months of the year.
> ➤ Taxpayer furnished over one-half the household expenses for the dependent mother's or father's, whether or not the dependent lived there.

Adoption Credit Code 197

If the taxpayer adopted a child and claimed the adoption credit on their federal return, if the child was from California, then the taxpayer could claim a credit. The credit is 50% of the cost. If the credit was more than $2,500 then the taxpayer would carryforward to future years. Adopting a child from another country or another state do not qualify. Included in the cost to claim for an adoption are:

> ➤ Department of Social Services or a licensed adoption agency fees.
> ➤ Unreimbursed medical insurances related to the adoption process.
> ➤ Travel expense for the adopting family.

Nonrefundable Renter's Credit (Line 46)

If the taxpayer paid rent on their principal California residence for at least six months of the tax year, and their California AGI is within certain limits, the taxpayer may qualify for this credit. The following conditions determine whether one qualifies for the Nonrefundable Renter's Credit:

> ➤ The taxpayer was a resident of California in the current tax year.
> ➤ The California income is $49,220 or less if the filing status is Single or Married/RDP filing separate, or $98,440 or less if Married/RDP Filing Jointly, Head of Household, or Surviving spouse with qualifying dependent.
> ➤ The taxpayer paid rent for at least half of the current tax year on their principal residence on California property.
> ➤ The taxpayer did not live with another person for more than half the year (such as a parent) who claimed them as a dependent in the current tax year.
> ➤ The taxpayer is not a minor living under the care of a parent, foster parent, or legal guardian.
> ➤ For more than half the year, the taxpayer rented property that was not exempt from California property tax in the current tax year.
> ➤ If married, neither the taxpayer nor the spouse was granted a homeowner's property tax exemption during the current tax year. The taxpayer can still qualify for the credit even though their spouse claimed a homeowner's exemption if each of them maintained a separate residence for the entire current tax year.

If the taxpayer meets the requirements to claim the credit, the amount is as follows:

> ➤ Single/Married or RDP filing separately $60

➢ Married/RDP Filing Jointly	$120
➢ Head of Household or Surviving spouse	$120

Credit for Taxes Paid to the Other States, Code 187

California taxpayers may qualify to receive a credit against the California tax paid to another state. Not all states allow California income to use 540 Schedule S to avoid double taxation. If using Schedule S, make sure to enter Code 187 in the appropriate box.

The credit is intended to be applied when a California resident is taxed by the other state as a nonresident of that state, but not to a situation in which the resident is taxed by both states. This residency rule does not apply to certain U.S. government officials considered California residents. This exception is to ensure that certain officials will not be denied credit when they are treated as residents of the other state, as well as California.

If the taxpayer is a nonresident who earned income from California, they must file a California nonresident income tax return in addition to their resident state return. This situation would mean that the income could be taxed twice: once by California and once by the taxpayer's resident state. The taxpayer could use Californian Schedule S to reduce the tax on the earned income to avoid the double taxation. Nonresident taxpayers can only claim the California credit if their resident state does not allow a credit on the income for the same reason.

State Taxes Withheld

Enter the total California income tax withheld from the following sources on Form 540, line 71:

> ➢ Form(s) W-2, box 17.
> ➢ Form(s) W-2G, box 15.
> ➢ Form(s) 1099-MISC, box 16.
> ➢ Form(s) 1099-R, box 12.
> ➢ Form(s) 1099-DIV, box 14.
> ➢ Form(s) 1099-INT, box 15.
> ➢ Form(s) 1099-OID, box 12.

Do not include any city or county tax withheld or any tax withheld by other states.

Part 1 Review Questions

To obtain the maximum benefit from this chapter, LTP recommends that you complete each of the following questions and then compare them to the answers with feedback that immediately follow. Under governing self-study standards, vendors are required to present review questions intermittently throughout each self-study course.

These questions and explanations are not part of the final examination and will not be graded by LTP.

CPTC1.1

Which state form is used to claim the state dependent care credit?

    a. Form 8863
    b. Form 3506
    c. Form 8812
    d. Form 3008

CPTC1.2
Gabby moved to California in February. How many months does she need to pay rent to qualify for renter's credit?

    a. 3 months
    b. 9 months
    c. 6 months
    d. 12 months

CPTC1.3
Which of the following best describes California's child and dependent care expense credit?

    a. Refundable credit
    b. Nonrefundable credit
    c. Partially refundable credit
    d. Expired credit

CPTC1.4
California Child and Dependent care expenses are only available for taxpayers with a federal AGI of what amount?

    a. $250,000 or less
    b. $125,000 or less
    c. $100,000 or less
    d. Unlimited income

CPTC1.5
A taxpayer with income less than $40,000 will qualify for the Child and Dependent Care credit percentage.

    a. 75%
    b. 50%
    c. 43%
    d. 34%

CPTC1.6
Joan, 65, cares for her daughter, Pati. Which income would not allow her to claim Senior Head of Household?

    a. Joan's AGI is $89,999.
    b. Joan's AGI is $75,931.
    c. Joan's AGI is $89,132.
    d. Joan's AGI is $90,125.

CPTC1.7
Freddy has provided for Junior for the last 6 months of the year. Which filing status will allow Freddy to claim the Joint Custody Head of Household?

    a. Freddy is filing Married/RDP Filing jointly.
    b. Freddy is filing HOH.
    c. Freddy is filing Surviving Spouse.
    d. Freddy is filing unmarried.

CPTC1.8
Which expenses could the taxpayer claim for the adoption credit?

    a. Adoption agency fees.
    b. Travel to Mexico to see a child.
    c. Unreimbursed medical bills for the parents.
    d. Travel to Nevada to see a child.

CPTC1.9
Alex goes yearly to Yuma, AZ during November – December for business. He receives wages earned in Arizona on his W-2. Which form would he need to file with his California return to report taxes paid to another state?

    a. CA Schedule 540
    b. Schedule P
    c. Schedule S
    d. Schedule D

CPTC1.10
Which box on the W-2 reports California income tax?

    a. Box 15
    b. Box 17
    c. Box 16
    d. Box 14

Part 1 Review Questions Answers

CPTC1.1
Which state form is used to claim the state dependent care credit?

    a. Form 8863
    b. Form 3506
    c. Form 8812
    d. Form 3008

Feedback: Review section *Child and Dependent Care Expanse Credit.*

CPTC1.2
Gabby moved to California in February. How many months does she need to pay rent to qualify for renter's credit?

    a. 3 months
    b. 9 months
    c. 6 months
    d. 12 months

Feedback: Review section *Nonrefundable Renter's Credit.*

CPTC1.3
Which of the following best describes California's child and dependent care expense credit?

    a. Refundable credit
    b. Nonrefundable credit
    c. Partially refundable credit
    d. Expired credit

Feedback: Review section *Child and Dependent Care Expense Credit.*

CPTC1.4
California Child and Dependent care expenses are only available for taxpayers with a federal AGI of what amount?

    a. $250,000 or less
    b. $125,000 or less
    c. $100,000 or less
    d. Unlimited income

Feedback: Review section *Child and Dependent Care Expense.*

CPTC1.5
A taxpayer with income less than $40,000 will qualify for the Child and Dependent Care credit percentage.

    a. 75%
    b. 50%
    c. 43%
    d. 34%

Feedback: Review section *Child and Dependent Care Expense.*

CPTC1.6
Joan, 65, cares for her daughter, Pati. Which income would not allow her to claim Senior Head of Household?

    a. Joan's AGI is $89,999.
    b. Joan's AGI is $75,931.
    c. Joan's AGI is $89,132.
    d. Joan's AGI is $90,125.

Feedback: Review section *Credit for Senior Head of Household.*

CPTC1.7
Freddy has provided for Junior for the last 6 months of the year. Which filing status will allow Freddy to claim the Joint Custody Head of Household?

    a. Freddy is filing Married/RDP Filing jointly.
    b. Freddy is filing HOH.
    c. Freddy is filing Surviving Spouse.
    d. Freddy is filing unmarried.

Feedback: Review section Joint Custody for Head of Household.

CPTC1.8
Which expenses could the taxpayer claim for the adoption credit?

    a. Adoption agency fees.
    b. Travel to Mexico to see a child.
    c. Unreimbursed medical bills for the parents.
    d. Travel to Nevada to see a child.

Feedback: Review section *Adoption Credit*.

CPTC1.9
Alex goes yearly to Yuma, AZ during November – December for business. He receives wages earned in Arizona on his W-2. Which form would he need to file with his California return to report taxes paid to another state?

    a. CA Schedule 540
    b. Schedule P
    c. Schedule S
    d. Schedule D

Feedback: Review section *Credit for Taxes Paid to the Other States*.

CPTC1.10
Which box on the W-2 reports California income tax?

    a. Box 15
    b. Box 17
    c. Box 16
    d. Box 14

Feedback: Review section *State Taxes Withheld*.

Part 2 California EITC (CalEITC) and Other Credits and Payments

California residents may qualify for a refundable state EITC. Refundable California Earned Income Tax Credit (CalEITC) can be claimed by using FTB Form 3514 and is designed to help low-income working taxpayers receive more money to help with everyday essentials. Eligible sources of earned income are wages, self-employment, salaries, tips, and other employee compensation subject to state withholding. The maximum income to claim CalEITC is $30,000 for tax year 2022, and investment interest cannot exceed $4,389 for the year. California conforms to the federal classifications for investment and interest income.

The qualifications required to claim the EITC in California differ from federal law in the following ways:

➤ The state credit is allowed for wage income earned in California that is subject to California withholding.
➤ California allows eligible individuals and their spouse who have a valid ITIN or who have qualifying children who have a valid federal ITIN.
➤ Nonresidents must have earned wage income from California.
➤ California income is less than $30,001.
➤ The nontaxable military combat pay may be included for California purposes whether it was chosen on the federal return or not.

➢ Taxpayer may exclude In Home Supportive Services (IHSS) payments and Medicare waiver payments from their earned income.
➢ California does not include self-employment income as earned income for the EITC.

The following five FTB notices were created to help administer CalEITC and explain to the taxpayer the process if they were denied or need information from the taxpayer.

FTB 4502, *Additional Documentation Required*: This notice is sent to clarify information provided on the tax return. This notice will detail the specific instructions to the taxpayer on which specific documents must be sent to validate their claim for CalEITC, such as:

➢ Copies of W-2 statements.
➢ Copies of the last two paycheck stubs.
➢ Business bank statements and credit card statements to corroborate the reported business income.
➢ Any certification, license, permit, or registration required for the business (e.g., taxi, cosmetology, food service, contractor, vendor).
➢ Any federal Schedule K-1 from a partnership.

If the taxpayer claims a qualifying child, the FTB may request documentation that the child lived with the taxpayer. If the taxpayer does not return the requested documentation to substantiate the claim, the CalEITC claim will be denied.

The taxpayer will receive another notice, FTB 5818, *Notice of Tax Return Change*, advising them that their refund has changed. If the documentation is received and the claim is substantiated, the refund will be sent to the taxpayer within eight weeks, and no adjustment will need to be made.

FTB 4513, *Earned Income Tax Credit Acceptance Letter*: This notice is sent to the taxpayer after submitting the documentation and their claim was substantiated. This letter only serves as a notice for the year on the letter.

FTB 4514, *Annual Documentation Required*: This notice is sent when the FTB has already sent the taxpayer the CalEITC. The FTB has determined insufficient information to confirm that the taxpayer qualifies to claim CalEITC. The taxpayer has 30 days to comply with the notice and send the required documents to the FTB.

If the documentation is not received timely or does not substantiate the claim, the FTB will send the fifth notice, FTB 4515, *Earned Income Tax Credit-Adjustment Made*, which notifies the taxpayer of the specific reasons the qualifying child or the documentation was not accepted. The taxpayer can disagree with the FTB and file a Formal Claim for Refund to state why they disagree along with any relevant documentation.

As with the federal return, paid tax professionals must exercise due diligence to determine the taxpayer's eligibility for CalEITC. With all returns claiming the CalEITC, a paid preparer will complete the California due diligence questionnaire, FTB Form 3596, *Paid Preparer's California Earned Income Tax Credit Checklist*. If the taxpayer is audited regarding the validity or credit eligibility for EITC, Form FTB 4502, *Additional Documentation Required*, will be sent to the taxpayer to complete and submit with the documentation requested to prove their claim for EITC. If the paid tax professional fails to complete their due diligence requirements, the Franchise Tax Board could assess a $500 penalty for each failure to do so. The IRS assesses a penalty of $560 per failure, in addition to the penalty assessed by the FTB, adding up to a penalty of $2,740. If you wish to avoid this penalty, make sure you have completed ALL the due diligence.

Young Child Tax Credit

If the taxpayer qualifies for CalEITC and has a child(ren) under the age of 6 at the end of the year, the individual could be eligible for up to $1,083. Qualifying ITIN holders are eligible to receive the $1,083 for the qualifying child under 6. Income thresholds are more than $25,000 and phases out at $30,000.

California's College Access Tax Credit (CATC)

The College Access Tax Credit (CATC) will be available for taxable years 2018 to 2027. To claim the credit, the taxpayer must contribute to the CATC Fund administered by the California Educational Facilities Authority (CEFA). Taxpayers who contribute must receive a certificate from CEFA documenting the amount of the contribution and the credit amount to claim the credit on the state tax return. The allocated credit amount must be no more than 50% of the amount contributed in the previous tax year and must be certified by CEFA for the taxpayer.

The federal charitable deduction and the CATC credit cannot be used to reduce a taxpayer's AGI at the same time. If the federal charitable deduction was used to reduce the AGI on the federal return, the now-reduced AGI could not be the amount reduced by the CATC credit on the state return. This is known as "double-dipping" and is a fraudulent tax practice. If a taxpayer wishes to use the CATC credit on their state return, they must "un-reduce" the AGI and use the amount of AGI before the charitable deduction reduces it and then apply the CATC credit reduction to that larger amount. If the reduced AGI from the federal return is lower than after being reduced by the CATC credit, the taxpayer does not have to take the CATC credit and can continue to use the AGI amount from the federal return. Either way, however, the taxpayer cannot apply both the CATC and the federal charitable deduction simultaneously. See R&TC Section 17275.4.

Example: Juana Dee applied for a CATC reservation on October 31, 2021. Her proposed contribution is $10,000. CEFA grants a $5,000 credit reservation (50% of $10,000) on November 7. Juana made a $10,000 contribution to the fund on November 22, 2021. CEFA sends the credit certification to Juana on December 1. Juana may claim a $5,000 credit on her 2021 California tax return. She may claim a $10,000 charitable contribution on her federal return. However, she will not be able to claim both the charitable contribution and the CATC credit on her California return; she must choose one or the other, and since the charitable contribution deduction is greater than the credit, it would be in Juana's best interest to not use the CATC and keep the federally-deducted amount.

California Estimated Tax and Other Payments

California estimated tax and other payments are reported on Form 540, line 72.

71	California income tax withheld. See instructions	● 71		.00
72	2022 California estimated tax and other payments. See instructions	● 72		.00
73	Withholding (Form 592-B and/or Form 593). See instructions	● 73		.00
74	Excess SDI (or VPDI) withheld. See instructions	● 74		.00
75	Earned Income Tax Credit (EITC). See instructions	● 75		.00
76	Young Child Tax Credit (YCTC). See instructions	● 76		.00
77	Foster Youth Tax Credit (FYTC). See instructions	● 77		.00
78	Add line 71 through line 77. These are your total payments. See instructions	⊙ 78		.00

Payments

Portion of Form 540

Reporting the Estimated Payments Paid or Rollover

> ➢ All estimated tax payments were made using the 2022 Form 540-ES.
> ➢ Overpayments from 2021 that were applied to 2022.
> ➢ Payments sent by the taxpayer to the FTB with Form 3519 (extension).

Estimated Tax Payments

California estimated tax payments are similar to the federal system and are due on the same dates. Individuals who are required to make estimated payments and whose 2023 California AGI is more than $150,000 (or $75,000 if Married or RDP filing separately) must figure the estimated tax (including AMT) based on 90% of the tax paid for. Farmers and fishermen are excluded from this rule. Taxpayers whose California adjusted gross income is equal to or greater than $1,000,000 ($500,000 if Married/RDP filing separately) must use the amount of taxes imposed in the previous tax year to estimate how much tax might be imposed for the next year.

Taxpayers are required to pay 30% of the estimated payment for the first and fourth installment. The second installment will be 40% of the estimated payment. There is no third installment.

Payment Due Dates

Quarterly installments are due on the same days as the federal: April 15, June 15, and January 15. If the 15th of the month falls on a Saturday, Sunday, or legal holiday, the due date is the next business day. The fourth estimated payment due January 15 can be filed with the tax return by January 31. Suppose the taxpayer qualifies or is considered a farmer or fisherman. In that case, the taxpayer can pay all their estimated payments on January 15 or can file and pay the tax by March 1 and pay no estimated penalties. Taxpayers must pay estimated payments electronically once the payment exceeds $20,000, or the tax liability is over $80,000.

Amount of Estimated Tax Applied

The taxpayer can apply none, all, or a portion of their tax refund shown on line 97 toward the following year's tax liability. The election to "rollover" a portion of the refund is made on line 98. Once the taxpayer makes this election, the overpayment cannot be applied to a deficiency once the return's due date has passed.

Excess SDI or VPDI Withheld

For tax year 2022, the employee's California State Disability Insurance (CASDI) or Voluntary Plan (VPDI) maximum rate is 1.1% of wages up to a maximum withholding for CASDI of $1,601.60 (1.10% of the California wage limit of $145,600). If the taxpayer had more than one employer during 2022 and the various employers withheld a combined total of more than $1,601.60, the taxpayer may claim the amount over the withholding limit as a credit toward their state tax liability. If the taxpayer only had one job, they cannot claim the excess amount as credit and must instead recover from the employer the excess SDI or VPDI amount that was withheld. For a joint return, the taxpayer and his spouse would calculate the excess SDI or VPDI individually.

For tax year 2023, the SDI withholding is 0.9% on the taxable wage of $153,164. The maximum is $1,378.48.

Excess SDI or VPDI Worksheet: Use Whole Dollars Only

Follow the instructions below to figure the amount of income tax to enter on Form 540, line 74. If the taxpayer files as Married/RDP Filing Jointly, each individual must figure the excess separately.

Excess SDI (or VPDI) Worksheet
Use whole dollars only.

Follow the instructions below to figure the amount of excess SDI to enter on Form 540, line 74. If you are married/RDP and file a joint return, you must figure the amount of excess SDI (or VPDI) separately for each spouse/RDP.

	You	Your Spouse/RDP
1. Add amounts of SDI (or VPDI) withheld shown on your federal Forms W-2. Enter the total here 1		
2. 2022 SDI (or VPDI) limit. 2	$1,601.60	$1,601.60
3. Excess SDI (or VPDI) withheld. Subtract line 2 from line 1. Enter the results here. Combine the amounts on line 3 and enter the total, in **whole dollars only** on line 74 3		

If zero or less, enter -0- on line 74.

Excess SDI Worksheet

Overpaid Tax

The tax return needs to be accurate to avoid a refund delay. Correct numbers must be entered on lines 93-97.

Overpaid Tax/Tax Due	93 Payments balance. If line 78 is more than line 91, subtract line 91 from line 78 . . . . ⊙ 93	☐ . 00
	94 **Use Tax balance.** If line 91 is more than line 78, subtract line 78 from line 91 . . . . ⊙ 94	☐ . 00
	95 Payments after Individual Shared Responsibility Penalty. If line 93 is more than line 92, subtract line 92 from line 93. . . . . ⊙ 95	☐ . 00
	96 Individual Shared Responsibility Penalty Balance. If line 92 is more than line 93, subtract line 93 from line 92. . . . . ⊙ 96	☐ . 00
	97 Overpaid tax. If line 95 is more than line 64, subtract line 64 from line 95. . . . . ⊙ 97	☐ . 00

333   3103223   Form 540 2022 **Side 3**

Portion of Form 540

If the taxpayer has an amount on Form 540, line 78, that is more than the amount on line 91 of the same form, they have more payments and credits than the tax owed. Subtract the amount on Form 540, line 65, from Form 540, line 95, and enter the overpaid tax on Form 540, line 91. The taxpayer can choose from the following refund options, just like on the federal return:

➢ Direct deposit from the Franchise Tax Board into a checking or savings account.

➢ Refund check mailed to the taxpayer.
➢ Bank product administered by a paid tax preparer.
➢ Apply all or a portion of the refund to the following year's estimated tax payments.

Although the taxpayer has the same options for the federal and state returns, the taxpayer can make different selections on each return.

Amount Available

If the amount on Form 540, line 97, is more than the amount on line 64, the tax owed is less than the payments and credits. The taxpayer can have their entire amount refunded or make voluntary contributions. Voluntary contributions begin after line 100 and the codes are 400 to 446. These contributions lower the taxpayer's refund by the same amount they choose to contribute.

Portion of Form 540

Enter the amount from line 99 on line 115; if there are no entries on lines 110, 112, or line 113, the amount on line 115 is the taxpayer's refund. If there are entries on lines 100, 111, 112, or line 113, then the amounts on those lines must be added together to determine the amount of the tax liability that is due. Report the total amount due on line 114. If the amount on line 95 is less than line 64, subtract line 64 from line 95 and enter the difference on line 115; this is the refund amount.

The taxpayer can have the refund amount directly deposited into their accounts(s) by indicating the routing number (RTN) and the account number on the lines. The taxpayer can designate up to two accounts. Do not attach a voided check or deposit slip if mailing the return. Indicate whether the account is a checking or savings account by checking the relevant box on the line (shown above). As with the federal return, the routing numbers must be nine digits, and the first two digits must be 01 through 12 or 21 through 32.

Part 2 Review Questions

To obtain the maximum benefit from this chapter, LTP recommends that you complete each of the following questions and then compare them to the answers with feedback that immediately follow. Under governing self-study standards, vendors are required to present review questions intermittently throughout each self-study course.

These questions and explanations are not part of the final examination and will not be graded by LTP.

CPTC2.1
Refundable credits are considered payments to the state. Which of the following is a state refundable credit?

    a. Earned Income Tax Credit
    b. Excess CASDI or VPDI
    c. Additional Child Tax Credit
    d. American Opportunity Credit

CPTC2.2
Cara is a California resident and has earned income on her federal return. Which of the following credits would Cara most likely qualify for in California?

    a. Earned income tax credit
    b. Lifetime learning credit
    c. Social Security benefits
    d. Additional child tax credit

CPTC2.3
The FTB has created 5 notices to help administer CalEITC, which is not one of the notices?

    a. FTB 582
    b. FTB 4502
    c. FTB 4513
    d. FTB 4515

CPTC2.4
The Young Child Tax Credit is available for which of the following?

    a. Qualifying ITIN holders with income more than $30,000.
    b. Qualifying ITIN holders with a child and income of $25,963.
    c. Qualifying ITIN holders with less than $25,000.
    d. Qualifying ITIN holders with an income of less than $25,000 and a child 6 years of age.

CPTC2.5
College Access Tax Credit can be claimed on both the federal and state return.

    a. True
    b. False

CPTC2.6
California estimated tax payments must be paid on the following dates: April 15, June 15, September 15, and January 15 of the following year.

    a. True
    b. False

CPTC2.7
Which taxpayer would have to pay California estimated payments electronically?

    a. Jose's estimated payment is $15,000.
    b. Miguel's tax liability is $75,000.
    c. Caroline's tax liability is $91,123.
    d. Lydia's estimated payment is $1,943.

CPTC2.8
What is the CASDI amount for 2022?

    a. $1,601.60
    b. $1,378.48
    c. $1,347.60
    d. $2,040.20

CPTC2.9
What is the CASDI amount for 2023?

    a. $1,601.60
    b. $1,378.48
    c. $1,347.60
    d. $2,040.20

CPTC2.10
Can the current year overpayment of tax be rolled over to the following year?

    a. Yes
    b. No

Part 2 Review Questions Answers

CPTC2.1
Refundable credits are considered payments to the state. Which of the following is a state refundable credit?

    a. Earned Income Tax Credit
    b. Excess CASDI or VPDI
    c. Additional Child Tax Credit
    d. American Opportunity Credit

Feedback: Review section *California EITC (CalEITC)*.

CPTC2.2
Cara is a California resident and has earned income on her federal return. Which of the following credits would Cara most likely qualify for in California?

    a. Earned income tax credit
    b. Lifetime learning credit
    c. Social Security benefits
    d. Additional child tax credit

Feedback: Review section *California EITC (CalEITC)*.

CPTC2.3

The FTB has created 5 notices to help administer CalEITC, which is not one of the notices?

    a. FTB 582
    b. FTB 4502
    c. FTB 4513
    d. FTB 4515

Feedback: Review section *California EITC (CalEITC)*.

CPTC2.4

The Young Child Tax Credit is available for which of the following?

    a. Qualifying ITIN holders with income more than $30,000.
    b. Qualifying ITIN holders with a child and income of $25,963.
    c. Qualifying ITIN holders with less than $25,000.
    d. Qualifying ITIN holders with an income of less than $25,000 and a child 6 years of age.

Feedback: Review section *Young Child Tax Credit*.

CPTC2.5

College Access Tax Credit can be claimed on both the federal and state return.

    a. True
    b. False

Feedback: Review section *California's College Access Tax Credit*.

CPTC2.6

California estimated tax payments must be paid on the following dates: April 15, June 15, September 15, and January 15 of the following year.

    a. Truc
    b. False

Feedback: Review section *Estimated Tax Payments*.

CPTC2.7

Which taxpayer would have to pay California estimated payments electronically?

    a. Jose's estimated payment is $15,000.
    b. Miguel's tax liability is $75,000.
    c. Caroline's tax liability is $91,123.
    d. Lydia's estimated payment is $1,943.

Feedback: Review section *Estimated Tax Payments*.

CPTC2.8
What is the CASDI amount for 2022?

    a. $1,601.60
    b. $1,378.48
    c. $1,347.60
    d. $2,040.20

Feedback: Review section *Excess SDI or VPDI Withheld.*

CPTC2.9
What is the CASDI amount for 2023?

    a. $1,601.60
    b. $1,378.48
    c. $1,347.60
    d. $2,040.20

Feedback: Review section *Excess SDI or VPDI Withheld.*

CPTC2.10
Can the current year overpayment of tax be rolled over to the following year?

    a. Yes
    b. No

Feedback: Review section *Overpaid Tax.*

Takeaways

California differs from federal law in many ways; from income tax withholding and estimated payments to real estate withholding, there are many different types of tax payments. Certain types of income taxed at the federal level are exempt from tax in California, while other types are taxed in California but are not on the federal return. In California, tax credits are deducted directly from the tax amount due (not from the tax liability), making the deductions useful. The California tax preparer must know these differences and details by heart to always prepare accurate and ethical returns.

TEST YOUR KNOWLEDGE!
Go online to take a practice quiz.

Chapter 8 Itemized Deductions

Introduction

There are two personal deductions: Standard Deductions and Itemized Deductions. A *standard deduction* is a set amount that the taxpayer can claim based on their filing status. Itemized deductions are certain personal expenses the IRS allows taxpayers to deduct. Itemized deductions are computed on the tax return using Schedule A, *Itemized Deductions*. The taxpayer should choose whichever option is best for their tax situation.

Itemized deductions are beneficial if the total amount exceeds the standard deduction. Some taxpayers must itemize deductions because they do not qualify for the standard deduction. Taxpayers not eligible for the standard deduction include nonresident aliens and individuals who file a tax return for less than 12 months. When a married couple files individual returns, if one spouse itemizes deductions, the other spouse must also itemize deductions. Even if standard deductions deliver the best option for them. See Publication 501, *Exemptions, Standard Deduction, and Filing Information.*

Objectives

At the end of this chapter, the student will:

> ➢ Explain which deductions are limited to the 7.5% floor.
> ➢ Identify which taxpayer is eligible to use Form 2106 after December 31, 2017, until December 31, 2025.
> ➢ Classify which taxpayer is eligible to use Form 3903 after December 31, 2017, until December 31, 2025.

Resources

Form 1040	Publication 17	Instructions Form 1040
Form 2106	Publication 463	Instructions Form 2106
Form 4684	Publication 502	Instructions Form 4684
Form 4952	Publication 526	Instructions Form 4952
Form 8283	Publication 529	Instructions Form 8283
Schedule A	Publication 530	Instructions for Schedule A
Publication 1771	Publication 936	Tax Topics 501–506, 508–515
Publication 597		

Table of Contents

Part 1 Itemized Deductions

TCJA and Itemized Deductions

The Tax Cuts and Jobs Act (TCJA) has eliminated the overall limitation of itemized deductions based on the taxpayer's adjusted gross income. TCJA also changed the limitations that can impact the total itemized deduction amount; for example, the total amount that can be deducted from the state and local income tax on Schedule A, line 5, is now capped at $10,000 ($5,000 for MFS); taxpayers may not be able to claim all of their expenses as deductions.

For example, in 2017, George's itemized deductions for his state and local taxes was $17,000. George's financial situation did not change, and he expected to be able to deduct the same amount in 2018. However, even though George would still have qualified for a $17,000 itemized deduction under the old rules, George will only receive a $10,000 deduction on line 5 under the TCJA. His deduction amount is capped. Taxpayers should itemize or consider itemizing if they meet the following criteria:

➢ Taxpayer would get a higher amount of deductions by itemizing.
➢ The taxpayer had large unreimbursed medical or dental expenses that amounted to more than 7.5% of their adjusted gross income.
➢ The taxpayer paid mortgage interest.
➢ The taxpayer paid points to discount the interest rate.
➢ The taxpayer had casualty or theft losses that were declared during a federal disaster.
➢ The taxpayer made contributions to qualified charities and has receipts for recordkeeping.
➢ The total of the taxpayer's itemized deductions is higher than the standard deduction to which the taxpayer is entitled.
➢ The taxpayer paid state and local taxes (may be capped).
➢ The taxpayer paid property taxes (may be capped).

Itemizing While Married Filing Separate

If taxpayers are filing MFS and one spouse itemizes, the other spouse is obligated to itemize. This is true even if the spouse's total deductions may be less than the standard deduction to which the individual would otherwise be entitled. If one spouse later amends the return, the other spouse must also amend their return. To formally agree to the amendments, both taxpayers must file a "consent to assessment" for any additional tax that one might owe as a result of the amendment. In the case of a spouse who qualifies to file as Head of household, this rule will not apply. The spouse who qualifies as Head of household is not required to itemize deductions even if the spouse who is required to file MFS decides to itemize their deductions. However, if the spouse filing Head of household decides to itemize deductions, the spouse filing MFS is required to itemize deductions.

Medical and Dental Expenses

Medical care expenses can be deducted if amounts are paid for the diagnosis, cure, treatment, or prevention of a disease or condition affecting any part or function of the body. Procedures such as facelifts, hair transplants, hair removal, and liposuction are generally not deductible. Cosmetic surgery is only deductible if it is to improve a deformity arising from or directly related to a congenital abnormality, a personal injury from an accident or trauma, or a disfiguring disease. Medications are only deductible if prescribed by a doctor. The taxpayer can deduct any medical and dental expenses that exceed 7.5% of the taxpayer's AGI as shown on Form 1040, page 1, line 10. The 7.5% has been made a permanent floor.

Examples of deductible medical expenses include the following:

- Personal protective equipment (PPE)
    - Masks
    - Hand sanitizer
    - Wipes
- Medical insurance premiums
- Medicare
- Dental treatment
- Prescription medicines
- Medical service fees
- Medical mileage
- Taxi
- Ambulance
- Cost of other needed transportation
- Medical care
- Acupuncture
- Seeing eye guide dogs care cost
- Eye exams
- Eyeglasses
- Contact lenses
- Solutions to clean contact lenses
- Eye surgery for nearsightedness
- Hospital fees
- Lab fees
- X-rays
- Psychiatric care
- Hearing aids and batteries
- Other medical aids
- Nursing care
- Artificial limbs & teeth
- Birth control pills
- Chiropractor services
- Inpatient care meals

➤ Lodging during hospital treatments while away from home for inpatient and outpatient care
➤ Capital expenses for medical equipment

Some home improvements may be deducted if their main purpose is to provide a medical benefit. The deduction is limited to the difference between the increase in the fair market value of the home and the cost of the improvements.

Examples of nondeductible medical expenses include over-the-counter medications, bottled water, diaper services, expenses for general health items, health club dues (unless related to a specific medical condition), funeral expenses, illegal operations and treatments, weight-loss programs (unless recommended by a doctor for a specific medical condition), and swimming pool dues. However, prescribed therapeutic swimming costs are deductible.

Other nondeductible items are insurance premiums paid for life insurance; loss of earnings, limbs, or sight; guaranteed payments for days the taxpayer is hospitalized for sickness or injury; and the medical insurance coverage portion of the taxpayer's auto insurance. Cafeteria plans are not deductible unless the premiums are included in box 1 of Form W-2.

The medical mileage rate for 2022 is 18 cents per mile from January to June and 22 cents per mile from July to December. For 2023 the rate is the same: 22 cents per mile.

Spouse and Dependent Medical Expenses

The taxpayer is allowed to claim medical expenses that were paid for their spouse. To claim the expenses, they must have been married at the time the spouse received medical treatment. If the taxpayer and spouse do not live in a community property state and file separate returns, each would claim only their paid medical expenses. If the taxpayer and spouse live in a community property state and file separate returns, the medical expenses must be divided equally if they were paid out of community funds.

The taxpayer is allowed to claim medical expenses that were paid for their dependent(s). To claim these expenses, the individual must have been a dependent at the time the medical treatment was completed or when the expenses were paid. An individual would qualify as a dependent if all the following are true:

➤ The individual was a qualifying child or a qualifying relative.
➤ The individual was a U.S. citizen or a resident of the United States, Canada, or Mexico.
➤ The dependent gross income was $4,400 or more.

Medical expenses can be deducted for any individual who is a dependent of the taxpayer, even if the taxpayer cannot claim the exemption for the individual on his or her return.

Example: James, age 66, has an AGI of $35,000; 7.5% of $35,000 is $2,625.00, and James had medical expenses of $2,700; therefore, James would be able to deduct $75.00 for medical expenses. The $75.00 is the difference between his expenses and the 7.5% "floor" needed to deduct medical expenses.

Example: Ryan, age 35, has an AGI of $40,000; 7.5% of $40,000 is $3,000, and Ryan had medical expenses of $2,500; therefore, Ryan will not be able to deduct his medical expenses since they are not over $3,000.

Medical Expense Reimbursement

Taxpayers can deduct only their medical amounts paid during the taxable year. If the taxpayer receives a reimbursement for a medical expense, the taxpayer must reduce their total medical deduction for the year. If taxpayers are reimbursed for more than their medical expenses, they may have to include the excess as income. If the taxpayer paid the entire premium for medical insurance, the taxpayer would not include the excess reimbursement as gross income.

Premiums paid for qualified long-term care insurance contracts can be deducted within limits for long-term care insurance.

Qualified long-term care premiums are limited to the following and are reported on Schedule A for 2022:

Age 40 or under	$450
Age 41–50	$850
Age 51–60	$1,690
Age 61–70	$4,510
Age 71 or over	$5,640

2023 Long-Term Care rates are.

Age 40 or under	$480
Age 41–50	$890
Age 51–60	$1,790
Age 61–70	$4,770
Age 71 or over	$5,940

Fees paid to retirement or nursing homes designed for medical care and/or psychiatric care are deductible. Meals, lodging, and prescriptions are deductible only if the individual is in the home primarily to get medical care. If the main reason the individual is in the home is personal, meals and lodging are not deductible.

Improvements made to the taxpayer's home due to a medical condition may increase the fair market value of the house. Some examples are:

➢ Construction of entrance or exit ramps
➢ Widening doorways or hallways
➢ Lowering cabinets and countertops
➢ Installing lifts
➢ Modifying stairways
➢ Adding handrails or grab bars in the home

If the cost of the improvement is more than the new fair market value, then the difference is a medical expense.

Example: Caroline had a lift installed in her two-story house for medical reasons. The cost of the lift was $12,000. The increase in her fair market value was $10,000. Therefore, she can deduct $2,000 as a medical expense.

Taxes Paid

Certain taxes such as state, local, or foreign taxes, real estate taxes, and personal property taxes can be deducted by the taxpayer. Property taxes can only be deducted by the owner of the property. Real estate taxes are deductible on Schedule A for all property owned by the taxpayer; it is not limited to personal residences like mortgage interest. Deeded time-shares may have a deductible real estate tax as well.

State and Local General Sales Tax (SALT)

State and local tax amounts withheld from wages are reported on line 5 of Schedule A, and the taxpayer may deduct the amounts of the following state and local taxes to reduce the taxpayer's federal tax liability:

> ➤ State and local taxes withheld from wages during the current tax year.
> ➤ State estimated tax payments made during the current year.
> ➤ State and local taxes paid in the current tax year for a prior tax year.
> ➤ Mandatory contributions made to the California, New Jersey, or New York Non-occupational Disability Benefit Fund.
> ➤ Mandatory contributions made to the Rhode Island Temporary Disability Fund or Washington State Supplemental Workmen's Compensation Fund.
> ➤ Mandatory contributions to the Alaska, California, New Jersey, or Pennsylvania state unemployment funds.
> ➤ Mandatory contributions to state family leave programs such as the New Jersey Family Leave Insurance (FLI) program and the California Paid Family Leave program.

Interest and penalties for paying taxes late are never a deduction. For tax returns after December 31, 2017, and before January 1, 2026, the state and local tax (SALT) is capped at $10,000 or $5,000 if the taxpayer is married filing separate.

General Sales Tax

If the taxpayer selects to deduct state and local sales tax, the taxpayer will check box 5a on Schedule A. The taxpayer can deduct either actual expenses or an amount figured using the Optional State Sales Tax Tables. If the Optional State Sales Tax Tables is chosen, taxpayer must check the sales tax tables for their local jurisdictions and follow the calculation instructions found at www.irs.gov/individuals/sales-tax-deduction-calculator. If the filing status is MFS and one spouse elects to use the sales tax, the other spouse must use the sales tax method as well. Actual receipts showing general sales taxes paid should be kept. See Schedule A Instructions.

Señor 1040 Says: The taxpayer can either deduct state and local general sales taxes or state and local income taxes; not both.

Real Estate Taxes

State, local, or foreign real estate taxes paid for real estate owned by the taxpayer are deducted on line 5b of Schedule A, only if the taxes are based on the assessed value of the property. If the taxpayer's real estate taxes are included in the mortgage and paid out of an escrow account, the amount paid by the mortgage company is the deductible amount.

After December 31, 2017, the taxpayer is no longer able to deduct foreign personal or real property taxes. If the taxes are based on the assessed value of the property, state and local real estate taxes paid on real estate owned by the taxpayer are deducted on line 5b of Schedule A. Items such as leasing solar equipment that has been added to the taxpayer's property tax bill is not a real estate tax deduction.

If the monthly mortgage payment includes an amount placed in an escrow account for real estate taxes, the taxpayer may not be able to deduct the total amount placed in escrow. Only deduct the real estate taxes that the third party actually paid to the taxing authority. If the third party does not notify the taxpayer of the amount of real estate tax paid, the taxpayer should contact the third party or the taxing authority to report the correct amount on the return. If the taxpayer bought or sold real estate during the year, the real estate taxes charged to the buyer should be reported on the settlement statement and in box 5 of Form 1099-S.

Personal Property Taxes

Personal property taxes are deducted on line 5c of Schedule A. The taxpayer should deduct state or local tax that is imposed yearly based on the value of the property. After December 31, 2017, the taxpayer must deduct personal property taxes on line 5c of Schedule A. The taxpayer should be careful not to include refunds, rebates, interest, or penalties as taxes paid.

Example: Lourdes pays a yearly registration fee for her car. Part of her fee is based on value, and the other part is based on the weight of the car. Lourdes can only deduct the part of the fee that was based on the value of the car, not the part based on the weight of the car.

Other Taxes

The taxpayer can claim a credit for foreign taxes as a nonrefundable credit on Form 1040, Schedule 3, line 1, or take it as an itemized deduction on Schedule A under "other taxes." The taxpayer may or may not have to complete Form 1116, *Foreign Tax Credits*. After December 31, 2017, the taxpayer must deduct other taxes on line 6 of Schedule A. Other taxes consist of foreign taxes earned from overseas investments and not from real property owned abroad.

Nondeductible Taxes and Fees

Nondeductible miscellaneous taxes and fees:

➢ Federal income tax and most excise taxes.
➢ Employment tax, such as Social Security, Medicare, federal unemployment, and railroad retirement taxes.
➢ Federal estate tax.
➢ Fines and penalties.
➢ Gift tax.
➢ License fees (such as for a marriage or driver's license).
➢ Certain state and local taxes such as the gasoline tax, car inspections, and other improvements to personal property.

Home Mortgage Interest and Points

Home acquisition debt is a mortgage that a taxpayer took out to buy, build, or substantially improve a qualified home. A qualified loan is a loan used to acquire the taxpayer's primary residence or a second home, and the loan must be secured by the individual property.

A home mortgage is any loan that is secured for the taxpayer's main home or second home. To make the mortgage interest deductible, the loan must be secured and can be a first or second mortgage, a home improvement loan, or a home equity loan. The deductibility of interest expense is determined based on how the loan proceeds are used, otherwise referred to as interest tracing. For loans acquired before the TCJA went into effect on December 15, 2017, the interest on up to $1 million of debt ($500,000 for Married filing separately) that was used for acquiring, constructing, or substantially improving the residence is deductible.

If the taxpayer has a primary home and a second home, the home acquisition and home equity debt dollar limit apply to the total mortgage on both homes.

For home loans secured after December 15, 2017, the deductible amount is limited to $750,000 ($375,000 for Married filing separately). Taxpayers may use the 2017 threshold amounts if the following are true:

➢ if the home acquisition debt was taken on prior to December 16, 2017
➢ if they entered into a written, binding contract on or before December 15, 2017, in order to close on a principal residence before January 1, 2018
➢ if they purchased the property before April 1, 2018.

If a taxpayer refinances a home acquisition loan that was acquired before the TCJA went into effect, the refinanced loan is subject to the same provisions as the original, pre-TCJA loan, but only up to the amount of the balance of the original loan. Any additional debt not used to buy, build, or substantially improve the home is not a home acquisition debt. For example, Cheryl took out a home equity line of credit for $100,000. She used $10,000 to redo the master bedroom and then used the rest to go on a world cruise. The $10,000 could be used as home acquisition debt, she is unable to use the world cruise as home acquisition debt. That could be considered income to Cheryl. See Publication 936.

Grandfathered Debt

If the taxpayer took out a mortgage on their home before October 14, 1987, or refinanced the loan, it may qualify as grandfathered debt. Grandfathered debt does not limit the amount of interest that can be deducted. All the interest paid on this loan is fully deductible home mortgage interest. However, the grandfathered debt amount could limit the home acquisition debt. For example, Sergio took out a first mortgage of $200,000 to buy a house in 1986. The mortgage was a 7-year balloon note, and the entire balance on the note was due in 1993. Sergio refinanced the debt in 1993 with a new 30-year mortgage. The refinanced debt is treated as grandfathered debt for the entire 30 years of the loan.

The main home is the property where the taxpayer lives the most. The second home is a similar property. The main or second home could be a boat or recreational vehicle, both must provide basic living accommodations, which include a sleeping space, a toilet, and cooking facilities. Mortgage interest and points are reported to the taxpayer on Form 1098 and entered on line 8 of Schedule A.

Form 1098, *Mortgage Interest Statement*, usually includes the paid amounts of mortgage interest, real estate taxes, and points (defined below). Mortgage companies will often "sell" mortgages during the year. If this occurs, the taxpayer could receive a Form 1098 from each mortgage company.

Señor 1040 Says: Remember to ask your clients if they paid more than one mortgage company. If they have more than one Form 1098, ask if this was for a second mortgage or if they bought and sold homes during the year.

Mortgage interest paid to an individual not issued on Form 1098 is reported on line 8b of Schedule A. The recipient's name and Social Security number or employer identification number is required. Failure to provide this information may result in a $50 penalty.

Points, often called loan origination fees, maximum loan charges, loan discounts, or discount points, are prepaid interest. Points that the seller pays for on behalf of the borrower are treated as being paid by the borrower. This allows the borrower, not the seller, to deduct these points as interest.

The full amount of paid points cannot be 100% deducted in the year of purchase or refinance. Points are considered prepaid interest and are generally deducted over the life of the mortgage on an annual basis. Form 1098 points need to meet the following conditions:

1. Points are clearly designated on HUD-1 or HUD Closing Settlement points with titles
    a. loan discount
    b. discount points
    c. points
2. Points were computed as a percentage of the specified principal loan amount
3. Charged under a business practice of charging points where the loan was issued and does not exceed the generally charged in the area
4. Points were paid for the acquisition of the taxpayer's principal residence
5. Points were paid directly by the taxpayer. Points were paid directly if either one applies:
    a. Funds were not borrowed from the lender by the taxpayer
    b. The seller paid the points on behalf of the taxpayer

Points paid when borrowing money for a refinance are normally deductible over the life of the loan. If the taxpayer pays off a mortgage early, the taxpayer can deduct the remaining points in the year the loan was paid off. Points are currently deductible only if paid from the taxpayer's funds. Financed points must be deducted over the life of the loan. If the taxpayer refinances and ends the loan, the remaining points are deducted when the life of the loan ends.

Mortgage Insurance Premiums

Beginning January 1, 2022, mortgage insurance premiums is no longer a deduction.

Form 1098

The IRS has made the mortgage interest statement evergreen.

Form 1098

Part 1 Review Questions

To obtain the maximum benefit from this chapter, LTP recommends that you complete each of the following questions, and then compare them to the answers with feedback that immediately follow. Under governing self-study standards, vendors are required to present review questions intermittently throughout each self-study course.

These questions and explanations are not part of the final examination and will not be graded by LTP.

IDP1.1
Pam is 65; at which percentage will she begin deducting her federal medical expenses?

    a. More than 10% of her adjusted gross income.
    b. More than 8% of her adjusted gross income.
    c. She cannot claim medical expenses because of her age.
    d. 7.5% of her adjusted gross income.

IDP1.2
Which of the following is not a deductible medical and dental expense?

    a. Artificial limbs
    b. False teeth
    c. Eyeglasses
    d. Maternity clothes

IDP1.3
John and his wife Cynthia are filing MFS. John is itemizing his deductions. Which of the following is true?

    a. Cynthia must file single and take the standard deduction.
    b. Cynthia must file head of household.
    c. Cynthia must itemize her deductions.
    d. Cynthia must itemize only if she has enough deductions.

IDP1.4
Which of the following taxes can be deducted on federal Schedule A, lines 5-7?

    a. Fines and penalties
    b. Real estate taxes
    c. Federal income tax withholding
    d. Tattoo removal

IDP1.5
Catherine's total taxes paid on Schedule A, line 5e, are $14,500. How much will she deduct?

    a. $10,000
    b. $14,500
    c. $12,200
    d. $24,400

IDP1.6
Which of the following can be claimed as a medical expense? (Provided the taxpayer qualifies to itemize his or her medical deductions).

    a. Recreational marijuana
    b. Cosmetic surgery
    c. Hair removal
    d. Medical miles

IDP1.7
State and local taxes withheld from the taxpayer's wages can be deducted on _____.

    a. Schedule A, line 11
    b. Schedule A, line 6
    c. Form W2, box 17
    d. Schedule A, line 5a

IDP1.8
Which interest payment may be deducted in full in the current tax year on Form 1040, Schedule A, line 11?

    1. Mortgage prepayment penalty
    2. Interest relating to tax exempt interest income
    3. Installment plan interest for work clothes purchases
    4. Mortgage interest
    5. Credit investigation fees

a. 3 and 4
b. 1 and 4
c. 2, 4, and 5
d. 1, 3, and 4

IDP1.9

Which of the following taxes can be deducted on Form 1040, Schedule A?

a. A tax on a motor vehicle based on vehicle weight.
b. Primary residence real estate taxes.
c. Transfer taxes on the sale of a residence.
d. All of the answers are correct.

IDP1.10

Which of the following costs are deductible on Form 1040, Schedule A, as taxes in 2015?

1. Personal property tax on a primary home
2. Garbage pickup itemized on the real estate bill
3. Taxes for local benefits
4. Real estate tax on property owned in Canada

a. 1, 2, and 4
b. 1,2, 3, and 4
c. 1 and 4
d. 2 and 3

Part 1 Review Questions Answers

IDP1.1

Pam is 65; at which percentage will she begin deducting her federal medical expenses?

a. More than 10% of her adjusted gross income.
b. More than 8% of her adjusted gross income.
c. She cannot claim medical expenses because of her age.
d. 7.5% of her adjusted gross income.

Feedback: Review section *Medical and Dental Expenses.*

IDP1.2

Which of the following is not a deductible medical and dental expense?

a. Artificial limbs
b. False teeth
c. Eyeglasses
d. Maternity clothes

Feedback: Review section *Medical and Dental Expenses.*

IDP1.3

John and his wife Cynthia are filing MFS. John is itemizing his deductions. Which of the following is true?

    a. Cynthia must file single and take the standard deduction.
    b. Cynthia must file head of household.
    c. Cynthia must itemize her deductions.
    d. Cynthia must itemize only if she has enough deductions.

Feedback: Review section *Itemizing While Married Filing Separate*.

IDP1.4

Which of the following taxes can be deducted on federal Schedule A, lines 5-7?

    a. Fines and penalties
    b. Real estate taxes
    c. Federal income tax withholding
    d. Tattoo removal

Feedback: Review section *Real Estate Taxes.*

IDP1.5

Catherine's total taxes paid on Schedule A, line 5e, are $14,500. How much will she deduct?

    a. $10,000
    b. $14,500
    c. $12,200
    d. $24,400

Feedback: Review section *State and Local General Sales Tax (SALT)*.

IDP1.6

Which of the following can be claimed as a medical expense? (Provided the taxpayer qualifies to itemize his or her medical deductions).

    a. Recreational marijuana
    b. Cosmetic surgery
    c. Hair removal
    d. Medical miles

Feedback: Review section *Medical Expense Reimbursement.*

IDP1.7

State and local taxes withheld from the taxpayer's wages can be deducted on _____.

    a. Schedule A, line 11
    b. Schedule A, line 6
    c. Form W2, box 17
    d. Schedule A, line 5a

Feedback: Review section *State and Local General Sales Tax (SALT)*.

IDP1.8
Which interest payment may be deducted in full in the current tax year on Form 1040, Schedule A, line 11?

1. Mortgage prepayment penalty
2. Interest relating to tax exempt interest income
3. Installment plan interest for work clothes purchases
4. Mortgage interest
5. Credit investigation fees

a. 3 and 4
b. 1 and 4
c. 2, 4, and 5
d. 1, 3, and 4

Feedback: Review section *Home Mortgage Interest and Points*.

IDP1.9
Which of the following taxes can be deducted on Form 1040, Schedule A?

a. A tax on a motor vehicle based on vehicle weight.
b. Primary residence real estate taxes.
c. Transfer taxes on the sale of a residence.
d. All of the answers are correct.

Feedback: Review section *Real Estate Taxes*.

IDP1.10
Which of the following costs are deductible on Form 1040, Schedule A, as taxes in 2015?

1. Personal property tax on a primary home
2. Garbage pickup itemized on the real estate bill
3. Taxes for local benefits
4. Real estate tax on property owned in Canada

a. 1, 2, and 4
b. 1,2, 3, and 4
c. 1 and 4
d. 2 and 3

Feedback: Review section *Real Estate Taxes*.

Part 2 Charity and Casualty and Theft Losses

There are two ways to donate to a qualifying organization: cash and noncash. The taxpayer could receive a tax benefit based on the amount of the contribution and the taxpayer's adjusted gross income. Casualty is when the taxpayer has lost property by destruction that is sudden or unexpected. Theft is when an individual takes another individual's belongings with the intent to deprive the owner.

Gifts to Charity

Contributions made to "qualified domestic organizations" by individuals and corporations are deductible as charitable contributions. Contributions of money or property, such as clothing, to qualified organizations may be deducted. Dues, fees, or bills to clubs, lodges, fraternal orders, civic leagues, political groups, for-profit organizations, or similar groups are not deductible. Gifts of money or property given to an individual are also not deductible, even if they were given for noble reasons. Raffle tickets or church bingo games would not be a deductible expense (they may count as gambling expenses). Another nondeductible item are Super Bowl squares by qualified domestic organizations. If the taxpayer received a benefit (for example, a gift of $60) from the donation, the donation amount must be reduced by the value of the benefit.

Cash Contributions

Cash contributions include those paid by cash, checks, electronic funds transfer, debit card, credit card, or payroll deduction. Cash contributions are not deductible regardless of the amount unless the taxpayer keeps one of the following:

> ➢ A bank record that shows the name of the eligible organization, the date of the contribution, and the amount of the contribution. Bank records may include:
>> o A canceled check.
>> o A bank or credit union statement.
>> o A credit card statement.
> ➢ A receipt or a letter or other written communication from the qualified organization showing the name of the organization, the date of the contribution, and the amount of the contribution.
> ➢ The payroll deduction records, or a pledge card or other document prepared by the organization. The document from the organization must show the name of the organization.

The tax professional should not overlook charitable contributions made through payroll deductions; they would appear on the taxpayer's last check stub or W-2. Make sure that the payroll deductions are not pretax contributions. Pretax contributions are not deductible. Advise your clients to make donations with checks, not cash. Make sure they get a receipt for all cash donations.

For payroll deduction contributions, one must keep the following:

> ➢ A pay stub, Form W-2, or other document furnished by the taxpayer's employer that shows the date and amount of the contribution.
> ➢ A pledge card or other document prepared by or for the qualified organization that shows the name of the organization.

The written communication must include the name of the charity, the date of the contribution, and the amount of the contribution. If the contribution was more than $250, the taxpayer should receive a statement from the charitable organization. When figuring $250 or more, do not combine separate donations. The charitable organization must include the following on the letter or statement:

> ➢ The amount of money that was contributed and a description of any property that was donated.
> ➢ Whether or not the organization provided goods or services to the taxpayer in return; a description and estimate value of the taxpayer's contribution must be included.

If the taxpayer overstates their charitable deductions and that results in understating their tax liability, the taxpayer could be assessed a penalty of 20% of the total deduction amount if more than 10% of the amount is owed. The taxpayer could also have to pay the underpayment of penalty for understating the amount if more than $5,000.

Other Than by Cash or Check

If the taxpayer gives items such as clothing or furniture, the taxpayer will be able to deduct the fair market value (FMV) at the time of the donation. The FMV is what a willing buyer would pay to purchase when both the buyer and seller are aware of the condition of the sale. If the noncash deduction amount is over $500, the taxpayer must fill out Form 8283. If the contribution is a motor vehicle, boat, or airplane, the organization accepting the donation must issue the taxpayer Form 1098-C with the required information for the taxpayer to attach it to Form 8283. If the deduction is over $5,000, for one item, the taxpayer must get an appraisal of the donated property. The vehicle identification number (VIN) must be reported on Form 8283, and if the car was sold in an auction the amount of the contribution is what the vehicle was sold for. See Instructions Form 8283.

When taxpayers donate noncash items, they must keep a list of the items donated as well as obtain and keep the receipt. Donated items are priced according to their resale value, not the price of the item when it was purchased. See Instructions Schedule A.

If noncash charitable contributions are made with a value of more than $500, the taxpayer is required to complete Form 8283, *Noncash Charitable Contributions*, and attach it to the return. Use Section A of Form 8283 to report noncash contributions for which the taxpayer claimed a deduction of $5,000 or less per item (or group of similar items). Also, use Section A to report contributions of publicly traded securities. Complete Section B, Form 8283, for each deduction over $5,000 claimed for one item or group of similar items. A separate Form 8283 must be submitted for separate contributions over $5,000 to different organizations. The organization that received the property must complete and sign Part IV of Section B.

The IRS may disallow deductions for noncash charitable contributions if they are more than $500 and if Form 8283 is not submitted with the return. See Publication 526 and Schedule A Instructions.

Contributions of Property Placed in Trust

When property has been placed in a trust and the trustees make a charitable deduction from the trust, the deduction is not allowed. If the property was placed in a remainder trust, then the deduction would be allowed. See IRC Code Section 170(f)(13).

Car Expenses

If the taxpayer claims expenses directly related to the use of their car when providing services to a qualified organization, the taxpayer must keep reliable written records of expenses. For example, the taxpayer's records might show the name of the organization the taxpayer was serving and the dates the car was used for a charitable purpose. The taxpayer would use the standard mileage rate of 14 cents a mile; records must show the miles driven for charitable purposes.

Canadian, Israeli, and Mexican Charities

The taxpayer may be able to deduct contributions to certain charitable organizations under the income tax treaty United States has with Mexico, Canada, and Israel. These organizations must meet tests like the ones used to qualify U.S. organizations to receive deductible contributions. The organization would be able to tell the taxpayer if they meet the necessary test. See Publication 526.

Taxpayer Must Keep Records

Records prove the amount of the contributions one makes during the year. The types of records to keep depends on the amount of the contributions and whether they include any of the following:

> ➤ Cash contributions.
> ➤ Noncash contributions.
> ➤ Out-of-pocket expenses when volunteering.

Organizations are usually required to give a written statement if they receive a payment that is more than $75 and is partly a contribution and partly a payment made in exchange for goods or services. The statement should be kept with the taxpayer's records. See Revenue Procedure 2006-50, 2006-47 I.R.B. 944.

Adjustments for Charitable Cash Contributions Nonitemizers has not Been Extended.

The above line charitable contribution has not been extended for 2022 for taxpayers who were unable to itemize their deductions. The charitable amount was $300 for single and $600 for married filing jointly tax return.

Other Itemized Deductions

The following items can be claimed on Schedule A, line 16:

> ➤ Gambling losses up to the extent of gambling winnings.
> ➤ Casualty and theft losses from income-producing property.
> ➤ An ordinary loss attributable to a contingent payment debt instrument or an inflation-indexed debt instrument.
> ➤ Amortizable premiums on taxable bonds purchased before October 23, 1986.
> ➤ Certain unrecovered investments in a pension.
> ➤ Impairment-related work experience of persons with disabilities.
> ➤ Federal estate tax on income with the respect of a decedent.
> ➤ Deductions for repayment of amounts under a claim of right if over $3,000. See Publication 525.

See Instructions Schedule A.

Gambling Losses

The taxpayer must report the full amount of any gambling winnings for the year. The taxpayer will deduct gambling losses for the year on line 16, Schedule A (Form 1040). The taxpayer may claim gambling losses up to the amount of gambling winnings. Taxpayers cannot reduce gambling winnings by gambling losses and report the difference; they must report the full amount of their winnings as income and claim their losses up to the amount of winnings as an itemized deduction. Therefore, the taxpayer's records should show winnings separately from losses. The taxpayer must keep an accurate diary or similar record of losses and winnings. The diary should contain at least the following information:

➢ The date and type of specific wages or wagering activity.
➢ The name and address or location of the gambling establishment.
➢ The names of other people present with the taxpayer at the gambling establishment.
➢ The amount(s) won or lost.

Casualty and Theft Losses

A casualty is the damage, destruction, or loss of property resulting from an identifiable event that is sudden, unexpected, or unusual. A loss on deposits can occur when a bank, credit union, or other financial institution becomes insolvent or bankrupt. When property is damaged or destroyed as a result of hurricanes, earthquakes, tornadoes, fires, vandalism, car accidents, and similar events, it is called a casualty loss. A casualty loss must be sudden and unexpected, so damage that occur over time do not qualify. Theft is the unlawful taking and removing of money or property with the intent to deprive the owner.

Before January 1, 2018, if theft occurred, the taxpayer completed Form 4684, *Casualty and Theft*, and attach it to the return. The loss calculated on Form 4684 was transferred to line 15 of Schedule A. The IRS allowed taxpayers who used Schedule A to deduct these losses with limited coverage.

A casualty loss amount equals the least of the following:

➢ The decrease in the fair market value (FMV) of the property as result of the event (in other words, the difference between the property's fair market value immediately before and after the casualty).
➢ The adjusted basis in property before the casualty loss, minus any insurance reimbursement.

After figuring a casualty or theft loss and subtracting any reimbursements, one must figure how much of the loss is deductible. To claim a loss as a deduction, each loss amount must have been greater than $100 or greater than 10% of the amount on Form 1040, line 8b, reduced by $100.

After December 31, 2017, theft losses can no longer be claimed, and casualty losses can only be claimed if they are the result of an event that was officially declared a federal disaster by the President of the United States. Apart from this, casualty losses are still calculated using the same methods explained above. Form 4684, *Casualty and Theft*, must still be attached to the tax return. If the taxpayer has a net qualified disaster loss on Form 4684, line 15, and has not itemized deductions, the taxpayer may qualify for an increased standard deduction.

Disasters and Casualties

If damage from a casualty is to personal, income-producing, or business property, taxpayers may be able to claim a casualty loss deduction on their tax return. Taxpayers must generally deduct a casualty loss in the year it occurred. However, if the property was damaged as a result of a federally declared disaster, taxpayers can choose to deduct that loss on their return for the tax year immediately preceding the year in which the disaster happened. A federally declared disaster is a disaster that took place in an area declared by the President to be eligible for federal assistance. Taxpayers can amend a tax return by filing Form 1040X, *Amended U.S. Individual Income Tax Return.*

Disaster Relief

The following website is where a taxpayer and tax professional can find the list of presidentially declared disaster areas: https://www.irs.gov/newsroom/tax-relief-in-disaster-situations.

Reconstructing Tips for the Disaster Claim

Reconstructing records after a disaster may be essential for tax purposes and for obtaining federal assistance or insurance reimbursement. After a disaster, taxpayers might need certain records to prove their loss. The more accurately a loss is estimated, the more loan and grant money may be available.

Below are tips to help the taxpayer gather the necessary information to reconstruct their records regarding their personal residence and real property. A piece of real estate is not just the land but is also anything built on, growing on, or attached to the land.

> - Take photographs or videos as soon as possible after the disaster. This establishes the extent of the damage.
> - Contact the title company, escrow company, or bank that handled the purchase of the home to get copies of the original documents. Real estate brokers may also be able to help.
> - Use the current property tax statement for land-versus-building ratios if available. If they are not available, owners could get copies from the county assessor's office.
> - The basis or fair market value of the home needs to be established. This can be completed by reviewing comparable sales within the neighborhood or by contacting an appraisal company or visiting a website that provides home valuations.
> - The mortgage company copies of appraisals or other information needed regarding cost or fair market value in the area.
> - Insurance policies list the value of the building, which initiates a base figure for replacement value insurance.
> - If improvements were made to the home, contact the contractors who did the work to see if records are available. Get statements from the contractors that state their work and its cost.
>   - ○ Get written accounts from friends and relatives who saw the house before and after any improvements. See if any of them have photos taken at get-togethers.
>   - ○ If there is a home improvement loan, get paperwork from the institution that issued the loan. The amount of the loan may help establish the cost of the improvements.
> - For inherited property, check court records for probate values. If a trust or estate existed, contact the attorney who handled the estate or trust.
> - If no other records are available, check the county assessor's office for old records that might address the value of the property.

Business Records

- ➤ To create a list of lost inventories, get copies of invoices from suppliers. Whenever possible, the invoices should date back at least one calendar year.
- ➤ Check for photos on mobile phones, cameras, and videos of buildings, equipment, and inventory.
- ➤ Gathering information about income, get copies from the bank statements. The deposits should reflect what the sales were for the given time period.
  - o Get copies of last year's federal, state, and local tax returns. This includes sales tax reports, payroll tax returns, and business licenses from the city or county. These should reflect gross sales for a given time period.
- ➤ If there are no photographs or videos available, sketch an outline of the inside and outside of the business location and then start to fill in the details of the sketches. For example, for the inside of the building, record where equipment and inventory were located. For the outside of the building, map out the locations of items such as shrubs, parking, signs, and awnings.
  - o If the business was pre-existing, go back to the broker for a copy of the purchase agreement. This should detail what was acquired.
  - o If the building was newly constructed, contact the contractor or a planning commission for building plans.

Other Helpful Agencies

There are several agencies that can help determine the fair market value of most cars on the road. The following are available online resources:

- ➤ Kelley Blue Book: www.kbb.com.
- ➤ National Automobile Dealers Association: www.nadaguides.com.
- ➤ Edmunds: www.edmunds.com.

Call the car dealer where the vehicle was purchased and ask for a copy of the contract. If this is not available, give the dealer the details and ask for a comparable price. If the taxpayer is making payments on the car, another source is the lien holder.

It can be difficult to reconstruct records showing the fair market value of some types of personal property. Here are some things to consider when categorizing lost items and their values:

- ➤ Look on mobile phones for pictures that were taken in the home that might show the damaged property in the background before the disaster.
- ➤ Check websites that could establish the cost and fair market value of lost items.
- ➤ Support the valuation with photographs, videos, canceled checks, receipts, or other evidence.
- ➤ If items were purchased using a credit or debit card, contact the credit card company or bank for past statements.

If there are no photos or videos of the property, a simple method to help remember which items were lost is to sketch pictures of each room that was impacted:

- ➤ Draw a floor plan showing where each piece of furniture was placed – include drawers, dressers, and shelves.
- ➤ Sketch pictures of the room looking toward any shelves or tables showing their contents.
- ➤ These do not have to be professionally drawn, just functional.
- ➤ Take time to draw shelves with memorabilia on them.

➢ Be sure to include garages, attics, closets, basements, and items on walls.

Figuring Loss

Taxpayers may need to reconstruct their records to prove a loss and the amount thereof. To compute loss, determine the decrease in FMV of the property resulting from the casualty or disaster or determine the adjusted basis of the property – this is generally the amount that the property is now worth after disaster events have added to or lessened the value of the amount that was originally paid for the property.

Taxpayers may deduct whichever of these two amounts is smaller after subtracting the amount of any reimbursement provided the taxpayer. If the reimbursement is larger than the adjusted basis of the loss, then the taxpayer will have a gain and not a subtraction. Certain deduction limits apply. See Publication 547, *Casualties, Disasters and Thefts*, for details on limits and Publication 551, *Basis of Assets*, for basis information.

If the casualty loss deduction causes a taxpayer's deductions for the year to be more than their income for the year, there may be a net operating loss. For more information, see Publication 536, *Net Operating Losses (NOLs) for Individuals, Estates and Trusts*.

Determining the Decrease in Fair Market Value

Fair market value (FMV) is generally the price for which the property could be sold to a buyer. The decrease in FMV used to figure the amount of a casualty loss is the difference between the property's fair market value immediately before and after the casualty. FMV is generally determined through an appraisal.

Casualty and Theft Losses of Income-Producing Property

Taxpayers can no longer claim a business casualty loss of income-producing property as an itemized deduction. If preparing a tax return from before 2018, use the following information to complete Form 4684:

➢ Loss from other activities from Schedule K-1 (Form 1065-B), box 2.
➢ Federal estate tax on income with respect to a decedent.
➢ Amortizable bond premium on bonds acquired before October 23, 1986.
➢ Deduction for repayment of amounts under a claim of right if over $3,000 (see Publication 525).
➢ Certain unrecovered investments in a pension.
➢ Impairment-related work expenses for a disabled person (see Publication 529).

The loss of income-producing property, such as a rental, is calculated depending on if the property was stolen or destroyed. The loss minus the adjusted basis of the property, any salvage value, and the insurance reimbursements expected to receive.

Insurance Payments

If a taxpayer receives funds from an insurance contract for daily living expenses due to damage, destruction, or denied access to their primary residence, such amounts received compensate or reimburse the living expenses for the taxpayer and their household. See IRC Code Section 123.

Investment Interest Form 4952

Form **4952**	**Investment Interest Expense Deduction**	OMB No. 1545-0191
Department of the Treasury Internal Revenue Service	Go to *www.irs.gov/Form4952* for the latest information. Attach to your tax return.	**2022** Attachment Sequence No. **51**

Name(s) shown on return		Identifying number

Part I   **Total Investment Interest Expense**

1	Investment interest expense paid or accrued in 2022 (see instructions)	**1**
2	Disallowed investment interest expense from 2021 Form 4952, line 7	**2**
3	**Total investment interest expense.** Add lines 1 and 2	**3**

Portion of Form 4952

Investment income is income that comes from interest payments, dividends, and capital gains collected upon the sale of a security or other assets, and any other profit made through an investment vehicle of any kind. Generally, individuals earn most of their total net income each year through regular employment income.

An investment interest expense is any amount of interest that is paid on loan proceeds used to purchase investments or securities. Investment interest expenses include margin interest used to leverage securities in a brokerage account and interest on a loan used to buy property held for investment.

The deductions for investment expenses could be limited by the at-risk rules and the passive activity loss limits. It does not include any interest related to passive activities or to securities that generate tax-exempt income. Investment expense deduction is limited to investment income. An example of investment income is interest and ordinary dividend income. Property held for investment purposes includes property that produces interest, dividends, annuities, or royalties that were not earned in the ordinary course of a trade or business. Alaska Permanent Fund dividends are not investment income.

Investment interest does not include any qualified home mortgage interest or any interest taken into account in computing income or loss from a passive activity. The deduction for investment interest expense is limited to the amount of net investment income.

Example: Sandy had interest income in the amount of $800. She also had ordinary dividend income in the amount of $325. Sandy's investment interest expense for the year was $695. Sandy will be allowed to deduct the full amount of investment interest expense on her Schedule A since her investment income exceeds her investment interest expense.

When claiming investment interest, Form 4952 should be completed and attached to the tax return. Form 4952 does not have to be completed if the following apply:

➢ Taxpayer interest expense is not more than the investment income from interest and ordinary dividends minus qualified dividends.
➢ The taxpayer has no other deductible investment expenses.
➢ The taxpayer had non-disallowed interest expense for the year.

Report Investment interest on Schedule A, line 9. See Publication 550.

Señor 1040 Says: Alaska Permanent Fund dividends, including those reported on Form 8814, are not investment income.

Fines or Penalties

The taxpayer cannot deduct their fines or penalties paid to a governmental unit for violating a law. This includes all fines and penalties paid in an actual settlement or a potential liability. Fines or penalties include parking tickets, tax penalties, and penalties deducted from teachers' paychecks after an illegal strike.

Part 2 Review Questions

To obtain the maximum benefit from this chapter, LTP recommends that you complete each of the following questions, and then compare them to the answers with feedback that immediately follow. Under governing self-study standards, vendors are required to present review questions intermittently throughout each self-study course.

These questions and explanations are not part of the final examination and will not be graded by LTP.

IDP2.1
Alberta has the following records of charitable contributions: $1,200 check to her church; $600 payroll after-tax dollars to local charity; and $400 fair market value of household items to a qualifying homeless shelter. How much can she deduct for her cash contributions on Schedule A, Itemized Deductions?

    a. $1,200
    b. $400
    c. $1,800
    d. $2,200

IDP2.2
Which of the following is not a type of investment income?

    a. Interest earned
    b. Dividend distributions
    c. Capital gains
    d. Interest paid on a loan

IDP2.3
Alyssa has received several W-2G's totaling $10,500. Alyssa shows proof of his gambling losses totaling over $22,000. What amount of her gambling loss can Alyssa deduct?

    a. She can deduct all her losses.
    b. She can deduct up to the amount of winnings.
    c. She can deduct none of her losses.
    d. She does not need to report any gambling winnings or the losses.

IDP2.4

Which form needs to be completed and attached to the tax return when claiming a "Casualty and Theft Loss"?

   a. Form 2106
   b. Form 8889
   c. Form 4684
   d. Form 3903

IDP2.5

Matthew has received several W-2G's totaling $17,000. Matthew shows proof of his gambling loss totaling over $22,000. What amount of his gambling loss can Matthew deduct?

   a. He can deduct $22,000 on his current year tax return.
   b. He can deduct $17,000 on his current year tax return.
   c. He can deduct $17,000 on his current year tax return and the remaining $5,000 the following year.
   d. He does not have to report the winnings or the losses.

IDP2.6

Bob and Alice are married and file a joint return. They both have items to include as itemized deductions. Which of the following *cannot* be deducted on Schedule A, line 16?

   a. Nursing association dues
   b. Hard hat required for job
   c. Fines or penalties
   d. Home office expense

IDP2.7

In the event of a casualty or disaster loss client records need to reconstruct their records. Which of the following companies could help with the taxpayer's information?

   1. Title company
   2. Mortgage company
   3. Property tax statement
   4. Neighbor

   a. 1, 2, and 4
   b. 4
   c. 1, 2, and 3
   d. 2 and 3

IDP2.8

Anet has the following records of charitable contributions she made in 2022. How much can she deduct on her Schedule A, Itemized Deductions?

   ➢ $200 check to local church
   ➢ $600 nontaxable payroll deduction of $50 per month to the United Way
   ➢ $400 fair market value of furniture to a qualifying shelter

   a. $200
   b. $400
   c. $600
   d. $1,200

IDP2.9
Which charitable contribution is not deductible?

    a. A donation to your local church
    b. A donation to the Boys & Girls Club of America
    c. A donation to your Homeowner's Association
    d. All the answers are correct

IDP2.10
Which form reports Investment Interest?

    a. Form 1098
    b. Form 2106
    c. Form 4952
    d. Form 1098-T

Part 2 Review Questions Answers

IDP2.1
Alberta has the following records of charitable contributions: $1,200 check to her church; $600 payroll after-tax dollars to local charity; and $400 fair market value of household items to a qualifying homeless shelter. How much can she deduct for her cash contributions on Schedule A, Itemized Deductions?

    a. $1,200
    b. $400
    c. $1,800
    d. $2,200

Feedback: Review section *Gifts to Charity*.

IDP2.2
Which of the following is not a type of investment income?

    a. Interest earned
    b. Dividend distributions
    c. Capital gains
    d. Interest paid on a loan

Feedback: Review section *Investment Interest.*

IDP2.3
Alyssa has received several W-2G's totaling $10,500. Alyssa shows proof of his gambling losses totaling over $22,000. What amount of her gambling loss can Alyssa deduct?

    a. She can deduct all her losses.
    b. She can deduct up to the amount of winnings.
    c. She can deduct none of her losses.
    d. She does not need to report any gambling winnings or the losses.

Feedback: Review section *Gambling Losses.*

IDP2.4

Which form needs to be completed and attached to the tax return when claiming a "Casualty and Theft Loss"?

  a. Form 2106
  b. Form 8889
  c. Form 4684
  d. Form 3903

Feedback: Review section *Casualty and Theft Losses*.

IDP2.5

Matthew has received several W-2G's totaling $17,000. Matthew shows proof of his gambling loss totaling over $22,000. What amount of his gambling loss can Matthew deduct?

  a. He can deduct $22,000 on his current year tax return.
  b. He can deduct $17,000 on his current year tax return.
  c. He can deduct $17,000 on his current year tax return and the remaining $5,000 the following year.
  d. He does not have to report the winnings or the losses.

Feedback: Review section *Gambling Losses*.

IDP2.6

Bob and Alice are married and file a joint return. They both have items to include as itemized deductions. Which of the following ***cannot*** be deducted on Schedule A, line 16?

  a. Nursing association dues
  b. Hard hat required for job
  c. Fines or penalties
  d. Home office expense

Feedback: Review section *Fines or Penalties*.

IDP2.7

In the event of a casualty or disaster loss, client records need to reconstruct their records. Which of the following companies could help with the taxpayer's information?

  1. Title company
  2. Mortgage company
  3. Property tax statement
  4. Neighbor

  a. 1, 2, and 4
  b. 4
  c. 1, 2, and 3
  d. 2 and 3

Feedback: Review section *Reconstructing Tips of the Disaster Claim*.

IDP2.8

Anet has the following records of charitable contributions she made in 2022. How much can she deduct on her Schedule A, Itemized Deductions?

> ➢ $200 check to local church
> ➢ $600 nontaxable payroll deduction of $50 per month to the United Way
> ➢ $400 fair market value of furniture to a qualifying shelter

a. $200
b. $400
c. $600
d. $1,200

Feedback: Review section *Gifts to Charity*.

IDP2.9

Which charitable contribution is not deductible?

a. A donation to your local church
b. A donation to the Boys & Girls Club of America
c. A donation to your Homeowner's Association
d. All the answers are correct

Feedback: Review section *Gifts to Charity*.

IDP2.10

Which form reports Investment Interest?

a. Form 1098
b. Form 2106
c. Form 4952
d. Form 1098-T

Feedback: Review section *Investment Interest*.

Part 3 Form 2106: Employee Business Expenses and Other Expenses

Prior to January 1, 2018, the following section is no longer reported on the federal return. This section is to help those who prepare returns where the states did not conform to the Tax Cuts and Jobs Act. The Schedule A is still used to calculate the state deduction amount. The following states did not conform:

> ➢ Alaska
> ➢ Arkansas
> ➢ California
> ➢ Georgia
> ➢ Hawaii
> ➢ Iowa
> ➢ Minnesota
> ➢ Montana
> ➢ New York

Form 2106 is still used by Armed Forces reservists, qualified performing artists, fee-basis state or local government officials, and employees who will be claiming impairment-related work expenses such as traveling more than 100 miles from home to perform their services. See Instructions Form 2106.

The suspension of miscellaneous itemized deductions under section 67(a), employees, who do not fit into the above classifications may not use Form 2106. The information in the next section has been provided to assist those preparing taxes in the states that did not conform to section 67(a) and still need to calculate the federal deduction to arrive at the state deduction amount.

An employee may deduct unreimbursed expenses that are paid and incurred during the current tax year. The expenses must be incurred for conducting trade or business as an employee, and the expenses must be ordinary and necessary. An expense is considered ordinary if it is common and necessary in the taxpayer's trade or business. Self-employed taxpayers do not use Form 2106 to report their business expenses.

An employee may deduct the following unreimbursed business expenses on Schedule A as a miscellaneous deduction subject to the 2% AGI limitation:

➢ Employee's business bad debt.
➢ Education that is employment related.
➢ Licenses and regulatory fees.
➢ Malpractice or professional insurance premiums.
➢ Occupational taxes.
➢ Passport for a business trip.
➢ Subscriptions to professional journals and trade magazines related to the taxpayer's trade or business.
➢ Travel, transportation, entertainment, gifts, and car expenses related to the taxpayer's trade or business.
➢ Tools used in a trade or business.
➢ Memberships for professional associations.
➢ Uniforms, work clothing, or protective wear, as well as their cleaning and maintenance.

Do not include any educator expenses on Form 2106.

Taxing Employee Expenses

Tax treatment of employee business expenses depends on whether the expenses are categorized as reimbursed expenses or non-reimbursed expenses. Business expenses incurred by an employee under a reimbursement arrangement with an employer are normally not shown on the tax return. Unreimbursed business expenses are deductible as miscellaneous itemized deductions. The definition of trade or business does not include the performance of services as an employee.

The taxpayer may deduct certain expenses as miscellaneous itemized deductions on Schedule A. The taxpayer may deduct the expenses that exceed 2% of their adjusted gross income. The calculation is determined by subtracting 2% of the AGI from the total amount of qualifying expense.

Tax Home

The taxpayer's main place of doing business is considered their tax home. If the taxpayer does not have a regular or main place of business due to the nature of work, the taxpayer's tax home may be the place where one regularly lives. To determine one's main place, the length of time must be taken into consideration. See Tax Topic 511.

Temporary Assignment or Job

The taxpayer may regularly work at their tax home and at another location. If the assignment is temporary, the taxpayer's tax home does not change. If the assignment is indefinite, the taxpayer must include in any income amounts received from his or her employer for living expenses, even if they were considered travel expenses. An indefinite assignment is a job that is expected to last a year or more, even if it does not end up lasting that long.

To determine the difference between a temporary and an indefinite assignment, look at when the taxpayer began working. A temporary assignment usually lasts for one year or less, although a temporary assignment could turn into an indefinite assignment, requiring the tax home to change. An indefinite assignment can be a series of short assignments to the same location for a certain amount of time. If the time spent at that location becomes a sufficiently lengthy period of time, then the temporary could turn to indefinite.

If the taxpayer is a federal employee participating in a federal crime investigation or prosecution, the taxpayer is not limited to the one-year rule but must meet other requirements to deduct the expenses.

If the taxpayer returns home from a temporary assignment, the taxpayer is not considered to be away from home. If the taxpayer takes a job that requires a move with the understanding that they will keep the job after the probationary period, the job is considered "indefinite." The expense for lodging and meals is not deductible.

Meals

Deductions can be determined by using the actual meal expense for the standard meal allowance. If there is no reimbursement for meal expenses, then only 50% of the standard meal allowance is deductible, and that 50% is subject to the 2% floor. Employees who travel out of town for extended periods of time may elect to take a per diem rate. The federal per diem rate depends on the location.

A transportation worker is defined as an individual whose work involves moving people or goods by plane, bus, ship, truck, etc. Transportation workers can deduct a special per-day allowance for meals and incidentals if their work requires that they travel away from home to areas with different federal per diem rates. Unlike other traveling employees, a Department of Transportation (DOT) worker is allowed to deduct up to 80% of the meal.

Travel and Transportation Expenses

If the taxpayer travels away from their tax home for business, the expenses could be deducted on Form 2106. Business-related travel expenses must be ordinary and necessary expenses of traveling away from home for the business or job. Expenses cannot be lavish or extravagant. A taxpayer is traveling away from home if:

> ➤ The taxpayer's duties require one to be away from the general area of their tax home for substantially longer than an ordinary day's work.
> ➤ The taxpayer needs sleep or rest to meet the demands of his or her work while away from home.

Travel by airplane, train, or bus is generally deductible. Fares paid for taxis, airport limousines, buses, or other types of transportation used between the airport, bus station or hotel, can be deducted including those used between the hotel and the client visited. Necessary trips are also deductible. Cleaning expenses, business calls, tips, and other necessary expenses related to the trip are also deductible.

Employees who drive their own vehicles are permitted to deduct either the actual expenses or the standard mileage rate for unreimbursed mileage. If the taxpayer is partially reimbursed, only the portion that is unreimbursed is reportable. See Publication 463, *Travel, Entertainment, Gift, and Car Expenses*.

Entertainment

Entertainment expenses must be ordinary and necessary. This includes activities generally considered to provide entertainment, recreation, or amusement to clients, customers, or employees. Expenses for entertainment that are lavish or extravagant are not deductible. An expense is not considered lavish or extravagant if the expense is reasonably based on facts and circumstances related to the business.

Entertainment expense deductions are limited to 50% of the actual expense and are further reduced by the 2% floor. "Entertainment" includes any activity that generally is considered to provide diversion, amusement, or recreation. It does not include club dues and membership fees to country clubs, airline clubs, and hotel clubs. The taxpayer may deduct entertainment expenses only if they are ordinary and necessary. Deducting entertainment expenses must meet either the "directly related" test or the "associated" test.

The "directly related" entertainment test, must meet the following conditions:

> ➤ Expenses must be directly related to business either before, during, or after the entertainment or associated with the active conduct of business.
> ➤ The taxpayer and client engaged in business during the entertainment period.
> ➤ The entertainment was more than a general expectation of getting income or some other specific business benefit in the future.

To meet the "associated" test, the entertainment must be associated with the active conduct of the taxpayer's trade or business and occur directly before or after a substantial business discussion. Daily lunch or entertainment expenses with subordinates or coworkers are not deductible, even if business is discussed.

Business Gifts

Gifts can be given to the client directly or indirectly. The taxpayer can deduct up to $25 per client per year for business gifts. Items do not include those that cost $4 or less, have the taxpayer's name imprinted on them, and are distributed (for example, pens, pencils, cases, etc.). Any item that could be considered a gift or entertainment is considered entertainment. Packaged food and beverage items are treated as gifts.

Business Recordkeeping

If audited, taxpayers must prove their deductions to the IRS. It is important to keep all receipts related to the tax return. Records of expenses should include the following:

➢ Amount paid.
➢ Time, date, and place.
➢ The purpose of the business discussion or the nature of the expected business benefit.
➢ People in attendance.

Reimbursements

Reimbursements paid by an employer's accountable plan are not reported in box 1 of Form W-2. Excess reimbursements paid by a nonaccountable plan are included in the employees' wages in box 1 of the W-2. See Instructions Form 2106.

Other Expenses

The taxpayer can deduct certain other expenses as miscellaneous itemized deductions subject to the 2% of adjusted gross income limit. The following are examples of deductible expenses:

➢ Expenses to manage, conserve, or maintain property held for producing taxable gross income (such as office space rented to maintain investment property).
➢ Attorney fees and legal expenses paid to collect taxable income.
➢ Appraiser fees to determine the value of a donated party.
➢ Fees paid to determine the value of a casualty loss.

The taxpayer can deduct investment fees, custodial fees, trust administration fees, and other expenses paid for managing investments that produce taxable income.

Tax Preparation Fees

Tax preparation fees are deductible to the taxpayer. If the taxpayer paid the preparation fee by using a debit or credit card and a convenience fee was charged, the taxpayer cannot deduct the convenience fee as a part of the overall cost of preparing the return.

Education

The taxpayer can deduct qualifying education tuition and expenses. The education must be required by the employer or the law to keep one's salary, status, or job or to maintain or improve skills required in the taxpayer's present job in order to be deductible. Education that qualifies the taxpayer for his or her first job in a specific field is not deductible on Schedule A, nor is education that enables the taxpayer to change jobs; however, these may be deductible as a lifetime learning credit.

Deductible expenses include tuition, textbooks, registration fees, supplies, transportation (standard mileage or actual expenses), lab fees, the cost of writing papers or dissertations, student cards, insurance, and degree costs.

Part 3 Review Questions

To obtain the maximum benefit from this chapter, LTP recommends that you complete each of the following questions, and then compare them to the answers with feedback that immediately follow. Under governing self-study standards, vendors are required to present review questions intermittently throughout each self-study course.

These questions and explanations are not part of the final examination and will not be graded by LTP.

IDP3.1

Which form is used to report employee business expenses for years prior to 2018?

    a. Form 2441
    b. Form 2106
    c. Schedule C
    d. Form 1040-EZ

IDP3.2

Which of the following states did not conform to TCJA?

    a. Alaska, Arkansas, Alabama, and California
    b. New York, New Jersey, Montana, and Iowa
    c. Hawaii, Arkansas, Montana, and Georgia
    d. Minnesota, Georgia, Texas, and Florida

IDP3.3

Which of the following best describes "Tax Home"?

    a. Taxpayer does not work regularly at their tax home.
    b. Taxpayers' employment was in a different city for 42 weeks.
    c. Taxpayer worked regularly at a temporary assignment.
    d. Taxpayer is a federal employee investigating crimes.

IDP3.4

Which form is unable to report federal employee business expenses?

    a. Form 2441
    b. Form 2106
    c. Schedule C
    d. Form 1040-EZ

IDP3.5

What is the limit for business gifts?

    a. $4 per client
    b. $15 per employee
    c. $25 per client
    d. No limit

Part 3 Review Questions Answers

IDP3.1
Which form is used to report employee business expenses for years prior to 2018?

    a. Form 2441
    b. Form 2106
    c. Schedule C
    d. Form 1040-EZ

Feedback: Review section *Form 2106 Employee Business Expenses.*

IDP3.2
Which of the following states did not conform to TCJA?

    a. Alaska, Arkansas, Alabama, and California
    b. New York, New Jersey, Montana, and Iowa
    c. Hawaii, Arkansas, Montana, and Georgia
    d. Minnesota, Georgia, Texas, and Florida

Feedback: Review section *Form 2106 Employee Business Expenses.*

IDP3.3
Which of the following best describes "Tax Home"?

    a. Taxpayer does not work regularly at their tax home.
    b. Taxpayers' employment was in a different city for 42 weeks.
    c. Taxpayer worked regularly at a temporary assignment.
    d. Taxpayer is a federal employee investigating crimes.

Feedback: Review section *Form 2106 Employee Business Expenses.*

IDP3.4
Which form is unable to report federal employee business expenses?

    a. Form 2441
    b. Form 2106
    c. Schedule C
    d. Form 1040-EZ

Feedback: Review section *Form 2106 Employee Business Expenses.*

IDP3.5
What is the limit for business gifts?

    a. $4 per client
    b. $15 per employee
    c. $25 per client
    d. No limit

Feedback: Review section *Form 2106 Employee Business Expenses.*

Takeaways

The taxpayer must decide to use the itemized deduction or the standard deduction. The standard deduction is a dollar amount that reduces the amount of income on which the taxpayer is taxed. The itemized deduction can be greater than the standard deduction. Some taxpayers must itemize their deductions because they do not qualify to use the standard deduction or because one's spouse chose to itemize their deductions.

TEST YOUR KNOWLEDGE!
Go online to take a practice quiz.

California Itemized Deductions

Introduction

The Tax Cuts and Jobs Act made some changes to the Internal Revenue Code (IRC) that California did not adopt. California does conform with IRC regulations established on and before January 1, 2015. California residents will need to account for the differences between state and federal tax law on 540 Schedule CA. California did not conform to the 2021 American Rescue Plan Act (ARPA) changes.

The California tax professional needs to understand which federal laws California does not adopt; changes are made on 540 Schedule CA. Common state differences are depreciation, social security, unemployment, and the phasing out of itemized deductions.

Objectives

At the end of this lesson, the student will:

➢ Explain the differences between federal and California itemized deductions.
➢ Understand how to compute California lottery losses.
➢ Recognize how voluntary contributions affect the taxpayer's refund or tax liability.

Resources

FTB Form 540	FTB Publication 1001	FTB Instructions Form 540
FTB 540 Schedule CA	FTB Form 3526	FTB 540 Instructions Schedule CA

Table of Contents

Part 1 540 Schedule CA: Itemizing Deductions

To calculate California itemized deductions, begin with the federal itemized deductions. To arrive at the California itemized deductions, the federal Schedule A must be entered even if the taxpayer is not able to use it for their federal return. California uses the federal information to either add or subtract based on California law. 540 Schedule CA would be used.

The taxpayer's itemized deductions could be limited on the California return. If the amount on Form 540, line 13, is one of the below amounts or greater, then the taxpayer would have to complete the *Itemized Deductions Worksheet* found in the Instructions 540 Schedule CA:

Single or married/RDP filing separately	$229,908
Head of Household	$344,867
Married/RDP filing jointly or Surviving spouse	$459,581

California did not conform to the following TCJA changes:

- ➢ Combat zone extended to Egypt's Sinai Peninsula.
- ➢ Moving expenses and reimbursements.
- ➢ Limitation on deduction of business interest.
- ➢ Limitation on wagering losses.
- ➢ Sexual harassment settlements.
- ➢ Qualified equity grants.
- ➢ Expanded use of 529 account funds.
- ➢ California Achieving a Better Life Experience (ABLE) Program.
- ➢ Living expenses for members of Congress.
- ➢ Limitation on state and local tax deduction (SALT).
- ➢ Mortgage & home equity indebtedness interest deduction.
- ➢ Limitation on charitable contribution deduction.
- ➢ College athletic seating rights.
- ➢ Casualty or disaster loss(es).
- ➢ Miscellaneous itemized deductions.

This chapter will cover the most common adjustments needed for itemized deductions to prepare an accurate California return. Remember, there are differences between California and federal law; California does not always conform to federal tax law changes.

Moving Expenses Before the TCJA

To claim California moving expenses as an adjustment to income, the taxpayer must meet the following requirements:

- ➢ The move is closely related to the start of work.
- ➢ The taxpayer meets the distance test.
- ➢ The taxpayer meets the time test.

Señor 1040 Says: Recordkeeping is vital to maintaining an accurate record of expenses for a move. The taxpayer should save receipts, bills, canceled checks, credit card statements, and mileage logs to correctly report the amount of moving expense.

The California taxpayer who has moved for a job will use the pre-TCJA rules to claim moving expenses. The distance between the old home and the new workplace must be at least 50 miles more than the old home to the old workplace. If the taxpayer did not have any reimbursed moving expenses, they could report the expenses in the year they were incurred. The following moving expenses could be claimed as adjustments to income before the TCJA:

> ➢ The cost of packing and moving household goods and personal effects.
> ➢ The cost of storing and insuring household goods once 30 days have passed.
> ➢ The cost of connecting and disconnecting utilities.
> ➢ The cost of one trip, including lodging but not meals, to the new home.
> ➢ The cost of tolls and parking fees.

The taxpayer would report the moving expenses on California form FTB 3913. Reimbursed expenses reported with code *P* do not have to be reported on the tax return. Taxpayers who were reimbursed for the moving expenses cannot double-dip and claim moving expenses as adjustments to income on their federal tax return. If line 3 is more than line 4 on Form 3913, the taxpayer does not qualify to claim moving expenses.

540 Schedule CA Part I Adjustments to Federal Itemized Deductions

Although the TCJA suspended gambling losses, California did not conform. California lottery losses are entered on 540 Schedule CA, Section B, line 8b. If the taxpayer has other gambling losses such as an Indian casino, that is taxable income and no adjustment is needed. California does conform to the federal 7.5% medical and dental expense deduction, no adjustment needed. California does not conform to the 2% floor for unreimbursed employee expenses, taxpayer would use Form 2106 and attach it to their 540.

Section B – Additional Income Continued	A Federal Amounts (taxable amounts from your federal tax return)	B Subtractions See instructions	C Additions See instructions
8 Other income:			
a Federal net operating loss........8a	( )		
b Gambling............8b			

Schedule CA, Section B

Adjustments to Federal Itemized Deductions Part II

Part II Adjustments to Federal Itemized Deductions			
Check the box if you did NOT itemize for federal but will itemize for California			
	A Federal Amounts (from federal Schedule A (Form 1040))	B Subtractions See instructions	C Additions See instructions
Medical and Dental Expenses See instructions.			
1 Medical and dental expenses 1			
2 Enter amount from federal Form 1040 or 1040-SR, line 11.. 2			
3 Multiply line 2 by 7.5% (0.075).... 3			
4 Subtract line 3 from line 1. If line 3 is more than line 1, enter 0 4			
Taxes You Paid			
5 a State and local income tax or general sales taxes. .5a			

Schedule CA, Part II

Line 1 - 4 Medical and Dental Expenses

Medical, dental, and other expenses that are medical deductions are reported on line 1. Some items that can be reported are prescription glasses, hearing aids, dental work, and other qualifying medical procedures.

Line 5 Taxes Paid (State, Local, and Foreign Income)

California does not allow the state and local income tax, nor does it allow for the deduction of State Disability Insurance (SDI) or Voluntary Plan Disability Insurance (VPDI). The SDI and the VPDI would have been listed on Form 1040, Schedule A, line 5. An adjustment is made on 540 Schedule CA, Part II, line 5, to remove these amounts from the California return. If a California taxpayer has tax liability balance due for some previous tax year, payment of that balance can be claimed as a deduction on the federal return in the year paid. California law does not allow a deduction for sales or state taxes. Adjustments are made on 540 Schedule CA, Part II, line 5b. California did not conform to the $10,000 state and local taxes limitation. The adjustment is required on 540 Schedule CA.

Sales and Use Tax

The California Department of Tax and Fee Administration (CDTFA) administers sales and use tax. Retailers who conduct business in California must register with CDTFA and have a Seller's Permit. Sales tax applies to the sale of merchandise in California. Use tax applies to the use, storage, or other consumption of merchandise in the state. When buyers purchase goods online the seller needs to add the state tax for the buyer to pay at the time of purchase. If not, then the buyer would pay the use tax on their tax return, whether it was personal or a business transaction. California law requires in-state purchases, and out-of-state purchased items, be taxed in California. Form 540, line 91 reports Use Tax.

Line 8-9: Home Mortgage Interest Paid

Schedule CA, Lines 8 and 9

TCJA changed the mortgage interest deduction from $1,000,000 to a maximum of $750,000. For Married filing separate, the maximum was $500,000 and now it is $375,000. California does not conform, and the adjustment is made on line 8a, column C. California also did not conform to the federal suspension of the paid interest deduction on home equity loans.

Taxpayers who reduce their federal mortgage interest must increase the California itemized deductions by the same amount to return the paid interest to its original amount. This allows the California taxpayer to claim the full amount of interest paid as an itemized deduction and reduce their tax liability more than they could on their federal return. Enter the amount of federal mortgage interest credit as a positive number on 540 Schedule CA, Part II, line 8a, column C.

The California deduction for investment interest expenses may be different than the federal deduction. Form FTB 3526, *Investment Interest Expense Deduction*, should be used to figure the amount to enter on 540 Schedule CA, Part II, line 9, column B or C.

Line 11 Gifts to Charity

Charitable contributions can only be deducted on the California return if the client itemized deductions on the federal return. Proper documentation is always needed to prepare an accurate return. Most deductions are generally limited to 50% of the federal AGI. Remember, direct payments to individuals are never a charitable contribution.

If the taxpayer filed Federal Form 8283, *Noncash Charitable Contributions*, with their tax return and claimed a deduction for a contribution greater than $5,000, a qualified appraisal is needed. This does not have to be included with the tax return. If the property is more than $500,000, the qualified appraisal must be included with the tax return.

If the taxpayer is deducting a prior year's charitable contribution carryover and if the California carryover is larger than the federal carryover, increase the California itemized deductions by entering the additional amount as a positive number on 540 Schedule CA, Part II, line 11, column C. California does not conform to federal law regarding athletic seats and still allows taxpayers to deduct them as a charitable contribution, even if seats are offered in return.

California did not conform to the above the line charitable deduction for nonitemizers.

Line 15 Casualty and Theft Losses

Schedule CA, Lines 15

Federal law allows a deduction for any personal casualty and disaster loss that resulted from a presidentially declared disaster area. California, however, does not conform and still allows personal casualty theft loss and disaster loss to be deducted, regardless of any presidential declaration. The taxpayer would need to complete a separate federal Form 4684 and enter the resulting numbers on 540 Schedule CA, Part II, line 15, either column B or C.

Between January 1, 2014, and January 1, 2024, taxpayers may deduct a disaster loss for any loss sustained in any city and county in California that has been declared by the California Governor as a state of emergency or declared a disaster area.

California law usually follows federal law regarding the treatment of losses incurred because of a casualty or a disaster. However, for California purposes, a casualty loss becomes a disaster loss when both of the following occur:

> ➢ The loss is sustained in an area the President of the United States, or the Governor of California, declares a state of emergency.
> ➢ The loss is sustained because of the declared disaster.

For information on how to deduct a loss from a disaster, see FTB Publication 1034, *Disaster Loss: How to Claim a State Tax Deduction*. Pub. 1034 includes a chart of declared disasters that is revised as needed. When claiming a disaster loss, the taxpayer may have to use the following forms:

Federal Forms:

> ➢ Completed Form 4684, *Casualties and Disasters*, use California amounts.
> ➢ Copy of Form 1040 or 1040X.
> ➢ Any supporting federal schedules that verify the taxpayer's deduction.

California Forms:

> ➢ Schedule D-1, *Sales of Business Property.*

Form FTB 3505V, *Net Operating Loss (NOL), Computation and NOL and Disaster Loss Limitations, Individuals, Estates and Trusts.*

Attach a clearly written statement to the loss documentation that indicates:

> ➢ The date of the disaster.
> ➢ The location of the disaster (city, county, and state).
> ➢ Decision to deduct the loss in the taxable year or the year before the disaster occurred.

Photos of the damaged property would be good recordkeeping. For more information on claiming a California disaster loss, see FTB Publication 1034.

Taxpayers who may need a copy of their prior year tax returns should file Form FTB 3516, *Request for Copy of Tax Return*. Disaster victims can receive their copies for no charge by writing the year of the disaster and its name in red ink at the top of the form.

Line 16 Other Itemized Deductions

California did not conform to the suspension of Form 2106 for tax years 2018 through 2025. There are only a few differences between federal and California law regarding employee business expenses. For example, federal law has suspended the 2% floor of job expenses and certain miscellaneous deductions; yet, California does not conform. Federal employee business expenses would be listed on Form 2106 and be carried forward to Schedule A. If there are differences and the federal amount is larger, the difference would be entered as a negative number on 540 Schedule CA. If the California portion is larger, the difference is entered as a positive number.

California does not allow a business expense deduction for club(s) that restrict membership use of its services; or facilities that discriminate based on age, sex, race, religion, color, ancestry, national origin, sexual orientation, and other forms of discrimination covered generally by antidiscrimination laws.

Example: Bud joined the Traveling Boomers Club. The club restricts membership for those over the age of 65. Bud paid $1,500 in dues and $2,500 in business entertainment expenses. Bud cannot deduct the $1,500 for dues for either federal or California purposes because Bud is paying for a privilege.

California does not conform to the suspension and still allows the deduction of tax preparation fees; it also does not conform to the suspension of the 2% floor. California adjustments will need to be made for the following deductions:

- ➢ Adoption related expenses.
- ➢ Nontaxable income expenses.
- ➢ State legislator's travel expenses.
- ➢ Interest on loans from utility companies.

Claim of Right

California has its own unique claim of right adjustment. A taxpayer that claims a deduction on the federal return but claims a credit in lieu of the deduction on the California return, must make an adjustment on the California return. The adjustment is made by entering the federal deduction as a negative amount on 540 Schedule CA, line 41. The credit amount is added on Form 540, line 44, the total payment line. Taxpayer should write IRC 1341 and the amount of the credit to the left of the total.

Under the claim of right provision, an individual may recompute their personal income tax liability if they included it in their adjusted gross income for a prior year. The income amount needs to be more than $3,000 and the amount was repaid during the taxable year.

California allows a claim of right adjustment similar to the adjustment allowed under federal law. Depending on whether a federal credit is taken in lieu of a deduction, an addition or subtraction adjustment may be required for state personal income tax.

Deductions of repaid amounts that were previously included in income are exempt from the 2% floor. See FTB Publication 1001.

Investment Interest Expense

Investment interest expense could also be called margin interest found on Form 1099-DIV or Form 1099-INT. California did not conform to TCJA regarding this deduction.

Voluntary Contributions

California allows taxpayers to make voluntary contributions to various charitable causes. These contributions can be designated on page 4 of Form 540. Unlike the federal Presidential Election Fund on the federal return, these voluntary contributions will increase the taxpayers' tax liability or decrease their refund by the amount contributed on their California return.

Charitable contributions can be made from the California tax return to the charitable organizations listed below. If the taxpayer wants to contribute to one of these funds, additional research may be necessary to determine the contribution minimums, maximums, and eligibility criteria.

- Alzheimer's Disease/Related Disorders Fund
- California Breast Cancer Research Fund
- California Cancer Research Fund
- California Community and Neighborhood Tree Voluntary Tax Contribution Fund
- California Firefighters' Memorial Fund
- California Peace Officer Memorial Foundation Fund
- California Sea Otter Fund
- California Senior Citizen Advocacy Voluntary Tax Contribution Fund
- California Seniors Special Fund (No expiration date)
- Emergency Food for Families Voluntary Tax Contribution Fund
- Keep Arts in Schools Fund
- Mental Health Crisis Prevention Voluntary Tax Contribution Fund
- Native California Wildlife Rehabilitation Voluntary Tax Contribution Fund
- Prevention of Animal Homelessness and Cruelty Fund
- Protect Our Coast and Oceans Fund
- Rape Kit Backlog
- Rare and Endangered Species Preservation Program
- Schools Not Prisons
- School Supplies for Homeless Children Fund
- State Parks Protection Fund/Parks Pass Purchase
- Suicide Prevention Voluntary Tax Contribution Fund

Part 1 Review Questions

To obtain the maximum benefit from this chapter, LTP recommends that you complete each of the following questions, and then compare them to the answers with feedback that immediately follow. Under governing self-study standards, vendors are required to present review questions intermittently throughout each self-study course.

These questions and explanations are not part of the final examination and will not be graded by LTP.

CIDP1.1
California generally conforms to federal medical expense deductions.

    a. True
    b. False

CIDP1.2
California Voluntary Contributions allow taxpayers to make voluntary contributions to various state causes. These contributions will affect their tax liability or refund if applicable.

    a. True
    b. False

CIDP1.3
When the President of the United States has declared a disaster area in California the resident may be able to claim on of the following?

    a. Disaster loss
    b. Disaster gain
    c. Expense credit
    d. Tuition credit

CIDP1.4
What should Jessica do if her California charitable contribution carryover is larger than her federal charitable contribution carryover?

    a. Jessica should exclude the difference from her California tax return.
    b. Jessica should do nothing.
    c. Jessica should increase her California itemized deduction.
    d. Jessica should decrease her California itemized deduction.

CIDP1.5
The purpose of 540 Schedule CA is for the California resident taxpayer to___.

    a. increase exemptions based on California law
    b. adjust their federal adjusted gross income
    c. increase the taxpayer's tax refund
    d. decrease the taxpayer's tax refund

Part 1 Review Questions Answers

CIDP1.1
California generally conforms to federal medical expense deductions.

    a. True
    b. False

Feedback: Review section *540 Schedule CA: Itemizing Deductions.*

CIDP1.2
California Voluntary Contributions allow taxpayers to make voluntary contributions to various state causes. These contributions will affect their tax liability or refund if applicable.

    a. True
    b. False

Feedback: Review section *Voluntary Contributions.*

CIDP1.3
When the President of the United States has declared a disaster area in California the resident may be able to claim which of the following?

    a. Disaster loss
    b. Disaster gain
    c. Expense credit
    d. Tuition credit

Feedback: Review section *Casualty and Theft Losses.*

CIDP1.4

What should Jessica do if her California charitable contribution carryover is larger than her federal charitable contribution carryover?

    a. Jessica should exclude the difference from her California tax return.
    b. Jessica should do nothing.
    c. Jessica should increase her California itemized deduction.
    d. Jessica should decrease her California itemized deduction.

Feedback: Review section *Gifts to Charity*.

CIDP1.5

The purpose of 540 Schedule CA is for the California resident taxpayer to___.

    a. increase exemptions based on California law
    b. adjust their federal adjusted gross income
    c. increase the taxpayer's tax refund
    d. decrease the taxpayer's tax refund

Takeaways

Knowing when California law conforms to federal law is important when preparing the state return, especially with the suspension of so many federal tax laws through 2025. Tax law is constantly changing, and a good tax professional will always do research and not rely on software for answers. Taxpayers must be able to substantiate deductions claimed on the tax return if requested by either the IRS or the FTB. Taxpayers can normally substantiate tax deductions by providing documentation, such as receipts, invoices, and canceled checks.

Remember, when taxpayers live in a community property state and file a separate return, both income and expenses are added together and then divided between the two tax returns. The taxpayer and spouse do not claim their individual income and expenses separately.

TEST YOUR KNOWLEDGE!
Go online to take a practice quiz.

Chapter 9 Schedule C

Introduction

This chapter presents an income and expenses overview of Schedule C. Business income or loss is reported on Schedule C then flows to Schedule 1, line 3. Sole proprietorship is not a legal entity; it is a popular business structure due to its simplicity, ease of setup, and nominal start-up costs. A sole proprietor would register the business name with the state and city, obtain local business licenses, and then open for business. A drawback of being a sole proprietor is that the owner is 100% personally liable for the business's income and/or debt.

Objectives

At the end of this lesson, the student will:

> ➢ Identify the differences between accounting periods and accounting methods.
> ➢ Understand the guidelines between an independent contractor and an employee.
> ➢ Recognize what determines start-up costs.
> ➢ Identify how to classify employees.

Resources

Form 1040	Publication 15	Instructions Form 1040
Form 1099-NEC	Publication 15-A	Instructions Form 1099-NEC
Form 3115	Publication 334	Instructions Form 3115
Form 4562	Publication 463	Instructions Form 4562
Form 4797	Publication 535	Instructions Form 4797
Form 8829	Publication 536	Instructions Form 8829
Schedule C	Publication 538	Instructions for Schedule C
Schedule SE	Publication 544	Instructions Schedule SE
	Publication 551	Publication 946
	Publication 560	Publication 527
	Publication 587	

Table of Contents

Part 1 Business Entity Types

There are many different types of business entities with their own sets of rules, regulations, and guidelines within the U.S. tax laws. The following entity type could apply to Schedule C, E, and/or F.

Sole Proprietorship

A sole proprietor is an individual owner of a business or a self-employed individual. Taxable income is reported on Schedule C and flows to Form 1040, Schedule 1, line 3. A business owner could have to pay self-employment tax reported, which is reported on Schedule SE.

A sole proprietorship reports the income and expenses from the owner's business on Schedule C, *Profit or Loss from a Business*. An individual is self-employed if the following apply:

> ➢ Conducts a trade or business as a sole proprietorship.
> ➢ Is an independent contractor.
> ➢ Is in business for themself.

Self-employment can include work in addition to regular full-time business activities. It can also include certain part-time work done at home or in addition to a regular job.

Minimum Income Reporting Requirements for Schedule C Filers

If the taxpayer's net earnings from self-employment are $400 or more, the taxpayer is required to file a tax return. If net earnings from self-employment were less than $400, the taxpayer may still have to file a tax return if they meet other filing requirements.

Husband and Wife Qualified Joint Venture (QJV)

A husband and wife cannot be sole proprietors of the same business. If they are joint owners, they are partners and should file a partnership return using Form 1065, *U.S. Partnership Return of Income.* They can be partners, but "sole" means one, and for the purposes of a business, the IRS does not recognize spouses as one.

If the taxpayer and spouse each materially participated in the business as the only members of a jointly owned and operated business, and if they file a joint return, they can elect to be taxed as a qualified joint venture (QJV) instead of a partnership. This election does not generally increase the total tax on the joint return, but it does give the self-employment credit for each taxpayer's Social Security earnings.

To make the QJV election, the spouses must divide all their income and expenses between them and file two separate Schedule Cs. Once the election has been made, it can only be revoked with IRS permission. The election will remain in effect if the spouses file as a qualified joint venture. If the taxpayer and spouse do not qualify in one year, then they will need to resubmit the paperwork to qualify as a qualified joint venture for the next year.

If the spouses own an unincorporated business and if they live in a state, foreign country, or a U.S. possession that has community property laws, the income must be treated as either a sole proprietorship or a partnership. Alaska, Arizona, California, Idaho, Louisiana, Nevada, New Mexico, Texas, Washington, and Wisconsin are the only states with community property laws.

Single-member Limited Liability Company (LLC)

For federal income tax purposes, a single-member LLC is not a separate entity. The single-member LLC would report income directly on the related Schedule as a sole-proprietor. A sole member of a domestic LLC would need to submit Form 8832 to the IRS prior to filing a corporation return if it is electing to treat the LLC as a corporation.

Accounting Periods

An accounting period is the fixed time that covers the company's financial statements. A tax year is an annual accounting period used for keeping records as well as for reporting income and expenses. An accounting period cannot be longer than 12 months, and options include:

➢ The standard calendar year.
➢ A fiscal year, which is a 12-month period that can end on the last day of any month except December.

Taxpayers generally choose the calendar-year accounting period for their individual income tax returns. Business owners must choose their accounting period before filing their first business tax return.

Calendar Year

A calendar tax year is the 12 consecutive months from January 1st to December 31st. Sole proprietors must adopt the calendar year if any of the following apply:

➢ The taxpayer does not keep books or records.
➢ The taxpayer has no annual accounting period.
➢ The taxpayer's present tax year does not qualify as a fiscal year.
➢ The taxpayer's use of the calendar tax year is required under the Internal Revenue Code (IRC) or the Income Tax Regulations.

Fiscal Year

A fiscal year is 12 consecutive months ending on the last day of any month except December. A "52 to 53-week tax year" is a fiscal year that varies from 52 to 53 weeks. It does not have to end on the last day of the month. For more information on fiscal years, who might choose them, and why, see Publication 538.

Change in Tax Year

To change the type of tax year used, the taxpayer would file Form 1128, *Application to Adopt, Change, or Retain a Tax Year*. See Instructions Form 1128.

Accounting Methods

Accounting methods are sets of rules used to determine when income and expenses are reported on a return. The accounting method chosen for the business must be used throughout the life of the business. If the owner wants to change the accounting method, approval from the IRS must be obtained. The two most common methods are cash and accrual. Businesses that have inventory must use the accrual accounting method.

The following are acceptable accounting methods:

- ➢ The cash method.
- ➢ The accrual method.
- ➢ Special methods of accounting for certain items of income and expenses.
- ➢ The combination (hybrid) method, using elements of two or more of the above.

F	Accounting method:	**(1)** ☐ Cash	**(2)** ☐ Accrual	**(3)** ☐ Other (specify)			
G	Did you "materially participate" in the operation of this business during 2022? If "No," see instructions for limit on losses					☐ Yes	☐ No
H	If you started or acquired this business during 2022, check here					☐	
I	Did you make any payments in 2022 that would require you to file Form(s) 1099? See instructions					☐ Yes	☐ No
J	If "Yes," did you or will you file required Form(s) 1099?					☐ Yes	☐ No

Portion of Schedule C

Taxpayers should choose whichever system best reflects their income. If the taxpayer does not choose an accounting method that clearly reflects their income, the IRS may recalculate the income to reflect the correct accounting method, which could involve penalties and interest. Taxpayers must use the same accounting method when figuring their taxable income and keeping their books. However, business owners can use a different accounting method for each business they operate. See Publication 538, *Accounting Periods and Methods*.

Cash Method

If one uses the cash method, all items must be reported as income in the year in which they are actually or constructively received. Income is constructively received when it becomes or is made available to the taxpayer without restrictions, such as through a bank account; the income does not necessarily have to be in the taxpayer's physical possession.

When using the cash method, all expenses are deducted in the year they are paid. This is the method most individual taxpayers use. Exceptions to the rule include prepaid expenses—for example, insurance or tuition. If expenses were paid in advance, they are generally deductible only in the year to which the expense applies.

Example: In the beginning of 2022, Chandler paid his business insurance expenses in advance for 2022, 2023, and 2024. For his 2022 tax return, he will only be able to claim the portion of those expenses that were used for 2022. He will only be able to claim the portion of the expense used for 2023 and 2024 on his tax returns for those respective years.

Cash method is the simplest accounting method, and taxpayers must use this method if they do not keep regular or adequate books.

The following three types of taxpayers are unable to use the cash method:

- ➢ C corporations.
- ➢ Partnerships that have a C corporation as a partner.
- ➢ Tax shelters.

Accrual Method

If the accrual method is used, income is reported when earned, whether it has been actually or constructively received. Similarly, expenses are deducted when acquired rather than when paid. Businesses with inventory are required to use the accrual method to track the business' cost-of-goods-sold. Once this accounting method has been chosen, the taxpayer cannot change to a different accounting method without IRS permission.

If a business owner chooses the accrual method, the amount of gross income would be reported at the earliest of the following events:

➢ When payment was received.
➢ When the income is due.
➢ When the business earned the income.
➢ When title was passed to the business.

Example: Ruben is a calendar-year taxpayer who uses the accrual method and owns a dance studio. He received payment on October 1, 2022, for a one-year contract for 48 one-hour lessons beginning on October 1, 2022. Ruben gave eight lessons in 2022. Ruben would include one-sixth (8/48) of the payment in his 2022 income and the remaining five-sixths (40/48) would be reported in his 2023 tax year because, under the accrual method, income is reported when it has been earned, not when it has been actually or constructively received.

Combination (Hybrid) Method

The taxpayer can choose any combination of cash, accrual, and special methods of accounting if the combination clearly shows the taxpayer's income and expenses and if the method is used consistently. The combination (or hybrid) method is often used when a company possesses some kind of inventory that is not essential to accounting for income. The combination method cannot be used in the following cases:

➢ If inventory is necessary to account for income, the accrual method must be used.
➢ If the cash method for figuring income is used, the cash method must also be used for expenses. It cannot be combined with another method.
➢ If the taxpayer uses an accrual method for reporting expenses, then the accrual method of income must be used for everything else as well.
➢ If the taxpayer uses a combination method that includes the cash method, treat that combination method as the cash method.

Independent Contractors

An independent contractor is an individual who is hired by employers on a per-contract basis where the employer only has the right to control or direct the result of the work but cannot dictate what or how the result will be achieved. This classification permits the taxpayer to certain tax benefits and full responsibility for their employment taxes. An independent contractor can itemize all ordinary and necessary business expenses by using the appropriate schedule.

To be considered an independent contractor, the taxpayer should set their own hours and work schedule, be responsible for having their own tools or equipment, and usually work for multiple individuals or companies.

If a taxpayer is an independent contractor, the taxpayer would not fill out Form W-4, *Employee's Withholding Allowance Certificate,* nor will taxes be withheld from the taxpayer's paycheck. The independent contractor is responsible for paying self-employment tax (Social Security and Medicare) and making estimated tax payments to cover both the self-employment tax and their income tax.

Taxpayers are considered employees and not independent contractors if the following apply:

➢ Must comply with their employer's work instructions.
➢ Receive training from the employer or the employer's designee.
➢ Provide services that are integral to the employer's business.
➢ Provide services that are personally rendered.
➢ Hire, pay, and supervise workers for the employer.
➢ Have an ongoing working relationship with the employer.
➢ Must follow set hours of work.
➢ Work full time for the employer.
➢ Work on the employer's premises.
➢ Work in a sequence set by the employer.
➢ Submit regular reports to the employer.
➢ Receive payments of regular amounts at regular intervals.
➢ Receive payments for business or travel expenses.
➢ Rely on employer to provide tools and materials.
➢ Do not have a major investment in resources for providing services.
➢ Do not make a profit or suffer a loss from services provided.
➢ Work for one employer at a time.
➢ Do not offer services to the general public.
➢ Can be fired by the employer.
➢ May quit anytime without incurring liability.
➢ Are statutory employees.

If one qualifies as a statutory employee for income tax purposes, the box titled "Statutory Employee" on Form W-2, *Wage and Tax Statement*, will be checked. Income and expenses must be ordinary and necessary business expenses, and are reported on Schedule C.

Statutory Employees

A statutory employee is an independent contractor who is nevertheless still treated as an employee due to some statute. This applies to the following occupational groups, all of whom qualify as statutory employees under U.S. law:

➢ Agent drivers or commissioned drivers limited to those who distribute food, beverages (other than milk products), and laundry or dry-cleaning services for someone else.
➢ Full-time life insurance salespeople who work for one company.
➢ A home worker who follows the guidelines of his or her employer using materials furnished by that employer and returning them as designated by the employer.
➢ Traveling or city salespeople who sell for one principal employer. The goods sold must be merchandise for resale or supplies for use in the buyer's business operation. The customers must be retailers, wholesalers, contractors, or operators of hotels, restaurants, or other businesses dealing with food or lodging.

To make sure the salespeople are employees under the usual common-law rules, individuals must be evaluated separately. If a salesperson does not meet the tests for a common-law employee, then they may be considered a statutory employee. See Publication 15 and Publication 535.

A statutory employee is very limited and must meet specific criteria to meet the definition. Tax preparers should watch for incorrectly marked Forms W-2 and advise people with incorrectly marked forms to have their employers reissue a corrected Form W-2. If the taxpayer does not wish to do this, the tax professional should prepare the return using the information reported on Form W-2.

Statutory Nonemployees

Statutory nonemployees are treated as self-employed for federal tax purposes, including income and employment taxes. The following are considered statutory nonemployees:

➢ Direct sellers.
➢ Qualified real estate agents.
➢ Certain types of caretakers.

Identification Numbers

Taxpayers can use their SSN or taxpayer identification number (TIN) on the appropriate schedule. However, the taxpayer must have an employer identification number (EIN) if either applies:

➢ The taxpayer pays wages to one or more employees.
➢ The taxpayer files pension or excise tax returns.

Taxpayers can obtain an EIN by completing Form SS-4, *Application for Employer Identification Number*. A new EIN must be obtained if either the entity type or the ownership of the business changes. If the business has employees, the employer (or their delegate) must see the SSN to verify the name and number as it appears on the Social Security card. The employer (or their delegate) must have each employee complete Form W-4. See Publication 17 and SS-4 Instructions.

Schedule SE: Self-Employment Tax

Social Security and Medicare taxes become a little more complicated for self-employed taxpayers. Normally, the standard 12.4% tax for Social Security and 2.9% tax for Medicare is split between employees and their employer; an employee pays half this amount, and the employer matches it. Self-employed individuals, however, are simultaneously the employee and the employer and thus must pay the full 15.3% tax for Social Security and Medicare by themselves. This is called the self-employment tax (SE), and self-employed taxpayers must pay it because they do not have Social Security and Medicare taxes withheld from their earnings.

The self-employment tax is not as overwhelming as it might seem. For example, the 15.3% self-employment tax is figured from 92.35% of the taxpayer's net profit; it is not figured from their gross income or even from their total net profit, just 92.35% of it. Taxpayers who have net profit of $400 do not need to pay self-employment tax. If net earnings are more than $400, self-employment tax needs to be paid. Self-employed taxpayers are allowed to deduct half of the self-employment tax as an adjustment to income on Schedule 1, line 15.

Reported on Schedule 2, line 4, the SE tax applies to everyone who has self-employment income with net earnings of $400 or more. Self-employment income consists of income from self-employed business activities that are reported on Schedule C, E, and F, as well as income received by clergy and employees of churches and religious organizations. There are three ways to figure net earnings from self-employment:

➢ The regular method.
➢ The nonfarm optional method.
➢ The farm optional method.

The regular method must be used unless the taxpayer qualifies to use either one or both optional methods. To calculate net earnings (sometimes referred to as "actual earnings") using the regular method, multiply the self-employment earnings by 92.35% (.9235).

Taxpayers who would like to make estimated tax payments to cover the self-employment tax they expect to owe must send the estimated tax payments on the following due dates:

➢ April 15th.
➢ June 15th.
➢ September 15th.
➢ January 15th of the upcoming calendar year.

If any of these dates fall on a holiday or weekend, the payment is due the next business day.

Schedule C

Schedule C, *Profit or Loss from Business*, is used for the sole proprietor or the sole owner of an LLC to report the business income and expenses for the current tax year. If the business owner owns multiple businesses, then a separate Schedule C must be filed for each business.

Completing Schedule C

Schedule C is a very detailed form that categorizes the income and expense of the business. The first portion requires basic information about the business and its type.

Line A: Enter the business or professional activity that provided the principal source of income reported on line 1 of the Schedule C. If the taxpayer owned more than one business, each business must complete a separate Schedule C or appropriate form. If the general field or activity is wholesale or retail trade or services connected with production services, state the type of customer or client. For example, "wholesale of hardware to retailers," or "appraisal of real estate for lending institutions."

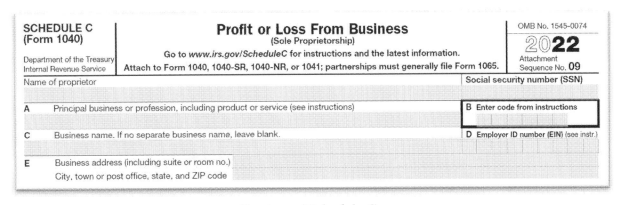

Portion of Schedule C

Line B: Enter the six-digit code found in the instructions for Schedule C to designate the type of business. If the taxpayer's company-type is not listed, find a similar principal business or professional activity code. No matter how unsure you are about which code to use, try not to use business code 999999, *Unknown Business*; businesses with this code are significantly more likely to be audited by the IRS due to the lack of information provided by using that code.

Line C: Enter the business name.

Line D: Enter the employer ID number (EIN). The taxpayer would have obtained this number by filling out and submitting Form SS-4 online to the IRS. If there is no EIN, enter the taxpayer's SSN at the top of the page where indicated. Remember: as a sole proprietorship, the company only needs an EIN in the following cases:

➢ The company has a qualified retirement plan.
➢ The company is required to file an employment, an excise, or an alcohol, tobacco, or firearms return.
➢ At least part of the company involves paying gambling winnings.

Line E: Business address. Enter the physical address of the business, not a P.O. Box number. If the business has a suite or room number, make sure that it is entered as well. If the business was conducted from the taxpayer's home, and if it is the same address used on Form 1040, page 1, do not complete this line.

Line F: Select which accounting method was used by the business during the tax year.

Line G: Material Participation

"Material participation" is when an owner of a passive activity takes part in the business's operations even though they typically wouldn't. A business is a passive activity if the owner does not regularly participate in the day-to-day operations of the business. Rental activity is the most common type of passive activity, but it is far from the only kind. If the business experienced a passive activity loss, the loss may be limited by reducing the percentage of the business's income that can be taxed, but only if the taxpayer can show that they materially participated in the business.

To be able to limit losses by claiming "material participation", the taxpayer must meet any of the seven material participation tests from the requirements listed below. These generally cover any work done in connection with an activity in which one owned an interest at the time the work was completed. However, work is considered participation if it is work that the owner would not customarily do in the same type of activity, and if one of the main reasons for doing the work was to avoid the disallowance of losses or credits from the activity under the passive activity rules.

If the taxpayer meets any of these tests, check "Yes" on line G; otherwise, check "No." For the purposes of the passive activity rules, any of the following requirements must be met to be considered to have materially participated:

1. The taxpayer substantially participated in the activity on a regular and continuous basis for more than 500 hours during the tax year.
2. The taxpayer substantially participated in the activity of all individuals, even including those who do not own an interest in the activity.

3. The taxpayer participated during the tax year as much as any other person in the company.
4. Taxpayer participated for more than 100 hours during the tax year but did not materially participate.
5. The taxpayer materially participated in the activity for any 5 of the prior 10 tax years.
6. The taxpayer is in a personal service activity in which the taxpayer materially participated for any three prior tax years. A personal service activity is an activity that involves performing personal services in the fields of health, law, engineering, architecture, accounting, consulting, or any other trade or business in which capital is not a material income-producing factor.
7. Taxpayer meets the test if any person other than the taxpayer did the following:
   a) Received compensation for performing management services in connection with the activity.
   b) Spent more hours during the tax year doing other activities than he or she spent performing management services in connection with the activity, regardless of whether the person was compensated for the service.

Line H: If the business was started or acquired in the current tax year, check the box.

Line I: If the taxpayer made any payments that would require the taxpayer to file Form(s) 1099, check yes; otherwise, check no.

Schedule C, Part I, Income

Part I	Income	
1	Gross receipts or sales. See instructions for line 1 and check the box if this income was reported to you on Form W-2 and the "Statutory employee" box on that form was checked ☐	1
2	Returns and allowances	2
3	Subtract line 2 from line 1	3
4	Cost of goods sold (from line 42)	4
5	**Gross profit.** Subtract line 4 from line 3	5
6	Other income, including federal and state gasoline or fuel tax credit or refund (see instructions)	6
7	**Gross income.** Add lines 5 and 6	7

Portion of Schedule C

Gross Income Receipts

Self-employment income is income earned from the performance of personal services that cannot be classified as wages because an employer-employee relationship does not exist between the payer and the payee because they are the same person. Self-employment tax is imposed on any U.S. citizen or resident alien who has self-employment income. If one is self-employed in a business that provides services (where products are not a factor), the gross income goes on line 7 of Schedule C and includes amounts reported on Form 1099-MISC, Form 1099-K, and Form 1099-NEC.

Different Kinds of Income

The taxpayer must report on their tax return all income received in business unless it is excluded by law. In most circumstances, income will be in the form of cash, checks, and credit card charges. Bartering is another form of income, and its fair market value must be included as income.

Example: Ernest operates a plumbing business and uses the cash method of accounting. Jim owns a computer store and contacts Ernest to discuss fixing the clogged pipes in his store in exchange for a laptop for Ernest's business. This is business-to-business bartering. If Ernest accepts the deal, he must report the fair market value of the laptop as income because it was the "income" he received in exchange for his service.

Miscellaneous Income

If one is self-employed in a business involving manufacturing, merchandising, or mining, the gross income on line 7 of Schedule C is the total sales from that business, minus the cost of goods sold, and plus any income from investments and incidental or outside operations or sources. If the taxpayer is involved in more than one business, a separate Schedule C is filed for each business (for example, newspaper delivery and computer consulting). Other income commonly includes bank interest, rebates, and reimbursements from government food programs for a daycare provider.

Line 1: Enter the gross receipts for the year from the trade or business. Include all amounts received, even if the income was not reported on Form(s) 1099.

Line 2: Enter returns and allowances for the year from the trade or business. Even though this amount will be subtracted later, make sure it is entered here as a positive number. A sales return is a refund given to the taxpayer's customers who returned defective, damaged, or unwanted products.

Line 6: Report all amounts from finance reserve income, scrap sales, bad debts recovered, interest (on notes and accounts receivable), state gasoline or fuel tax refunds received in 2021. Prizes and awards related to the trade or business and other miscellaneous business income are also reported on line 6.

Schedule C, Part II, Expenses

To be a deductible business expense, the tangible or nontangible item must be either ordinary or necessary. An ordinary expense is an expense that is common, standard, and accepted in the taxpayer's industry. A necessary expense is one that is helpful and appropriate for the taxpayer's trade or business. An expense does not have to be indispensable to be considered necessary. The taxpayer needs to keep records of their expenses no matter how minimal the payment is. Documentation is the key if the taxpayer is ever audited for proof of expenses.

Part II	Expenses. Enter expenses for business use of your home **only** on line 30.				
8	Advertising	8	18	Office expense (see instructions)	18
9	Car and truck expenses (see instructions)	9	19	Pension and profit-sharing plans	19
10	Commissions and fees	10	20	Rent or lease (see instructions):	
11	Contract labor (see instructions)	11	a	Vehicles, machinery, and equipment	20a
12	Depletion	12	b	Other business property	20b
13	Depreciation and section 179 expense deduction (not included in Part III) (see instructions)	13	21	Repairs and maintenance	21
			22	Supplies (not included in Part III)	22
			23	Taxes and licenses	23
			24	Travel and meals:	
14	Employee benefit programs (other than on line 19)	14	a	Travel	24a
15	Insurance (other than health)	15	b	Deductible meals (see instructions)	24b
16	Interest (see instructions):		25	Utilities	25
a	Mortgage (paid to banks, etc.)	16a	26	Wages (less employment credits)	26

Portion of Schedule C

The following examples are expenses that can be deducted:

Line 8: Advertising. Advertising is communicating with the general public to promote a product or service that the business provides. All advertising expenses can generally be deducted if the expense is related to the business. Advertising for purposes of influencing legislation is not deductible as this is considered lobbying.

Line 9: Car and Truck Expenses. Expenses used for business can be deducted as a business expense. Vehicle expenses include gasoline, oil, repairs, license tags, insurance, and depreciation. For 2022 the rate is 58.5 cents per mile from January to June and 62.5 cents per mile from July to December. For tax year 2023 the business travel rate is 65.5 cents per mile. Standard mileage rate for each business mile can be used for the taxpayer's owned or leased vehicle. The standard mileage rate cannot be used if five or more cars or light trucks are used at the same time. Five or more cars are considered to be a fleet.

The taxpayer may choose between using the actual expenses incurred by using the vehicle or using the standard mileage rate. Report the expense amount on Schedule C, Part II, line 9. The taxpayer should include the following in their daily business mileage log:

➢ Beginning mileage.
➢ Ending mileage.
➢ Commuting mileage.

Business meals for 2022 are 100% deductible only if the properly applied rules from Revenue Procedure 2019-48 are used. The rule is for expenses incurred after December 31, 2020, and before January 1, 2022, the food and/or beverages must be provided by a restaurant. A restaurant means a business that prepares and sells food and beverages to retail customers for immediate consumption, regardless of whether the food or beverages are consumed on the restaurant's premises. A restaurant does not include a business that primarily sell prepackaged food or beverages not for immediate consumption, such as:

➢ A grocery store
➢ Specialty food store
➢ Beer, wine, or liquor store
➢ Drugstore
➢ Convivence store
➢ Newsstand
➢ A vending machine or kiosk

See Notice 2021-25.

When determining the 100% meal deduction, the following applies:

➢ Business meals that don't qualify for the 100% deduction, such as those that were purchased from a grocery store, may still qualify for the 50% deduction.
➢ The 100% meals deduction applies to amounts paid or incurred after December 31, 2020, and before January 1, 2023.

Remember, ordinary business-related meals are 50% deductible if business travel is either overnight or long enough to require the taxpayer to stop for sleep or rest to properly perform his or her duties. The taxpayer should note the destination and the reason for travel on a daily business mileage document.

Business meals for 2023 revert back to prior to 2021 rules, which is 50% deductible, and most entertainment expenses are not deductible at all.

Line 10: Commissions and Fees. A commission is a service charge for providing advice on an investment purchase for the taxpayer. The commission must be ordinary and necessary for the type of business the taxpayer claims. Expenses paid for services rendered by a nonemployee could be considered commissions or fees. If more than $600 is paid to one individual, Form 1099-NEC and/or 1099-MISC must be filed, and a copy of the form should be issued to the independent contractor by January 31st of the following year. A copy of the form must be sent to the taxpayer who rendered the work; a copy must also be sent to the IRS along with Form 1096. See Instructions Form 1099(s).

Line 11: Contract Labor. Contract labor includes payments to individuals that are not employees, such as independent contractors. Report the payment amounts on this line.

Line 12: Depletion. Depletion is only deducted when a taxpayer has an economic interest in mineral property such as oil, gas, and standing timber reported on this line.

Line 13: Depreciation. Depreciation is the annual deduction that is allowed or allowable on all qualified business property reported on this line. If the taxpayer has timber depletion, they will use Form T. See Publication 535.

Line 14: Employee Benefit Programs. Employee benefit programs are an expense for the business owner and include retirement plans, disability insurance, life insurance, education assistance, and vacation and holiday pay. Expenses for employees such as accident plans, health plans, dependent-care expenses, and group life insurance plans can be deducted on this line.

Line 15: Insurance. The following business insurance premiums may be deducted on this line:

- ➢ Liability insurance.
- ➢ Malpractice insurance.
- ➢ Casualty insurance, such as fire or theft.
- ➢ Workers' compensation insurance.
- ➢ Disability insurance that covers the business's overhead expenses if the sole proprietor becomes unable to work.
- ➢ Bond insurance.
- ➢ Insurance to cover inventory and merchandise.
- ➢ Credit insurance.
- ➢ Business interruption insurance.

One who is self-employed may qualify to deduct up to 100% of the medical insurance premiums paid for themselves and qualifying family members. To take the deduction, the insurance plan must be established under the business, and the business must make a profit. See Publication 535.

Line 16: Interest. The following are examples of deductible interest reported on this line:

- ➢ The portion of mortgage interest related to the business.
- ➢ If auto is used in business, business percentage of the auto loan interest.
- ➢ Interest capitalization.
- ➢ Interest on business purchases.

See Publication 535.

Line 17: Legal and professional fees. The following are examples of deductible legal and professional expenses on this line:

➢ Bookkeeping and accounting fees.
➢ Tax preparation fees for business tax preparation.
➢ Business-related attorney's fees.

See Publication 334 and 535.

Line 18: Office Expense. Office expenses that are not included in office-in-home expenses are deducted here. The following are examples of deductible expenses on this line:

➢ Postage
➢ Office supplies

Line 19: Pension and profit-sharing plans. Deduct the contribution portion of an employee's pension or profit-sharing plan that is paid as a benefit to the employee using this line. See Publication 560.

Line 20: Rent or lease. Schedule C, Part II, line 20a, is used for the lease of vehicles, machinery, and equipment rentals. Part II, line 20b, is used for leasing other rental property, such as rent for an office, building, or warehouse. See Publication 560.

Line 21: Repairs and maintenance. Repairs and maintenance of equipment, offices, buildings, or structures are deductible expenses and should include the cost of labor and supplies on this line.

Line 22: Supplies. Ordinary and necessary expenses that are not included in inventory should be deducted on this line.

Line 23: Taxes and licenses. The following are examples of deductible expenses on this line:

➢ License and regulatory fees for the trade or business.
➢ Real estate and personal property taxes on business assets.
➢ State and local sales taxes imposed for the selling of goods or services.
➢ Social Security and Medicare taxes paid to match employee wages.
➢ Paid federal unemployment tax.
➢ Federal highway use tax.
➢ Contributions to a state unemployment insurance fund or to a disability benefit fund if the contributions are considered taxes under state law.

Do not deduct the following:

➢ Federal income tax, including the self-employment tax.
➢ Estate and gift taxes.
➢ Taxes used to pay for improvements, such as paving and sewers.
➢ Taxes on the taxpayer's primary residence.
➢ State and local sales taxes on property purchased for use in the business.
➢ State and local sales taxes imposed on the buyer that were required to be collected and paid to state and local governments.
➢ Other taxes and licenses fees not related to the business.

See Publication 535.

Line 24a: Travel. The following are examples of ordinary and necessary business travel expenses that can be deducted on this line:

➢ Business airfare.
➢ Hotels for business trips.
➢ Taxi fares and tips while on business.

Example: Gladys lives in Seattle, Washington, and is a paid tax practitioner. She went to the Latino Tax Fest to learn the latest tax law and updates. The Fest was held on Tuesday, Wednesday, and Thursday. Gladys flew from Seattle to Las Vegas, Nevada, on Sunday and then flew home on Friday. Her ordinary and necessary expenses are the above costs that were incurred during the days of the convention, not the costs that were incurred on Sunday, Monday, and Friday. Her meals and hotel room on Sunday, Monday, and Friday are not a business expense. See Publication 463.

Line 24b: Meals. Include expenses for meals while traveling away from home. Meals must be food or beverage provided by a restaurant.

Line 25: Utilities. Utility expenses include water, gas, electric, and telephone costs. Business telephone expenses do not include the base rate for any personal phone lines into the taxpayer's house, even if they are used for business. If the taxpayer has additional costs related to the business use of the phone, such as long-distance calls, the taxpayer can deduct those expenses. If the taxpayer has a dedicated second phone line for business, all expenses may be deducted regarding the second phone line.

Line 26: Wages. The gross amount paid in wages (minus employment credits) to employees is deducted from the business' gross income. If the self-employed taxpayer paid themselves out of the profits of the business, those "wages" are not deductible as an expense on line 26. This is considered a draw and is not a deductible expense.

Line 27: Other Expenses. Other expenses are deducted in Part V of Schedule C, and the total amount of any deductions in Part V is reported here. Other expenses include any expense that is not described elsewhere and is both ordinary and necessary in the operation of the taxpayer's business.

Part 1 Review Questions

To obtain the maximum benefit from this chapter, LTP recommends that you complete each of the following questions, and then compare them to the answers with feedback that immediately follow. Under governing self-study standards, vendors are required to present review questions intermittently throughout each self-study course.

These questions and explanations are not part of the final examination and will not be graded by LTP.

SCP1.1
Which of the following best describes a self-employed taxpayer?

a. An in-home caregiver who is paid by the family.
b. An individual who owns their own corporate company.
c. An individual who owns their own company.
d. An individual who is the general partner of a partnership.

SCP1.2
Which business entity may be required to pay self-employment tax?

    a. Partnership
    b. Corporation
    c. Schedule C filer
    d. Qualified Joint Ventures

SCP1.3
Which accounting period ends in December?

    a. Calendar
    b. Fiscal
    c. Both
    d. None

SCP1.4
Which of the following would require a self-employed individual to obtain an Employer Identification Number (EIN)?

    a. Pays wages to his employees.
    b. Files Schedule C.
    c. Files Form 1099-MISC.
    d. Pays independent contractors.

SCP1.5
Which of the following is not considered a legal and professional fee?

    a. Bookkeeping
    b. Accounting fees
    c. Tax preparation fees
    d. Home mortgage interest

SCP1.6
Which of the following is considered a legal and professional fee?

    a. Business-related attorney's fees
    b. Postage
    c. Office supplies
    d. Taxes and licenses

SCP1.7
Which of the following is not an accounting method?

    a. Cash method
    b. Accrual method
    c. Combination method
    d. First in, first out

SCP1.8

Which of the following is not a description of a self-employed taxpayer?

1. Conducts a business as a sole proprietorship.
2. Receives income from his employer.
3. Is an independent contractor.
4. Is in business for himself in any other way.

a. 1, 3, and 4
b. 2 only
c. 3 and 4
d. 1 and 2

SCP1.9

Which form is used to obtain an EIN?

a. W-4
b. I-9
c. SS-4
d. W-2

SCP1.10

Which insurance is not deducted on Schedule C?

1. Liability insurance
2. Malpractice insurance
3. Workers' compensation insurance
4. Self-employed health insurance

a. 4 only
b. 1, 2, and 3
c. 2 and 4
d. 1 and 3

Part 1 Review Questions Answers

SCP1.1

Which of the following best describes a self-employed taxpayer?

a. An in-home caregiver who is paid by the family.
b. An individual who owns their own corporate company.
c. **An individual who owns their own company.**
d. An individual who is the general partner of a partnership.

Feedback: Review section *Sole Proprietorship.*

SCP1.2
Which business entity may be required to pay self-employment tax?

 a. Partnership
 b. Corporation
 c. Schedule C filer
 d. Qualified Joint Ventures

Feedback: Review section *Schedule SE: Self-Employment Tax.*

SCP1.3
Which accounting period ends in December?

 a. Calendar
 b. Fiscal
 c. Both
 d. None

Feedback: Review section *Accounting Periods.*

SCP1.4
Which of the following would require a self-employed individual to obtain an Employer Identification Number (EIN)?

 a. Pays wages to his employees.
 b. Files Schedule C.
 c. Files Form 1099-MISC.
 d. Pays independent contractors.

Feedback: Review section *Identification Numbers.*

SCP1.5
Which of the following is not considered a legal and professional fee?

 a. Bookkeeping
 b. Accounting fees
 c. Tax preparation fees
 d. Home mortgage interest

Feedback: Review section *Line 17: Legal and Professional Fees.*

SCP1.6
Which of the following is considered a legal and professional fee?

 a. Business-related attorney's fees
 b. Postage
 c. Office supplies
 d. Taxes and licenses

Feedback: Review section *Line 17: Legal and Professional Fees.*

SCP1.7
Which of the following is not an accounting method?

 a. Cash method
 b. Accrual method
 c. Combination method
 d. First in, first out

Feedback: Review section *Accounting Methods*.

SCP1.8
Which of the following is not a description of a self-employed taxpayer?

  1. Conducts a business as a sole proprietorship.
  2. Receives income from his employer.
  3. Is an independent contractor.
  4. Is in business for himself in any other way.

 a. 1, 3 and 4
 b. 2 only
 c. 3 and 4
 d. 1 and 2

Feedback: Review section *Sole Proprietorship*.

SCP1.9
Which form is used to obtain an EIN?

 a. W-4
 b. I-9
 c. SS-4
 d. W-2

Feedback: Review section *Identification Numbers*.

SCP1.10
Which insurance is not deducted on Schedule C?

  1. Liability insurance
  2. Malpractice insurance
  3. Workers' compensation insurance
  4. Self-employed health insurance

 a. 4 only
 b. 1, 2, and 3
 c. 2 and 4
 d. 1 and 3

Feedback: Review *Section C, Part II, Expenses*.

Part 2 Business Use of the Home

Report the total amount of expenses from business use of the home on Line 30 of Schedule C. If the taxpayer chooses to use the simplified method, they cannot claim more than 300-square-feet for storage of inventory or product samples. If the taxpayer runs a daycare, then use Form 8829.

Form 8829: Office in the Home

Self-employed taxpayers may be able to use Form 8829, *Expenses for Business Use of Your Home*, to claim deductions for certain expenses for business use of their home. To qualify for these deductions, the taxpayer must show that they used a space (such as an office) in the home exclusively and regularly for business. The amount of deduction a taxpayer can receive is based on what percent of the house's total square footage is being used for the business.

Example: Monica has an office she uses exclusively to manage and run her catering business. To receive a deduction for her home business expenses, Monica would divide the square footage of her office by the total square footage of her home to find the percentage of expense she can deduct. If her office is 130-square-feet and her home is 1,000-square-feet, then the percentage of her expenses she can deduct would be 13%.

Daycare providers would use Form 8829 to report expenses based on the number of hours spent caring for children or disabled dependents. The time also includes time spent cleaning the house before and after children arrive or leave as well as time spent preparing activities for the children.

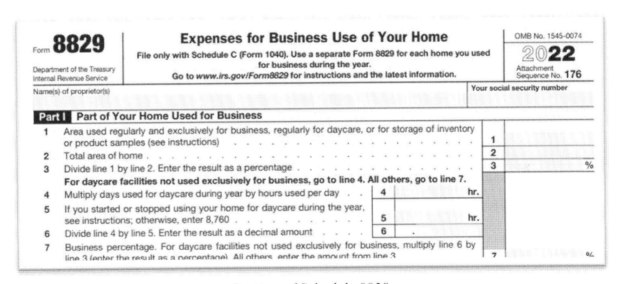

Portion of Schedule 8829

If childcare providers do not use their entire home for childcare, they will use a combination of hours and square feet to determine business use. The home portion does not have to meet the exclusive-use test if the use is for an in-home daycare facility.

Business expenses that apply to a part of the taxpayer's home may be a deductible business expense if the part of the home was exclusively used on a regular basis in all of the following ways:

> ➤ As the principal place of business for any of the taxpayer's trade or business.

> ➤ As a place of business used by patients, clients, or customers to meet or deal during the normal course of trade or business.
> ➤ In connection with the trade or business if the office is a separate structure that is not attached to the taxpayer's home.

Some exceptions to the "space rule used on a regular basis" are certain daycare facilities and storage spaces used for inventory or product samples. The tax professional must determine whether the office in the home qualifies as the taxpayer's principal place of business.

To qualify the office in the home as the primary place of business, the following requirements must be met:

> ➤ The taxpayer uses the home exclusively and regularly for administrative or management activities of the taxpayer's trade or business.
> ➤ The taxpayer has no other fixed location where the taxpayer conducts substantial administrative or management activities of his or her trade or business.

Administrative or Management Activities

There are many activities that can be considered administrative or managerial in nature. Some of the most common include:

> ➤ Billing customers, clients, or patients.
> ➤ Keeping books and records.
> ➤ Ordering supplies.
> ➤ Setting up appointments.
> ➤ Writing reports or forwarding orders.

If the following activities are performed at another location, the taxpayer would be disqualified from being able to claim the home office deduction:

> ➤ The taxpayer conducts administrative or management activities at other locations other than the home.
> ➤ The taxpayer conducts administrative or management activities at places that are not fixed locations, such as in a car or a hotel room.
> ➤ The taxpayer occasionally conducts administrative or management activities at an outside location.
> ➤ The taxpayer conducts substantial non-administrative or non-management business activities at another fixed location other than home.
> ➤ The taxpayer has suitable space to conduct administrative or management activities outside of their home but choose to work at home.

Example: Fernando is a self-employed plumber. Most of Fernando's time is spent installing and repairing plumbing at customers' homes and offices. He has a small office in his home that he uses exclusively and regularly for the administrative or management activities of his business, such as calling customers, ordering supplies, and keeping his books. Fernando writes up estimates and records of work completed at his customers' premises but does not conduct any substantial administrative or management activities at any fixed location other than his home office. Fernando does not do his own billing. He uses a local bookkeeping service to bill his customers.

Because it is the only fixed location where he does his administrative and managerial activities, Fernando's home office qualifies as his principal place of business for deducting expenses for its use. The fact that a bookkeeper does his billing is not important, as it does not change or impact where Fernando does his business administrative and managerial activities.

Simplified Option for Home Office Deduction

Taxpayers may use a simplified option to figure the home office business deduction. Revenue Procedure 2013-13 provides an optional safe harbor method that taxpayers may use, which is an alternative to the calculation, allocation, and substantiation of actual expenses for purposes of satisfying the Internal Revenue Code section 280A. These rules do not change the home office criteria for claiming business use but instead simplify the ruling for recordkeeping and calculation.

The major highlights of the simplified option are as follows:

➢ Standard deduction of $5-per-square-foot of home used for business with a maximum 300-square-feet.
➢ Allowable home-related itemized deductions claimed in full on Schedule A.
➢ No home depreciation deduction or later recapture of depreciation for the years the simplified option is used.

When selecting a method, the taxpayer must choose to use either the simplified method or the regular method for any taxable year and can make that choice by using their selected method on their tax return. However, once the method has been chosen for the year, it cannot be changed. If the methods are used in different tax years, the correct depreciation table must be used. Year-by-year determination is acceptable.

The deduction under the safe harbor method cannot create a net loss; it is limited to the business' gross income reduced by deductions unrelated to the home office deduction. Any excess is disallowed and cannot be carried over or back, unlike the carryover of unallowed expenses that is available to offset income from that activity in the succeeding year when using the actual expense method.

Regardless of the method that is used to claim the home office, the space must be regularly and exclusively used as the taxpayer's principal place of business. If the taxpayer used the simplified method for tax year 2022, and they chose not to use it for 2023, taxpayer may have an unallowed expense from a prior year carryover to the current year. See Instructions Form 8829.

Regular and Exclusive Use

The portion of the home that is used must be used exclusively for conducting business.

Example: Nadine teaches piano lessons in her home. She has a piano in her spare bedroom and a grand piano in her living room. She uses the piano in her spare bedroom to teach her students and the grand piano for the students' recitals. Nadine does not use the spare bedroom for anything else except teaching students and storing music books related to her students. Her spare bedroom is used exclusively and regularly for business, but her grand piano is not; it is only used for recitals for her students. Therefore, she would only be able to claim the spare bedroom as a deduction and not the living room.

Like everything with tax law there are exceptions to the rule; the taxpayer does not have to meet the exclusive use test if either of the following applies:

> ➤ If the taxpayer uses part of their home for storage of inventory or sample product(s), they may deduct business use of the home expense if the following conditions are met:
>> ○ The taxpayer sells products wholesale or retail as their trade or business.
>> ○ The taxpayer keeps inventory in his or her home for the trade or business.
>> ○ The home is the only fixed location for the trade or business.
>> ○ The storage space is used on a regular basis.
>> ○ The space used can be identifiable as a separate suitable space for storage.
> ➤ The taxpayer uses part of the home as a daycare facility.

Principal Place of Business

If the taxpayer conducts business outside of the home and uses their home substantially and regularly to conduct business, they may qualify for a home office deduction. The taxpayer can also deduct expenses for a separate freestanding structure such as a studio or a barn, but the regular and exclusive use test must apply. To determine if the place used is the primary place of business, the following factors must be considered:

> ➤ The relative importance of the activities performed at each location where the taxpayer conducts his or her business.
> ➤ The amount of time spent at each location where the taxpayer conducts business.

Expenses

When using Form 8829, there are two categories for expenses direct and indirect. The direct expenses are for the business portion of the home. Indirect expenses are for keeping up and running the home.

Direct expenses include:

> ➤ Business portion of casualty losses.
> ➤ Insurance: indirect insurance covers the entire home while direct insurance covers the business. A direct insurance policy is referred to as an umbrella policy.
> ➤ Business rent.
> ➤ Business repairs for the home.
> ➤ Business portion of real estate taxes.
> ➤ Business portion of home mortgage interest.

Indirect expenses include:

> ➤ *Security system:* The cost to maintain and monitor the system is considered an indirect cost. However, the taxpayer may depreciate the percentage of the system that relates to his business.
> ➤ *Utilities and services:* Including electricity, gas, trash removal, and cleaning services.
> ➤ *Telephone:* The basic local service charge, including taxes for the first line into the home, is a nondeductible personal expense. Long-distance phone calls and the cost of a secondary home phone line used exclusively for business are both deductible expenses.

> ➤ *Depreciation:* If the taxpayer owns the home, the business portion could be depreciable. See Publication 587. Before calculating the depreciation deduction, the following information is needed:
>   - o The month and year the taxpayer began using the home for business.
>   - o The adjusted basis and fair market value of the home at the time the taxpayer began using it for business; the cost of the home plus any improvements, minus casualty losses or depreciation deducted in earlier years; land is never considered part of the adjusted basis.
>   - o The cost of improvements before and after the taxpayer began using the home for business.
>   - o The percentage of the home used for business.

The following expenses are not deductible:

- ➤ Bribes and kickbacks.
- ➤ Charitable contributions.
- ➤ Demolition expenses or losses.
- ➤ Dues paid to business, social, athletic, luncheon, sporting, airline, and hotel clubs.
- ➤ Lobbying expenses.
- ➤ Penalties and fines paid to a governmental agency for breaking the law.
- ➤ Personal, living, and family expenses.
- ➤ Political contributions.
- ➤ Repairs that add value to the home or increase the property life.

Business Auto Expenses

Taxpayers can deduct ordinary and necessary transportation expenses if they incur them while procuring income. If taxpayers use a personal vehicle for maintaining business activities, the deduction of the expenses is either by actual expenses or the standard mileage rate. For tax year 2023 the business travel rate is 65.5 cents per mile. Standard mileage rate for each business mile can be used for the taxpayer's owned or leased vehicle.

The taxpayer can deduct the ordinary and necessary business-related expenses of traveling away from home. The taxpayer must properly allocate expenses between rental and nonrental activities. Information needed to record auto expenses accurately:

- ➤ Beginning mileage
- ➤ Ending mileage
- ➤ Commuting mileage
- ➤ Business mileage (notes about the destination and reason for travel should be made)

Schedule C, Part III, Cost of Goods Sold

The cost of goods sold is used when a business has inventory or produces a product. Inventory must be calculated at the beginning and end of the year.

Schedule C (Form 1040) 2022   Page **2**

Part III   **Cost of Goods Sold** (see instructions)

33   Method(s) used to value closing inventory: a ☐ Cost   b ☐ Lower of cost or market   c ☐ Other (attach explanation)

34   Was there any change in determining quantities, costs, or valuations between opening and closing inventory? If "Yes," attach explanation   ☐ Yes   ☐ No

35   Inventory at beginning of year. If different from last year's closing inventory, attach explanation   **35**

36   Purchases less cost of items withdrawn for personal use   **36**

37   Cost of labor. Do not include any amounts paid to yourself   **37**

38   Materials and supplies   **38**

39   Other costs   **39**

40   Add lines 35 through 39   **40**

41   Inventory at end of year   **41**

42   **Cost of goods sold.** Subtract line 41 from line 40. Enter the result here and on line 4   **42**

Portion of Schedule C

The following items are used to calculate a business's cost of goods sold:

Line 35: Beginning inventory. The beginning inventory is the closing inventory from the prior year. If this is the taxpayer's first business year, then beginning inventory is the amount of cost of goods purchased.

Line 36: Purchases. The amount of reported purchases is the completed products or raw materials used for manufacturing, merchandising, or mining plus the cost of shipping minus the cost of items for personal use.

Line 37: Cost of labor. The cost of labor used in the actual production of the goods. The cost of labor is not wages, which are reported on Schedule C, Part II, line 26, *Wages*. The cost of labor is mainly used in manufacturing or mining, since the labor can be properly charged to the cost of goods sold. A manufacturing business can properly allocate indirect and direct labor to the expense of the cost of goods. A direct expense would be the labor to fabricate raw material into a saleable product.

Line 38: Materials and Supplies. Materials used in the actual production or processing of the goods such as hardware and chemicals are charged to the cost of goods sold.

Line 39: Other Costs. A proportion of overhead expenses related to creating a product. Containers and freight used for raw materials are examples of other costs.

Line 41: Ending Inventory. The counted inventory at the end of the tax year is used as the beginning inventory for the following year's return.

Inventory is an itemized list of goods, with valuations, held for sale or consumption in a manufacturing or merchandising business. Inventory should include all finished or partly finished goods and only those raw materials and supplies that have been acquired for sale or that will physically become a part of merchandise intended for sale. How companies valuate inventory varies from business to business. See Publication 334.

Schedule C, Part IV, Information on Your Vehicle

Part IV Information on Your Vehicle. Complete this part **only** if you are claiming car or truck expenses on line 9 and are not required to file Form 4562 for this business. See the instructions for line 13 to find out if you must file Form 4562.

43 When did you place your vehicle in service for business purposes? (month/day/year) __ / __ / __

44 Of the total number of miles you drove your vehicle during 2022, enter the number of miles you used your vehicle for:

a Business _____ b Commuting (see instructions) _____ c Other _____

45 Was your vehicle available for personal use during off-duty hours? ☐ Yes ☐ No

46 Do you (or your spouse) have another vehicle available for personal use?. ☐ Yes ☐ No

47a Do you have evidence to support your deduction? ☐ Yes ☐ No

b If "Yes," is the evidence written? ☐ Yes ☐ No

Portion of Schedule C

The taxpayer would enter the information of the vehicle in Part IV to be able to claim the related expenses. Commuting is generally considered travel between home and work. Part IV is used to calculate the standard mileage rate for the taxpayer's vehicle. If more than one vehicle was used, attach a statement containing the same information included in Schedule C, Part IV. The following circumstances may not meet the commuting rules:

➢ The taxpayer has at least one regular location away from home, and the travel is to a temporary work location in the same trade or business. See Pub 463.
➢ The travel is to a temporary work location outside the location where he or she lives and normally works.
➢ The home is the principal place of business, and the travel is to another work location in the same trade or business, regardless of whether the location is regular or temporary and regardless of the distance. See IRC Section 280A(c)(1)(A).

For more information on recordkeeping rules for vehicles, see Publication 463.

Schedule C, Part V, Other Expenses

Other expenses are deducted in Part V, Schedule C. Other expenses include any expense that is not included elsewhere and is ordinary and necessary in the operation of the taxpayer's business. Once all other expenses have been reported, figure the total amount, and report it on line 48 and line 27a.

Any ordinary and necessary business expense that was not deducted elsewhere on Schedule C would be reported in this section. List the type and amount of each expense separately in the spaces provided. If more space is needed, use another sheet of paper. Other expenses can include the following:

➢ Amortization that began in 2022; Form 4562 will need to be attached.
➢ Bad business debt that was previously reported as income. If the bad debt is paid off after writing the amount off as a deduction or expense, the business must include the reduction amount that they had received as income on their next return.
➢ At-risk loss deduction.
➢ Business start-up costs.
➢ Costs of making commercial buildings energy efficient.

➢ Deductions for removing barriers to individuals with disabilities and the elderly.
➢ Excess farm loss.
➢ Film and television production expenses.
➢ Forestation and reforestation costs.

Do not include the following as other expenses:

➢ Charitable contributions.
➢ Cost of business equipment or furniture.
➢ Replacements or permanent improvements to property.
➢ Personal, living, and family expenses.
➢ Fines or penalties paid to a government for violating any law.

Bad Debts from Sales or Services

The business owner accrues bad debt when the sales or service becomes uncollectable from a customer. Bad debt that is unrelated to business is not a reportable entry. When using the cash method of accounting, bad debts cannot be deducted unless the amount was previously included as income.

Start-Up Costs

Start-up costs are the expenses incurred before a business begins due to starting or purchasing a business. Taxpayers can elect to deduct up to $5,000 of start-up costs and up to $5,000 of organizational expenditures that were paid or incurred during the tax year in which the trade or business began. Start-up or organizational expenditures that are not deductible in the year in which the trade or business began must be capitalized and amortized over the course of the 15 years following the business or trade's beginning. See Publication 535.

The following are examples of start-up costs:

➢ Survey of market.
➢ Advertisements for the opening of the business.
➢ Training wages.
➢ Travel and other expenses incurred to secure distributors, suppliers, etc.
➢ Consulting fees and professional fees connected with starting a business.
➢ Legal fees.
➢ Net operating loss (NOL).

A net operating loss is incurred when business expenses and expenditures exceed business income. Sometimes the loss is great enough to offset income from other tax years. For more information, see Publication 536, *Net Operating Losses (NOLs) for Individuals, Estates and Trusts*.

Work Opportunity Tax Credit (WOTC)

An employee may claim the work opportunity credit for wages paid to workers from ten targeted groups. See IRC Code section 51 and 52 for a description of targeted groups. The credit is calculated on Form 5884 and reduces the taxpayer's deduction for wages and salaries. The work opportunity credit is a business credit, and the credit can be claimed against both regular and alternative minimum tax liabilities.

The credit is normally 40% of the first $6,000 of qualified wages during the first year of employment, then reduced to 25% of the first $6,000 if the employee works less than 400 hours. The employee needs to work at least 120 hours for the employer to qualify. See IRC code section 51.

This credit has been extended to 2020 and before 2026 for qualifying wages. Qualifying wages do not include:

> ➢ Wages paid to or earned for any employee during any period the employee was paid by a federally-funded on-the-job training program.
> ➢ Wages paid for a summer youth employee for services performed when the employee lived outside an empowerment zone.
> ➢ Wages paid to a designated community resident for services by a summer youth employee before or after any 90-day period between May 1 and September 15.

See Instructions Form 5884.

Research Credit

A sole proprietor, partnership, or corporation that does not have publicly-traded stock could claim the research credit. Any unused credit will be carryforward and deducted in the next year. To be able to claim this credit the research must relate to new or improved function, performance, reliability, or quality of a function purpose for the company. Capitalized expenses are reduced by the amount of the research credit that exceeds the amount of the allowable as a deduction for the expenses. For expenditures paid or incurred in the tax year 2022, the amount is capitalized and eligible for amortization over five years and is reduced by the excess (if any) of the research credit for the tax year.

Part 2 Review Questions

To obtain the maximum benefit from this chapter, LTP recommends that you complete each of the following questions, and then compare them to the answers with feedback that immediately follow. Under governing self-study standards, vendors are required to present review questions intermittently throughout each self-study course.

These questions and explanations are not part of the final examination and will not be graded by LTP.

SCP2.1
Which federal form is used with Schedule C to report home office expenses?

    a. Form 2106
    b. Form 8829
    c. Form 4562
    d. Form 8889

SCP2.2
Which of the following is not a major highlight of the new federal simplified option method?

   a. Standard deduction of $15-per-square-foot of home used for business, with a maximum of 300-square-feet.
   b. Allowable home-related itemized deductions claimed in full on Schedule A.
   c. No home depreciation deduction or later recapture of depreciation for the years the simplified option is used.
   d. Standard deduction of $5-per-square-foot of home used for business, with a maximum of 300-square-feet.

SCP2.3
Which of the following is not used to calculate cost of goods?

   a. Beginning and ending inventory
   b. Vehicle mileage
   c. Cost of labor
   d. Materials

SCP2.4
Which of the following is not used to calculate cost of goods?

   a. Cost of labor
   b. Materials and supplies
   c. Ending inventory only
   d. Bad debts

SCP2.5
Which of the following is a simplified option for the home office deduction?

   a. Standard deduction of $5-per-square-foot with a maximum of 300-square-feet
   b. Claiming a home depreciation deduction on Form 8829
   c. All home-related itemized deductions are claimed on the Schedule C
   d. Setting up business appointments

SCP2.6
Which of the following is not a simplified option for the home office deduction?

   a. Standard deduction of $5-per-square-foot with a maximum of 300-square-feet
   b. Cannot claim a home depreciation deduction
   c. All home-related itemized deductions are claimed on the Schedule A
   d. Billing customers, clients, or patients

SCP2.7
Which of the following are administrative or management activities?

   1. Billing customers, clients, or patients.
   2. Keeping books and records.
   3. Ordering supplies.
   4. Setting up appointments.
   5. Ordering pizza for dinner.

a. 1, 2, 3, and 5
b. 1, 2, and 4
c. 1, 2, 3, 4, and 5
d. 1, 2, 3, and 4

SCP2.8

To determine the principal place of business the activities performed must be relative.

a. True
b. False

SCP2.9

Form 8829 has 2 expense categories, indirect and direct.

a. True
b. False

SCP2.10

Which of the following is not a deductible expense on Schedule C?

a. Telephone
b. Depreciation
c. Charitable contributions
d. Repairs that do not add value to the property

Part 2 Review Questions Answers

SCP2.1

Which federal form is used with Schedule C to report home office expenses?

a. Form 2106
b. Form 8829
c. Form 4562
d. Form 8889

Feedback: Review section *Form 8829: Office in the Home.*

SCP2.2

Which of the following is not a major highlight of the new federal simplified option method?

a. Standard deduction of $15-per-square-foot of home used for business, with a maximum of 300-square-feet.
b. Allowable home-related itemized deductions claimed in full on Schedule A.
c. No home depreciation deduction or later recapture of depreciation for the years the simplified option is used.
d. Standard deduction of $5-per-square-foot of home used for business, with a maximum of 300-square-feet.

Feedback: Review section *Simplified Option for Home Office Deduction.*

SCP2.3
Which of the following is not used to calculate cost of goods?

    a. Beginning and ending inventory
    b. Vehicle mileage
    c. Cost of labor
    d. Materials

Feedback: Review section *Schedule C, Part III, Cost of Goods Sold.*

SCP2.4
Which of the following is not used to calculate cost of goods?

    a. Cost of labor
    b. Materials and supplies
    c. Ending inventory only
    d. Bad debts

Feedback: Review section *Schedule C, Part III, Cost of Goods Sold.*

SCP2.5
Which of the following is a simplified option for the home office deduction?

    a. Standard deduction of $5-per-square-foot with a maximum of 300-square-feet.
    b. Claiming a home depreciation deduction on Form 8829.
    c. All home-related itemized deductions are claimed on the Schedule C.
    d. Setting up business appointments.

Feedback: Review section *Simplified Option for Home Office Deduction.*

SCP2.6
Which of the following is not a simplified option for the home office deduction?

    a. Standard deduction of $5-per-square-foot with a maximum of 300-square-feet.
    b. Cannot claim a home depreciation deduction.
    c. All home-related itemized deductions are claimed on the Schedule A.
    d. Billing customers, clients, or patients.

Feedback: Review section *Simplified Option for Home Office Deduction.*

SCP2.7
Which of the following are administrative or management activities?

    1. Billing customers, clients, or patients.
    2. Keeping books and records.
    3. Ordering supplies.
    4. Setting up appointments.
    5. Ordering pizza for dinner.

    a. 1, 2, 3, and 5
    b. 1, 2, and 4
    c. 1, 2, 3, 4, and 5
    d. 1, 2, 3, and 4

Feedback: Review section *Administrative or Management Activities.*

SCP2.8
To determine the principal place of business the activities performed must be relative.

    a. True
    b. False

Feedback: Review section *Principal Place of Business.*

SCP2.9
Form 8829 has 2 expense categories, indirect and direct.

    a. True
    b. False

Feedback: Review section *Expenses.*

SCP2.10
Which of the following is not a deductible expense on Schedule C?

    a. Telephone
    b. Depreciation
    c. Charitable contributions
    d. Repairs that do not add value to the property

Feedback: Review section *Expenses.*

Part 3 Qualified Business Income

Qualified Business Income (QBI)

Qualified business income deduction (QBI) is a tax deduction that allows eligible self-employed and small-business owners to deduct up to 20% of their qualified business income on the tax return. Taxpayers' total taxable income for 2022 must be under $170,100 for all filers except married filing joint. The joint filers income needs to be less than $340,100 to qualify.

Qualified Business Income (QBI) is the net amount of income, gain, deduction, and loss with respect to any qualified business of the taxpayer. Qualified items of income, gain deduction, and loss include items that are effectively connected with the conduct of a U.S. trade or business and are included in determining the business's taxable income for the tax year.

The Section 199A Qualified Business Income Deduction, enacted as part of the Tax Cuts and Jobs Act in 2017, was meant to provide a tax benefit to smaller flow-through businesses in response to the large decrease in the C corporation tax rate from 35% to 21%.

The initial step in calculating the Sec. 199A deduction begins with determining the QBI, which is determined separately for each of the taxpayer's qualified businesses. Certain investment items are excepted from QBI, including short-term and long-term capital gains and losses, dividends, and interest income not properly allocable to a trade or business. QBI also does not include reasonable compensation payments to a taxpayer for services rendered to a qualified business, guaranteed payments to a partner for services rendered to a business, and, to the extent provided in regulations, a Sec. 707(a) payment to a partner for services rendered to the business (Sec. 199A(c)).

20% Deduction for a Pass-Through Qualified Trade or Business

The combined QBI amount serves as a placeholder: it is the amount of the Section 199A deduction before considering a final overall limitation. Under this overall limitation, a taxpayer's QBI deduction is limited to 20% of the taxpayer's taxable income in excess of any net capital gain. The combined QBI amount is the sum of the deductible QBI amounts for each of the taxpayer's qualified businesses. The deductible QBI amount of a qualified business is generally 20% of its QBI, but the deductible QBI amount may be limited when the business is a specified service trade or business or by a wage and capital limitation. See Sec. 199A(b).

The calculation of a taxpayer's Sec. 199A deduction depends on whether the taxpayer's taxable income is below a lower taxable income threshold ($170,100, or $340,100 if filing a joint return). When computing taxable income for this purpose, the Sec. 199A deduction is ignored.

If a taxpayer has income below the lower threshold, calculating the Sec. 199A deduction is straightforward. The taxpayer first calculates the deductible QBI amount for each qualified business and combines the deductible QBI amounts to determine the combined QBI amount. If the taxpayer has only one qualified business, the combined QBI amount is the deductible QBI amount for that business. The taxpayer then applies the overall taxable income limitation to the combined QBI. Thus, the taxpayer's Sec. 199A deduction is equal to the lesser of the combined QBI amount or the overall limitation (20% × taxpayer's taxable income in excess of any net capital gain).

Issues in Calculating the Deduction

If the taxpayer has taxable income above the higher threshold amount, two issues arise in the calculation of the Sec. 199A deduction. First, a business of the taxpayer will not be treated as a qualified business, and the income of the business of the taxpayer will not be included in QBI if the business meets the definition of a specified service trade or business (see below). Thus, the Sec. 199A deduction will be denied in full for the business. Second, if a business is a qualified business (i.e., it is not a specified service trade or business), the deductible QBI amount for the business is subject to a W-2 wage and capital limitation. Taxpayers with taxable income that is over the phaseout amount are unable to use Sec. 199A deduction for the business income that is a specified service trade or business.

Specified Service Trade or Business

A specified service trade or business is defined in Sec. 199A(d)(2) as "any trade or business which is described in section 1202(e)(3)(A) (applied without regard to the words 'engineering, architecture,') ... or which involves the performance of services that consist of investing and investment management, trading, or dealing in securities (as defined in section 475(c)(2)), partnership interests, or commodities (as defined in section 475(e)(2))."

Sec. 1202(e)(3)(A) defines a "qualified trade or business" as:

> "…any trade or business involving the performance of services in the fields of health, law, engineering, architecture, accounting, actuarial science, performing arts, consulting, athletics, financial services, brokerage services, or any trade or business where the principal asset of such trade or business is the reputation or skill of 1 or more of its employees or owners."

Thus, service trades or businesses (e.g., engineering, architecture, manufacturing, etc.) that are not specified service trades or businesses are eligible for the deduction regardless of the taxpayer's taxable income, but businesses providing specified services (e.g., law, accounting, consulting, investment management, etc.) of taxpayers who have taxable income above the higher taxable income threshold limit are excluded from the deduction.

Taxpayers with Income Above the Threshold

If a taxpayer has taxable income above the higher taxable income threshold and owns a business that is not a specified service trade or business, the QBI deductible amount for the business is subject to a limitation based on W-2 wages or capital (capital here is measured as the unadjusted basis of certain business assets) (Sec. 199A(b)(2)(B)). The deductible QBI amount for the business is equal to the *lesser* of 20% of the business's QBI or the *greater* of 50% of the W-2 wages for the business or 25% of the W-2 wages plus 2.5% of the business's unadjusted basis in all qualified property. Thus, two alternative limitations under Sec. 199A(b)(2) may limit the deductible QBI amount for each business that is included in a taxpayer's combined QBI amount (a pure 50% wage test or a combined 25% wage and capital test).

QBI and the W-2

W-2 wages are total wages subject to wage withholding, elective deferrals, and deferred compensation paid during the tax year that are attributable to QBI (Sec. 199A(b)(4)). However, amounts not properly included in a return filed with the Social Security Administration on or before the 60th day after the due date (including extensions) for that return are not included (Sec. 199A(b)(4)(C)). A partner's allocable share of W-2 wages is required to be determined in the same manner as the partner's share of wage expenses.

QBI and Property

The basis of qualifying property is calculated as the unadjusted basis immediately after acquisition of that property. Qualifying property is tangible property or depreciable property that was held by and available for use in the business at the close of the tax year, or was used in the production of QBI at any time during the year and the "depreciable period" has not ended before the close of the tax year (Sec. 199A(b)(6)).

The depreciable period starts on the date the property is first placed in service and ends the last day of the last full year of the applicable recovery period under Sec. 168 (disregarding Sec. 168(g)) or 10 years after the beginning date, whichever is later. This rule allows "qualified property" to include property that has exhausted its modified accelerated cost recovery system (MACRS) depreciation period if it is still in its first 10 years of service. The statute directs Treasury to provide anti-abuse rules to prevent the manipulation of the depreciable period of qualified property through related-party transactions and for determining the unadjusted basis immediately after the acquisition of qualified property in like-kind exchanges and involuntary conversions.

Service Trade Disqualifier

A taxpayer potentially loses all or part of the Sec. 199A deduction if taxable income rises too high and the income is from a specified service business. The income phase-out amounts are as follows (adjusted for inflation in 2022):

- ➢ All other $170,050 - $220,050 partial phase out of Sec. 199A
  $220,051 + complete phase out of Sec. 199A
- ➢ MFJ $340,100 - $440,100 partial phase out of Sec. 199A
  $440,101+ complete phase out of Sec. 199A

A taxpayer potentially loses all or part of the Sec. 199A deduction if taxable income rises too high and the income is from a specified service business. This includes "fields of health, law, accounting, actuarial science, performing arts, consulting, athletics, financial services, brokerage services, or any trade or business where the principal asset of the business is the reputation or skill of one or more of its employees or owners."

Taxpayer earnings under the threshold amount could qualify for the Sec. 199A deduction even if the income is from a specified service business.

- ➢ All other   < $170,050
- ➢ MFJ   < $340,100

Taxpayer earnings over the threshold amount qualify for a lesser amount or for none of the Sec. 199A deduction.

- ➢ Single $220,051+
- ➢ MFJ $440,101+

The terminology "within the United States" means taxpayers only receive the 20% deduction on business income earned exclusive in the U.S. and on rental income from property located inside the U.S. The taxpayer only counts W-2 wages for businesses or real estate located within the U.S. If depreciable property figures into the formula, the property must be located inside the U.S. Therefore, if an entrepreneur has qualified business income from within and outside the U.S., separate the two before calculating Sec. 199A deduction.

Pass-Through Entities

The pass-through deduction is available regardless of which deduction method is chosen—itemized or standard deduction. The deduction cannot exceed 20% of the excess of a taxpayer's taxable income over net capital gain. If QBI is less than zero, it is treated as a loss from a qualified business in the following year.

For pass-through entities other than sole proprietorships, the deduction cannot exceed whichever of the following is greater:

- ➢ 50% of the W-2 wages with respect to the qualified trade or business ("W-2 wage limit").
- ➢ The sum of 25% of the W-2 wages paid with respect to the qualified trade or business *plus* 2.5% of the unadjusted basis of all "qualified property" immediately after acquisition.

Qualified property is any tangible, depreciable property that is held by and available for use in a qualified trade or business.

For a partnership or S corporation, each partner or shareholder is treated as having W-2 wages for the tax year in an amount equal to his or her allocable share of the W-2 wages of the entity for the tax year. A partner's or shareholder's allocable share of W-2 wages is determined in the same way as the partner's or shareholder's allocable share of wage expenses. For an S corporation, an allocable share is the shareholder's pro rata share of an item. However, the W-2 wage limit begins phasing out in the case of a taxpayer with taxable income exceeding $340,100 for married individuals filing jointly ($170,050 for other individuals). The application of the W-2 wage limit is phased in for individuals with taxable income exceeding the thresholds.

Sec. 199A Overview

To get the savings, a business owner may want to make operational, legal, and accounting changes early in the year.

The three major concepts with the Sec. 199A deduction are as follows:

> It benefits the following "pass-through entities":
>   o Sole proprietorships.
>   o Partnerships.
>   o S corporations.
>   o Real estate investment trusts (REITs).
>   o Qualified cooperatives.
> It shelters taxable income that would otherwise be taxed as ordinary income subject to the highest individual tax rates.
> The bigger the benefit, the more complex the rules.

Reporting and Taxability of Form 1099-K, Payment Card, and Third-Party Network Transactions

Third-party settlement organizations charge a fee for being the facilitator of the transaction. The reporting requirements are $600 or more.

Effective January 1, 2022, third-party payment providers must begin reporting to the IRS business transactions totaling $600 or more, (ARPA section 9674(a); IRC section 6050W(e)). This new provision is meant to apply transactions for goods and services only, but an individual taxpayer may receive a 1099-K for a nontaxable personal transaction. How do the new reporting guidelines determine what is business and personal?

When an individual sets up their third-party network transaction app such as PayPal, Zelle, Venmo, etc., they choose either a personal or a business account. When a payment is made to a personal profile, the payor could tag that transaction as payment for goods and services, which would be determined to be a business transaction, and yet it could be a personal payment for goods and services.

Employee Retention Credit

An employer may qualify for a refundable employment tax equal to 50% of qualified wages. The eligible employer who pays employees after March 21, 2020, and before December 31, 2021, may qualify for the Employee Retention Credit. The credit is 50% of the employees' wages up to $10,000 per employee. To receive the refunded money, the employer will need to file Form 7200, *Advance of Employer Credits Due to COVID-19*. This credit has expired but the taxpayer can still amend their 2021 tax return and 941s. See Instructions Form 7200.

Recordkeeping

This section will cover basic recordkeeping for all business returns. A tax professional should emphasize to their clients the importance of recordkeeping and to keep business and personal accounts separate. If a taxpayer has a loss on their business return, remind the taxpayer of the hobby rules. The taxpayer does not want to lose expense deductions due to poor recordkeeping; this is where the tax professional should spend time with their clients to educate them on how to track income and expenses. A good recordkeeping system includes a summary of all business transactions. These transactions in books are called journals and ledgers and can be kept electronically or as hard copies (paper). If paper records are kept, they must be locked up. The electronic records must be backed up in case of a computer crash and should be password protected.

Benefits of Recordkeeping

Everyone in business must keep appropriate and accurate records. Recordkeeping will help the taxpayer:

- ➤ Monitor the progress of their business.
- ➤ Prepare an accurate financial statement.
- ➤ Classify receipts.
- ➤ Track deductible business expenses.
- ➤ Prepare the tax return.
- ➤ Support reported income and expenses on the tax return.

Records show the taxpayer if the business is improving, which items sell the best, and insights to increase the success of the business. Records are needed to prepare accurate financial statements, which include profit and loss, balance sheets, and any other financial statements. Taxpayers should identify receipts at the time of purchase. It is easier to get into the habit of tracking receipts when received rather than dealing with them when preparing the tax return. A tax professional should teach clients how to identify and track receipts.

Kinds of Records to Keep

The taxpayer should choose the recordkeeping system that is best for their business. The system should match the accounting method of the taxpayer's tax year. The recordkeeping system should include a summary for all the taxpayer's business transactions. For example, recordkeeping should show gross income as well as deductions and credits for the business. Supporting documentation for consistent transactions, such as purchases, sales, and payroll, should be maintained. It is important to retain documentation that supports the entries in the journal, ledgers, and the tax return. Records for travel, transportation, and gift expenses fall under specific recordkeeping rules. For more information see Publication 463. There are also specific employment tax records the employer must keep. See Publication 51 (Circular A).

Assets used in business can be property, such as machinery and equipment used to conduct business. Records of the asset are used to figure depreciation and the gain or loss when the asset is sold. Records should show the following information:

> ➢ When and how the business asset was acquired.
> ➢ The purchase price of the business asset.
> ➢ The cost of any business improvements.
> ➢ Section 179 deduction.
> ➢ Business deductions taken for depreciation.
> ➢ Business deductions taken for casualty losses, such as losses resulting from fires, storms, or natural disasters.
> ➢ How the business asset was used.
> ➢ When and how the business asset was disposed.
> ➢ The selling price of the asset or the business.
> ➢ The expense of the business asset.

The following are examples of records that might show the information from the above list:

> ➢ Purchase and sales business invoices.
> ➢ Business purchase of real estate closing statements (HUD-1).
> ➢ Canceled business checks.
> ➢ A business' bank statements.

Maintaining Records

Tax records should be kept as needed for the administration of any provision of the Internal Revenue Code. Business records should be kept that support an item of income or deduction appearing on the return until the period of limitations is finished. Generally, that time frame is a 3-year period, although certain records must be kept longer than 3 years.

Employment records must be kept for at least 4 years after the date the tax becomes due or is paid. Records that pertain to assets such as property should be kept if the taxpayer owns the business asset. Other creditors, such as an insurance company, may require the business records to be kept longer than the IRS.

Part 3 Review Questions

To obtain the maximum benefit from this chapter, LTP recommends that you complete each of the following questions, and then compare them to the answers with feedback that immediately follow. Under governing self-study standards, vendors are required to present review questions intermittently throughout each self-study course.

These questions and explanations are not part of the final examination and will not be graded by LTP.

SCP3.1

Jade started a new business in 2022. Which of the following is not considered to be self-employment income?

  a. Income from Schedule E
  b. Income from Schedule F
  c. Income from Schedule C
  d. Income from wages

SCP3.2

Which of the following chooses the recordkeeping system?

  a. Taxpayer
  b. Internal Revenue Service
  c. Franchise Tax Board
  d. Taxpayer's banker

SCP3.3

Which of the following best describes how long to keep records?

  a. Employment records need to be kept for at least 6 years.
  b. Business records should be kept if an item of income or deduction appear on the tax return.
  c. Business records that pertain to property should be kept for at least 10 years.
  d. Computer software that was purchased for the business does not need to be kept.

SCP3.4

What is the beginning QBI phaseout for the MFJ taxpayer?

  a. $170,100
  b. $340,100
  c. $220,050
  d. $440,100

SCP3.5

What is the beginning QBI phaseout for all filers?

  a. $170,100
  b. $340,100
  c. $220,050
  d. $440,100

SCP3.6

What is the maximum QBI phaseout for all filers?

  a. $170,100
  b. $340,100
  c. $220,050
  d. $440,100

SCP3.7
What is the maximum QBI phaseout for MFJ?

    a. $170,100
    b. $340,100
    c. $220,050
    d. $440,100

SCP3.8
A taxpayer who uses cash apps to purchase items will receive Form 1099-K if their transactions are what amount?

    a. $400
    b. $600
    c. $800
    d. $1,000

SCP3.9
Which Congress Act reversed IRS Notice 2020-32?

    a. Additional Coronavirus Response and Relief Act
    b. Paycheck Protection Program
    c. Consolidated Appropriations Act
    d. American Rescue Plan Act

SCP3.10
Which Congress Act created the Restaurant Revitalization Fund Grant?

    a. Additional Coronavirus Response and Relief Act
    b. Employee Retention Credit
    c. Consolidated Appropriations Act
    d. American Rescue Plan Act

Part 3 Review Questions Answers

SCP3.1
Jade started a new business in 2022. Which of the following is not considered to be self-employment income?

    a. Income from Schedule E
    b. Income from Schedule F
    c. Income from Schedule C
    d. Income from wages

Feedback: Review section *Schedule C, Part I, Income.*

SCP3.2
Which of the following chooses the recordkeeping system?

    a. Taxpayer
    b. Internal Revenue Service
    c. Franchise Tax Board
    d. Taxpayer's banker

Feedback: Review section *Kinds of Record to Keep.*

SCP3.3
Which of the following best describes how long to keep records?

    a. Employment records need to be kept for at least 6 years.
    b. Business records should be kept if an item of income or deduction appear on the tax return.
    c. Business records that pertain to property should be kept for at least 10 years.
    d. Computer software that was purchased for the business does not need to be kept.

Feedback: Review section *How long to Keep Records.*

SCP3.4
What is the beginning QBI phaseout for the MFJ taxpayer?

    a. $170,100
    b. $340,100
    c. $220,050
    d. $440,100

Feedback: Review section *Qualified Business Income.*

SCP3.5
What is the beginning QBI phaseout for all filers?

    a. $170,100
    b. $340,100
    c. $220,050
    d. $440,100

Feedback: Review section *Qualified Business Income.*

SCP3.6
What is the maximum QBI phaseout for all filers?

    a. $170,100
    b. $340,100
    c. $220,050
    d. $440,100

Feedback: Review section *Qualified Business Income.*

SCP3.7
What is the maximum QBI phaseout for MFJ?

    a. $170,100
    b. $340,100
    c. $220,050
    d. $440,100

Feedback: Review section *Qualified Business Income*.

SCP3.8
A taxpayer who uses cash apps to purchase items will receive Form 1099-K if their transactions are what amount?

    a. $400
    b. $600
    c. $800
    d. $1,000

Feedback: Review section *Qualified Business Income*.

SCP3.9
Which Congress Act reversed IRS Notice 2020-32?

    a. Additional Coronavirus Response and Relief Act
    b. Paycheck Protection Program
    c. Consolidated Appropriations Act
    d. American Rescue Plan Act

Feedback: Review section *Paycheck Protection Program*.

SCP3.10
Which Congress Act created the Restaurant Revitalization Fund Grant?

    a. Additional Coronavirus Response and Relief Act
    b. Employee Retention Credit
    c. Consolidated Appropriations Act
    d. American Rescue Plan Act

Feedback: Review section *Restaurant Revitalization Fund Grants*.

Takeaways

Business income is derived from a multitude of sources using Schedules C, E, and F. How business income is calculated, and which deductions and expenses are reported can vary based on the type of business, the accounting method used, and many other considerations. It is fundamental that the tax professional be familiar with the concepts when preparing business returns. There are four common tax errors for business taxpayers:

1. Not paying enough estimated tax.
2. Depositing employment taxes.
3. Filing tax returns and payroll returns late.
4. Not separating business and personal expenses.

See Publication 15, 505, 535, and Circular E for more information.

TEST YOUR KNOWLEDGE!
Go online to take a practice quiz.

California Schedule C

Introduction

This chapter will present the differences between federal tax law business income and California tax law. This includes self-employment income, self-employment tax, withholding issues for self-employed nonresidents, common law employees, statutory employees, and contractors.

Objectives

At the end of this lesson, the student will:

> ➤ Explain how California treats self-employment income.
> ➤ Understand the differences between *employees* and *independent contractors.*
> ➤ Identify who qualifies as a statutory employee.
> ➤ Recognize the reporting requirements for independent contractors.

Resources

FTB Form 540 FTB Form 3801 FTB Form 3805V 540 or 540NR Schedule CA Form DE 231 (edd.ca.gov)	FTB Publication 984 FTB Publication 1001 FTB Publication 1060 DE 38 DE 44 Publication 287	Instructions FTB Form 540 Instructions FTB Form 3801 Instructions FTB Form 3805V Instructions 540 or 540NR Schedule CA

Table of Contents

Part 1 Key Differences Between California and Federal Business Income

There are differences from the federal in how California manages and taxes businesses and their income. Some of the most common differences will be covered in this part.

Principal Business Activity Code (PBA)

The Principal Business Activity code must be written on both the federal Schedule C and the state return. It is a 6-digit number that represents or best describes the primary business activity. The PBA code is used to identify business type to measure economic activity in the United States, Canada, and Mexico. The PBA Code is a necessary element in processing an accurate state tax return.

Self-Employment Income

California law conforms to federal law regarding self-employment income and most expenses. Self-employed individuals need to pay estimated payments if they owe at least $500 ($250 if married or RDP filing separately). California conforms to federal guidelines regarding both estimated payments and the due dates on April 15, June 15, and January 15 of the following year. California does not require a third-quarter payment. The percentage amount that needs to be paid is 30% for the first and fourth quarter and 40% for the second quarter.

The most common difference for business owners is depreciation. Use Form FTB 3885A to figure the adjustment for the difference between the amount of depreciation and amortization allowed as a deduction using California law. The difference is carried to Part I of California 540 or 540NR Schedule CA. Depreciation will be studied in a later chapter.

Start-up Expenses

California conforms to a new business electing to deduct up to $5,000 of start-up costs in the year the business begins. When California conforms, the tax preparer should refer to the IRS instructions or publications for guidance. For start-up costs see IRS Publication 535.

Net Operating Loss (NOL)

Another difference between federal and California tax law is that California does not always adopt the changes made at the federal level regarding Net Operating Losses (NOL). For 2022 taxable year, the NOL suspension has been repealed. The suspension does not apply to the following:

➤ Individual taxpayers who have business income or modified adjusted gross income of less than $1 million.
➤ Corporate taxpayers who have California taxable income is less than $1 million.

California NOL carryback and carryforward differs between the federal and state. Taxpayers with disaster loss carryovers were not affected by the NOL suspension from the TCJA. For more information regarding California and federal law, visit the FTB website at www.ftb.ca.gov and search for conformity. See FTB Publication 1001.

Nonresident Withholding Issues

A self-employed nonresident taxpayer is subject to required withholdings for California state taxes on income received from services performed in California. The entities making payments to the self-employed individuals are known as the withholding agents. Withholding is required when making payments to nonresident independent contractors for services performed in California.

Withholding agents are required to withhold from all payments or distributions with Californian sources that were made to a nonresident when the payments or distributions are greater than $1,500 for the calendar year. The only time the withholding agents may not withhold is upon receiving authorization for a waiver or a reduced withholding rate from the California Franchise Tax Board. The rate at which the withholding agent is required to withhold is 7% of gross payments made to nonresident independent contractors for services performed in California. See FTB Publication 1017.

The ABC Test for Employees

The Employment Development Department (EDD) has created guidelines to determine when a worker is legally considered an employee. These guidelines should be followed by all contractors and employees that are being treated as independent contractors.

On September 18, 2019, AB5 was signed into law and the common law rules were replaced with the ABC test.

- A. The person is free from the control and direction of the hiring entity in connection with the performance of the work, both under the contract for the performance of the work and in fact.
- B. The person performs work that is outside the usual course of the hiring entity's business.
- C. The person customarily is engaged in an independently established trade, occupation, or business of the same work performed.

The ABC test determines the following to be employees:

1. Any officer of a corporation.
2. Any worker who is an employee under the ABC Test.
3. Any worker whose services are specifically covered by law.

California does not conform to the federal "Safe Harbor" provisions. The employer needs to classify independent contractors properly. See DE 44 and DE 38.

AB5

California adopted the ABC test in AB5 and was signed into law September 2019 in which states that a worker will be considered an employee unless all the following three circumstances are met:

1. The worker is free from control and direction of the hiring entity in connection with the performance of the work, both under the contract of the work and in fact, commonly known as the *Borello* "control test".
2. The worker performs work that is outside the usual course of the hiring entity's business.
3. The worker is customarily engaged in an independently established trade, occupation, or business of the same nature as the work performed.

As per to any law there are exceptions to the above. A tax preparer is not permitted to give advice on classifying an individual as an employee or independent contractor. See CA Labor Code Section 226.8

Statutory Employees

A statutory employee is defined as an employee by law under specific statutes, whereas most individuals are determined to be an employee under *common law* (see Form DE 231). Certain groups of workers have been specifically covered by the law for unemployment insurance, employment training, tax, and disability insurance purposes.

California personal income tax withholding is not required if a statutory worker does not meet the common law tests for an employee; however, tax withholding is required for statutory employees in the construction industry and corporate officers who are residents of California or nonresidents performing services in California.

Statutory workers include individuals working for an employer in a continuing relationship in any of the following ways:

➢ An agent-driver or commission-driver engaged in distributing meat, vegetables, fruit, bakery products, beverages (other than milk), or laundry and dry-cleaning services for the principal.
➢ A traveling or city salesman (other than an agent or commission driver) working full time on behalf of the principal (except for sideline activities on behalf of some other person), taking orders from wholesalers, retailers, contractors, or operators of hotels, restaurants, or other similar establishments for merchandise for resale or supplies to be used for their own business operations.
➢ A home worker working according to their employer's specifications using materials or goods furnished by said employer, which must be returned to them.

See Section 621(c)(1)(C).

Services provided by the groups listed above are covered if the following apply:

➢ A substantial amount of the work is performed personally.
➢ The person performing the work does not have a substantial investment in the facilities used in the performance of those services (other than the facilities for transportation).
➢ The services are not paid for by way of a single transaction.
See DE 231N.

Independent Contractor Reporting Requirements

If a business is required to file federal Form 1099-MISC or 1099-NEC for services performed by an independent contractor, it should follow the reporting requirements for independent contractors. The IRS will automatically send a copy of Form 1099-NEC to the FTB. Forms 1099-NEC that were filed for tax year 2020 were mailed by the businesses; the IRS did not automatically send a copy.

Paycheck Protection Program (PPP) Loans and Forgiveness

The program provided cash-flow assistance through 100 percent federally guaranteed loans to employers who maintain their payroll during COVID-19. If employers maintain their payroll, the loans would be forgiven, which would help workers remain employed, as well as help affected small businesses and our economy snap-back quicker after the crisis. Small businesses and other eligible entities were able to apply if they were harmed by COVID-19 between February 15, 2020, and June 30, 2020.

Eligible loan recipients can have all or a portion of their PPP loans forgiven if the loan proceeds are used for specific purposes. This includes both first and second draws PPP loans. Borrowers can apply for forgiveness any time up to the maturity date of the loan. However, if borrowers do not apply for forgiveness within 10 months after the last day of the covered period, then PPP loan payments are no longer deferred, and borrowers must begin making loan payments to their PPP lender.

After the CARES Act was passed in March 2020, the IRS stated that taxpayers could not deduct expenses paid with forgiven PPP funds. The Additional Coronavirus Response and Relief Act (ACRRA), passed as part of the Consolidated Appropriations Act of 2021 (CAA) reversed IRS Notice 2020-32 and allowed businesses to deduct expenses paid with forgiven PPP loans.

Economic Injury Disaster Loan Grants (EIDL)

The American Rescue Plan Act (ARPA) authorized an additional $15 billion for targeted EIDL grants. The EIDL grants were an additional grant of up to $5,000 to business with not more than 500 employees that suffered a reduction in gross receipts of greater than 50%.

These grants are excluded from gross income on the federal return, and no deduction may be denied, no tax attribute reduced, and no basis increase denied by reason of such exclusion. This means that for grant income excluded on a partnership or S corporation return, the amount excluded is treated as tax-exempt income for purposes of IRC sections 705 and 1366.

Homeless Hiring Tax Credit (HHTC)

Assembly Bill 150 was passed July 16, 2021, which allows qualified pass-through entities to make an annual election to claim the credit. The credit is available for eligible employees and the employer could receive $2,500 - $10,000 per certified employee based on their actual work hours. Employers could claim up to $30,000 per year. Employers need to make a reservation with the certifying organization, which includes the Continuum of Care (Co) program provider. This credit is available from January 1, 2022, to December 31, 2026. Unused credits may be carried forward for 3 taxable years after the year the credit was generated. This credit will not be able to be filed on an amended return.

To claim the credit the employer needs to:

> Obtain an HHTC certificate from a certifying organization.
> Wages paid need to be greater than 120% of their local California minimum wage.
> Make a provisional credit within 30 days of completing the New Hire report with the EDD.

See (AB) 150.

Main Street Small Business Tax Credit I and II

Main Street Small Business Tax Credit was created in Senate Bill 1447. Small businesses can use the credit against income taxes or apply the credit against sales and use taxes. For the employer to qualify for the credit they must:

- ➢ On December 31, 2019, had 100 or less employees.
- ➢ Compare from April - June 2020 to April - June 2019 the company's gross receipts and have a decrease of 50% decrease in gross receipts.
- ➢ Apply with CDTFA (California Department of Tax and Fee Administration) for a tentative credit reservation during December 1, 2020 – January 15, 2021.
- ➢ Not be mandated or certified to be included in a combined report.

All businesses whether the taxpayer is electing to use the credit to offset qualified sales and use tax or applying the tax credit must reduce any qualified wages by the amount of the credit allowed.

The changes from I to II are:

- ➢ Fewer than 500 employees on December 31, 2020, whose wages are subject to California withholding laws.
- ➢ Gross receipts have decreased by 20% or more; calendar year compare 2020 to 2019.
- ➢ Fiscal filers compare fiscal year 2019-2020 to 2018-2019.
- ➢ New business began after January 1, 2019, but before January 1, 2020, will be determined by gross receipts from January 1, 2020 – February 28, 2020, and multiply by 1.5 of gross receipts from April 1, 2020 – June 30, 2020.
- ➢ Apply to CDTFA for a tentative credit reservation November 1, 2021 – November 30, 2021.
- ➢ Not be mandated or certified to be included in a combined report.

The credit equals to $1,000 for each net increase in the monthly average number of employees, as measured in full-time employee equivalents. Employer is limited to $100,000 for this credit. Use FTB Form 3866 to claim the credit. See AB 150 & 1447.

Pass-through Entity (PTE) Elective Tax

Qualifying PTEs may elect to pay an entity level state tax on income for years beginning January 1, 2021, through January 1, 2026. A qualifying PTE is one that is not publicly traded or required or permitted to be in a combined reporting group. The nonrefundable credit will be claimed on the shareholder's individual tax return. Any unused credits can be carried forward for up to 5 years. The elective tax is 9.3% of the entity's qualified net income.

Business entities must make elective payments by using the FTB free web pay or mail the check to the FTB. FTB Form 3893 must be included with the check. Payment 1 is due on or before June 15th. Payment 1 is $1,000 or 50% of the elective tax paid for the prior taxable year. Payment 2 is due on or before the due date of the original return without extensions. Payment 2 is the remaining dollar amount if any.

Research Credit

California does not conform to this credit. An adjustment needs to be made to 540 Schedule CA Part II.

Business Licenses

Any business owner living in California must obtain a general business license in the city or county (and sometimes both) in which the business will operate. Be aware that some cities refer to a business license as a "business tax certificate". Businesses that operate in unincorporated areas must acquire the tax certificate or license through the county of residence. The cost of the license or tax certificate varies depending on the specific business and the type of business entity. Depending upon the type of sales that the business conducts, the entity may need a sales tax permit even if the business entity only operates online. Sales taxes must still be charged on certain items such as retail. For more information regarding who needs a business license, go to www.ca.gov/service.

Qualified Business Income

California did not conform to Section 199A Deduction.

Assembly Bill (AB) 150 allows the business entity to have a workaround from the SALT $10,000 cap. California allows the S corporation or a partnership to elect to pay 9.3% state income tax, and their owners to claim a credit on their personal return equal to the tax entities pay.

Cannabis Nonconformity

Federal law allows small businesses to claim business expense for a trade or business, except for cannabis. Federal law does not allow any cannabis business to claim their business expenses. California did not conform.

Food Trucks and Sales Tax

Food truck operators and other mobile food vendors must register with the California Department of Tax and Fee Administration (CDTFA) and must file the *Sales and Use Tax Form*. If the vendors include sales tax in the price of the menu item, there must be a notice posted for customers that states, "*All prices of taxable items include sales tax.*" Sales tax should be reported at the rate in effect at the sales location. See Publication 287.

Part 1 Review Questions

To obtain the maximum benefit from this chapter, LTP recommends that you complete each of the following questions, and then compare them to the answers with feedback that immediately follow. Under governing self-study standards, vendors are required to present review questions intermittently throughout each self-study course.

These questions and explanations are not part of the final examination and will not be graded by LTP.

CSCP1.1
California food truck cart owners must register with which agency?

    a. Franchise Tax Board
    b. California Department of Tax and Fee Administration
    c. COVID-19.CA.GOV
    d. Employment Development Department

CSCP1.2
Which individual will have an additional 7% withheld from their gross payments?

    a. Nonresident
    b. California resident
    c. Wage earner
    d. Nanny

CSCP1.3
Which of the following income is not "constructively received"?

    a. Paul earned income that was received by his agent but not received by Paul.
    b. Lori was informed that her check for services rendered was available, but she did not pick it up.
    c. Jacque bought a nine-month CD in November 2021 and earned $200 interest. She can withdraw the principal and interest in the current year if she pays an early withdrawal penalty equal to one month of interest ($100).
    d. A payment on the sale of real property was placed in escrow pending settlement, at which time the title would be conveyed.

CSCP1.4
What amount of start-up costs can a business owner write off in the year the business started?

    a. $500
    b. $2,500
    c. $3,000
    d. $5,000

CSCP1.5
California conformed with the IRS regarding net operating loss.

    a. True
    b. False
    c. Sometimes
    d. All the time

CSCP1.6
Which of the following credits did California not conform to?

    1. Homeless Hiring Tax Credit
    2. Qualified Business Income
    3. Paycheck Protection Act
    4. Research Credit

    a. 1, 3, and 4
    b. 2, 3, and 4
    c. 2 and 4
    d. 1

CSCP1.7
Food trucks must be registered with which California Agency?

    a. Franchise Tax Board
    b. California Department of Tax and Fee Administration
    c. Secretary of State
    d. Employment Development Department

CSCP1.8
Who is the withholding agent for a nonresident working in California?

    a. The business entity
    b. The Franchise Tax Board
    c. The Employment Development Department
    d. California Department of Tax and Fee Administration

CSCP1.9
Which of the following is not a statutory worker?

    a. A commission-driver
    b. A traveling salesperson
    c. A home worker that purchases their own supplies
    d. An agent-driver

CSCP1.10
Which agency administers the ABC test for employees?

    a. Franchise Tax Board
    b. California Department of Tax and Fee Administration
    c. Secretary of State
    d. Employment Development Department

Part 1 Review Questions Answers

CSCP1.1
California food truck owners must register with which agency?

    a. Franchise Tax Board
    b. California Department of Tax and Fee Administration
    c. COVID-19.CA.GOV
    d. Employment Development Department

Feedback: Review section *Food Trucks and Sales Tax.*

CSCP1.2

Which individual will have an additional 7% withheld from their gross payments?

    a. Nonresident
    b. California resident
    c. Wage earner
    d. Nanny

Feedback: Review section *Nonresident Withholding Issues.*

CSCP1.3

Which of the following income is not "constructively received"?

    a. Paul earned income that was received by his agent but not received by Paul.
    b. Lori was informed that her check for services rendered was available, but she did not pick it up.
    c. Jacque bought a nine-month CD in November 2021 and earned $200 interest. She can withdraw the principal and interest in the current year if she pays an early withdrawal penalty equal to one month of interest ($100).
    d. A payment on the sale of real property was placed in escrow pending settlement, at which time the title would be conveyed.

Feedback: Review section *Accounting Methods.*

CSCP1.4

What amount of start-up costs can a business owner write off in the year the business started?

    a. $500
    b. $2,500
    c. $3,000
    d. $5,000

Feedback: Review section *Start-up Expenses.*

CSCP1.5

California conformed with the IRS regarding net operating loss.

    a. True
    b. False
    c. Sometimes
    d. All the time

Feedback: Review section *Net Operating Loss.*

CSCP1.6
Which of the following credits did California not conform to?

      1. Homeless Hiring Tax Credit
      2. Qualified Business Income
      3. Paycheck Protection Act
      4. Research Credit

  a. 1, 3, and 4
  b. 2, 3, and 4
  c. 2 and 4
  d. 1

Feedback: Review section *Key Differences Between California and Federal.*

CSCP1.7
Food trucks must be registered with which California Agency?

  a. Franchise Tax Board
  b. California Department of Tax and Fee Administration
  c. Secretary of State
  d. Employment Development Department

Feedback: Review section *Food Trucks and Sales Tax.*

CSCP1.8
Who is the withholding agent for a nonresident working in California?

  a. The business entity
  b. The Franchise Tax Board
  c. The Employment Development Department
  d. California Department of Tax and Fee Administration

Feedback: Review section *Nonresident Withholding Issues.*

CSCP1.9
Which of the following is not a statutory worker?

  a. A commission-driver
  b. A traveling salesperson
  c. A home worker that purchases their own supplies
  d. An agent-driver

Feedback: Review section *Statutory Employees.*

CSCP1.10
Which agency administers the ABC test for employees?

    a. Franchise Tax Board
    b. California Department of Tax and Fee Administration
    c. Secretary of State
    d. **Employment Development Department**

Feedback: Review section *The ABC Test for Employees*.

Takeaways

The tax professional needs to realize California does not always conform to federal law, but there are times when California does conform with federal law. Knowing and being willing to do research to answer taxpayers' questions gives the tax professional confidence and could bring in more clients. California conforms with the federal on worldwide income. The tax professional needs to recognize which types of income and expenses are ordinary and necessary for each business entity.

TEST YOUR KNOWLEDGE!
Go online to take a practice quiz.

Chapter 10 Schedule E

Introduction

Rental income is any payment received for the use or occupation of real estate or personal property. The payment that is received is taxable to the taxpayer and is generally reported on Schedule E. Each Schedule E can report three properties. If the taxpayer has more than three properties, additional Schedule Es would be used. Schedule E is not used to report personal income and expenses. The taxpayer should not use Schedule E to report renting personal property that is not a business. To report other income, use Schedule 1, lines 8 – 24b.

Objectives

At the end of this lesson, the student will:

> ➢ Know the types of income reported on Schedule E.
> ➢ Realize the difference between repairs and improvements.
> ➢ Recognize where to find the rental property depreciation chart.

Resources

Form 1040	Publication 17	Instructions Form 1040
Form 4562	Publication 527	Instructions Form 4562
Form 4797	Publication 534	Instructions Form 4797
Form 6198	Publication 544	Instructions Form 6198
Form 8582	Publication 925	Instructions Form 8582
Schedule E	Publication 946	Instructions for Schedule E
		Tax Topics 414, 415, 425, 704

Table of Contents

Part I Reporting Rental Income

If the taxpayer rents buildings, rooms, or apartments and provides heat and electric, trash collection, etc., the taxpayer should report the income and expenses in Part I of Schedule E. Do not use Schedule E to report a not-for-profit activity.

If the taxpayer provided significant services primarily for the tenant's convenience, such as regular cleaning, changing linens, or maid service, the taxpayer reports the rental income and expenses on Form 1040, Schedule E, *Supplemental Income and Loss.* Significant services do not include the furnishing of heat and light, cleaning of public areas, trash collection, etc. If the taxpayer provides significant services, the taxpayer may have to pay self-employment tax on the income.

Types of Rental Income

		Properties:		
Income:		A	B	C
3	Rents received			
4	Royalties received			

Portion of Schedule E

Cash or the fair market value of property received for the use of real estate or personal property is taxable rental income. Individuals who operate on the "cash basis" report their rental income as income when it is constructively received and deduct expenses as they are paid. In addition to normal rent, many other things may be considered rent.

Advance Rent

Advance rent is any amount collected by the taxpayer before the time it is due. This income is reported in the year the taxpayer receives it, regardless of the accounting method and when the income was due.

Example: On March 18, 2022, Matthew signed a 10-year lease to rent Martha's property. During 2022, Martha received $9,600 for the first year's rent and $9,600 as rent for the last year of the lease. Martha must include $19,200 as rental income in 2022 ($9,600 + $9,600 = $19,200).

Canceling a Lease

If the tenant paid the landlord to terminate the lease, the amount received is considered rent. The amount paid by the tenant is included in the year received, regardless of the accounting method.

Expenses Paid by Tenant

If the occupant pays any of the owner's expenses, the payments are rental income. The taxpayer must include them as income and can deduct the rental expenses if they are deductible.

Example: Anet pays the water and sewage bill for Fernando's rental property and deducts the amount from her rent payment. Under her terms of the lease, Anet is not required to pay those bills. Fernando would deduct the amount Anet paid for the water and sewage bill as a utility expense and include the amount as rental income.

Property or Services (instead of rent)

If the taxpayer receives property or services as rent instead of money, the fair market value of the property or service is included as rent income.

Example: Lynn enjoys painting and she is Leonard's tenant. Lynn offers to paint the rental property in lieu of paying two months' rent. Leonard accepts the offer. Leonard will include in his rental income the amount that Lynn would have paid for two months' rent. Leonard can deduct the same amount that was included as rent as a rental expense.

Security Deposits

Do not include a security deposit as income when received if the owner returns it at the end of the lease. If the owner keeps part or all the security deposit during any year because the tenant did not perform under the terms of the lease, the owner must include the amount in income for that year. If a security deposit is to be used as the final rent payment, it is advance rent. The taxpayer would include it in income in the year received.

Rental Property Also Used as Home

If the taxpayer rented their primary residence for fewer than 15 days yearly, do not include the rent received as income. Rental expenses are not deductible either.

Fair Rental Value of Portion of Building Used as a Home

Fair rental value for property is an amount that a person who is not related to the owner would be willing to pay for rental use. If any part of the building or structure is occupied by the taxpayer for personal use, the gross rental income includes the fair rental value of the part occupied for personal use. See Publication 946, *Residential Rental Property*.

Room Rental

If a taxpayer rents out rooms of their primary residence, expenses that arise from the rental activity must be ordinary and necessary and to be deductible. All income is taxable. The taxpayer needs to prorate expenses based on the room's square footage. To get the percentage, take the entire square footage of the home and divide by the room's square footage. For example, Jenny's home is 1,800-square-feet, and the room she rents out is 180-square-feet. The percentage she would use to deduct expenses is 10%. 180/1,800=10%.

Part Interest

If the taxpayer is a partial owner in a rental property, the taxpayer must report their percentage of the rental income from the property.

Lease with Option to Buy

If the rental agreement offers the tenant the right to purchase the property, the payments received under the agreement are considered rental income. If the tenant exercises the right to purchase the property, the payments received for the period after the date of sale are considered part of the selling price.

SCHEDULE E (Form 1040)	Supplemental Income and Loss	OMB No. 1545-0074
	(From rental real estate, royalties, partnerships, S corporations, estates, trusts, REMICs, etc.)	2022
Department of the Treasury Internal Revenue Service	Attach to Form 1040, 1040-SR, 1040-NR, or 1041. Go to *www.irs.gov/ScheduleE* for instructions and the latest information.	Attachment Sequence No. 13

Name(s) shown on return	Your social security number

Part I   Income or Loss From Rental Real Estate and Royalties

Note: If you are in the business of renting personal property, use **Schedule C**. See instructions. If you are an individual, report farm rental income or loss from **Form 4835** on page 2, line 40.

A   Did you make any payments in 2022 that would require you to file Form(s) 1099? See instructions . . . . . ☐ Yes ☐ No
B   If "Yes," did you or will you file required Form(s) 1099?   . . . . ☐ Yes ☐ No

1a   Physical address of each property (street, city, state, ZIP code)

A	
B	
C	

Portion of Schedule E

Husband and Wife Qualified Joint Venture (QJV)

A husband and wife cannot be sole proprietors of the same business. If they are joint owners, they are partners and should file a partnership return on Form 1065, *U.S. Return of Partnership Income.* They can be partners, but "sole" means one. For purposes of a business, the IRS does not recognize spouses as one.

If the taxpayer and spouse each materially participated in the business as the only members of a jointly owned and operated business and file a joint return, they can elect to be taxed as a qualified joint venture instead of a partnership. Generally, this election does not increase the total tax on the joint return, but it gives the credit for each taxpayer's social security earnings. If Form 1065 was filed for a prior year, the partnership terminates the year immediately preceding the year the joint venture election takes effect.

To make the election, the taxpayers must divide all income and expenses and file two separate Schedule E. Once the election is made, it can only be revoked with IRS permission. The election remains in effect for as long as the spouses file as a qualified joint venture. If the taxpayer and spouse do not qualify in one year, then the next year they will need to redo the paperwork to become a qualified joint venture.

Community Income Exception

If the spouses own an unincorporated business and they live in a state, foreign country, or a U.S. possession that has community property laws, the income and deductions are reported as follows:

1. If only one spouse participates in the business, all the income from that business is self-employment earnings of the spouse who carried the business.
2. If both spouses participate, the income and the deductions are allocated to the spouses based on their distributive shares.
3. If either or both spouses are partners in a partnership, see Publication 541.
4. If the taxpayer and spouse elected to treat the business as a qualifying joint venture, both taxpayer and spouse must file separate Schedule E and a separate Schedule SE.

Community property law states are Arizona, California, Idaho, Louisiana, Nevada, New Mexico, Texas, Washington, and Wisconsin.

Types of Property

Portion of Schedule E

Like determining a filing status, rental property(s) need to be classified as well. Single family residence means any building situated on one lot with a single dwelling, and sharing no common wall, foundation, or other interconnection. Types of single-family residences are mobile homes, homes, and mansions. Use code 1 for these structures.

Multi-family residence is a classification of housing where multiple separate housing units for residential inhabitants are contained within one building. This includes duplex, tri-plex, condos, and/or apartments. Use code 2 for these structures.

Commercial buildings include offices, hotels, malls, retail stores, etc. Use code 4 for these structures.

Land is never depreciated, but property may need to report income for renting out the land. Use code 5 for this use. Items considered rent income include renting the land to a farmer to grow crops; this would not be reported on Schedule F, but Schedule E. Basis for land is the price determined by the county as land value. It is also found on the property statement.

A royalty payment is income derived from the use of the owner's property. It must relate to the use of a valuable right. A valuable right could be items such as precious minerals (gold, silver, etc.) and crude oil.

Self-rental is when the owner of the property rents the business to their business. This is regarded as materially participates, therefore any net income for the property is deemed to be nonpassive.

Types of Expenses

Portion of Schedule E

Deductible rental expenses are expenditures that are incurred in renting the property. The taxpayer would deduct all ordinary and necessary expenses such as:

Advertising – line 5

Advertising is considered an ad in a local paper, online, or other means of advertising to cause a potential renter to inquire about the property. The price paid is the amount entered on line 5.

Auto and Travel – line 6

Taxpayers can deduct ordinary and necessary auto and travel expenses related to the rental activity. The taxpayer should keep track of the miles to and from the rental. Ordinary and necessary mileage is when the owner collects rent, works on the rental, etc. The standard mileage rate is used for the current tax year. Taxpayer can claim the mileage only if they:

1. Owned the vehicle and used the standard mileage rate for the first year placed in service.
2. Leased the vehicle and are using the standard mileage rate for the entire lease period.

Señor 1040 Says: The taxpayer cannot deduct car rental or lease payments, depreciation, or the actual auto expense if the standard mileage rate is used.

Cleaning and Maintenance – line 7

The day-to-day maintenance of the property is an allowed expense provided it is only for common areas and day-to-day cleanliness. These expenses are also limited to the days that are allowable rental days and not personal use days.

Commissions – line 8

Fees or commission paid to agents who collect the rent, maintain the rental, or find tenants could be reported on line 8.

Insurance – line 9

Insurance for the rental property and the rider policy if the taxpayer has one.

Legal and Other Professional Fees – line 10

You can't claim legal fees charged as part of buying or selling the property. The taxpayer can claim fees paid to an accountant for managing their accounts and the tax return preparation and tax advice. Fees involved for setting up the rental property are not a deduction.

Management Fees – line 11

Property management services are reported on line 11 and may lower the taxpayer's liability. The taxpayer may claim the entire cost of the services but must keep all invoices or statements the property management company issues as evidence of the deduction's eligibility.

Part of property management is to maintain the paperwork between the tenant and the landlord. This can come in handy during tax season, especially for landlords who are not particularly organized or good at bookkeeping. When the management company prepares the paperwork for the tax preparer, it can deliver a more accurate tax return.

Mortgage Interest Paid to Banks – line 12

The taxpayer can claim the interest charged on money borrowed to buy the rental property, but not the entire mortgage payment. If the taxpayer borrowed money against the rental and did not use it for the rental, the interest is not a deduction on Schedule E.

Other Interest – line 13

If the taxpayer paid interest on the rental income to an individual and did not receive Form 1098, enter the amount on line 13 and not on line 12. Attach to the return a statement that shows the name and address of the person who received the income. On the dotted line next to line 12 enter "See attached."

Repairs – line 14

The taxpayer can claim costs for repairs to the property or general maintenance. Nevertheless, if the taxpayer is doing the work themselves, only claim the materials and not the time it took to repair the property. If the work is more of an improvement than a repair, then the taxpayer cannot claim the cost as an expense. The cost would be considered an asset and will be covered in the depreciation chapter.

Supplies – line 15

"Materials and supplies" are tangible property used or consumed in the business operations that fall within any of the following categories:

> ➢ Tangible items that cost less than $200.
> ➢ Personal property with an economic useful life of 12 months or less.
> ➢ Spare parts that have been acquired to maintain or repair a unit of tangible property.

The cost of such items may be deducted in the year the item is used or consumed. To use this deduction, the taxpayer should keep records of when items are used or consumed for the rental property.

Cleaning and repair supplies are fully deductible, and some materials are as well. Supplies used in maintenance or to complete repairs are reported under supplies and not added to line 14. Materials on the other hand are generally not "used up" and sometimes become a part of the property. Materials used for improvements are usually depreciated, but materials used for repairs are considered supplies and can be deducted.

For example, the taxpayer changed the roof on their rental property. Nails and tar would be considered repair supplies, while roof shingles would be considered an improvement. The supplies get deducted, and the materials are added to the basis and depreciated separately over 27.5 years.

If the roof replacement was a repair and not an improvement (replacing a leaky roof), the roof shingles would be considered repair supplies, and would be deducted in the year the expenses were incurred.

Taxes – line 16

This line reports the property tax paid on the property. Like the primary home, one cannot claim bonds or other add-on taxes that are not related to the property.

Utilities – line 17

Utilities that can be claimed are what the taxpayer pays, such as water, electricity, etc. If the renter is the one paying these expenses, it is not a landlord deduction.

Depreciation – line 18

Depreciation is the annual deduction one must take to recover the cost or other basis of business or investment property having a useful life. Depreciation starts when the taxpayer puts the property into service. Property ends when the owner has sold or discontinued the property.

Other Expenses – line 19

What is claimed on this line is any ordinary and necessary expenses not included in lines 5 - 18.

Expenses That Cannot be Claimed

The taxpayer cannot claim deductions for capital expenses, private expenses, or expenses that do not relate to the rental. Capital expenses are the costs of buying a capital asset or increasing its value; for example, the cost of buying the property and making improvements. Private expenses are things purchased for their own benefit, rather than to generate rental income.

Rental income expenses that are unable to be used on the taxpayer's personal income tax return:

- ➤ Purchase price of a rental property.
- ➤ Capital portion of mortgage repayments.
- ➤ Interest on money borrowed for any purpose other than financing a rental property.
- ➤ The costs of making additions or improvements to the property.
- ➤ The costs of repairing or replacing damaged property, if the work increases the property's value.
- ➤ Real estate agent fees (commissions) charged as part of buying or selling the property.

Claiming Deductions When Renting Out the House or Part of the Home

The usual rule is to claim expenses related to the rental activity only. One cannot claim private living costs or capital expenses. Private living costs include the taxpayer's day-to-day costs, such as food, electricity, or gas. Capital expenses include buying furniture for the rented room or the cost of improving that portion of the property. The taxpayer can claim depreciation on capital expenses. Expenses the taxpayer may be able to claim include electricity, gas, telephone and internet, insurance, or rates that are related to the rental portion. If the taxpayer is living in the house, these expenses will need to be apportioned.

Renting Out the House - Apportionment

If the taxpayer rents out the house on an occasional basis, the taxpayer can claim the percentage of expenses for the time the house is rented. This may apply where the taxpayer rents out the house or property while away for a short period of time. The percentage of expenses claimed must match the amount of time in the tax year the house was rented out.

Renting Out a Room - Apportionment

If the taxpayer is renting out part of the home, the taxpayer can only claim expenses that relate to that part of the property. The taxpayer can only claim expenses for the time the room was rented out and occupied. Expenses could be claimed as a percentage based on the total area of the home and the rented room area.

Expenses Lines 5 - 19

Expenses reported on Schedule E are:

➢ Advertising
➢ Cleaning and maintenance
➢ Depreciation
➢ Rental insurance premiums
➢ Real estate taxes

Transportation and Travel Expenses, Line 6

Taxpayers can deduct ordinary and necessary local transportation expenses if they incur them while collecting rental income or to manage, conserve, or maintain the rental property. If taxpayers use a personal vehicle for maintaining rental activities, the deduction of the expenses is either by actual expenses or the standard mileage rate. For tax year 2022, the rate is 58.5 cents per mile from January to June and 62.5 cents per mile from July - December. For tax year 2023 the business travel rate is 65.5 cents per mile.

The taxpayer can deduct the ordinary and necessary expenses of traveling away from home if the primary purpose of the trip was to collect rental income or to manage, conserve, or maintain rental property. The taxpayer must properly allocate expenses between rental and nonrental activities. Information needed to record auto expenses accurately:

➢ Beginning mileage
➢ Ending mileage
➢ Commuting mileage
➢ Business mileage (notes about the destination and reason for travel should be made)
➢ Separate records for each rental property

If the taxpayer rents only part of the property, the expenses must be allocated between the part rented and the part that is not rented.

Insurance Premiums Prepaid, Line 9

If the owner prepays an insurance premium for more than one year in advance, the payment will be applied for the year it was used.

Example: Gary paid $1,200 for his insurance on April 15, 2022, for 2022 and 2023. Gary will apply $600 for insurance in 2022 and $600 for insurance in 2023. He cannot take the entire amount in 2022.

Legal and Other Professional Fees, Line 10

These fees include legal and other professional fees such as tax preparation and expenses paid to resolve a tax underpayment related to rental activities. Federal taxes and penalties are not deductible.

Mortgage Interest, Line 12

Mortgage interest paid on the rental building could be deducted in the year paid. If the taxpayer owns a partial interest in a rental property, part of the rental expenses for that property can be deducted based on the taxpayer's percentage interest.

Points

Points are used to describe certain charges paid or treated as paid by a borrower to obtain a home mortgage. Points are not added to the basis of the property. Points can also be called loan origination fees.

Taxes Line 16

State and local, real estate taxes paid for rental income owned by the taxpayer are deducted on line 16 of Schedule E. If the taxpayer's real estate taxes are included in the mortgage and paid out of an escrow account, the amount paid by the mortgage company is the deducted amount.

Depreciation Line 18

Depreciation is a capital expense. Depreciation begins when the property has been placed in service.

Depreciation is the annual deduction for recovery of the purchase price of the fixed-asset expenditure. Property used for business should be depreciated. The amount of depreciation taken each year is determined by the basis of the property, the recovery period for that property, and the depreciation method. The recovery period for residential rental property under MACRS is 27.5 years and is used for property placed in service after 1986.

Depreciation for rental property (in the year placed in service) is reported on Form 4562, *Depreciation and Amortization*, and flows to Schedule E.

Depreciation that was not taken in one year cannot be taken in a following year. But an amended return (Form 1040X) can be filed for the year in which it was not taken (if no more than three years prior). If depreciable property is sold, its basis for determining gain or loss will be reduced by depreciation "allowed or allowable," even if not deducted. Land is never depreciated.

Section 179 deductions cannot be used to depreciate rental property. The rental property can be depreciated if all the following requirements are met:

> - The taxpayer owns the property.
> - The taxpayer uses the property as an income-producing activity.
> - The property has a determinable useful life.
> - The property is expected to last more than one year.

Property That Can Be Depreciated

Most types of tangible property can be depreciated. Examples of tangible property are:

➢ Buildings
➢ Vehicles
➢ Machinery
➢ Furniture
➢ Equipment
➢ Storage facilities

Land is tangible property and can never be depreciated. Some intangible items that can be depreciated are:

➢ Copyrights
➢ Patents
➢ Computer software if life value is more than one year.

Property that needs to be depreciated must meet the following requirements:

➢ Must be the taxpayer's own property.
➢ Must be used in the taxpayer's business or income-producing activity.
➢ Property must have a determinable useful life.
➢ The property is expected to last more than one year.

Passive Activity Limits

Passive activity is when the taxpayer did not materially participate during the tax year. The two types of passive activity are:

1. Trade or business not materially participated in during the tax year.
2. Rental activities, regardless of the taxpayer participation.

Material participation is the involvement in the activity of the business on a regular, continuous, and substantial basis. The taxpayer can claim a passive loss only against active income. Any excess passive activity loss can be carried forward to future years until used, or until it can be deducted in the year when the taxpayer disposes of the activity in a taxable transaction.

Rental real estate activities are passive activities; exceptions may apply for certain real estate professionals. Rental activity is when the taxpayer receives income mainly for the use of tangible property, rather than for services. Deductions or losses from passive activities are limited. Taxpayers cannot offset their income with passive activity income; passive activity income can only offset passive activity loss. The excess loss or credit is carried forward to the next tax year.

At-Risk Rules

The at-risk rules place a limit on the amount that can be deducted as a loss from rental real estate activity. Losses from holding real property (other than mineral property) placed in service before 1987 are not subject to the at-risk rules.

Generally, any loss from an activity subject to the at-risk rules is allowed only to the extent of the total amount at risk in the activity at the end of the tax year. The taxpayer is considered at-risk in an activity to the extent that cash and the adjusted basis of other property contributed to the activity and certain amounts borrowed for use in the activity.

The taxpayer may need to complete Form 6198 to figure their loss if:

> ➢ The taxpayer has a loss from the activity that is a trade or business or for production of income.
> ➢ The taxpayer is not at-risk in this activity.

Active Participation

If a taxpayer owned at least 10% of the rental property and made management decisions in a significant and bona fide sense, he or she is considered to have active participation. Management decisions include approving new tenants, deciding on rental terms, approving expenditures, and similar decisions. In most cases, all rental real estate activities are passive activities. For this purpose, a rental activity is an activity from which income is received mainly for the use of tangible property rather than for services.

Example: Christian is single and had the following income and losses during the tax year:

Salary	$56,954
Lottery winnings	$10,000
Rental loss	($3,450)

The rental loss resulted from a residential rental house that Christian owned. Christian made all the management decisions including collecting rent, making repairs, or hiring someone to complete the repairs, and approving the current tenant. Christian actively participated in the rental property management; therefore, he can use the entire loss of $3,450 to offset his other income.

Local Benefit Taxes

A deduction cannot be taken for charges of local benefits that increase the value of the rental property. Examples of such charges are putting in streets, sidewalks, or water and sewer systems. These charges are capital expenditures that cannot be depreciated. The charges may be added to the basis of the property. Local benefit taxes may be deducted if they are for maintenance, repairing, or paying interest charges for the benefits.

Expenses Accrued While Fixing the Rental

The taxpayer can deduct ordinary and necessary expenses for managing, supporting, or maintaining rental property from the time it is made available for rent.

Rental of Equipment

The taxpayer could deduct the rent paid for equipment that is used for rental purposes. But, if the lease contract is a purchase contract, the taxpayer cannot deduct these payments.

Uncollected Rent

If the taxpayer uses the cash-basis, the taxpayer cannot deduct uncollected rent since the cash-basis taxpayer was never included in income. If the taxpayer is an accrual-basis taxpayer, the taxpayer must report the income when it is earned. If the taxpayer is unable to collect the rent, one may be able to deduct it as a bad-debt business expense.

Vacant Rental Property

If the taxpayer holds property for rental purposes, the taxpayer may be able to deduct ordinary and necessary expenses for managing, sustaining, or maintaining rental property from the time it became available for rent. Loss of rental income is not deductible.

Repairs and Improvements

Repairs

Maintaining the condition of the rental property. Repairs do not add to the value of the property or substantially prolong its life. The following are examples of repairs:

> ➢ Repainting the property inside and out.
> ➢ Fixing gutters or floors.
> ➢ Fixing leaks.
> ➢ Plastering a hole in a wall.
> ➢ Replacing broken windows.

If repairs are made during an extensive remodeling of the property, the whole job is an improvement. Improvements add value to the property and prolong the property's useful life. Improvements to property must be capitalized. The capitalized costs can generally be depreciated as if the improvements were separate property.

Example: Janice purchased an old Victorian house. The house needed many repairs, such as re-plastering, repainting, replacing broken windows, replacing roof tiles, and fixing leaks. After taking several months to complete the repairs, Janice was finally able to place the property on the market for rent. The remodeling of the property is considered an improvement, not a repair.

Improvements

Any expense that is paid to improve the property must be capitalized. An improvement adds value or prolongs the property life, restores the property, and/or adapts the property to a new or different use. Examples include:

> *Betterment* includes expenses for fixing a pre-existing defect or condition or for enlarging or expanding the property.

> *Restoration* includes expenses for replacing a substantial structural part of the property, repairing damage to the property, or rebuilding the property to a like-new condition.

> *Adaptation* includes expenses for altering the property to a use that is not consistent with the intended ordinary use of the property.

Recordkeeping

Keeping records is a way to show proof of any deduction that has been claimed on the tax return. Taxpayers should keep the tax records for at least five years from the date of filing the tax return and claiming the deduction. The individual should keep all receipts, loan documents, buyers closing statement of the assets that are claimed on the tax return.

Keeping records is a way to show proof of any deduction that has been claimed on the tax return. Taxpayers should keep the tax records for at least five years from the date of filing the tax return and claiming the deduction. The individual should keep all receipts, loan documents, and the buyers closing statement of the assets that are reported on the tax return.

The taxpayer must also keep records regarding expenses and days of rental use. Records should be kept if the taxpayer or a member of the family used the rental property for personal purposes. The taxpayer should keep records of dates and times they personally spent on repairing or maintaining the property.

Not Rented for Profit

If the property is not rented with the intent of making a profit, the expenses can be deducted only up to the amount of income. In this situation, the income is reported on Schedule 1, line 8a - z. The mortgage interest, real estate taxes, and casualty losses are deducted on the appropriate lines of Schedule A. If the taxpayer rents the home fewer than 15 days a year, the taxpayer does not need to report any of the rental income and cannot deduct any of the expenses.

Fair Rental Price

A fair rental price for property is an amount that a person who is not related to the taxpayer would be willing to pay. The rent charged is not a fair rental price if it is substantially less than rent charged for other similar properties. Ask the following questions when comparing one property to another:

> - Is it used for the same purpose?
> - Is it approximately the same size?
> - Is it in approximately the same condition?
> - Does it have similar furnishings?
> - Is it in a similar location?

If any one of the answers are no, the properties are not similar.

Use as Main Home Before or After Renting

Do not count personal days when the property was used as a main home or after renting or offering it for rent in either of the following:

1. The taxpayer rented or tried to rent the property for 12 or more consecutive months.
2. The taxpayer rented or tried to rent the property for a period of less than 12 consecutive months, and the period ended because the property was sold or exchanged.

This special rule does not apply when dividing expenses between rental and personal use.

Dividing Expenses for Property Changed to Rental Use

If an expense is for both personal and rental use, the expense must be divided between personal and rental use. Any reasonable method can be used to divide the expense. For example, it may be reasonable to divide the cost of some items, such as water, based on the number of people using them. However, the two most common methods for dividing expenses are:

1. Dividing an expense based on the number of rooms in the home.
2. Dividing an expense based on the square footage of the home.

Property Changed to Rental Use

If the taxpayer converts their primary home or other property (or a part of it) to rental use at any time other than at the beginning of the year, the taxpayer must divide the yearly expenses (such as depreciation, taxes, and insurance) between rental use and personal use. The taxpayer can deduct as rental expenses only the portion of the expenses that was for the part of the year the property was used or held for rental purposes. The taxpayer cannot deduct insurance or depreciation for the part of the year the property was held for personal use. The taxpayer can deduct home mortgage interest and real estate taxes as an itemized deduction on Schedule A for the part of the year the property was used for personal purposes.

Rental of Vacation Homes and Other Dwelling Units

If the taxpayer uses a dwelling as both a home and a rental unit, expenses must be divided between personal use and rental use. The taxpayer uses a dwelling as a home if one uses it for personal use more than the greater of:

➢ 14 days
➢ 10% of the total days it is rented to others at a fair rental price

Personal use consists of any day the unit is used by:

➢ The taxpayer or other person who has an interest in the home unless rented to another owner as the main home under a shared equity financing agreement.
➢ A family member or member of any other family who has an interest in the home unless the family member uses the dwelling as their main home and pays fair rental price.
➢ Anyone under an arrangement that lets the taxpayer use some other dwelling unit even if that person pays a fair rental price.
➢ Anyone who uses the dwelling at less than a fair rental price.

Days spent substantially working full time to repair or maintain the property do not count as personal days. If any part of a building or structure is occupied by the taxpayer for personal use, its gross rental income includes the fair rental value of the part occupied for personal use.

Dividing Expenses for Vacation Homes and Other Dwelling Units

If a unit is used for both rental and personal use, the expenses must be divided between the two. Any day that the unit is rented at the fair market value and used for both rental and personal use, the expenses are considered business use. Any day that the unit is available for rent but not actually rented is not a day of rental use.

Example: A ski lodge is available for rent from November 1 through March 31 (a total of 151 days, using 28 days for February). The taxpayer's family uses it for 14 days in October. No one rents it in the first week of November or at any time in March. The person who rented it the first week in December was called home for a family emergency. The taxpayer's daughter used it for two days. The remainder of the year the lodge was closed and not used by anyone.

Rental Days: 151 − 38 = 113

The lodge was available for 38 days in which it was not rented. Days used by taxpayer and/or the taxpayer's family on which fair rental price was received count as rental days. The use by the taxpayer's daughter in December is recorded as rental days.

Total Use: 113 + 14 = 127

Personal Use: Percentage on rental is 113/127 = 89%. The deductible portion of any expenses is 89%. If the taxpayer does not have a profit from the rental, deductible expenses are limited.

Real Estate Professional

Generally, rental activities are passive activities even if the taxpayer materially participates. However, the activity may not be passive if all of these are true:

> - The taxpayer is a real estate professional.
> - During the year the individual materially participated in the rental activities.
> - Participates more than 750 hours in performing personal services in the trade or business.
> - Spends half of the time performing personal services in real property.

Qualified activities include developing, redeveloping, constructing, reconstructing, acquiring, converting, operating, managing, leasing, or selling real property. A taxpayer materially participates in an activity if for the tax year the taxpayer was involved in its operation on a regular, continuous, and substantial basis during the year. If the taxpayer meets these requirements, the rental business is not a passive activity. If the taxpayer has multiple properties, each one is treated separately unless the taxpayer chooses to treat them as one activity. Personal services that were performed as an employee cannot be counted. If the taxpayer files a joint return, the hours cannot be added together to fulfill the requirements.

Limited Partnership Interests

If the taxpayer held property in a limited partnership as a limited partner, the taxpayer does not materially participate in rental real estate. Failure to meet the minimum-hours threshold may result in the passive activity amount being limited. Proper recordkeeping is the key to making sure that if the taxpayer is ever audited, the taxpayer does not lose their passive activity loss (PAL).

Rental Property Sales

When rental property or other business assets are sold, the gain or loss must be reported on Form 4797, *Sales of Business Property.* If the property sold includes land, both the land and the property must be reported on Form 4797. Each property is reported separately in the appropriate part of Form 4797. The different sections of Form 4797 are as follows:

Part I: Used to report sales of the section 1231 portion of a real estate transaction. This includes land and all long-term property sold at a loss. A transaction reported here is not required to report in Part III.

Part II: Used to report sales of business property that are not reported in Part I or Part III.

Part III: Used to calculate the recapture of depreciation and certain other items that must be reported as ordinary income on the disposition of property. The property includes sections 1245, 1250, 1252, 1254, and 1255 property sales. This includes most long-term property that was depreciated and sold at a gain.

Depreciation should be calculated (and deducted on the appropriate form) for the period prior to the sale. If the taxpayer sells or exchanges property used partly for business or rental purposes and partly for personal purposes, the taxpayer must figure the gain or loss on the sale or exchange as though two separate pieces of property were sold. The taxpayer must divide the selling price, selling expenses, and the basis of the property between the business or rental part and the personal part. The taxpayer must subtract depreciation that was taken or could have taken from the basis of the business or rental part. Gain or loss on the business or rental part of the property may be a capital gain or loss or an ordinary gain or loss. Any gain on the personal part of the property is a capital gain. The taxpayer cannot deduct a loss on the personal part.

Depreciation is the annual deduction that allows taxpayers to recover the cost or other basis of their business or investment property over a certain number of years. Depreciation begins when a taxpayer places property in service for use in a trade or business or to produce income. The property ceases to be depreciable when the taxpayer has fully recovered the property's cost or other basis or when the property has been retired from service, whichever comes first.

Property Owned

To claim depreciation, one must be the owner of the property, even if the property has debt. Leased property can be claimed only if ownership in the property includes the following:

➢ The legal title to the property.
➢ The legal obligation to pay for the property.
➢ The responsibility to pay maintenance and operating expenses.
➢ The duty to pay any taxes on the property.
➢ The risk of loss if the property is destroyed, condemned, or diminished in value through obsolescence or exhaustion.

Example: Amanda made a down payment on a rental property and assumed Terrance's mortgage. Amanda owns the property and can depreciate it.

If the property is held as a business or investment property as a life tenant, the taxpayer may depreciate the property.

Property Having a Determinable Useful Life

Property must have a determinable useful life to be depreciated. It must be something that wears out, decays, is used up, becomes obsolete, or loses its value from natural causes.

Property Lasting More than One Year

To depreciate property, the useful life must be one year or more.

Example: Ms. Lady maintains a library for her tax business. She purchases yearly technical journals to use in her tax business. The library would be depreciated, but the technical journals do not have a useful life of more than one year. The technical journals can be taken as a yearly business expense.

Property used in Business or Income-Producing Activity

To claim depreciation on property one must use it in their business or an income-producing activity. If the taxpayer uses the property to produce an investment use, then the income is taxable. One cannot depreciate property that one uses solely for personal activities.

If the property has multiple use business and personal purpose, the portion used as business will be depreciated. For example, the taxpayer cannot deduct deprecation on a car used only for commuting to and from work or used for personal shopping trips and family vacations. Records must be kept showing business and personal use of the property.

Inventory cannot be depreciated. Inventory is any property that is held primarily for sale to customers in the ordinary course of business. If the owner is in the rent-to-own business, certain property held in that business may be considered as depreciable instead of inventory. See Publication 946.

Containers for the products one sells are part of inventory and are not depreciable. Containers used to ship products can be depreciated if the life expectancy is more than one year and meet the following requirements:

1. Qualify as property used in business
2. Title to the containers does not pass to the buyer

Property That Cannot Be Depreciated

Land does not wear out; therefore, it cannot be depreciated. The cost of land generally includes clearing, grading, planting, and landscaping. Although land is never depreciated, certain improvements to the land can be depreciated, such as landscaping.

Excepted Property

The following property cannot be depreciated even if the requirements are met:

1. Property placed in service and disposed of in the same year.
2. Equipment used to build capital improvements.
3. Section 197 intangibles that must be amortized.
4. Certain term interests.

The Beginning and Ending of Depreciation

Depreciation begins when the property is placed in service for use in a trade or business or to produce income. Depreciation ends when the cost (or other basis) has been fully recovered or when it has been retired from service, whichever comes first.

Placed in Service

Property is placed in service when it is ready and available for a specific use for a business activity, an income-producing activity, a tax-exempt activity, or a personal activity. Even if the property is not being used, it is still placed in service when it is ready and available for its specific use.

Example 1: Joel purchased a machine in December of last year for his business. The machine was delivered but not installed. Joel had the machine installed and ready for use in February of the current tax year. The machine would be placed in service in February of the current year.

If the property has been converted from personal to business use, the "placed in service" date is the date it was converted to business use or to an income-producing activity. In other words, depreciation begins when the property has been placed in service.

Example 2: Nicolas purchased a home as his primary residence in 2016, and in 2021 he converted it to a rental property. He placed the home in service in 2021; therefore, Nicolas would start depreciation when it was placed in service as an income-producing property.

Royalties

Portion of Schedule E

Royalty income is reported on Schedule E as ordinary income. The following are examples of royalty income:

➢ Copyrights on literary, musical, or artistic works.
➢ Patents on inventions.
➢ Gas, oil, and mineral properties.
➢ Depletion, if the taxpayer is the owner of an economic interest in mineral deposits or oil and gas wells.
➢ Coal and iron ore.

Like rental income, expenses reduce this income. If the taxpayer was self-employed as a writer, inventor, artist, etc., income and expenses should be reported on Schedule C.

If the taxpayer is in business as a self-employed writer, artist, or musician, or if they hold an operating oil, gas, or mineral interest, the income and expenses would be reported on Schedule C. Royalties from copyrights and patents, oil and gas, and mineral properties are taxable as ordinary income and are reported on page 1 of Schedule E.

Taxable rental income and taxable income from royalties are reported on Schedule E and reported on Schedule 1, line 5. However, income from renting hotel rooms or other retail property where the renter provides significant additional services is not reported on Schedule E; it is reported as business income on Schedule C.

Partnership or S Corporation Income

Part II	**Income or Loss From Partnerships and S Corporations**

Note: If you report a loss, receive a distribution, dispose of stock, or receive a loan repayment from an S corporation, you **must** check the box in column **(e)** on line 28 and attach the required basis computation. If you report a loss from an at-risk activity for which **any** amount is **not** at risk, you **must** check the box in column **(f)** on line 28 and attach **Form 6198**. See instructions.

| 27 | Are you reporting any loss not allowed in a prior year due to the at-risk or basis limitations, a prior year unallowed loss from a passive activity (if that loss was not reported on Form 8582), or unreimbursed partnership expenses? If you answered "Yes," see instructions before completing this section . . . . ☐ **Yes** ☐ **No** |

28	(a) Name	(b) Enter P for partnership; S for S corporation	(c) Check if foreign partnership	(d) Employer identification number	(e) Check if basis computation is required	(f) Check if any amount is not at risk
A			☐		☐	☐
B			☐		☐	☐
C			☐		☐	☐
D			☐		☐	☐

Portion of Schedule E

Income a taxpayer receives from a partnership, or an S corporation is taxable. Neither the partnership nor the S corporation pays taxes. The taxes are "passed through" to the partners or shareholders, who report the income, as well as some of the expenses, on their individual tax returns. This income is reported on Schedule E, page 2.

Taxpayers should receive a Schedule K-1 from the partnership or S corporation, which will show the income and expenses the taxpayers would report on their individual returns.

Part II on page 2 of Form 1040, Schedule E is used to report partnership and shareholders of a subchapter S corporation income from the Schedule K-1. If the taxpayer actively participates in their partnership's business, it is nonpassive income or nonpassive loss. Partnership income is reported to each partner on Schedule K-1.

Part I Review Questions

To obtain the maximum benefit from this chapter, LTP recommends that you complete each of the following questions, and then compare them to the answers with feedback that immediately follow. Under governing self-study standards, vendors are required to present review questions intermittently throughout each self-study course.

These questions and explanations are not part of the final examination and will not be graded by LTP.

SEP1.1

Marlene paid $4,000 for real estate taxes on her rental property located at 1850 Happy Street, Jersey City, New Jersey. She paid $6,850 of real estate taxes on her primary residence. Marlene has household employees for whom she paid social security taxes of $1,300 and state income tax of $2,500. What amount of real estate tax will Marlene deduct on her Schedule E?

a. $14,650
b. $6,850
c. $4,000
d. $1,300

SEP1.2
Candy paid her landlord $3,000 to cancel her lease. What amount is included in her landlord's income for the year?

   a. $1,500
   b. $2,000
   c. $3,000
   d. $0

SEP1.3
Property _____ to be depreciable when the taxpayer has fully recovered the property's cost or other basis.

   a. ceases
   b. contains
   c. commences
   d. completes

SEP1.4
Royalty income is reported on which of the following as ordinary income?

   a. Schedule E, page 1
   b. Schedule E, page 2
   c. Royalty income is not reportable
   d. Form 1040, line 21

SEP1.5
Depreciation is a(n) _____ allowance for the wear and tear of the property.

   a. annual
   b. monthly
   c. quarterly
   d. taxpayer's choice

SEP1.6
Which of the following is **not** considered to be rent?

   a. Advance rent
   b. Security deposit used as last month's rent
   c. Expenses paid by the tenant in lieu of rent
   d. Royalty income

SEP1.7
Which of the following could increase the value of the property?

   a. Advertising fees paid to market the rental property.
   b. Insurance fees paid to insure the rental property.
   c. Adding a room to the rental property.
   d. Depreciation of the rental property.

SEP1.8
Which of the following is not depreciable?

    a. Buildings
    b. Furniture
    c. Land
    d. Machinery

SEP1.9
Which of the following best describes when depreciation begins?

    a. When the property is placed in service
    b. When the property has used up its useful life
    c. When the property has not been converted from personal to business use
    d. When the property has not been placed in service

SEP1.10
Which of the following scenarios best describes when property is retired from service?

    a. When the property has been permanently withdrawn from its use in trade or business
    b. When the property has been temporarily withdrawn from use in trade or business
    c. When the property has not been converted to business use
    d. When the property has not been permanently withdrawn from its use in trade or business

Part 1 Review Questions Answers

SEP1.1
Marlene paid $4,000 for real estate taxes on her rental property located at 1850 Happy Street, Jersey City, New Jersey. She paid $6,850 of real estate taxes on her primary residence. Marlene has household employees for whom she paid social security taxes of $1,300 and state income tax of $2,500. What amount of real estate tax will Marlene deduct on her Schedule E?

    a. $14,650
    b. $6,850
    c. $4,000
    d. $1,300

Feedback: Review section *Taxes Line 16*.

SEP1.2
Candy paid her landlord $3,000 to cancel her lease. What amount is included in her landlord's income for the year?

    a. $1,500
    b. $2,000
    c. $3,000
    d. $0

Feedback: Review section *Canceling a Lease*.

SEP1.3

Property _____ to be depreciable when the taxpayer has fully recovered the property's cost or other basis.

    a. ceases
    b. contains
    c. commences
    d. completes

Feedback: Review section *Depreciation*.

SEP1.4

Royalty income is reported on which of the following as ordinary income?

    a. Schedule E, page 1
    b. Schedule E, page 2
    c. Royalty income is not reportable
    d. Form 1040, line 21

Feedback: Review section *Royalties*.

SEP1.5

Depreciation is a(n)_____ allowance for the wear and tear of the property.

    a. annual
    b. monthly
    c. quarterly
    d. taxpayer's choice

Feedback: Review section *Depreciation*.

SEP1.6

Which of the following is **not** considered to be rent?

    a. Advance rent
    b. Security deposit used as last month's rent
    c. Expenses paid by the tenant in lieu of rent
    d. Royalty income

Feedback: Review section *Royalties*.

SEP1.7

Which of the following could increase the value of the property?

    a. Advertising fees paid to market the rental property.
    b. Insurance fees paid to insure the rental property.
    c. Adding a room to the rental property.
    d. Depreciation of the rental property.

Feedback: Review section *Improvements*.

SEP1.8
Which of the following is not depreciable?

    a. Buildings
    b. Furniture
    c. Land
    d. Machinery

Feedback: Review section *Depreciation*.

SEP1.9
Which of the following best describes when depreciation begins?

    a. When the property is placed in service
    b. When the property has used up its useful life
    c. When the property has not been converted from personal to business use
    d. When the property has not been placed in service

Feedback: Review section *Depreciation*.

SEP1.10
Which of the following scenarios best describes when property is retired from service?

    a. When the property has been permanently withdrawn from its use in trade or business
    b. When the property has been temporarily withdrawn from use in trade or business
    c. When the property has not been converted to business use
    d. When the property has not been permanently withdrawn from its use in trade or business

Feedback: Review section *Depreciation*.

Takeaways

There are two types of residential activities: rental-for-profit activity and not-for-profit rental activity. This chapter discussed the types of income and expenses reported on Schedule E and the different property types. Special rules limit the amount of rental expense deductions that may be taken by an individual taxpayer on a residence that is rented out for part of a year and used for personal use during other parts of the year. For passive activity rules, income is required to be classified as active, passive, or non-passive. Active income is attributable to the direct efforts of the taxpayer such as salary, commissions, wages, etc.

TEST YOUR KNOWLEDGE!
Go online to take a practice quiz.

California Schedule E

Introduction

This chapter gives an overview of the basic rental property differences from the federal and state. California has conformed to the Internal Revenue Code (IRC) concerning passive activity loss since January 1, 2010. California normally conforms to the federal law concerning passive activity loss limitations. California passive activity loss is normally different than the federal. Two major California differences in rental property law are:

1. In 1994, the federal government decided that rental real estate activities conducted by persons in a real property business are not automatically treated as passive activities. California did not conform to this provision in the federal law.
2. Depreciation: California basis could be different.

Form FTB 3885A is used to figure the adjustment for the difference between the amount of depreciation and amortization allowed as a deduction using California law. Carry the difference to Part I of the California 540 Schedule CA. Calculate any adjustment for the passive activity then carry the difference to Part I of the California 540 Schedule CA.

Objectives

At the end of this lesson, the student will:

➤ Understand California law regarding substandard rentals.
➤ Characterize California conformity to federal passive activity loss.
➤ Identify California depreciation basis difference between federal and state.
➤ Distinguish who needs to file Schedule S.

Resources

540 Schedule CA	FTB 3801	Instructions 540 Schedule CA
Schedule S	FTB 3885A	Instructions Schedule S

Table of Contents

Part I – California Rental Income

California residents who own rental properties are taxed on all rental income. For example, Maria is a California resident and owns two rentals in Arizona. Maria reports her Arizona property on her California return. She may need to pay Arizona tax depending upon her rental properties earned income in Arizona. Edwardo lives in Missouri and owns a rental in California. Edwardo is a nonresident for California and reports his rental earned income to California. Both scenarios could qualify for the double tax credit. Taxpayers would need to file Schedule S, *Other State Tax Credit*.

Passive Activity Losses

Passive activity includes trade or business in which the taxpayer does not materially participate such as rental income. A business is a passive activity if the owner does not regularly participate in the day-to-day operations of the business. Rental activity is the most common type of passive activity, but it is far from the only kind. California law conforms to the Internal Revenue Code (IRC) as of January 2005. However, there are continuing differences between California and federal law. When California conforms to federal tax law changes, they do not always adopt all the changes made at the federal level. Passive activity losses are reported on FTB 3801.

The following may affect the computation of a corporation's passive activity loss and credit limitation:

> Passive loss rules IRC Section 469(c)(7): Beginning in 1994, and for federal purpose only, rental real estate activities of taxpayers engaged in a real property business are not automatically treated as passive activity. California did not conform to this provision.

For California purposes, all rental activities are passive activities regardless of the level of participation.

> Amortization of certain intangibles (IRC Section 197): Property classified as IRC Section 197 property under federal law is also IRC Section 197 property for California purposes; there is no separate California election required or allowed. For California purposes, in the case of IRC section 197 properties acquired before January 1, 1994, the California adjusted basis as of January 1, 1994, must be amortized over the remaining federal amortization period.

The following passive-loss rules in IRC section 469(c)(7) may affect the computation of the corporation's passive activity loss and credit limitation:

> Beginning in 1994, and for federal purpose only, rental real estate activities of taxpayers engaged in a real property business are not automatically treated as passive activity. California did not conform to this provision.

Pass-Through Entity (PTE) Elective Tax and Other State Tax Credit

Beginning January 1, 2022, and before January 1, 2026, the calculation of the other state tax credit has changed. California allows a qualified partner, member, or shareholder to increase the net tax payable by the amount of the allowed PTE tax credit for the taxable year. See R&TC section 17052.10. California nonresident individuals, estates, or trusts that are residents of Arizona, Guam, Oregon, and Virginia may claim the state credit. California nonresidents who are resident of any state or U.S. possession not mentioned above may not claim the tax credit. See Instructions for Schedule S.

Material Participation in Real Property Business IRC Section 469(c)(7)

Beginning in 1994, and for federal purposes only, rental real estate activities of taxpayers engaged in real property business are not automatically treated as passive activity. California did not conform to this provision. For California purposes, all rental activities are passive activities.

Capitalization and Repair Regulations

Repairs and maintenance expenses are normally not capitalized. Using the *Generally Accepted Accounting Principles* (GAAP) the expenses must be recorded on the business financial statement. The type of expenditure should be expenses and not capitalized, regardless of cost. Equipment repairs and/or purchased or parts over $5,000 that increases the value of the property can be capitalized.

Substandard Rental

If the State of California or a local regulatory agency declares a rental house in violation of building codes, the landlord has six months to achieve compliance. If the owner does not reach compliance, they will receive the *Notice of Property Noncompliance* within 30 days.

A copy of the notice is also sent to the FTB. The notice of noncompliance includes an explanation of the tax consequences for an owner deriving income from substandard housing and is recorded with the appropriate county recorder. The regulatory agency charges the substandard housing owner a fee to recover the cost of recording and releasing the notice of noncompliance.

Upon receipt of a notice of noncompliance, the FTB must identify the taxpayer. The FTB then audits the corporate, partnership, fiduciary, or individual income tax return and disallows any deductions for interest, taxes, depreciation, or amortization that are claimed on the substandard rental property for the period of noncompliance. If the period of noncompliance is less than a year, the expenses are disallowed on a prorated basis.

Real Estate Terms

Real Estate Escrow Person (REEP)

The REEP is anyone involved in closing the real estate transaction, which includes any attorney, escrow company, title company, QI, or anyone else who receives and disburses payment for the sale of real property.

Remitter

The person who will remit the withheld tax on any disposition from the sale or exchange of California real estate and file the prescribed forms on the buyer's/transferee's behalf with the FTB.

Seller

The term "seller" includes the seller or any other transferor of real property. (i.e., Seller/Transferor.)

Buyers/Transferees

The term "buyer" includes the buyer or any other transferee of real property. (i.e., Buyer/Transferee.) Buyers/Transferees are required to withhold on the principal portion of all payments made following the close of the real estate transaction, unless an approval letter for elect out method is received.

Like-Kind Exchanges

California requires taxpayers who exchange property located in California for like-kind property located outside of California and meet all of the requirements of the IRC Section 1031, to file an annual information return with the FTB. For more information, get Form FTB 3840, California Like-Kind Exchanges, or go to ftb.ca.gov and search for like kind.

Installment Sales: The REEP reports the sale or transfer as an installment sale if there will be at least one payment made after the tax year of the sale. The withholding is 3 1/3% (.0333) of the down payment during escrow.

Real Estate Withholding

Real estate withholding is a prepayment of income tax due from sellers on the gain of a sale of real property in California. Income tax from the sale of a property is withheld at a percentage rate of 3.3% of the gross sale and is reported by the withholding agent to the taxpayer on Form 593 (or on Form 592-B if it was an income-producing property). The buyer is responsible for the withholding, but the withholding agent (i.e., the real estate escrow individual) can withhold on the buyer's behalf. Real estate withholding is required whenever a transfer occurs on real property in California. Examples of real property include:

> - Sales or transfers of real property (including exchanges and gifts).
> - Leaseholds or options, which are beyond the scope of this course.
> - Short sales.
> - Easements.
> - Personal property sold with real property if a distinction is not made at the time of sale.
> - Deferred exchanges, which are beyond the scope of this course.
> - Vacant land.

The amount of state income tax withheld from the real estate sale is entered on Form 540, line 73, from either Form 593 or Form 592-B. Because this only applies in California, do not include withholding from federal Forms W-2, W-2G, 1099, or the partner's tax from Schedule K-1 (568), line 15e.

Real Estate Withholding Penalties

Information Return from Owner of Real Property

California will penalize owners and transferors who do not file the required information relating to interest in real property within the due date. Reasonable cause and not willful neglect may be an exception. If the failure is due to an intentional disregard of the requirement, the penalty is greater of $500 or 10% of the required withholding.

Real Estate Penalties

An individual who is required to withhold tax and fails to withhold may be assessed a penalty. The penalty is the greater of the actual amount withheld or the payee's total tax liability not to exceed 7% of the required withholding. See R&TC §18668(a).

An individual who is required to withhold tax from a real estate sale but fails to withhold will be responsible for the penalty. If the failure is due to an intentional disregard of the requirement, the penalty is greater of $500 or 10% of the required withholding. See R&TC §18668(d).

A seller or transferor who intentionally avoids the withholding requirements and executes a false certificate is liable for a penalty of $1,000 or 20% of the required withholding, whichever is greater. See Instructions Form 593 and R&TC §18668(e).

If the escrow person failed to provide written notification of withholding requirement to the transferee/buyer the penalty is the greater of $500 or 10% of the required amount. The exception is reasonable cause. See R&TC §18668(d).

A transferor of real property who deliberately misrepresent the exemption certificate (Form 593-C) to avoid withholding will be penalized the greater of $1,000 or 20% of the amount required to withhold. See R&TC §18668(e)(5).

The successor on a sale, transfer, or disposition of a business for failing to pay required withholding amounts will be penalized 10% of the amount not paid. See R&TC §18669.

Like-Kind Exchange

Property received by a partnership in exchange for §704(c) property in a non-recognition transaction is treated as a §704(c) property for the purposes of the seven-year rule. [Treas. Reg. §1.704-4(d)(1)]

A partnership can distribute a §704(c) property to a partner other than the contributing partner and within the §1031 rules to the contributing partner no later than the earlier of:

➢ 180 days after the date of the distribution
➢ Or the due date of the contributing partner's income tax return for the current taxable year of the distribution. See Treas. Reg. §1.704-4(d)(3).

Part 1 Review Questions

To obtain the maximum benefit from this chapter, LTP recommends that you complete each of the following questions, and then compare them to the answers with feedback that immediately follow. Under governing self-study standards, vendors are required to present review questions intermittently throughout each self-study course.

These questions and explanations are not part of the final examination and will not be graded by LTP.

CSEP1.1
Which of the following is **not** rental income?

    a. Advance rent
    b. Expenses paid by the tenant
    c. Canceling a lease
    d. Mortgage interest

CSEP1.2
Which of the following is rental income?

    a. Cindy who purchased the paint and painted the kitchen of her rented apartment.
    b. Glenda who paid her mortgage interest on her personal home.
    c. Andrew who purchased a rug for his gramma's house she rents.
    d. Missy who is signing a lease at the property manager's office.

CSEP1.3
Rental income is reported on which federal form?

    a. Schedule C
    b. Schedule E
    c. Schedule D
    d. Schedule F

CSEP1.4
Which of the following is **not** considered to be rent?

    a. Property or service paid by tenant in lieu of rent.
    b. Payment for canceling a lease.
    c. Rent received to use primary residence for 10 days.
    d. Income received from selling dogs.

CSEP1.5
If a California landowner is receiving income from their substandard rental housing, what are their consequences?

    1. A notice of noncompliance may be issued to the owner by the regulatory authority.
    2. The notice of noncompliance will include tax consequences.
    3. The notice of noncompliance is recorded with the county recorder.
    4. The landowner could be fined.

    a. 1 and 4
    b. 2 and 3
    c. 1, 2, 3, and 4
    d. 2, 3, and 4

CSEP1.6

A partnership can distribute a §704(c) property to a partner other than the contributing partner and within the §1031 rules to the contributing partner no later than:

    a. 180 days after the date of the distribution
    b. 90 days after the date of the distribution
    c. 120 days after the date of the distribution
    d. 60 days after the date of the distribution

CSEP1.7

Schedule E rental losses are_____ .

    a. passive activity losses
    b. capital losses
    c. ordinary losses
    d. always deductible

CSEP1.8

Which IRC section gives the rules regarding a like-kind exchange?

    a. §704(c)
    b. §1.704-4(d)(1)
    c. §1031
    d. §1032

CSEP1.9

An individual who does not withhold taxes could be assessed which percentage?

    a. 2.5%
    b. 3%
    c. 7%
    d. 20%

CSEP1.10

Repairs and maintenance expenses are normally not _____?

    a. depreciated
    b. capitalized
    c. amortized
    d. transferred

Part 1: Review Questions Answers

CSEP1.1

Which of the following is **not** rental income?

    a. Advance rent
    b. Expenses paid by the tenant
    c. Canceling a lease
    d. Mortgage interest

Feedback: Review *Reporting Rental Income.*

CSEP1.2
Which of the following is rental income?

    a. Cindy who purchased the paint and painted the kitchen of her rented apartment.
    b. Glenda who paid her mortgage interest on her personal home.
    c. Andrew who purchased a rug for his gramma's house she rents.
    d. Missy who is signing a lease at the property manager's office.

Feedback: Review *Reporting Rental Income.*

CSEP1.3
Rental income is reported on which federal form?

    a. Schedule C
    b. Schedule E
    c. Schedule D
    d. Schedule F

Feedback: Review *Reporting Rental Income.*

CSEP1.4
Which of the following is **not** considered to be rent?

    a. Property or service paid by tenant in lieu of rent.
    b. Payment for canceling a lease.
    c. Rent received to use primary residence for 10 days.
    d. Income received from selling dogs.

Feedback: Review *Reporting Rental Income.*

CSEP1.5
If a California landowner is receiving income from their substandard rental housing, what are their consequences?

    1. A notice of noncompliance may be issued to the owner by the regulatory authority.
    2. The notice of noncompliance will include tax consequences.
    3. The notice of noncompliance is recorded with the county recorder.
    4. The landowner could be fined.

    a. 1 and 4
    b. 2 and 3
    c. 1, 2, 3, and 4
    d. 2, 3, and 4

Feedback: Review section *Substandard Rental.*

CSEP1.6
A partnership can distribute a §704(c) property to a partner other than the contributing partner and within the §1031 rules to the contributing partner no later than:

    a. **180 days after the date of the distribution**
    b. 90 days after the date of the distribution
    c. 120 days after the date of the distribution
    d. 60 days after the date of the distribution

Feedback: Review section *Like-Kind Exchange*.

CSEP1.7
Schedule E rental losses are_____.

    a. **passive activity losses**
    b. capital losses
    c. ordinary losses
    d. always deductible

Feedback: Review section

CSEP1.8
Which IRC section gives the rules regarding a like-kind exchange?

    a. §704(c)
    b. §1.704-4(d)(1)
    c. **§1031**
    d. §1032

Feedback: Review section *Like-Kind Exchange*.

CSEP1.9
A seller or transferor who does not withhold taxes could be assessed which percentage?

    a. 2.5%
    b. 3%
    c. 7%
    d. **20%**

Feedback: Review section *Real Estate Penalties*.

CSEP1.10
Repairs and maintenance expenses are normally not _____?

    a. **depreciated**
    b. capitalized
    c. amortized
    d. transferred

Feedback: Review section *Depreciation*.

Takeaways

This chapter gives an overview of the basic rental property differences from the federal and state. California has conformed to the Internal Revenue Code (IRC) concerning passive activity loss since January 1, 2010. California normally conforms to the federal law concerning passive activity loss limitations. California passive activity loss is normally different than the federal. California residents who own rental properties are taxed on all rental income. Nonresident taxpayers who own property in California will report their income on Form 540NR.

TEST YOUR KNOWLEDGE!
Go online to take a practice quiz.

Chapter 11 Schedule F

Introduction

Income received from the operation of a farm or from rental income from a farm is taxable. Farmers determine their taxable income from farming and related activities by using Schedule F. Profit or loss from farm income is first reported on Schedule F and then "flows" to Form 1040, Schedule 1, line 6. A farm could qualify to be a qualified joint venture (discussed in Schedule C chapter).

Objectives

At the end of this lesson, the student will:

> ➢ Understand basic farm income.
> ➢ Know when a taxpayer should file Schedule F.

Resources

Form 1040	Publication 17	Instructions Form 1040
Form 4797	Publication 51 (Circular A)	Instructions Form 4797
Form 4835	Publication 225	Instructions Form 4835
Form 8990	Publication 334	Instructions Form 8990
Schedule F	Publication 463	Instructions Schedule F
	Publication 536	
	Publication 538	

Table of Contents

Part I: Schedule F

Livestock income from breeding, draft, sport, or dairy purposes such as beef, pork, and racehorses, is reportable on Schedule F. Individuals who breed dogs, or cats to sell need to report their income and expenses for the domestic animals on Schedule F.

Taxpayers are in the business of farming if they cultivate, operate, or manage a farm for profit, either as an owner or tenant. A farm can include livestock, dairy, poultry, fish, fruit, and truck farms. It can also include plantations, ranches, ranges, and orchards. See Publication 225.
A farmer must keep records to prepare an accurate tax return. Tax records are not the only type of records needed for a farming business. The taxpayer should keep records that measure the farm's financial performance.

Income reported on Schedule F does not include gains or losses from sales or other farm assets dispositions such as:

> Land
> Depreciable farm equipment
> Buildings and structures
> Livestock held for draft, breeding, sport, or dairy purposes

Taxpayers are in the business of farming if they cultivate, operate, or manage a farm for profit, either as an owner or tenant. A farm can include livestock, dairy, poultry, fish, and fruit farms. It can also include plantations, ranches, ranges, and orchards. See Publication 225.
A farmer must keep records to prepare an accurate tax return. Tax records are not the only type of records needed for a farming business. The taxpayer should keep records that measure the farm's financial performance.

Where to Report Sales of Farm Products

When livestock, produce, grains, or other products raised on the taxpayer's farm are for sale or bought for resale, the entire amount received is income and reported on Schedule F.

When farm products are bought for resale, the profit or loss is the difference between the selling price and the basis in the product. The year that the payment was received is the year that the income is reported.

Item Sold	Schedule F	Form 4797
Farm products raised for sale	X	
Farm products bought for resale	X	
Farm products not held primarily for sale, such as livestock held for draft, breeding, sport, or dairy purposes (bought or raised)		X

Example: Avery purchased 20 feeder calves for $6,000, in the prior tax year, with the intent to resell them. Avery sold them in current tax year for $11,000. The $11,000 sale is reported as sales, and the $6,000 purchase price is reported as basis, resulting in $5,000 reported as profit on the current tax return.

$11,000   Sales price (reported on Schedule F, line 1a)
–$ 6,000   Purchase price (basis, reported on Schedule F, line 1b)
$5,000   Profit (reported on Schedule F, line 1c)

Livestock held for draft, breeding, sport, or dairy purposes may result in ordinary capital gain or loss when sold depending upon the circumstances and needs to be reported on Form 4797. Animals that are not held for primary sale are considered business assets of the farm.

Completing Schedule F

Portion of Schedule F

As with any return, interviewing the taxpayer before entering the information is necessary. The SSN or the EIN must be entered in the appropriate area. Line B is the principal agricultural activity codes. Like a Schedule C, Schedule F has specific codes. Select the code that best describes the taxpayer's majority source of income. For example, Allen owns a dairy farm. He receives income from milk production and selling male calves. Allen receives most of the income from the dairy cattle and milk production. The code is used to determine where the farmer makes most of the income. Principal Agricultural Activity Codes are located on Schedule F, Part IV.

Line C Accounting Method: The two accounting methods are Cash and Accrual. Hybrid is not an option for farm income. Check the appropriate box. Using the cash accounting method, the taxpayer would complete Parts I and II. Income is reported in the year in which it was actually or constructively received. If payment on an expenditure such as prepaid expense creates an intangible asset that has a useful life that extends beyond 12 months of the end of the taxable year, that expense may not be deductible. See Publication 225.

If the accrual method is used, Parts II, III, and Part I, line 9 must be completed. Income is reported in the year it was earned, and expenses are deducted in the year they are incurred, even though they were paid in a prior year. Taxpayers who use the accrual method will use the cash basis for deducting business expense owed to a related cash-basis taxpayer. See Publication 538.

Certain farming collectives are unable to use the cash method of accounting.

A farming syndicate may be a partnership, LLC, S corporation, or any other enterprise other than a C corporation if:

> ➤ The interests in the business have at any time been offered for sale in a way that would require registration with any federal or state agency.
> ➤ More than 35% of the losses during any tax year are allocable to limited partners or limited entrepreneurs. A limited partner is one who can lose only the amount invested or required to be invested in the partnership. A limited entrepreneur is a person who does not take any active part in managing the business.

Line E is a yes or no question. Line E asks if the taxpayer materially participated in the activity. The taxpayer must meet the seven tests to qualify for material participation. To qualify for farming material participation, the taxpayer must own an interest at the time work is performed in connection with the activity.

Line F asks if any payments made in the current tax year require Form 1099s to be filed. See General Instructions for Certain Information Returns if more information is needed. If the taxpayer paid more than $600 in rents, services, and prizes, then see the specific instructions for the individual Form 1099-MISC or 1099-NEC.

Schedule F Profit or Loss Framing

Like Schedule C & E, farm income has specific line items for income and expenses that are industry related. This section is designed for the tax preparer to become aware of types of farm income. For more information, see Instructions Schedule F.

Part I: Farm Income Cash Method

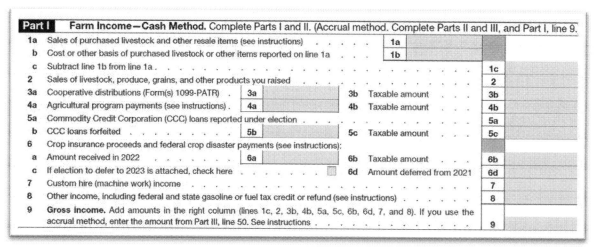

Part I	Farm Income—Cash Method. Complete Parts I and II. (Accrual method. Complete Parts II and III, and Part I, line 9.						
1a	Sales of purchased livestock and other resale items (see instructions)			1a			
b	Cost or other basis of purchased livestock or other items reported on line 1a			1b			
c	Subtract line 1b from line 1a					1c	
2	Sales of livestock, produce, grains, and other products you raised					2	
3a	Cooperative distributions (Form(s) 1099-PATR)	3a		3b	Taxable amount	3b	
4a	Agricultural program payments (see instructions)	4a		4b	Taxable amount	4b	
5a	Commodity Credit Corporation (CCC) loans reported under election					5a	
b	CCC loans forfeited	5b		5c	Taxable amount	5c	
6	Crop insurance proceeds and federal crop disaster payments (see instructions):						
a	Amount received in 2022	6a		6b	Taxable amount	6b	
c	If election to defer to 2023 is attached, check here			6d	Amount deferred from 2021	6d	
7	Custom hire (machine work) income					7	
8	Other income, including federal and state gasoline or fuel tax credit or refund (see instructions)					8	
9	**Gross income.** Add amounts in the right column (lines 1c, 2, 3b, 4b, 5a, 5c, 6b, 6d, 7, and 8). If you use the accrual method, enter the amount from Part III, line 50. See instructions					9	

Portion of Schedule F

Sales Caused by Weather-Related Conditions

If the farmer sells or exchanges more livestock, including poultry, than normal due to a drought, flood, or other weather-related conditions, the farmer may qualify to postpone the reporting until the following year. All the conditions must be met:

> ➤ The principal trade or business is farming.
> ➤ The accounting method is the cash method.
> ➤ The taxpayers must be able to show that under their usual business practices, they would not have sold or exchanged the additional animals in that year except for the weather-related conditions.
> ➤ The weather-related condition caused an area to be designated as eligible for assistance by the federal government.

If sales or exchanges were made before the area became eligible for federal assistance due to weather-related conditions, the taxpayer could qualify if the weather-related condition caused the area to be designated. To qualify for the disaster, the president of the United States must declare the area as a disaster.

> *Señor 1040 Says:* A weather-related sale or exchange of livestock (other than poultry) held for draft breeding or dairy purposes may be an involuntary conversion. See Publication 225.

Example: Bernie is a calendar-year taxpayer, and he normally sells 100 head of beef cattle a year. As a result of the disaster, Bernie sold 250 head during the current tax year. Bernie realized $70,200 from the sale. As a result of the drought, the affected area was declared a disaster area eligible for federal assistance in the same year. Bernie can postpone a portion ($42,120) of the income until the following year. ($70,200 ÷ 250 = $280.80 × 150 = $42,120).

Rents (Including Crop Share)

Rent received for farmland is rental income and not reported on Schedule F. However, if the farmer materially participates in the farming operations on the land, the rent received is farm income. If the taxpayer pastures someone else's livestock and takes care of them for a fee, the income is from the farming business. That income must be reported as "other" income on Schedule F. If the pasture is strictly rented out without providing services, the income is to be reported on Schedule E as rental income.

Rent received in the form of crop shares is income in the year the shares were converted to money or the equivalent. The accounting method used—cash or accrual—does not matter. Whether the material participation in operating the farm is crop sharing or livestock, the rental income is included in self-employment income.

Crop-sharing lease arrangements that involve a loss may be subject to the limits under the passive-loss rules.

Income Averaging for Farmers

Taxpayers can use income averaging to figure their tax for any year in which they were engaged in a farming business as an individual, a partner in a partnership, or a shareholder in an S corporation. Services performed as an employee are disregarded in determining whether an individual is engaged in a farming business. However, a shareholder of an S corporation engaged in a farming business may treat compensation received from the corporation that is attributable to the farming business as farm income. Corporations, partnerships, S corporations, estates, and trusts cannot use income averaging.

Elected Farm Income (EFI)

EFI is the amount of income from the farming business that is elected to be taxed at base-year rates. EFI can be designated as any type of income attributable to the farming business. However, EFI cannot be more than the taxable income, and EFI from a net capital gain attributable to the farming business cannot be more than the total net income. If the taxpayer is using income averaging, that is figured on Schedule J. See Publication 225.

Line 1 Sale of Purchased Livestock and Other Resale Items

Income from farming reported on Schedule F includes amounts taxpayers receive from cultivating, operating, or managing a farm for gain or profit, either as an owner or tenant. Income is included but not limited to:

➢ Income from operating a nursery specializing in growing ornamental plants.
➢ Income from the sale of crop shares if the taxpayer materially participated in producing the crop.
➢ Operating a stock, dairy, poultry, fish, fruit, or truck farm and income from operating a plantation, ranch, range, orchard, or grove.

Both the actual cash received, and the fair market value of goods or income constructively received, are reported on lines 1 through 8. If the taxpayer ran the farm and received rents based on crop share or farm production, that income is reported as rents. If the taxpayer sold livestock due to drought, flood, or other weather-related conditions, the taxpayer could elect to report the income from the sale in the year after the year of sale.

For example, Caleb uses the cash method, and sold three Holstein heifers due to weather-related circumstances in the current tax year. Caleb chose to report the income in the next year after the sale. For Caleb to make the election, all the following must apply:

1. Caleb's main business is farming.
2. Caleb can show he sold the livestock due to a weather-related event.
3. Caleb's farm area qualified for federal aid.

Items Purchased for Resale

If the cash method is used, deduct the ordinarily deducted cost of the livestock and other items purchased for resale only in the year of sale. Deduct this cost, including freight charges for transporting the livestock to the farm, on Part I of Schedule F.

Example: The cash method of accounting is used in the current year Sandy purchased 50 steers, which she will sell in the next year. She cannot deduct the cost of the steers on her current return. She will deduct the cost in Part I of her next year Schedule F.

Line 3 Cooperative Distributions

Distributions from a farm cooperative are reported on Form 1099-PATR on line 3a. Taxpayer may receive multiple Form 1099-PATR if so, report the total distribution from all cooperatives. Distributions include:

➢ Patronage dividends
➢ Nonpatronage distributions
➢ Per-unit retain allocations
➢ Redemptions of nonqualified written notices of allocation
➢ Per-unit retain certificates

Line 4 Agriculture Payments

Government payments received on Form 1099-G or Form CCC-1099-G are reported on line 4a. Any of the following sources are reported:

➢ Price loss coverage payments.
➢ Agriculture risk coverage payments.
➢ Coronavirus Food Assistance Program Payments.
➢ Market Facilitation Program Payments.
➢ Market gain from the repayment of a secured Commodity Credit Corporation (CCC) loan for less than the original loan amount.
➢ Diversion payments.
➢ Cost-share payments.
➢ Payments in the form of materials (such as fertilizer or lime) or services (such as grading or building dams).

The taxpayer reports crop insurance proceeds in the year received. Federal crop disaster payments are treated as proceeds for crop insurance proceeds. If 2021 was the year of the crop damage, the taxpayer can elect to include certain proceeds in their 2022 income. To make this election, check the box on 6c.

Crop insurance proceeds received in a prior year, and elected to be treated in the current year's income, would be reported on line 6d. All other income that does not have a designated line on which to report is reported on line 8. Types of income could include, but are not limited to:

> ➢ Illegal federal irrigation subsidies
> ➢ Bartering income
> ➢ Income from Form 1099-C
> ➢ State gasoline or fuel tax refunds received in current tax year

See Schedule F Instructions for a complete list.

Line 5 CCC (Commodity Credit Corporation Loans)

Loans are generally not reported as income. However, if the production was pledged in part to secure a CCC loan, then treat the loan as if it were a sale of the crop and report the loan proceeds as income in the year received. Approval is not needed from the IRS to adopt this method of reporting CCC loans. Once the CCC loan is reported as income for the year received, all CCC loans in that year and subsequent years are reported the same way.

If pledged crops are forfeited to the CCC in full payment of the loan, then the individual may receive a Form 1099-A, *Acquisition or Abandonment of Secured Property*. In box 6 of Form 1099-A, one would see "CCC," and the amount of the outstanding loan would also be indicated on the form. See Publication 225.

Line 8 Other Types of Income

> ➢ Bartering income.
> ➢ Income from canceled debt.
> ➢ State gasoline or fuel tax refunds received.
> ➢ Income from line 2 that includes Biofuel Producer Credit (Form 6478).
> ➢ Income from line 8 that includes Biodiesel and Renewable Diesel Fuels Credit (Form 8864).
> ➢ The amount of credit for federal tax paid on fuels claimed on the 2021 Schedule 3.
> ➢ Recapture of excess depreciation on listed property, including Section 179 expense deduction.
> ➢ Inclusion amount on leased property when the business drops 50% or less.
> ➢ Any recapture of a deduction or credit for clean-fuel vehicle.
> ➢ Any income from breeding fees.
> ➢ Gain or a loss on commodity sales.
> ➢ Any payroll tax credit amount from the employer payroll.

Income from the farming business is the sum of any farm income or gain minus any farm expenses or losses allowed as deductions in figuring taxable income. However, it does not include gain or loss from the sale or other disposition of land or from the sale of development rights, grazing rights, or other similar rights.

Canceled Debt

If a debt is canceled or forgiven other than as a gift or bequest to the taxpayer, the individual must include the canceled amount in gross income for tax purposes. Discharge of qualified farm indebtedness is one of the exceptions to the general rule. It is excluded from taxable income; report the canceled amount on Schedule F, line 10, if the canceled debt was incurred in the farming business. If the debt is a nonbusiness debt, report the canceled amount as "other income" on Schedule 1, line 8c. See Publication 225 and 982.

Schedule F Part II Farm Expense Cash and Accrual Method

Part II reports expenses that are typically deductible. Current costs are expenses that do not have to be capitalized or included in inventory costs. The deduction for the cost of livestock feed and certain other supplies may be limited. If the taxpayer has an operating loss, the taxpayer may not be able to deduct the loss.

Certain expenses paid throughout the year may be part personal and part business. Some shared expenses could include expenses for gasoline, oil, fuel, water, rent, electricity, telephone, automobile upkeep, repairs, insurance, interest, and taxes. Shared expenses need to be allocated correctly between personal and business. The personal portion is not deductible; the business portion would be deducted on Schedule F.

Ordinary and necessary costs of operating a farm for profit are deductible business expenses. Current costs are expenses that do not have to be capitalized or included in inventory costs. However, the deduction for the cost of livestock feed and certain other supplies may be limited. If the taxpayer has an operating loss, the taxpayer may not be able to deduct this loss. The following are not deductible:

➢ Personal or living expenses.
➢ Expenses used to raise a family.
➢ Animal expenses used by the taxpayer to raise the animal.
➢ Repaid expenses.
➢ Inventory losses.
➢ Personal losses.

Portion of Schedule F

Prepaid farm supplies are amounts paid during the tax year for the following items:

> ➢ Feed, seed, fertilizer, and similar farm supplies not used or consumed during the year. Do not include amounts paid for farm supplies that would have been consumed if not for a fire, storm, flood, other casualty, disease, or drought.
> ➢ Poultry (including egg-laying hens and baby chicks) bought for use (or for both use and resale) in the farm business. Include only the amount that would be deductible in the following year if the taxpayer had capitalized the cost and deducted it ratably over the lesser of 12 months or the useful life of the poultry.
> ➢ Poultry bought for resale and not resold during the year.

Line 10, Car and Truck Expenses

Only expenses that are used for business can be deducted as a business expense. Items include gasoline, oil, repairs, license tags, insurance, and depreciation. For 2022 the rate is 58.5 cents per mile from January to June and 62.5 cents per mile from July to December. For tax year 2023 the business travel rate is 65.5 cents per mile. The standard mileage rate for each mile of business use can be used for the taxpayer's owned or leased vehicle. The standard mileage rate cannot be used if five or more cars or light trucks are used at the same time. See Instructions Schedule F.

Line 14, Depreciation

When property is acquired to be used in the farm business and expected to last more than one year, do not deduct the entire cost in the year. The cost is recovered over more than one year and deducted each year on Schedule F as depreciation or amortization. Depreciation will be covered in a later chapter. See Instructions Form 4562.

Line 17, Fertilizer and Lime

In the year paid or incurred, the cost of fertilizer, lime, and other materials applied to farmland to enrich, neutralize, or condition the land can be an expense. The cost to apply the raw material is also an expense.

Line 19, Gasoline, Fuel, and Oil

Some expenses paid during the tax year are part personal and part business. These can include expenses for gasoline, fuel and oil, water, utilities, automobile upkeep, repairs, insurance, and taxes. The taxpayer cannot mix business and personal portions to be reported. The business portion is deductible on the tax return.

Line 20, Insurance

Ordinary and necessary cost of insurance for the farm business is a business expense. Premiums can include payment for the following types of insurance:

> ➢ Fire, storm, crop, theft, liability, and other insurance on farm business assets
> ➢ Health and accident insurance on farm employees
> ➢ Workers' compensation insurance set by state law that covers claims for job-related bodily injuries or diseases suffered by employees on the farm, regardless of fault
> ➢ Business interruption insurance
> ➢ State unemployment insurance on farm employees (deductible as taxes if they are considered taxes under state law)

Self-employed health insurance can be deducted as well as medical, dental, and qualified long-term care insurance coverage for the taxpayer, the spouse, and dependents when figuring adjusted gross income. See Publication 535.

Line 21, Interest

Interest paid on farm mortgages and other obligations incurred in the farm business can be deductible. If the cash method of accounting is used, deduct interest paid during the tax year. Interest paid with other funds received from the original lender through another loan, advance, or other arrangement similar to a loan cannot be deducted until payments are made on the new loan. Under the cash method, if interest is prepaid before it is due, the deduction is taken in the tax year in which the interest is due. See Instructions Form 8990.

Line 22, Labor Hired

Reasonable wages paid for regular farm labor, piecework, contract labor, and other forms of labor hired to perform the farming operations can be paid in cash or in noncash items such as inventory, capital assets, or assets used in business. The cost of boarding farm labor is a deductible labor cost. Other deductible costs incurred for farm labor could include health insurance, workers' compensation insurance, and other benefits. Reduce the tax deduction that was claimed on the following:

- ➤ Form 5884, Work Opportunity Credit
- ➤ Form 8844, Empowerment Zone Employment Credit
- ➤ Form 8845, Indian Employment Credit
- ➤ Form 8932, Credit for Employer Differential Wage Payments
- ➤ Form 8994, Employer Credit for Paid Family and Medical Leave

Line 25, Repairs and Maintenance

Most expenses for repair and maintenance are deductible. However, repairs or an overhaul to depreciable property that increases the asset's value or adapts it to a different use is a capital expense. See Publication 225.

Line 29, Taxes

Real estate and property taxes on farm business assets such as farm equipment, animals, farmland, and farm buildings can be deducted in the year paid. The taxes on the part of the farm used for personal use are not a deductible expense on the business; those expenses may be deductible on Schedule A.

State and local general sales tax on non-depreciable farm business items are deductible as part of the cost of those items. Include state and local general sales tax imposed on the purchase of the assets for use in the farm business as part of the cost that is depreciable.

Individuals cannot deduct state and federal income taxes as farm business expenses. Individuals can deduct state and local income taxes only as an itemized deduction on Schedule A. Federal income tax is not a deduction. One-half of the self-employment tax is figured as an adjustment to income on Form 1040. See Instructions Schedule F.

Line 32 Other Expenses

Travel Expenses

Ordinary and necessary expenses can be deducted if they are incurred while traveling away from home for farm business. Lavish and extravagant expenses cannot be deducted. For tax purposes, the farm business's location is considered the location of the farm and the taxpayer is traveling away from the farm if:

➢ Duties require the taxpayer to be absent from the farm for substantially longer than an ordinary workday
➢ Sleep and rest are required to meet the demands of work while away from home

Following are some examples of deductible travel expenses:

➢ Air, rail, bus, and car transportation
➢ Meals and lodging
➢ Dry cleaning and laundry
➢ Telephone and fax
➢ Transportation between hotel and temporary work or business meeting location
➢ Tips for any expenses

Remember, ordinary business-related meals are deductible if business travel is overnight or long enough to require the taxpayer to stop for sleep or rest to properly perform his or her duties.

The following list is not a complete list but includes some expenses that may be deducted as farm expense on Part II of Schedule F. These expenses must be for business purposes and paid in the year used (if using the cash method) or incurred (if using the accrual method).

➢ Accounting fees
➢ Advertising
➢ Business travel and meals
➢ Commissions
➢ Consultant fees
➢ Crop-scouting expenses
➢ Dues to cooperatives
➢ Educational expenses (to maintain and improve farming skills)
➢ Farm-related attorney fees
➢ Farm magazines
➢ Ginning
➢ Insect sprays and dusts
➢ Litter and bedding
➢ Livestock fees
➢ Marketing fees
➢ Milk assessment
➢ Record-keeping expenses
➢ Service charges
➢ Small tools expected to last one year or less
➢ Stamps and stationery
➢ Subscriptions to professional, technical, and trade journals that deal with farming

Marketing Quota Penalties

Marketing quota penalties can be deducted as an "other expense" on Schedule F. These penalties are paid for marketing crops in excess of farm marketing quota. If the penalty is not paid but the purchaser of the crop deducts it from the payment, include the payment in gross income. Do not take a separate deduction for the penalty. See Publication 225.

Capital Expenses

A capital expense is a payment, or a debt incurred for the acquisition, improvement, or restoration of an asset that is expected to last more than one year. Include the expense in the basis of the asset. Uniform capitalization rules also require the asset to be capitalized or included in certain inventory expenses. See Publication 225.

Business Use of Home

Business use of the home can be deducted if part of the home is exclusively and regularly used as:

> ➢ The principal place of business for any trade or business.
> ➢ A place to meet or deal with patients, clients, or customers in the normal course of the trade or business.
> ➢ In connection with a trade or business, if using a separate structure that is not attached to the home.

An office in the home will qualify as the principal place of business for deducting expense for its use if both of the following requirements are met:

> ➢ The taxpayer uses it exclusively and regularly for the administrative or management activities of the trade or business.
> ➢ The taxpayer has no other fixed location where one conducts substantial administrative or management activities of the trade or business.

The IRS has provided a simplified method to determine the expense use of the home. This was covered in Schedule C chapter. See Publication 587.

Business Start-Up and Organizational Costs

The taxpayer can elect to deduct up to $5,000 of business start-up costs and $5,000 of organizational costs paid or incurred after October 22, 2004. The $5,000 deduction is reduced by the amount of the total start-up or organizational costs exceeding $50,000. Any remaining costs must be amortized. See Publication 225.

Crop Production Expenses

The uniform capitalization rules require the taxpayer to capitalize expense incurred in producing plants. However, for certain taxpayers who are required to use the accrual method of accounting, the capitalization rules do not apply to plants with a pre-productive period of two years or less. See Publication 225.

Timber

Capitalize the cost of acquiring timber; do not include the cost of the land. Generally, one must capitalize the direct costs incurred in reforestation; however, one can elect to deduct some forestation and reforestation costs.

Christmas Tree Cultivation

If the taxpayer is in the business of planting and cultivating Christmas trees to sell when they are more than 6 years old, capitalize expense incurred for planting and stump culture and add them to the basis of the standing trees. The taxpayer would recover these expenses as part of the adjusted basis when the trees are sold as standing trees, or as a depletion allowance when the trees are cut.

Breeding Fees

If the accrual method is used, breeding fees need to be capitalized and allocated to the cost of the basis of the calf, foal, etc. Breeding fees can be an expense on Schedule F. If the breeder guarantees live offspring or other veterinary procedure costs as the cost basis of the offspring.

Other Nondeductible Expenses

Personal expenses and certain other items on the tax return cannot be deducted even if they are farm related. The taxpayer cannot deduct certain personal and living expenses, including rent and insurance premiums paid on property used as the taxpayer's primary residence. The cost of maintaining personal vehicles or other items used for personal use or the cost of purchasing or raising produce or livestock consumed by the taxpayer and his or her family is not deductible.

Losses from Operating a Farm

If the farm expenses are more than the farm income, the taxpayer has a loss from the operation of the farm. The amount of the loss one can deduct when figuring the taxable income may be limited. To figure the deductible loss, the following limits must be applied:

> ➢ The at-risk limits
> ➢ The passive activity limits

If the deductible loss after applying the limits is more than the income for the year, there may be a net operating loss. See Publication 536.

Not-for-Profit Farming

If the taxpayer operates a farm for profit, all ordinary and necessary expenses of carrying on the business of farming can be deducted on Schedule F. If the farming activity or other activity the taxpayer is engaged in or invests in is not-for-profit, the income from the activity is reported on Schedule 1, line 6. The expenses are no longer deducted on Schedule A. Losses from not-for-profit farming can be limited.

Estimated Payments Exception

If the taxpayer files their tax return yearly by March 1 and do the following, the penalty will be waived.

1. File the tax return and pay the tax due by March 1.
2. Taxpayers had no liability for the prior year and the current year was for the 12 months.
3. Taxpayers would not be charged a penalty if the total tax on the current year minus the amount of withholding tax paid is less than $1,000.

Benefits of Recordkeeping

Everyone in business must keep appropriate and accurate records. Recordkeeping will help the taxpayer:

➤ Monitor the progress of their business.
➤ Prepare an accurate financial statement.
➤ Classify receipts.
➤ Track deductible business expenses.
➤ Prepare the tax return.
➤ Support reported income and expenses on the tax return.

Records show the taxpayer if the business is improving, which items sell the best, and insights to increase the success of the business. Records are needed to prepare accurate financial statements, which include profit and loss, balance sheets, and any other financial statements. Taxpayers should identify receipts at the time of purchase. It is easier to get into the habit of tracking receipts when received rather than dealing with them when preparing the tax return. A tax professional should teach clients how to identify and track receipts.

Kinds of Records to Keep

The taxpayer should choose the recordkeeping system that is best for their business. The system should match the accounting method of the taxpayer's tax year. The recordkeeping system should include a summary for all the taxpayer's business transactions. For example, recordkeeping should show gross income as well as deductions and credits for the business. Supporting documentation for consistent transactions, such as purchases, sales, and payroll, should be maintained. It is important to retain documentation that supports the entries in the journal, ledgers, and the tax return. Records for travel, transportation, and gift expenses fall under specific recordkeeping rules. For more information see Publication 463. There are also specific employment tax records the employer must keep. See Publication 51 (Circular A).

Assets used in business can be property, such as machinery and equipment used to conduct business. Records of the asset are used to figure depreciation and the gain or loss when the asset is sold. Records should show the following information:

➤ When and how the business asset was acquired.
➤ The purchase price of the business asset.
➤ The cost of any business improvements.
➤ Section 179 deduction.
➤ Business deductions taken for depreciation.
➤ Business deductions taken for casualty losses, such as losses resulting from fires, storms, or natural disasters.
➤ How the business asset was used.

➢ When and how the business asset was disposed.
➢ The selling price of the asset or the business.
➢ The expense of the business asset.

The following are examples of records that might show the information from the above list:

➢ Purchase and sales business invoices.
➢ Business purchase of real estate closing statements (HUD-1).
➢ Canceled business checks.
➢ A business' bank statements.

Maintaining Records

Tax records should be kept as needed for the administration of any provision of the Internal Revenue Code. Business records should be kept that support an item of income or deduction appearing on the return until the period of limitations is finished. Generally, that time frame is a 3-year period, although certain records must be kept longer than 3 years.

Employment records must be kept for at least 4 years after the date the tax becomes due or is paid. Records that pertain to assets such as property should be kept if the taxpayer owns the business asset. Other creditors, such as an insurance company, may require the business records to be kept longer than the IRS.

Part 1 Review Questions

To obtain the maximum benefit from this chapter, LTP recommends that you complete each of the following questions, and then compare them to the answers with feedback that immediately follow. Under governing self-study standards, vendors are required to present review questions intermittently throughout each self-study course.

These questions and explanations are not part of the final examination and will not be graded by LTP.

SFP1.1
Which of the following farm assets could produce a gain or a loss for the taxpayer?

   a. Land
   b. Depreciable farm equipment
   c. Buildings and structures
   d. Livestock

SFP1.2
When farm products are sold, they are reported on_____.

   a. Schedule F
   b. Form 4797
   c. Form 8949
   d. Form 1040

SFP1.3

Where do dog breeders report their income from sales?

    a. Schedule A
    b. Schedule C
    c. Schedule E
    d. Schedule F

SFP1.4

EFI stands for _____.

    a. Electronic filing income
    b. Electronic farm income
    c. Elected farm income
    d. Elected filing income

SFP1.5

Cattle breeding sales are reported on which form?

    a. Schedule A
    b. Schedule C
    c. Schedule E
    d. Schedule F

Part 1 Review Questions Answers

SFP1.1

Which of the following farm assets could produce a gain or a loss for the taxpayer?

    a. Land
    b. Depreciable farm equipment
    c. Buildings and structures
    d. Livestock

Feedback: Review section *Schedule F, Farm Income.*

SFP1.2

When farm products are sold, they are reported on_____.

    a. Schedule F
    b. Form 4797
    c. Form 8949
    d. Form 1040

Feedback: Review section *Farm Income.*

SFP1.3
Where do dog breeders report their income from sales?

    a. Schedule A
    b. Schedule C
    c. Schedule E
    d. Schedule F

Feedback: Review section *Farm Income*.

SFP1.4
EFI stands for _____.

    a. Electronic filing income
    b. Electronic farm income
    c. Elected farm income
    d. Elected filing income

Feedback: Review section *Elected Farm Income*.

SFP1.5
Cattle breeding sales are reported on which form?

    a. Schedule 1
    b. Schedule C
    c. Schedule E
    d. Schedule F

Feedback: Review section *Farm Income*.

Takeaways

Taxpayers are in the business of farming if they cultivate, operate, or manage a farm for profit, either as an owner or tenant. A farm includes livestock, dairy, poultry, fish, fruit, and truck farms. The farm can also include plantations, ranches, ranges, and orchards.

TEST YOUR KNOWLEDGE!
Go online to take a practice quiz.

California Farm Income

Introduction

California considers Schedule F to be business income. Schedule F conforms to the same guidelines as Schedule C. California law complies with federal law regarding self-employment income and, in most fields, regarding expenses. The most common difference is depreciation.

Objectives

At the end of this lesson, the student will:

> ➤ Know the California conformity to the federal farm income and expenses.
> ➤ Understand the nonconformity of the federal income and expenses.
> ➤ Realize the conformity and nonconformity treatment of farm assets.

Resources

Form 540	FTB Publication 984	Instructions Form 540
540 Schedule CA	FTB Publications 1001	540 Instructions Schedule CA
FTB Form 3801	R & TC Section 17250	Instructions FTB Form 3801
FTB Form 3801C		Instructions FTB Form 3801C
Form 3885A		Instructions FTB Form 3885A

Table of Contents

Part I Farm Income

Farm Income or Loss

Adjustments to federal income or loss are reported in column A of 540 Schedule CA and are necessary when there is a difference between California and federal law relating to depreciation methods, special credits, and accelerated write-offs. As a result, the recovery period or basis the taxpayer uses to figure their California depreciation. Taxpayers need to make an adjustment to their farm income or expenses. Taxpayers will make the adjustments on 540 Schedule CA column B and column C, line 12. On 540 Schedule CA column A is the federal amounts, column b is the subtractions, and column C is the additions. The most common differences are amortization of intangibles, grapevines subject to Phylloxera or Pierce's disease, additional depreciation, startup costs, IRC Section 179 election, and IRC Section 181, which are the expensing rules for certain productions. To make the necessary adjustments, use Form 3801, side 2 if the taxpayer has the following:

➢ One or more passive activity that produce a loss
➢ One or more passive activity that produce a loss and any nonpassive activity reported on federal Schedule F (Form 1040)

Form 3801 needs to be attached to the taxpayers' California return. See Form 3801 Instructions.

Form FTB 3885A is used to figure the adjustment of depreciation and amortization if the taxpayer has:

➢ Only nonpassive activities that produce either gains or losses (or a combination of gains and losses)
➢ Passive activities that produce gains

Automobile Differences

Passenger automobiles that are not trucks or vans depreciation limitations are:

1st Year	$3,460
2nd Year	$5,600
3rd Year	$3,350
Succeeding Year	$1,975

For trucks and vans the depreciation limitations are:

1st Year	$3,960
2nd Year	$6,300
3rd Year	$3,750
Succeeding Year	$2,275

Business Use of Home

California allows business use of home for farmers. To determine the deduction, it is the same as the federal as long as the use is exclusively and regularly used for business and meets one of the 3 IRS qualifications discussed in the Schedule C chapter. To adjust the loss or income use 540 Schedule CA.

Estimated Payments Exception

If the taxpayer files their tax return yearly by March 1 and do the following the penalty will be waived.

1. File the tax return and pay the tax due by March 1.
2. Taxpayers had no liability for the prior year and the current year was for the 12 months.
3. Taxpayers total tax on the current year including the tax paid though withholding is less than $1,000.

The difference in estimated payments from the federal is that California has 3 estimated payments. The following are the dates and percentage amount for the payments:

1.	April 18, 2023	30%
2.	June 15, 2023	40%
3.	September 15, 2023	0%
4.	January 16, 2024	30%

Part 1 California Farm Income Review Questions

To obtain the maximum benefit from this chapter, LTP recommends that you complete each of the following questions, and then compare them to the answers with feedback that immediately follow. Under governing self-study standards, vendors are required to present review questions intermittently throughout each self-study course.

These questions and explanations are not part of the final examination and will not be graded by LTP.

CSFP1.1
If a California taxpayer needs to adjust the federal income or loss, where are the adjustments reported?

    a. Form 3801
    b. Schedule CA (540)
    c. Form 3885A
    d. FTB 1001

CSFP1.2
California generally conforms to the federal law in regard to farm income. Which of the following is not one of the differences in federal and state law?

    a. Depreciation method
    b. Accelerated write-offs
    c. Special credits
    d. IRA distribution

CSFP1.3
How many estimated payments does California require?

    a. 4
    b. 3
    c. 0
    d. 2

CSFP1.4
What is the automobile depreciation for the first year?

    a. $3,460
    b. $5,600
    c. $3,350
    d. $1,975

CSFP1.5
What is the depreciation for trucks and vans for the first year?

    a. $3,960
    b. $6,300
    c. $3,750
    d. $2,275

Part 1 California Farm Income Review Questions Answers

CSFP1.1
If a California taxpayer needs to adjust the federal income or loss, where are the adjustments reported?

    a. Form 3801
    b. 540 Schedule CA
    c. Form 3885A
    d. FTB 1001

Feedback: Review section *Part 1 Farm Income.*

CSFP1.2
California generally conforms to the federal law in regard to farm income. Which of the following is not one of the differences in federal and state law?

    a. Depreciation method
    b. Accelerated write-offs
    c. Special credits
    d. IRA distribution

Feedback: Review section *Part 1 Farm Income.*

CSFP1.3
How many estimated payments does California require?

    a. 4
    b. 3
    c. 0
    d. 2

Feedback: Review section *Part 1 Farm Income.*

CSFP1.4
What is the automobile depreciation for the first year?

    a. $3,460
    b. $5,600
    c. $3,350
    d. $1,975

Feedback: Review section *Part 1 Farm Income.*

CSFP1.5
What is depreciation for trucks and vans for the first year?

    a. $3,960
    b. $6,300
    c. $3,750
    d. $2,275

Feedback: Review section *Part 1 Farm Income.*

Takeaways

California generally conforms to federal law regarding farm income or loss. There are differences between California laws and federal laws relating to depreciation methods, special credits, and accelerated write-offs. Due to the differences, recovery periods could be different. The taxpayer would adjust the farm income or loss on 540 Schedule CA. See 540 Schedule CA Instructions.

TEST YOUR KNOWLEDGE!
Go online to take a practice quiz.

Chapter 12 Depreciation

Introduction

Depreciation is an annual deduction that allows taxpayers to recover the cost or other basis of their business or investment property over a specified number of years. Depreciation is an allowance for the wear and tear, decline, or uselessness of a property and begins when a taxpayer places property in service for use in a trade or business. The property ceases to be depreciable when the taxpayer has fully recovered the property's cost or other basis or when the property has been retired from service, whichever comes first. Depreciation is reported on Form 4562.

Objectives

At the end of this lesson, the student will:

> ➢ Describe when property cannot be depreciated.
> ➢ Recognize when depreciation begins and ends.
> ➢ Identify which method of depreciation to use for the property.

Resources

Form 1040	Publication 534	Instructions Form 1040
Form 3115	Publication 544	Instructions Form 3115
Form 4562	Publication 551	Instructions Form 4562
Form 8866	Publication 946	Instructions Form 8866

Table of Contents

Part 1 Defining Depreciation and Depreciation Methods

Depreciation is an annual allowance for the wear and tear of certain property that includes the process of allocating the cost of a tangible asset to expense over its estimated useful life. To be depreciable, tangible property must have a limited life. Tangible property can be divided into two categories: real property and personal property. Real property is land, land improvements, buildings, and building improvements. Land does not have a limited life; therefore, it does not qualify for depreciation. Personal property is usually business machinery and equipment, office furniture, and fixtures. The term "personal property" should not be confused with property owned by an individual for personal use.

Depreciation

Depreciation is a way of accounting for the costs associated with durable goods used in a business, for investment, or for a hobby. The recovery period is determined by the IRS and the taxpayer deducts the cost of the item over the property class life. Only the percentage of the cost corresponding to the percentage of use attributable to deductible purposes can be depreciated; costs attributed to personal use can never be depreciated. Depreciation starts when the asset is placed into service and ends when the property is disposed or worn out.

Basis is a way of determining the cost of an investment in property and is decided by how it was acquired. If the property was purchased, the purchase price is the basis. Any improvements made to the property are then added to that basis. The purchase price plus improvements constitutes the adjusted basis. Other items that add to the basis are the expenses of acquiring the property (commissions, sales tax, and freight charges). There are also items that reduce the basis, which include depreciation, nontaxable distributions, and postponed gain on home sales. This is also referred to as "cost basis."

Depreciation is reported on Form 4562.

Form **4562**	**Depreciation and Amortization** (Including Information on Listed Property) Attach to your tax return. Go to *www.irs.gov/Form4562* for instructions and the latest information.	OMB No. 1545-0172
Department of the Treasury Internal Revenue Service		**2022** Attachment Sequence No. **179**
Name(s) shown on return	Business or activity to which this form relates	Identifying number

Portion of Form 4562

Section 179

Section 179 is an internal revenue code that allows the taxpayer an immediate deduction on certain business assets. Business owners can take the purchase price of business equipment in the year of purchase and depreciate the asset 100%. Federal law allows an expense election up to $1,050,000 of the cost of certain business property. For the tax year 2022 the limits are $1,080,000 with a total purchase of $2,700,000. For the tax year 2023 the limits are $1,160,000 with a total phaseout at $2,890,000.

Taxpayers can choose to take a portion of Section 179 instead of the entire amount of the asset. For example, Solomon purchased a tractor for his farming business. The tractor cost $45,000, and Solomon decided to use 50% of the cost as Section 179. The remaining $22,500 would be used as a yearly depreciation deduction.

Section 179 is reported on Form 4562, part I.

Part I   **Election To Expense Certain Property Under Section 179**
Note: If you have any listed property, complete Part V before you complete Part I.

1	Maximum amount (see instructions)	**1**	
2	Total cost of section 179 property placed in service (see instructions)	**2**	
3	Threshold cost of section 179 property before reduction in limitation (see instructions)	**3**	
4	Reduction in limitation. Subtract line 3 from line 2. If zero or less, enter -0-	**4**	
5	Dollar limitation for tax year. Subtract line 4 from line 1. If zero or less, enter -0-. If married filing separately, see instructions	**5**	

6	(a) Description of property	(b) Cost (business use only)	(c) Elected cost

7	Listed property. Enter the amount from line 29 **7**		
8	Total elected cost of section 179 property. Add amounts in column (c), lines 6 and 7	**8**	
9	Tentative deduction. Enter the **smaller** of line 5 or line 8	**9**	
10	Carryover of disallowed deduction from line 13 of your 2021 Form 4562	**10**	
11	Business income limitation. Enter the smaller of business income (not less than zero) or line 5. See instructions	**11**	
12	Section 179 expense deduction. Add lines 9 and 10, but don't enter more than line 11	**12**	
13	Carryover of disallowed deduction to 2023. Add lines 9 and 10, less line 12 **13**		

Note: Don't use Part II or Part III below for listed property. Instead, use Part V.

Portion of Form 4562

Line 1 reports the maximum amount of Section 179.

Line 2 reports total cost of Section 179 that was placed in service in the current tax year.

Line 3 reports the maximum amount the taxpayer would elect to claim. The amount could be reduced based on taxpayer.

Line 4 reports the reduction limitation.

Line 5 reports the dollar limitation for the current tax year.

Bonus Depreciation

Bonus depreciation was designed to stimulate investment in business property that is not land or buildings. IRC section 168(k) is the code that provides the explanation of the accelerated depreciation. The IRS sometimes refers to bonus depreciation as a "special depreciation allowance." For tax year 2022, the allowable depreciation is 100% of qualified business property. The immediate deduction is eligible for property that has been placed in service between September 27, 2017, and January 1, 2023. After January 1, 2023, the phaseout amounts are:

2023: 80%
2024: 60%
2025: 40%
2026: 20%

Property that qualifies for bonus depreciation must have a useful life of 20 years or less. The property must also be new for the taxpayer. If the taxpayer leased the equipment, prior to purchase, the property is disqualified for bonus depreciation.

Part II reports Special Depreciation Allowance and other Depreciation, such as bonus depreciation.

Part II	Special Depreciation Allowance and Other Depreciation (Don't include listed property. See instructions.)		
14	Special depreciation allowance for qualified property (other than listed property) placed in service during the tax year. See instructions.	14	
15	Property subject to section 168(f)(1) election	15	
16	Other depreciation (including ACRS)	16	

Portion of Form 4562

The Beginning and End of Depreciation

Depreciation begins when the property is placed in service for use in the trade or business or for the production of income. Depreciation ends when the cost and added basis, if any, have been fully recovered or when the property is retired from service, whichever comes first.

Property is placed in service when it is ready and available for a specific use for a business activity, an income-producing activity, a tax-exempt activity, or a personal activity. Even if the property is not being used, it is still placed in service when it is ready, available, and capable of performing its specific use.

When a taxpayer places an improvement or addition in service after the original asset was placed in service, the improvements or addition is a separate asset. For example, Gabriela placed her rental in service and then made some major improvements. The improvements were more than the purchase price of the rental. The improvements will be a separate line item to be depreciated and could have a different class life. See §1.263(a)-3T(e)(3) or (e)(5) for more information.

Example 1: Joel purchased a copy machine in December of last year for his printing business. The machine was delivered in January but not installed. Joel had the machine installed and ready for use in February of the current tax year. The machine would be considered to be placed in service in February of the current year, and not December or January, because it wasn't until it was installed in February that the machine became ready to be placed in service.

If the property has been converted from personal to business use, the "placed in service" date is the date it was converted to business use or to an income-producing activity. In other words, depreciation begins when the property has been placed in service.

Example 2: Nicolas purchased a home as his primary residence in 2010, and on February 10, 2022, he converted it to a rental property. Therefore, depreciation begins the day it was placed into service as an income-producing property.

Property That Can Be Depreciated

Most types of tangible property can be depreciated. Examples of tangible property are:

➤ Buildings
➤ Vehicles
➤ Machinery
➤ Furniture
➤ Equipment
➤ Storage facilities

Some intangible items that can be depreciated include:

➤ Copyrights
➤ Patents
➤ Computer software (if the software life value is more than one year)

Property that can be depreciated must meet the following requirements:

➤ Must be the taxpayer's own property.
➤ Must be used in the taxpayer's business or income-producing activity.
➤ Property must have a determinable useful life.
➤ The property is expected to last more than one year.

Property Owned

To claim depreciation, one must be the owner of the property, even if the property has debt. Leased property can be claimed only if ownership of the property includes the following:

➤ The legal title to the property.
➤ The legal obligation to pay for the property.
➤ The responsibility to pay maintenance and operating expenses.
➤ The duty to pay any taxes on the property.
➤ The risk of loss if the property is destroyed, condemned, or diminished in value through obsolescence or exhaustion.

Example: Amanda made a down payment on a rental property and took over Tom's mortgage payments. Amanda owns the property and can depreciate it.

If the property is held as a business or as an investment property as a life tenant, the taxpayer may depreciate the property.

Property Having a Determinable Useful Life

Property must have a determinable useful life to be depreciated. It must be something that wears out, decays, gets used up, becomes obsolete, or loses its value from natural causes.

Property Lasting More than One Year

To be able to depreciate property, the useful life should extend significantly beyond the year the property was placed in service.

Example: Ms. Wilson maintains a library for her tax business and purchases yearly technical journals for its use. The library would not be depreciated because the technical journals do not have a useful life of more than one year. The technical journals should be taken as a yearly business expense.

Property Used in Business or an Income-Producing Activity

To claim depreciation on property, the income-producing activity must be used in business. If the taxpayer uses the property to produce an investment use, then the income is taxable. Personal property cannot be depreciated.

If the property is used for business and personal use, the portion used as business may be depreciated. For instance, the individual cannot deduct depreciation on a car used only for commuting to and from work or for personal shopping trips and family vacations. Taxpayer must keep records showing business and personal use of the property.

Containers used for the products one sells are considered inventory and cannot be depreciated. Containers used to ship products can be depreciated if they have a life expectancy of more than one year and meet the following requirements:

➢ Qualify as property used in business.
➢ Title to the containers does not pass to the buyer.

To determine if the above requirements are met, the following things need to be considered:

➢ Does the sales contract, sales invoice, or some other type of order acknowledgement indicate whether the taxpayer has retained the title of the containers?
➢ Does the invoice treat the containers as a separate item?
➢ Do the taxpayer's records indicate the basis of the containers?

Auto Depreciation Limits

Maximum deprecation for passenger vehicles acquired after September 27, 2017, and placed in service in 2022 and taxpayer did not opt in for special depreciation. The depreciation is:

First year $19,200
Second year $18,000
Third year $10,800
Fourth year and later $6,460

For sport utility vehicles (SUV) placed in service beginning 2022, the maximum deduction is $27,000. For passenger automobiles placed in service for 2022, it is $19,200, if special depreciation is allowed, or $11,200 if special depreciation is applied. For IRS purposes an SUV is different than a passenger automobile because the depreciation limits are based on the vehicle weight.

Property That Cannot Be Depreciated

Land does not wear out; therefore, it cannot be depreciated. The cost of land generally includes clearing, grading, planting, and landscaping. Although land is never depreciated, certain improvements to the land can be depreciated, such as landscaping and improvements to a building.

The following exceptions are property that cannot be depreciated even if the requirements are met:

➢ Property placed in service and disposed of in the same year.
➢ Equipment used to build capital improvements.
➢ Section 197 intangibles that must be amortized.
➢ Certain term interests.

Inventory is not depreciated. Inventory is any property that is held primarily for sale to customers in the ordinary course of business. If the taxpayer is in the rent-to-own business, certain property held for business may be considered as depreciable instead of inventory. See Publication 946.

Property Acquired by Like-kind Exchanges

Like-kind property is property of the same nature, character, or class. Quality or grade does not matter. For example, real property that is improved with a residential rental house is like-kind to vacant land. Most common like-kind exchanges are real property, or better known as a 1031 exchange.

A 1031 exchange gets its name from Section 1031 of the U.S. Internal Revenue Code, which allows you to postpone paying capital gains taxes when you sell an investment property and reinvest the proceeds from the sale within certain time limits in a property or properties of like-kind and equal or greater value.

Like-kind exchanges completed after December 31, 2017, are limited to real property exchanges not held primarily for sale. See IRC Section 1.168(i)-6.

De minimis Safe Harbor Election

The taxpayer can elect to deduct small dollar amounts for expenditures for acquiring or manufacturing of property that generally needs to be capitalized under the general rules. The amount spent needs to be ordinary and necessary expenses to carry on the trade or business for the taxpayer. Costs include materials, supplies, repairs, and maintenance usually under $2,500. See IRC Section 1.263.

Depreciation Methods

Depreciation methods consist of modified accelerated cost recovery system, along with straight-line and accelerated cost recovery system (ACRS). ACRS was used prior to 1987. The IRS now uses MACRS and straight-line.

Modified Accelerated Cost Recovery System (MACRS)

The Modified Accelerated Cost Recovery System (MACRS) is the current depreciation method used in the United States to calculate depreciable assets. MACRS should be used to depreciate property. MACRS is not used in the following circumstances:

➢ Property placed in service before 1987.
➢ Property owned or used in 1986.
➢ Intangible property.
➢ Films, video tapes, and recordings.
➢ Certain corporate or partnership property that was acquired in a nontaxable transfer.
➢ Property that has been elected to be excluded from MACRS.

Property Placed in Service Before 1987

If property was placed in service before 1987 (unless the taxpayer elected to use MACRS after July 31, 1986) it must use ACRS or Straight Line. See Publication 534.

MACRS is generally used to depreciate property that was acquired for personal use before 1987 but placed in service after 1986. Improvements made to the property placed in service before 1986 is depreciated as a separate entry using MACRS depreciation.

Certain property that was acquired and placed in service after 1986 may not qualify for MACRS. In any of the following personal property situations, MACRS cannot be used:

➢ The taxpayer or someone related to the taxpayer owned or used the property in 1986.
➢ The taxpayer acquired the property from a person who owned it in 1986; and, as a part of the transaction, the user of the property did not change.
➢ The taxpayer leased the property to a person (or someone related to them) who owned or used the property in 1986.
➢ The taxpayer acquired the property in a transaction in which the following took place:
   o The user of the property did not change.
   o The property was not a MACRS property in the hands of the person from whom the taxpayer acquired it due to one of the reasons above.

A taxpayer cannot depreciate Section 1250 property using MACRS in any of the following situations:

➢ The taxpayer or someone related to the taxpayer owned the property in 1986.
➢ The taxpayer leased the property to a person who owned the property or to someone related to that person in 1986.
➢ The taxpayer acquired the property in a like-kind exchange, involuntary conversion, or repossession of property that was owned by the taxpayer, or someone related to the taxpayer in 1986.

MACRS only applies to the part of basis in the acquired property that represents cash paid or unlike property exchanged. It does not apply to the carried-over part of the basis.

Exceptions to the above include the following:

> ➢ Residential rental property or nonresidential real property.
> ➢ Any property if, in the first tax year that it is placed in service, the deduction under Accelerated Cost Recovery System (ACRS) is more than the deduction under MACRS using the half year convention. See Publication 534.

The following are related persons who cannot depreciate Section 1250 property:

> ➢ An individual and a member of their family, including only a spouse, child, parent, brother, sister, half-brother, half-sister, ancestor, and lineal descendant.
> ➢ A corporation or an individual who directly or indirectly owns more than 10% of the value of the outstanding stock of that corporation.
> ➢ Two corporations that are members of the same controlled group.
> ➢ A trust fiduciary and a corporation if more than 10% of the value of the outstanding stock is directly or indirectly owned by or for the trust or grantor of the trust.
> ➢ The grantor and fiduciary; and the fiduciary and beneficiary of any trust.
> ➢ The fiduciaries of two different trusts and the fiduciaries and beneficiaries of two different trusts if the same person is the grantor of both trusts.
> ➢ A tax-exempt educational or charitable organization and any person (or a member of that person's family) who directly or indirectly controls the organization.
> ➢ Two S corporations, an S corporation and a regular corporation, if the same individual owns more than 10% of the value of the outstanding stock of each corporation.
> ➢ A corporation and a partnership if the same persons own both of the following:
>   o More than 10% of the value of the outstanding stock of the corporation.
>   o More than 10% of the interest gained from the capital or profits of the partnership.
> ➢ The executor and beneficiary of any estate.
> ➢ Two partnerships, if the same person directly or indirectly owns more than 10% of the capital or profits of each.
> ➢ The related person and a person who is engaged in trades or businesses under common control. See IRC section 52(a) and 52(b).

The buyer should determine the nature of a relationship before the property is acquired.

Intangible Property

Intangible property is anything of value that can be owned that has no corresponding physical object (e.g., a patent, copyright, or partnership interests). These are generally depreciated using the straight-line method. The taxpayer may choose to depreciate intangible property by using the income forecast method, which is not covered in this course. See Publication 946.

Straight Line Method

The straight-line method of depreciation allows the taxpayer to deduct the same amount each year over the useful life of the property. To determine the deduction, first determine the adjusted basis, salvage value, and estimated useful life of the property. Subtract the salvage value, if any, from the adjusted basis. The balance is the depreciation that can be taken for the property. Divide the balance by the number of years in the useful life. This is the yearly depreciation deduction. To use the straight-line method, prorate the depreciation deduction by dividing the value proportionally based on a unit of time or number of months in use.

Example: Francisco purchased a patent in August for $5,100 that is defined in Section 197. Francisco will depreciate the patent using the straight-line method. The useful life for a patent is 17 years with no salvage value. Francisco would divide the $5,100 basis by 17 years to get the yearly depreciation of $300. In the first year of business, Francisco only used the patent for 9 months so he would have to multiply the $300 x 9/12 to get his deduction of $225 for the first year. Over the next full year, Francisco would claim the $300 depreciation deduction.

Computer software is generally a Section 197 tangible and cannot be depreciated if the taxpayer acquired it in connection with the acquisition of assets constituting a business. However, when it meets the following tests, computer software that is not a Section 197 intangible can be depreciated even if it's acquired in a business acquisition:

➢ It is readily available for purchase by the general public.
➢ It is subject to a nonexclusive license.
➢ It has not been substantially modified.

If the software meets the above test, it may also qualify for Section 179. If computer software can be depreciated, use the straight-line method over a useful life of 36 months.

Part 1 Review Questions

To obtain the maximum benefit from this chapter, LTP recommends that you complete each of the following questions, and then compare them to the answers with feedback that immediately follow. Under governing self-study standards, vendors are required to present review questions intermittently throughout each self-study course.

These questions and explanations are not part of the final examination and will not be graded by LTP.

DP1.1
Which of the following is the current tax depreciation system in the United States?

a. MACRS
b. ACRS
c. Half-year convention (HY)
d. Mid-month convention (MM)

DP1.2
Depreciation is a(n)____ allowance for the wear and tear of certain property.

a. recovery period
b. annual
c. monthly
d. quarterly

DP1.3
Which of the following is not tangible property?

a. Buildings
b. Machinery
c. Furniture
d. Cell phones

DP1.4

Bonus depreciation was designed to stimulate investment in business property that is not land or buildings. The IRS sometimes refers to bonus depreciation as a "special depreciation allowance." For tax year 2022, the allowable depreciation is what percent of qualified business property?

a. 100%
b. 50%
c. 60%
d. 75%

DP1.5

If the taxpayer does not take the first-year bonus depreciation for a passenger vehicle acquired Sept 27, 2017, what is the allowable depreciation for the first year?

a. $19,200
b. $18,000
c. $10,800
d. $6,460

Part 1 Review Questions Answers

DP1.1

Which of the following is the current tax depreciation system in the United States?

a. MACRS
b. ACRS
c. Half-year convention (HY)
d. Mid-month convention (MM)

Feedback: Review section *Modified Accelerated Cost Recovery System (MACRS).*

DP1.2

Depreciation is a(n)____ allowance for the wear and tear of certain property.

a. recovery period
b. annual
c. monthly
d. quarterly

Feedback: Review section *Depreciation.*

DP1.3

Which of the following is not tangible property?

a. Buildings
b. Machinery
c. Furniture
d. Cell phones

Feedback: Review section *Property That Can Be Depreciated.*

DP1.4

Bonus depreciation was designed to stimulate investment in business property that is not land or buildings. The IRS sometimes refers to bonus depreciation as a "special depreciation allowance." For tax year 2022, the allowable depreciation is what percent of qualified business property?

   a. **100%**
   b. 50%
   c. 60%
   d. 75%

Feedback: Review section *Bonus Depreciation.*

DP1.5

If the taxpayer does not take the first-year bonus depreciation for a passenger vehicle acquired Sept 27, 2017, what is the allowable depreciation for the first year?

   a. **$19,200**
   b. $18,000
   c. $10,800
   d. $6,460

Feedback: Review section *Bonus Depreciation.*

Part 2 Depreciation Basis and Depreciation under MACRS

To the beginner tax professional, depreciation and basis can be overwhelming, but when one understands the basics, then depreciation and basis are easy to determine.

Basis of Depreciable Property

To calculate the depreciation deduction, you must know the basis of the property. To determine the basis of the property, you must know the cost of the property.

Cost Basis

The basis of property that has been purchased is the cost plus the amounts paid for certain items. The cost includes the amount paid in cash, debt obligations, other property, or services. Some items that might be added to basis are:

- Sales tax
- Freight charges
- Installation fees
- Testing fees
- Settlement costs such as:
  - Legal and recording fees
  - Abstract fees
  - Survey charges
  - Owner's title insurance
  - Amounts the seller owes that the buyer agrees to pay, such as back taxes, interest, recording or mortgage fees, charges for improvements or repairs, and sales commissions.

Other Basis

Other basis refers to the way the owner of the property received the property. Was the property acquired by a like-kind exchange, as payment for services performed, as a gift, inheritance, or some other way? See Publication 551.

Adjusted Basis

Certain adjustments, whether an increase or a decrease, may have to be made to determine the adjusted basis in property. These events occur between the time that the property was acquired and placed into service. The events could include any of the following:

- ➢ Installing utility lines
- ➢ Paying legal fees for perfecting the title
- ➢ Setting zoning issues
- ➢ Receiving rebates
- ➢ Incurring a casualty or theft loss

Reduce the basis of property by the depreciation allowed or allowable, whichever is greater. "Depreciation allowed" is depreciation that the taxpayer was entitled to and has already deducted as a tax benefit. "Depreciation allowable" is depreciation that the taxpayer was entitled to but did not yet deduct. See Publication 551.

Figuring Depreciation Under MACRS

The Modified Accelerated Cost Recovery System (MACRS) is used to recover the basis of most business and investment property placed in service after 1986. MACRS consists of two depreciation systems: the General Depreciation System (GDS) and the Alternative Depreciation System (ADS). These two systems provide different methods and recovery periods to figure deductions. The most common method used is GDS unless the law requires the ADS method to be used, or the taxpayer has elected to use ADS.

If the taxpayer is required to use ADS to depreciate the property, no special depreciation allowance can be claimed on the property. Although the property may qualify for GDS, the taxpayer can elect to use ADS. The election must cover all property in the same property class that was placed in service during the same year.

GDS Property Classifications

There are nine property classifications under GDS. The classifications are divided by the length of the depreciation period and by the type of property being depreciated. Most of the classifications have the same recovery period as the title of the year. The following are some samples of the type of asset for each classification. See Publication 946.

(a) Classification of property	(b) Month and year placed in service	(c) Basis for depreciation (business/investment use only—see instructions)	(d) Recovery period	(e) Convention	(f) Method	(g) Depreciation deduction
Section B—Assets Placed in Service During 2022 Tax Year Using the General Depreciation System						
19a 3-year property						
b 5-year property						
c 7-year property						
d 10-year property						
e 15-year property						
f 20-year property						
g 25-year property			25 yrs.		S/L	
h Residential rental property			27.5 yrs.	MM	S/L	
			27.5 yrs.	MM	S/L	
i Nonresidential real property			39 yrs.	MM	S/L	
				MM	S/L	
Section C—Assets Placed in Service During 2022 Tax Year Using the Alternative Depreciation System						
20a Class life					S/L	
b 12-year			12 yrs.		S/L	
c 30-year			30 yrs.	MM	S/L	
d 40-year			40 yrs.	MM	S/L	

Portion of Form 4562

Classification One, 3-year Property:

- Tractor units for over-the-road use.
- Racehorses that were over 2 years old when placed in service.
- Any other horses that were over 12 years old when placed in service.
- Qualified rent-to-own property

Classification Two, 5-year Property:

- Automobiles, taxis, buses, and trucks.
- Office machinery such as calculators, copiers, and computers.
- Dairy cattle and breeding cattle.
- Appliances, carpets, solar, and wind energy property

Classification Three, 7-year Property:

- Office furniture and fixtures such as desks, chairs, and a safe.
- Railroad tracks.
- Any property that does not have a class life and has not been designated by law as being in any other class.
- Certain motorsports entertainment complex property.

Classification Four, 10-year Property:

- Any tree or vine bearing fruit or nuts.
- Any single-purpose agricultural or horticultural structure.
- Vessels, barges, tugs, and similar water transportation equipment.
- Qualified small electric meter and qualified grid system placed in service on or after October 3, 2008.

Classification Five, 15-year Property:

- Certain improvements made directly to land or added to land, such as shrubbery, fences, roads, sidewalks, and bridges.
- Any municipal wastewater treatment plant.

➢ The initial clearing and grading for land improvements for gas utilities.
➢ Electric transmission section 1245 property, used in the transmission at 69 or more kilovolts of electricity placed in service after April 11, 2005.

Classification Six, 20-year property:

➢ Farm buildings, other than single-purpose agricultural or horticultural structures.
➢ Initial clearing and grading land improvements for electric utility transmission and distribution plants.
➢ Municipal sewers not classified as 25-year-property.

Classification Seven, 25-year Property:

➢ Property that is an integral part of the gathering, treatment, or commercial distribution of water; all other property regarding water would be 20-year property.
➢ Municipal sewers other than property placed in service under a binding contract in effect at all times since June 9, 1996.

Classification Eight, Residential Rental Property:

Rental property includes any building or structure such as rental income, which includes dwelling units and mobile homes. A dwelling unit is an apartment or house that provides living accommodations in a building or structure. Motels, hotels, and other similar establishments that use more than 50% of the rooms for transients are not included; for these, the property class-life is 27.5 years.

Classification Nine, Nonresidential Real Property:

This is Section 1250 property, such as an office building, store, or warehouse that is not a residential rental property or a property with a class life of less than 27.5 years. There are always exceptions to the rules. If this is the case, one must do research related to the particular situation. Any other GDS recovery periods that are not listed above can be found in Appendix B of Publication 946.

Which Convention Applies?

A convention method is established under MACRS to determine the portion of the year to depreciate property both in the year the property was placed in service and in the year of disposition. The convention used determines the number of months for which one can claim depreciation. The three methods are: Mid-month (MM), Mid-quarter (MQ), and Half-year (HY).

Mid-month convention is used for nonresidential real property, residential real property, and any railroad grading or tunnel bore. Under this convention, one-half month of depreciation is allowed for the month the property was placed in service or disposed of.

Example: Josue uses the calendar year accounting method and placed nonresidential real property in service in August. The property is in service for 4 months (September, October, November, and December). Josue's numerator is 4.5 (4 months plus 0.5). Josue would multiply the depreciation for a full year by 4.5/12, or 0.375.

If the taxpayer does not use the asset solely for business, then the asset must be multiplied by the business percentage for the year, and then multiply the result by the fraction found in the MACRS depreciation tables.

Example: In February 2022, Jennifer purchased office furniture for $2,600. She used the office furniture for her business only 50% of the time. Furniture is a 7-year property. The depreciation percentage is taken from Table A-2 found in Publication 946. Since Jennifer purchased the furniture in the first quarter of the year, she would use the mid-quarter convention placed in service in the first quarter. The amount Jennifer could depreciate her first year would be the cost of the furniture ($2,600) times the percentage of its use for business (50%) times the percentage provided from the depreciation table (25%), which amounts to $325.00.

The Mid-quarter convention is used if the Mid-month convention does not apply, and the total depreciable basis of MACRS property placed in service is in the last 3 months of the tax year. If the Mid-quarter convention is used for a particular year, each item of depreciable personal property placed in service during that year must be depreciated using the Mid-quarter convention for its entire recovery period.

Nonresidential real property, residential rental property, railroad grading or tunnel bore property placed in service and disposed of in the same year, and property that is being depreciated under a method other than MACRS are all excluded from using the Mid-quarter convention. Under this convention, treat all property placed in service or disposed during any quarter of the tax year as placed in service. This means that 1½ months of depreciation is allowed for the quarter the property is placed in service or disposed.

The Half-year convention is used if neither the Mid-quarter nor the Mid-month convention applies. Under this convention, treat all property placed in service or disposed of during a tax year as placed in service or disposed of at the midpoint of the year. This means that one-half year of depreciation is allowed for the year the property is placed in service or disposed.

When the taxpayer elects to use the half-year convention, a half-year of depreciation is allowed in the first year their property is placed in service, regardless of when the property is placed in service during the tax year. For each of the remaining years of the recovery period, the taxpayer can claim a full year of depreciation. If the property is held for the entire recovery period, a half-year of depreciation is claimed for the year following the end of the recovery period. If the property is disposed before the recovery period ends, a half-year of depreciation is allowable for the year of disposition.

If the personal property has been placed into a farming business after 1988, and before 2018, the taxpayer must depreciate by using 150% of GDS. The exception to the rule is if the farmer must depreciate real property using the straight-line method. For 3-, 5-, 7-, or 10-year property placed in the farming business after 2017 no longer have to use the 150% declining balance.

Changing Accounting Methods

To change the accounting method used for depreciation, the taxpayer needs to file Form 3115, *Application for Change in Accounting Method,* to be approved by the IRS.

The following are examples of a change in the method of accounting used for depreciation:

➢ A change from an impermissible method of determining depreciation for property if it was used in two or more consecutively filed tax returns.
➢ A change in the treatment of an asset from non-depreciable to depreciable, or vice versa.
➢ A change in the depreciation method, period of recovery, or convention of a depreciable asset.

➤ A change from not claiming to claiming the special depreciation allowance if the election was made to not claim the special allowance.

➤ A change from claiming a 50% special depreciation allowance to claiming a 100% special depreciation allowance for qualified property acquired and placed in service after September 27, 2017, if the election was not made under IRC section 168(k)(10) to claim the 50% special allowable depreciation.

Changes in depreciation that are not a change in method of accounting are as follows:

➤ An adjustment in the useful life of a depreciable asset for which depreciation is determined under Section 167.

➤ A change in use of an asset in the hands of the same taxpayer.

➤ Making a late depreciation election or revoking a timely valid depreciation election, including the election not to deduct the special depreciation allowance.

➤ Any change in date of when a depreciable asset was placed in service.

If the taxpayer does not qualify to use the automatic procedure by filing Form 3115, then he or she must use the advance consent request procedures. See Instructions Form 3115.

Idle Property

Depreciation can still be claimed on property that is placed in service, even if a property is temporarily idle and not being used. For instance, if Emilio owns a printing press but has not used it for six months of the current tax year because he has no jobs that require the machine, then he can continue claiming depreciation on his printing press.

Cost or Other Basis Fully Recovered

Stop depreciating property when the property has fully recovered its cost or other basis.

Retired from Service

When the property has been retired from service, depreciation stops. Property is retired from service when it has been permanently withdrawn from use in trade or business; in production of income; or if the property has been sold or exchanged, converted to personal use, abandoned, transferred to a supply, or destroyed. Disposition of an asset includes the sale, exchange, retirement, physical abandonment, or destruction of an asset.

Understanding the Table of Class Lives and Recovery Periods

There are two sections in the *Table of Class Lives and Recovery Periods* for depreciation. Table B-1 is *Specific Depreciable Assets Used in All Business Activities, Except as Noted*; this table lists the assets used in all business activities. Some items included could be office furniture; information systems such as computers; and secondary equipment, like printers or computer screens.

Table B-2 is used for all other activities, such as those involving agriculture, horse racing, farm buildings, and single purpose agricultural or horticultural structures.

Use the tables in numerical order. Look on Table B-1 first; if you do not find the asset you are looking for, then check Table B-2. Once the asset has been located, use the recovery period shown in the table. However, if the activity is specifically listed in Table B-2 under the type of activity in which it is used, then use the recovery period for that activity in that table.

Each table gives the asset class, the class life, and the recovery period in years. Understanding these tables is vital for the beginner tax professional. A tax professional does not have to memorize the tables – just know where to find the information and how to use it correctly.

If the property is not listed in either table, check the end of Table B-2 to find *Certain Property for Which Recovery Periods Assigned*. Generally, non-listed property has a recovery period of 7 years GDS or 12 years ADS.

Example: Peter Martinez owns a retail clothing store. During the year, he purchased a desk and cash register for business use. Peter finds "office furniture" in Table B-1, under asset class 00.11. Cash register is not listed in Table B-1. Peter then looks in Table B-2 and finds the activity "retail store" under asset class 57.0, *Distributive Trades and Services*, which includes assets used in wholesale and retail trade. The asset class does not specifically list office furniture or a cash register. Peter uses asset class 00.11 for the desk. The desk has a 10-year class life and a 7-year recovery period for GDS. Peter elects to use ADS; the recovery period is 10 years. For the cash register, Peter uses asset class 57.0 because a cash register is not listed in Table B-1, but it is an asset used in the retail business. The cash register has a 9-year class life and a 5-year recovery period for GDS. If Peter elects to use the ADS method, the recovery period is 9 years.

Part 2 Review Questions

To obtain the maximum benefit from this chapter, LTP recommends that you complete each of the following questions, and then compare them to the answers with feedback that immediately follow. Under governing self-study standards, vendors are required to present review questions intermittently throughout each self-study course.
These questions and explanations are not part of the final examination and will not be graded by LTP.

DP2.1
To determine the basis of property, which of the following should be added to the cost?

1. Sales tax
2. Testing fees
3. Survey charges
4. Settlement costs

a. 1 and 2
b. 2, 3, and 4
c. 3 and 4
d. 1, 2, 3, and 4

DP2.2
The General Depreciation System (GDS) has___property classifications.

a. 5
b. 7
c. 9
d. 12

DP2.3
Andres would like to change his accounting method. Which form would he submit to receive the IRS approval?

    a. Form 8829
    b. Form 3115
    c. Form 8867
    d. Form 8849

DP2.4
Which of the following depreciation method(s) is a component of MACRS?

    a. Global Depreciation System and Accelerated Cost Recovery System
    b. Another Depreciation System and Accelerated Cost Recovery System
    c. Accelerated Cost Recovery System and Alternative Depreciation System (ADS)
    d. General Depreciation System (GDS) and Alternative Depreciation System (ADS)

DP2.5
James needs to change his accounting method. Which form would he need to file?

    a. Form 3115
    b. Form 8332
    c. Form 4797
    d. Form 6252

DP2.6
What does the acronym MACRS mean?

    a. Modified Accelerated Custom Recreation Study
    b. Modified Accelerated Cost Recovery System
    c. Modified Adjusted Cost Recovery System
    d. Modified Adjusted Certain Recovery System

DP2.7
Which of the following can be depreciated?

    a. Idle property
    b. Land
    c. Property that has not been placed into service
    d. Idle property and property that has not been placed into service

Part 2 Review Questions Answers

DP2.1
To determine the basis of property, which of the following should be added to the cost?

    1. Sales tax
    2. Testing fees
    3. Survey charges
    4. Settlement costs

a. 1 and 2
b. 2, 3, and 4
c. 3 and 4
d. 1, 2, 3, and 4

Feedback: Review section *Basis of Depreciable Property.*

DP2.2

The General Depreciation System (GDS) has___property classifications.

a. 5
b. 7
c. 9
d. 12

Feedback: Review section *GDS Property Classifications.*

DP2.3

Andres would like to change his accounting method. Which form would he submit to receive the IRS approval?

a. Form 8829
b. Form 3115
c. Form 8867
d. Form 8849

Feedback: Review section *Changing Accounting Methods.*

DP2.4

Which of the following depreciation method(s) is a component of MACRS?

a. Global Depreciation System and Accelerated Cost Recovery System
b. Another Depreciation System and Accelerated Cost Recovery System
c. Accelerated Cost Recovery System and Alternative Depreciation System (ADS)
d. General Depreciation System (GDS) and Alternative Depreciation System (ADS)

Feedback: Review section *GDS Property Classifications.*

DP2.5

James needs to change his accounting method. Which form would he need to file?

a. Form 3115
b. Form 8332
c. Form 4797
d. Form 6252

Feedback: Review section *GDS Property Classifications.*

DP2.6
What does the acronym MACRS mean?

    a. Modified Accelerated Custom Recreation Study
    b. Modified Accelerated Cost Recovery System
    c. Modified Adjusted Cost Recovery System
    d. Modified Adjusted Certain Recovery System

Feedback: Review section *Figuring Depreciation Under MACRS.*

DP2.7
Which of the following can be depreciated?

    a. Idle property
    b. Land
    c. Property that has not been placed into service
    d. Idle property and property that has not been placed into service

Feedback: Review section *Idle Property.*

Takeaways

Although depreciation may seem overwhelming, this subject must be understood to prepare accurate business tax returns. Depreciation is used to benefit the taxpayer; the IRS has defined the convention and class type and has figured the percentage amount. All the tax professional needs to do is find the correct class type and percentage amount to calculate the correct depreciation amount for the taxpayer. A tax professional should not rely on software to do the calculation but understand depreciation to make sure the software is calculating the depreciation correctly.

TEST YOUR KNOWLEDGE!
Go online to take a practice quiz.

California Depreciation and Amortization

Introduction

California law has not always conformed to federal law regarding depreciation methods, special credits, or accelerated write-offs. In general, California law conforms to the Internal Revenue Code as of January 1, 2015; however, recovery periods and basis on which depreciation is calculated may be different from the amounts used for federal purposes. Reportable differences occur if the asset was placed in service at the following times:

➢ Zero-Emissions Nuclear Power Production Credit that produces electricity and sold after 12/31/2023 and before 01/01/2033. Inflation Reduction Act.
➢ Nonconformity for the Inflation Reduction Act (IRA) of 2022. The elections related to the beginning of the 12-year period of credit, facility or equipment placed in service after 12/31/2022. This applies to carbon capture equipment. Inflation Reduction Act.
➢ Alternative fuels sold or used beginning on January 1, 2022, and ending on the calendar quarter beginning August 16, 2022, credits are allowed. Refunds or payments attributable to the credits will be determined by the Secretary of the Treasury.
➢ Extensions of Second-Generation Biofuel Incentives after 12/31/2022.
➢ On or after September 11, 2001: California does not conform to the Job Creation and Worker Assistance Act of 2002. Taxpayers could take an additional 30% additional depreciation on their federal return.
➢ On or after January 1, 1987: California provides special credits and accelerated write-offs that affect the California basis for qualifying assets. California does not conform to all the changes to federal law enacted in 1993. Therefore, the California basis or recovery period may be different for some assets.
➢ Before January 1, 1987: California disallowed depreciation under the federal Accelerated Cost Recovery System (ACRS). Continue to calculate California depreciation in the same manner as in prior years for those assets.

Find more nonconformity on the FTB website and search for the term "conformity". Additional information can be found in FTB Publication 1001, *Supplemental Guidelines to California Adjustments*; the instructions for 540 or 540NR Schedule CA; and the *Business Entity* tax booklets.

Objectives

At the end of this lesson, the student will be able to do the following:

➢ Understand the differences between California and federal depreciation.
➢ Know the differences between California and federal Section 179 deductions.
➢ Recognize how California does not conform to ACRS or MACRS.

Resources

FTB Form 3805V 540 or 540NR Schedule CA FTB Form 3885A	FTB Publication 984 FTB Publication 1001 FTB Publication 1060	Instructions Form 3805V Instructions 540 or 540NR Schedule CA Instructions Form 3885A

Table of Contents

Part 1: Depreciation Under California Tax Law

Depreciation is the annual deduction allowed to recover the cost or other basis of business or income-producing property with a determinable useful life of more than one year (as with federal depreciation, land is not depreciable). *Amortization* is an amount deducted to recover the cost of certain capital expenses over a fixed period.

Use Form 3885A to figure the adjustment for the difference between the amount of depreciation and amortization allowed as a deduction under California law. Carry the difference to Part I of 540 or 540NR California Schedule CA. Do not use Form 3885A to report depreciation expense from federal Form 2106, *Employee Business Expenses*.

Section 179 Expense Deduction

Federal law allows an expense election up to $1,050,000 of the cost of certain business property in lieu of depreciation. California allows an expense election up to $25,000 and limits it to $200,000. The federal Section 179 property cost phase out begins at $2,890,000. Federal law allows a Section 179 expense election for off-the-shelf software and certain qualified real property. California does not comply with this. To report the deduction difference, use Form 3885A.

ACRS or MACRS Depreciation

California has not adopted the federal depreciation methods known as the Accelerated Cost Recovery System (ACRS) or the Modified Accelerated Cost Recovery System (MACRS). If those systems are used for federal purposes, state adjustments are required to adjust depreciation to the amount allowable under California law. To figure the adjustments, use Form 3885A, which is then used on 540 or 540NR Schedule CA to adjust the taxpayer's income; the specific rules for both ACRS and MACRS should be researched if additional information is necessary to reconcile differences between state and federal regulations.

Accrual Basis Rule

When moving in or out of California, the taxpayer should be sure to apply the accrual basis rule described in FTB 1001 and Instructions FTB Form 3885A. When using the accrual method, the taxpayer should know what the basis is of any and all assets, inventory, and incoming or outgoing cash for the period in which the taxpayer was a resident of California.

California Nonconformity to Depreciation

California does not conform to federal depreciation, which results in numerous substantive changes to both the personal and business tax law. California conforms to federal tax law that was passed as of September 30, 2015. California does not conform to the following federal depreciation changes made after September 30, 2015:

➤ The enhanced IRC Section 179 expensing election.
➤ IRC Section 168(k) relating to the 50% bonus depreciation for certain assets.
➤ The additional first-year depreciation of certain qualified property placed in service after October 3, 2008; and the election to claim additional research and minimum tax credits in lieu of claiming the bonus depreciation.
➤ Zero-Emissions Nuclear Power Production Credit that produces electricity and sold after 12/31/2023 and before 01/01/2033. Inflation Reduction Act.
➤ Nonconformity for the Inflation Reduction Act (IRA) of 2022. The elections related to the beginning of the 12-year period of credit, facility or equipment placed in service after 12/31/2022. This applies to carbon capture equipment. Inflation Reduction Act.
➤ Alternative fuels sold or used beginning on January 1, 2022, and ending on the calendar quarter beginning August 16, 2022, credits are allowed. Refunds or payments attributable to the credits will be determined by the Secretary of the Treasury.
➤ Extensions of Second-Generation Biofuel Incentives after 12/31/2022.

Señor 540 Says: When the taxpayer has depreciation differences, make sure that the differences are tracked. If the taxpayer has a large subtraction from income on 540 Schedule CA, the taxpayer could get a letter from the FTB questioning the difference.

For more information see FTB 1001.

Federal and State Differences for Depreciation Purposes

Use Form FTB 3885A only if there is a difference between the amount of depreciation and amortization allowed as a deduction using California law and the amount allowed using federal law. California and federal law have not always allowed the same depreciation methods, special credits, or accelerated write-offs. As a result, the recovery periods and the basis on which the depreciation is figured for California may be different from the amounts used for federal purposes. There will likely be the following reportable differences if all or part of the assets were placed in service:

➤ Before January 1, 1987: California did not allow depreciation under the federal Accelerated Cost Recovery System (ACRS), and the taxpayer continues to figure California depreciation for those assets in the same manner as in prior years.
➤ On or after January 1, 1987: California provides special credit and accelerated write-offs that affect the California basis of qualifying assets. California did not conform to all changes to federal law enacted in 1993, which causes the California basis or recovery periods to be different for some assets on or after September 11, 2001.
➤ California has not conformed to the federal Job Creation and Worker Assistance Act of 2002, which permits a 30% additional depreciation for federal purposes and allows taxpayers to take an additional first-year depreciation deduction and alternative minimum tax (AMT) depreciation adjustment for property placed in service on or after September 11, 2001.

➢ California generally conforms to the federal 2003 increase (IRC section 280F) for the limitation on luxury automobile depreciation. California does not conform to IRC section 168(k) provisions (30% and 50% additional first-year depreciation). In addition, SUVs and minivans that are built on a truck chassis are not included in the definition of *trucks and vans* when applying the 6,000-pound differences between depreciation on the federal and California gross weight limit. See IRC section 280F.

➢ The TCJA increased the amount of the additional first-year depreciation from 50% to 100% for certain qualified property acquired and placed in service after September 27, 2017, and before January 1, 2023. California did not conform.

Differences may occur for other less common reasons, and the instructions for 540 Schedule CA lists them on the line for the types of income likely to be affected. See FTB Publication 1001 regarding figuring and reporting these adjustments.

Part 1 Review Questions

To obtain the maximum benefit from this chapter, LTP recommends that you complete each of the following questions, and then compare them to the answers with feedback that immediately follow. Under governing self-study standards, vendors are required to present review questions intermittently throughout each self-study course.

These questions and explanations are not part of the final examination and will not be graded by LTP.

CDP1.1
Which form would a California taxpayer use to report the difference in federal and state depreciation?

    a. FTB Form 3885
    b. FTB Form 3885A
    c. FTB Form 3805V
    d. FTB Form 3506

CDP1.2
Federal law allows a taxpayer to claim up to _____ for a Section 179 deduction and California allows the taxpayer to claim up to _____.

    a. $1,050,000/$1,000,000
    b. $1,050,000/$200,000
    c. $1,050,000/$25,000
    d. $2,620,000/$200,000

CDP1.3
Which federal depreciation method does California not conform to?

    a. ACRS
    b. MAGI\
    c. ADR
    d. AMT

CDP1.4

Which federal depreciation method does California not conform to?

a. MAGI
b. ADR
c. MACRS
d. SSA

CDP1.5

California does not conform with which of the following federal items?

a. Gross income
b. Business expenses
c. Bonus depreciation
d. Indirect depreciation

Part 1 Review Questions Answers

CDP1.1

Which form would a California taxpayer use to report the difference in federal and state depreciation?

a. FTB Form 3885
b. FTB Form 3885A
c. FTB Form 3805V
d. FTB Form 3506

Feedback: Review section *Depreciation and Amortization.*

CDP1.2

Federal law allows a taxpayer to claim up to _____ for a Section 179 deduction and California allows the taxpayer to claim up to _____.

a. $1,050,000/$1,000,000
b. $1,050,000/$200,000
c. $1,050,000/$25,000
d. $2,620,000/$200,000

Feedback: Review *Section 179 Expense Deduction.*

CDP1.3

Which federal depreciation method does California not conform to?

a. ACRS
b. MAGI
c. ADR
d. AMT

Feedback: Review *ACRS or MACRS Depreciation.*

CDP1.4
Which federal depreciation method does California not conform to?

    a. MAGI
    b. ADR
    c. MACRS
    d. SSA

Feedback: Review *ACRS or MACRS Depreciation.*

CDP1.5
California does not conform with which of the following federal items?

    a. Gross income
    b. Business expenses
    c. Bonus depreciation
    d. Indirect depreciation

Feedback: Review *California Nonconformity to Depreciation.*

Takeaways

In general, for taxable years on or after January 1, 2015, California law conforms to the Internal Revenue Code. However, there are continuing differences between California and federal law. When California conforms to federal tax law changes, not all the changes have been adopted at the federal level. For more information on depreciation and conformity, see FTB Publication 1001, *Supplemental Guidelines to California Adjustments,* the instructions for California Schedule CA (540 or 540NR), and the Business Entity tax booklets.

TEST YOUR KNOWLEDGE!
Go online to take a practice quiz.

Chapter 13 Capital Gains and Losses

Introduction

Almost everything a taxpayer owns and uses for personal or investment purposes is a capital asset. When a capital asset is sold, the difference between the basis in the asset and the amount the item is sold for is either a capital gain or a capital loss. A capital gain is the profit that results from selling an investment (stocks, bonds, or real estate) for a higher price than it was purchased. Capital gains may refer to investment income that arises in relation to real assets (such as property), financial assets (such as shares of stocks or bonds), and intangible assets (such as goodwill). A capital loss arises if the proceeds from the sale of a capital asset are less than the purchase price. The taxpayer can deduct up to a $3,000 loss ($1,500 if filing MFS). The capital loss that exceeds the limit amount may be taken in future years.

Objectives

At the end of this lesson, the student will:

➢ Explain the holding periods for different types of property.
➢ Understand the difference between short-term and long-term capital gains.
➢ Identify capital assets.
➢ Determine basis before selling an asset.
➢ Establish when the primary residence is excluded from capital gain.

Resources

Form 1040	Publication 17	Instructions Form 1040
Form 1099-B	Publication 523	Instructions Form 1099-B
Form 4797	Publication 544	Instructions Form 4797
Form 6252	Publication 551	Instructions Form 6252
Form 8949	Tax Topic 409, 703	Instructions Form 8949
Schedule D		Instructions for Schedule D

Table of Contents

Part 1 Capital Assets

Capital assets are items held for personal use, pleasure, or investment purposes. Some examples of capital assets are:

> ➤ Stocks or bonds held in a personal account.
> ➤ A house owned and used by the taxpayer and family.
> ➤ Household furnishings.
> ➤ A car used for pleasure and/or work.
> ➤ Coin or stamp collections.
> ➤ Gems and jewelry.
> ➤ Gold, silver, or other metal types.
> ➤ Timber grown on taxpayer personal property or investment property.

A capital asset can be any property held by the taxpayer; however, the following would be considered noncapital assets:

> ➤ Property held mainly for sale to customers or property that will physically become a part of merchandise for sale to customers (e.g., inventory).
> ➤ Depreciable property used in trade or business, even if 100% depreciated.
> ➤ Real property used in trade or business.
> ➤ Accounts or notes receivable acquired in the ordinary course of a trade or business for services rendered, or the sale of stock in trade or other property included in inventory.
> ➤ A copyright, a literary, musical, or artistic composition, a letter or memorandum, or a similar property that is as follows:
>> o Created by personal efforts.
>> o Prepared or produced for the taxpayer in the case of a letter, memorandum, or similar property.
>> o Received from an individual who created the property or for whom the property was prepared under circumstances entitling the taxpayer to the basis of the person who created the property, or for whom it was prepared or produced.
> ➤ U.S. government publications received from the government for free or for less than the normal sales price.
> ➤ Any financial instruments for commodities derivative held by a commodities derivatives dealer.
> ➤ Hedge fund transactions, but only if the transaction is clearly identified as a hedging transaction before the close of the day on which it was acquired or originated.
> ➤ Supplies of a type regularly used or consumed in the ordinary course of trade or business.

> ➤ Property deducted under the de minimis safe harbor for tangible property.

The rate at which the gain on the sale of a capital asset will be taxed depends on the type of capital asset, the holding period, and the taxpayer's tax bracket. If the taxpayer has a capital loss, the loss will be netted against any realized gain. If the taxpayer has a net loss in excess of $3,000, he or she will be able to deduct up to $3,000 of the loss against the taxpayer's ordinary income in the year of the sale. The unused capital loss would then be carried forward to subsequent years and used to help offset net capital gains or ordinary income up to $3,000 a year until the loss is depleted. If the taxpayer is filing as Married filing separately, the limit is $1,500.

Basis of Property

Basis is a way of determining the cost of an investment in property and is decided by how it was acquired. If the property was purchased, the purchase price is the basis. Any improvements made to the property are then added to that basis. The purchase price plus improvements constitutes the adjusted basis. Other items that add to the basis are the expenses of acquiring the property (commissions, sales tax, and freight charges). There are also items that reduce the basis, which include depreciation, nontaxable distributions, and postponed gain on home sales. This is also referred to as cost basis.

Basis is the amount of the investment in the asset for tax purposes. To calculate the gain or loss, basis is needed on the sale or disposition of the asset. Recordkeeping must be accurate to adjust the basis of the property when it is sold.

If a single transaction includes multiple properties, the total cost must be allocated among the separate properties according to the fair market value established by each property's basis. As a result of the allocation, the basis that each property takes is the original unadjusted basis for tax purposes. This rule applies in determining basis for depreciation purposes or a gain or loss, on a transaction.

Holding Period

The holding period (the length of time an individual "held" or owned a property) determines whether the capital gain or loss is short-term or long-term. To determine the holding period, start counting on the day after the date the taxpayer acquired the property. Holding periods end on the day the taxpayer sold the property. Short-term property is property held for one year (365 days) or less. Long-term property is property held for more than one year. For example, if the taxpayer purchased property on September 20, 2021, and sold it on September 20, 2022, the taxpayer would have a short-term capital gain or loss. However, if the taxpayer waited one more day and sold the property on September 21, 2022, the transaction would be a long-term capital gain or loss. It is important to correctly determine the holding period because the maximum tax rate is based on the holding period. To calculate the total net gain or loss, combine the net short-term gains or losses with the net long-term gains or losses.

Capital Gains Distributions

Capital gains distributions are paid to the taxpayer by brokerage firms, mutual funds, and investment trusts. The capital gains distributions from mutual funds are long-term capital gains regardless of how long the taxpayer owned the stock. Distributions of net-realized short-term capital gains are reported on Form 1099-DIV as ordinary dividends.

Adjusted Basis

To arrive at the adjusted basis, the taxpayer must make allowable adjustments to the basis of the property. The taxpayer would figure the gain or loss on a sale, exchange, or other disposition of property, or would figure the allowable depreciation, depletion, or amortization. The result is the property's adjusted basis.

Increases to Basis

To increase the property basis, the improvements must have a useful life of more than 1 year. Examples of capital improvements that would increase the property basis are an addition to the primary home, replacing the entire roof, and paving the driveway. Each one of these items may have a different class life for depreciation. Each would have to be depreciated by the rules for their property. Each depreciation class should have a separate set of recordkeeping.

Decreases to Basis

There are certain items that will cause the property to decrease its basis. Those items include certain vehicle credits, IRC section 179 deductions, residential energy credits, casualty and theft losses, and insurance reimbursement. See Publication 551.

Determining Capital Gains and Losses

Capital gains or losses are either short-term or long-term. If the property was disposed of and it was inherited, the basis is generally the fair market value of the property at the date of the owner's death. Nonbusiness bad debt is treated as a short-term capital loss.

Form 1099-DIV

The reported amount is found on Form 1099-DIV, box 2a, and entered on Schedule D, line 13, no matter how long the investment was held. The amount in box 2b is reported on line 11 of the *Unrecaptured Section 1250 Gain Worksheet.* The amount in 2c is reported on *Exclusion of Gain on Qualified Small Business Stock* (QSB). The amount in 2d is reported on line 4 of the *28% Rate Gain Worksheet.*

If the taxpayer earns dividends from an account that is held by a commercial company even though the account is held in the taxpayer's name, the commercial account will distribute Form 1099-DIV to the taxpayer in the amount of their capital gains distributions. This transaction is reported on Schedule D, line 13.

Sale of Stocks and Mutual Funds

The taxpayer should receive Form 1099-B, which reports the total proceeds from the sale of stock or mutual funds. The proceeds are reported on Form 8949.

To determine the capital gain on stocks or mutual funds, the taxpayer must know the cost basis. The cost basis is the purchase price plus any costs related to its purchase and/or to any paid commissions. The cost basis is subtracted from the selling price to determine the capital gains. This information, along with the purchase date and sales date, is included on Form 8949. The trade date—not the settlement date—is used to determine whether the transaction is long-term or short-term.

The cost basis of a mutual fund is the cash investment amount plus any reinvested dividends and capital gains minus any returns of capital that were received. If it is less than the entire value of the funds sold, then one must figure the cost basis of the shares sold. To use the average cost per share, the taxpayer must have acquired the shares at various times and various prices and must have left the shares on deposit in an account that is handled by a custodian or agent who acquires or redeems those shares.

Sale of Personal Residence

The Taxpayer Relief Act of 1997 repealed IRC section 1034, *Deferral of Gain on Sale of Residence*, and amended section 121, *The Once-in-a-Lifetime Exclusion of Gain*. Previously, IRC section 1034 allowed taxpayers to defer the gain on the sale of a principal residence if a replacement residence was purchased within two years and if the replacement residence's price was equal to or exceeded the adjusted selling price of the former residence. Now, however, the current law under IRC section 121 is considerably more generous. The sale of the primary residence is reported on the taxpayer's tax return only if there is a taxable gain or if the property was used for business.

To qualify for the exclusion, the taxpayer must meet the following "ownership and use" tests during the last five-year period ending on the date of the sale:

  ➢ Owned the home for at least two years (the ownership test).
  ➢ Lived in the home as the main home for at least two years (the use test).

A taxpayer can meet the ownership and use test during different two-year periods if they meet both tests during the five years before the date of the sale.

Exclusion

If all the following are true, a taxpayer can exclude the entire gain of the sale of their main home up to $250,000 or up to $500,000 if Married Filing Jointly or a Surviving Spouse:

➢ The taxpayer is married and filing a joint return for the year.
➢ Either the taxpayer or the spouse meets the ownership test.
➢ Both the taxpayer and the spouse meet the use test.

If the taxpayer's divorce decree allows the taxpayer's former spouse to live in the home the taxpayer owns, the taxpayer is considered to have also lived there for the purposes of claiming the exclusion. The exclusion is limited to one sale every two years on sales after May 6, 1997.

Other Facts and Circumstances for a Partial Exclusion

The amount of gain a taxpayer can exclude must be prorated if the sale of a home is due to a job relocation, health reasons, or other unforeseen circumstances of the homeowner (or the homeowner's spouse if they file a joint return), and if any the following are also true:

➢ Both spouses meet the residence and look-back requirements and one or both spouses meet the ownership requirement.
➢ Taxpayer meets the residence, ownership, and look-back requirements.
➢ A widow(er) taxpayer:
   1. Sells the home within 2 years of the spouses' death.
   2. Widow(er) has not remarried when the house is sold.
   3. Neither the spouse nor the late spouse has taken the home exclusion in the past 2 years before the current home sale.
   4. The taxpayer meets the 2-year ownership and residence requirements (including the late spouse's times of ownership and residence, if relevant).

Use worksheet in Publication 523, to determine if the taxpayer qualifies.

Sales of residences other than the taxpayer's main residence are treated differently than sales of primary residences for tax purposes. If the taxpayer sells a residence that is not their principal residence, a capital gain or loss would be reported on Form 8949. While a loss on a main residence is not deductible, a loss on a residential rental house may be deductible.

Because the exclusion only pertains to residences, if the taxpayer used part of their home for business or rental purposes, some of the gain may not qualify for the exclusion. Any gain due to depreciation claimed after May 6, 1997, cannot be excluded.

Example: Bill Burns had taken depreciation in prior years for an office in the home before changing it back to a bedroom and using it for personal purposes for two out of the five years prior the sale. In this instance, Mr. Burns can exclude all the gain from the sale of the house, except for gain from depreciation after May 6, 1997.

If the taxpayer cannot exclude all of the gain, you would treat the sale as two transactions: one business and one personal.

Example: On February 1, 2019, Amy bought a house. She moved in on that date and lived in it until May 31, 2020, when she moved out of the house and put it up for rent. The house was rented from June 1, 2020 to March 31, 2021. Amy moved back into the house on April 1, 2021, and lived there until she sold it on January 31, 2022. During the five-year period ending on the date of the sale (February 1, 2019 to January 31, 2022), Amy owned and lived in the house for more than two years.

Five-Year Period	Used as Home		Used as Rental
2/1/19 – 5/31/20	16 months		
6/1/20 – 3/31/21			10 months
4/1/21 – 1/31/22	10 months		
	26 months		10 months

Because she lived in the home for more than two years, Amy can exclude gain up to $250,000. However, as mentioned above, she cannot exclude the part of the gain equal to the depreciation she claimed for renting the house after May 6, 1997.

Surviving Spouse Taxpayer

The Mortgage Forgiveness Debt Relief Act of 2007 allows a surviving spouse to exclude up to $500,000 of the gain from the sale of a principal residence owned jointly. The sale needs to occur within two years from the death of the spouse. Exceptions apply.

Incapacitated Taxpayers

Taxpayers who own a residence are still considered to reside in that residence even if they become physically or mentally incapable of self-care and are placed in a care facility licensed by a state or governmental subdivision such as a nursing home. However, the taxpayer must have owned and used the residence as a principal residence for a period of at least one year during the five years preceding the sale to qualify for IRC section 121 exclusion.

Divorced Taxpayers

If the taxpayer is divorced, and the primary residence is transferred to the taxpayer, the time during which the taxpayer's former spouse owned the residence is added to the taxpayer's period of ownership. A taxpayer who owns a residence is considered to have used it as a principal residence while the taxpayer's spouse or former spouse is granted use of the residence under the terms of the divorce or separation instrument.

Calculating the Sales Price

Anytime the taxpayer sells a home, land, stock, or other security, the taxpayer will receive either Form 1099-S, *Proceeds from Real Estate Transactions*, or Form 1099-B, *Proceeds from Broker and Barter Exchange Transactions*.

Forms 1099-S and 1099-B are "reporting documents" that provide the gross proceeds or sales price. If the taxpayer sold one stock several times, Form 1099-B might only report the gross proceeds together. The taxpayer can divide the gross proceeds by the total number of shares sold to arrive at an average price per share. The taxpayer can then multiply the price per share by the number of shares sold on each occasion to arrive at the sales price.

Installment Sales

An installment sale is a sale of property in which the taxpayer receives a payment after one year of the sale. An installment sale is an arrangement where some or the entire selling price is paid in a later year. Owners who sell homes and finance the purchase themselves often do so as an installment sale. This is beneficial because the taxpayer does not have to pay taxes on the entire gain in the year of sale. It can also benefit the taxpayer by keeping the gain from pushing them into a higher tax bracket. For taxpayers looking for a steady stream of income over a period of time, the installment sale can provide this income.

The gain from an installment sale is usually reported in the year it is received. However, the taxpayer can elect to report all of the gain in the year of sale, which can be beneficial if the taxpayer had other capital losses to offset the gain. The income from the sale is reported on Form 6252, *Installment Sale Income.* Interest income is reported on Schedule B as it is received. The gain is reported on Form 4797 if it is a business gain. Personal gain is reported on Form 8949.

If a taxpayer has a loss, it cannot be reported as an installment sale. Personal losses are not deductible. If it is a business loss, the entire loss will be reported on Form 4797 in the year of the sale. The interest earned is still reported on Schedule B.

Inherited Property

The basis of inherited property is the property's fair market value (FMV) at the date of death or at an alternate valuation date if chosen by the executor of the estate. The election to use the alternate valuation date is irrevocable. The alternate date is generally six months after the decedent's death or some earlier date of sale or distribution. Alternate valuation can be elected only if the property use decreased both the value of the gross estate and the combined estate and a generation-skipping transfer of tax liability. The holding period is always considered long-term regardless of how long the taxpayer actually owned the property because it includes the holding period of the deceased.

Gift of Property

To determine the basis of property received as a gift, it is necessary to know the donor's adjusted basis of the gift when given to the taxpayer, the fair market value at the time it was given to the taxpayer, and the amount of gift tax that was paid. The taxpayer's basis for figuring gain at the time of the sale or for figuring the disposition of the asset at the time of the sale is the donor's adjusted basis, plus or minus any changes during the period the taxpayer held the property. The taxpayer's basis for figuring loss is the fair market value when received, plus or minus any required adjustments to the basis made during the period the taxpayer held the asset.

The amount of paid gift tax to be included in the basis of the asset depends on the date the gift was received.

Example: Jess received an acre of land as a gift. At the time the gift was given, the land had a fair market value of $8,000. Ezra purchased the land for $10,000, making the property's adjusted basis. Jess received the property; no events occurred to increase or decrease the basis. Jess is thinking of selling the property for $12,000; if Jess sells the land, he will have a $2,000 gain. Jess must use Ezra's adjusted basis ($10,000) at the time of the gift as the basis to figure gain. If Jess sells the property for $7,000, he will have a $1,000 loss because he must use the fair market value ($8,000) at the time of the gift to figure loss. If the sales price is between $8,000 and $10,000, he will have neither a gain nor a loss.

Form 8949: Reporting Capital Gains and Losses

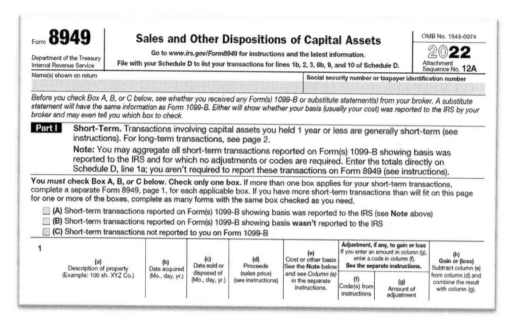

Portion of Form 8949

Form 8949 is used to report the sales and exchanges of capital assets. It also allows the taxpayer and the IRS to reconcile what has been reported to the IRS on Forms 1099-B or 1099-S.

Individual taxpayers report the following information on Form 8949:

➢ The sale or exchange of a capital asset.
➢ Gains from involuntary conversions.
➢ Nonbusiness bad debts.
➢ Worthless stocks or bonds.

When using Form 8949, the taxpayer separates the short-term and long-term capital gains and losses. If the disposed property was inherited, it is treated as a long-term asset. Remember, when figuring the holding period, the calculation starts one day after the property has been received. Short-term losses and gains are reported on Form 8949, Part I. Long-term losses and gains are reported on Form 8949, Part II.

Example: Rachel purchased 300 shares of Imperial Soap for $1,000. She sold the stock this year for $1,200. Rachel realized a gain of $200, not the $1,200 in proceeds she received from the sale. Only the $200 is included in gross income since the $1,000 is Rachel's return of capital.

Codes for Form 8949

Below are the definitions that tell the IRS if the sale was a short-term or long-term. The codes also determine if the asset basis was reported to the IRS or not. The taxpayer received either Form 1099-B or a substitute statement with the codes. These codes are used for Box A-F on Form 8949.

A   Short-term basis reported to the IRS.

B   Short-term basis not reported to the IRS.

C   Short-term basis not reported on Form 1099-B.

D   Long-term basis reported to the IRS.

E   Long-term basis not reported to the IRS.

Capital Assets Held for Personal Use

When a taxpayer sells their primary residence, it could be a reportable transaction. Factors that could trigger the transaction are:

1. Sales amount
2. Filing status
3. Claiming a portion of the house as a home office.

If the taxpayer and spouse sold their primary residence and the gain was over $500,000 ($250,000 all other filing status) the amount is reported on Schedule D. If the gain is less than $500,000 ($250,000 all other filing status) it may not be taxable. See IRC section 121.

If the taxpayer converted the depreciable property to personal use, all or part of the gain on the sale or exchange would be recaptured as ordinary income. Recaptured means the gain realized by the sale of capital property that is depreciable and must be reported. A loss from the sale or exchange of personal use asset is not deductible.

Example: Sally sold her main home in 2022 for $320,000 and received Form 1099-S showing the $320,000 gross proceeds. The selling expense was $20,000 and her home basis was $100,000. Sally would be able to exclude the entire $200,000 gain from her income.

$ 320,000	Sales price
– $ 100,000	Basis
– $ 20,000	Selling expenses
$ 200,000	**Capital gain (excluded from income)**

Digital Assets

The IRS defines "virtual currency" (VC) as a digital representation of value that functions as a medium of exchange, a unit of account and a store of value other than a representation of the United States dollar or a foreign currency. Convertible virtual currency is virtual currency (VC) that has an equivalent value in real currency, or that acts as a substitute for real currency. Cryptocurrency is generally referred to as coins or tokens and is a type of virtual currency that utilizes cryptography to secure transactions that are digitally recorded on a distributed ledger, such as a blockchain. A taxpayer has gross income when the individual receives the cryptocurrency (i.e., recorded on the distributed ledger) and has dominion and control over it.

Virtual currency received as payment for goods or services is considered income equal to the fair market value (FMV) on the date received. Payment by virtual currency is included as income, the FMV is determined by the United States dollar (USD). Employers paying VC as compensation for services constitute wages for employment tax purposes and is subject to Federal tax withholding. VC payments are subject to the same information reporting as other payments (e.g., Forms W-2, 1099, 1042 – Misc., etc.). See Notice 2014-21, 2014-16, and IRB 938.

Payments made by VC are subject to back-up withholding rules to the same extent as other payments. A taxpayer who successfully "mines" virtual currency has gross income equal to the fair market value of the virtual currency as of the date of receipt.

Form 1040 has a question that is to be asked of all taxpayers: "did you receive, sell, exchange, or otherwise dispose of any financial interest in any virtual currency?"

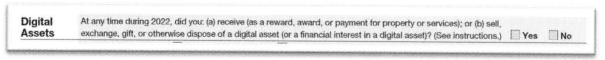

Portion of Form 1040

As the tax professional, do not assume the answer is no; ask the taxpayer and mark the appropriate box, based on their answer.

Not reporting the sale or exchange of virtual currencies could resort in a tax consequence. See Publication 544.

Part 1 Review Questions

To obtain the maximum benefit from this chapter, LTP recommends that you complete each of the following questions, and then compare them to the answers with feedback that immediately follow. Under governing self-study standards, vendors are required to present review questions intermittently throughout each self-study course.

These questions and explanations are not part of the final examination and will not be graded by LTP.

CGLP1.1
Which scenario could make a taxpayer pay a capital gains tax on their primary residence?

 a. The taxpayer lived in the main house for two of the last five years.
 b. The taxpayer's gain on his primary residence is less than $250,000.
 c. The taxpayer and his or her spouse have lived in the house for two of the last five years.
 d. The taxpayer sold the house in 18 months because they found a house they liked more.

CGLP1.2
Which of the following best describes basis?

 a. Basis is the amount of investment in the asset for tax purposes.
 b. Basis includes inventory.
 c. Basis includes land.
 d. Basis is a capital asset.

CGLP1.3
Is virtual currency subject to back-up withholding?

 a. True
 b. False

CGLP1.4
James was paid in virtual currency by his employer. How does he report the income?

    a. James does not have to claim virtual currency as income.
    b. James needs to report the payment as the fair market value on the date received.

Part 1 Review Questions Answers

CGLP1.1
Which scenario could make a taxpayer pay a capital gains tax on their primary residence?

    a. The taxpayer lived in the main house for two of the last five years.
    b. The taxpayer's gain on his primary residence is less than $250,000.
    c. The taxpayer and his or her spouse have lived in the house for two of the last five years.
    d. The taxpayer sold the house in 18 months because they found a house they liked more.

Feedback: Review section *Sale of Personal Residence.*

CGLP1.2
Which of the following best describes basis?

    a. Basis is the amount of investment in the asset for tax purposes.
    b. Basis includes inventory.
    c. Basis includes land.
    d. Basis is a capital asset.

Feedback: Review section *Basis of Property.*

CGLP1.3
Is virtual currency subject to back-up withholding?

    a. True
    b. False

Feedback: Review section *Virtual Currency.*

CGLP1.4
James was paid in virtual currency by his employer. How does he report the income?

    a. James does not have to claim virtual currency as income.
    b. James needs to report the payment as the fair market value on the date received.

Feedback: Review section *Digital Assets.*

Takeaways

The original basis for property is its cost, except as otherwise provided by law. The cost is the amount paid for such property in cash or other property. The basis includes acquisition costs such as commissions, legal fees, recording fees, and sales taxes, as well as installation and delivery costs. The cost of property includes not only the amount of money or other property paid, but also the amount of paid mortgage or liability costs in connection with the purchase. It makes no difference whether the taxpayer assumes the liability by taking over the payments or merely purchases the property at the asking price. When the property is disposed, any remaining amount of mortgage or liability of which the seller is relieved is treated as part of the amount realized. Real estate taxes are included as part of the property's basis if the buyer assumes the seller's obligation to pay them.

Capital gains and losses are classified as long-term or short-term. If the asset has been held for more than one year before the asset was disposed, it is considered to be a long-term capital gain or loss. If the asset is held for less than one year, it is considered a short-term capital gain or loss.

TEST YOUR KNOWLEDGE!
Go online to take a practice quiz.

California Capital Gains and Loss

Introduction

California law complies with federal law regarding capital gains and losses and requires no adjustments to complete the state return. If the California basis of the taxpayer's assets differs from the federal, adjustments would be required using the California Schedule D. The amount of capital loss limitation for California taxpayers is also the same as the federal limitation. Depending on the taxpayer's California tax bracket their capital gains tax could be 1% to 13.3%.

Objectives

At the end of this lesson, the student will:

> ➢ Recognize the basis difference between federal and California laws.
> ➢ Understand how California treats the sale of a taxpayer's primary residence.
> ➢ Know the state withholding rate for sales of real property.

Resources

FTB Form 593-I	FTB Publication 1004	Instructions Form 593-I
FTB Form 593-C	FTB Publication 1016	Instructions Form 593-C
FTB 593-E Booklet	FTB Publication 1017	Instructions Form 3805-E
FTB Form 3805-E	Schedule D (540 or 540NR)	Instructions Schedule D (540 or 540NR)

Table of Contents

Part 1 Sales and Property

Sale or Exchange of Personal Residence

For sales or exchanges after May 6, 1997, federal law allows an exclusion of gain on the sale of a personal residence in the amount of $250,000 or $500,000 if Married Filing Jointly. The taxpayer must have owned and occupied the residence as a personal residence for at least two of the last five years before the sale. California conforms to this provision.

If there is a difference between the amounts excluded (or depreciated, if recapture applies) for federal and state purposes, complete 540 or 540NR California Schedule D to reconcile the differences. To calculate the taxpayer's total income, transfer the reconciled amount from California Schedule D to 540 or 540NR Schedule CA.

What is Recapture?

Recapture refers to a situation in which a taxpayer must add back a deduction that was taken in a prior year.

Installment Sales

Under the installment method, gains are reported in periods subsequent to the year of sale. In contrast, the entire gross receipts from installment sales are included in the sales factor in the year of sale. In the subsequent periods when the gains from the installment sales are recognized, those gains are apportioned using the factors from the year of sale. The taxpayer should use Form FTB 3805-E to report an installment sale.

The taxpayer must allow for withholding on an installment sale; the seller is to withhold from each payment based on the principal portion received. The FTB requires the seller to report the installment sale income and claim the related withholding credit in each year that installment payments have been received.

Inherited Property

Capital gains or losses on inherited property prior to January 1, 1987, may have a depreciation difference on the federal return. For property that was inherited on or after January 1, 1987, the depreciation will be the same as the federal tax return. Report the amount of California capital gains and losses on 540 or 540NR California Schedule D.

If a taxpayer inherited real property, the fair market value of the property on date of death is now the property value for the taxpayer. For example, Paul and Jim inherited their parents' house on their date of death. Their parents purchased the home in 1962 for $21,000. The fair market value, at date of death, was $525,000. That is the new basis for Jim and Paul. California does not have an inheritance tax.

Withholding on Resident and Nonresident Sales of Real Property

Every time that real property has a transfer of title, California law requires withholding. The buyer, qualified intermediary (QI), or the real estate escrow person (REEP) are the party responsible for the withholding. The qualified intermediary is also known as an accommodator or buyer. The real estate escrow person refers to any attorney, escrow company, or title company responsible for closing the transaction. Like any law, there are exceptions to the withholding rule. If any of the following apply, real estate withholding is not required on the transfer of title.

- ➢ The total sales price is $100,000 or less.
- ➢ Multiple sellers are involved in the transaction; the withholding is determined by the total sales price, not by the individual seller's portion.
- ➢ The sales of multiple parcels or family units (such as triplex or duplex) are considered one transaction. Withholding is required when the combined sales amount is $100,000.
- ➢ The property is being foreclosed upon in any of the following ways:
    - o Sold according to a power of sale under a mortgage or deed of trust.
    - o Sold according to a decree of foreclosure.
    - o Acquired a deed in place of foreclosure.
- ➢ The transferor is a bank acting as a trustee and not a deed of trust.
- ➢ The seller or transferor certifies that there is an exemption on Form 593-C.

Real Estate Foreclosures and Short-Sale Transactions

Withholding is required for real estate foreclosures and short-sale transactions unless any exemptions certified on Form 593-C apply or if the sale qualifies for one of the following exclusions:

- ➢ The total sale price is $100,000 or less.
- ➢ The seller is a bank acting as a trustee, other than a trustee of a deed of trust.
- ➢ The buyer is acquiring the property as part of a foreclosure.

In the case of a foreclosure, the buyer must acquire the property under one of the following conditions for the seller to be excluded from withholding:

- ➢ A power of sale required under a mortgage or deed of trust.
- ➢ A decree requiring foreclosure.
- ➢ A deed in lieu of foreclosure.

Withholding Rates

California requires a withholding of 3.33% of the total sales price on all real estate transactions. The taxpayer may elect to withhold on the gain of the sale and apply the following applicable rates:

- ➢ 12.3% for individuals, non-California partnerships, and trusts, grantor or non-grantor.
- ➢ 8.84% for corporations.
- ➢ 10.84% for banks and financial corporations.
- ➢ 13.8% for S corporations.
- ➢ 15.8% for financial S corporations.

Certain sellers may be exempt from the withholding. See Instructions Form 593-C.

Stocks and Capital Changes

Qualifying or Disqualifying Dispositions

If the taxpayer exercises an option under an employee stock purchase plan while a nonresident and then later sells the stock in a qualifying or disqualifying disposition after becoming a California resident, the ordinary income and capital gain are taxable by California. See FTB Publication 1004.

Example: On March 5, 2010, Mark was a resident of New York, and his employer granted him options at a discount under the employee stock option plan. On March 5, 2021, Mark exercised his options. On December 2, 2021, Mark permanently moved to California; and on April 1, 2022, he sold the options for a gain. California will tax the ordinary income and capital gain because Mark was a California resident when the stock was sold. If Mark pays New York taxes, California may allow a credit against his California taxes for the taxes Mark paid to New York on the double-taxed ordinary income.

California Qualified Stock Options

California Revenue and Taxation Code (R&TC) section 17502 states that a stock option specifically designated as *California qualified* will receive the favorable tax treatment applicable to incentivize stock options and employee stock purchase plans. To receive this treatment, the following conditions must be met:

- ➢ The option was issued after January 1, 1997, and before January 1, 2002.
- ➢ The earned income of the employee to whom the option was issued did not exceed $40,000 in the tax year in which the option was issued.
- ➢ The number of shares of stock granted under the option does not exceed 1,000 units and the value of the shares does not exceed $100,000.
- ➢ The employee must be employed by the company at the time the option was granted or must have been employed within three months (one year if permanently disabled) of the date the option was granted.

If section 17502's provisions of R&TC are met, federal law treats a California qualified stock option as a non-statutory stock option (stock purchased in a company that is not on the open market). The taxpayer would make an adjustment to their federal adjusted gross income for the California qualified stock option wage income included on their federal return and on the California return by using 540 or 540NR Schedule CA. In the year in which the taxpayer sells the stock, the individual should report any capital gain or loss differences on California Schedule D, *California Capital Gain or Loss Adjustment*. If the provisions of R&TC section 17502 are not met, the stock option is treated as a non-statutory stock option.

Exclusion of Deferral and Gain on the Sale of Qualified Small Business Stock

Under IRC section 1045 as well as IRC section 1202, the federal code allows deferral and exclusion of 100% of the gain on the sale of qualifying small business stock originally issued after August 10, 1993, that was held for more than five years. California does not conform to this provision. To report the exclusion and deferral from the federal return, use 540 or 540NR California Schedule D.

Undistributed Capital Gains for Regulated Investment Company (RIC) Shareholders

Federal law requires certain undistributed capital gains reported on federal Form 2439 to be included in the gross income of the mutual fund shareholder and allows a tax credit for the capital gains tax to be paid for by the regulated investment company. California does not have a similar provision. Do not enter the amount of undistributed capital gains on 540 or 540NR California Schedule D. Instead enter the amount of distributed capital gain dividends. California taxes the undistributed capital gain from a Regulated Investment Company (RIC) in the year distributed rather than in the year earned.

Part 1 Review Questions

To obtain the maximum benefit from this chapter, LTP recommends that you complete each of the following questions, and then compare them to the answers with feedback that immediately follow. Under governing self-study standards, vendors are required to present review questions intermittently throughout each self-study course.

These questions and explanations are not part of the final examination and will not be graded by LTP.

CCGLP1.1
Who is responsible for withholding on a nonresident California real estate sale?

    a. Buyer
    b. Seller
    c. Title company
    d. Real estate professional

CCGLP1.2
Hunter and Julie inherited a house from Julie's grandmother on her date of death. What is their tax consequence on this transaction?

    a. Hunter and Julie may not have any tax consequence since the house is inherited.
    b. Hunter and Julie would have a tax consequence since the house is inherited.
    c. Hunter and Julie would need to divide the proceeds of the inherited house.
    d. Hunter and Julie would be able to purchase another house in two years from her grandmother's date of death.

CCGLP1.3
What is the withholding rate on California real estate sales for nonresidents?

    a. 3.33%
    b. 1.5%
    c. 7%
    d. 6.25%

CCGLP1.4
If the total sales price exceeds a certain amount; California real estate withholding is required. What is the amount?

    a. $10,000
    b. $100,000
    c. $250,000
    d. $1,000,000

CCGLP1.5
Which of the following best describes when the taxpayer would need to complete California Schedule D?

    a. Sergio sold an asset where the federal capital gain was the same as California.
    b. Enrique sold an asset where the federal capital loss was different than California.
    c. Jan sold a capital asset where the federal capital loss was the same as California.
    d. Yesenia sold her rental home in California for a loss.

Part 1 Review Questions Answers

CCGLP1.1
Who is responsible for withholding on a nonresident California real estate sale?

    a. Buyer
    b. Seller
    c. Title company
    d. Real estate professional

Feedback: Review section *Withholding on Resident and Nonresident Sales of Real Property*.

CCGLP1.2
Hunter and Julie inherited a house from Julie's grandmother on her date of death. What is their tax consequence on this transaction?

    a. Hunter and Julie may not have a tax consequence since the house is inherited.
    b. Hunter and Julie would have a tax consequence since the house is inherited.
    c. Hunter and Julie would need to divide the proceeds of the inherited house.
    d. Hunter and Julie would be able to purchase another house in two years from her grandmother's date of death.

Feedback: Review section *Inherited Property*.

CCGLP1.3
What is the withholding rate on California real estate sales for nonresidents?

    a. 3.33%
    b. 1.5%
    c. 7%
    d. 6.25%

Feedback: Review section *Withholding on Resident and Nonresident Sales of Real Property*.

CCGLP1.4
If the total sales price exceeds _____; California real estate withholding is required. What is the amount?

    a. $10,000
    b. $100,000
    c. $250,000
    d. $1,000,000

Feedback: Review section *Withholding on Resident and Nonresident Sales of Real Property*.

CCGLP1.5

Which of the following best describes when the taxpayer would need to complete California Schedule D?

    a. Sergio sold an asset where the federal capital gain was the same as California.
    b. Enrique sold an asset where the federal capital loss was different than California.
    c. Jan sold a capital asset where the federal capital loss was the same as California.
    d. Yesenia sold her rental home in California for a loss.
    e. Yesenia sold a capital gain was not different than California.

Feedback: Review section *California Qualified Stock Options*.

Takeaways

The reduction of a previously reported capital gain is a capital loss subject to the same limitations as other capital losses. California law generally follows federal law with respect to basis. To report sales or exchanges of property other than capital assets, including the sale or exchange used in a trade or business and involuntary conversions (other than casualties and thefts), use California Schedule D-1, *Sales of Business Property*. California does not have a special capital gain tax rate. California basis may be different from the federal return based on the differences in the federal and state law, which will affect the gain or loss on a disposition.

TEST YOUR KNOWLEDGE!
Go online to take a practice quiz.

Chapter 14 Extensions and Amendments

Introduction

If taxpayers are unable to file their federal individual tax returns by the due date, they may be able to qualify for an automatic six-month extension of time to file. The taxpayer can either electronically file or mail Form 4868 to the IRS to file for the extension. If the taxpayer has filed a return and realizes that a mistake was made, they would file an amended return by using Form 1040-X.

Objectives

At the end of this lesson, the student will:

➢ Realize when to use Form 4868.
➢ Understand when an amendment must be filed.
➢ Identify when the installment agreement should be used.

Resources

Form 1040	Publication 17	Instructions Form 1040
Form 1040-X	Publication 54	Instructions Form 1040-X
Form 4868	Tax Topic 308	Instructions Form 4868
Form 9465		Instructions Form 9465
Form 13884		Instructions Form 13844

Table of Contents

Part 1 Form 4868: Extension of Time to File

File Form 4868, *Application for Automatic Extension*, to file for an automatic six-month extension for filing a federal return. The extension is for filing the tax return only. If the taxpayer has a balance due, the payment must be paid by April 15 or the due date of the return. There are three ways to request an automatic extension:

> ➢ File Form 4868 electronically.
> ➢ Pay all or part of the estimated income tax due using the Electronic Federal Tax Payment System (EFTPS) or a credit or debit card.
> ➢ Mail Form 4868 to the IRS and enclose the tax payment.

To qualify for the extension for extra time, taxpayers must estimate their tax liability as accurately as possible and enter it on Form 4868, line 4, before filing Form 4868 by the regular due date of the return. If the IRS does not accept the extension of time, the taxpayer will receive a letter of denial stating the need to file his or her tax return and how much time they have to file. If the application was accepted, the taxpayer can file any time prior to the extension's due date.

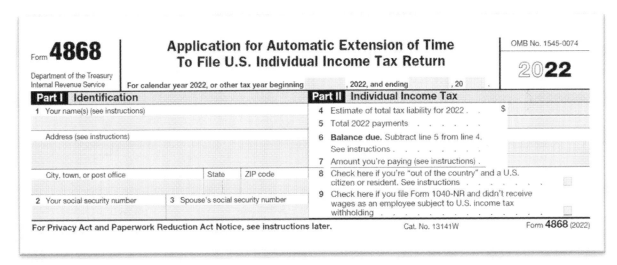

Form 4868

If the taxpayer, who is a U.S. citizen or resident, is out of the country, the extension is valid for four months. Part I of Form 4868 is used to identify the taxpayer. Part II is for information about how the tax return should be filed.

Late Payment Penalty

The taxpayer may be charged a late payment penalty of $\frac{1}{2}$% of 1% of any tax (except estimated tax) not paid by the regular filing deadline. An additional monthly penalty with a maximum rate of 25% of the unpaid amount is charged on any unpaid tax. If the taxpayer can show reasonable cause for not paying on time, a statement should be attached to the return (not to Form 4868), and the late penalty payment will not be charged. Both of the following requirements must be met to be considered reasonable cause:

> ➢ Paid at least 90% of the tax liability before the regular due date of the return via withholding, estimated payments, or payments made with Form 4868.
> ➢ The remaining balance is paid with tax return on the extended due date.

If the taxpayer has a balance due, interest is accrued on the unpaid balance. The penalty is 5% of the amount due for each month or part of a month the return is late. If the return is more than 60 days late, the minimum penalty is $450 or the balance of the tax due on the return, whichever is smaller. The maximum penalty is 25%.

Making Extension Payments

For extensions, payments can be made electronically by credit card, debit card, money order, the Electronic Federal Tax Payment System (EFTPS), a direct transfer from a bank account using Direct Pay, or an ACH from the taxpayer's checking or savings account. When making a payment with the extension, remember to include the payment amount on Form 1040, Schedule 3, Part 2, line 13z. EFTPS can also be paid via phone. The taxpayer must write down the confirmation number he or she received when making an electronic payment. If the electronic payment has been designated as an extension payment, then do not file Form 4868.

Señor 1040 Says: If the taxpayer and spouse filed separate Form 4868s with payments and then chose to file the tax return as married filing jointly, make sure to include both payment amounts on Form 4868, line 5.

When paying by check or cashier's check, Form 4868 should be included and mailed to the address on Form 4868. Make sure the check or money order is made payable to United States Treasury. The taxpayer should include their SSN and write Form 4868 in the memo on the check. Do not send cash. Checks over $100 million or more are not accepted, so any payments exceeding that amount will have to be split into two or more payments. The $100 million limit does not apply to other payment methods (such as electronic payments). As with Form 1040, there are specific mailing addresses to mail extension payments. To find which mailing address should be used, see Instructions Form 4868, page 4. The address is determined based on where the taxpayer lives.

Installment Agreement Request (Form 9465)

If a taxpayer owes the federal government more than can be paid at one time, the taxpayer can file Form 9465, *Installment Agreement Request*, which asks permission to pay the taxes on a monthly basis. The IRS charges a late-payment penalty of 25% per month. If the return was not filed in a timely manner, the late payment penalty is 5% per month. The IRS usually notifies the taxpayer within 30 days of approval or denial of the proposed payment plan.

The user fee for new installment agreements is $225. The taxpayer can also set up a payroll deduction installment agreement, and that fee is $225. If the taxpayer uses an online payment portal, the user fee would be $31.00; if using credit card, check or money order the payment set-up fee is $149.00. If the taxpayer's income is below a certain level (250% of the annual poverty level), the installment agreement may be reduced to $43. Form 13844 must be completed to qualify. Form 13844, *Application for Reduced User Fee For Installment Agreements*.

Form 9465
(Rev. September 2020)
Department of the Treasury
Internal Revenue Service

Installment Agreement Request

▶ Go to *www.irs.gov/Form9465* for instructions and the latest information.
▶ If you are filing this form with your tax return, attach it to the front of the return.
▶ See separate instructions.

OMB No. 1545-0074

Tip: If you owe $50,000 or less, you may be able to avoid filing Form 9465 and establish an installment agreement online, even if you haven't yet received a tax bill. Go to *www.irs.gov/OPA* to apply for an Online Payment Agreement. If you establish your installment agreement using the Online Payment Agreement application, the user fee that you pay will be lower than it would be with Form 9465.

Part I   Installment Agreement Request

This request is for Form(s) (for example, Form 1040 or Form 941) ▶

Enter tax year(s) or period(s) involved (for example, 2018 and 2019, or January 1, 2019, to June 30, 2019) ▶

1a Your first name and initial | Last name | Your social security number

If a joint return, spouse's first name and initial | Last name | Spouse's social security number

Current address (number and street). If you have a P.O. box and no home delivery, enter your box number. | Apt. number

City, town or post office, state, and ZIP code. If a foreign address, also complete the spaces below (see instructions).

Foreign country name | Foreign province/state/county | Foreign postal code

1b If this address is new since you filed your last tax return, check here . . . . ▶ ☐

2 Name of your business (must no longer be operating) | Employer identification number (EIN

3 Your home phone number | Best time for us to call | **4** Your work phone number | Ext. | Best time for us to call

5 Enter the total amount you owe as shown on your tax return(s) (or notice(s)) . . . . | **5**

6 If you have any additional balances due that aren't reported on line 5, enter the amount here (even if the amounts are included in an existing installment agreement) . . . . | **6**

Portion of Form 9465

If the taxpayer elects to use the installment agreement, interest and a late-payment penalty will still apply on the unpaid amount by the due date. In agreeing to an installment payment, the taxpayer also agrees to meet all future tax liabilities. If the taxpayer does not have adequate withholding or make estimated payments so their tax liability will be paid in full on a timely filed return, the taxpayer will be considered in default of the agreement, and the IRS can take immediate action to collect for the entire amount. Form 9465 can be filed electronically with the taxpayer's tax return. Penalties and interest can be avoided if the tax bill is paid in full on the due date.

If the taxpayer can make the payment in full in 120 days, to avoid the installment agreement fee, the taxpayer can call the IRS or apply online and ask for a payment agreement. See Instructions Form 9465, *Installment Agreement Request.*

By completing Form 9465 the taxpayer agrees to the following terms. The terms of the installment agreement are:

➢ The Installment agreement will remain in effect until all liabilities (including penalties and interest) are paid in full.
➢ Taxpayer will make each payment monthly by the due date that was chosen on Form 9465. If unable to make a monthly payment, the taxpayer will notify the IRS immediately.
➢ The agreement is based on current financial condition. IRS may modify or terminate the agreement if the taxpayer's information changes. When requested, taxpayer will provide current financial information.
➢ Must file all federal tax returns and pay on time any federal taxes owed.

> ➤ IRS will apply federal refunds or overpayments to the entire amount owed, including the shared responsibility payment under the ACA, until paid in full.
> ➤ If the taxpayer defaults on the installment agreement, an additional $89 reinstatement fee will be charged to reinstate the installment agreement. IRS has the authority to deduct this fee from the first payment after the agreement was reinstated. Since January 1, 2019, the fee would be $10 if the agreement was restructured through an online payment agreement (OPA).
> ➤ IRS will apply all payments made on this agreement in the best interest of the United States. Generally, IRS will apply the payment to the oldest collection period.

IRS can terminate the installment agreement if the taxpayer does not make the monthly payment as agreed. If the agreement is terminated, the IRS could collect the entire amount owed, except the Individual Shared Responsibility Payment under the ACA, by levying the taxpayers' income, bank accounts, or other assets, and even seizing property. If the tax collection is in jeopardy, the IRS may terminate the agreement. The IRS may file a Notice of Federal Tax Lien, if not already been filed.

Part 1 Review Questions

To obtain the maximum benefit from this chapter, LTP recommends that you complete each of the following questions, and then compare them to the answers with feedback that immediately follow. Under governing self-study standards, vendors are required to present review questions intermittently throughout each self-study course.

These questions and explanations are not part of the final examination and will not be graded by LTP.

EAP1.1
Which of the following is true when filing Form 4868?

    a. Interest is charged on the tax that was not paid by the due date of the return, even if an extension was filed.
    b. Electronic filing cannot be used to file an extension of time to file.
    c. Any U.S. citizen who is out of the country on April 16, 2023, is allowed an automatic six-month extension of time to file his or her return and pay any federal balance due.
    d. Filing Form 4868 provides an automatic two-month extension to file and pay income tax.

EAP1.2
Which scenario is correct?

    a. Marie filed Form 4868 on April 16, 2023, but did not pay the amount due. Marie may be charged a late penalty.
    b. Paul died on April 1, 2022, and did not file a return. Paul will be charged death taxes on his 2021 tax return.
    c. Pedro did not file Form 4868 and will receive a refund. Pedro will be charged a late penalty on the refund amount.
    d. Reed filed his tax return timely and will be charged a penalty for filing on time.

EAP1.3
Faith has a balance due on her 2022 federal tax return and needs to make monthly payments to the IRS. Which of the following would she use?

    a. Form 4868
    b. Form 1040X
    c. Form 9465
    d. Form 1040

EAP1.4
If you do not file your return by the due date (including extensions), you may have to pay a failure-to-file penalty. The maximum penalty is____of the unpaid balance for each month or part of a month that a return is late.

    a. 7%
    b. 10%
    c. 15%
    d. 25%

EAP1.5
The IRS will charge _____ to set up the Installment Agreement if Form 9465 is filed with the tax return.

    a. 10% of the unpaid tax
    b. $225
    c. $89
    d. $10

Part 1 Review Questions Answers

EAP1.1
Which of the following is true when filing Form 4868?

    a. **Interest is charged on the tax that was not paid by the due date of the return, even if an extension was filed.**
    b. Electronic filing cannot be used to file an extension of time to file.
    c. Any U.S. citizen who is out of the country on April 16, 2023, is allowed an automatic six-month extension of time to file his or her return and pay any federal balance due.
    d. Filing Form 4868 provides an automatic two-month extension to file and pay income tax.

Feedback: Review section *Form 4869: Extension of Time to File.*

EAP1.2
Which scenario is correct?

    a. **Marie filed Form 4868 on April 16, 2023, but did not pay the amount due. Marie may be charged a late penalty.**
    b. Paul died on April 1, 2022, and did not file a return. Paul will be charged death taxes on his 2021 tax return.
    c. Pedro did not file Form 4868 and will receive a refund. Pedro will be charged a late penalty on the refund amount.
    d. Reed filed his tax return timely and will be charged a penalty for filing on time.

Feedback: Review section *Late Payment Penalty.*

EAP1.3

Faith has a balance due on her 2022 federal tax return and needs to make monthly payments to the IRS. Which of the following would she use?

    a. Form 4868
    b. Form 1040X
    c. Form 9465
    d. Form 1040

Feedback: Review section *Installment Agreement.*

EAP1.4

If you do not file your return by the due date (including extensions), you may have to pay a failure-to-file penalty. The maximum penalty is____of the unpaid balance for each month or part of a month that a return is late.

    a. 7%
    b. 10%
    c. 15%
    d. 25%

Feedback: Review section *Installment Agreement*.

EAP1.5

The IRS will charge _____ to set up the Installment Agreement if Form 9465 is filed with the tax return.

    a. 10% of the unpaid tax
    b. $225
    c. $89
    d. $10

Feedback: Review section *Installment Agreement*.

Part 2 Amended Returns

Form 1040-X is available to be e-filed as long as the original return was filed electronically. A tax professional should always double check the IRS website to ensure the mailing address is accurate. This could affect the taxpayer's payment, tax return, or communication with the IRS. Remember, the corresponding address is determined by taxpayer address, not the tax professional.

Form **1040-X**	Department of the Treasury—Internal Revenue Service **Amended U.S. Individual Income Tax Return** ▶ Use this revision to amend 2019 or later tax returns. ▶ Go to *www.irs.gov/Form1040X* for instructions and the latest information.	OMB No. 1545-0074
(Rev. July 2021)		

This return is for calendar year (enter year) _____ **or fiscal year** (enter month and year ended) _____

Your first name and middle initial	Last name	Your social security number

If joint return, spouse's first name and middle initial	Last name	Spouse's social security number

Current home address (number and street). If you have a P.O. box, see instructions.	Apt. no.	Your phone number

City, town or post office, state, and ZIP code. If you have a foreign address, also complete spaces below. See instructions.

Foreign country name	Foreign province/state/county	Foreign postal code

Amended return filing status. You must check one box even if you are not changing your filing status. **Caution:** In general, you can't change your filing status from married filing jointly to married filing separately after the return due date.

☐ Single   ☐ Married filing jointly   ☐ Married filing separately (MFS)   ☐ Head of household (HOH)   ☐ Qualifying widow(er) (QW)

If you checked the MFS box, enter the name of your spouse. If you checked the HOH or QW box, enter the child's name if the qualifying person is a child but not your dependent ▶

Enter on lines 1 through 23, columns A through C, the amounts for the return year entered above. Use Part III on page 2 to explain any changes.	**A. Original amount** reported or as previously adjusted (see instructions)	**B. Net change—** amount of increase or (decrease)— explain in Part III	**C. Correct amount**

Portion of Form 1040-X

When an original return must be corrected and the corrections will alter the current tax calculations, an amended tax return must be filed. An amended return cannot be filed unless the original return has been completed, but once it has been filed, an amended return becomes the new tax return for the taxpayer. The amended return is used to change items that were previously claimed and now need adjusting because they were originally over- or understated.

For example, if the taxpayer needs to report additional income from a W-2 that arrived after the taxpayer filed the original return or if the taxpayer needs to remove a dependent because they were not eligible to claim them, the taxpayer will file an amended return. Taxpayers who wish to receive a refund from an amended return must file the amendment within three years (including extensions) of the date the original return was filed or within two years of the date the tax was paid, whichever was later.

Example: Isabella filed her original return on March 1 of the current tax year, and her return was due April 15 of the same year. Isabella is considered to have filed her return by April 15. However, if Isabella had filed for an extension until October 15 and filed her return on July 1, her return is considered to be filed on July 1.

Other reasons a taxpayer might need to file an amendment are:

> ➤ To add or remove dependents.
> ➤ To report the proper filing status.
> ➤ To report additional income from a W-2, Form 1099, or some other income statement.
> ➤ To make changes in above-the-line deductions, standard deductions, or itemized deductions.
> ➤ To add or remove tax credits.
> ➤ To report bad debt or worthless security.
> ➤ To report foreign tax credit or deduction.

The status of an amended return can be tracked using the web portal "Where's My Amended Return?" on the IRS website after providing one's identification number (SSN, ITIN, etc.), date of birth, and zip code.

Do not file Form 1040-X in the following situations:

➢ The taxpayer is requesting a refund of penalties and interest or an addition to tax that has already been paid. Instead, use Form 843, *Claim for Refund and Request for Abatement*.
➢ The taxpayer is requesting a refund for their share of a joint overpayment that was offset against a past-due obligation of the spouse. Instead, file Form 8379, *Injured Spouse Allocation*.

Interest and penalties will also be charged from the due date of the return for failure to file, negligence, fraud, substantial valuation misstatements, substantial understatements of tax, and reportable transaction understatements.

Complete Form 1040-X

The following content is how to file the 1040-X when not using software. Most software will have the preparer add Form 1040-X, and then save the form to the return, then make changes on the form that was added or removed from the original return. For example, Jimmy received an additional W-2. Tax preparer would enter the W-2 as an additional form, and software will flow the information to Form 1040-X. Filing the form electronically helps since one does not need to mail the return and information.

Part I of the 1040-X is where the taxpayer would make changes that affect lines 1-31 of the original tax return. Part II is where the taxpayer can choose to have $3 go to the Presidential Election Campaign Fund. This must be done within 20.5 months after the original due date of the return. Part III is for the explanation of changes. The IRS wants to know what was changed on the return and why the taxpayer is filing Form 1040-X.

The three columns on Form 1040-X are as follows:

➢ Column A: The original return amount.
➢ Column B: The Net Change. Enter the change in amount for each line that is altered.
➢ Column C: The correct amount. Add or subtract column B (if there is an entry) from column A and enter amount in column C.

Example: Robert reported $41,000 as his adjusted gross income on the Form 1040 of the current year. He then received another Form W-2 for $500 after he had already filed his return. He should complete line 1 of Form 1040-X as follows:

	Column A	Column B	Column C
Line 1	$41,000	$500	$41,500

Enter on lines 1 through 23, columns A through C, the amounts for the return year entered above. Use Part III on page 2 to explain any changes.		A. Original amount reported or as previously adjusted (see instructions)	B. Net change— amount of increase or (decrease)— explain in Part III	C. Correct amount
Income and Deductions				
1 Adjusted gross income. If a net operating loss (NOL) carryback is included, check here ▶ ☐	1			
2 Itemized deductions or standard deduction	2			
3 Subtract line 2 from line 1	3			
4a Reserved for future use	4a			
b Qualified business income deduction	4b			
5 Taxable income. Subtract line 4b from line 3. If the result is zero or less, enter -0-	5			

Portion of Form 1040-X

On Form 1040-X, input the income, deductions, and credits as originally reported on the return in Column A, input the changes being made in Column B, and place the difference or sum in Column C. Next, figure the tax on the corrected amount of taxable income and calculate the amount owed or to be refunded. If the taxpayer owes taxes, the taxpayer should pay the full amount with Form 1040-X. The tax owed will not be subtracted from any amount credited to estimated tax.

If the taxpayer cannot pay the full amount due on the amended return, the individual can ask to make monthly installment payments using Form 9465. If the taxpayer overpaid taxes, they would receive a refund. The overpayment refunded based on the amended return is different and separate from any refund gained from the original return.

When assembling an amended return to be mailed, make sure that the schedules and forms are behind Form 1040-X and that the taxpayer (and spouse if filing jointly) sign the 1040-X. If the amendment was prepared by a paid tax preparer, the tax preparer must sign as well.

Señor 1040 Says: Make sure to use the correct form for the year that is being amended. To find the forms you need, go to www.irs.gov, and choose the correct form(s) to amend the tax return.

Attach forms to the front of Form 1040-X that support changes made on the return. Attach to the back of Form 1040-X any Form 8805, *Foreign Partner's Information Statement of Section 1446 Withholding Tax*, that supports the changes made.

When sending a check or money order to the IRS for payments of taxes due, do not attach the check to the return. Instead, enclose it in the envelope and make sure the check is made out to "United States Treasury."

Superseded Tax Return

A superseding return is a return filed subsequent to the originally filed return and filed within the filing period (including extensions). A superseding return must be a complete filing of the entire return, with all the required forms and attachments such as XML or PDF. Taxpayer filing this type of return must indicate on the form it is a superseded return.

State Tax Liability

If a return is changed for any reason, it may affect the state income tax liability. This includes changes made as a result of an examination of the return by the IRS. The IRS will inform the taxpayer's state if adjustments are made on the federal tax return.

Part 2 Review Questions

To obtain the maximum benefit from this chapter, LTP recommends that you complete each of the following questions, and then compare them to the answers with feedback that immediately follow. Under governing self-study standards, vendors are required to present review questions intermittently throughout each self-study course.

These questions and explanations are not part of the final examination and will not be graded by LTP.

EAP2.1
Which scenario is true?

    a. The taxpayer has two years to make any corrections that result in additional tax refunds, including extensions after the date the original return was filed or within 3 years after the date the tax was paid, whichever was later.

    b. The taxpayer has four years to make any corrections that result in additional tax refunds, including extensions after the date the original return was filed or within 2 years after the date the tax was paid, whichever was later.

    c. The taxpayer has three years to make any corrections that result in additional tax refunds, including extensions after the date the original return was filed or within 2 years after the date the tax was paid, whichever was later.

    d. The taxpayer is not allowed to make any corrections on previous year tax returns.

EAP2.2
Which of the following is used to file a federal amended return?

    a. Form 1040
    b. Form 1040-X
    c. Form 4868
    d. Form 2241

EAP2.3
Which of the following would not be a valid reason to file an amendment?

    a. Taxpayer changing personal exemptions.
    b. Taxpayer claiming their cousins' dependents.
    c. Taxpayer reporting additional income.
    d. Taxpayer claiming additional tax credits.

EAP2.4
Lorena filed her original tax return on April 15 and was scheduled to receive a tax refund on May 9. Lorena realized she forgot income from her summer job. She files an amended return on May 3. The amended tax return resulted in Lorena having a balance due. Lorena paid her balance due on May 3. Which scenario is true?

    a. Lorena is not subject to a penalty because she paid her tax due on May 3.
    b. Lorena is subject to a penalty for not paying her tax due by April 15.
    c. Lorena is subject to a penalty for amending her tax return.
    d. Lorena does not have to report the income from her summer job.

Part 2 Review Questions Answers

EAP2.1
Which scenario is true?

    a. The taxpayer has two years to make any corrections that result in additional tax refunds, including extensions after the date the original return was filed or within 3 years after the date the tax was paid, whichever was later.

    b. The taxpayer has four years to make any corrections that result in additional tax refunds, including extensions after the date the original return was filed or within 2 years after the date the tax was paid, whichever was later.

    c. The taxpayer has three years to make any corrections that result in additional tax refunds, including extensions after the date the original return was filed or within 2 years after the date the tax was paid, whichever was later.

    d. The taxpayer is not allowed to make any corrections on previous year tax returns.

Feedback: Review section *Part 2: Amended Returns.*

EAP2.2
Which of the following is used to file a federal amended return?

    a. Form 1040
    b. Form 1040-X
    c. Form 4868
    d. Form 2241

Feedback: Review section *Part 2: Amended Returns.*

EAP2.3
Which of the following would not be a valid reason to file an amendment?

    a. Taxpayer changing personal exemptions.
    b. Taxpayer claiming their cousins' dependents.
    c. Taxpayer reporting additional income.
    d. Taxpayer claiming additional tax credits.

Feedback: Review section *Part 2: Amended Returns.*

EAP2.4
Lorena filed her original tax return on April 15 and was scheduled to receive a tax refund on May 9. Lorena realized she forgot income from her summer job. She files an amended return on May 3. The amended tax return resulted in Lorena having a balance due. Lorena paid her balance due on May 3. Which scenario is true?

    a. Lorena is not subject to a penalty because she paid her tax due on May 3.
    b. Lorena is subject to a penalty for not paying her tax due by April 15.
    c. Lorena is subject to a penalty for amending her tax return.
    d. Lorena does not have to report the income from her summer job.

Feedback: Review section *Part 2: Amended Returns.*

Takeaways

This chapter gives a brief understanding of extensions and amendments. The paid tax professional must understand who should file for an extension and when to file an amendment as these are two separate processes.

If more time is needed to file the tax return, the individual should file for an extension. However, an extension of time to file *is not an extension of time to pay*. Payment is still owed by the April 15th deadline or the taxpayer will pay late payment penalties. An extension of time to file does not change this. Although an extension of time to pay and various payment plans do exist, these should not be confused with extensions of time to file.

TEST YOUR KNOWLEDGE!
Go online to take a practice quiz.

California Extensions and Amendments

Introduction

If taxpayers are unable to file their California individual tax return by the due date, they may be able to qualify for an automatic six-month extension of time to file by electronically filing or mailing Form 3519 to the FTB. If the taxpayer has filed a return and realizes that a mistake was made, they would need to file an amended return using Schedule X.

Objectives

At the end of this lesson, the student will:

➢ Know when to use Form 3519.
➢ Understand when to file a California amendment.
➢ Identify when to use and file the Schedule X.

Resources

Form 540	Schedule X	FTB Form 3519

Table of Contents

Part 1 Form 3519: Extension of Time to File

Form 3519 is used when the taxpayer needs to file an extension and they have a balance due for the state return. Form 3519 cannot be used in conjunction with Form 540 2EZ. Payments can also be made online at www.ftb.ca.gov/pay.

DETACH HERE

Save the stamp – pay online with Web Pay!
IF NO PAYMENT IS DUE, DO NOT MAIL THIS FORM — — — — — — DETACH HERE — —

(Calendar year filers – File and Pay by April 18, 2023) (Fiscal year filers – see instructions)

TAXABLE YEAR   CAUTION: You may be required to pay electronically. See instructions.   CALIFORNIA FORM

2022   Payment for Automatic Extension for Individuals   3519 (PIT)

For calendar year 2022 or fiscal year beginning (mm/dd/yyyy) _____ , and ending (mm/dd/yyyy) _____

Your first name	Initial	Last name		Your SSN or ITIN
If joint payment, spouse's/RDP's first name	Initial	Last name		Spouse's/RDP's SSN or ITIN
Address (number and street, PO box, or PMB no.)				Apt. no./ste. no.
City			State	ZIP code

IF PAYMENT IS DUE, MAIL TO:

FRANCHISE TAX BOARD
PO BOX 942867
SACRAMENTO CA 94267-0008

If amount of payment is zero, do not mail this form } ▶

Amount of payment

_____ . 00

For Privacy Notice, get FTB 1131 EN-SP.   1221223   FTB 3519 2022

Form 3519

California allows an automatic six-month extension, without the need of a written request, if taxpayers are due a refund but cannot file their tax return by the April due date. To qualify for an automatic extension, taxpayers must file their return by the October due date. An extension of time to file the return is *not* an extension of time to pay the tax. To avoid paying any late payment penalties and interest, taxpayers must pay 100% of their tax liability by the April due date even if they file for an extension. Late payment penalty may be waived based on reasonable cause. A reasonable cause is presumed when 90% of the tax was paid by the original due date. However, the obligation of interest is mandatory.

If the taxpayer is living or traveling outside the United States on the April due date, the deadline to file and pay the tax is June 15, although this will not stop interest from accruing on any amount owed. If additional time is needed to file the return, an automatic six-month extension will be allowed without filing a request. To avoid late penalties, 100% of the liability must be paid by June 15. When taxpayers file their returns, they should attach a statement to the front of their tax returns indicating that they were outside of the United States on the April due date.

If the taxpayer owes the state for the current tax year and needs to file for an extension, they should file FTB Form 3519 to file the extension and to pay the amount that is due on the April due date. Do not mail Form 3519 to the FTB if using Web Pay. If no tax is owed, Form 3519 does not need to be filed, but the tax return must be filed by October due date of the current tax year. The taxpayer can make a payment using Web Pay for individuals, a credit card, or a check or money order (as long as it was mailed by the due date). Web Pay can be set up in advance at www.ftb.ca.gov, and the payments can be scheduled at any time throughout the year. Credit card payments can be processed by ftb.ca.gov/e-pay. A convenience fee will be charged for using the service. Checks or money orders can be mailed to the FTB with Form 3519. Money orders must be payable in U.S. dollars via a U.S. financial institution.

Payment Plans

California has payment plans that may take up to 90 days to process the request. The cost to set-up the agreement is $34 for individuals and the taxpayer has 3 to 5 years to pay off the balance. To be eligible for the agreement, the taxpayer should owe less than $25,000 and pay the amount owed within 60 months. Taxpayer must be current on their tax returns and if not, they would need to file 5 years of prior tax returns. If a taxpayer has a current installment agreement or wage garnishment, bank levy, or other collection order, they cannot apply for a current year payment plan. They would need to call the FTB (800.689.4776) to apply.
https://www.ftb.ca.gov/pay/payment-plans/index.asp

Part 1 Review Questions

To obtain the maximum benefit from this chapter, LTP recommends that you complete each of the following questions, and then compare them to the answers with feedback that immediately follows. Under governing self-study standards, vendors are required to present review questions intermittently throughout each self-study course.

These questions and explanations are not part of the final examination and will not be graded by LTP.

CEAP1.1
Which of the following is true when filing FTB Form 3519?

a. Taxpayers can pay their amount due in cash.
b. Electronic filing cannot be used to file an extension of time to file.
c. Any United States citizen who is out of the country on April 16, 2023, is allowed an automatic six-month extension of time to file his or her return and pay any federal balance due.
d. Filing FTB Form 3519 provides an automatic two-month extension to file and pay income tax.

CEAP1.2
Which of the following best describes when to use Form 3519?

a. Omar returned from out of the country on April 14 and has a balance due; he needs to file Form 3519 to pay his balance due.
b. Andres used Web Pay to pay his balance due; he will mail Form 3519 to the FTB.
c. Viviana wants to file for an extension and has a balance due; she will mail her check with Form 3519 to the FTB.
d. Brittni used her credit card to pay her balance due; she will mail Form 3519 to the IRS.

CEAP1.3
Which of the following is needed to qualify for an installment agreement?

a. 5 years of prior tax returns.
b. Payment amount of more than $25,000.
c. Pay the required fee of $134.
d. Have no bank levy.

Part 1 Review Questions Answers

CEAP1.1
Which of the following is true when filing FTB Form 3519?

a. Taxpayers can pay their amount due in cash.
b. Electronic filing cannot be used to file an extension of time to file.
c. Any United States citizen who is out of the country on April 16, 2023, is allowed an automatic six-month extension of time to file his or her return and pay any federal balance due.
d. Filing FTB Form 3519 provides an automatic two-month extension to file and pay income tax.

Feedback: Review section *Form 3519: Extension of time to file.*

CEAP1.2

Which of the following best describes when to use Form 3519?

   a. Omar returned from out of the country on April 14 and has a balance due; he needs to file Form 3519 to pay his balance due.
   b. Andres used Web Pay to pay his balance due; he will mail Form 3519 to the FTB.
   c. Viviana wants to file for an extension and has a balance due; she will mail her check with Form 3519 to the FTB.
   d. Brittni used her credit card to pay her balance due; she will mail Form 3519 to the IRS.

Feedback: Review section *Form 3519: Extension of time to file.*

CEAP1.3

Which of the following is needed to qualify for an installment agreement?

   a. 5 years of prior tax returns.
   b. Payment amount of more than $25,000.
   c. Pay the required fee of $134.
   d. Have no bank levy.

Feedback: Review section *Payment Plans.*

Part 2 Schedule X and Amended Returns

Schedule X, *California Explanation of Amended Return Changes*, has replaced Form 540X, *Amended Individual Income Tax Return*. California's e-file program has accepted e-file amended returns for individuals since tax year 2017. For tax year 2016 and earlier, amended individual returns must still be paper filed using Form 540X. If you are an individual filing an amended personal income tax return, use Schedule X to provide reason(s) for amending and to determine any additional amount you owe or if you are due a refund. Attach Schedule X to your amended tax return when filing a paper return.

Portion of Schedule X

For taxable years beginning on January 1, 2020, and before January 1, 2023, California law allows an exclusion from gross income for grant allocations received by a taxpayer through the California Microbusiness COVID-19 Relief Program. For taxable years beginning September 1, 2020, and before January 1, 2030, California allows an exclusion from gross income for grant allocations received by a taxpayer from the California Venues Grant Program. See FTB Pub 1001.

The following content shows how to file the Schedule X when not using software. Most software will have the preparer add the Schedule X, and save the return, then make changes on the form that was added or removed from the original return. The key is making the changes after you have saved the Schedule X. For example, Jimmy received an additional W-2. Tax preparer would enter the W-2 as an additional form and software will flow the information to Schedule X. Filing the form electronically helps since there is no need to mail the return and the additional documents.

To complete Schedule X, read the lines for Part 1. For Line 1, enter the amount owed, and for line 2, enter the amount if the taxpayer would receive a refund. When using software, these lines should be auto-filled when making the necessary corrections on the original tax return.

Schedule X, Part II is for choosing the boxes for the reason of the amended return. For example, an error on the original return, which could result in an amount owed or refund, depending on the error.

California does not conform to the changes to the amendment process made by the TCJA, but it has streamlined its amendment process to make it easier than it was in previous years. Schedule X, Part I is the reconciliation of the financial adjustments, which is where the calculations are made to determine if the taxpayer will receive a refund or owe additional tax.

Statute of Limitations

If the taxpayer is requesting a refund of previously paid penalties, they have two options, one file an amended return or use the reasonable cause form. For individual taxpayers use Form 2917 *Reasonable Cause – Individual and Fiduciary Claim for a Refund* and business Form 2924 *Reasonable Cause – Business Entity Claim for a Refund*. State law allows the taxpayer 4 years to claim the refund.

Amended returns statute of limitations is 1 year from the date of overpayment or 4 years after the original return due date to file the claim.

When the IRS has a final determination on an audited tax return.

California requires the taxpayer to make any adjustment within six months after the federal determination becomes final. California does not conform to the federal Tax Equity and Fiscal Responsibility Act (TEFRA), that allows partnerships to provide adjustments to the individual partners.

Schedule X, Part II: Reason for Amending

Check all applicable boxes to specify why the taxpayer is filing an amendment. Line 2 should include detailed information about the item being changed and the reason the change was needed. List or attach the documents used to support the claim in the explanation. Any federal schedules that were changed need to be attached to the state amendment, as do any documents that support any of the changes; this can include corrected form(s) such as the W-2, 1099s, escrow documents, etc.

Part II Reason(s) for Amending

1 Check all that apply:

- ⦿ a ☐ Protective claim for refund. See instructions.
- ⦿ b ☐ Reservation source income adjustments
- ⦿ c ☐ Pass-through entity adjustments
- ⦿ d ☐ Federal audit and/or adjustments
- ⦿ e ☐ FTB audit contact

- ⦿ f ☐ NOL carryback. See instructions.
- ⦿ g ☐ Error on original return
- ⦿ h ☐ Credit adjustment
- ⦿ i ☐ Earned income tax credit/ Young child tax credit/Foster youth tax credit

- ⦿ j ☐ Disaster loss
- ⦿ k ☐ Military HR 100
- ⦿ l ☐ Informal claim
- ⦿ m ☐ Other. See instructions.

2 Provide further explanation of reason(s) for amending below. If needed, attach a separate sheet that includes your name and SSN or ITIN. See instructions.

Portion of Schedule X

The taxpayer's refund could be denied or delayed if the explanation does not include sufficient detail about the changes that were made or if supporting documents and revised forms were not attached and are missing. Attach additional pages as needed to provide a clear, detailed explanation. Be sure to include the taxpayer's name and SSN or ITIN on each attachment and make sure that the taxpayer, and spouse (if filing jointly), and the paid tax preparer sign the return in the designated space provided. Also provide the name, best time to call, and phone number of the person that the FTB should contact for questions regarding the amended return. This will allow the FTB to provide better service when processing the amended return.

Exception for Filing a Separate Tax Return

A married couple who filed a joint federal tax return may file separate state tax returns if either spouse was an active member of the United States armed forces (or any auxiliary military branch) during the year being amended, or if they were nonresidents for the entire year and had no income from California sources during the year being amended. If taxpayers change their filing status on their federal amended tax return, they must also change their filing status on the California return by filing Schedule X.

The taxpayer cannot change from married or RDP filing jointly to married or RDP filing separately after the due date of the tax return even if it hasn't yet been filed. However, for taxable years 2000 and after, a married couple that meets the "exception for filing a separate tax return" may change from joint to separate tax returns after the due date of the tax return. If the taxpayer, spouse, or RDP filed a separate tax return, they can generally change their filing status to a joint tax return at any time within four years of the original due date of the separate tax return(s). To change to a joint tax return, the taxpayer and spouse or RDP must have been legally married or an RDP on the last day of the taxable year being amended.

California Statute of Limitations

Taxpayers who need to file a claim for a refund have four years after the original due date of the tax return, or one year after the date of overpayment to claim the refund, whichever period expires later. If the original tax return was filed within the extension period, April due date to October due date, the taxpayer can file a claim for refund by filing an amended tax return within four years of the original due date of the tax return or within one year of the date of overpayment, whichever expires later. If the original tax return was filed after October due date and if the taxpayer is filing a claim for refund, they must file the claim within four years of the original due date of April 15 or within one year of the date of overpayment, whichever expires later. If the taxpayer is filing an amended return after the normal statute of limitations period (four years after the due date of the original return), a statement of explanation must be attached to explain why the normal statute of limitations does not apply to the filing.

Part 2 Review Questions

To obtain the maximum benefit from this chapter, LTP recommends that you complete each of the following questions, and then compare them to the answers with feedback that immediately follow. Under governing self-study standards, vendors are required to present review questions intermittently throughout each self-study course.

These questions and explanations are not part of the final examination and will not be graded by LTP.

CEAP2.1
Which of the following forms is used to file an amended state return?

    a. FTB 540 Schedule X
    b. Form 1040-X
    c. Form 4868
    d. FTB Form 3519

CEAP2.2
The FTB will verify the taxpayer's eligibility when he or she submits an installment agreement. The taxpayer will not qualify for the installment agreement if which condition applies?

    a. Tax liability is over $25,000.
    b. The installment period for payment does not exceed 60 months.
    c. The taxpayer has filed all required valid personal income tax returns.
    d. The taxpayer does not have an existing installment agreement.

CEAP2.3
To be able to apply for a California Payment Plan the amount should be less than _____.

    a. $100,000
    b. $75,000
    c. $25,000
    d. Everyone is eligible

Part 2 Review Questions Answers

CEAP2.1
Which of the following forms is used to file an amended state return?

    a. FTB 540 Schedule X
    b. Form 1040-X
    c. Form 4868
    d. FTB Form 3519

Feedback: Review section *Part 2: Schedule X and Amended Returns.*

CEAP2.2

The FTB will verify the taxpayer's eligibility when he or she submits an installment agreement. The taxpayer will not qualify for the installment agreement if which condition applies?

a. **Tax liability is over $25,000.**
b. The installment period for payment does not exceed 60 months.
c. The taxpayer has filed all required valid personal income tax returns.
d. The taxpayer does not have an existing installment agreement.

Feedback: Review section *Part 2: Schedule X and Amended Returns.*

CEAP2.3

To be able to apply for a California Payment Plan the amount should be less than _____.

a. $100,000
b. $75,000
c. **$25,000**
d. Everyone is eligible

Feedback: Review section *Payment Plans.*

Takeaways

California allows automatic paperless extensions. Taxpayers are granted a six-month extension of time to file a return. For federal purposes, extensions are not automatic. The taxpayer must file an extension either electronically or on paper, estimating the balance due. Both the IRS and FTB require a taxpayer to pay the amount of tax due by the first due date of the return. If the taxpayer does not pay the amount due, both IRS and FTB will charge the taxpayer a late payment penalty and interest on a return not filed timely.

The penalty amounts are as follows:

➤ Federal: 0.5% per month for each month, or a fraction thereof if not paid, and a maximum of 25%.
➤ California: 5% flat fee, and 0.5% per month with a maximum of 25%.

TEST YOUR KNOWLEDGE!
Go online to take a practice quiz.

Chapter 15 Electronic Filing

Introduction

Electronic filing (also referred to as e-file and e-filing) is the process of submitting tax returns over the internet via approved tax software. The e-file system has made tax preparation significantly easier, and the IRS notifies software users within 24-48 hours if the tax return was accepted or rejected. E-filing is not available year-round but begins in January and ends in October; the IRS determines when e-filing begins and ends each year, and states follow the IRS dates. An electronic return originator (ERO) is the individual who originates the electronic submission of the tax return. To file a return electronically, the individual needs to be an Authorized IRS e-file Provider.

Objectives

At the end of this lesson, the student will:

> ➤ Understand the different e-filing options.
> ➤ Know which form(s) to use when the taxpayer opts-out of e-filing.
> ➤ Identify which forms are unable to be e-filed.

Resources

Form 8453	Publication 17	Instructions Form 8453
Form 8878	Publication 1345	Instructions Form 8878
Form 8878-A	Publication 3112	Instructions Form 8878-A
Form 8879	Publication 4164	Instructions Form 8879
Form 9325	Publication 4557	Instructions Form 9325

Table of Contents

Part 1 Electronic Return Originator (ERO)

An electronic return originator (ERO) is an authorized IRS e-file provider that originates submissions of returns he or she either prepares or collects from taxpayers who want to e-file their returns. An ERO originates the electronic submission of a return after the taxpayer authorizes the e-filing of the tax return. The ERO must have either prepared the return or collected it from a taxpayer. An ERO originates the electronic submission by one of the following methods:

➢ Electronically sending the return to a transmitter that will transmit the return to the IRS.
➢ Directly transmitting the return to the IRS.
➢ Providing the return to an intermediate service provider to transmit it to the IRS.

Obtaining, Handling, and Processing Return Information from Taxpayers

If the return was prepared by a paid preparer, the ERO must always identify the paid preparer in the proper field of the electronic record and include the paid preparer's following information:

➢ Name
➢ Address
➢ EIN (if a member of a firm)
➢ PTIN

An ERO who chooses to originate returns that have not been prepared by the firm becomes the tax preparer when, entering the data, the ERO discovers errors that require substantive changes and makes the changes. A non-substantive change is a correction limited to a transposition error, a misplaced entry, a spelling error, or an arithmetic correction. The IRS considers all other changes substantive, and the ERO becomes the tax preparer if corrections are made.

e-File Providers

An authorized IRS e-file provider is a business or organization authorized by the IRS to participate in their e-file program. A Provider may be an Electronic Return Originator (ERO), an Intermediate Service Provider, a Transmitter, a Software Developer, a Reporting Agent, or an Affordable Care Act (ACA) Provider. These different roles are not mutually exclusive, and one person or entity can have more than one. For example, a Provider may be an ERO while also being a Transmitter or a tax return preparer. Even though the activities and responsibilities for IRS e-file and return preparation are distinct and different from each other, one person can possess both titles, duties, and responsibilities at the same time.

A Transmitter is the person, entity, or software that literally sends the return data electronically directly to the IRS. A Provider is one who has been authorized by the IRS to file tax returns electronically, typically through a third-party transmitter such as a tax software provider; filing a return is not the same thing as sending it.

Becoming an e-File Provider

To become an e-file provider, an individual must submit a completed application to the IRS requesting the proper authorization, a process that usually takes 45 days. To complete the application quickly, the individual should have the following information prepared:

➢ Know which Provider options can be furnished to taxpayers.
➢ Enter identification information for the company.
  • Employer Identification Number.
  • Name of the company.
  • Enter the name, date of birth, Social Security number, current professional information, and citizenship status of the organization's Principal and Responsible Official. Mark if either or both are an attorney, certified public accountant, enrolled agent, officer of a publicly traded corporation, or a bonded bank official.

Who are Principals and Responsible Officials?

Anyone who is a Principal or Responsible Official must:

1. Be a U.S. citizen or an alien who has permanent residence as covered in 8USC 110(a)(20)(1994).
2. Be at least 18 years old at the time of completing the application.
3. Meet applicable state and local licensing and bonding requirements to be able to prepare and collect tax returns.

The Principal is the individual who is ultimately responsible for anything and everything that occurs regarding e-filing at the firm. Although a firm can have more than one "Responsible Official", there can be only one Principal, and the individual designated as the Principal must be on the application. Any of the following individuals that participate in the e-file operations of the company are eligible to be designated as the Principal:

➢ A sole proprietor of the business. For sole proprietorships, the sole proprietor must be the Principal.
➢ A partner who has at least 5% or more interest in the partnership. If no partner has 5% or more, the Principal needs to be an individual who is authorized to act for the partnership in legal or tax matters.
➢ The President, Vice-President, Secretary, or Treasurer of a corporation are all eligible to be a Principal.
➢ The Principal for an entity that is not any of the above needs to be an individual with the authority within the company to act on behalf of the entity in legal or tax matters.

If any of the above individuals are not involved in the e-file operation of the company, then a large firm with multilayered management can substitute a "Key Person" who participates substantially in the firm's electronic filing operations as the principal for the e-file application.

Unlike the Principal, who is a single person responsible for e-file matters across the whole company, Responsible Officials are the people in charge of the day-to-day e-file operations at specific locations such as offices. They are the first point of contact with the IRS and have the authority to sign and revise IRS e-file applications. Responsible Officials must set the revenue procedures for e-filing and for all publications and notices thereof and ensure that employees follow them. Responsible Officials can oversee the operations at more than one office, and though there can be more, each firm must have at least one Responsible Official, although it can always add more later; the Principal can also be the Responsible Official.

Step One: Accessing the Application

Before starting the e-file application process, the individual must create an account with IRS Secure Access. To do this, the individual will register using a two-factor authentication process at irs.gov. After this, the taxpayer will be asked to provide the following information to create the account:

➢ Full legal name
➢ Home address
➢ Social Security number
➢ Date of birth
➢ Phone number
➢ Email address

Any other individuals that the firm wishes to appoint as either the Principal or as Responsible Officials must also create e-services accounts. Account creators must return to the e-Services site within 28 days of receiving the confirmation code to confirm the registration and thus allow the firm to continue the application process.

Step Two: Complete and Submit the Application

Once all relevant individuals have confirmed their e-Services accounts, the firm can apply to become an authorized IRS e-file provider. The next steps of the application process are as follows:

1. Log in to e-Services and access the online application to become an IRS e-file provider.
2. Select the e-file provider type (Transmitter, ERO, etc.).
3. Enter the identification information of the firm and services provided.
4. Enter the name, home address, SSN, DOB, and citizenship status for each principal and responsible party for the firm.
5. Enter the Principal and Responsible Official(s) current professional status (attorney, certified public accountant, enrolled agent, etc.) and any other requested information.
6. Each Principal and Responsible Official must answer several personal questions and sign the Terms of Agreement (TOA) using the PIN they selected when creating their e-services accounts.
7. Each Principal and Responsible Official must declare under penalty of perjury that all the personal information they entered is true.

Submit the IRS e-file application and retain the tracking number provided after the submission of the application was successful.

Any individuals appointed to become the Principal or a Responsible Official who are not an EA, CPA, or attorney must pass a background check before the application can continue. To do this, first request a fingerprint card from the IRS by calling their toll-free number (1-866-255-0654). Once the IRS has mailed the cards, take them to a trained professional at your local police department or to a company certified to provide that service. They will perform the fingerprinting of each Principal and Responsible Official, who must each sign the card that contains their fingerprints.

Suitability Check

Once the IRS has received, processed, and reviewed the application, they will conduct a "suitability check" to determine if the firm qualifies to become an e-file provider. The "suitability check" consists of the following checks on the firm, on each person listed as a principal or responsible official on the application, and on all documents related to the application:

➢ A credit check.
➢ A tax compliance check.
➢ A criminal background check.
➢ A check for prior noncompliance with IRS e-file requirements.

If the firm passes the suitability check they will receive their acceptance letter from the IRS with the electronic filing identification number (EFIN), which should not be confused with the firm's EIN.

Denial to Participate in IRS e-File

If the firm, a Principal, or a Responsible Official fails the suitability check, the IRS will notify the applicant of denial to participate in the program, the date they may reapply, and if they may reapply sooner if the suitability issues are resolved.

Acceptance to Participate in IRS e-File

After an applicant passes the suitability check and the IRS completes the processing of the application, the IRS will notify the applicant of their acceptance or rejection to participate in the program. A provider does not have to reapply unless the IRS suspends the provider from participation in the program for a violation. If any of the information on the original application changes, the provider will have 30 days to update the information by resubmitting the application with the assorted changes.

If the professional status of a Principal or Responsible Official changes, the firm must update its e-file application and resubmit the individual's fingerprints for a new background check. If a Principal or a Responsible Official dies, the Provider must remove or replace the deceased within 30 days by resubmitting the application. If this is not done, the IRS will remove the deceased individual(s) from the e-file application themselves, which may result in rejected returns because of leaving one of the firm's offices uncovered. The IRS will also remove Providers if they are unable to contact the provider or if the IRS' mail is returned to them as undeliverable because the Provider failed to update their physical mailing address, in which case the IRS will reject all returns submitted by the Provider until the Provider updates their information.

Monitoring

The IRS monitors Providers by visiting the locations where one performs IRS e-file activities and by reviewing the e-file records the IRS requires them to keep. Monitoring may include, but is not limited to, the following:

- Reviewing the quality of e-file submissions for rejects and other defects.
- Checking adherence to signature requirements on returns.
- Scrutinizing advertising material.
- Examining records.
- Observing office procedures.
- Conducting periodic suitability checks.

The IRS monitors the regulations put in place by the Providers to ensure they are in compliance with IRC §6695(g).

Revocation

The IRS will revoke participation from an authorized Provider, Principal, or Responsible Official if so ordered by a federal court or a federal or state legal action. If the legal action expires or is reversed, the revoked Provider may reapply to participate in IRS e-file after the legal action expires or is reversed.

Sanctioning

IRS e-file violations may result in warning or sanctioning an authorized IRS e-file Provider, a Principal, or a Responsible Official. Sanctioning may take the form of a written reprimand, a suspension, or an expulsion from participating in the e-file program. In most circumstances, a sanction is effective 30 days after the date of the letter informing individuals of a sanction against them or the date that the reviewing officers or the Office of Appeals affirms the sanction, whichever is later. If a Provider, Principal, or Responsible Official is suspended or expelled from participation in e-filing, every entity that listed the suspended or expelled Principal or Responsible Official on their e-file application may also be suspended or expelled. Although notice must be given eventually, the IRS has full authority to immediately suspend or expel anyone without a prior warning or notice.

Infractions

The IRS categorizes the seriousness of infractions in three different levels.

Level One Infractions are infringements of IRS e-file rules and requirements that have little-to-no harmful effect on the quality of the returns or on the IRS e-file program. This infraction could result in a written reprimand but may not lead to a suspension or expulsion.

Level Two Infractions are violations of IRS e-file rules and requirements that have an unfavorable impact upon the quality of the returns or on the IRS e-file program. The repeating Level One Infractions after the IRS has notified the person about the current violation could cause an increase to Level Two Infraction. Depending on the nature of the infraction, the IRS may limit participation in IRS e-file or suspend the authorized IRS e-file Provider from participation in IRS e-file for a period of one year.

Level Three Infractions are violations of IRS e-file rules and requirements that have a significant adverse impact on the quality of tax returns. Level Three Infractions include continued Level Two Infractions after the IRS has brought the Level Two Infraction to the attention of the Provider. A Level Three Infraction may result in suspension from participation in IRS e-file for two years or, depending on the severity of the infraction (such as fraud, identity theft, or criminal conduct), in removal without the opportunity for future participation. The IRS reserves the right to suspend or expel a Provider prior to administrative review for Level Three Infractions. See Publication 3112.

Safeguarding Taxpayer Information

"Taxpayer information" is any piece of information that has been furnished for or by the taxpayer in any form or manner such as in person, over the phone, by mail, or by fax for the purpose of preparing the taxpayer's tax return. It includes, but is not limited to, the following pieces of information:

➢ Name
➢ Address
➢ Identification number
➢ Income
➢ Receipts
➢ Deductions
➢ Dependents
➢ Tax liability

Criminal and monetary penalties may be imposed on individuals preparing taxes or providing tax preparation services. This includes tax preparers that knowingly or recklessly make unauthorized disclosures with the preparation of income tax returns. See Title 26 IRC §301.7216.1 and §6713. Some common safeguarding strategies are:

➢ Lock doors to restrict access to files.
➢ Passwords to access computer files.
➢ Encrypting electronically stored taxpayer data.
➢ Keep a backup of electronic data for recovery purposes. Backup files regularly.
➢ Shred taxpayer information.

For more information about safeguarding personal information, go to the official website of the Federal Trade Commission at www.ftc.gov.

Nonstandard Document Awareness

The IRS has identified key indicators of potential abuse and fraud such as altered, forged, or fabricated Forms W-2, W-2G, and 1099-R, especially when prepared by hand. Information on the reporting forms should never be altered. If the employer must make any changes, the employer should provide the employee with a corrected document, and a corrected reporting form should be sent to the IRS and the SSA. Any time the tax professional has a questionable income document, report it to the IRS.

Verifying Taxpayer Identification Numbers (TINs)

To help safeguard taxpayers from fraud and abuse, the tax preparer should confirm the identity and identification number of taxpayers, spouses, and dependents listed on every tax return prepared. Taxpayer Identification Numbers include SSNs, EINs, adopted taxpayer identification numbers (ATINs), and individual taxpayer identification numbers (ITINs). To confirm identities, the paid preparer should request to see both a current government-issued photo ID and the taxpayer's original identification number.

If the identification card does not have the same address as the one on the tax return, ask additional questions to verify the taxpayer's identity. Although the addresses are not required to match, confirming the identity of the taxpayer is a fundamental part of a tax professional's due diligence. Using an incorrect identification number or the same number on multiple returns or an incorrect name with the wrong identification number are some of the most common reject causes of e-filed returns. To minimize rejections, the preparer should verify the taxpayer's name and identification number prior to submitting the tax return electronically to the IRS.

Client Protection

The IRS has created several basic security guidelines for tax preparers to follow while preparing returns, which will make clients' data and their businesses safer:

- ➢ Learn to recognize phishing emails, especially those that look like they originated from the IRS. Never open an embedded link or attachment from an email that looks suspicious.
- ➢ Create a data security plan using the guidelines found in Publication 4557, *Safeguarding Taxpayer Data*.
- ➢ Review internal controls:
  - o Install anti-malware and anti-virus security software on all devices (laptops, desktops, routers, tablets, phones, etc.) and keep the software up to date.
  - o Use strong passwords of 8 or more characters with a mixture of upper and lowercase letters, numbers, and special symbols that do not start or end with a space or include common phrases or the names of loved ones or pets.
  - o Encrypt all sensitive files and emails and use strong password protections.
  - o Back up sensitive data to a safe and secure external source that is not connected to a network full-time.
  - o Wipe, clean, or destroy old hard drives or printers containing sensitive data.
  - o Limit access to taxpayer data exclusively to individuals who need to know.
  - o Perform weekly checks on the number of returns filed with the company's EFIN through the eServices account and compare that number with the number of returns the firm has actually prepared to make sure no one is fraudulently using their EFIN to e-file returns without one's knowledge. Individuals can do the same thing via their PTIN account.
- ➢ Report any data theft or data loss to the appropriate IRS Stakeholder Liaison.
- ➢ Sign up on the IRS website to receive email notices from e-News for Tax Professionals, Quick Alerts, and Social Media.

The Gramm-Leach-Bliley Act

Enacted by Congress in 1999, the Gramm-Leach-Bliley Act implemented various safeguard rules and the financial privacy rule to protect taxpayers' private information. Safeguard rules require tax return preparers, data processors, transmitters (ERO), affiliates, service providers, and others to ensure the security and confidentiality of customer records and information. The financial privacy rule requires the following to give their customers privacy notices that explain the financial institution's information collection and sharing practices:

- ➢ Tax return preparers
- ➢ Data processors
- ➢ Transmitters
- ➢ Affiliates
- ➢ Service providers
- ➢ Anyone significantly engaged in providing financial products or services that include the preparation or filing of tax returns

Reporting Security Incidents

Online Providers of individual tax returns shall report any adverse event or threat of an event that could result in an unauthorized disclosure, misuse, modification, or destruction of information. These types of incidents can affect the confidentiality, integrity, and availability of taxpayer information or the ability for a taxpayer to prepare or file a return. Types of incidents include theft of information, loss of information, natural disasters (such as floods, earthquakes, or fires that destroy unrecoverable information), and computer system or network attacks using such tools as malicious code or denials of service. If the tax professional experiences a security incident or is hacked, report it to the IRS immediately.

Part 1 Review Questions

To obtain the maximum benefit from this chapter, LTP recommends that you complete each of the following questions, and then compare them to the answers with feedback that immediately follow. Under governing self-study standards, vendors are required to present review questions intermittently throughout each self-study course.

These questions and explanations are not part of the final examination and will not be graded by LTP.

EFP1.1
What does the acronym ERO stand for?

- a. Electronic Return Originator
- b. Electric Refund Option
- c. Electronic Return Operator
- d. Electronic Refund Originator

EFP1.2
A provider, as defined by the IRS, includes all of the following, **except?**

- a. Electronic Return Originator (ERO)
- b. A Software Developer
- c. A Reporting Agent
- d. An Enrolled Agent

EFP1.3
Which of the following best describes an Electronic Return Originator (ERO)?

   a. Originates the electronic submission of tax returns to the IRS
   b. Issues the tax refund
   c. Accepts tax liability payments
   d. Issues an extension on the taxpayer's behalf

EFP1.4
Which of the following best describes the Principal?

   a. Javier, who works for XYZ Company and e-files all returns.
   b. Alyssa, who handles all e-filing responsibilities.
   c. Lexa, who is a receptionist.
   d. Spencer, who does not prepare or e-file tax returns.

EFP1.5
Who is most likely to be the Responsible Official?

   a. Taylor, who runs the electronic day-by-day operations.
   b. Abigail, who is the receptionist.
   c. Jess, who prepares and e-files his returns electronically.
   d. Landon, who is the electronic filing marketing manager.

EFP1.6
If the individual who is appointed as the Principal or the Responsible Official is not an EA, CPA, or attorney, which of the following must the individual pass before the application moves forward?

   1. Background check
   2. Fingerprint card
   3. Credit check
   4. Tax compliance check

   a. 1 only
   b. 1 & 4
   c. 2 only
   d. 1, 3, & 4

EFP1.7
Which of the following will help the ERO and/or tax professional safeguard against fraud by determining and confirming the taxpayer's identity?

   a. Viewing a taxpayer's birth certificate
   b. Viewing a taxpayer's government issued photo ID
   c. Viewing a taxpayer's medical records
   d. Viewing a taxpayer's cancelled check

EFP1.8
A Responsible Official is an individual with authority over the Provider's IRS e-file operation at a location. The IRS will conduct a suitability check on the Responsible Official. Which of the following is not included in the suitability check?

    a. A credit check
    b. A tax compliance check
    c. A passport check
    d. A criminal background check

EFP1.9
The IRS conducts a suitability check on e-file applicants and on all Responsible Officials listed on the application. Suitability checks do not include which of the following?

    a. A criminal background check
    b. A credit history check
    c. A tax compliance check
    d. A citizenship status check

EFP1.10
Carlos is the ERO for his company. His paid preparer Yesenia needs to be identified. Which of the following information is not needed to identify Yesenia?

    a. Name
    b. Address
    c. PTIN
    d. Phone number

Part 1 Review Questions Answers

EFP1.1
What does the acronym ERO stand for?

    a. Electronic Return Originator
    b. Electric Refund Option
    c. Electronic Return Operator
    d. Electronic Refund Originator

Feedback: Review section *Part 1: Electronic Return Originator.*

EFP1.2
A provider, as defined by the IRS, includes all of the following, **except?**

    a. Electronic Return Originator (ERO)
    b. A Software Developer
    c. A Reporting Agent
    d. An Enrolled Agent

Feedback: Review section *Part 1: Electronic Return Originator.*

EFP1.3
Which of the following best describes an Electronic Return Originator (ERO)?

a. Originates the electronic submission of tax returns to the IRS
b. Issues the tax refund
c. Accepts tax liability payments
d. Issues an extension on the taxpayer's behalf

Feedback: Review section *Part 1: Electronic Return Originator.*

EFP1.4
Which of the following best describes the Principal?

a. Javier, who works for XYZ Company and e-files all returns.
b. Alyssa, who handles all e-filing responsibilities.
c. Lexa, who is a receptionist.
d. Spencer, who does not prepare or e-file tax returns.

Feedback: Review section *Who are the Principals and Responsible Officials.*

EFP1.5
Who is most likely to be the Responsible Official?

a. Taylor, who runs the electronic day-by-day operations.
b. Abigail, who is the receptionist.
c. Jess, who prepares and e-files his returns electronically.
d. Landon, who is the electronic filing marketing manager.

Feedback: Review section *Who are the Principals and Responsible Officials.*

EFP1.6
If the individual who is appointed as the Principal or the Responsible Official is not an EA, CPA, or attorney, which of the following must the individual pass before the application moves forward?

1. Background check
2. Fingerprint card
3. Credit check
4. Tax compliance check

a. 1 only
b. 1 & 4
c. 2 only
d. 1, 3, & 4

Feedback: Review section *Who are the Principals and Responsible Officials.*

EFP1.7
Which of the following will help the ERO and/or tax professional safeguard against fraud by determining and confirming the taxpayer's identity?

    a. Viewing a taxpayer's birth certificate
    b. Viewing a taxpayer's government issued photo ID
    c. Viewing a taxpayer's medical records
    d. Viewing a taxpayer's cancelled check

Feedback: Review section *Safeguarding Taxpayer Information*.

EFP1.8
A Responsible Official is an individual with authority over the Provider's IRS e-file operation at a location. The IRS will conduct a suitability check on the Responsible Official. Which of the following is not included in the suitability check?

    a. A credit check
    b. A tax compliance check
    c. A passport check
    d. A criminal background check

Feedback: Review section *Who are Principals and Responsible Officials*?

EFP1.9
The IRS conducts a suitability check on e-file applicants and on all Responsible Officials listed on the application. Suitability checks do not include which of the following?

    a. A criminal background check
    b. A credit history check
    c. A tax compliance check
    d. A citizenship status check

Feedback: Review section *Suitability Check*.

EFP1.10
Carlos is the ERO for his company. His paid preparer Yesenia needs to be identified. Which of the following information is not needed to identify Yesenia?

    a. Name
    b. Address
    c. PTIN
    d. Phone number

Feedback: Review section *Electronic Return Originator (ERO)*.

Part 2 Transmitting Returns

Electronic filing was introduced by the IRS in 1986. Filing electronically, and having a refund deposited directly into a bank account, is the fastest and greenest way of filing the return. If the taxpayer has a balance due, the amount owed could be withdrawn from a bank account as well. Electronic filing saves the snail mail waiting time for sending or receiving a paper check.

Electronic filing is mandatory for tax preparers who file 11 or more Form 1040 returns during any calendar year. If the firm has more than one preparer, all individual returns prepared by the firm contribute to that number. For example, Javier is the owner of a tax preparation company and does not prepare returns. His employee, Rosemarie, prepares five tax returns that contain a Schedule C. Oscar prepares 10 returns, and Mario prepares 100 individual tax returns. Javier's company needs to file the returns electronically because the firm prepared more than 11 returns.

All authorized IRS e-file providers must ensure that returns are promptly processed on or before the due date of the return (including extensions). An ERO must ensure that stockpiling returns do not occur at the company. "Stockpiling" is both collecting returns from taxpayers prior to official acceptance in the IRS e-file program and waiting more than three calendar days to submit a return to the IRS once the ERO has all the necessary information for an e-file submission. Tax professionals who are EROs must advise their clients that they cannot transmit returns to the IRS until the IRS begins accepting transmissions. Tax returns held prior to that date are not considered "stockpiled."

Filing the Completed Return

Once the return has been completed and signed by all the necessary parties (taxpayer, preparer, etc.), it is time to file the return to the IRS. If sending the return by mail, one must acquire an envelope and postage of sufficient size and amount and mail it to the address designated by the IRS. When mailing the tax return or payment voucher, make sure to use the correct address based on the taxpayer's address not the preparer's address.

Submission of Paper Documents

As discussed throughout this course, there are a multitude of forms that may need to be completed and attached to a taxpayer's return for submission to the IRS. Some software companies allow forms to be attached as PDFs to the tax return prior to submission. If the software company does not support this feature, the documents need to be attached to Form 8453 (which does not need to be signed) and mailed to the IRS using the address on page 2 of Form 8453. The following is a list of the supporting documents that will need to be mailed with Form 8453 if the software does not allow PDF attachments to the return:

➤ Form 1098-C: Contributions of Motor Vehicles, Boats, and Airplanes
➤ Form 2848: Power of Attorney
➤ Form 3115: Application of Change in Accounting Method
➤ Form 3468: Investment Credit, Historical Structure Certificate
➤ Form 4136: Certificate for Biodiesel and Statement of Biodiesel Reseller
➤ Form 5713: International Boycott Report
➤ Form 8283: Noncash Charitable Contributions, Section B Appraisal Summary
➤ Form 8332: Release of Claim to Exemption for Children of Divorced or Separated Parents
➤ Form 8858: Information Return of U.S. Persons with Respect to Foreign Disregarded Entities
➤ Form 8885: Health Coverage Tax Credit
➤ Form 8864: Certificate for Biodiesel and Statement of Biodiesel Reseller
➤ Form 8949: Sales and Other Dispositions of Capital Assets, or a statement with the same information

Providing Information to the Taxpayer

The ERO must provide a complete copy of the return to the taxpayer. EROs may provide this copy in any medium—electronic or another form that is acceptable to both the taxpayer and the ERO. The copy does not need the Social Security number of the paid preparer, but the preparer's PTIN is required. A complete copy of a taxpayer's return includes, when applicable, Form 8453 and any other documents that the ERO cannot electronically transmit in addition to the electronic portion of the return.

The electronic portion of the return can be printed onto a copy of an official form or in some unofficial form. However, on an unofficial form, the ERO must match data entries with the relevant line numbers or with the descriptions found on official forms. If the taxpayer provided a completed paper return for electronic filing, and the information on the electronic portion of the return is identical to the information provided by the taxpayer, the ERO does not have to provide a printout of the electronic portion of the return to the taxpayer. The ERO should advise the taxpayer to retain a complete copy of their return and all supporting material. The ERO should also advise taxpayers that amended returns beginning 2019 can be e-filed. All others prior to 2019 must be filed as paper returns and mailed to the IRS submission processing center.

Processing Return Information from Taxpayers

Before an ERO can originate the electronic submission of a return, they must first either prepare the return or collect the already completed return and its various documents from the person who prepared it. If the return was prepared by someone else, the ERO must always identify the paid preparer in the appropriate field. EROs may either transmit the return directly to the IRS or transmit it through another provider. An authorized IRS e-file provider may disclose tax return information to other providers for the purpose of preparing a tax return under Reg. 301.7216. For example, an ERO may pass on return information to an intermediate service provider or a transmitter for the purpose of having an electronic return formatted or transmitted to the IRS.

File Accurate Tax Return to Receive Timely Refund

An electronically filed tax return is the best way for the tax professional to file an accurate tax return. To ensure the tax return is processed quickly, the ERO should take the following steps:

- ➢ File electronically.
- ➢ Submit an accurate, complete, error-free return.
- ➢ Verify that the Social Security number(s) or Taxpayer Identification Number(s) are accurate for all individuals included on the tax return.
- ➢ Provide the taxpayer's correct mailing address in case the IRS mails a refund check.
- ➢ Use correct bank account and routing number for a direct deposit.

Resubmitting Rejected Tax Returns

If the taxpayer's tax return is rejected by the IRS, the ERO has 24 hours to explain to the taxpayer the reason for the rejection. If the return can be fixed and resubmitted, then the return can be retransmitted. The taxpayer could decide to mail the tax return instead of retransmitting the return. If the taxpayer chooses to mail the return, they will need a paper copy to send to the IRS. If the taxpayer chooses not to have the electronic portion of the return corrected and transmitted to the IRS or if it cannot be accepted for processing by the IRS, the taxpayer must file a new paper return. This must be filed by the due date of the return or within 10 calendar days after the date the IRS gave notice of the return's rejection, whichever of the two is later. The paper return should include an explanation of why the return is being filed after the due date.

Electronic Postmark

When a tax return is e-filed, a transmitter will electronically postmark it to show when it was filed. The postmark is created at the time the tax return is submitted and includes the date and time of the transmitter's time zone. An e-filed tax return is a timely filed return if the electronic postmark is on or before the filing deadline.

Acknowledgment of Transmitted Returns

The IRS electronically acknowledges the receipt of all transmissions and will either accept or reject the transmitted returns for specific reasons. Accepted returns meet the processing criteria and are considered "filed" as soon as the return is signed electronically or by hand. Rejected returns fail to meet processing criteria and are considered "not filed." See Publication 1345, *Handbook for Authorized IRS e-File Providers of Individuals Tax Returns*.

The acknowledgment record of accepted returns contains other useful information for originators, such as: if the IRS accepted a PIN, if the taxpayer's refund will be applied to a debt, if an elected electronic funds withdrawal was paid, and if the IRS approved a request for extension on Form 4868. EROs should check the acknowledgment records stored by their tax software regularly to identify returns that require follow-up action and then take reasonable steps to address the issues specified in those records. For example, if the IRS does not accept a PIN on an individual income tax return, the ERO must provide a completed and signed Form 8453 for the return.

Rejected returns can be corrected and retransmitted without new signatures or authorizations if changes do not differ from the amount in the electronic portion of the electronic return by more than $50 to "total income" or AGI of more than $14 to "total tax," "federal income tax withheld," "refund," or "amount owed." The taxpayer must be given copies of the new electronic return data if changes are made. If the required changes are greater than the amounts discussed above, new signatures will be required, and the taxpayer must be given copies of their new signatures.

Balance Due Returns

Taxpayers who owe additional tax must pay their balances due by the original due date of the return or be subject to interest and penalties. An extension of time to file may be filed electronically by the original due date of the return, but it is an extension of time to file the return, not an extension of time to pay a balance due. Tax professionals should inform taxpayers of their obligations and options for paying balances due. Taxpayers have several choices when paying taxes owed on their returns as well as paying estimated tax payments.

As discussed previously, tax returns with amounts due can still be filed electronically, and the payment can also be made directly to the IRS via ACH withdrawals. The taxpayer can schedule a payment on or before the tax payment deadline. If a balance due return was submitted after the due date, the payment date must be the same day the Provider transmitted the return. Taxpayers can make payments by Electronic Fund Withdrawal for amounts due from the following forms:

> ➤ Current year Form 1040.
> ➤ Form 1040-ES, *Estimated Tax for Individuals*. When filing the tax return, the taxpayer can select all four dates to electronically make the payment.
> ➤ Form 4868, *Application for Automatic Extension of Time to File U.S. Individual Income Tax Return*.
> ➤ Form 2350, *Application for Extension of Time to File U.S. Income Tax Return for Citizens and Resident Aliens Abroad Who Expect to Qualify for Special Tax Treatment*.

The tax professional needs to make sure the client's banking information is accurate and includes the routing transit number (RTN), the bank account number, the account type (checking or savings), the date the payment will be withdrawn (year, month, and day), and the amount of the payment. If the payment is being made after the due date, this should include interest and penalties as well.

As discussed previously, there are other ways to pay the balance due, such as IRS Direct Pay, via credit or debit card (though some credit card companies may charge an additional fee called a "cash advance" to use this method), using the Electronic Federal Tax Payment System (EFTPS), by check or money order, or through an installment agreement.

Pay by Check

Taxpayers may still mail their payment due to the IRS, but the payment should be accompanied with Form 1040-V. The paid preparer must supply taxpayers with copies if they mail Form 1040-V with their check or money order. Taxpayers must mail the payment due by April due date, even if the return was electronically filed earlier.

Form 1040-V is a statement that is sent with a check or money order for any balance due on the taxpayer's current tax year. If the taxpayer files electronically, the voucher and payment are sent together. Most tax preparation software will generate Form 1040-V automatically.

Electronic Funds Withdrawal

Taxpayers can authorize an electronic funds withdrawal (EFW) when they e-file their return if they have a balance due on the return. Taxpayers who choose this option must provide the tax professional with the account number and routing transit number for a savings or checking account. If the financial institution is unable to locate or match the numbers entered in a payment record with account information given on the tax return for the taxpayer, the institution will reject the direct debit request and return the money back to the sender.

Credit or Debit Card Payments

Taxpayers may also pay electronically using a credit or debit card. Taxpayers can make credit or debit card payments when e-filing, or by telephone, or the Internet. A third-party provider may charge a service fee to process the payment.

Electronic Federal Tax Payment System (EFTPS)

Individual taxpayers who make more than one payment per year should enroll in EFTPS. After the taxpayer has been enrolled, they will receive two separate mailings. One is the confirmation or update form; the second is a letter that includes the taxpayer's enrollment trace number, PIN, and instructions on how to obtain an Internet password. Payments on EFTPS can be made 24 hours, 7 days a week; however, to make a timely payment, it must be submitted before 8:00 p.m. EST at least one calendar day prior to the tax due date. Taxpayers can schedule payments up to 365 days in advance.

Returns Not Eligible for IRS e-File

The following individual income tax returns and related return conditions must be paper filed and they cannot be processed using IRS e-file:

> ➢ Tax returns with fiscal-year tax periods.

> ➢ Amended tax returns prior to 2019.
> ➢ Returns containing forms or schedules that cannot be processed by IRS e-file.

Refund Delays

Before giving a taxpayer a refund, the IRS will verify that the taxpayer does not owe any past taxes or other debts such as child support, student loans, unemployment compensation, or any state income tax obligation. If the taxpayer or spouse owes, the refund amount will be applied to their amount owed before any refund amount is paid to the taxpayer. If the amount owed is greater than the amount of refund, then the entire amount of that refund and any future refunds will be applied to offset the amount owed until it has been paid in full.

The following are other reasons a refund could be delayed:

> ➢ The return has errors, is incomplete, or needs further review.
> ➢ The return includes a claim for refundable credits and was held until Feb 15.
> ➢ The return is impacted by identity theft or fraud.
> ➢ The tax return includes Form 8379, Injured Spouse Allocation, which can take up to 14 weeks to process and review.
> ➢ Errors in the direct deposit information that cause the refund to be sent by check.
> ➢ Financial institution's refusal of direct deposit, which will result in the refund being sent by check.
> ➢ The estimated tax payments differ from the amounts reported on a tax return.
> ➢ Bankruptcy.
> ➢ Inappropriate claims for EITC.
> ➢ Recertification to claim EITC.

When the refund is delayed, the IRS will send a letter to the taxpayer explaining the issue(s) and how to resolve them. The letter or notice contains the telephone number and address for the taxpayer to use or to acquire further assistance. If there is a delay, the taxpayer can search for the needed information on the IRS website discussed in the "Where's My Refund?" section.

Refund Offsets

When taxpayers owe a prior-year balance, the IRS will offset their current-year refund to pay the balance due on the following items:

> ➢ Back taxes.
> ➢ Child support.
> ➢ Federal agency non-tax debts such as student loans.
> ➢ State income tax obligations.

If taxpayers owe any of these debts, their refund will be offset until the debt has been paid off or the refund has been spent, whichever occurs first.

Where's My Refund?

"Where's My Refund?" is a portal on the IRS website that provides information about a taxpayer's refund status. This system is updated once every 24 hours (usually at night), and the taxpayer can begin checking where their refund is within 24 hours after the IRS has acknowledged the tax return—not the date that the provider transmitted the tax return.

Taxpayers will need the following information to track their refund:

- ➢ SSN
- ➢ Filing status
- ➢ The full refund amount

To receive assistance from the IRS or a Taxpayer Assistance Center (TAC) over the phone or in person, a return must have been filed electronically and also have a refund. Otherwise, they will not be able to help. IRS personnel can only research tax returns that were filed at least 21 days before. If the return was mailed, the taxpayer must wait at least 6 weeks for the return to be processed.

The Protecting Americans from Tax Hikes Act, or PATH Act, of 2015 allowed Congress to hold refunds from tax returns with refundable credits until February 15 to reduce the potential for fraud by giving the IRS more time to process and check those returns. Any refunds from tax returns with refundable credits that were held will be released after February 15 in the order that they were received and electronically approved. If the taxpayer is claiming a refundable credit, they should only call the IRS when the "Where's My Refund?" portal directs them to call.

Bank Products

Tax-related bank products are another way for a taxpayer to receive their refund and can be offered to clients to defray the cost of tax preparation fees. The most common types of bank products are as follows:

- ➢ Bank Cards: When the deposit is loaded on a bank card to be used like a debit card. Additional fees may apply to the taxpayer.
- ➢ Cashier's Check: A paper check that the taxpayer can either cash at a check cashing service or deposit into their personal checking or savings account.
- ➢ Refund Advance Loans: A loan from the bank that is based on the taxpayer's refund or a flat amount.

The advantage of using a third-party bank is that the tax preparer's fee can be deducted from the taxpayer's refund. While tax-related bank products are a convenient option for many taxpayers, there are additional fees associated with each bank product, which can vary from bank to bank.

If the tax professional marks a tax return for electronic filing when preparing a tax return using software, he or she will be prompted to choose how they would like to receive their refund. There are additional fees charged by the bank and filing software for each type of bank product. The remaining balance will be distributed to the taxpayer by direct deposit, prepaid debit card, or check. Each bank offers different products, so determine which products are best for your clients. The downside to using a bank product is that if the taxpayer owes child support, back taxes, student loans, or other debts, these debts will be paid before the tax professional receives their preparation fees, which could create an additional fee for taxpayers from their preparers who will now have to collect the fees themselves.

E-File Guidelines for Fraud and Abuse

A "fraudulent return" is a return in which an individual is attempting to file using someone else's name or SSN or in which the taxpayer is presenting documents or information that have no basis in fact. A potentially abusive return is a return that the taxpayer is required to file but which contains inaccurate information that may lead to an understatement of a liability or the overstatement of a credit that could result in a refund to which the taxpayer may not be entitled.

Providers must be on the lookout for fraud and abuse. EROs must be particularly diligent because they are the first point of contact with taxpayers' personal information, and they are the ones who compile their information to prepare and file the returns. An ERO must be diligent in recognizing fraud and abuse, reporting it to the IRS and preventing it whenever possible. Providers must cooperate with the IRS's investigations by making information and documents related to returns with potential fraud or abuse available to the IRS upon request. An ERO, who is also the paid preparer, should exercise due diligence in the preparation of all returns involving refundable tax credits, as those credits are the popular target for fraud and abuse. The Internal Revenue Code requires paid preparers to exercise due diligence in determining a taxpayer's eligibility for the credit.

Double Check the Taxpayer's Address

Tax professionals should inform taxpayers that the address on the first page of the return, once processed by the IRS, will be used to update the taxpayer's recorded address. The IRS will use the taxpayer's address of record for notices and refunds.

Avoiding Refund Delays

Tax professionals should make sure that all the information is current when they e-file a tax return to avoid refund delays. The tax professional should also inform clients how to avoid delays by having their information correct – encouraging them to double-check the info they provide. Tax preparer should be aware of the following to help avoid delays:

➢ Make sure to see the actual Social Security card and other forms of identification for all taxpayers and dependents.
➢ Double-check the data entry of all information prior to submission for e-file.
➢ Don't allow the taxpayer to insist upon filing erroneous tax returns (if the taxpayer does, return their documents and do not complete the return).
➢ If the client is new, ask if they filed electronically in the past.
➢ Keep track of the issues that result in a client's refund delays, document the delays, and add the documentation to the client's files.

Signing an Electronic Tax Return

As with an income tax return submitted to the IRS in paper form, an electronic income tax return is signed by both the taxpayer and the paid preparer. The taxpayer would sign electronically. The taxpayer must sign and date the "Declaration of Taxpayer" to authorize the origination of the electronic submission of the return to the IRS prior to its transmission. The taxpayer must sign a new declaration if the electronic return data on an individual's income tax return is changed after the taxpayer signed the Declaration of Taxpayer and if the amounts differ by more than $50 to "total income" (or AGI) or $14 to "total tax," "federal income tax withheld," "refund," or "amount owed."

Electronic Signature Methods

Individual income tax returns are signed using PIN numbers generated in one of two ways: the taxpayers can pick it themselves, or the paid tax preparer can generate one for them. Both methods allow the taxpayer to use a personal identification number (PIN) to sign the various forms, although self-selecting a PIN requires the taxpayer to provide their prior year adjusted gross income (AGI) amount so the IRS can confirm the taxpayer's identity, link it with the taxpayer's other returns from across the years, and detect any returns fraudulently filed under the taxpayer's name in the future. Signature documents are not required when the taxpayer signs using the self-select method and enters their PIN directly into the electronic return. This does not apply to the practitioner-generated PIN. In all instances, the taxpayer must sign Form 8879, Signature Authorization Form, even if a practitioner-generated PIN was used.

IRS e-File Signature Authorization

When taxpayers are unable to enter their PINs directly into the electronic return, taxpayers must authorize the ERO to enter their PINs by completing Form 8879, *IRS e-file Signature Authorization.*

The ERO may enter the taxpayer's PIN in the electronic return record before the taxpayer signs Form 8879 or 8878, but the taxpayer must sign and date the appropriate form before the ERO originates the electronic submission of the return. In most instances, the taxpayer must sign and date Form 8879 or Form 8878 after reviewing the return and ensuring that the information on the form matches the information on the return.

The taxpayer who provides a completed tax return to an ERO for electronic filing may complete the IRS e-file signature authorization without reviewing the return originated by the ERO. The line items from the paper return must be entered on the application Form 8879 or Form 8878 prior to the taxpayer's signing and dating of the form. The ERO may use pre-signed authorizations as authority to input the taxpayer's PIN only if the information on the electronic version of the tax return agrees with the entries from the paper return.

The taxpayer and the ERO must always complete and sign Forms 8879 or 8878 for the practitioner PIN method for electronic signatures. The taxpayer may use the practitioner PIN method to electronically sign Form 4868, *Application for Automatic Extension of Time to File U.S. Individual Income Tax Return* if a signature is required. A signature is only required for Form 4868 when an electronic funds withdrawal is also being requested. The ERO must retain Form 8879 and Form 8878 for 3 years from the return's due date or the date received by the IRS, whichever is later. EROs must not send Form 8879 and Form 8878 to the IRS unless the IRS requests that they do so.

Guidance for Electronic Signatures

If the tax professional's software allows electronic signatures for Forms 8878 and 8879, the taxpayer can choose to sign it that way instead of using a PIN. Technology has created many different types of e-signatures. For tax preparation, it is not the specific technology that is important but rather that the acceptable signature method is used to capture the taxpayer's information. The following are examples of currently accepted methods by the IRS:

➢ A handwritten signature that is inputted on an electronic signature pad.
➢ A handwritten signature, mark, or command inputted on a display screen by means of a stylus device.
➢ A digitized image of a handwritten signature that is attached to an electronic record.
➢ A name typed in by the signer (for example, typed at the end of an electronic record or typed into a signature block on a website form).
➢ A digital signature.
➢ A mark captured as a scalable graphic.
➢ A secret code, password, or PIN used to sign the electronic record.

The software must record the following data for the e-signature to be valid:

➢ Digital image of the signed form.
➢ Date and time of the signature.
➢ Taxpayer's computer IP address; used for remote transactions only.
➢ Taxpayer's login identification (username); used for remote transactions only.

➢ Method used to sign the record (typed name) or a system log or some other audit trail that reflects the completion of the electronic signature process by the signer.
➢ Identity verification; taxpayer's knowledge-based authentication past results for in-person transactions and confirmation that government photo identification has been verified.

IRS e-File Security and Privacy Standards

The IRS has mandated security, privacy, and business standards to better serve taxpayers and protect the information collected, processed, and stored by Online Providers of individual income tax returns.

1. Extended validation of SSL Certificate and minimum encryption standards.
2. Periodic external vulnerability scan.
3. Protecting against bulk filing of fraudulent tax returns.
4. The ability to isolate and investigate in a timely manner the potential of information being compromised.

Part 2 Review Questions

To obtain the maximum benefit from this chapter, LTP recommends that you complete each of the following questions, and then compare them to the answers with feedback that immediately follow. Under governing self-study standards, vendors are required to present review questions intermittently throughout each self-study course.

These questions and explanations are not part of the final examination and will not be graded by LTP.

EFP2.1
Which of the following would the taxpayer not receive from the ERO?

 a. Form 8879
 b. Form W-2
 c. Copy of the return that was electronically filed
 d. Tickets to the Super Bowl

EFP2.2
When a tax return is prepared, the tax professional needs to verify the accuracy of which identification numbers?

 a. SSN, ITIN, and PTIN
 b. SSN, ITIN, and ATIN
 c. ITIN, EFIN, and PTIN
 d. ATIN, EFIN, and CTIN

EFP2.3
Which of the following copies should the taxpayer keep?

 1. Form 8879
 2. Income documents related to the tax return
 3. Copy of their driver's license
 4. The copy of the tax return that the preparer gave to them

a. 1 & 3
b. 3 only
c. 1 & 2
d. 1, 2, & 4

EFP2.4
If a tax return has been rejected and the ERO cannot rectify the issue, how soon does he need to notify the taxpayer?

a. Does not need to notify, just resubmit the tax return.
b. 24 hours of receiving the rejection notice.
c. 10 calendar days after the rejection notice.
d. 72 hours of receiving the rejection notice.

EFP2.5
Which form requires an ERO signature when filing a return electronically?

a. Form 8332
b. Form 3468
c. Form 8879
d. Form 5713

EFP2.6
Which of the following are the two electronic methods of signing an individual income tax return?

a. Self-Select PIN and Practitioner PIN
b. Self-Select PIN and Practitioner PTIN
c. PTIN and Third Party Designee PIN
d. EFIN and Third Party Designee PIN

EFP2.7
When must the ERO and/or tax professional provide a complete copy of the tax return to the taxpayer?

a. At the time the tax return has been paid for
b. At the time the tax return has been electronically filed
c. Within 48 hours from the time the tax return has been electronically filed
d. Within 24 hours from the time the tax return has been paid for

EFP2.8
Which of the following forms cannot be electronically filed?

a. Form 1040 prior to 2020
b. Form 1040X prior to 2019
c. Form 1040A prior to 2017
d. Form 1040 EZ prior to 2015

EFP2.9

Jan's tax return was electronically filed. The tax return was rejected. What must Dave, the ERO, do for Jan?

a. Inform Jan that her return was rejected within 24 hours
b. Resubmit the rejected return before informing Jan
c. Change the DCN to a new number
d. Sign the tax return for the taxpayer and resubmit the return

EFP2.10

Matt is the Responsible Official for his firm, Accounting 4 U. Matt was denied participation as an Authorized IRS e-file Provider. Which of the following is not a procedure to inform Matt of his denial?

a. Notify Matt, he failed the suitability check
b. Notify Matt of his denial to participate
c. Notify Matt the date he may reapply
d. Notify Matt of the Gramm-Leach-Bliley Act

Part 2 Review Questions Answers

EFP2.1

Which of the following would the taxpayer not receive from the ERO?

a. Form 8879
b. Form W-2
c. Copy of the return that was electronically filed
d. Tickets to the Super Bowl

Feedback: Review section *What the Taxpayer Should Receive.*

EFP2.2

When a tax return is prepared, the tax professional needs to verify the accuracy of which identification numbers?

a. SSN, ITIN, and PTIN
b. SSN, ITIN, and ATIN
c. ITIN, EFIN, and PTIN
d. ATIN, EFIN, and CTIN

Feedback: Review section *Verifying Taxpayer Identification Numbers (TINs).*

EFP2.3

Which of the following copies should the taxpayer keep?

1. Form 8879
2. Income documents related to the tax return
3. Copy of their driver's license
4. The copy of the tax return that the preparer gave to them

a. 1 & 3
b. 3 only
c. 1 & 2
d. **1, 2, & 4**

Feedback: Review section *What the Taxpayer Should Receive.*

EFP2.4
If a tax return has been rejected and the ERO cannot rectify the issue, how soon does he need to notify the taxpayer?

a. Does not need to notify, just resubmit the tax return.
b. **24 hours of receiving the rejection notice.**
c. 10 calendar days after the rejection notice.
d. 72 hours of receiving the rejection notice.

Feedback: Review section *Resubmitting Rejected Tax Returns.*

EFP2.5
Which form requires an ERO signature when filing a return electronically?

a. Form 8332
b. Form 3468
c. **Form 8879**
d. Form 5713

Feedback: Review section *Electronic Signature Methods.*

EFP2.6
Which of the following are the two electronic methods of signing an individual income tax return?

a. **Self-Select PIN and Practitioner PIN**
b. Self-Select PIN and Practitioner PTIN
c. PTIN and Third Party Designee PIN
d. EFIN and Third Party Designee PIN

Feedback: Review section *Electronic Signature Methods.*

EFP2.7
When must the ERO and/or tax professional provide a complete copy of the tax return to the taxpayer?

a. At the time the tax return has been paid for
b. **At the time the tax return has been electronically filed**
c. Within 48 hours from the time the tax return has been electronically filed
d. Within 24 hours from the time the tax return has been paid for

Feedback: Review section *Providing Information to the Taxpayer.*

EFP2.8
Which of the following forms cannot be electronically filed?

    a. Form 1040 prior to 2020
    b. Form 1040X prior to 2019
    c. Form 1040A prior to 2017
    d. Form 1040 EZ prior to 2015

Feedback: Review section *Returns Not Eligible for IRS e-File.*

EFP2.9
Jan's tax return was electronically filed. The tax return was rejected. What must Dave, the ERO, do for Jan?

    a. Inform Jan that her return was rejected within 24 hours
    b. Resubmit the rejected return before informing Jan
    c. Change the DCN to a new number
    d. Sign the tax return for the taxpayer and resubmit the return

Feedback: Review section *Resubmitting Rejected Tax Returns*.

EFP2.10
Matt is the Responsible Official for his firm, Accounting 4 U. Matt was denied participation as an Authorized IRS e-file Provider. Which of the following is not a procedure to inform Matt of his denial?

    a. Notify Matt, he failed the suitability check
    b. Notify Matt of his denial to participate
    c. Notify Matt the date he may reapply
    d. Notify Matt of the Gramm-Leach-Bliley Act

Feedback: Review section *The Gramm-Leach-Bliley Act*.

Takeaways

Electronic filing is one of the safest ways to file a tax return, and paid tax preparers are mandated to e-file federal tax returns if they prepare more than 11 returns. Title 26 can impose criminal and monetary penalties on any person who fraudulently engages in preparing or providing services in connection with the tax preparation business. A paid tax professional must guard their clients' information to avoid such penalties. The acceptance of e-filing has saved preparers time and resources. Although there are individuals who still prepare returns by hand, the vast majority use software and reap the benefits of all the advantages that come with being automated.

¡PON A PRUEBA TUS CONOCIMIENTOS!
Ve en línea para tomar una prueba de práctica.

California Electronic Filing

Introduction

California does not conform to the federal guidelines regarding electronic filing and the importance of safeguarding the taxpayer's personal identification information. California requires any tax preparer that uses software for tax preparation to file electronically if filing 1 or more tax returns. California has systems in place to perform these duties at the state level, and it is important for California tax professionals to know the difference. See California Revenue & Taxation Code Sections 18621.9 and 19170.

Objectives

At the end of this lesson, the student will be able to do the following:

 ➢ Understand the benefits of e-filing.
 ➢ Know the difference between federal and state e-filing requirements.
 ➢ Identify the e-file process.
 ➢ Recognize the importance of guarding taxpayer's personal identification information.

Resources

FTB Form 8453	FTB Publication 923	Instructions Form 8453
FTB Form 8879	FTB Publication 1345	Instructions Form 8879

Table of Contents

Part 1 The e-File Process

The process for preparing and submitting an e-file return is very similar to the paper return process:

 ➢ Prepare the client's tax return as normal.
 ➢ Provide your client with a copy of the return and a California e-file Return Authorization for Individuals or a California e-file Signature Authorization for Individuals form.

➢ Have the client sign and return FTB 8453, *California e-file Return Authorization for Individuals*, or FTB 8879, *California e-file Signature Authorization for Individuals*, to the tax preparer before the return is transmitted (a faxed copy is acceptable).

➢ Transmit the returns to the IRS and FTB; the state will approve the tax return after the IRS acknowledgment.

➢ Retrieve the acknowledgment (ACK) file that states if the FTB has accepted the return for further processing or if it has found an error. The state could reject the tax return even if the IRS has accepted the return.

➢ Correct any errors and retransmit the return to FTB. The return is not considered filed until the state issues an accepted ACK.

➢ Record the date the FTB accepted the return on Form FTB 8453 or FTB 8879.

➢ Retain a copy of Form FTB 8453 or FTB 8879 for 4 years after the return due date or for 4 years after the filing date, whichever is longer. This is different than the IRS.

See FTB Publication 1345, *Handbook for Authorized e-File Providers*.

Participating in the California individual e-file program has many benefits for the tax preparer and their clients. Filing electronically is very convenient and can be completed at any time of day, or any day of the week. The taxpayer who has a balance due could file the tax return and pay the balance due on April 15th. Taxpayers can submit an EFW request for extensions and payments just like on the federal return. IRS-approved Providers are automatically enrolled in the California e-file program. The FTB automatically receives any updates made to an individual's IRS account within 7-10 business days. California needs the provider to verify their EFIN and to confirm their identity before they can e-file any returns.

Mandatory e-File

California tax law requires all returns prepared by businesses or individuals who prepare California tax returns annually to be electronically filed. California allows a taxpayer to opt out of e-filing in favor of paper filing for any reason. Although a taxpayer is not required to list a reason for not e-filing, a preparer must list a reasonable cause for not e-filing if the return was not e-filed for any reason other than the taxpayer opt-out. The preparer should have the individual sign FTB 8458 for proof of opting out.

Differences Between the FTB and IRS e-File Programs

The FTB and the IRS both have their own Publication 1345, *Handbook for Authorized e-File Providers*, although California differs in the following ways:

➢ All state e-filed tax returns are transmitted directly to the FTB in Sacramento.

➢ No additional paper documents are sent to the FTB.

➢ FTB allows EROs and most online filers to use both pen-on-paper signatures (sometimes called wet signatures) and electronic signatures for Form 8453.

➢ The FTB 8453 series must be e-filed and kept by both the taxpayer and tax professional.

➢ Taxpayers must retain all Form 1040 series forms as well as copies of all their returns.

Acknowledgment Files and Error Resolution

Because most errors can be resolved electronically before the FTB accepts the return for processing, less than 1% of California e-file returns require special error handling. The FTB system performs up-front audits on all incoming e-file returns and will let the ERO know if it detects any errors. It will identify those errors and will allow the preparer time to make any corrections, reducing the need to repeatedly contact their clients. The FTB will also provide an electronic acknowledgment that the return has been accepted. If the return was rejected, the return is considered not filed, and it is the provider's responsibility to notify the client, correct the return, and retransmit it within 24 hours.

Acknowledgment (ACK) files are available 24 to 48 hours after the return has been transmitted. If the tax professional is missing a batch of ACK files, contact the transmitter for assistance before attempting to retransmit the returns or contacting the FTB. If the FTB finds an error in the initial processing of a return, it will reject the return and provide the tax professional with the information in the ACK file. Review "Common e-file Errors and Resolution Tips" on the FTB website to avoid common mistakes.

Quality Control and Fraud Prevention

Like at the federal level, California is very concerned with the potential for fraud committed by both tax professionals and the general public. A tax professional can help prevent and detect fraudulent tax return filings by following some of the same safeguards as the IRS:

> ➢ Verify the identity of new clients.
> ➢ Inform the clients that the FTB will scrutinize the information provided on the W-2 and Child and Dependent Care Expenses Credit.
> ➢ Verify the nonrefundable Child and Dependent Care Expenses Credit's supporting information by doing the following:
> > o Inspecting Social Security cards to verify each child's name and SSN.
> > o Obtaining proof of provided care, such as cleared checks.
> > o Review the taxpayer's (and spouse, if married) earned income to determine if the Child and Dependent Care Expense Credit requirements have been met.
> ➢ Ask questions about W-2 forms that look suspicious or have been altered.
> ➢ Identify repeated information provided on multiple returns from different "clients", such as refund amounts, number of dependents, and number of W-2s.
> ➢ Question individuals using the same address, or a P.O. Box, and are filing head of household.
> ➢ Ask to see all Social Security cards and related documentation for everyone on the return.

Before preparing or accepting returns for transmission, the tax professional should see two of the following forms of current photo identification from the client:

> ➢ Driver's license
> ➢ State Identification number
> ➢ Military identification
> ➢ Alien Registration Card
> ➢ Passport
> ➢ Veteran's ID Card

Each form of ID should include the same name and Social Security number for the individual filing the tax return. All documents need to be retained for four years after the return's due date or four years after the date the return was filed, whichever is longer.

Power of Attorney FTB 3912

FTB 3912 is intended to keep taxpayers informed of the relationship and level of online access to their online account. The level is full or limited access; this allows the taxpayer to control who has access or what one could see.

Form 3520

Form 3520 can be submitted either electronically or snail mail. The purpose of the form is to authorize an individual to represent the taxpayer before the FTB. The form can also allow the representative to receive and inspect the taxpayers' confidential documents and represent the taxpayer in all matters before the FTB.

Request for Appeal the Office of Tax Appeals

If the taxpayer does not agree with the FTB decision on their audit, they can appeal to the Office of Tax Appeals by using FTB 1037 *Request for Appeal the Office of Tax Appeals*. If taxpayer wants to appeal the decision they can by mail, fax, or email.

Recordkeeping

The general rule for how long tax records should be kept is when the period of limitations runs out for the tax return, which depends on the deductions taken on the return. The taxpayer should keep copies of their filed tax return and any computations made in the process of preparing an amended return. The taxpayer should keep records that are connected to property until the limitation expires for the year the property was disposed. For example, if the taxpayer owned a rental and disposed of the property in 2021, the records should be kept for 4 years after the date of disposal. The burden of proof is on the taxpayer to prove entries, deductions, and statements made on the tax return. The taxpayer should have substantiating evidence (for example, bookkeeping records) of their personal and business activities.

A California driver's license or state ID card is not required to e-file a state tax return. However, asking for the information on a voluntary basis may help process a tax return more efficiently and protect the taxpayer and their refund. A tax preparer should always look for ways to protect the taxpayer's confidential information, increase security, and minimize impact to the business. There are some states that do require a current government issued ID.

Part 1 Review Questions

To obtain the maximum benefit from this chapter, LTP recommends that you complete each of the following questions, and then compare them to the answers with feedback that immediately follow. Under governing self-study standards, vendors are required to present review questions intermittently throughout each self-study course.

These questions and explanations are not part of the final examination and will not be graded by LTP.

CEFP1.1
How many years does the ERO need to retain Form 8879 records?

    a. 4 years after the return due date
    b. 4 years after the filing date
    c. 4 years after the return due date or for 4 years after the filing date, whichever is longer
    d. Don't have to keep copies

CEFP1.2
Which of the following is a difference between the FTB and the IRS e-file program?

    a. State returns are e-filed directly to the FTB.
    b. IRS returns go directly to the IRS.
    c. FTB conforms to the IRS with sending additional documentation.
    d. IRS and FTB use software to transmit the returns.

CEFP1.3
Which of the following would not be an acceptable form of identification?

    a. Driver's license
    b. Matricula
    c. Military identification card
    d. Passport

Part 1 Review Questions Answers

CEFP1.1
How many years does the ERO need to retain Form 8879 records?

    a. 4 years after the return due date
    b. 4 years after the filing date
    c. 4 years after the return due date or for 4 years after the filing date, whichever is longer
    d. Don't have to keep copies

Feedback: Review section *Part 1: The e-File Process.*

CEFP1.2
Which of the following is a difference between the FTB and the IRS e-file program?

    a. State returns are e-filed directly to the FTB.
    b. IRS returns go directly to the IRS.
    c. FTB conforms to the IRS with sending additional documentation.
    d. IRS and FTB use software to transmit the returns.

Feedback: Review section *Part 1: The e-File Process.*

CEFP1.3
Which of the following would not be an acceptable form of identification?

    a. Driver's license
    b. Matricula
    c. Military identification card
    d. Passport

Feedback: Review section *Qualify Control and Fraud Prevention*.

Takeaways

Both federal and state tax laws require paid preparers to e-file. When e-filing a return, the paid tax preparer cannot just assume that once they hit the submit button (or transmit) that the return will automatically be accepted by the federal or state tax agency. The paid tax preparer should always have due diligence on their mind when it comes to tax returns. It is the responsibility of the paid tax professional to safeguard clients' personal information to help prevent identity theft.

TEST YOUR KNOWLEDGE!
Go online to take a practice quiz.

The Latino Tax Professionals Association (LTPA) is a professional association dedicated to excellence in serving tax professionals who work in all areas of tax practice, including individual practitioners, accounting and bookkeeping services, enrolled agents, certified public accountants, and immigration attorneys. Our unique, interactive e-book and online training system provides the only tax and bookkeeping training in both English y en español. Our mission is to provide knowledge, professionalism, and community to those who serve the Latino taxpayer, to help you grow your practice and increase your profits by attracting more Latino clients, and to provide the best tax preparation training available.

Latino Tax Professionals Association, LLC
1588 Moffett Street, Suite F
Salinas, California 93905
866-936-2587
www.latinotaxpro.com

For support: edsupport@latinotaxpro.org

Made in the USA
Monee, IL
08 July 2023

38545628R00396